Realism and International Relations

Realism and International Relations

A Graphic Turn Toward Scientific Progress

PATRICK JAMES

OXFORD
UNIVERSITY PRESS

Oxford University Press is a department of the University of Oxford. It furthers
the University's objective of excellence in research, scholarship, and education
by publishing worldwide. Oxford is a registered trade mark of Oxford University
Press in the UK and certain other countries.

Published in the United States of America by Oxford University Press
198 Madison Avenue, New York, NY 10016, United States of America.

© Oxford University Press 2022

All rights reserved. No part of this publication may be reproduced, stored in
a retrieval system, or transmitted, in any form or by any means, without the
prior permission in writing of Oxford University Press, or as expressly permitted
by law, by license, or under terms agreed with the appropriate reproduction
rights organization. Inquiries concerning reproduction outside the scope of the
above should be sent to the Rights Department, Oxford University Press, at the
address above.

You must not circulate this work in any other form
and you must impose this same condition on any acquirer.

Library of Congress Cataloging-in-Publication Data
Names: James, Patrick, 1957- author.
Title: Realism and international relations : a graphic turn toward
scientific progress / Patrick James.
Description: New York, NY : Oxford University Press, 2022. |
Includes bibliographical references and index.
Identifiers: LCCN 2022014934 (print) | LCCN 2022014935 (ebook) |
ISBN 9780197645024 (hardback) | ISBN 9780197645048 (epub) | ISBN 9780197645055
Subjects: LCSH: Political realism. | Science and international relations. | War (Philosophy)
Classification: LCC JZ1307 .J363 2022 (print) | LCC JZ1307 (ebook) |
DDC 327.101—dc23/eng/20220607
LC record available at https://lccn.loc.gov/2022014934
LC ebook record available at https://lccn.loc.gov/2022014935

DOI: 10.1093/oso/9780197645024.001.0001

1 3 5 7 9 8 6 4 2

Printed by Integrated Books International, United States of America

To Carolyn C. James—great scholar, teacher, wife, friend, and sphynx mommy

Contents

List of Figures ix
List of Tables xi
List of Appendixes xiii
Preface xv
Acknowledgments xvii

PART I. SETTING THE AGENDA

1. Realism, International Relations, and the World Today 3
2. Progress in International Relations 25

PART II. CREATING A METATHEORY OF PROGRESS FOR INTERNATIONAL RELATIONS

3. Introducing Components: Knowledge, Units, and Methods 53
4. Knowledge 76
5. Units 124
6. Methods 157
7. A Metatheory of Progress 212

PART III. IDENTIFYING REALISM

8. The Nature of Realism 231
9. Classifying Realist Theories of War 261
10. Classical Realism 284

PART IV. REALIST THEORIES OF WAR

11. Power Cycles 331

12. Structural Realism	355
13. Balance of Threat	386
14. Balance of Interests	417
15. Defensive Realism	448
16. Dynamic Differentials	479
17. Offensive Realism	494
18. Predation	517

PART V. THE WAY FORWARD

| 19. Dialogue for Realist Theories of War | 533 |
| 20. Realism and Progress in International Relations | 574 |

| *References* | 585 |
| *Index* | 617 |

Figures

1.1.	Systemism at a Glance: The Politics of Intervention in Latin America as a Region	21
2.1.	Perspectives on Progress	37
3.1.	Configuration of Elements from a Metatheory of Progress	73
4.1.	Shadows and Illumination	84
5.1.	War as an Empirical Problem	152
6.1.	International System and Region	185
6.2.	Neoclassical Realist Model of International Outcomes	197
6.A.	Types of Causal Connections	211
7.1.	The Metatheory as a Working System	214
8.1.	Realism as the Point of Origin for International Relations Theory: Anarchy, State-Centrism, Rationality, and Power Seeking	254
9.1.	Genealogy for Realist Theories of War	277
10.1.	Martin Wight on War	299
10.2.	Hans Morgenthau on War	302
10.3.	Henry Kissinger on War	307
10.4.	Arnold Wolfers on War	314
10.5.	Raymond Aron on War	319
11.A.	Power Cycle Theory	339
11.1.	Power Cycle Theory	344
12.1.	Structural Realism	370
12.2.	Hegemonic Stability	380
13.1.	Balance of Threat	397
13.2.	Revolution	407
14.1.	The Additive Model	424
14.2.	Extremely Incoherent States Model	433
14.3.	Polarized Democratic Model	439
15.1.	Stability	455
15.2.	Windows	465

15.3.	Offense-Defense	471
16.1.	Dynamic Differentials	486
17.1.	Offensive Realism	504
18.1.	Predation	525
19.1.	Combined Version for Balance of Interests	548
19.2.	A Defensive Realist Synthesis	550
19.3.	A Study of Crisis	562

Tables

2.1.	Criteria for Progress in International Relations	29
3.1.	Elements of a Metatheory for Scientific Progress, Summaries, and Visualizations	60
4.1.	Analytic Eclecticism and Implementation	105
5.1.	Systems of Explanation	136
6.1.	Conditions for the Axiomatic Basis of a Research Enterprise: Stages of Identification	160
6.2.	Ideas about Cause and Effect	176
6.3.	Systemist Notation	190
6.4.	Neoclassical Realism at a Glance	196
8.1.	The Realist Worldview	235
8.2.	Candidates for the Axiomatic Basis of Realism	244
9.1.	Typologies of Realism	266
9.2.	Taxonomies of Realism	273
9.3.	Classifying Realist Theories of War	282
10.1.	Classical Realism at a Glance	287
10.2.	Properties of Variables in the Great Books	323
11.1.	Power Cycles at a Glance	335
12.1.	Structural Realism at a Glance	357
12.2.	Variable Types and Connections for Structural Realist Theories	376
13.1.	Balance of Threat at a Glance	389
13.2.	Variable Types and Connections for Balance-of-Threat Theories	405
14.1.	Balance of Interests at a Glance	420
14.2.	Variable Types and Connections for Balance-of-Interests Theories	431
15.1.	Defensive Realism at a Glance	450
15.2.	Variable Types and Connections for Defensive Realist Theories	463
16.1.	Dynamic Differentials at a Glance	480
17.1.	Offensive Realism at a Glance	496
18.1.	Predation at a Glance	518
19.1.	Profiling Realist Theories	536

Appendixes

Appendix 6.A.	Implementation of Systemism	209
Appendix 8.A.	Independent and Essential Axioms	260
Appendix 11.A.	The Power Cycle	354
Appendix 14.A.	Models of Foreign Policy from Balance-of-Interests Theory	447

Preface

This book puts forward a point of view about progress for International Relations in general and realism in particular. If borne out, the arguments contained in this study could have far-reaching consequences for International Relations and even beyond. Over the course of a century, many thousands of books, articles and other publications have accumulated about international relations. I have come to believe that translation of such information into knowledge requires a greater emphasis on communication beyond words alone. This is true already for realism, with its vast corpus of academic research in place, and increasingly accurate as an assessment of other schools of thought in International Relations as well. Realism is the "canary in the coal mine" for International Relations; its embattled status is a story foretold with regard to the field as a whole. In sum, information accumulates at a rapid pace and comprehension of it lags behind, which does not bode well for overall progress in an academic discipline.

Given the challenges posed by existing and intensifying information overload, a call is made in this book for a new vision of progress with a solid foundation in the philosophy of inquiry. At the center of this outlook is argument for a *visual* turn in communication. Realist scholarship in the post–World War II era is the natural domain of application for systemism, a graphic form of expression with straightforward rules for portrayal of cause and effect within theories. Systemism thereby also facilitates comparative analysis. A review of realist theories about the causes of war over the course of more than seven decades reveals the value of visual representations based on systemism. These graphics bring order out of what critics tend to describe, with some justification, as chaos. While realists respond at times to their critics, it is fair to say that all participants have become dissatisfied with results from exchanges in words alone. Constructive engagements for realists and those who identify with other schools of thought seem to be diminishing with time. Thus a graphic turn is in order for realism in particular and theories of world politics in general. Progress otherwise is likely to remain elusive.

Realism is a research enterprise that will create scientific value only if it moves forward in a more integrated manner. The argument of this book is that advancement for realism requires a graphic turn. Application of systemism, a visualization technique borrowed from the philosophy of science and adapted to present purposes, reveals the shortcomings, contributions, and potential of realism. Through graphic representation of cause and effect, as here applied to respective theories about war, systemism creates the potential for more productive communication within and beyond the realist school of thought. This type of visual presentation is essential for realism as well as other approaches in the quest for a scientific International Relations.

The University of Southern California is one of the world's great universities. I am fortunate to have such fine people around me—faculty, students, and staff—and that facilitates a great life of research and teaching. The contents of this study have been influenced by any number of seminars and hallway conversations at USC. In sum, I have enjoyed writing this book and am solely responsible for any errors within its pages.

Patrick James, Ventura, California, 18 October 2021

Acknowledgments

This work has benefited greatly from support provided by various institutions and advice obtained from many friends. I am grateful to the School of International Relations (SIR) and Center for International Studies (CIS) at USC, each of which contributed valuable resources along the way. David Kang, Director of CIS, 2015–18, Saori Katada, Director of CIS, 2018–19, 21–, and Joshua Aizenman, Director of CIS, 2019–21, made possible the outstanding research assistance I have received from Miriam Barnum, Sarah Gansen and Evgeniia Iakhnis. Stefanie Neumeier helped out with much-needed translation work. The SIR, with Wayne Sandholtz as Director, 2015–18, and Linda Cole as Office Manager, helped in ways too numerous to mention; work study students and other personnel played a significant role in moving this project forward. SIR helped especially in providing support for research carried out so effectively by Gabrielle Cheung, Sarah Gansen, Edward Gonzalez, Michael Pfonner, and Ian Solano. I have received the same high level of support from the Department of Political Science and International Relations since its founding in 2019, with Saori Katada as the Chair, 2019–20, Ange-Marie Hancock Alfaro as the Chair, 2020–2022, and Cathy Ballard as Senior Administrator. A manuscript review at the Department of Government, Dartmouth University, accelerated development of the project via thoughtful critiques for Chapters 3 and 4 in April 2017. I thank Stephen G. Brooks, Jeffrey A. Friedman, William C. Wohlforth, and other participants from the seminar at Dartmouth for their outstanding ideas.

Carolyn C. James gave an insightful reading of this manuscript that improved it greatly in preparation for the CIS manuscript review of May 2017; she provided multiple and invaluable commentaries at later stages as well. I am grateful once again to David Kang, Director of CIS, for encouraging and implementing an assessment of the manuscript at an important stage of work in progress. Participants in the manuscript review of the first eight chapters, which included Andrew Bertoli, Benjamin Graham, Joey Huddleston, Jonathan Markowitz, Wayne Sandholtz, and others, offered excellent ideas that are reflected in the pages of this book. In particular, I appreciate the extraordinarily thoughtful readings from James Lebovic and John A. Vasquez, who came to the CIS event in 2017 from their respective institutions as designated discussants.

Any number of friends have read either chapters or specific parts of my manuscript. I appreciate the good ideas provided along the way by Miruna Barnoschi, Stuart J. Kaufman, Mark Raymond, Veronica Ward, and Jeff Wright.

Jeffrey W. Taliaferro and Charles F. Doran provided an especially important consultations on Chapters 9 and 11, respectively. Angharad (Harry) Buxton and Brian Rathbun read through a complete draft of the manuscript, and I am grateful for their valuable insights, which have made the result much better than otherwise. Annette Freyberg-Inan provided an extraordinary reading of this study just before it went out for review, with a great and favorable impact on both the content and how ideas have been conveyed. A reading by Jack Donnelly of my article in *ISQ* (2019) led to several improvements of the manuscript.

I also appreciate the time and effort spent by creators of respective realist theories, or experts contacted in instances without the original author being available, in consultations about graphic representation via systemism. I have benefited very much from exchanges with Dale C. Copeland, Charles F. Doran, Steven E. Lobell, John J. Mearsheimer, Norrin M. Ripsman, Randall L. Schweller, and Joshua R. Itzkowitz Shifrinson about their theories. The following scholars provided great insight into the theories of those noted in parentheses: Annette Freyberg-Inan (Raymond Aron, Arnold Wolfers), Stefano Guzzini (Hans Morgenthau), Ewan Harrison (Martin Wight), Arie Kacowicz (Robert Gilpin), and Harvey Starr (Henry Kissinger).

Nuffield College, Oxford, which hosted me for the Trinity Term in 2016 and 2018, provided an ideal setting for research and writing at very important stages of work. I am grateful to Duncan Snidal for sponsoring my visits. Sarah Das provided valuable staff assistance. During the visit to Nuffield in 2018, I gained invaluable insights from presenting Chapter 8 of this book to the IR Research Colloquium. I am grateful to Angharad (Harry) Buxton, Todd Hall, Jonathan Maynard, Duncan Snidal, and other participants in the colloquium for reading through my manuscript and helping to improve it in many ways. I also presented drafts of Chapters 6 and 8 to faculty and doctoral students at Nuffield and appreciate thoughtful commentaries from Duncan Snidal, Annette Stimmer, and Jeffrey Wright.

David McBride, Social Sciences at Oxford University Press, is an outstanding editor. I am very grateful to David, along with two referees that he selected, for insights that significantly improved the final version of this manuscript. Suganya Elango, Project Manager at Newgen Knowledge Works, did excellent work at the stage of copy editing for this manuscript.

Even while busy with books of his own, the late and great Michael Brecher somehow found time to read through this manuscript multiple times and provide a wealth of valuable ideas for its improvement. His grasp of scientific principles and extraordinary insights have combined to make this volume much better than it ever would have been without such generosity. When all is said and done, exchanging views on so many manuscripts—back and forth with Michael as the years have went by—will be one of my favorite memories. I am grateful to him for our collaboration on many things, most notably the International Crisis Behavior Project, which he founded with my dissertation adviser, Jonathan Wilkenfeld. Jon continues to be a great mentor and friend to this day. His guidance and encouragement have been invaluable throughout my career.

This book is dedicated to Carolyn C. James. She has been a wonderful partner and advocate throughout the long process of writing this book. I continue to be grateful for all of the wonderful things she does for me and our family.

PART I
SETTING THE AGENDA

Part I of this book begins in Chapter 1 with the assertion that political realism, by far the most time-honored idea in the study of international relations (IR), must enter into compliance with scientific principles. The focal point for reassessment will be respective theories of war in the era following on from classical realism, which provides the foundation for research that continues to this day. Chapter 1 identifies a graphic turn in communication as essential for realism to obtain scientific viability as it continues to investigate the causes of war and other empirical problems. The chapter includes an outline of the rest of the volume, which consists of a vision of progress, a metatheory directed toward achievement of that goal, identification of realism as a research enterprise based on a combination of inductive and deductive criteria, graphic representation and evaluation of respective realist theories about war, comparative analysis of these frameworks with each other, and an overall assessment of realism today.

Chapter 2 focuses on the meaning of scientific progress for the discipline of IR. An inductive and sociological approach is used to identify characteristics and results that would be desirable for research. A deductive and rationalist assessment produces a verdict in favor of scientific realism as the most promising overall frame of reference in the quest for knowledge. Comparative analysis produces the conclusion that scientific realism is the pragmatic choice both on its own merits and when reviewed in the context of preferred traits for characteristics and outcomes of research.

Source: Photo by Martin Farrell.

1
Realism, International Relations, and the World Today

Realism is obviously a human software package with deep-seated appeal.

—Mearsheimer (1994–95: 45)

Collectively the realist mainstream has set up a situation that provides a very narrow empirical basis on which to falsify the paradigm.

—Vasquez (2003a: 41)

Overview

Realism is a worldview with ancient origins, long before anyone imagined an academic discipline of International Relations (IR).[1] It makes sense that a viewpoint in which power is central to human life would gain adherents from time immemorial and maintain support even through today. With a sense of order in antiquity based on empires such as Greece, China, India, Persia, and Rome, military capabilities became the arbiter of decisions. Threat and use of force mattered above all else. Social institutions existed only in embryonic form.[2]

Foundational texts from ancient times include *The Art of War* from Sun Tsu, *History of the Peloponnesian War* by Thucydides, and Kautilya's *Arthashastra*. These studies created a tradition of realist philosophy upon which thousands of academics and practitioners have built over the millennia. It might be more accurate to observe that realists have projected that mission into these classics retroactively—a projection that likely would result in a never-ending debate. Notable realist signposts in the early modern era include *The Prince* from

---

[1] "International Relations" (IR) refers to the academic discipline, whereas "international relations" is taken to mean the subject matter. The terms "international relations," "international politics," and "world politics" will be used interchangeably in this volume. For an authoritative history of IR as a discipline, which helps with understanding its terminology and research accomplishments, see Knutsen (2016).

[2] For a fascinating window into the beginning of international diplomacy in ancient Egypt, see Cohen and Westbrook (2002).

Realism and International Relations. Patrick James, Oxford University Press. © Oxford University Press 2022.
DOI: 10.1093/oso/9780197645024.003.0001

Machiavelli and *Leviathan* from Hobbes.[3] Often written against the backdrop of war, those books and others introduced ideas essential to the theory and practice of what became known as power politics. For example, *Leviathan* is recognized for identifying the state as the "primordial form of delineation of politics" (Lizée 2011: 29). At the same time, it is appropriate to note that readings that transcend realism also are possible for these great books.[4] Thus other traditions are able to lay claim to such classics as well.

Ancient and early modern studies associated with realism continue to exert influence over the conduct of international relations and even life in general (Donnelly 2008: 194; see also Elman and Jensen 2014). Consider, for example, the idea of Machiavellianism, which refers to acts of manipulation in pursuit of enhanced personal power. On the academic front, realist theories in the modern era are "grounded in an understanding of international politics, and politics more generally, as a constant struggle for, and conflict over, power and security" (Frankel 1996c: ix; see also Fozouni 1995: 496). Realists, Van Evera (1999: 256) adds, are "right to make strong claims for the virtues of their paradigm." In sum, many still look at the world as one of power politics, even as they hope for better things to come.[5]

From its origins onward, realism's exponents have argued that the politics of power will never go away. The epigraph from Mearsheimer refers to overwhelming intuition that realism represents a logic of life with ongoing relevance. Many others concur, and a few examples from realists are sufficient to make the point. Realism is referred to as the "most important school of thought in the study of international politics" (Layne 2006: 15). According to Snyder and Lieber (2008: 185), realism is "thriving, both in theory and in practice." Realism, moreover, stands as the "default setting" for IR theory (Brown 2012: 857; see also Elman and Jensen 2014: 12). Wohlforth (2008: 131) adds that the study of international politics "is in an important sense inexplicable without a grounding in realism." Walt (1998: 43) further observes that, "[although] academics (and more than a few policymakers) are loathe to admit it, realism remains the most compelling

---

[3] Numerous translations of the preceding works are available; examples include Sun Tzu (1963) [500–450 BCE], Thucydides (1972) [431 BCE], Kautilya (1992) [n.d.], Machiavelli (2003) [1532], and Hobbes (1982) [1651].

[4] For example, a thoughtful rendering of *The Peloponnesian War* from Welch (2003) locates Thucydides outside of a realist framework. A few passages, Welch (2003) asserts, have received too much emphasis and, in turn, caused readers to see the history of the ancient war as an affirmation of realism.

[5] One of the terms used interchangeably with realism, "realpolitik," will not appear in that way within this volume. The term should not be equated with Machiavellianism, the national interest, or other associated concepts; instead, realpolitik originates with August Ludwig von Rochau, a German liberal activist and journalist (Bew 2016: 6). In his 1853 treatise, *Foundations of Realpolitik*, Rochau denoted a method for "analyzing complex political problems" rather than a philosophical position associated with power politics (Bew 2016: 6).

general framework for understanding international relations." Regardless of its precise level of support at any given time, variants of realism are ever-present within IR.[6]

Even critics acknowledge the centrality of realism in development of IR.[7] "Realism," as Guzzini (1998: 212) observes, "is alive in the collective memory and self-understanding of our (i.e., Western) foreign policy élite and public," and therefore "we cannot but deal with it." The realist approach, as Lizée (2011: 19; see also Vasquez 1998: 42) notes, "is in fact always the starting point in the study of the field." Freyberg-Inan (2016: 81) asserts that "realism seems to have been around forever without ever losing all of its plausibility as an interpretive lens." Adherents agree and add that realism "provides a foil against which many other schools of thought define themselves and their contributions" (Wohlforth 2008: 131). According to Elman and Jensen (2014: 3), even critics "acknowledge that humankind has, in most times and in most places, lived down to realism's very low expectations." Thus realism continues to be regarded as relevant among both supporters and skeptics to this very day.

Some critics, however, question the continuing viability of realism. Among others, Vasquez (1983, 1998) and Legro and Moravcsik (1999) emphasize the failings of realism as a would-be scientific approach to international relations. The epigraph from Vasquez, which focuses on whether realism is in line with scientific principles for testing, must not be ignored. Such critiques are fundamental and should combine to create a sense of urgency among realists regarding the future relevance of their school of thought. While some have replied to the science-oriented critics, still lacking is a book-length response that begins from the ground up in reassessing and revising realism from an *advocate's* point of view. Given the ongoing problems identified by those who reject realism as a rigorous foundation for the study of international relations, such an effort in fact is overdue.

For such reasons, this volume reassesses realism in terms of its relevance to developing a scientific account of international relations. From an evaluation conducted on the basis of scientific criteria, realism emerges as problematic in its current state but with potential for contributing significantly to progress in IR. To cite perhaps the most obvious example, serious work is needed to obtain compliance with the criterion of logical consistency. Difficulties faced by realism today, moreover, will apply to other schools of thought with virtual certainty in the passing of time. This is because the problems experienced by contemporary realism derive, to a significant degree, from its *sheer size as a body of work*. The

---

[6] Among many collections that convey the wide range of options available within realist theory, representative examples are Frankel (1996a, 1996d) and Elman and Jensen (2014).
[7] A wide range of critiques about realism, such as those from constructivists that focus on material determinism, are taken up at various points later in this book.

difficulties take the form of self-contradiction and related impediments to scientific progress. And all of that is compounded by problems that derive from the sociology of the discipline—notably incentives to stand by prior commitments.

These challenges are anticipated to grow for other approaches as well because theory and evidence expand with time across the board. There is no immunity to the onset of chaos and confusion within any given frame of reference if countermeasures are not taken. After gaining popularity, terms with previously agreed-upon meaning "become carelessly used and cease to communicate with accuracy" (Schelling 2006: 39). IR is building up immensely in volume, and thus all of its sectors become vulnerable to such problems. For example, Raymond (2019) points out that constructivism is troubled by a proliferation of theoretical mechanisms that have been put forward for creating and revising intersubjective knowledge. Instances already in place would include strategic social construction, argument, persuasion, contestation, learning, and others. How such concepts relate to each other, along with associated questions, still awaits answers from constructivists (Raymond 2019). Mutual intelligibility is a principal casualty of both the overall expanse of the discipline and its increasing internal complexity.

Consider just some of the data presented by Saideman (2018) in a comprehensive review of publications from the field of IR; in particular, more articles are being published than ever before in an accumulating number of premier outlets. In addition, a greater variety of material with varying vocabularies is in print, which leads to the expectation that conversations within circles will continue but without "fruitful communications across the discipline" (Saideman 2018: 701). Taken together, data from this survey of the field reinforce the argument in favor of a new approach to promote effective exchange of ideas.

After a century of IR, it is natural to reflect on its accomplishments and set priorities for future research. The philosophical basis of the quest for progress is *pragmatism*. The pragmatic school of thought in modern times can be traced to the writings of Charles Sanders Peirce in the 19th century (Burch 2014).[8] While it is beyond the scope of the current exposition to introduce the pragmatic school of thought in detail, basic principles from Peirce and William James (from the early 20th century), will be sufficient to identify the philosophical basis of the present study.

From a pragmatic point of view, concept formation "must have some sort of experiential 'cash value,' must somehow be capable of being related to some sort of collection of possible empirical observations under specifiable conditions" (Burch 2014: 8). Furthermore, "At any temporal point in the process of scientific

---

[8] Burch (2014) provides a highly accessible exposition of Peirce that will be used here to present ideas that are relevant to arguments developed in the current study.

inquiry we are only at a provisional stage of it and cannot ascertain how far off we may be from the limit to which we are somehow converging" (Burch 2014: 10). James (1907) concurs: "The 'absolutely' true, meaning what no further experience will ever alter, is that ideal vanishing-point towards which we imagine that all of our temporary truths will some day converge." Ideas, moreover, become true in light of events (James 1907). The overall message is one of modesty about what is known, with an emphasis on beliefs justified by evidence as opposed to an ideology that sees some kind of end state toward which life is converging.

Pragmatism can be identified in IR as well, with a few key illustrations to follow. In a classic exposition, Almond and Genco (1977: 522) assert that, to make scientific progress, "the social disciplines require their own philosophy of science based on explanatory strategies, possibilities, and obligations appropriate to human and social reality." Almond and Genco (1977) endorse a middle ground between the polar points of inductive and deductive reasoning. On the one hand, according to Almond and Genco (1977: 500), in a deductive-nomological model, "Something is explained when it has been shown to be a member of a more general class of things." On the other hand, Almond and Genco (1977: 500–501) observe that "there will be exceptions to any generalizations we might form about the phenomena that are of interest to us." Thus a pragmatic approach will pursue breadth and depth of explanation, with deductive and inductive foundations, respectively. For such reasons, "Methods are fit to the subject matter rather than subject matter being truncated or distorted in order to fit it to a preordained notion of 'scientific method'" (Almond and Genco 1977: 510). All of these admonitions are in line with a pragmatic approach toward social science in general and IR in particular.

More explicit advocacy for pragmatism in IR is developed convincingly in Bauer and Brighi (2009). Pragmatism, according to Bauer and Brighi (2009: 159) "can indeed offer a new avenue for IR, one that has been surprisingly neglected so far." Moreover, "Pragmatism encourages us to consider academia not only as an activity, but as a *community of scholars* brought together by similar (and yet always distinctive) intellectual interests and, even more crucially, by a sense of belonging to (and duty towards) society" (Bauer and Brighi 2009: 159). Thus Bauer and Brighi (2009: 161) assert that "IR scholars should stop preaching about the necessity of dialogue and of the encounter with the 'other,' and start embodying these ideals, making them a practice" and thereby "avoid division into theoretical feuds." Bauer and Brighi (2009) also provide a figurative Ten Commandments for an IR pragmatist, each of which, if reviewed in further detail, would be fully in line with the metatheory of progress that is forthcoming in Chapters 3–7.[9]

---

[9] The full list is as follows (Bauer and Brighi 2009): (1) "believe in the primacy of practice: that is, IR pragmatists will begin not by questioning what a thing 'is' or what (and how) we 'think' it is, but

This study therefore develops and implements a metatheory of scientific progress for IR—a pragmatic response to developments over the course of decades that have made the discipline huge and beset with communication-related challenges that go down to the foundations of its work. Conveyed in both words and images based on a graphic technique to convey explanations, a metatheory integrates knowledge, units of analysis, and methods into an overall perspective on scientific progress.

For reasons covered at a later point in this chapter, the metatheory developed in this volume is applied to realism since World War II.[10] Realist theorizing about the causes of war is the specific subject of investigation. The purpose of this exercise is to address the problems associated with size and incoherence, which currently make realism less than viable as a scientific endeavor and bedevil the entire field. The metatheory of scientific progress is multifaceted and introduced in stages, but a key aspect to note at the outset is that it includes a model of cognition that calls for a *visual* turn.[11] This refers specifically to a shift toward graphic representation of theorizing, realist or otherwise, to facilitate communication. The overarching goal is to improve comprehension of theory and evidence associated with realism, in a collective sense, with special attention to the matter of logical consistency. In this way, it is argued, realism in the 21st century can move into an era of scientific progress. If successful in the context of realism, moreover, the metatheory and associated visual turn could be applied throughout IR and perhaps beyond.

This chapter unfolds in three additional sections. The next section introduces the question of realism as a school of thought in relation to principles from the philosophy of inquiry. These reflections set the agenda for more in-depth analysis in forthcoming chapters. The third section offers a plan of work, through

---

with an inquiry into practices and actions, whatever their source"; (2) "consider all knowledge of the world as a human creation, and hence language-mediated, socially based and historically grounded"; (3) "take this knowledge merely as a means to navigate the world"; (4) "profess that theory and practice are always interlaced"; (5) "resist the temptation of radical skepticism and, by letting go of the anxiety caused by it, learn to move on and 'cope' "; (6) "[assert that] knowledge does not exist outside experience and judgment"; (7) "honour the diversity of methods and perspectives by exercising eclecticism in their research, not being afraid of 'trespassing' disciplinary boundaries"; (8) "[be] committed to dialogue within the community of scholars to which they belong"; (9) "[undertake] inquiry . . . geared toward the idea of emancipation and betterment of the community to which they belong"; and (10) "believe in the open-endedness of the social world, in the possibility of creative action, and in the emergence of new practices to which they themselves, as a social scientist and social actor, will contribute."

[10] In a book-length assessment of power politics, Guzzini (1998: 31) observes that the realist worldview tries for pragmatism, in contrast with the cynicism sometimes attributed to its adherents.

[11] The emphasis in this volume is on visualization of cause and effect for respective theories in order to facilitate comparison of them with each other and thereby enhance prospects for explanation. For a different sense of visualization, which emphasizes a turn to graphic representation of subject matter in an effort to promote understanding of global politics, see Bleiker (2018a, 2018b).

chapter-based outlines, for the rest of the volume. A fourth and final section reiterates the basic points from this chapter and leads into Chapter 2.

Realism and the Philosophy of Inquiry

This section carries out four tasks. The first goal is to introduce realism as it exists today. Second will come a consideration of IR, realism, and the quest for explanation. A third objective is to consider how realism and scientific progress currently relate to each other. Fourth and finally, the realist response to the call for scientific advancement will be assessed.

Realism Today

Beyond a basic worldview that emphasizes power politics, what does realism have to offer in terms of theorizing and explanation? An answer to that question entails exploration of how realism can be connected to science and the idea of progress for IR.

With regard to realism as a theory put forward in a way that goes beyond a worldview or *gestalt* type of meaning, Smith (1986: 1) provides a good point of departure:

> In the realm of international politics, states are the only major actors, and no structure of power or authority stands above them to mediate their conflicts; nor would they peacefully consent to the creation of such a structure, even if it could be shown to be workable. States act according to their power interests, and these interests are bound at times to conflict violently. Therefore, even if progress toward community and justice is possible *within* states, the relations *between* them are doomed to a permanent competition that often leads to war. However deplorable, this permanent competition remains an unavoidable reality that no amount of moral exhortation or utopian scheming can undo. Only by appreciating its source and its permanence can interstate conflict be moderated.

Smith (1986: 1–2) further observes that realism possesses three main features that theorists emphasize in varying ways: realism (a) is a general theory of international politics; (b) is used to evaluate policies for respective states; and (c) is applied as a solution to the problem of moral considerations in foreign policy. For this volume, point (a) is of primary importance because the focus will be on assessment and reformulation of realism in a quest for improved explanation.

Points (b) and (c), which are policy-related and normative, become secondary.[12] On the one hand, these goals lie beyond the scope of a project that applies a metatheory to realism in order to assess and potentially enhance its performance in the context of science. On the other hand, improved explanations for international politics cannot be without at least some valuable implications for policy. A few ideas are taken up about that subject toward the end of this book.

Various meanings have accumulated within and beyond the preceding categories for realism over a very long time—a point that will come up often in this study. An essential goal, therefore, is to zero in on a conception of realism that is compatible with scientific advancement.

Even as it continues to boast of many adherents, realism gathers as many or more critics.[13] Rothstein (2005: 418), for example, draws attention to an "overly narrow conception of politics," along with "antiquated notions of sovereignty, Great Power dominance and the autonomy of foreign policy"—none of which seems consistent with the world of today. Critics see realism as "fundamentally flawed," with a theoretical structure "in need of modernization yet oblivious to the modern currents of scholarship that might inform it" (Wayman and Diehl 1994a: 3, 4; see also Diehl and Wayman 1994: 262). In such instances, the context of criticism is a belief that realism is not well suited, in the absence of substantial revision, to pursuit of scientific progress in IR.

From the standpoint of the skeptics, realism is a vast congeries of confusing ideas and applications. Fozouni (1995: 508) even claims that the discipline has been "mesmerized by a false theory!" Rosecrance and Steiner (2010: 343; see also Freyberg-Inan 2004: 159) observe that realism cannot be falsified due to its expansive, even ecumenical, character. Thus realism violates an essential rule for any would-be scientific explanation—potential for refutation in the face of evidence. Miller (2004: 37) dismisses realism altogether:

> Realist theory is based on erroneous and arbitrary assumptions. The existence of international anarchy is contradicted by the existence of international institutions possessing varying degrees of sovereignty; states are not "like units" and do not behave as "unitary rational agents"; and the organization of sovereignty on the domestic level, in addition to international systemic factors, affects the international behavior of states.

---

[12] For discussion of realism in the context of morality, notably its lack of appeal to American public opinion, see Smith (1986), Mearsheimer (1994–95), and Van Evera (1999: 41).

[13] A sample of the many expositions that criticize realism at a general level would include Vasquez (1983, 1998, 2003a, 2003b), Ashley (1984), Onuf (1989), Griffiths (1992), Rothstein (2005), Diehl and Wayman (1994), Schroeder (1994), Wayman and Diehl (1994a, 1994b), Fozouni (1995), Guzzini (1998, 2004), Legro and Moravcsik (1999), Wendt (1999), Freyberg-Inan (2004, 2006), Schroeder (2003), Miller (2004), Schmidt (2007), Wagner (2007), Barkin (2010), Rosecrance and Steiner (2010), Fearon (2011), and Bew (2016).

The preceding list of reasons has become standard among opponents of realism. If its assumptions are invalid, how can realism be expected to explain international relations?

Realists have produced thousands of expositions about world politics, so there is a lot to talk about, favorably or otherwise. Political realism, as Schweller (1997: 927) observes, continuously has been "revised, reformulated and amended for the purposes of (1) better explanations and more determinate predictions, (2) refinement and clarification of the research program's theoretical concepts, and (3) extension of the research program to cover new issue areas." Rather than a single instance, Frankel (1996c: ix; see also Mastanduno 1997: 50; Wohlforth 2008: 131) asserts that there instead exists a "family of realist theories and explanations" that vary in terms of the importance assigned to respective variables, such as domestic institutions or polarity of the international system. As this quantity of research continues to expand, so do potential and even realized instances of self-contradiction within the corpus of realism.

This is where the epigraph from Vasquez, a well-established and convincing critic of realism, comes into play. Vasquez (2003b: 107) observes that "many emendations, decades of discourse (if not centuries), and lack of clear corroboration of the original proposition are not indicators of good health" (see also Fozouni 1995: 492). Among many other points of criticism directed at would-be realist explanations are an inability to account for change, an erroneous treatment of human nature, and an inaccurate sense of direction with regard to international history (Schroeder 2003: 125). So is realism, which seems at odds with a quest for scientific explanation, worthy of further implementation in IR?

Controversy rages on about whether realism is a viewpoint with lasting value and further potential or instead is a way of thinking that has run its course. One prominent dividing line in the debate, as articulated by Vasquez (1983, 1998), is whether realism complies with conventional standards for scientific inquiry. Exponents of realism see the tradition as alive and well, with valuable contributions in place and continuing to accumulate, whereas critics tend to look at the same thing and see an unscientific quagmire instead.

All of that leads into a more encompassing question: Can or even should there be a *science* of IR? An answer to that query is essential before taking on the issue of scientific status for realism in particular. In a highly visible rejection several decades ago, Hoffmann (1977: 51) argued that the quest for scientific progress in IR had run into multiple, quite serious, and even overwhelming problems. As a would-be science, IR theory had come to depend on the concept of power, which does not function in the same way as money in economics and therefore cannot play a parallel role in developing rigorous theories; in addition, the discipline still seemed to lack consensus about what to explain and how to go about doing it (Hoffmann 1977: 51, 52, 54). Great debates in IR—or at least several controversies recognized as such within the field—have converged on more fundamental issues related to knowledge itself (Lapid 1989). Lack of resolution for these controversies would seem to vindicate the skepticism of Hoffmann (1977), expressed several decades ago, about a purportedly scientific IR. Arguments about viability for a science of IR continue to this day, with an increasingly abstract character and no sign of coming to a resolution.

IR, Realism, and the Quest for Explanation

One way to approach the controversy over the identity of IR as a discipline is to pose a more general question: What is it that scientists *do*? An answer to this point of inquiry should help to decide whether IR can or should proceed in a scientific direction, with obvious implications for realism as well.

Some responses from within IR about the nature of scientific inquiry are encouraging. "Science," according to Wight (1996: 309; see also Wight 2019: 70), "is an active, intentional examination, and possible intervention, into nature or some aspect of the world" and carried out by people "using taught and/or acquired skills in order to deepen existing knowledge through the transformation of existing knowledge." If that is what scientists do, then IR scholars would qualify for such status. In addition, Haas (2017: 1) asserts that "scientists make observations, engineer changes in the real world, and calibrate measuring instruments" and "search for relationships between two or more variables across several cases in order to establish generalizations." Thus scientists seek a certain kind of explanation for empirical findings—one that stands up to further scrutiny and becomes more credible with time through successful application. There is no reason to rule this activity out of hand for IR. At the same time, it would be unwise to ignore skeptics who warn that challenges to scientific inquiry about the social world ultimately could prove to be overwhelming, with IR as no exception.

Questions about science underlie the controversy over realism in particular—a long-standing approach but seen as lacking in demonstrated value by persistent critics throughout IR. The multifaceted query about whether IR can be a science is answered in every imaginable way by those in the field. Although challenged by alternative modes of thinking, the most commonly adopted—albeit usually implicit—perspective on how to study IR over its initial century of existence is neopositivism. The neopositivist outlook is associated with belief in fully objective reality.

Within a comprehensive and influential exposition on philosophy of inquiry, Jackson (2011, 2016a, 2016b) provides a thought-provoking treatment of what science means and the connection of this concept to IR. An essential aspect of his exposition is to challenge self-designated exclusive scientific status among neopositivists. Science, for Jackson (2016: 26), is "equivalent to systematic inquiry designed to produce factual knowledge." Its specific characteristics follow naturally from that definition; science is "systematic, worldly inquiry subject to public criticism intended to improve its results" and also "factual, explanatory, *impersonal*, and *detached* in a specific sense" (Jackson 2017: 17). These traits add up to an inclusive sense of science and provide the foundation for an argument against pride of place for neopositivism, the point of view associated most closely with empirical observation. From Jackson's (2011, 2016a, 2016b) perspective, neopositivism is narrowly focused and should not be permitted to claim the mantle of science to the exclusion of other options provided via the philosophy of inquiry. As the present study unfolds, a position on this issue is developed that regards neopositivism as an end state worth striving for, as opposed to something that can or should be a requirement for research on international relations in particular or the world in general. Thus an assessment of realism with standards imposed from neopositivism would be impractical—theorizing in IR across the board, in fact, would be found wanting in those terms.

Critiques of neopositivism as a guiding principle often come from a sociological point of view. Jackson (2016a: 28), for instance, draws attention to "a persistent problem: the bias of the 'Science' gesture itself tilts the field in such a way that neopositivists can take advantage of their rhetorical position and claim to be the truest representatives of Scientific knowing." The process described by Jackson might be compared to the way verbal conflict played out between the self-designated majority, the Bolsheviks, and those they labeled "Mensheviks" (i.e., "the minority"), during the Russian Revolution of 1917. This tactic worked well for the Bolsheviks—their Menshevik rivals lost influence and ultimately disappeared. In Jackson's frame of reference, neopositivists attempt to marginalize rival philosophies of inquiry in the same way—in this context through a labeling process that designates others as unscientific.[14] In other words, since neopositivism always commands more adherents than alternative approaches—or appears to do so via control over key resources such as academic journals—this staying power suggests that it deserves to be seen as the most compelling philosophy of science. In contrast, from Jackson's point of view, scientific status should not be decided by a simple count of hands.

While the exposition from Jackson (2011, 2016a, 2016b) is convincing in some ways, it is expansive enough to risk missing the essence of science: explanation. Put simply, science entails explanation expressed in terms of cause and effect, with an empirical basis. While not an endorsement of neopositivism, this

---

[14] For example, see Steele (2013), who introduces a symposium on the place of constructivism within IR as carried out in the United States. While constructivism is a "key part of the international relations field," some exponents continue to be troubled by success coming to the approach as a by-product of "neopositivist reframing" and other aspects linked to conformity (Steele 2017: 71, 72).

position—developed further in Chapter 2—identifies priorities for research. Theorizing with pragmatic value includes an element of accounting for processes and outcomes. Theories entail "connected propositions" toward an explanation (Freyberg-Inan 2016a: 77; see also Knutsen 2016: 3). Explanatory theory therefore cannot be constructed without at least some minimal belief in objective reality. Progress through more convincing explanations over time otherwise would be supplanted by endless cycles of argument with no anchor to reality.

What, then, does IR try to explain? For IR, war is the most long-standing topic on the agenda. Its destruction of life and property make war a natural point of curiosity. Why does it happen? Can it be prevented? These questions about international politics have stimulated many thousands of studies over a very long time. With regard to concept formation, interstate war is a point of consensus, with due credit to the Correlates of War (COW) Project. An interstate war involves two or more recognized states and results in at least 1,000 battle-related casualties. While this might sound contrived to some degree, the definition, it is irresistible to say, is battle tested. Historians tend to produce lists of interstate wars that implicitly use the criteria from COW (Small and Singer 1982). In later chapters, realism will be assessed in terms of the explanations its various theories offer for the causes of interstate war. Collectively speaking, are these theories of scientific value?

Consider a dynamic tension that will keep coming up in the pages of this volume, within which scientific inquiry is a principal concern (Knutsen 2016: 1):

> What is it that distinguishes International Relations scholars from anybody else who talks and thinks about international politics? Briefly put, International Relations scholars are, first, active members of an academic community. Second, they obey a scientific methodology. Third, they are self-conscious about theory and about their places in a long theoretical tradition.

On the one hand, Knutsen describes a community of scholars—a sociological designation for IR as a discipline. On the other hand, members of that commonality are identified with—even obedient to—a scientific methodology and are oriented toward theory and traditions associated with it. All of this can be true, but only if science is designated in the highly exclusive sense that Jackson (2011, 2016a, 2016b) urged against a moment ago. A problem, however, immediately arises in light of the reality in IR. Many of those under the umbrella just put up by Knutsen mean very different things when they refer to a scientific methodology. These differences are a matter of kind rather than mere degree. Moreover, the range of opinion appears to be expanding over time.

One pragmatic and inclusive way out of this problem is to focus on the logic of confirmation versus discovery. Standards for these tasks do not have to be the same (Freyberg-Inan, Harrison, and James 2017b: 182, 183). The logic of discovery can be quite inclusive; to put it differently: Does the source of a good idea really matter? The same cannot be said for the logic of confirmation. From the standpoint of science, causal mechanisms supported by reproducible evidence are essential. (This terminology leaves aside, for the moment, fundamental questions about whether a more modest designation, such as provisional or tentative support, would be more appropriate.) This is the basic meaning of explanation and is out of line with some options nevertheless described as scientific by Jackson.

With regard to the logic of discovery, consider the impact of Morgenthau (1946) on IR. *Scientific Man and Power Politics* conceived of human history as a cycle of conflict rather than ascending progress. The realist exposition from that book stimulated sustained debate about human nature in relation to world politics. All of this followed on from a study of international relations that had more of a philosophical than scientific bent. Among many others that could be cited, this example reinforces the idea that the logic of discovery can and should be inclusive. The same cannot be said, however, with regard to the logic of confirmation. Rather than speculation about processes of the mind, as in the case of Morgenthau (1946) long ago, the logic of confirmation demands an avowedly scientific approach as put forward above by Knutsen (2016). An example, within the same basic subject area, is the rapidly accumulating research on neuroscience in relation to conflict processes.[15]

Realism and Scientific Progress

Consider, in light of discussion about the logic of discovery versus confirmation, a set of specific but still quite encompassing queries: If IR could be scientific, is there a place for *realism* within that effort? To what extent does realism, at present, offer a scientific account of international relations? How might realist explanations be improved in light of criteria regarding science? The purpose of this study is to answer the preceding questions about realism and IR in a constructive and forward-looking way. The volume assesses whether realism, which today is seen by many as falling short of standards for scientific inquiry, possesses the potential to contribute effectively under certain conditions of renewal. After a particular kind of reconstruction is carried out in this volume, realism will be able to play a more effective role in advancement of IR. The means

---

[15] This type of research includes experimentation—a long-standing method in natural science that made its way into IR much more recently. For an example of neuroscientific research on trust in relation to international cooperation and conflict, with an emphasis on evidence from experiments, see Kugler and Zak (2017).

toward a scientifically viable realism include adoption of a *visual* turn in conveying and reassessing its ideas—something that also applies to IR in general. Given the vast accumulation of studies based on realism, words alone are not enough to move in a scientific direction, which entails logical consistency within explanation. Instead, as detailed in later chapters, graphic presentation of would-be cause and effect is the recommended way forward for realism. This argument obviously applies even more readily to the totality of contemporary IR, which is an order of magnitude greater in scope and complexity than even the vastness of the realist school.

Debate over the scientific character and viability of IR, of course, is nothing new. A look in the rear-view mirror at these exchanges will offer insight for the future. Intense arguments date back to the 1960s. Advocates of a scientific IR, designated as behavioralists, participated in vitriolic intellectual debates with those who became known as traditionalists (Kaplan 1966; Bull 1966). Much of the argument raged back and forth about consequences from appropriation of terminology and techniques associated with the natural sciences.[16] The debates came to no real conclusion but instead stimulated new theoretical frameworks and schemes of evaluation (Ruane and James 2008, 2012). Virtually without exception, realists flocked to the traditional banner during and after arguments from the behavioral era. Creation in the 1970s of *International Security*, a journal understood informally and pervasively as the premier realist academic outlet, reflected alienation from the behavioral revolution and the trend toward mathematical and statistical analyses in its aftermath.

What about the scientific status of realism? Many of its adherents continue to reject quantitative methods and other things associated with the trappings of science. Realists have attracted the ire of any number of science-oriented critics, but expositions from Vasquez (1983, 1998) have had the greatest intensity and sustained impact. Vasquez (1998: 91), moreover, drew attention to the dominance of realism in theory and research about IR (Walker and Morton 2005: 342). The central critique from Vasquez (1983, 1998) depicted the vast corpus of realism as lacking especially in internal consistency, with troubling implications for any lasting value in terms of explanation. Moreover, when tested, realist propositions perform poorly in comparison with those from outside of its boundaries (Vasquez 1998: 149, 153; see also Vasquez 1979: 225). Wayman and Diehl (1994a: 26; see also Freyberg-Inan 2004, 2006; Wivel 2005: 373) sum up many years of critiques from a social scientific point of view:

---

[16] See Vasquez (1998: 43); a prominent example of such debate, which focused on deductive versus inductive theorizing as a foundational issue, involved Young (1969) versus Russett (1969).

Scientific study of realism is difficult because it is not often specific enough to be falsifiable. Rather, it is a cluster of models, assumptions, hunches, hypotheses, and parameter estimates, held together by their common focus on concepts including and related to national material capabilities, power, perceived power, major power status, revisionist and status quo powers, coalition formation via the balance of power, resolve, and commitment.

Realists have replied to the compelling assault from those committed to the scientific study of IR and continue to do so. While various respondents have claimed to refute Vasquez (1983, 1998) and other critics, their answers—covered in detail during later chapters—tend to be dismissive rather than scientifically convincing.[17] Why not reply, instead, by embracing the value of science and making its standards a priority for the realist research enterprise?

This study constitutes a response, from a new point of view, to the wide range of critiques regarding realism. So far, the arguments against realism from Vasquez are the only ones introduced in any detail, but others will join in the fray as well. A compelling reply to those who point out the shortcomings of realism begins with the creation of a metatheory of progress for IR. A metatheory combines ideas about knowledge, units of analysis, and methods to provide a foundation for research. Only with such a framework in place can effective dialogue between advocates and critics ensue for realism or any other school of thought. To some extent, debates have been intensely worded and unproductive because they take place across a currently incommensurable gulf between rival ideas about what research is supposed to accomplish for IR. A central idea within the metatheory, intended to meet that problem head on, is a graphic turn with regard to communication. The emphasis on visual representation of theory responds to difficulties in comprehension that have accumulated as views are exchanged through words alone that focus on massive and ultimately overwhelming amounts of material.[18]

A Realist Response to the Call for Scientific Advancement

Five characteristics of this study as a system-oriented response to challenges from science-based critiques should be acknowledged before going further.

---

[17] Vasquez (2003b: 95), for instance, is quite critical of Waltz for responding to both qualitative and quantitative data in a manner "so dismissive that one wonders whether any evidence will ever be sufficient to test his proposition."

[18] What if, however, the issues are less about understanding and more concerned with sincere differences, notably assumptions about ontology? A graphic turn still would be deemed relevant as a potential means toward translation of arguments back and forth between rival positions on being and existence, which would have to use basic logic to communicate.

First, given the vast size of realism in conjunction with this study's concern with scientific inquiry, for pragmatic reasons the investigation focuses on the post–World War II era. Realism is the long-standing dominant approach in IR since World War II (Wohlforth 1993: 2). Although its "market share" has declined as rival approaches gained adherents, the timeline is by far the longest, and thus realism serves as the most complete paradigmatic case available for investigation. Among many other schools of thought, realism therefore becomes the natural priority for application of the metatheory of progress.

Realism stood in 1945 "against the perceived ills of excessive utopianism, legalism, and sentimentalism, which, it was claimed, had characterized Woodrow Wilson's foreign policy" (Bew 2016: 187; see also Freyberg-Inan 2004: 69). This way of thinking became known as classical realism. Before World War II, realist expositions took a primarily philosophical form. During the postwar period, efforts toward theory-based explanations of international politics began to appear, at least implicitly, in classical realist studies. While classical realist studies from approximately the first two decades after the war still tilted toward reflection rather than rigor, potential exists for insight from reassessing their contents when translated into a visual form. Even with the limitation to the years from 1945 onward, the amount of material referenced in this study—from classical realism to the present—is substantial. In fact, there are enough realist theories to create the need for a scheme of organization among them to facilitate comparison. This frame of reference is developed in Chapter 9.

Second, this study looks at realism as an account of how things work. It is not intended as a guide regarding foreign policy. Thus the agenda is focused on assessment of realism as an explanation, rather than a set of normative principles, with respect to international relations. At the same time, the results of this review will not be without relevance to policy. Consider the question posed by Wight (2016: 32) about scholarship in general: "Why should policymakers and publics struggling to make complex policy choices turn to academics if the research is not scientific?" If realism seeks relevance to matters of policy, an initial step must be to assess its value from a rigorous point of view.

Third, this volume takes on the causes of war as a substantive problem. This is the most established agenda item for realism; the major works from ancient and early modern times referenced at the outset of this chapter all focus on why wars occur. The realist literature on the causes of war is vast and more than sufficient for the purpose of conveying arguments in a graphic form that facilitates comparison and building upon what is known already. While realism includes explanations directed toward many other things, to be viable it must succeed in the most intuitively obvious domain of application, which is accounting for war.

Fourth, this study stands as an internal rather than external critique of realism. The goal is to reinvigorate rather than dispose of realism. Thus what follows in this volume can be understood as an instance of "voice"—a call for change that comes from within—as articulated in the classic work from Hirschman (1970). Of course, the possibility exists that the visual turn will suggest that the time has come to move beyond realism. Hirschman (1970) would call that an "exit." No conclusion should be ruled out ahead of time, but the point of departure is response from an internal voice to ongoing concerns about the scientific standing of realism.

Fifth, this volume is characterized by an incremental approach toward introduction of concepts. For example, after an initial chapter that provides a general introduction, the components and their elements for the metatheory of progress are introduced in detail across three more chapters. Each chapter develops two or three elements within each component. A fifth chapter in the sequence then combines the elements into an overall framework in graphic form. This modus operandi is in line with research from educational psychology, referenced at greater length in Chapter 4, which takes the academic world to task—in a constructive way—with regard to how it communicates. Many studies simultaneously introduce and manipulate myriad concepts. The overall result is that the reader becomes overwhelmed and cannot grasp and retain the content. Surprisingly, perhaps, even the most erudite audience can experience this effect when too much is put forward all at once. Thus the chapters that follow, for pragmatic reasons, introduce and manipulate concepts a few at a time and also include a relatively high amount of visual representation along the way to facilitate understanding and retention of major points.

Plan of Work

Part I of this book continues with Chapter 2, which focuses on the meaning of scientific progress for IR as a discipline. Advancement is identified with growth of knowledge achieved though explanations that have become more convincing over time. Among overarching positions from the philosophy of inquiry, scientific realism is seen as best equipped to facilitate progress. While committed to the existence of objective reality, scientific realism recognizes that unobservables can play a role in theorizing about the social world. A scientific realist point of view emphasizes accounts based on reproducible evidence but, importantly, does not assert that an ultimate truth can be obtained. Instead, increasing approximations to an explanation of the world can be achieved as research proceeds—think, perhaps, of a line that steadily approaches but never reaches some point above it (i.e., an asymptote). Specific criteria associated with progress also are identified and organized in a way that couples characteristics with results. Examples of specific characteristics for research associated with progress include rigor and identification of cause and effect, while desirable aspects of findings include a greater range of explanation and predictive value. These criteria turn out to be compatible with scientific realism as a unifying point of view about research on IR.

Part II of the volume develops a metatheory of scientific progress. This process spans Chapters 3 through 7. It begins with an overview of the elements for each component of the metatheory. The components correspond to knowledge, units and methods. Respective elements for each component are (a) scientific realism, analytic eclecticism, and a model of cognition (knowledge); (b) instrumental rationality and the research enterprise as a system of explanation (unit); and (c) identification of axioms for a research enterprise and systemism (method).

Part III consists of Chapters 8–10. The meaning of realism is conveyed in an overarching sense, along with identification of a set of axioms for the school of thought as a whole. Realist theories about the causes of war are placed into a typology and a taxonomy, respectively, to facilitate comparison. This approach reflects the combination of deductive and rationalist, along with inductive and sociological, analysis that will be a consistent feature for the volume as a whole. This part of the book finishes up with a review of the classical approach as the foundation for realist research that continues to this day.

Part IV, which includes Chapters 11–18, converts respective realist theories about the causes of war into systemist graphics. The theories covered include power cycle, structural realism, balance of threat, balance of interests, defensive realism, dynamic differentials, offensive realism, and predation. The visualizations produced along the way make it possible to identify priorities for improvement that otherwise might not have been detected.

Finally, Part V consists of Chapters 19 and 20. One chapter engages realist theories with each other, along with a major exposition on crisis escalation to war from beyond the domain of realism. The other chapter sums up the intended contributions of this volume and offers a few ideas about future research.

Given the priority placed in this study on a visual approach to international relations, one graphic item is included in this introductory chapter to give a sense of what will be introduced more systematically later on. Thus Figure 1.1 foreshadows the more programmatic presentation of systemism in Chapter 6. The purpose of the figure is to show what a systemist-inspired visualization of cause and effect looks like in a basic way, with elaboration later on. For example, systemist figures, supplemented with shapes and colors, distinguish different kinds of variables from each other. The notation is explained fully in Chapter 6. Figure 1.1 contains only generic variables, designated with plain boxes, to keep things simple at this point of introduction. The figure also is presented in full rather than being developed in stages (i.e., one or a few connections at a time in each respective sub-figure), which is the standard approach for systemist

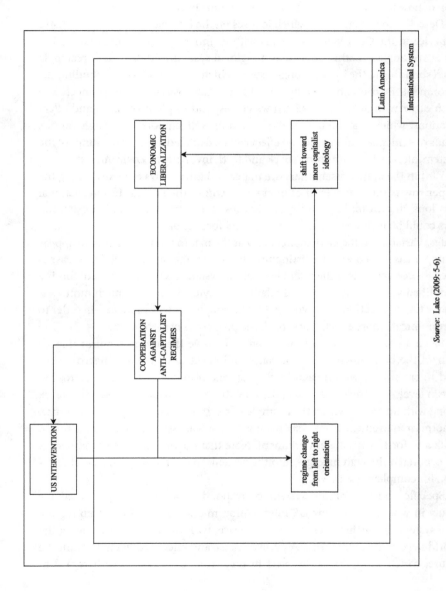

Source: Lake (2009: 5-6).

Figure 1.1 Systemism at a Glance: The Politics of Intervention in Latin America as a Region

applications to respective realist theories that take place from Chapter 6 onward. Thus the system and environment included in Figure 1.1 are not put forward as a definitive treatment of the subject matter but rather, literally, as an initial illustration of how to shift analysis in words into graphic form.[19]

Description of Figure 1.1, which focuses on the international politics of Latin America in the Cold War era, begins with its inner and outer boundaries. The inner rectangle is Latin America as a regional system, with the outer rectangle corresponding to the international system, which constitutes its surrounding environment. Boxes within the figure, which contain variables, are connected to each other with arrows. These arrows correspond to putative cause-and-effect relations, which may be new and untested or well supported through various kinds of evidence. Thus cause and effect can be depicted as inner workings of the system, along with connections back and forth involving its environment.

Within the system itself, there are upper and lower rows of boxes. Along the upper row is the *macro* level of interaction within the system. In international relations, this means beyond the boundaries of the state. States and nonstate actors could be included alike. The *micro* level focuses on what takes place within states. Variables in the environment and at the macro level of the system appear in upper case as a means to distinguish them from the micro level. Lowercase is used for connections at the micro level of the system. As per above, all of this is a simplified vision of international relations—obviously there is much more to it than a few connections involving states and properties within them—in order to communicate more effectively some basic properties of systemism.

From a systemist point of view, comprehensive theorizing requires that all four of the basic possibilities for cause and effect in a system—macro-macro and micro-micro, within each level, plus macro-micro and micro-macro, between levels—be included. Figure 1.1 contains arrows leading across each level, along with up and down, so the example of a system is satisfactory in that sense. Another requirement from systemism is that at least some connection is made, back and forth, with the environment. Note that the box in the environment is incorporated through linkages into the system, so the figure satisfies that criterion for completeness as well.

Specific contents of the system correspond to arguments, presented initially in words, about how US intervention might play out in a given region. The system in this instance is Latin America, with the environment being the world beyond its boundaries. A cycle of cause and effect is depicted within the figure, which summarizes the brief history from Lake (2009) with regard to

---

[19] Aspects such as functional form for a given connection that is displayed—meaning incremental versus other possibilities—will be introduced during the more complete presentation of systemism in Chapter 6.

the Dominican Republic in relation to the United States. A natural point of departure is with the linkage from the environment of the system into its micro level: "US INTERVENTION" → "regime change from left to right orientation." One such example concerns the United States and the Dominican Republic, with assassination of the uncooperative president Rafael Trujillo in 1961 (Lake 2009: 6).[20] An effect from that action ensues at the micro level, within the state concerned: "regime change from left to right orientation" → "shift toward more capitalist ideology." This, connection, in turn, stimulates a development at the macro level: "shift toward more capitalist ideology" → "ECONOMIC LIBERALIZATION." The trend toward capitalism induces a natural movement at the regional level away from state-led development. Now a change ensues within the macro level: "ECONOMIC LIBERALIZATION" → "COOPERATION AGAINST ANTI-CAPITALIST REGIMES." Thus an economic cause produces a political effect. The Dominican Republic, for example, supported the United States against the Soviet bloc during the Cold War, notably with regard to Fidel Castro's Cuba (Lake 2009: 6). At this point, two linkages ensue. The first points from the macro level into the environment: "COOPERATION AGAINST ANTI-CAPITALIST REGIMES" → "US INTERVENTION." This makes sense in light of the United States feeling "welcome" to do more of the same within the region. In addition to this feedback into the environment, a connection also goes down from the macro to the micro level of the system: "COOPERATION AGAINST ANTI-CAPITALIST REGIMES" → "regime change from left to right orientation." A feature of the region thereby impacts individual states within it.

This cycle of cause and effect represents, in a graphic way, thinking among the foreign policy establishment of the United States during the Cold War—and perhaps even beyond that era—about Latin America. Over the course of the last century in Central America, for instance, US actions provide "little evidence of self-restraint in the absence of countervailing power" (Waltz 2002: 53). The point of this example is not to debate its normative implications or even credibility in terms of available evidence, but instead to show, using a simple example, how a line of argument in written or verbal form is translated into the framework of systemism. The format of Figure 1.1 facilitates criticism through a visualization of cause and effect—a picture worth, perhaps, even more than a thousand words. Much more complex arguments are amenable to this type of translation as well—a point addressed with greater detail in Chapter 6.

---

[20] Other instances, which antedate the Cold War, include US intervention with marines in the civil war of 1916. The United States' favored candidate subsequently won election as president in 1924. In sum, the Dominican Republic possesses "partial independence in return for signing a treaty which makes it an actual protectorate" (Lake 2009: 5).

Summing Up and Moving Forward

Why are there hippos on the page facing the start of this chapter? The answer to this query helps very much to set the agenda for the volume. The hippopotamus, to begin, is a huge animal—about 3,000 pounds on average. Note also that the pod (also known as a 'bloat') of hippos does not seem to be headed anywhere in particular. Taken together, these features—massive size and no obvious direction of movement—approximate the condition of contemporary IR.[21] Thousands of books and articles are published every year about IR. Given the range of terminology and methods encompassed in that work, it is reasonable to argue that specialization in the absence of integration is becoming a basic feature of the discipline. It would be very challenging at this time to enumerate points of overall convergence about either theory or substance for IR as a whole.

Massive size and a lack of direction are just fine for the hippo pod, lolling about in and around the water, but what about the scholars of IR? Is this condition desirable for an academic discipline? The basic answer is no. Thus the overall and interlocking objectives of the current study can be summarized as follows:

- Implementing a scientific realist foundation to promote progress.
- Taking a graphic turn, via systemism, to facilitate communication within the vastness of the discipline.[22]
- Focusing on political realism as the most long-standing school of thought in order to demonstrate the value of scientific realism in combination with a graphic approach toward subject matter.

The agenda just presented, of course, is a truncated version of the outline for Chapter 2, along with Parts II–V. It highlights the most important priorities within the work that follows.

Attention now turns to the meaning of progress in IR. Chapter 2 will review available ideas and ultimately conclude that scientific realism, an approach that emphasizes explanation and permits unobservables to play a role in research, provides the most promising foundation for progress in the discipline.

---

[21] This picture and the accompanying theme also appear in James (2019b).

[22] The graphic emphasis follows on from studies in educational psychology that are introduced in Chapter 4. These studies also provide the rationale for gradual introduction of major concepts, along with some degree of repetition, due to cognitive challenges created by new and in some instances highly abstract material. Thus each of Parts I–V is preceded by a brief overview of contents that will follow on in much greater detail.

2
Progress in International Relations

Overview

Pursuit of progress is what separates the sciences, including those like IR that reside in the social domain, from the arts. Take, for example, the obviously strange debate that would ensue in an effort to decide whether the Taj Mahal represents progress over the Sistine Chapel. Each of these great works stands as a major creative achievement in human history. On the basis of intuition alone, it therefore seems odd to label the later work of 1648 as somehow showing progress over the earlier one from 1483. The same could be said of efforts to compare music from different eras, and so on. By contrast, consider the contents of an academic journal from any given discipline that aspires to status in the natural or social sciences. What if it proved possible to shuffle volumes and read through them with little confusion as a result of random ordering? If that happened, it would be troubling because of the obvious question raised: does this field not have any *progress* to show for its efforts?

Scientific progress, based merely on the abstract example of a journal just above, entails comparison. A time element exists. If what appears at a given moment looks just as good as—or possibly even better than—what is available later, that is the antithesis of advancement. Such a state of affairs is quite acceptable for art, perhaps, but not regarding science: "What makes IR a science rather than art or poetry is that it attempts to provide accurate accounts and explanations of the phenomena under study" (Wight 2019: 79 n. 1). As Chernoff (2014: 28) observes, progress is "a hallmark of genuine science." The proposition of the people in Plato's Cave—seeing shadows and believing that they are real—is falsified through modern science and technology (Bunge 2003: 38). Movement forward, in the most basic sense, corresponds to *growth* of knowledge over time.

What, then, does progress mean for International Relations? Consensus on what advancement denotes for IR is lacking (Lake 2002: 135, 2013: 572). The story of IR, according to Jackson and Nexon (2009: 908), "is not unquestionably 'progressive' in the same way as physics or chemistry." This point is true at least in the sense that human agency pervades and complicates the subject matter of IR and, of course, the social disciplines in general. At the same time, it is "a given that international relations (IR) aspires to be a science" (Wight 2019: 79 n. 1). So reflection on the meaning of progress is a greater priority for IR than for any natural science.

Challenges for concept formation regarding progress are great, perhaps appropriately for something with such importance to IR. Anything approaching a standardized set of indicators for movement forward in the social sciences remains elusive (Sil and Katzenstein 2010c: 125–126). IR is no exception. "Progress is hard to measure," as Lake (2002: 135) observes, "especially in one's own era." Freyberg-Inan (2017: 74; see also Sil and Katzenstein 2010c: 125–162) agrees and offers further details reinforcing that position:

> I intentionally leave open the question of how "progress" in our field should be defined. It can mean cumulation of knowledge, to the extent that we can reach agreement that knowledge has cumulated. Yet progress can also legitimately be defined differently. In any instance, I hold that *there can be no objective criteria to measure progress, since as IR scholars we are engaged in an inherently social and political activity*. (Emphasis added)

Thus some observers are skeptical about assessment of progress per se for IR as a result of their views regarding the philosophy of inquiry.

Progress, however, cannot be sidestepped; its meaning must be established in at least some inclusive manner if IR is to be taken seriously as a scientific discipline. Perhaps the most obvious complicating factor for concept formation and assessment regarding advancement is the presence of competing schools of thought within IR. Consider the observations of Bennett (2013: 460):

> The IR subfield has also achieved considerable progress in the last few years in its theoretical and empirical understanding of important policy-relevant issues, including the inter-democratic peace, terrorism, peacekeeping, international trade, human rights, international law, international organizations, global environmental politics, economic sanctions, nuclear proliferation, military intervention, civil and ethnic conflicts, and many other topics.

Advancement, on the one hand, may have taken place in spite of paradigm-based conflict rather than because of it (Bennett 2013: 460). On the other hand, perhaps the overarching schools of thought are essential to guide research along an upward trajectory. Each side of this argument would seem to have some merit.

Whether their ideas are labeled as paradigms or something else, adherents of fundamentally different viewpoints are certain to clash over what is meant by movement forward. Intuition therefore suggests that the most basic sense of progress comes from convergence in thinking, wherever it is identified. Moreover, if fundamental matters such as epistemology (i.e., what is knowledge) and ontology (i.e., what units are to be studied) come up for debate less frequently over time, then that also would be evidence of advancement. So, too, would be increasing agreement on priorities for explanation, even if debates are ongoing about specific aspects of cause and effect.

All of this comes back to explanation as the point of convergence regarding advancement for IR in general and realism in particular. Even while cautious about meaning, Lake (2002: 136) is willing to go so far as to define progress as "improved understanding at one of two levels: general explanations that fit a variety of phenomena and cases more accurately and particular explanations that apply to a small number of phenomena or cases more fully." Accounts that combine to achieve breadth and depth of explanation thereby create overall movement forward.

This chapter seeks to go beyond intuition and obtain a more specific and operational sense of what progress means in the context of IR. The chapter unfolds in four further sections. Ideas about movement forward—built around a state-of-the art research effort from a diverse team of scholars—will be assessed in the second section. The third section focuses on overarching perspectives with regard to progress. Scientific realism, the general outlook recommended for IR, turns out to be compatible with the criteria for advancement identified in the preceding section. In the fourth section, scientific realism as a general perspective and specific ideas about moving forward are juxtaposed with each other. This section also explores more encompassing aspects related to adoption of scientific realism as a foundation for research. The fifth and final section sums up what it means to say that IR has moved forward and sets the agenda for Chapters 3–7 in Part II of this volume, where a metatheory of progress is developed.

Ideas about Progress

Results from a recent team effort provide a starting point for identifying criteria with regard to scientific progress (Freyberg-Inan, Harrison, and James 2017a; see also Vasquez 2003c: 423). This venture, which brought together a diverse collection of scholars for dialogue, reached closure on some major issues but not others. Significant and sustained points of divergence in thinking about progress reflected, at least to some degree, "terminological confusion" regarding matters of paradigm and epistemology (Barkin 2003: 326). For instance, constructivism sometimes is labeled as a paradigm, like realism, liberalism, and others, but that is inappropriate and reveals conceptual confusion. Constructivism is a point of view that focuses on what to study and how to do so—one that holds the position that, given the *social* nature of reality, *ideational* analysis is essential. Public opinion, for example, is an aggregate assessment of what people are thinking.

Culture is a more general manifestation of similar factors—a combination of ideas into an overall sense of identity. These examples are sufficient to establish that further attention to basic conceptual apparatus is warranted if IR seeks genuine advancement.

Some disagreements persist in spite of the team approach from Freyberg-Inan, Harrison, and James (2017a), along with various others, to defining progress. These points of discord go beyond issues potentially related to communication about the meaning of one term or another. Consider criteria for movement forward that have been cited by various subsets among more than a dozen participants in the above-noted project (Freyberg-Inan, Harrison, and James 2017a). It is possible to identify agreement, but in a limited way, on the meaning of scientific progress. Comprehensiveness, defined as the potential to explain a full range of subject matter within a field of study, is the only criterion to appear three times in the summary of contributors to that project (Freyberg-Inan, Harrison, and James 2017b: 174–175). Public exchange of views, identification of causal mechanisms, range of explanation, falsifiability, rigor, predictive value, and recognition of normativity are present twice within that same summing up. There also are numerous criteria that appear just once (Freyberg-Inan, Harrison, and Jame 2017b: 176).

Consensus primarily appears either within something that approaches a neopositivist context or among those who reject such a strongly empiricist point of view. One major exception is agreement on the importance of public exchange of views, which spans that division (Freyberg-Inan, Harrison, and James 2017b: 176). Science requires transparency, so a public exchange of views makes sense. Unrestricted comparison of ideas is essential; progress otherwise is certain to be impeded. Thus a public character to debate emerges as a necessary condition for progress. All of this is in line with philosophical pragmatism, for which the scientific method is "essentially public and reproducible in its activities" (Burch 2014: 9).

Analysis begins with the set of items mentioned at least twice in the collective effort toward identifying progress from Freyberg-Inan, Harrison, and James (2017a). This initial stage admittedly is sociological and inductive; it recognizes the existence of a self-aware community of scholars. The list of criteria will be cross-referenced with items available from other expositions about advancement in IR. This approach enables an assessment of convergence versus divergence in criteria identified with progress in the field that goes beyond the boundaries of the team effort from Freyberg-Inan, Harrison, and James (2017a, 2017b).

Criteria can be organized most clearly into categories of characteristics of, and results from, research. Table 2.1 therefore arranges items in that way to facilitate comparison of the team effort to other expositions on progress. Each criterion for characteristics and results from the team project Freyberg-Inan, Harrison, and

Table 2.1 Criteria for Progress in International Relations

a. Characteristics of Research

Criterion from the Team Project	Meaning	Advocates from Beyond the Team Project
Identifying causal mechanisms	Are we solving puzzles in a body of literature?	Zinnes (1980)
	Does the hypothesis satisfy our curiosity?	Van Evera (1999: 3)
	We suggest the following standards to evaluate causal importance: weight, depth and indispensability.	Schweller and Wohlforth (2000: 100–101)
	Our purpose as scholars is to increase understanding of world affairs, to help ourselves and others understand better how the world "works."	Lake (2002: 136)
Rigor and falsifiability	A theory should specify rigorously how it can be synthesized with other theories into a multicausal explanation consistent with tenets of fundamental social theory.	Moravcsik (1997: 516)
	Emphasis on deductive rigor.	Lake (2002: 138–139)
	Falsifiability; parsimony.	Elman and Vasquez (2003: 287 [Vasquez])
	Is the methodology employed consistent with the broad canons and argument in the social sciences?	Schweller (2003a: 315)
	At first we should seek parsimony and then gradually add complexity in order to enhance the explanatory power of the approach.	Wivel (2005: 363)
Comprehensiveness	Draw upon and integrate analysis into broader areas of theory.	Lake (2002: 138–139)
	Internal fertility: is a given research tradition able to refine its theoretical claims, while expanding (or in some cases, bounding) the range of phenomena to which they apply?	Walt (2002: 201)
	Does the research ask interesting and important questions, raising, for example, new theoretical or empirical puzzles?	Schweller (2003a: 315)

(*continued*)

Table 2.1 Continued

b. Results from Research

Criterion from the Team Project	Meaning	Advocates from Beyond the Team Project
Range of explanation	Empirical and pragmatic assessment of a theory.	Morgenthau (1959)
	Explanatory power: do theories drawn from this research tradition tell us useful things about political events in the real world?	Walt (2002: 201)
	Are plausible and compelling answers to these questions provided, that is, are the hypotheses and the theory or research program in which they are embedded reasonably supported by the evidence?	Schweller (2003a: 315)
	When evaluating an entire research program or body of theory, we must ask a basic Lakatosian question: is the research program producing cumulative knowledge?	Schweller (2003a: 315)
	Explanatory power.	Van Evera (1999: 3; Elman and Vasquez (2003: 287 [Vasquez])
	Any theory stands or falls by its capacity to explain against the known facts.	Haslam (2010: 339)
Predictive value	Empirical accuracy; progressive versus degenerative problem shifts.	Elman and Vasquez (2003: 287 [Vasquez])
	Perhaps a self-correcting science of making predictions about international relations is one path forward.	Ward (2018: 564)
Public exchange of views	Science today is a public proceeding, and it requires being communicable and intersubjectively transmissible.	Ferrarotti (1999: 548)
	Emphasis on open deliberation.	Sil and Katzenstein (2010a: passim)
	Consistency with what is known in other areas.	Elman and Vasquez (2003: 287 [Vasquez])
	A discipline debating the merits of competing paradigms is a community of scholars engaged in each other's work, still keeping an open mind, and learning from each other. We would think that such a community of scholars would also more quickly uncover their mistakes and illusions than one that devolved into a community of like-minded people.	Elman and Vasquez (2003: 303 [Elman and Vasquez])

Note: The structure of this table is based on Freyberg-Inan, Harrison, and James (2017a).

James (2017a, 2017b) is listed in the first column of Table 2.1a and 2.1b, respectively. The meaning of a given criterion as expressed in other expositions, along with citations of respective advocates from beyond the team project, appears in the second and third columns of Table 2.1a and 2.1b.[1]

Consider the characteristics of theorizing. As listed in Table 2.1a, a framework with the potential to generate progress should identify causal mechanisms. A causal mechanism begins with a declarative statement of the following type: "If x is true, then y is more likely than otherwise." Symbolically, this is expressed as "x → y." The mechanism also includes an *explanation* for why the presence of "x" contributes to the greater likelihood of "y."[2]

Emphasis on causal mechanisms from Freyberg-Inan, Harrison, and James (2017a, 2017b) triangulates with ideas expressed elsewhere about the appropriate focus of research. Examples in Table 2.1a include intellectual curiosity and solving puzzles in one area of academic literature or another, along with references to valuable properties, such as indispensability, exhibited by an effective presentation of cause and effect. Rigor and falsifiability go hand in hand as characteristics leading to progress. Table 2.1a lists several advocates who endorse these traits either directly or through related observations about favorable aspects of theorizing. For example, one meaning consistent with rigor and falsifiability takes the form of adding complexity, as needed, to improve explanatory power (i.e., advocated by Wivel 2005: 363). This stands as yet another affirmation of the well-known principle of Occam's razor. In addition, a theory should be comprehensive; a related meaning appears within the table in the form of internal fertility (i.e., advocated by Walt 2002: 201). Thus a given approach should be expected to refine its claims while also expanding the research agenda.

Table 2.1b contains criteria regarding results from Freyberg-Inan, Harrison, and James (2017a) that connect with other expositions. The focus is on products of a theory, as opposed to how it is constituted at the stage concerning characteristics of research. Results with merit include range of explanation, predictive value, and public exchange of views. Numerous expressions from IR scholarship triangulate well with range of explanation. This goes back to IR before the behavioral revolution of the 1960s—often summed up as the time of classical realism—with pragmatic assessment regarded as appropriate for theory and research.

Interestingly, even as the world changes, expressions about progress can remain well preserved. Predictive value, listed in Table 2.1b, refers to the worth of

---

[1] This tabular approach toward summarizing literature will be used throughout the present volume. Use of tables is intended to truncate expositions in words and facilitate understanding of the main points intended for communication. Thus the literature-based tables have the same rationale as the series of figures used to convey cause-and-effect relations from respective theories. See Chapter 4 for a model of cognition that justifies the shift in relative emphasis toward a graphic approach.

[2] This matter is taken up at greater length when systemism is presented in Chapter 6 as a method for conveyance of causal mechanisms.

a theory in terms of its ability to explain known facts and thereby anticipate the future. Note that empirical accuracy appears explicitly. Finally, public exchange of views is confirmed, for example, through a connection with what is known in other areas of research (i.e., advocated by Elman and Vasquez 2003: 207).

Characteristics in Table 2.1a can be linked directly and easily to results as depicted in Table 2.1b. Identification of causal mechanisms and comprehensiveness should be expected to expand range of explanation. Rigor and falsifiability, along with comprehensiveness, point toward predictive value. Public exchange constitutes a process as well as a result and feeds back into respective characteristics of research. For example, a public dialogue could cause a theory to become more rigorous and falsifiable in response to criticism.

What is the best way to apply the criteria to IR in general and realism in particular? Some items from the compilation in Freyberg-Inan, Harrison, and James (2017b: 177) appear two or even three times: recognition of (causal) complexity, use of diagrams, a call for pluralism, and rejection of the idea of scholarly neutrality. These criteria will come to life as a metatheory of progress is put together in the chapters from Part II. A few examples will show how that process is intended to work. Causal complexity is recognized through the model of cognition that, when presented in Chapter 4, calls for a visual turn in IR. Scholarly neutrality, moreover, is rejected to some extent but not to the point where it would create complications for the scientific status of research. As an example, the metatheory of progress introduced in Chapter 3 embraces scientific realism and its position on the essential nature of unobservables along the road to explanation. In that same chapter, furthermore, analytic eclecticism—a pragmatic approach to combining ideas from different frames of reference—is included within the knowledge component of the metatheory. A key aspect of analytic eclecticism is relevance to policy, which goes beyond pursuit of knowledge for its own sake. This position is in line with the nature of IR as a social science that seeks to inform foreign policy.

Consider realism in brief as related to characteristics and results of research as just enumerated. Characteristics and results are covered in turn.

Many realist expositions identify causal mechanisms, notably as related to how foreign policy actions and outcomes are impacted by the distribution of capabilities in the international system. Realism looks problematic in terms of rigor and falsifiability. The wide range of causes and effects identified by realists would seem consistent with almost any events that might ensue. With regard to comprehensiveness, many topics are covered—from grand strategy through specifics about how wars get underway—but the propositions, with their vast range, are not well integrated with each other.

What about results from research? Great controversy exists over range of explanation for realism. With regard to prediction, intense debates continue over realism's ability to anticipate major developments such as the end of the Cold War (Vasquez 1998: 317–368). Perhaps most troubling is the appearance of realism vis-à-vis the requirement for public exchange of views. As will become apparent, adherents of realism, like their peers in the discipline as a whole, communicate increasingly with those who are like-minded. The resulting silo effect is hazardous to the health of both realism and IR.

When characteristics and results of realism are considered in sum, room for improvement clearly exists. Overall outlooks on progress are identified next.

Overarching Views on Progress

Attention shifts from specific criteria to overarching perspectives on advancement. This new priority follows on from recognition that something beyond the preceding incremental approach is needed in concept formation about progress. The prior section took a sociological and inductive pathway toward identifying advancement in IR. To complement what emerged from that review, a deductive and rationalist agenda is pursued. Overarching perspectives on progress will be identified and assessed in terms of their value for guiding research. Thus the specific, inductively derived criteria are to be reviewed later in the context of the overall perspective that is obtained through deductive reasoning.

Comprehensive and well-argued, the exposition from Jackson (2011, 2016a, 2016b) provides an effective point of departure for dialogue about general perspectives on progress in IR. Jackson sets in motion a four-party debate, "with non-positivist conceptions of science offering a variety of alternatives" (Harrison, Freyberg-Inan, and James 2017a: 11). Two philosophical "wagers," each with a pair of possible results, are put forward to create four mutually exclusive and exhaustive perspectives on knowledge and, by association, scientific progress. A wager, in the context of the exposition from Jackson, is a bet on how much can be learned from research based on one general perspective versus another. The first philosophical wager is about mind and world: mind-world dualism versus monism (Jackson 2017: 25, 2016: 39). Put differently, this bet is about whether more can be understood about the world via assumption, respectively, of an objective existence beyond the mind itself (dualism) as opposed to a subjective sense of reality (monism). The second wager focuses on the relationship between knowledge and observation: transfactualism "holds out the possibility of going beyond the facts to grasp the deeper processes and factors that generate those facts"; by contrast, phenomenalism asserts that knowledge "is a matter of organizing past experiences so as to forge useful tools for the investigation of future, as-yet-unknown situations" (Jackson 2016: 40–41). This difference comes down to whether explanations permit *un*observables to play a role, with transfactualists saying yes and phenomenalists answering no.

When the two wagers, each with two possibilities, are combined, the result is the following four perspectives (Jackson 2017: 17):

- Neopositivism: dualist/phenomenal (objective and observable). The world is empirical and fully comprehensible.
- Critical (scientific) realism:[3] dualist/transfactual (objective and unobservables permitted). The world is empirical, but unobservables can and even must appear in explanations that are compelling.
- Analyticism: monist/phenomenal (subjective and observable). The world is observable but subject to interpretation due to the role of the mind.
- Reflexivity: monist/transfactual (subjective and unobservables permitted). The world is neither empirical nor fully comprehensible.

These polar points take a highly abstract form, so illustrations from IR are called for at this point to distinguish what the respective positions mean in practice. What follows is not intended as any type of systematic survey of the field. Instead, examples are used to give a sense of what research looks like when conducted in line with any one of the overarching viewpoints on the world.[4] This process also brings to light certain points of criticism with regard to the typology from Jackson, although its intrinsic value as a practical and revealing way to organize thinking about IR is preserved.

Positivism dates back centuries. In its most basic version, positivism is a sense of the world as purely factual (Ferrarotti 1999: 536; see also Ashley 1984: 253; Sil and Katzenstein 2010b: 416–417). It views social and natural science as the same in an important way—truth is found in the external object (Ashley 1984: 249, 253). As a result of refinements that are not relevant for present purposes, its position evolved, and exponents eventually became known as neopositivists. Katzenstein and Sil (2008: 111–112; see also Sil and Katzenstein 2010b: 416–417)

---

[3] While Jackson (2011) refers to the combination of world-mind dualism and transfactualism as critical realism, the literature from IR tends to use the label "scientific realism." This difference, to some degree, probably reflects Jackson's desire to avoid designating any one of the wagers as scientific in comparison to the others. Since that is not a concern in this study, the more conventional designation, scientific realism, is used from this point onward. Explanations for how critical and scientific realism relate to each other, with an emphasis on the former as either a synonym for, or one type of, the latter appear in MacDonald (2003: 553), Chernoff (2007: 400), Wight (2007: 381 n. 12), Kurki (2007: 364), and Gunnell (2011: 1455). For example, Wight (2007: 381) observes that critical realism "uses scientific realism to develop a particular approach to social science."

Note also that critical realism exists with yet another meaning in IR, referring in this new context to a school of thought (Buxton 2018). Chapter 20 includes reflection on the axiomatic basis of critical realism in comparison to realism per se as a scientific research enterprise.

[4] The illustrations that follow are the product of consultations with respective authors. However, none of the scholars cited is responsible for the way in which their work is described here.

introduce neopositivists as those who "generally gravitate toward a view of social inquiry in which patterns of human behavior are presumed to reflect *objective* principles, laws, or regularities that exist above and beyond the subjective orientations of actors and scholars, and that can be deduced, inferred, or falsified through the rigorous application of replicable methods and logics across a specified universe of cases." Neopositivist research therefore is carried out most effectively in a domain with well-confirmed concept formation and highly developed empirical referents. In sum, neopositivism is based on confidence that, in the fullness of time, the world is one that can be explained by a process of research analogous to that of natural science.

One example of neopositivism from IR is Mitchell and Prins (2004) on interstate rivalry and diversionary use of force.[5] The study begins with the assumption that key variables in the research design, such as domestic turmoil and conflict initiation, are subject to measurement and can be studied on the basis of reproducible evidence. A large "N" statistical approach is implemented to test propositions. One hypothesis, for example, is that domestic turmoil is more likely to result in initiation of a Militarized Interstate Dispute (MID) when the situation includes an opportunity-rich environment (Mitchell and Prins 2004: 947). Well-accepted sources and procedures for identifying and organizing conflict processes, such as the MID compilation and EUGene program, are used to construct a directed-dyad data set for 1960 to 2001 (Mitchell and Prins 2004: 947). Domestic turmoil is assessed via World Bank data—another highly verified source. Differenced data on the consumer price index are used to quantify the inflation-related dimension of domestic turmoil—a standard measurement and approach (Mitchell and Prins 2004: 949). Other metrics and data sources from this study of rivalry and diversionary use of force fit the same description: well accepted among those who study conflict processes.

Scientific realism begins with the premises that "there is nothing in the ontology of the social world that negates the attempt to study it in a scientific manner" (Wight 2007: 388; see also Gunnell 2011: 1452) and that "scientific theories correctly describe the nature of a mind-independent world" (Chakravarrty 2007: 4; see also Kydd 2008: 430). In this sense, scientific realism is aligned with neopositivism. Scientific realism, however, also "posits the existence of unobservable structures and generative mechanisms" (Joseph 2007: 346; see also MacDonald 2003: 554). Among the most influential social processes, from a scientific realist point of view, many are nonobservable (Wight 2007: 381; see also Kurki 2002: 28). As MacDonald (2003: 555) points out, "The majority of

---

[5] Among many examples of neopositivism available across a vast range of topics are Saideman (2001) on ethnic strife; Rhamey and Early (2013) on state competition for international status through Olympic medals; and a vast number of studies based upon Militarized Interstate Dispute (MID) and Correlates of War (COW) data that are reviewed in Geller and Singer (1998).

successful scientific theories rely on phenomena that are not directly observable by scientists such as atoms, quarks or gravity." The perspective of scientific realism therefore departs from neopositivism in a fundamental way.

Interesting to review, in the scientific realist context, is research on political economy from Boehmer and Sobek (2005) and Boehmer (2010).[6] These studies bring out the point that many *economic*, let alone political, variables feature aspects that are more abstract and even amorphous than what appears at the surface level of statistical compilations. This is true especially of the multidimensional concept of development. The ability to observe such processes directly—unlike coding for a military alliance or some other treaty-based variable, for instance—is impossible, at least so far. Based on a long-standing argument about hubris, economic expansion creates the potential for warlikeness; with a control in place for growth of military expenditure, the causal mechanism seems ideational and confidence-related rather than material (Boehmer and Sobek 2005; Boehmer 2010). There is no way to measure confidence or hubris on a cross-national basis over time, so this line of research appears likely to entail unobservables for many years to come.

Analyticism, which holds that the world is observable but subject to interpretation because of processes in the mind, is illustrated effectively through a study of collectivities of stakeholders from Raymond and DeNardis (2015).[7] Multistakeholderism is an institutional form in need of more effective concept formation to enhance its applicability to international politics. A taxonomy is developed and used by Raymond and DeNardis (2015) to designate five cases for purposes of illustration. Three instances focus on the internet, with the other two pertaining to securities regulation and corporate social responsibility. Governance is assessed in each instance, and the concept of multistakeholderism is elaborated as a result. The study from Raymond and DeNardis (2015) thereby constitutes an analyticist effort to move beyond the dichotomy over (un) observables. In more encompassing terms, if material aspects of the world are given priority, then the ideational agenda of constructivism is marginalized from the outset. However, it is appropriate to point out that many observable

---

[6] A wide range of subject areas have been investigated in IR under the auspices of scientific realism; a few examples would include Fordham (1998) on US national security policy during the Cold War; Sil (2002) on industrialization processes for Japan and Russia, with some attention to transnational diffusion of ideas and models; Lemke (2003) on insights from the international politics of Africa; Branch (2014) on cartography and development of the modern state; von Hlatky (2013, 2015) on alliances in time of war; Haglund (2015) on diaspora politics; Sandal (2017) on religious leaders and transformation of conflict; and Graham (2018) on the political economy of diaspora investment.

[7] Other studies classified as analyticist include Eichler (2012) on gender, conscription, and war in post-Soviet Russia; Mitchell (2012) on norms in relation to the democratic peace; Valeriano and Maness (2015) on cyber conflict; Steele (2013) on physical and shocking outcomes of violence in relation to accountability; and Paul (2018) on combination of soft balancing with institutional theory as a way to understand that tactic as a restraining strategy.

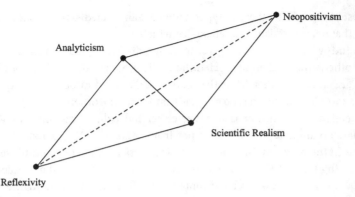

Figure 2.1 Perspectives on Progress

things are associated with the social world; the findings from Raymond and DeNardis (2015) illustrate that point well. Examples include speech—including justification and denial—along with aspects of behavior that can be regarded as referring to rules. All of that, from the standpoint of analyticism, is subject to interpretation.

Reflexivity entails subjectivity and acceptance of unobservables. One essential aspect of reflexivity concerns application of the same principles to scholar and subject matter alike. Another requirement is to bear in mind that all texts can be read at two levels—in terms of what is said and done, respectively. To clarify, authors can be quoted directly, word for word, but also are subject to interpretation. An exemplar here is Kessler (2016), which attempts to come to terms with collective imaginaries.[8] These unobservable entities—dwelling within minds—always structure the positionality of actors and thus what they can see and know. The purpose of Kessler (2016), which explores the "failure of failure," is to understand how knowledge and fields of study are co-constituted. Failure is conceptualized as a concept, as opposed to a result. The focus of the study of failure is on "its use, rather than on a definition," and an application to international political economy yields insights that stimulate further research (Kessler 2016: 366).

Figure 2.1 conveys the four perspectives on progress—neopositivism, scientific realism, analyticism, and reflexivity—in a visual form, to bring out properties implicit in the presentation so far on an individual basis.[9] The spatial

---

[8] Additional examples of reflexivity include Basu (2013) on the emancipatory potential in feminist security studies; Tickner (2013) on core, periphery, and (neo)imperialist IR; and a wide range of studies in *Millennium*, *International Political Sociology*, and other journals that access critical concepts developed primarily, but not exclusively, among social theorists outside of North America with explicitly normative research priorities.

[9] What follows is inferred from the contents of Jackson (2011, 2016a, 2016b).

representation shows the four types, but not at an equal distance from each other. Note that neopositivism and reflexivity, which hold exactly opposite beliefs along the mind/world and knowledge/observation dimensions, are more distant from each other. Analyticism and scientific realism, which differ along one dimension, are closer together. Thus the shape is a diamond rather than a square that instead would show each type as equidistant from the others.

Interesting to consider is whether either individual academics or works of scholarship are able to span the types from Jackson (2011, 2016a, 2016b) that appear in the diagram. In other words, is it possible to occupy points along the connecting lines of Figure 2.1? Obstacles certainly exist, as Sil and Katzenstein (2010c: 125) observe of a related context: "Trafficking in more than one research tradition typically takes considerable time and effort, requiring scholars not only to read widely but also to engage in shifting 'multilingual' conversations with diverse scholarly communities, each confidently speaking a single theoretical language that its members have been wedded to for their entire careers." Yet observe that five of the six possible connections in Figure 2.1 include a solid line, which is taken to represent a significant possibility for transition between these perspectives. Intuition suggests that the least-difficult movement back and forth would be for analyticism and scientific realism—hence the shortest distance in the figure separates them. The other connections are longer because a shift along the mind/world dimension is deemed more fundamental than with regard to knowledge versus observation. The sixth connection, for reflexivity and neopositivism, is represented with a broken line. This symbolizes the near-impossibility of direct movement back and forth between these belief systems because neopositivism and reflexivity stand apart along both dimensions. While the preceding points are speculative, the observations seem accurate in an approximate way with regard to the sociology of knowledge in IR.

While it is beyond the scope of the present study to pursue all cases in detail, instances of IR scholars spanning the types are not difficult to find. This possibility is acknowledged by Jackson (2016b: 230 n. 23).[10] For example, analyticism comes through in various studies from Starr and collaborators (Most and Starr 2015 [1989]; Friedman and Starr 1997), within which opportunity and willingness are central concepts. The analyticist designation comes from the strongly perception-based nature of willingness within that framework for explaining actions. Other works from Starr and coauthors (Starr 2002a, 2002b, 2005), however, reflect scientific realism as it plays a qualifying role regarding neopositivism. Unobservables are deemed essential with regard to complex concepts that can be conceptualized, measured, and operationalized through positing how the world

---

[10] Less likely and perhaps even impossible would be movement of a given study around the options, but that matter is even further afield and will not be take up here.

would function if the concept turned out to be valid. Some unobservables of special note include power, balance of power, foreign policy substitutability, and wealth.

All four of the combinations—neopositivism, critical realism, analyticism, and reflexivity—are regarded by Jackson (2011, 2016a, 2016b) as omnibus and viable options for conduct of research. The position adopted here, however, is more exclusive with regard to applications across the board. This is due to concerns about the logic of confirmation and accurate depiction of scientific inquiry as being consistent with one option more than the others. Two reasons combine to favor scientific realism as the foundation for IR and, by implication, a school of power politics with renewed vitality.[11]

First, consider the logic of confirmation. Subjective interpretation goes against the existence of objective reality. It is not essential to agree that a fully objective reality exists—obviously perceptions matter—only that at least *some* universal principles can be identified to provide an anchor for effective exchange of views. Classic expositions from Arrow (1951b) and Toulmin (1953), which respectively convey outlooks from economics and political science, are valuable here. Scientific knowledge, as Arrow (1951b: 130) observed, "should be interpersonally valid and transmittable and hence expressible in an objective, consistent language." Toulmin (1953: 13, 15) drew attention to what appears to be a challenge to that requirement but, after more thorough consideration, is not. "When a theory is developed," Toulmin (1953: 13) posited, "all kinds of phrases which in ordinary life are devoid of meaning are given a use, many familiar terms acquire fresh meanings, and a variety of new terms is introduced to serve the purposes of the theory." Thus, when adopted, a new theory entails a "*language-shift*, and one can distinguish between an account of the theory in the new terminology—in 'participant's language'—and an account in which the new terminology is not used but described—an account in 'onlooker's language'" (Toulmin 1953: 13). Diverse language thus follows on from innovative theorizing.

However, things still can turn out well from the standpoint of mutual understanding because, although the effort can be quite significant, it is possible to translate from one of these languages into the other (Toulmin 1953: 15). In the context of IR, Snidal and Wendt (2009: 5) observe that "theories sometimes are incompatible in whole or in part—although that still does not mean they cannot speak to each other at least by raising critiques of, and insofar as they share common empirical ground, posing substantive challenges to one another." Even across paradigms it is not impossible for communication, described perhaps as

---

[11] While their names are similar, it is essential to recognize that scientific realism and the realist outlook on international relations are separate from each other: "The former is a school of thought in epistemology; the latter is an approach to international politics" (Mearsheimer and Walt 2013: 450 n. 4; see also Diehl and Wayman 1994: 3; Wight 1996: 291; Gunnell 2011: 1457).

"intellectual arbitrage," to take place (Walt 1998: 43). At the same time, greater effort is required for such conveyance and, over the long term, it may not be sustained.

Without agreement on what has been said, there is nothing to stand in the way of *self-contradiction* in particular. This argument is pursued at greater length in Chapter 4 on the subject of knowledge, but for now it is sufficient to assert that objective thinking (i.e., world-mind dualism) is the wager made here regarding the logic of confirmation.

Second, consider accurate portrayal of research as a reason to favor scientific realism. Concerns in that area decide Jackson's other bet, figuratively speaking, in favor of transfactualism—belief that unobservables can and even must appear in explanations that are convincing. Phenomenalism, which excludes unobservables, legitimately can be held up as an ideal. However, it represents a belief, if acted upon in practice, that unintentionally could stand in the way of a more pragmatic and realistic path toward scientific progress. This conclusion is inexorable because unobservables play a role in every framework of analysis at its outset and then in a lesser way as advancement occurs. A *completely* observable world of cause and effect stands out as a polar point of perfection rather than something that is likely to be reached by research.

It might be said that neopositivism can hold true in a *local* sense—that is, among a limited network of highly confirmed empirical referents. Imagine, for example, variables X, Y, and Z that are familiar within a research community, with consensus on measurements in place for a long time. Research designs restricted to these variables could be described as neopositivist and successful. The addition, however, of W or some other variable that contains uncertainty about measurement would be sufficient to push the analysis into the realm of scientific realism rather than neopositivism.

Aspects of causal mechanisms seem certain to remain unobservable even as technologies reveal more than in the past (George and Bennett quoted in Sil and Katzenstein 2010b: 420). Instead, it makes sense to think of empirical referents as accumulating while, for any given type of theorizing, the journey of research unfolds. Convergence in terms of conceptualization, operationalization, and measurement represents progress, with new abstractions forming along the way as research moves forward. This is a familiar and dynamic process from the real experience of research in any would-be science.

Take, for example, perhaps the two most famous concepts from respective academic disciplines: (a) gravity in physics and (b) power in political science and IR. Each entity, in principle, is unobservable. Elaboration of these concepts will be pursued in turn.

Gravity, to this day, remains unseen—but neither is its existence denied. Over the course of centuries, the effects attributed to gravity have been observed enough to obtain high credibility. In one defense of scientific realism, gravity is noted as "an unobservable mechanism that is central to our understanding of the universe" (Mearsheimer and Walt 2013: 433). Universal gravitation is a concept that gained traction among scientists over time, even while unobservable, because theorizing associated with it worked in an uncanny way when put to the test. As experimental research accumulated over centuries, gravity increasingly became associated with empirical reality.

For political science and IR, power is the most time-honored among unobservable entities that are placed within the theories. While the concept long precedes Dahl (1957), his highly influential exposition stimulated rigorous thinking that articulates power in relational terms. Power is the ability of Actor A to get Actor B to do something that Actor A wants and that Actor B would be unlikely to do otherwise (Dahl 1957). Definitions in IR converged around this concept formation in the years that followed. For example, in a prominent realist exposition, Aron (1966: 47) defined power as "the capacity of a political unit to impose its will upon other units." Moreover, efforts to measure power for states across multiple dimensions, which ensued from the behavioral revolution onward, attempted to identify metrics that would permit one actor to influence the policies of another. This work built on elements of national power identified by Morgenthau (1959 [1948]) in qualitative terms. Sample components of such indices include GNP, military spending, population, and other traits likely to translate well into power at an operational level—that is, exerting influence through whatever means (Small and Singer 1982).

Components that help to explain conversion of potential to operational power continue to evolve at an empirical level. For example, wars in which a state with seemingly greater material power ends up losing can reveal previously hidden dimensions of capability. Unsuccessful wars fought by the United States in Vietnam and Iraq, in particular, establish the importance that psychological and political factors can possess in comparison to material capability in deciding the issue (Lebovic 2010). These events also reveal limitations that exist for use of certain kinds of capabilities, such as nuclear weapons.

Moreover, in the era of high technology, components of capability continue to evolve. Along with more long-standing metrics of power, new indicators, such as intellectual capital, educational systems, and others, become relevant (Rosecrance and Steiner 2010: 362, 363). Thus Dahl's version of power as a concept plays an ongoing role in stimulating empirical research about any number of subjects in IR, with deterrence as just one obvious example.[12]

---

[12] Realism tends to focus on material aspects of power, such as military capabilities or what can be converted into them. Among recent alternative visions of power with an ideational emphasis, see Barnett and Duvall (2005), Krebs and Jackson (2007), and Rubin (2014).

What does realism look like in the context of the respective wagers from Jackson (2011, 2016a, 2016b)? Clear positions exist. It is impossible to find anything in power politics, from classical realism to the present, that is grounded either in reflexivity or in neopositivism. Realists instead engage in heated debates with adherents of those positions. Reflexivists find realism off-putting from a normative point of view. Realists see their mission as fundamentally different from what postmodernism and some variants of constructivism emphasize (Ashley 1984; Gilpin 1984). In a word, realists seek explanations for how and why conflicts occur. At the other extreme, realists reject the hypothesis-testing agenda that is identified quite directly with neopositivism (Mearsheimer and Walt 2013). Perhaps a more nuanced position—notably, skepticism about statistical methods—would describe realists in general. To the extent that scholarship in power politics offers any explicit endorsement of a Jackson-style wager, the answer is scientific realism (Mearsheimer and Walt 2013: 432).

None of the preceding arguments in favor of scientific realism is meant to imply that work based in analyticism and reflexivity lacks intellectual worth. The conclusion instead is that such approaches possess value in terms of the logic of discovery rather than that of confirmation. Creative, normatively oriented analysis of international relations should not be discouraged but rather respected within the realm of political theory rather than a full-fledged science of IR. This proposed division of labor is in line with sentiments expressed long ago by Morgenthau (1964: 118)—often cited as an archetypal realist without interest in morality—who saw international relations as "something to be understood" and even "changed beyond the present limits of its political structure and organization." Thus analyticism and reflexivity might be expected to fit in more with the latter part of that statement, with its emphasis on imagination and change, and focus more effectively on the logic of discovery rather than confirmation.

Prominent realist expositions are in line with scientific realism. Human nature, featured in Morgenthau (1959 [1948]) and other classical realist studies, certainly qualifies as unobservable. So, too, does structure in later holistic versions of realism, such as Waltz (1979). Moreover, these studies refer to longstanding truths about world politics and clearly, if not explicitly, endorse the existence of objective reality.

With wagers regarding the philosophy of inquiry decided—and the reasons elaborated in subsequent chapters—the bet is placed upon scientific realism as the foundation for realism in IR. This is the perspective that combines world-mind dualism with transfactualism as a foundation for research (Gunnell 2011: 1448). Scientific realists therefore "maintain that theories make genuine claims about real-world existence" (Chernoff 2014: 32). With a touch of irony, given the controversy about IR's scientific status, this assertion could be made just as easily about a discipline such as physics or chemistry. Note that mathematics, which consists of abstract characters and equations, plays an essential role throughout the natural sciences.

Creation of a metatheory based upon scientific realism does not preclude development of alternatives corresponding to other basic visions. If anything, the work carried out toward that end is intended to encourage such efforts within IR—to provide the discipline with metatheoretical options in place of further debates that lack precision and lead nowhere.[13] The pod of hippopotamuses facing Chapter 1 comes to mind once again. If the goal is to move the figurative hippo pod of IR in a worthwhile direction, it becomes pragmatic to do so from within a scientific realist frame of reference.

A General Perspective, Specific Ideas, and Other Aspects of Progress

With a decision in favor of scientific realism, a question naturally arises: is this general perspective from the philosophy of science consistent with *specific* criteria for research progress identified inductively earlier in this chapter and summarized in Table 2.1? No problems emerge in responding affirmatively to that question. For the criteria pertaining to characteristics of research, the focus on identification of causal mechanisms is at the very center of a scientific realist point of view. Rigor and falsifiability, along with comprehensiveness—the other criteria regarding characteristics of investigation—are consistent with scientific realism. With regard to results from research, range of application and predictive value are not problematic, either. Finally, public exchange of views is an essential condition for all scientific inquiry.

Agreement is in place with regard to the meaning of progress in an inclusive sense. The survey from earlier in this chapter assembled specific ideas from the literature of IR about progress, with the recent collaborative effort from Freyberg-Inan, Harrison, and James (2017a, 2017b) as the anchor point for comparison. On the one hand, this exercise had an inductive and sociological makeup and identified a set of criteria about characteristics and results associated with scientific advancement. For example, identifying causal mechanisms (a characteristic) would be anticipated to lead toward predictive value (a result). On the other hand, a deductive and rationalist analysis of overarching perspectives about knowledge in a preceding section of this chapter settled on scientific realism as the appropriate choice for IR in general and the realist school of thought

---

[13] Interesting to note, however, is the explicit emphasis that scientific realism places on the search for metatheory (Gunnell 2011: 1469).

in particular. When put together, specific criteria from scholarship in IR are in line with scientific realism as an overall point of view on the subject of progress.

Among scholars of IR, advancement for research is identified as a process that converts characteristics into results. Causal mechanisms, rigor and falsifiability, and comprehensiveness are favorable characteristics for research, while range of explanation, predictive value, and public exchange of views constitute desirable aspects of results. The sets of criteria for characteristics and results are consistent with scientific realism as an overall point of view. Scientific realism also envisions (a) combination of (un)observables in theorizing and (b) gradual conversion into knowledge with an empirical basis. The process, envisioned already in terms of characteristics and results, is one that moves forward but without belief in some kind of ultimate truth. From the standpoint of scientific realism, there is no "end of history" or "end of theory and research." This is why neopositivism, for which the world is empirical and fully comprehensible, is regarded as an idealization rather than an accurate portrayal of what ultimately can be achieved in IR.

For an illustration of the observation just made, consider the complicated story with regard to balance of power from within the domain of realism. Both classical realists and those from entirely outside of power politics find the use of this term to be multifaceted and inconsistent. From a vantage point within classical realism, Claude (1962: 53) noted "some confusion as to whether Morgenthau believes that war is a phenomenon incident to the operation of the balance system, or an evil toward the suppression of which the system is supposed to contribute." Zinnes (1967), from outside of a realist perspective, identified multiple and not entirely consistent meanings for balance of power. Many years later, Vasquez (2003b: 92) observes that "what is and is not an instance of balancing must be delimited before conducting a test" and, in operational terms, claims that "resisting an open attack or invasion is not a valid indicator of balancing." Quite recently, a realist exposition confirmed the relevance of ongoing critiques when describing balance of power as a concept with "remarkable ambiguity" (Schweller 2018: 145). Balance of power therefore persists as a concept that defies the neopositivist sense of a fully empirical world.

Research, of course, continues. Thus the possibility of identifying a logically consistent set of meanings for balance of power that, in turn, would provide the foundation for effective research remains in place. Consider, for instance, an effort by Elman (2003: 9) to identify rigorous categories for balance of power based on outcome (intentional versus inevitable) and the dependent variable of interest (equilibrium in the system or countervailing state behavior). The resulting set of four categories provides the basis for more effective debate in the future among realists about the balance of power as a multifaceted concept.

Summing Up

Progress for IR is identified in two ways. One approach focuses on individual criteria for advancement, which are classified easily into characteristics and results. The other way, which looks at more comprehensive efforts to assess progress, decides in favor of a scientific realist point of view. As it turns out, the inductively identified scientific criteria for characteristics and results from research and the overarching and deductively based perspective of scientific realism are consistent with each other. Each is in line with a pathway toward the growth of knowledge through explanation based on causal mechanisms—the underlying meaning of scientific progress.

None of this is meant to deny the existence of competing, even inimical, points of view. The language of Jackson (2011, 2016a, 2016b), which sees positions on the philosophy of science as respective wagers, once again is helpful. The bet here is on scientific realism, an approach that already features enthusiastic advocates: "When stripped of false and misleading philosophies of science the social sciences could follow the lead of the natural sciences and become relentlessly realist" (Wight 2016: 33). The scientific realist wager is in line with an inclusive point of view regarding the logic of discovery, while strict about the logic of confirmation. Scientific realism also is more consistent, as opposed to other overarching perspectives, with IR as a discipline that includes an important role for unobservables throughout its history. In sum, while other wagers certainly can and will be made for IR, the present study is founded upon scientific realism because existing evidence in general, along with the characteristics of IR in particular, argues strongly in favor of this option among overarching perspectives.

Traits of IR, through a process of elimination, lead toward a priority on scientific realism and away from other options as, to borrow again the language of Jackson (2016a), the best wager. New people, ideas, and inventions come into the world as a steady stream. This process is comprehensible in and of itself but does not bode well for neopositivism in the larger sense. Will any given theory that exists now be able to account, without modification, for changes to come? An answer of yes would seem wildly optimistic. Thus scientific realism, with its capacity for unobservables in theorizing, is the more pragmatic choice in comparison to neopositivism. In addition, scientific realism is a better wager than either analyticism or reflexivity, which are singular with regard to the mind and world in connection to each other. The reason to prefer scientific realism is that the alternative—subjectivity (i.e., world-mind monism, in terms of either an individual or a culture)—is inherently self-limiting in light of the logic of confirmation. Without agreement on some degree of objective reality, what is the basis for supporting one set of ideas over another? Thus scientific realism emerges as the best wager, across the board, with regard to progress. It therefore should be adopted as the philosophical foundation for realist research in IR.

Part II of this volume turns to development of a metatheory of progress. Components of a metatheory, which entail knowledge, units, and methods, are introduced in Chapter 3. Each of these components, in turn, includes a set of elements. Chapters 4–6 introduce the elements of each component—knowledge, units, and methods, respectively—in greater detail. Chapter 7 then combines the elements from across the components into a working metatheory of progress. This sets the stage for application of the metatheory to realism that begins with Chapter 8 in Part III.

PART II
CREATING A METATHEORY OF PROGRESS FOR INTERNATIONAL RELATIONS

Part II of this volume will create a metatheory of progress that is intended for application to realism in particular and IR in general. Work on the metatheory is carried out in Chapters 3–7, which follow this overview. In line with the forthcoming model of cognition, the summary that precedes Part II, along with parallel expositions for Parts III through V, is intended to facilitate the grasp of a range of new and renovated concepts and arguments along the way.

Chapter 3 provides an overview of the three essential components for a metatheory of scientific progress—knowledge, units, and methods. These components refer, respectively, to epistemology, ontology, and methodology—long-standing concepts within philosophy. Given the complexity of elements within each component of the metatheory, the overview from Chapter 3 is reproduced here in abbreviated form, followed by outlines of the separate chapters devoted to knowledge, units, and methods in turn (i.e., Chapters 4 through 6).

Knowledge encompasses three elements (introduced at length in Chapter 4): (1) scientific realism, (2) analytic eclecticism, and (3) a model of cognition. Scientific realism recognizes that unobservables play essential roles in causal explanations. Perhaps the most obvious example is gravity within the domain of physics. Analytic eclecticism urges an inclusive approach toward developing such accounts. Rather than working within paradigmatic boundaries, analytic eclecticism endorses a wider range of hypothesizing as the best pathway to academic *and* policy relevance. An eclectic explanation could include, for instance, ideas associated with realism and other schools of thought, along with stand-alone hypotheses. A model of cognition emphasizes a *visual* turn for IR as a natural byproduct of its vast accumulation of theorizing and research findings. The shift refers specifically to graphic display of cause-and-effect relations from a putative explanation, as opposed to use of words alone. Somewhat familiar-looking box-and-arrow diagrams are to be implemented; however, importantly, each figure is created under formatting rules that facilitate comparative analysis and long-standing value as a reference.

Units of analysis identified for the metatheory (covered in detail by Chapter 5) are (1) rational actors and (2) systems of explanation. Instrumental rationality provides the *baseline* of expectations for human behavior. This type of approach from rational choice expects goal-directed action as opposed to representing a normative judgment regarding the ends pursued. A clear example of the difference is Stalinist totalitarianism. This repressive regime is recalled as one of the most odious of all time. Yet the specific policies associated with that dictatorship, such as extreme censorship and liquidation of political opponents, reflected instrumental rationality in light of the totalitarian goals pursued by Stalin. A system of explanation, the other unit of analysis, refers to how theories and evidence are organized in a coherent whole within a given academic discipline. Well-known instances of systems of explanation, such as paradigms and research programs, are reviewed, and the best features of each then are assembled into a synthesis designated as the research enterprise. The basic dividing line for systems of explanation, at least so far, is emphasis upon deductive versus inductive reasoning. A research enterprise, put forward as the preferred system of explanation, is distinguished through its use of both inductive and deductive logic to identify bodies of scholarship for comparative analysis.

Methods (detailed in Chapter 6) include (1) identification of axioms for a research enterprise, the preferred type of system of explanation, and (2) systemism, a technique for rigorous graphic display of cause and effect. A set of rules is put forward to identify assumptions for a research enterprise. Both (a) deductive and rationalist and (b) inductive and sociological variants are included. Rules of both kinds are needed in order to designate a research enterprise in a way that is rigorous but also legitimate in the eyes of its adherents. Systemism, a graphic approach toward depicting theories in terms of causal mechanisms, implements the visual turn noted above. A systemist approach emphasizes graphic presentation of cause and effect as identified within and across levels of analysis in a social system, along with connections to its environment. For example, the Caribbean could be the system of interest, with the rest of the world designated as its environment. Levels of analysis for the Caribbean could be defined as corresponding to interactions (a) within and (b) between and among its states and other actors, along with connections to and from the international system as the environment. Systemism emphasizes completeness and clarity in depicting cause and effect to form an explanation for war, trade, or any other subject of interest within IR.

Chapter 4 focuses on the three elements of knowledge—scientific realism, analytic eclecticism, and a model of cognition—in greater depth.

First, scientific realism is adopted to provide a foundation in the philosophy of science. Scientific realism incorporates both observables and unobservables into the research process. In that sense, it departs from neopositivism, which demands that all concepts refer directly to something that can be detected with the senses. A theory is evaluated in terms of its performance in accounting for what is observed. If explanations accumulate and become convincing, unobservables gain empirical meaning and obtain credibility. If not, the theory loses traction and attention turns to replacement. A classic case from the natural sciences is the fate of phlogiston theory, superseded by the modern chemistry of Lavoisier, who accounted for combustion through experiments that identified oxygen and hydrogen in 1778 and 1783, respectively. As a possibly amusing aside, critics inspired by constructivism might claim that realist ontology today looks about as convincing as phlogiston theory after Lavoisier's experiments.

Second, the epistemology also includes analytic eclecticism, which calls for combined efforts in research beyond paradigms. Analytic eclecticism is an intellectual position that can be adopted "when pursuing research that engages, but does not fit neatly within, established research traditions in a given discipline or field" (Sil and Katzenstein 2010b: 412). In IR today, analytic eclecticism could mean hybrid theorizing that involves ideas from varieties of realism, neoliberal institutionalism, the English school, and other designated approaches.[1]

Third, and perhaps most far reaching beyond the boundaries of IR, a model of cognition is developed. The model, which emphasizes challenges to comprehension resulting from the vastness of IR, advocates graphic representation of theorizing to enhance communication. Four types of relational reasoning—analogy, anomaly, antinomy, and antithesis—are put forward to clarify the further combination of verbal and visual expositions. The size-related problem becomes more acute with the passing of time, as books and articles continue to accumulate at a dizzying pace and defy efforts toward integration that are restricted to words alone. Consider, for example, proliferation of journals as an indicator of internal complexity for IR. A doctoral student preparing for comprehensive exams 50 years ago might have consulted *World Politics*, *Background* (the precursor to

---

[1] A wide range of paradigmatic entities exist in IR, and it is beyond the scope of this study to introduce anything other than realism at length. The English school is a way of thinking related to realism but with an emphasis on the role of international society in limiting power politics, while neoliberal institutionalism focuses on international organizations in much the same way. These and other encompassing viewpoints on IR are summarized for a general audience in Ruane and James (2012). Note that constructivism, which is regarded as a method rather than a paradigm, therefore does not appear on the list but instead receives separate consideration in a different context later on. Views on the nature of constructivism are diverse; to cite a few examples, it is designated as an ontology (Ripsman, Taliaferro, and Lobell 2016: 157), a general analytic perspective (Bertucci, Hayes, and James 2018a: 3), a theoretical approach (Bertucci, Hayes, and James 2018b: 244), a method, epistemology, social theory, ontology, or politics (Sjoberg and Barkin 2018: 233), and a process within distinct national and academic contexts of IR (McCourt 2018: 34).

International Studies Quarterly), and a few major journals from political science. While still worthwhile, these outlets fall far short of spanning the discipline of IR today.

Units are conveyed in detail in Chapter 5. Two units are included. The first concerns rationality, understood in the instrumental rather than normative sense. Actors within the metatheory are assumed to follow self-interest, that is, actions reflect instrumental rationality. This is in contrast to normative rationality, which would assess behavior on the basis of a moral standard. For example, collective loss to humanity from destruction of the environment could be described as irrational in a normative sense, even if many individual actions with that effect make sense at the time to those concerned.[2] Ongoing destruction of the Amazon rainforest—horrendous for humanity in an overall sense but expedient among those engaged in "slash and burn" agriculture—is an example that distinguishes normative from instrumental rationality. The second type of unit is the system of explanation, which refers to encompassing entities such as paradigms or research programs that provide an organizing principle for a given discipline. After a review of existing options regarding systems of explanation, a synthesis is developed: the research enterprise. The concept of a research enterprise brings together the best aspects of (i) inductive and sociological and (ii) deductive and rationalist predecessors among systems of explanation. For example, emphasis on rigor and falsification from Popper (2002 [1959]) and Lakatos (1970) through the concepts, respectively, of (a) methodology of falsification and (b) research program, are balanced with (c) a sociological outlook introduced by Kuhn via the idea of a paradigm (1970 [1962]) and (d) elaboration in Laudan (1977) with the research tradition as a frame of reference. Creation of the research enterprise as an amalgam of good, practical features from systems of explanation that have found significant application in IR reflects the commitment to analytic eclecticism that will be explained in further detail during Chapter 4.

Chapter 6 presents the two methods—identification of axioms for a research enterprise and systemism—entailed within the metatheory. The first of these methods focuses on how assumptions are designated to create the foundation for a given research enterprise within IR. Axioms are selected through a process that includes deductive and inductive reasoning. Examples of criteria for status as an axiom include logical consistency with other assumptions (deductively derived) and identification obtained from those outside of the research enterprise (inductively derived). In this way, rigorous standards for designating assumptions are combined with a realistic description of how members of a research community

---

[2] The classic exposition on how such a destructive process might occur appears in Hardin (1968), which introduces the tragedy of the commons as an overarching account; Ostrom (1990) offers a compelling solution that emphasizes the role of institutions.

see themselves. The other method introduced in Chapter 6, systemism, is a visual technique for conveying theories in a way that facilitates comparison and criticism. The systemist approach originates from within the philosophy of inquiry, brought into existence as a byproduct of reductionism and holism as predominant yet ultimately unsatisfactory regimes for theory construction throughout the social sciences (Bunge 1996). Systemism emphasizes completeness and logical consistency regarding cause and effect within and across levels of analysis, along with recognition of how a system and its environment are linked to each other. The chapter finishes up with an introduction to Systemist International Relations (SIR), which includes a method for graphic portrayal of expositions on an individual basis and in combination with each other.

Chapter 7 combines elements from the components covered in Chapters 4–6—knowledge (scientific realism, analytic eclecticism, and a model of cognition), units (rational choice and systems of explanation), and methods (identification of an axiomatic basis for research enterprise and systemism)—into a metatheory of scientific progress. The metatheory, which includes a visual turn, is regarded as optimal for growth of knowledge creation given the characteristics of IR as a discipline.

3
Introducing Components
Knowledge, Units, and Methods

What Do We Want?

Progress, in a word, is what the field of IR is after. How can realists obtain it? In its most basic form, progress refers to growth of knowledge. Chapter 2 worked through specific ideas and overarching perspectives on the meaning of progress and thereby set the stage for creation of a metatheory that can be applied to realism and beyond.

Among general outlooks, scientific realism emerged as the philosophical position with the best intrinsic opportunity to satisfy specific criteria about how to achieve advancement. Scientific realism asserts that objective reality exists, but convincing explanations will entail unobservables. Specific criteria for scientific progress, identified in two stages during Chapter 2, focus on characteristics and results of research and turn out to be compatible with scientific realism. A sociological and quite openly inductive first stage for designating specific criteria to discern scientific progress assembled ideas expressed among the community of scholars in IR. A second stage of work, deductive and rationalist in nature, concentrated on logical consistency among the criteria that had been identified for characteristics and results of research. Characteristics include identification of causal mechanisms, rigor and falsifiability, and comprehensiveness. Range of explanation, predictive value, and public exchange of views are the results hoped for from research, with some feedback via dialogue into the characteristics. Taken together, (a) specific criteria for characteristics and results and (b) scientific realism as an overarching perspective are consistent with each other in the quest for progress.

With scientific advancement as the objective, a metatheory of how to achieve it becomes the priority. In the quest for progress, "Metatheoretic choice *necessarily predates* other considerations" (Elman 2003: 4; see also Chernoff 2013: 359, 360, 2014: 24). This assertion is true for IR in particular and academic disciplines in general. Bennett (2013: 462) sums up the situation, with ongoing paradigm-based wars in IR as "another manifestation of out-of-date and problematic views on the philosophy of science." According to Checkel (2010: 26), those who build bridges "need to get real about philosophy, developing a meta-theoretical foundation for their plural and synthetic research efforts." Greater engagement would be worthwhile for the study of, respectively, metatheory and substantive matters within IR (Chernoff 2013: 359–360). Rather than a detour into abstractions, reflections on metatheory should be carried out with the objective of practical application in mind.

Along the path to success, bringing metatheory out into the open for discussion is an important step. "Every research program," asserts MacDonald (2003: 563), "requires a clear, coherent epistemological foundation that establishes the standards for testing and evaluating particular theories and for judging between competing theoretical paradigms." Chernoff (2013: 347) further observes that, while philosophical axioms do not need extensive treatment from IR scholars, "they should understand what those assumptions are, what the alternative positions are, and the strengths and weaknesses of those assumptions." Foundational discussions form "a proper and valuable part of the study of IR" (Chernoff 2009: 476; see also Chernoff 2013: 359–360). The alternative is to proceed without self-awareness and trust to fortune that things will turn out well for the discipline. Foundational work of this kind therefore is essential for a reinvigorated realism in IR.

Metatheoretical points of view in practice, however, tend either to remain implicit or to take the form of largely metaphorical rather than operational references. Assertions about the desirability of expanding empirical content or endorsement of other conceptual apparatus from Lakatos (1970)—unaccompanied by operationalization—are common in discussions of metatheory. This state of affairs is unsatisfactory and goes a long way toward explaining debates in IR over the merits of realism in particular and ostensible paradigms in general.

Consider, for example, arguments in IR about scientific status for one type of research versus another. Jackson (2016b: 210) argues that science "ought to stop functioning as a trump-card in our internecine debates, and perhaps we as a field can stop worrying so much about the ultimate status of our knowledge-claims and get on with our primary task of producing knowledge about world politics." This will require, however, a metatheory that is *operational and visual*, as opposed to what exists now. Only through such means can debates become more productive because words in general and metaphors in particular have proven insufficient to produce convergence.

Others have lamented the lack of a metatheory in various contexts. For example, Elman and Vasquez (2003: 282 [Elman]) assert that, "if IR theorists are going to be paradigmatists, any well-specified metatheory is to be preferred to none."[1] While convincing as far as it goes, a more expansive claim is viable.

---

[1] This source takes the form of a dialogue between the coauthors. In each instance, the author noted in brackets is the one to whom a particular statement should be attributed. A few other sources with that property are cited in the same way.

Even nonparadigmatically oriented scholars of IR must ground their work in a metatheory. Otherwise, research runs the risk of chaos in the worst sense—a Tower of Babel that is ruled out, a priori, from contending for status as a collectively convincing account of the subject matter. Wivel (2005: 357), to cite one example, draws attention to this type of danger in the context of developing a realist approach to foreign policy; it is deemed essential to put together structural and other factors in order to avert creation of a set of unintegrated arguments. In sum, metatheory is essential regardless of the mechanisms involved in carrying out subsequent research.

Metatheory also may be able to help with another problem in IR. This is a tendency to follow "fads and fashions" (Knutsen 2016: 3). This observation is not meant to denigrate any particular line of research, only to note that the division of labor at times may be inefficient because of a desire to "get in on something while it is hot." Development and implementation of a rigorous yet inclusive metatheory should help to set the agenda for research in IR in a way that is more forward-looking than before. In particular, a metatheory could guide realism—already a vast and even incoherent body of work—in designation of priorities that enhance its degree of integration and ongoing quest for scientific progress.

This chapter will identify components of a metatheory of progress. A *component* is defined as something that is essential for a metatheory to function. Thus knowledge, units, and methods are individually necessary and collectively sufficient to produce a working metatheory. How things are to be known, along with the subject matter for study and means toward investigation of it, combine to set a metatheory in motion. *Elements* are specific entities that collectively make up a component. For example, the elements of the method component of the metatheory include both rationality and a set of instructions for how to identify the axioms underlying a set of theories taken to be related to one another.

Thus the components of the metatheory, developed in sequence, are knowledge, units, and methods. Elements of the respective components are introduced here and then presented in much greater detail throughout Chapters 4–6. The metatheory, fully articulated in Chapter 7 and in line with an overarching pragmatic approach, is intended to facilitate progress in IR.

Application of the metatheory to the corpus of realist work on the causes of war, as it has developed since World War II, will occur in Part IV of this volume. The focus on realism in the post-1945 era is a product of multiple considerations, with two sufficient to reiterate for present purposes. One is that realism emerged as the reigning school of thought about international relations around the end of World War II. Academic and policy-related studies that emphasized power politics began to appear and have a self-reinforcing effect over time (Carr 1939; Morgenthau 1946, 1959 [1948]). The other consideration is that it is a prohibitively large venture for any single book to take on the vastness of realism from antiquity onward. Even a restriction to the era after World War II includes a wide range of studies on the causes of war that identify with the realist point of view. Thus, to prepare more effectively for the stage of evaluation, organization of theories into categories is carried out in Chapter 9 in Part III.

This chapter is completed in three further sections. The second section further identifies essential components of a metatheory: knowledge, units, and methods. The third section provides an overview of the elements within each of these components. The fourth and final section reflects on the chapter's accomplishments and leads into detailed presentation of elements within each component, along with their integration to form the metatheory, in Chapters 4–7.

Components of a Metatheory

Three components are essential to a metatheory of progress: knowledge, units, and methods. These components—representing fields known as epistemology, ontology, and methodology—are individually necessary and collectively sufficient to create a metatheory. This is because scientific research in its basic form consists of the quest for *knowledge* through application of *methods* to the study of *units*. Each component of the metatheory is introduced in turn.

Knowledge is a multifaceted concept. An authoritative treatment from the field of educational psychology puts forward the following set of items as representing knowledge: facts, procedures, concepts, strategies, and beliefs (Mayer 2010: 14). This sense of knowledge is in line with scientific realism. Both observables, such as facts, procedures, and strategies, and *un*observables, like concepts and beliefs, appear on the list. Knowledge grows as unobservables (such as beliefs) guide observables (like facts). Theorizing and research move forward, and, as a result, abstract concepts increasingly take on an observable form.

For IR the list would not necessarily be identical, but analogous, to that of educational psychology in the sense of including unobservables and empirical referents. Concepts such as power, state, utility, alliance, and many others play roles in IR theories of various kinds. Abstractions become more empirically grounded over time, with alliances as one example of elaboration of a concept through the study of treaties and compilation of data from them (Gibler 2009; Leeds 2017). A sign of difficulty for an area of research, with balance of power as discussed in the preceding chapters serving as one example, is when empirical referents proliferate and even diverge over time. This type of problem is especially worrisome for realism, a long-standing school of thought with many active adherents.

Units drive action. The conventional meaning in IR would be that states are primary units that carry out foreign policy and that nonstate actors (e.g., multinational corporations, international organizations, and transnational insurgencies) are secondary units of varying importance within a given frame of reference. Activity takes place in both observable and unobservable domains. Any ontology must specify what is expected from individuals, who can be seen going about their activities in the empirical world. At the same time, from a scientific realist point of view, unobservables must be theorized as well. As research accumulates, unobservables are confirmed, modified, or discarded as a result of becoming more or less credible over time.

Within a conventional exposition of IR as it developed over the years since World War II, units correspond with three levels of analysis: system, state, and individual (Waltz 1959). Unobservables play a role in theorizing about units at all levels. At the system level, for example, consider polarity and norms—key concepts that appear in a wide range of theories from IR.

With regard to polarity, the initial argument over its implications for stability took an abstract form but evolved into an empirically grounded debate, most directly about international systems with bipolar versus multipolar configurations (Waltz 1964; Deutsch and Singer 1964). The polarity debate also stimulated new concept formation and hypotheses about the distribution of capabilities among states and its connection with conflict processes (Niou, Ordeshook, and Rose 1989; James 2002b).[2] For example, Brecher, James, and Wilkenfeld (1990) elaborated on the standard categories of polarity, with polycentrism—a hybrid with two centers of power but a greater number of independent centers of decision—as an example found for a period after the peak of the Cold War. Consider, for example, the nonaligned-states movement, with leadership from states such as India and Ghana eschewing allegiance with the blocs led by the United States and USSR, respectively.

Norms operate in the ideational world and are unobservable within international relations. Precise measurement therefore proves to be elusive. Empirical referents accumulate, however, as constructivist scholars in particular assess the possible impact of norms on outcomes in various policy areas. A prominent example is the process leading up to the international land mines treaty (Finnemore 2003).

Unobservables factor into the process of concept formation with regard to organizing principles for IR, such as a paradigm or research program. The concept of a paradigm, which Kuhn (1970 [1962]) created without intending any application to the social sciences, entered academe in an amorphous state. With time and building interest, IR scholars linked the concept of a paradigm to realism, followed by liberalism, and then a host of other entities (Ruane and James

---

[2] The debate over polarity has unfolded over many years; an authoritative list of citations appears in Elman and Jensen (2014: 6).

2012). The concept of a research program, which Lakatos (1970) put forward in much greater detail than Kuhn vis-à-vis paradigms, also found its way into the vernacular of IR. A research program consists of a *series* of theories that is assessed on the basis of its trend line—either success in terms of expanding empirical content or failure to move in that direction. The quite abstract and even dense exposition from Lakatos (1970) on research progress eventually generated what may be the greatest number of references to any concept that IR ever borrowed from the philosophy of science. As will become apparent, however, efforts to identify and assess research programs within IR have remained in pre-operational form.

Consider the volume from Elman and Elman (2003b), which brought together a team of scholars and encompassed a number of research programs. This collaborative effort still stands as the most expansive and comparative connection of the framework from Lakatos (1970) to IR. However, as will become apparent as this book unfolds, nothing of the concept formation for knowledge in IR—paradigm, research program, or other options covered later—exists in a fully functional condition. Instead, assertions tend to be normative and lacking in specificity when it comes to applying frames of reference borrowed from the philosophy of inquiry to the domain of IR. The fact that all of the research programs from IR included in Elman and Elman (2003b) are pronounced as progressive should give pause with regard to the ability of the Lakatosian apparatus, such as empirical content, to offer an *operational* sense of performance.

Methods are linked to elements of both units and knowledge. A metatheory of progress requires a methodology to operate. As methods are applied to the study of units, knowledge accumulates and progress is achieved. When that process is stalled, interest turns toward reconsideration and even replacement of a metatheory.

This exposition is *not* about long-standing debates regarding qualitative versus quantitative methods. Instead, the argument made here is at a truly meta level. A method is needed to identify assumptions for any given family of theories—an axiomatic basis that is not open to question in a direct sense but instead gains or loses credibility on the basis of research that tests propositions. Thus a language is required for conveyance of causal mechanisms derived from combinations of axioms, that is, statements of the form "x causes y" or "x → y."[3] These propositions combine to form theories.

---

[3] This formulation goes beyond the founding principles from Hume, which focused in a more isolated way on whether change in one variable affected the probability of change in another. Chapter 6 will pursue the subject of causal mechanisms at some length.

This point regarding a meta-level argument comes through clearly when formal modeling, for instance, is offered as a possible solution to conveying ideas from IR more effectively. Communication based on mathematics, all other things being equal, certainly enhances rigor. Formal models, however, cannot provide an answer to the question of how to convey theories for purposes of comparison regarding cause and effect in a "user friendly" way. Formal models depict strategic interaction between and among actors, with sequential form game theory and attendant equilibria concepts resulting in a very successful approach. Barriers to entry for this type of research, however, are formidable; a reasonably good command of mathematics is required at the very least. The focus here instead is on communication of causal mechanisms through a visual means that entails minimal start-up costs. The recommended graphic method is systemism—introduced briefly through an example in Chapter 1 and at somewhat greater length below, with a detailed presentation forthcoming in Chapter 6 on methods.

Knowledge, units, and methods are individually necessary and collectively sufficient for a metatheory. The goal of science is explanation. It therefore is essential to specify how something is known, along with subject matter and the approach to gathering information about it. Within each component of the metatheory are elements. The elements within respective components of the metatheory will be introduced in turn.

Table 3.1 displays the set of elements for each component of the proposed metatheory of progress for IR. The table is in line with a graphic turn in terms of both explanation and understanding as priorities for IR (Hollis and Smith 1992). The priority on explanation as the principal goal of a science already has been made clear. However, understanding—defined briefly as comprehending the world from the standpoint of those who are actors within it—also is a valuable pursuit. Identified by Bleiker (2018a: 4; see also 2018b: 4), a visual turn in this sense emphasizes the value of aesthetics in obtaining greater understanding of IR: "not only to practices of art—from painting to music, poetry, photography and film—but also, and above all, to the type of insights and understandings they facilitate." Tufte (2006: 105) adds that "the one deep communality of science and art" is to "show the results of intense seeing." Table 3.1 therefore includes graphics to accompany its neologisms and uses of familiar terms in a new context; these illustrations, as will become apparent after insights from educational psychology appear in Chapter 4, also will assist with retention of respective concepts. The columns of Table 3.1 refer, respectively, to (a) placement of each element within a component of the metatheory of scientific progress, (b) the element itself, (c) a summary of meaning for the element, and (d) an associated visual symbol. The purpose of this overview is to introduce the respective elements in order to facilitate understanding of their eventual assembly into a metatheory of advancement in Chapter 7.

Table 3.1 Elements of a Metatheory for Scientific Progress, Summaries, and Visualizations

Chapter and Component	Element	Summary Meaning	Visual Symbol
Chapter 4, knowledge	Scientific realism	Scientific realism incorporates both observables and unobservables into the research process. A theory is evaluated in terms of its performance in accounting for what is observed. If explanations accumulate and become convincing, unobservables gain empirical meaning and the theory that incorporates them obtains credibility.	Ö
Chapter 4, knowledge	Analytic eclecticism	Analytic eclecticism calls for combined efforts in research beyond paradigms that focus on empirical problem-solving rather than adherence to a specific school of thought. The problem-oriented approach is anticipated to restore policy relevance to IR, which under paradigmatic rule has become arcane and out of touch with practical concerns.	Æ
Chapter 4, knowledge	Model of cognition	The model of cognition emphasizes use of graphic representation for theories. Four kinds of relational reasoning—analogy, antithesis, antinomy, and anomaly—will complement the combination of verbal and visual expositions. These respective measures are intended to counteract the pernicious effects of cognitive overload from a huge and rapidly expanding academic discipline that includes a wide range of terminologies and methods.	X
Chapter 5, units	Instrumental rationality	Instrumental rationality refers to pursuit of perceived self-interest under constraints of time and information. Ordinal rationality, in which beliefs about the best possible choice are adjusted in direction rather than in more exactly mathematical terms, is regarded as a realistic depiction of conventional human behavior.	β
Chapter 5, units	System of explanation; research enterprise	A system of explanation refers to encompassing entities such as paradigms or research programs that provide an organizing principle for a given discipline. The preferred type of system, which combines (a) inductive and sociological and (b) deductive and rationalist criteria, is the research enterprise. Rather than empirical content, a research enterprise is evaluated on the basis of ability to solve empirical problems relative to its degree of complexity.	Σ

Chapter 6, methods	Identification of axioms for a research enterprise	Axioms for a research enterprise are identified on the basic of nine criteria, which fall under (a) inductive and sociological and (b) deductive and rationalist headings, in order to provide a foundation that is acceptable to both exponents and those outside of its boundaries. Among the deductive criteria, logical consistency is one. Rejection of an assumption by a significant proportion of adherents to a school of thought is one of the inductive criteria. ↑
Chapter 6, methods	Systemism	Systemism is a perspective on theorizing that emphasizes completeness across levels of analysis, along with visual representation of cause-and-effect relations, to facilitate communication and scientific advancement. The systemist outlook is an alternative to holist and reductionist models that inappropriately implement a ceteris paribus clause rather than meeting the challenge to provide comprehensive explanations. The systemist method uses diagrams, created with clear formatting rules, to convey theories. ∫

Epistemology for the metatheory is grounded in scientific realism.[4] In philosophical terms, scientific realism holds that a world exists outside the mind.[5] It is associated with the story about Sir Isaac Newton's observing an apple fall straight down to the ground and an associated inference about gravitational force. (No evidence exists that an apple hit him on the head and caused the great scientist to think of gravity, although the anecdote continues to be entertaining centuries later.) Gravity arguably is the most famous unobservable in the history of science. The Cyrillic letter Ö resembles an apple and will serve as a graphic reminder of scientific realism.

Scientific realism entails mind-world dualism, that is, belief in an independent existence for each. In other words, objective reality exists. Theories therefore produce explanations that, as testing accumulates, either become more accepted as knowledge or head toward refutation. Unobservables can play a role in theorizing—a belief that separates scientific realism from neopositivism, with its emphasis on the empirical record above all else. Thus neopositivism emerges as an ideal—a polar point for research at which unobservables no longer are required—instead of an accurate depiction of research on IR at this time or any point in the foreseeable future. In no way does the scientific realist position imply that IR is primitive, with other disciplines inherently regarded as superior. Sustained unobservables from the natural sciences include magnetism and radio waves. A neopositivist world thus stands as an ideal state for scientific inquiry across the board.

Scientific realism—a philosophy of inquiry—holds that "the external world exists independently of our sense experience, ideation, and volition, and that it can be known" (Bunge 1993: 229; see also Gunnell 2011: 1452). A scientific realist accepts the need for unobservables to theorize effectively in a world of incomplete observation. It is not, however, a defeatist perspective. Science marches on, and unobservables come into the empirical world. An exemplar from international relations is the ability of a state to get things done—from a starting point of speculation to eventual explanation based on reproducible evidence. Some states are effective in war, for instance, while others perform poorly. Over the course of history, certain conflicts have produced a "surprise" winner. So is it magic that explains why results do not always reflect prior expectations about a struggle between states?

Initially puzzling war outcomes have become less mysterious over time as the concept of relative political capacity is brought to life through increasingly informative indicators of performance for states. With origins in the study of war

---

[4] The meaning of realism in IR, which is communicated most simply as power politics, is *not* the same as the usage in this context. For further explanation of this difference, see Wight (1996: 291) and Gunnell (2011: 1452, 1457).

[5] Recognition of this point in IR goes back at least to Herz (1951: 7).

(Organski and Kugler 1980), relative political capacity in state-of-the-art form is assessed on the basis of a government's control over its population, notably material extractive capacity (Kugler and Tammen 2012). With relative political capacity added into the equation, both figuratively and literally, previously surprising outcomes from conflict processes become comprehensible. One example is Israel's wartime victories when taking on coalitions of states with a collectively much larger population (Organski and Kugler 1980).

New technologies also assist with unobservables. Consider, for example, the revolution in neuroscience. Previously unobservable processes in the mind can be detected through imaging via use of micromanipulators, oscilloscopes, electrophysiology equipment, and other devices. The digital world promises to create technologies with the ability to move even more unobservables into empirical reality. At the same time, technological advances mean the potential exists for new unobservables to enter into explanations. For example, the field of cybersecurity—perhaps a different name eventually will take hold, but that label will suffice for now—is rising rapidly (Choucri 2012; Valeriano and Maness 2015).

Analytic eclecticism, which combines ideas from across paradigms, accompanies scientific realism as an element of the metatheory's knowledge component. Its visualization, the ligature Æ, also is a full-fledged letter within some Scandinavian languages. This perspective emphasizes diversity in the logic of discovery and eschews boundaries imposed by the paradigms of today. Analytic eclecticism "encourages scholarly practices aimed at generating creative forms of knowledge that engage adherents of different traditions in meaningful conversations about substantive problems in international life" (Katzenstein and Sil 2008: 111). "Meta-theoretical frameworks that accept incommensurability or are unable to outline the conditions of possibility for cross-paradigm conversation," Wight (1996: 314) observes, "must logically presuppose *that they alone hold the truth of the world they have created.*" This single observation is sufficient to create interest in moving beyond strict adherence to paradigms.

Analytic eclecticism is in line with increasing references to the value of bridge-building in IR (Checkel 2010: 5; Haas 2010b: 10). "The distinctiveness of analytic eclecticism," observe Sil and Katzenstein (2010b: 414), "arises from its effort to specify how elements of different causal stories might coexist as part of a more complex argument that bears on problems of interest to both scholars and practitioners." Bridge-building from the standpoint of analytic eclecticism therefore focuses on connection of "different theories in a middle-range sense to make better sense of some analytic puzzle" (Checkel 2010: 11). Sil and Katzenstein (2010c: 110–111) provide further details:

> What we refer to as analytic eclecticism is distinguished by the fact that *features of analyses in theories initially embedded in separate research traditions can*

be separated from their respective foundations, translated meaningfully, and recombined as part of an original permutation of concepts, methods, analytics, and empirics.

Analytic eclecticism is a problem-specific framework that connects normally isolated mechanisms and processes with each other (Sil and Katzenstein 2011: 484; see also Sil and Katzenstein 2010b: 415, 417, 2010c: 111). Such eclecticism, however, does not discard research products linked to existing paradigms but instead engages with them. Sil and Katzenstein (2011: 484; see also Sil and Katzenstein 2010c: 111 and Barkin and Sjoberg 2019: 142–143) observe that analytic eclecticism "requires engaging, not discarding, the research products associated with existing paradigms." Thus analytic eclecticism inherently is pluralistic in its view of research already in place about international relations.

Quite defensible anyway on intellectual grounds of pragmatism, analytic eclecticism becomes especially valuable in light of the current condition and trajectory of IR as a field. Clear changes have taken place in terms of paradigmatic dominance. More specifically, a survey of data-based articles from IR that spans 1995 to 2000 reveals that (a) realism represents less than 22 percent of activity; (b) liberalism covers 39 percent of what is going on; and (c) another 39 percent identify with neither realism nor liberalism (Walker and Morton 2005: 350). Rather than dominance of a paradigm, leaving aside the exact meaning of that term, the new trend might be labeled "theoretical diversity" (Walker and Morton 2005: 353).

While the study from Walker and Morton (2005) focuses on quantitative analysis in particular, it is possible to identify explicit movement away from paradigmatically inspired research in an overall sense as well. Taken from the Teaching, Research and International Policy (TRIP) Project, evidence suggests that "a great deal of the published articles in IR have been non-paradigmatic, in that the authors do not advance or advocate, and are not guided by, realism, liberalism, or Marxism" (Walker 2018: 203). Dissatisfaction with infighting increasingly is the norm and explains an expanding antiparadigmatic mindset. Both realism and constructivism, observes Barkin (2010: 154), "often suffer from a castle syndrome, in which they are seen as paradigms, as exclusive and self-contained research orientations for the study of international relations." This assessment could be offered for other paradigmatic entities as well and argues in favor of efforts to move beyond any number of stalemates in progress.

Relevance and application of research findings to policy also are emphasized by analytic eclecticism. This priority helps to explain movement away from research in IR carried on from within the confines of a paradigm—realism or whatever else. Intuition strongly supports the idea that the logic of discovery should be inclusive rather than exclusive. Insistence upon honoring the assumptions of a particular paradigm could come at the cost of missing important insights with practical application for IR. Put differently, as long as evaluation is rigorous, does the origin of an idea really matter?

Analytic eclecticism is not the same as theoretical synthesis; it does not call for a unified theory of IR (Sil and Katzenstein 2010c: 118). Instead, analytic eclecticism should be regarded as a "bridge-building effort" (Haas 2010b: 10). The focus of analytic eclecticism is on exploring, in combination, causal mechanisms that previously have been investigated in isolation from each other (Sil and Katzenstein 2010d: 23). Thus scope conditions for would-be relationships of cause and effect rise to the top of the priority list for research. Take, for example, the debate over absolute versus relative gains in the context of realism (Grieco 1988; Snidal 1991; Powell 1991). As opposed to arguing that one type will predominate, what about identifying specific conditions for each to take precedence? The initial debate over relative versus absolute gains made some headway on that point, but the issue of scope conditions should have been more of a priority for realism as a whole in subsequent years. In a more general sense, Brooks (1997: 463) adds that realism focuses on competition in world politics, but its adherents so far have "refrained from engaging in intellectual competition with each other regarding their theory's assumptions." The pattern instead looks like an accumulation of theorizing without much concern for achievement of a well-integrated approach.

Last among the elements in the knowledge component of the metatheory is a model of cognition. The model emphasizes graphic conveyance of cause and effect, along with application of four types of relational reasoning—analogy, antithesis, antinomy, and anomaly—to facilitate comprehension and communication in IR. Think of the classic "death by PowerPoint" slide as the antithesis to what is desired via graphic representation. The incomprehensible and awful slide helps us to keep in mind the importance of using visualization to improve, rather than hinder, an already challenging situation for the field of IR. To approximate the murkiness of such an image, the Cyrillic letter X appears to figuratively "cross it out"—a suitable graphic reminder for the model of cognition.

For the model of cognition, the focus is on an ability to process and retain abstract concepts and empirical information. An argument will be made that the long-standing approach to communication in IR, which emphasizes verbal and written debate, is in need of adjustment. Wight (2019: 66) notably observes that there exist "almost as many approaches as there are theorists." A turn toward *diagrammatic* exposition is required in order to facilitate cognition for such a vast field. This position is in line with well-established insights from educational psychology: "When combined, text and graphics can communicate relationships *among* or *between* the informational representations," and a great deal of evidence "indicates text comprehension can be improved through the addition of graphics" (Danielson and Sinatra 2017: 55, 56). In contrast to a language, which must be learned, Bleiker (2018b: 11) observes that "everyone can see and 'read' images, even though we might end up with different interpretations." Thus a visual shift becomes essential in order to make the most of diverse conceptual and substantive material that has accumulated in IR over a long period. Progress otherwise is likely to be impeded.

Even a cursory glance at the volume of writings about realism, through use of an internet search, brings the problem of expansiveness into bold relief. When "realism international relations" is entered into Google, for example, there are approximately 2.21 billion results. The same effort for "realism" produces about 113 million results. Use of additional search engines and combinations of words would raise these numbers to even higher levels. It would take a long time to collate this material, let alone read it, even allowing for the fact that many items would turn out to be irrelevant to realist IR as understood in an academic context.

Insights from research on learning support the idea that more should be done, through visual means, to enhance communication and facilitate mutual understanding in IR. While learning is at least somewhat area-specific, general principles or strategies "can apply within a particular domain" (Mayer 2010: 21). Research from the field of education suggests that a structure for organizing new information is especially helpful to learning (Ambrose et al. 2010: 53). The advantages of graphic presentation for purposes of understanding and retention are consistent with both intuition and research findings.

Research from the natural sciences reveals a relatively high proportion of visual materials. "In modern scientific research," Tufte (2006: 83) observes, "25% of published materials are graphs, tables, diagrams and images; the other 75% are words (in 2,850 articles we randomly sampled from the 10 most-cited scientific journals, 1951–2000)." Even a quick survey is enough to suggest that research in IR does not maintain such an average. Some journals—perhaps those oriented toward quantitative methods that entail graphs and tables to convey data analysis—might rival or even exceed the proportion just noted. However, the dearth of graphic portrayal for *theorizing* virtually guarantees a significantly lower proportion of visual presentations, on the whole, for IR.

One way for IR to respond to insights from learning theory, along with practices from the natural sciences, is with a graphic turn. The saying "A picture is worth a thousand words" comes to mind. While the appropriate ratio can be expected to vary by context, there can be little doubt, based on research in psychology, about the value of graphic presentation as a complement to what appears in words. This assertion becomes more credible when the academic task of a "literature review" is the focal point. *Unlike any other component of a research design, the process of assembling prior studies into an integrated whole lacks a methodological primer.* This gap becomes more troubling with time because research findings accumulate in every area and increasingly challenge the ability of the human mind to synthesize what exists into an integrated sense of the whole. Checkel (2010: 24–25) notes the existence of "proliferating lists" with regard to variables and causal mechanisms. "Unless we have theories to make sense of them," observe Mearsheimer and Walt (2013: 450), "we cannot even keep track of all the hypotheses that scholars keep piling up." Yet even this assertion turns out to be too optimistic. There are many theories, as well, along with vast amount of research findings that reside within IR. The volume of information—theory and evidence, taken together—seems overwhelming as IR enters its second century. All of this points toward visualization of cause and effect as a way to put together information as knowledge and thus more effectively guide future research in IR. If anything, the advice is even more pressing for realism, the most long-standing school of thought in the discipline.

With elements of the knowledge component now introduced, attention turns to units for the metatheory. The ontology will include a commitment to individual rather than collective consciousness. Explication of elements for units of the metatheory therefore begins with the idea of rationality. This is a vision of choice as a product of acting out of perceived self-interest under constraints of time and information. In particular, *ordinal* rationality is regarded as the most realistic sense of what, on average, people exhibit in their behavior. Beliefs and actions are adjusted in the direction of new information, but not in an exact, mathematical, and highly demanding way in terms of cognition. Chancellor Otto von Bismarck, renowned (or perhaps even notorious) for ruthless and highly effective pursuit of Prussian interests, is the graphic reminder of instrumental rationality.[6] The Greek letter beta, β, serves as a graphic reminder of *B*ismarck as the standard bearer for instrumental rationality.

Consider the evolution of rationality as a concept. "Rational actor theory," as Monroe (2001: 152) observes, "originated in the classical microeconomics of Adam Smith. In its purest form, rationality refers to behavior by an individual actor—a person, a firm, or a political entity—designed to further the actor's perceived self-interest, subject to information and opportunity costs." Rational choice today is a concept that has been elaborated significantly since its origins in economics. Instrumental rationality "prescribes weighing costs and benefits of alternative decisions to reach desired outcomes" (Haas 2017: 107). In particular, rational choice is taken to reflect constraints "imposed both by the external situation and by the capacities of the decision-maker" (Monroe 2001: 154; see also Milner 1991: 70). Rationality, in other words, does not imply any unrealistic sense of perfection about *how* choices are made.

---

[6] Rathbun (2019), for example, identifies Bismarck as a memorable exemplar for the practice of rational choice in the history of world leaders.

Instrumental rationality is the operational form of the individual decision-making element. Means rather than ends, in other words, are the focus of rationality as incorporated in the metatheory of progress. It is understood that departures from instrumental rationality occur, but the baseline assumption for individuals remains pursuit of self-interest. Thus, in the world of international relations, the individual acting out of perceived self-interest is the most basic unit of analysis. This position is grounded in, rather than at odds with, psychology—a point established convincingly by Mercer (2005). Rationality demands, for example, an attentive actor (Rathbun 2019). Thus in emotive terms, an individual must care enough about a decision to pay attention to it; otherwise, the apparatus of rational choice becomes irrelevant as outcomes reflect the mindset "Who cares?"

Consistent with instrumental rationality, the other element within the unit component of the metatheory, is the concept of a system of explanation. The Greek letter Σ, coterminous with summation, is an appropriate visual aid in this context. This concept refers to how a network of constructs is combined to describe and evaluate a sector of substantive research within an academic discipline such as IR. The research enterprise, which emerges as the preferred system of explanation, relies upon both (a) inductive and sociological and (b) deductive and rationalist criteria in order to identify respective approaches toward IR that would meet with approval from both those inside and outside of such efforts. A research enterprise is accessed in terms of its ability to solve empirical problems in comparison to its degree of internal complexity.

Most prominent among systems of explanation as applied within IR are the paradigm and research program (Kuhn 1970 [1962]; Lakatos 1970; see also Ball 1976). A paradigm is the set of beliefs and practices that identify, in an inductive and sociological way, a community of researchers within a discipline. A research program, by contrast, designates a series of theories that possess common foundations that can be deduced objectively from outside the boundaries of those carrying out the work. All of these entities, of course, are unobservables. Systems of explanation are assemblies of concepts—"Lego buildings" in the mind.

Consider realism as a system of explanation in IR today. It could be designated through either inductive or deductive means. On the one hand, the concepts associated with realism could be assembled into something through an inductive process. Balance of power, the security dilemma, and other constructs could be put together to tell a realist story about the world. On the other hand, a deductive approach could take the form of designating as realist all theories that are based on a common set of axioms. Given the evolution of realism over the years, the first of these processes would be likely to generate thousands of incoherent pages, while in contrast the second would not have any obvious starting point. Thus there is much to be said for coming up with an operational approach, which includes both deductive and inductive features, to define realism in a way that is acceptable to advocates, critics, and those who are not sure what to make of it.

Taken together, the units of the metatheory include two elements: (a) individuals who act upon instrumental rationality and (b) systems of explanation that convey theory and evidence.[7] The system of explanation that ultimately appears in the metatheory is referred to as a *research enterprise*—a concept that brings together the most practical elements from preceding examples of its kind such as paradigm and research program.

Given its multifaceted composition, a research enterprise thereby reflects an analytic eclecticist approach as well. For example, like a paradigm from Kuhn (1970 [1962]), the foundation of a research enterprise—its axiomatic basis—is identified partially through an inductive survey of literature from a self-identified research community. This process is complemented by deductive reasoning about what should be included among the axioms to facilitate explanation—more in tune with the idea of a research program as put forward by Lakatos (1970). Thus the research enterprise as a "finished product" will be in line with instrumental rationality, the other element within the unit component of the metatheory, because it combines the most effective parts of preceding systems of explanation.

Methods include two elements. One is a set of rules for identifying the axioms of a research enterprise. Axioms are "things that we may accept without proof" (Priest 2017). The rules for designating axioms are enumerated in four stages: the first and fourth are inductive and sociological, with the second and third being deductive and rationalist. For this process of identification, the visualization is an arrow pointing upward (↑). This image connects with *Social Choice and Individual Values*, which conveys the Arrow Impossibility Theorem (Arrow 1951a). This theorem continues to influence the social sciences seven decades later. A few seemingly innocuous criteria, once combined with each other, cannot be satisfied by any method of collective choice. Thus the Arrow Impossibility Theorem combines rigor with relevance to the real world and thereby serves as a role model for processes such as the one implemented here to identify axioms for a research enterprise.

Axioms for a research enterprise are identified in a way that consults the views of those inside its boundaries while also recognizing criteria from outside that are essential to progress. The initial, sociological stage includes a review of academic works that (a) self-identify with a given approach to research and an associated agenda and (b) exist outside of it. For example, neoliberal institutionalist

---

[7] Element (a) applies to social scientists as well as their subject matter—a feature in line with reflexivity as it contributes to the logic of discovery. Development of element (b) will be consistent with the assumption just noted.

studies—with origins traced back to the exposition from Keohane (1989)—could be cataloged and surveyed regarding their axioms in the same way as realism within this volume. The second and third deductive stages of identification apply selection criteria to candidate axioms on an individual and combined basis, respectively. An example from Stage III is the requirement of logical consistency, with assumptions out of compliance being eliminated. A fourth and final stage, once again sociological and inductive, deletes axioms to which a critical mass of adherents have objected.

Once the axiomatic basis of a research enterprise is identified, theories can be articulated and conveyed through systemism. The systemist method relies upon diagrams to convey cause and effect for a theory (Bunge 1996). These graphics are created with clear rules in place for formatting, which is anticipated to improve comparability and communication. Systemism, unlike holism or reductionism, calls for comprehensive specification of cause-and-effect relations across levels of analysis. Use of diagrams to show theories is anticipated to reveal more directly the contradictions and limitations that can remain hidden in words alone. As a visualization, the symbol from calculus for an integral, $\int$, can help here. This graphic not only resembles the letter S, but also denotes a process of integration that is an analogue to what occurs with implementation of systemism.

Recognition and implicit endorsement of principles in line with systemism can be detected over decades and continue to build within IR. Neither structure nor agency, to use terms familiar in IR, should be studied in isolation. Motives among actors, Donnelly (2000: 51; see also Lake 2013: 574) asserts, should be incorporated into structural theories. When examining potential connections from the individual to the group and vice versa, Schelling (2006: 14) urges caution about reaching conclusions too quickly. A wide range of expositions, such as Kurki (2002: 32) about structural influence on intentional action and Best and Walter (2013) on the idea of studying the "productive tension" within an actor network, call for more comprehensive thinking about structure and processes in relation to each other.

Since it facilitates communication and especially comparison of complementary and competing theories, systemism is anticipated to contribute effectively to progress. Systemism depicts causal mechanisms using box-and-arrow diagrams that, on the surface, appear to be much the same as those often seen in the past. Figures based on systemism, however, result from application of terminology and rules that facilitate intelligibility. A system consists of macro and micro levels, along with boundaries and thus also an environment. Systemist graphics are unlike the visualizations sometimes implemented to summarize a study's argument, which show little consistency with each other in terms of format. Figures based on systemism are created according to a set of rules, covered in Chapter 6, that maximize logical consistency and completeness in representing theoretical statements.

Systemism, for example, insists that at least one causal mechanism reside in each potential type of linkage: macro to macro and micro to micro, but also *across* levels of aggregation, that is, macro to micro and micro to macro. Effects back and forth for the system and environment must be included as well. To simplify matters for the moment, in IR the preceding terminology usually would mean (a) a region as the macro level, (b) the state as the micro level, and (c) the environment as everything outside the system, such as the world beyond a given region.[8] A geographic domain is designated to some degree in an arbitrary way, based on density of interaction. Thus for one study it might make sense to treat East Asia as the system, while for others either Southeast Asia or Thailand might be preferred, with more of the world thereby placed into the environment.

One immediate insight from systemism, once applied, is that many theories in the social sciences avoid dealing with at least one type of linkage from those on the preceding list through use of a ceteris paribus clause (Bunge 1996). An assumption that one or more among the types of connection can be held constant is commonplace within theorizing about IR. Omission of one or more categories of linkage constitutes a defect from the standpoint of scientific explanation—unintentionally mystifying aspects of an operating system. Sustained research on the democratic peace, for example, took place overwhelmingly in micro-to-macro terms, with a nearly exclusive emphasis on experiences of interstate dyads as related to composition in terms of regime types.[9] A highly progressive work about the dynamics of democratic diffusion at the level of the global system has introduced new energy to the study of regime type through exploration of the previously neglected matter of the international system as a whole (Harrison and Mitchell 2014). In other words, what happens when democracies become more common around the globe? Will the world turn out to be increasingly pacific, or are more complex developments to be expected? Answers to these and related questions transcend prior research on the democratic peace that focused on outcomes of specific interstate conflicts.

Research on the psychology of learning favors adoption of either systemism or some other visual technique that includes its most essential properties. The idea of a "concept map" is put forward within learning theory as a way to organize knowledge. "Concept mapping," as described by Ambrose et al. (2010), "is a technique that helps people represent their knowledge organizations

---

[8] The focus of a given theory will determine what is designated as system versus environment, but points (a) through (c) represent a commonly encountered profile. Within the state, if instead it is designated as the system, the macro and micro levels will correspond, respectively, to government and society.

[9] In this context the state- or micro-level entity refers to democratic regimes. When these states interact at the macro level, cooperation is anticipated as more likely than conflict. This belief is due to how democracy is expected to impact bargaining and factors that will tend to lower risk of escalation (Maoz and Russett 1993).

visually." This type of map is a graphic way to organize and represent what is known. These maps are "drawn as nodes and links in a network structure in which nodes represent concepts, usually enclosed in circles or boxes, and links represent relationships, usually indicated by lines drawn between two associate nodes. Words on the line, referred to as linking words or linking phrases, specify the relationship between the two concepts" (Ambrose et al. 2010: 228). All of that reinforces the argument in favor of implementing systemism.[10]

Figure 3.1 shows the configuration of the seven elements from within the knowledge, units, and methods components that make up the metatheory. The figure, in sum, is about *how to study international relations*. The *dynamics* of Figure 3.1, expressed via arrows that connect the elements, will be introduced in Chapter 7. (Shapes that distinguish roles played by elements also will be explained in Chapter 7 when the metatheory is put forward as a working system.) It is deemed important at this point, given emphasis on visualization throughout the entire book, to provide the figure in simplified form as an entrée to explaining its contents at greater length in Chapters 4–6. The inner box represents the academic system that includes the seven elements from across the three components enumerated in this chapter. This is the world of IR as an academic discipline. The outer box, the environment, is where scientific progress resides. This is the public domain.

Within the academic system, macro and micro levels are depicted in the top and bottom rows, respectively. Upper- and lowercase letters are used to represent, in turn, macro- and micro-level variables. The macro level contains the three elements from the knowledge component: SCIENTIFIC REALISM, ANALYTIC ECLECTICISM, and MODEL OF COGNITION. Elements of knowledge are designated as macro level because these are not particular to a given person but instead exist at the level of the system. For example, a model of cognition is available in a systemwide manner once it is published in some format. At the micro level are found the four elements from the unit and methods components: rationality, identification of axioms for a research enterprise, research enterprise, and systemism. Each of these items either represents individuals or refers to their actions and therefore is designated as micro level. The seven elements at the macro and micro levels are deemed individually necessary and collectively sufficient to form a metatheory of progress for IR.

---

[10] Use of concept maps in the field of education shows consilience, in the sense of Whewell (1840), with the argument in favor of systemism to assist IR with communication of cause-and-effect relations. In each instance, experience—an inductive process—points toward a parallel type of outcome, namely, use of a visualization technique to solve an intellectual problem. The consilience is found in the "jumping together" of inductions from different contexts (Whewell 1840).

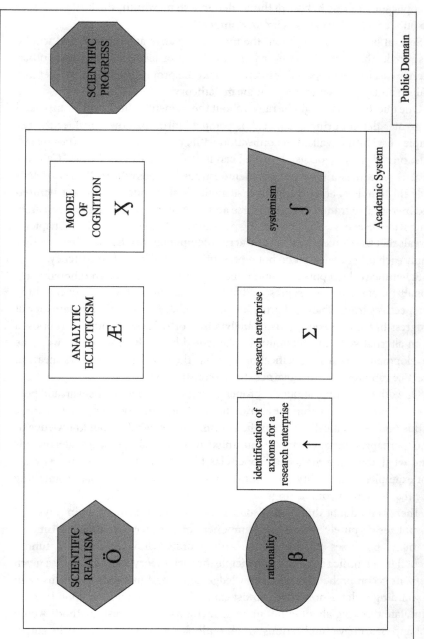

Figure 3.1 Configuration of Elements from a Metatheory of Progress

One item, SCIENTIFIC PROGRESS, appears in the public domain. This refers to application of research from the academic system, within which IR resides, to the public realm that exists as its environment.

Several basic questions about the metatheory arise at this point and will be answered. These queries concern compatibility of elements with each other, alternatives to the proposed framework, and the proper placement of scientific realism and other elements within the metatheory.

One question that might be raised about the elements, which will be answered in greater detail during Chapter 7, is compatibility. For now, consider the example of scientific realism in connection with analytic eclecticism. These elements, on at least one occasion, have been linked in an essential way: "Calls for 'analytic eclecticism' must not only demonstrate that scientific realism is a defensible epistemology amenable to diverse methods; they must provide a structured and memorable framework for diverse and cumulative theorizing and research, field-wide discourse, and compelling pedagogy" (Bennett 2013: 459). Chapter 7 reveals that the elements within and across components of the metatheory either imply each other or at least do not represent a threat to logical consistency.

Scientific realism puts in motion one set of possibilities for an inherently rationalist metatheory of progress. What if, instead, one of the other overarching perspectives from Chapter 2 provided the foundation instead? A metatheory of progress based on neopositivism, analyticism, or reflexivity could be proposed as an alternative to the apparatus implemented here. These would be welcome developments because specification of what the respective concepts mean in practice can only help to move debate in a constructive direction.

One other question, about the proper placement of scientific realism and possibly other elements within the knowledge, unit, and method components, arises at this point. Specifically, is scientific realism a set of beliefs about knowledge or also, perhaps, a point of view about units? If so, how should it be categorized? And what about the matter of proper classification for other elements as well? For example, is rationality a position adopted about units or perhaps something else that is more encompassing?

There is no doubt that at least some elements can be articulated in ways that do not reside purely within one component or another. Scientific realism, for example, possesses implications regarding units. Unobservables are fundamental to scientific realism. The principle the metatheory uses to classify a given element is comprehensiveness. Knowledge, units, and methods are inclusive in descending order. Knowledge is most expansive, and an outlook upon it could stimulate thinking about either units or methods. By contrast, methods would not appear to have implications for an outlook on knowledge. Units lie somewhere in between.

INTRODUCING COMPONENTS   75

One point should be reiterated about the style of presentation that will ensue as components of the metatheory are presented, through their respective elements, in Chapters 4–6. Research from educational psychology, with particular reference to cognitive load theory, supports the idea that concepts from a relatively complex network should be introduced in manageable subsets. In addition, manipulation of such concepts is especially challenging and should be attempted only after substantial preexisting explanation of each constituent.[11] These insights from educational psychology explain the sequential and gradual way in which elements are introduced in subsets corresponding to each component and then assembled into a working system via Chapter 7. The advice from the psychology of education is worth taking because much of the ensuing discussion of the metatheory takes place at an abstract level.

Summing Up the Components

This chapter has identified individually necessary and collectively sufficient elements of a metatheory with three components: knowledge, units, and methods. Each component, in turn, encompasses multiple elements. Knowledge includes commitment to scientific realism, analytic eclecticism, and a model of cognition as its elements. Rational individuals and systems of explanation (with a research enterprise as the preferred type) are the elements of the unit component. The method component entails identification of axioms for a research enterprise and use of systemism to facilitate communication regarding causal mechanisms as its elements. Respective elements then can be assembled to form a working system. Conveyed in graphic form, the working system includes the preceding elements in connection to scientific progress. Respective elements for knowledge, units, and methods are covered at greater length in Chapters 4–6 and then combined into the metatheory as a working system in Chapter 7.

---

[11] Among the studies with theory and evidence that support the approach adopted for communication of the metatheory are Rohrer and Bjork (2009), Mayer (2010), Rohrer and Pashler (2012), Kirschner, Kirschner, and Paas (2016), and Danielson and Sinatra (2017).

4
Knowledge

Knowledge as a Component of the Metatheory of Progress

Epistemology is the science of knowledge. A viable metatheory of progress for IR must include a compelling epistemology. While no exposition will answer all questions that might arise, minimal requirements can be identified. A brief review of the two preceding chapters will help to set the agenda for this one, which presents elements of the knowledge component in detail. And all of this works toward the ultimate goal of reformulating realism in a way that promotes advancement of knowledge.

Chapter 2, on scientific progress, enumerated criteria for advancement designated as characteristics (i.e., identifying causal mechanisms, rigor and falsifiability, and comprehensiveness) and results (i.e., range of explanation, predictive value, and public exchange of views) of research, respectively. The question of an overall perspective, identified along dimensions of (a) objectivity versus subjectivity and (b) a fully observable world as opposed to one including unobservables, also received an answer in Chapter 2. Among four basic possibilities, scientific realism emerged as preferred in terms of prospects for advancement. Scientific realism is the pragmatic choice because it embraces objective reality while also allowing a role for unobservables in the process of explanation. When compared, the specific criteria for research and the overarching perspective on progress, scientific realism, turn out to be fully consistent with each other.

Scientific realism, which combines belief in objective reality (world-mind dualism) with a role for unobservables in explanation (transfactualism), is the element that anchors the knowledge component of the metatheory of progress introduced in Chapter 3. Two other elements fill out the knowledge component; Chapter 3 described these as well. One of these elements is concerned with how explanations are to be constructed. Should research be paradigm-based or eclectic? Analytic eclecticism is the response given by the metatheory to that question because the logic of discovery argues against restricting exploration of ideas or evidence. Finally, as posed in the subtitle of a recent collective effort to conceptualize and assess progress in IR, "How do you know?" Along those lines, the third element of the knowledge component includes a model of cognition that argues in favor of a *visual* turn for IR. Given the size and scope of IR now and even more so in the future, the logic of confirmation demands an enhanced ability regarding synthesis of panoramic information into applicable knowledge. This observation applies even more to realism, the most sustained school of thought in the discipline.

Figure 3.1 from Chapter 3 provided a visual summary of elements from the metatheory, to be developed into a working system. Elements of knowledge—scientific realism, analytic eclecticism, and a model of cognition—occupied the macro level of the academic system in that figure. The micro level of the diagram included elements from the unit and methods components. For units and methods, respectively, these elements are (a) rationality and (b) research enterprise (units); and (c) identification of axioms for a research enterprise and (d) systemism (methods). Scientific progress, which exists in the public domain that constitutes the system's environment, completed the graphic representation of the metatheory in Figure 3.1.

This chapter elaborates on the elements of the *knowledge* component from the metatheory: scientific realism, analytic eclecticism, and a model of cognition. The chapter proceeds in four additional sections. The second section conveys scientific realism, a philosophy of inquiry that emerges as especially well suited to IR. The third section focuses on analytic eclecticism, an approach to developing theory that is gaining attention in response to disappointment in IR with results, over the long term, of efforts based on paradigmatic research. This observation applies to realism as much as anything else. The fourth section conveys a model of cognition based on insights from the fields of education and psychology, which point in the direction of a graphic turn for IR. The preceding elements combine to form the knowledge component, to accompany units and methods, covered in detail by Chapters 5 and 6, respectively. Composed of knowledge, units, and method, the metatheory then is assembled into a working system in Chapter 7. The fifth and final section of this chapter summarizes its accomplishments and sets the stage for work to continue on units for the metatheory in Chapter 5.

Scientific Realism (Ö)

Two tasks are completed in this section. First, the meaning of scientific realism is established. Second, alternative points of view about knowledge are assessed.

What Does It Mean?

This project adopts *scientific realism* as its foundation in the quest for knowledge. As summed up by Wight (2016: 37; see also Gunnell 2011: 1452), scientific realism is "a philosophy of and for science." Bunge (1993: 231) introduces scientific realism in further detail:

> In addition to the ontological and epistemological postulates of realism, it asserts (a) the methodological principle that scientific research is the best (most rewarding) mode of inquiry into any matters of fact, even though it is not infallible, and (b) the article of (justified) meliorist faith that scientific research, though fallible, can give us increasingly true representations of the world. These two additional principles can jointly be called *scientism*.

Scientific realism is committed to the idea that theories provide knowledge of the world, which in turn includes aspects that at least so far are unobservable (Chakravartty 2011: 1; Wight 2007: 381, 2016: 37). Unobservables are "things one cannot perceive with one's unaided senses, and this category divides into two subcategories. Some unobservables are nonetheless detectable through the use of instruments with which one hopes to 'extend' one's senses, and others are simply undectable" (Chakravartty 2007: 4). Thus, even as research moves forward, some limitations can be expected to persist.

Bennett (2013: 466) takes up that point in the context of IR:

> Instruments of observation may improve to the point that we take them to be relatively straightforward, but this just pushes back the horizon that demarcates the many remaining things we cannot unproblematically observe. There are always obscured, discrete, or distant mechanisms that we cannot directly observe, including the ideas in other people's heads.

Scientific theories that include statements about unobservables "are true or false by virtue of the extent to which they correspond to such a reality" (Gunnell 2011: 1448; see also Joseph 2007: 346; Kydd 2008: 430). These observable implications can be tested "against the predictions of our theories even though we cannot directly observe mechanisms of causation" (Bennett 2013: 466). Consider, for example, norms within constructivist theorizing. Beginning in the 20th century, a norm in favor of conservation and environmental protection gained traction around the globe. An example of how this unobservable translated into the objective world is the purchase of carbon offsets or credits as a measurement of adherence to a pro-environment position. Growth of knowledge, from a scientific realist point of view, is a process through which unobservables guide research and obtain empirical meaning as results accumulate. Scientific progress therefore is understood in pragmatic terms.

Perhaps the most obvious example of the above-noted process in the domain of IR is government declassification of material, which in turn affects the possibilities for research. In some instances information may come to light long after events. For example, in 2000, Oxford University made available all but one box of documents related to the abdication of Edward VIII in 1936. The remaining box is scheduled to be unsealed in 2037. While speculation is rampant about what embarrassing item(s) may be contained in that final collection, there is no way of knowing for sure until the time comes. Potentially important causal mechanisms leading up to abdication remain concealed. The same could be said of classified material in the case of the Cuban Missile Crisis and other major political events, which tends to become available in stages as events recede or governments change.

Scientific realism's point of view can be understood through use of an antinomy, the "mystification of residuals"—a belief that some things lie beyond the realm of explanation and thus are not worth studying (Babbie 2001). From a scientific realist point of view, unobservables create priorities for empirical research in the quest for knowledge. Thus explanation, rather than mystification, is the mindset concerning that which is not yet grounded in the empirical world. Astronomy rather than astrology holds the status of a science for precisely this reason. Unobservables in astronomy generate falsifiable explanations that are well supported as research accumulates, whereas astrology provides amusement but not an account of reality that stands up to testing.

One important nuance should be added to this argument before moving ahead. The call for rigor does *not* constitute an endorsement of quantitative over qualitative methods. The choice between these two approaches to data analysis constitutes, as Brecher (1999) accurately labeled it, a flawed dichotomy. It is possible to implement virtually any method in a manner consistent with the principles of scientific testing. Success in that way depends on research design, as opposed to the degree of aggregation for data.

Scientific realism entails three dimensions that collectively define objective reality: metaphysical, semantic, and epistemological (Chakravartty 2011: 2):

- Metaphysical—objective (i.e., mind-independent) existence of the world investigated by the sciences
- Semantic—literal interpretation of scientific claims about the world
- Epistemological—theoretical claims constituting knowledge of the world.

These traits combine to create a rationalist, as opposed to primarily constructivist, view of the world. Existence of objective reality makes it possible for theorizing to progress in the sense of developing superior explanations over time. Thus "specification of the objects (ontology) must come prior to attempts to validate claims about the objects" (Wight 2016: 37). Once units are agreed upon, methods can be implemented and research findings accumulate and become subject to debate over their greater meaning.

Consider scientific realism in the context of realist IR. A concept such as the state—central to all variants of realism—begins as an abstraction. Its origin in social science invariably is traced back to Weber (Gerth and Mills 1946). Understanding of an unobservable concept's meaning increases through empirical research, debate, and refinement. Enlightening works about the state as a concept along its path of development include Evans, Rueschmeyer, and Skocpol (1985) on its importance as an actor in and of itself, Spruyt (1996) regarding effects from various contingencies on the meaning of sovereignty, and Migdal (2001) in terms of influence back and forth with society. Contributions from comparative politics as carried out within the discipline of political science, in combination with theorizing and research in IR, turn the initial concept formation from Weber (see Gerth and Mills 1946) about the state into a well-grounded empirical referent a century onward. This process of elaboration, moreover, would be easy to detail for any number of concepts from IR and constitutes the essence of scientific realism in action.[1]

Theories, from a scientific realist point of view, are "approximately true" because their success otherwise would have to be explained by a miracle (Chakravartty 2011: 3). The logic behind that position about theory is Bayesian; beliefs are adjusted in light of evidence.[2] As explanations accumulate, it becomes more probable that they are not just a result of good fortune.[3]

Instead of being the product of coincidence, accumulating evidence is an outcome anticipated from consistent application of scientific principles.[4] A detailed treatment of scientific principles is beyond the scope of this study, but a few basic traits are easy to convey. The process of scientific investigation, understood in general terms, commences with a research question that may arise from either inductive or deductive thinking. A review of prior research on the query, to the extent it exists, is used to identify priorities for work to get underway. A hypothesis of the form "If x, then y is more likely than otherwise" is formulated to guide further efforts to answer the question. (The proposition may take a compound form, with a set of variables rather than a single "x" being put forward as

---

[1] A few examples of this type of progress are with respect to alliances (von Hlatky 2013: 5), appeasement (Ripsman and Levy 2008: 181), and realpolitik (Bew 2016: 308).

[2] Bayes' theorem is explained at greater length as the foundation for instrumental rationality in Chapter 5. The basic meaning is that people are expected to update their beliefs about the world in response to experience that produces relevant new data about the probability of occurrence for a given event.

[3] This position is in line with scientific realism, for which "baseline theories are crucial because they help scientists adjudicate between theories" and "ensure that theoretical programs, rather than individual empirical predictions, are at the center of scientific development" (MacDonald 2003: 560).

[4] For scientific realists, there is no specific method entailed for carrying out research; tools become relevant on the basis of a problem rather than in principle (Wight 2007: 385; see also Maradi 1990: 154).

the explanation for "y.") Specific orderings of events and mechanisms are identified as processes (Grzymala-Busse 2011: 1268). Data gathering then takes place to evaluate the hypothesis, about which confidence either increases or decreases as results are obtained from analysis.[5] The process then goes through a new cycle. Confidence in a theory, which consists of a logically interconnected set of hypotheses derived from an axiomatic basis, is enhanced or diminished on the basis of empirical research.

One objection to the preceding line of reasoning is that the argument concerning miracles might make sense for a discipline like physics or chemistry but is not convincing with regard to the social sciences (Chernoff 2007: 404). As Ripsman, Taliaferro, and Lobell (2016: 105) observe, "It is far more complex to measure social phenomena, such as self-esteem or international norms." While IR may not have anything as well supported as the periodic table among its repertoire, it is possible to point to concepts and associated data that command general confidence. Take, for example, interstate war as a concept. The Correlates of War (COW) data set, in existence for over 50 years, is the definitive source. Over the course of decades, the COW definition of war, with two or more recognized state entities and a minimum of 1,000 battle-related casualties, stands as one of the most strongly implemented and verified concepts in IR (Small and Singer 1982). In addition, the concept formation of COW has expanded to include Militarized Interstate Disputes (MIDs), along with categories of war beyond interstate alone (Correlates of War Project 2017).

Various scholars compare theories to maps and thereby facilitate understanding of the viewpoint held by scientific realism (Mearsheimer and Walt 2013: 430–432; Wight 2016 45). Like a theory, a map is "an abstract representation organized in particular ways" and goes beyond an accumulation of data—an exact replica (Wight 2017: 44; see also Jackson and Nexon 2009: 922; Mearsheimer and Walt 2013: 430). This comparison makes more sense than looking at a theory as a mirror of reality (Mearsheimer and Walt 2013: 431; Wight 2017: 49). The principal reason is that the representation of interest is not just an exhaustive *description* of what is observed. Instead, the goal is to highlight features that matter in a given context. "Our judgment of how good a map is," as Wight (2017: 46) points out, "relates to how well it enables us to carry out the task." Assessment of a map's utility thereby entails a sociological element.

---

[5] Experts in methods of inquiry and IR alike increasingly emphasize the importance of identifying and evaluating causal mechanisms. For recent examples, see Mearsheimer and Walt (2013: 448) and Beach (2016: 18, 19); a classic exposition appears in Nurmi (1974: 34). For one treatment of challenging issues associated with a focus on mechanistic evidence, see Beach (2016: 20). Note also that explanation or y-oriented research is fundamentally different from the quest for context-based understanding as enumerated in Hollis and Smith (1992).

Validity depends upon the degree of consensus among users of maps and theories that, respectively, they are fulfilling the function desired (Wight 2017: 47). A map's function often is to locate something or plan a route, while a theory's purpose is explanation. The pragmatic and to some degree sociological aspects of how theories rise and fall, most famously identified by Kuhn (1970 [1962]) in terms of paradigmatic persistence and change, remain relevant to this day and are considered in detail within Chapter 5.

A map's value depends primarily on how well it gives directions. Old maps may provide aesthetic enjoyment, but virtually all maps go out of date at some point. New maps of a city, for instance, will show streets, bridges, and tunnels that have been added over time. In the world of IR, a theory regarded as an effective "map" at one time does not necessarily become outdated because it cannot initially account for new developments that come to be seen as anomalies. If a theory can adapt to explain ongoing events, especially those of a major and jarring nature, it is regarded as resilient and remains viable.

Challenges to realism and other approaches to IR can be explained, in the preceding way, by what seems like unsatisfactory coping with significant shocks. Prominent surprises in recent decades include the end of the Cold War, the attacks against the United States on 9/11, and the revolutions in the Middle East and North Africa that (somewhat misleadingly) are referred to in the aggregate as the "Arab Spring." (Differences among events in Tunisia, Libya, and Egypt arguably outweigh their common traits.) To stay relevant as maps for IR, figuratively speaking, theories must be able to cope with important events such as these in a satisfactory way, at least in comparison to alternative frameworks.

Scientific realism, as summarized by one advocate, "rests upon the explication of basic assumptions, the logical derivation of propositions from those assumptions, the deduction of observable implications, and the testing of implications through carefully designed quasi-experiments" (Lake 2002: 136). Implementation of scientific realism, as just described, results in transformation of unobservable concepts into working systems of explanation for the empirical world. Consider, to return to an earlier example, the concept of the state as implemented within IR. Two well-known expositions will be sufficient to show how this concept became more elaborate and gained empirical referents over time (Allison 1971 [see also Allison and Zelikow 1999]; Putnam 1988).

One treatment, which focused on alternative visions of the Cuban Missile Crisis, demonstrated that the state could be examined in ways that transcended previous applications of a unitary rational actor framework (Allison 1971; see also Allison and Zelikow 1999). Allison's (1971) study of what is considered the most intense Cold War crisis—one that became more disturbing to recall after declassified sources showed that a level of danger had existed greater than contemporary accounts revealed—did not discard instrumental rationality but instead showed how a more complete story of state action had to include organizational processes and bureaucratic politics. This elaboration of the state as a concept set the agenda for a wide range of investigations that focus on both crisis and noncrisis situations to investigate the interplay of top leaders, bureaucrats, and government organizations with regard to the process of decision-making about foreign policy.

Consider the idea that decision-makers for a state, figuratively speaking, are playing more than one game at the same time (Putnam 1988). A leader could see one policy as best from a foreign policy standpoint but might not be willing to move in that direction because of countervailing factors within the state. Thus rational decision-makers choose from among policies that fall within their "win set," that is, options that possess at least minimal acceptability across all of the games being played at the time (Putnam 1988). With regard to trade liberalization, for example, it is essential for leaders of respective states to reach agreement with each other while also maintaining a coalition at home that is sufficient to stay in power (Lusztig 2004). It also is possible, of course, for a decision-maker to end up in a place where there is a null win set—no single policy meets even the most basic needs in an area of policy, trade, or otherwise. In sum, the "two-level game" concept from Putnam (1988) continues to influence the way in which the state is incorporated in studies of bargaining at the international level.

Taken together, the expositions from above (Allison 1971; Allison and Zelikow 1999; Putnam 1988) are sufficient to reveal elaboration of the state as a concept. Further examples could be provided for development of this concept, as well as others that are used heavily in IR, notably among realists.[6]

Scientific realism offers a pathway toward knowledge that emphasizes the existence of objective reality in tandem with unobservables that can obtain high credibility via accumulation of research-based evidence. The state—from its advent with Weber through to present applications in realism and beyond—serves as one obvious example of a concept in IR.

Alternative Points of View

Some observers, however, do not find this scientific realist vision to be compelling for *any* academic discipline and prefer various alternative unifying perspectives. Scientific realists embrace the existence of an objective world, whereas antirealists believe that reality is subjective, and this is the focal point

---

[6] Informative expositions on the state as applied in IR include Mastanduno, Lake, and Ikenberry (1988), Taliaferro (2006: 470, 486, 2009b: 198), Lake (2008: 41, 50–51), and Rathbun (2008: 315).

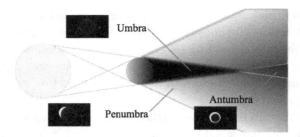

Figure 4.1 Shadows and Illumination

for disagreement. The principal antirealist alternatives in IR, with regard to the philosophy of inquiry, are postmodernism and some variants of constructivism.

Debates between scientific realists and antirealists can be quite arcane and seem unlikely to be resolved any time soon.[7] Rather than an attempt to end the argument, the goal instead is to identify competing positions clearly and move forward on the basis of a scientific realist foundation. Use of a metaphor may help to distinguish, for present purposes, scientific realism from antirealist alternatives. The metaphor concerns shadows and illumination. Shadows result from an object blocking a light source, with the most easily communicated version concerning the sun and objects in orbit around it. Figure 4.1 displays the possibilities regarding shadows and illumination. A full shadow, known as the umbra, results when all light from the sun is cut off due to full interposition of one item in front of another. The penumbra refers to the partial shadow that is cast when the position of one object results in only a partial blockage of light for the other. The antumbra is a shadow that results when the blocking object is far enough in front that some light begins to emerge around its edges.

How do antirealists see the quest for knowledge? Responses vary in the IR context and can be communicated with help from the metaphor regarding illumination and shadows.

For postmodernists, the social scientific enterprise is doomed from the outset. Accumulation of knowledge on such terms is deemed impossible. An interpretive understanding of the world, from the postmodernist standpoint, prevents the existence of objective knowledge. Since people possess different, unique perspectives on reality—or perhaps instead process what their senses tell them within a cultural context—pursuit of what social scientists would call "progress"

---

[7] Chakravatty (2011: 9; see also Gunnell (2011: 1465–1466) and Wight (2016: 34) in the context of IR) observes that arguments back and forth show "every symptom of a perennial philosophical dispute." It should be noted once again that realism and antirealism in this context refer to positions about the philosophy of science and do not correspond to usage of these terms within IR. See Gunnell (2011: 1457).

KNOWLEDGE 85

on the basis of objective knowledge becomes a fool's errand. Thus within Figure 4.1, the umbra is what postmodernists expect to persist, with its darkness representing the nonresults from social scientific efforts toward explanation. None of that empirical work is anticipated to be illuminating; instead, knowledge exists in the minds of individuals as processed from within their point of view—moderated perhaps by subjectivities induced from residing within a given culture—and cannot be added together toward some greater whole. From a postmodernist perspective, illumination is possible, but takes a very different form—best pursued through contextual knowledge.[8] IR's quest should be for understanding rather than explanation, as communicated through the dichotomy famously articulated by Hollis and Smith (1992).[9] All of this may be summed up as a position about knowledge in line with anthropological approaches that emphasize context-based understanding over presumably vain efforts toward generalized explanations.

Full subjectivity (i.e., monism with regard to mind and world), however, collapses under its own inherent contradictions when taken to an extreme. An anecdote from Lake (2002: 149 n. 1) effectively introduces the basic problem entailed by antirealism:

> A colleague once asked a postmodern theorist of international relations how he would evaluate two works on the same topic. If he had to decide which was better, how would he choose? After a brief pause, the theorist replied that he would prefer the one that revealed the most hidden power. My colleague was too polite to ask the obvious follow-up: how would he know this result?

It is clear from the anecdote alone that every scholar must acknowledge the existence of some minimal amount of objective reality in order for productive dialogues, rather than pointless monologues, to occur. Wight (2016: 31–32) points out that, if all claims are relative, why should one take precedence over another? The full-fledged relativism of postmodernism, especially regarding the logic of confirmation, becomes self-defeating because of this straightforward insight. There must be at least some amount of agreement on objective reality in order to create even minimal potential for communication. The result otherwise is debate without conclusion.[10]

---

[8] A classic exposition of this viewpoint, which emphasizes the difficulties associated with inferring meaning from action and thereby challenges the overall mission of the social sciences, appears in Schutz (1967).

[9] Understanding refers to learning about how things are seen from inside a given perspective and tends to be associated with nonpositivist research, while explanation is more about an outsider-based account of cause and effect and is connected to neopositivism in a general way. This dichotomy continues to be influential as an ongoing principle within IR.

[10] Bunge (1993: 220) forcefully asserts that "hermeneutic philosophy has nothing to teach social scientists." Freyberg-Inan, Harrison, and James (2017b: 183; see also Barkin 2010: 182–183) point out

Social constructivists also are skeptical about scientific explanation based on some objective frame of reference, but vary in the intensity of that belief. These critics thereby differ from postmodernists, who fully reject the existence of objective reality. "The term 'social construction' refers," as defined by Chakravartty (2011: 8), "to any knowledge-generating process in which what counts as a fact is substantively determined by social factors, and in which different social factors would likely generate facts that are inconsistent with what is actually produced." The concept of the penumbra, which varies in size as a function of the positioning of the three objects, is useful in applying the metaphor depicted in Figure 4.1 to articulate the social constructivist point(s) of view. Social constructivists can be thought of as varying in how they see the size of the illuminated area in Figure 4.1—that which can be grasped via the scientific method—as opposed to the penumbra that will evade such efforts and remain in partial darkness. Intersubjective agreement can be obtained on the same matters, leading to illumination. At the same time, social constructions of reality may not fully overlap.

Nuances certainly exist within constructivist thinking about the matters above and should be acknowledged. For example, Wendt (1999) regards scientific realism and constructivism as compatible. This is because constructivism accepts the existence of a world of ideas in an *objective* sense. Such a world can be detected and studied. More specifically, while culture, norms, and values are created within the mind, results from that process can be seen in terms of communication. At the same time, other strains of constructivism would object to this line of reasoning and adopt the position that the uniqueness of each person's point of view refutes the concept of objective reality.

Consider, in the context of constructivism, the question of why wars occur. From a social constructivist point of view, degeneration of conflict into warfare can be explained, at a general level, through variation in how issues are conceptualized and assessed from one group to the next. The story of war therefore is fundamentally ideational. One causal mechanism identified via constructivism, for example, is securitization (Buzan, Wæver, and de Wilde 1998). If the leadership of one state can convince its public that another state poses a threat, such a belief can be used to mobilize and initiate conflict. A constructivist explanation for the democratic peace therefore can be based on the extreme difficulty of securitization processes between and among such states (Hayes 2009, 2015). Many other examples could be provided for constructivist research that seeks to explain observations of international politics.

---

that the postmodernist position is undermined by Russell's paradox: "A common illustration of the Paradox is a barber who shaves exactly all those men who do not shave themselves. After brief reflection of the two basic scenarios—the barber either shaves himself or he does not—Russell's Paradox emerges. The statement is a contradiction in terms." This position is consistent with recognition that some aspects of life are subjective—just not everything.

Contrary to postmodernism and constructivism, consider the scientific realist position in this metaphor about shadow and illumination. The antumbra is the concept that helps in understanding scientific realism. As the point of view recedes further away from the object that is interposed, the antumbra diminishes in Figure 4.1. Illumination begins as a ring outside the circular antumbra and expands as distance increases. Once the distance becomes great enough, the antumbra diminishes to a vanishingly small size—eventually, just a point. This metaphor works nicely for the scientific realist view because it incorporates the idea of becoming more distant from subject matter in order to achieve greater comprehension of it. In an academic context this does not mean increasing physical distance but instead movement toward objectivity. Illumination becomes greater with the distance that is achieved, metaphorically speaking, through accumulation of research findings and thus a greater sense of what is known.

While unobservables are included under the banner of scientific realism, no mystification is intended. Instead, the quest for explanation either (a) increases the credibility of unobservables if expectations based on theorizing about them are supported by empirical observations over time; or (b) leads to reformulation otherwise. Sil (2000a: 366–367) is worth quoting at length to explain further the role of the unobservable in any scientific analysis:

> Where a materialist account of social phenomena invokes explanatory factors that are not directly observable, the immediate *effects* of these factors can be taken as proxies in establishing their ontological status and justifying their epistemological relevance. For example, while the actual calculus of a gain-maximizing rational individual may not itself be observed, it is taken to be directly and proportionately evident in the individual's behavior and in the immediate results of that behavior. Similarly, while not all structuring principles are evident in written rules or observable coordination among members of social networks, their existence is presumed to be directly and proportionately evident in observable factors such as income distribution, the actual exercise of decision-making authority, or the rule-following behavior of individuals. In neither situation do unobservable aspects of a social process pose problems for the interpretation of that process since such aspects have direct, observable consequences.

One follow-up to this effective presentation of scientific realist thinking concerns the role of prediction. Successful forecasting increases the confidence that causal mechanisms from a theory, even one that includes unobservable elements, really are at work.

For example, expected utility models effectively forecast the interstate dyads most at risk of conflict escalation, which in turn increases confidence in the underlying explanation grounded in rational choice (Bueno de Mesquita et al. 2003). Moreover, the concept of utility continues to evolve within that setting, with initial efforts at measurement focusing on the degree of overlap in alliances for a pair of states and later versions incorporating other metrics such as the amount of convergence in voting records within an international organization (Bueno de Mesquita 1981; Gartzke 2005). All of this breathes life into utilitarian thinking as it developed within the boundaries of philosophy, with Bentham and Mill as the starting point in the 19th century, and radiated outward into political economy and beyond.

Recall the discussion from Chapter 2 about the choice of scientific realism, as opposed to neopositivism, the other perspective that entails world-mind dualism. Neopositivism, in one sense, stands as an unobtainable polar point of complete knowledge; that is, unobservables are not required because everything is in the empirical realm.[11] Rather than alternatives, as described by Jackson (2011, 2016a, 2016b), neopositivism and scientific realism might be thought of, respectively, as entities to seek and live within. To return momentarily to Figure 4.1 and the metaphor derived from it: neopositivism implies eventual full illumination. From a scientific realist point of view, this is hoping for too much.[12] The practice of empirical research on international relations, with its combination of deductive and inductive reasoning (Blagden 2016), along with theories that succeed to varying degrees in their quest for explanation, is in line with scientific realism rather than neopositivism.

Scientific realism looks favorably upon finding unobservables through "different means of detection" (Chakravartty 2011: 4). In the context of IR, this process of discovery plays out in terms of assessing potential causal mechanisms through various types of data analysis. Take, for example, the idea that settled borders are the reason behind pacific relations when assessed in terms of interstate dyads (Gibler 2012). Aggregate data analysis confirms part of the causal story, namely, conjunction of presumed cause and effect. While the connection is not perfect, data analysis on peace achieved through settled borders surpasses all conventional standards for statistical association. To complement this success, attention naturally turns to the playing out of individual dyads, to see if the process matches the aggregate data point. A positive and high-profile example is the Alaskan border settlement between Britain (which at the time represented

---

[11] Coleman (1990: 719) identifies a perfect social system as one that includes rational actors, absence of structures that impede use of resources, and no transaction costs or free rider problems. This system stands as a goal to be pursued but not obtained—an analogue to the argument made here about a full and final explanation of the world sans unobservables.

[12] It should be acknowledged that not all scientific realists would see neopositivism as an ideal to be achieved. Some instead might be comfortable even with in-principle unobservables (Freyberg-Inan 2020).

Canada) and the United States. Significant friction had developed after discovery of gold. The Alaska border agreement ended tensions permanently in 1903. The border between the Alaskan territory of the United States and Canadian province of British Columbia had been the last remaining source of apprehension of its kind for those states.[13] Accumulation of confirming instances, carried out in compliance with best practices identified for case studies (King, Keohane, and Verba 1994; Gerring 2007), would (a) strengthen confidence in the mechanism theorized for peace based on borders and (b) triangulate findings from aggregate data analysis already in place.

Refutation is a natural part of the process of research and should not be taken as evidence of futility. It is important to avoid "pessimistic induction" in particular. Pessimistic induction refers to the inference that, because previous theories have been falsified and replaced, those currently in use must be flawed as well (Chakravvarty 2011: 6).[14] From a scientific realist point of view, theories naturally arise and are replaced from within or outside of a given research enterprise when something better becomes available. This includes an expectation that future theoretical developments are likely to build on frameworks already in place. Thus it makes sense to improve upon, rather than eliminate, realism as an outlook on world politics. This school of thought contains basic insight about international relations and, from a scientific realist viewpoint, can provide the foundation for more effectively theorizing in the future.

Consider research on deterrence as an example of an approach that succeeded in producing more convincing explanations over time. Schelling (1960) introduced strategic analysis through game-theoretic expositions, followed soon after by data analysis from Russett (1963) that attempted to identify the key determinants of extended deterrence. Games of imperfect information, inspired by Selten (1974), improved correspondence with reality by introducing player types. The study of deterrence today features highly sophisticated models that identify equilibria that would have been virtually unimaginable at the time the initial game-theoretic analysis took place. Models of strategic interaction based on game theory produce any number of well-supported propositions about the dynamics of conflict processes (Quackenbush 2015; Zagare 2019).

Reinforcing favorable assessment of scientific realism is an important idea from formal logic (Priest 2017): "What Gödel showed was that, though there

---

[13] Canada and the United States, however, do continue to disagree about the status of Arctic archipelago waters, and matters could intensify if either a Northwest Passage becomes a practical sea lane or energy could be accessed more easily (James 2016, 2021).

[14] One example that comes to mind as a potential contradiction is replacement of Newtonian mechanics with those of Einstein. The framework from Newton, however, continues to work well except under conditions of very high velocity. Something similar is to be expected as theories supplant each other in IR. Those of the past are not so much "wrong" as not entirely right.

may be axiom systems capturing *some* of the truths of arithmetic, there is no axiom system capturing *all* of them. As logicians say, any axiom system must be *incomplete*." Gödel's theorem triangulates with scientific realism as an outlook on knowledge for IR. The reason is that some truths will remain elusive—unobservables will persist and new ones will be proposed—even as learning accumulates via empirical research and ideas arise about causal mechanisms for further testing. The preceding example of deterrence and conflict processes as studied via game theory works well here. Another way of putting this is to say that neopositivism might encourage a mistaken belief, from the standpoint of science, that there is an "end of history." At some point all truths will be revealed. Scientific realism, by contrast, is more in line with the logic of Gödel's theorem as it exists within the domain of mathematics—incompleteness is to be expected even as knowledge accumulates.

One example of this way of thinking in the realm of IR appears in Doran (1991: 15–16): "The most precise causal explanation of the question under study, let us call it 'truth,' may be thought of (to borrow the idiom of abstract mathematics) as the 'limit point' of investigation which is approached through such cumulative theoretical understanding." Around the limit point, analysis identifies a neighborhood that is "as large as are the irrelevances and imprecisions and other weaknesses of the perspective" (Doran 1991: 16). Putting together "bridges and commonalities" of respective studies will result in greater proximity to the limit point (Doran 1991: 16). This line of reasoning is consistent with Gödel's theorem; it encourages pursuit of knowledge about international relations while also showing awareness of limitations on what ultimately can be learned.

Further support for the intuition derived from Gödel, in relation to IR, is provided through the analysis of paradigms—understood in the Kuhnian, sociological sense—from Barkin (2010). According to Barkin (2010: 4), paradigms are not able to serve the "function of complete sets of assumptions that suffice as starting points for research into international politics" because, among other reasons, each constitutes a belief about one specific aspect of the subject matter. This inference about limitations for paradigm-based research parallels the sense of incompleteness derived from Gödel's theorem. Sil and Katzenstein (2010c: 420) reinforce the point: "Although George and Bennett (2005) acknowledge that new technologies may make 'unobservable' elements 'observable' at a later time, they nonetheless assert: 'No matter how far down we push the border between the observable and the unobservable, some irreducibly unobservable aspect of causal mechanisms remains.'" The observations from this paragraph about limitations on what can be known combine to form an excellent point of transition into the subject of analytic eclecticism, which seeks a path to knowledge beyond the paradigms of IR.

Analytic Eclecticism (Æ)

This section carries out four tasks. First, problems with paradigms are identified. The second task is to assess prospects for constructive engagement across paradigms. Third, analytic eclecticism is put forward as an alternative to paradigm-based research and introduced in substantive terms via a classic work from realism. The fourth task is to assess the "balance sheet" with regard to the viability of analytic eclecticism as part of the way forward.

Paradigmatic Problems

Over the course of the last decade and perhaps longer, a sense has grown that paradigmatic allegiance may not be the best path toward progress for IR.[15] On the one hand, paradigms "have gathered groups of theories about causal mechanisms together in ways that have proved memorable and easy to convey" (Bennett 2010: 7). Placing the field in the context of "the isms has proven a useful shorthand for classroom teaching and field-wide discourse" (Bennett 2013: 461). Moreover, with focus comes greater coherence (Barkin 2010: 155; see also Haas 2017: 46). Perhaps, then, the burden of proof should be on advocates of intellectual pluralism (Wight 1996: 294; see also Checkel 2010: 24; Bennett 2010: 7). On the other hand, application of paradigms to provide structure for inquiry is criticized on both substantive and pedagogical grounds (Barkin and Sjoberg 2019: 40). Devotion to paradigms can entail impediments to progress, such as dwelling on separate islands of theory and appropriating "universal truth and virtue" (Lake 2011: 466; see also Lake 2002: 139–141; Bew 2016: 298). Paradigms even control research "by suggesting issues, methods and possible solutions at the expense of others" (Guzzini 1998: 12). Rathbun (2019: 303–305) adds that simplification via paradigms can lead to irrationality. Wight (2019: 69) connects the preceding problems with paradigmatic research under the heading of "fragmented adhocracy," within which IR features "a low degree of reputational interdependency between competing research groups, with few organisational impediments regarding the choice of theoretical framework, research methodology or even core problematic." In sum, any number of reasons exist for IR to look beyond research guided exclusively by paradigms.

One exposition on the value of paradigms detects a trend toward middle-range explanations (Sil and Katzenstein 2011: 483). Opinion increasingly favors "a concern with problem solving and the human relevance of our research

---

[15] For a partially dissenting view, see Legro and Moravcsik (1999: 8); a polemic against eclecticism in general, written from a postmodernist point of view, is put forward by Scott (2005).

efforts" (Freyberg-Inan 2004: 171). Data from a survey taken in 2011, however, reveals that "only 25 percent see themselves as not working within a paradigm, which suggests that the paradigms themselves are still quite robust" (Saideman 2018: 698). What, then, is a viable middle ground for IR?

Periodic "great debates" (Lapid 1989) tend to harden positions and exacerbate disagreements about IR. Resulting divisions often are "reified by turning a deaf ear to any differing voices" and even sometimes resemble "tribal affiliation" (Walker 2018: 199, 206). Consider, for example, the long period of confrontation involving rationalists versus critics of various kinds, notably structuralists and culturalists (Sil 2000a: 353). Eventually, at least some members of each side became more willing to "emphasize problem-focused research, permitting explanatory power rather than theoretical polemic to decide the contest" (Kahler 1998: 922). Along the same lines, Lake (2002: 148, 149) identifies key problems with "paradigm warriors" who stand in the way of overall progress: the tendency to argue about the truth of axioms rather than building bridges across approaches, along with a neglect of research design. These observations are prescient and reveal the degree to which IR would benefit from change in the direction of greater pluralism. It almost goes without saying that the record of confrontation in IR does not suggest that such a shift could be achieved easily.

With a medieval visage, the metaphor below from Barkin (2010: 1) throws down the gauntlet against paradigm-driven research:

> In the sociology of science, paradigms are a bit like castles. Scientists are knights in this metaphor, and assumptions are the liege-lords that the knights/scientists are sworn to defend. The strength of a paradigm can be measured by how many scientists are willing to defend its ramparts. Scientists tend to retain allegiance to their assumptions, so that the paradigmatic castles defend their inhabitants successfully, until those inhabitants die off. In this metaphor, it is in the nature of paradigms to be mutually exclusive—as a knight/scientist, one is more concerned about defending one's castle/paradigm, and in defeating others, than in building bridges among them. Paradigms, in other words, are distinct from, and in opposition to, each other.

Thus, figuratively speaking: expect moats rather than bridges between paradigms in IR. "Instead of a diverse discipline," observes Walker (2018: 205), "IR might be better characterized by indifference or hostility between various theoretical and methodological sects." To the medieval metaphor might be added, as a relevant but also humorous extension of the set of actors, those who might be designated as serfs in the IR of today: policymakers and bureaucrats. These actors are more distant and peripheral with time as the academic study of international relations moves away from its more peace- and policy-oriented origins in the aftermath of World War I, so serfdom seems about right if any recognition is given in our metaphorical world.

According to Barkin (2010: 2), the overall effect of the paradigmatic mindset is to encourage an insular and difference-oriented approach toward dialogue. "Meaningful interactions between distinct research sects in IR," Walker (2018: 196) points out, "appear to be very rare." A self-limiting form of purity ends up being valued over gains that might accrue from combining ideas associated with one paradigm or another. To some extent, the intensity of such conflict reflects its often abstract form—at an increasing distance from matters of application to policy in particular.[16] A return to the classical realist tradition, in this context at least, would be a welcome development.

When advancement with academic and policy-related aspects does take place, it arguably tends to look eclectic. Take, for example, the promising line of research on territorial issues and conflict processes. Research identifies territory as the issue with the greatest potential for escalation of an interstate dispute (Huth 1998; Senese and Vasquez 2008). Subsequent investigations suggest that the causal mechanism behind peaceful interstate relations is a product of stable borders or, put differently, the resolution of territorial strife (Gibler 2012). For example, settlement of the Polish border with Germany is identified as foundational with regard to European stability (Sarotte 2011).

While convincing and at the very least a stimulus to productive debates over why some conflicts escalate while others do not, the line of research on territory and conflict is not identified with a paradigm. It corresponds to neither realism nor liberalism, to cite two of the most visible schools of thought, and the variables incorporated in research designs on territorial conflict and peace through stable borders go beyond paradigmatic boundaries.

Assumptions outside of a given paradigm, in principle, are likely to become essential in addressing any number of empirical problems. "Paradigmatism," Hellman (Feaver et al. [Hellman] 2000: 173) adds,[17] "therefore shows the wrong way if one is seriously interested in advancing understanding of international politics. This is not to say, however, that *paradigmatic pragmatism* may not be useful." Paradigms, as Ripsman, Taliaferro, and Lobell (2016: 8) observe, "can help us understand the dynamics of international politics and its regularities in a holistic manner, rather than simply focusing on largely disconnected empirical results." Abandonment of paradigmatic research might leave chaos in its wake.

---

[16] Instances of highly charged exchanges are easy to find. An example involving realists and their critics appears in Feaver et al. (2000). Intense debates may reflect the presence of cognitive-affective maps that cause adversaries to transform debate into what becomes a de facto exchange of ideological positions that possesses very little possibility of consensus. For an introduction to cognitive-affective maps, see Homer-Dixon et al. (2013).

[17] This symposium included a large number of authors. In each instance the specific contributor making a given point is indicated in brackets.

A paradigm might guide research—as a way of proceeding, which resembles one of its meanings from the dictionary—but not become a Procrustean bed that rules out helpful innovations from outside of its boundaries. Thus a paradigm could anchor research on an empirical problem, such as the causes of war, while also connecting with hypotheses that are derived from axioms not entirely within its domain. A key role for the paradigm in this scenario is to rule out incorporation of axioms—and subsequent derivation of hypotheses—that create logical inconsistency. Auxiliary hypotheses, in other words, could be linked with an existing paradigm, but not if that entails calling upon assumptions that contradict one or more of those already in place.[18]

Calls for eclectic thinking permeated research grounded in realism during the years after 9/11 shocked the world.[19] These realist expositions have combined to stimulate another way of rethinking basic principles in IR. Adherence to a "rigorously defined set of coherent and distinct core assumptions," identified with a paradigm, "may be neither possible nor desirable" (Feaver et al. [Hellman]: 2000: 172). "Scholars do not sign a loyalty oath when they work within a particular theoretical tradition," observes Walt (2002: 199), "and no methodological laws are broken when a scholar draws on more than one theoretical tradition when seeking to explain some particular phenomenon." Christensen and Snyder (2003: 66–67) assert that at least some realists "have generated insights into international politics that can be employed as tools in our broader, more eclectic research programs" and that dogmatic political realism and antirealism both "prove crippling in understanding many aspects of international relations." In some instances, realist explanations can be expected to recede into the background: "Ideology, institutions, domestic politics, and interdependence may indeed combine in various ways that make balance of power considerations irrelevant to various regions or bilateral relationships" (Christensen and Snyder 2003: 710). Glaser (2003: 274; see also Brecher 1999) adds that

> there is no reason that an analyst who works with structural theory should not combine it with other levels of analysis and/or with other structural or rational theories. There will be a trade-off with parsimony, but sometimes the real world will make trading complexity for parsimony a good deal. While there are strong reasons to be very clear about moves between levels of analysis and

---

[18] The preceding analysis goes against the vision from Kuhn (1970 [1962]) regarding research as inherently paradigm-driven and essentially incommensurable across such boundaries. However, this is more of an assumption than a confirmed finding and may apply in only a selected way, that is, to some fields of study and not others. So pursuit of progress in ways that transcend paradigmatic boundaries is worthy of consideration for IR—a discipline also not among the natural sciences that served as the focal point for Kuhn.

[19] For a dissenting view, which sees pluralism as limited, see Rengger (2015: 16–17).

assumptions about types of states, there is no good reason for theorists to lock themselves into too narrow a box.

Mearsheimer and Walt (2013: 430) add that "a diverse theoretical ecosystem is preferable to an intellectual monoculture." These and many other observations among those identified with realism could be cited as generally negative reactions to sustained, paradigm-based warfare within IR.

Consider additional assessments of realism in this context, but from observers beyond its boundaries. In a review of classical realism, Williams (2004: 659) observes that Morgenthau engaged with "complex political and analytical traditions often ignored in understandings of realism today." In addition, "While Morgenthau's realism has often been cast in opposition to a constructivist approach, enquiring more fully into his understanding of politics reveals a deep and challenging contribution to contemporary discussions over the development of constructivist thinking" (Williams 2004: 660). For example, Williams (2004: 638) observes that power and interest, as applied by Morgenthau, "are actually remarkably flexible and indeterminate concepts." Thus at least one view from outside contemporary realism sees a pernicious trend toward intellectual orthodoxy and even parochialism. Realism, from that perspective, might benefit from greater engagement with constructivism and other frames of reference normally regarded as beyond its boundaries. Such a process could prove beneficial—facilitating a return to more inclusive and intuitively appealing roots in the classical tradition.

Objections to paradigm-based conflict and openness to diverse theorizing, however, may reflect awareness and alarm about losing ground as the contest continues. One prominent exposition challenged realists to focus on greater coherence or move away from "social scientific concepts and language—paradigms, assumptions, theory testing, and so on" (Feaver et al. [Legro and Moravcsik] 2000: 190). Regardless of their motivation for the shift in thinking, there is value for realists, just like others, in taking an eclectic turn.

Progress, understood as growth of knowledge, cannot occur without resolution of differences between contending schools of thought (Chernoff 2017: 89). So, then, what about synthesis as an option? Is this the answer for realists as well as adherents of other paradigms? From one point of view, IR does not need theoretical integration, and thus "pluralism and openness—alongside an embrace of real-life complexity which leads away from the grand theoretical hang-ups discussed earlier—are productive for our field" (Freyberg-Inan 2017a: 84).[20] Perhaps improved communication among adherents of diverse approaches

---

[20] For a compelling argument against synthesis, developed in the context of attempts with regard to constructivism and critical theory, see Barkin and Sjoberg (2019).

could produce sufficient coherence and avert the problems associated with moving away from paradigmatic allegiance.

Rather than pursue great debates, IR should move in a more pragmatic direction. This line of reasoning, which emphasizes engagement rather than competition, can be summed up as "sociable pluralism" (Freyberg-Inan 2017). When reflecting upon the degree of confrontation embedded in long-standing conflicts over paradigms, an idea like sociable pluralism seems quite appealing. Wight (2019: 65, 68) follows up with a call for "integrative pluralism"—an attempt to connect theories and use alternative views to re-examine one's own theoretical position—that would combine insights to expand the substantive knowledge base of IR.

Increasing confrontation and resulting divisions, by contrast, are likely to stand in the way of progress for IR. This inference can be supported through application of the concept of social capital, which Putnam (1993) imported from sociology into the study of politics. Social capital takes two forms: (a) bonding, which is exclusive and assessed in terms of intragroup cohesion; and (b) bridging, which is inclusive and measured on the basic of intergroup connections (Putnam 1993). Bridging capital plays an unequivocally positive role in a society, forming a virtuous cycle with trust. Bonding capital, by contrast, can become pernicious when members of increasingly insular groups develop hostile inclinations toward those regarded as outsiders. A more nuanced treatment of social capital is beyond the scope of this study, but what appears already is sufficient to create concern about the role of paradigms within IR. Bonding capital increases, while bridging capital decreases, as paradigmatic allegiance becomes more intense among members of IR as a society. This trend, increasingly recognized as harmful, contributes to incommensurability, as described by Kuhn (1970 [1962]) and thus reduces prospects for moving forward as a discipline. It also undermines the trust (see Uslaner 2002) that is essential for collaboration between and among diverse research traditions.

Observers increasingly see IR as a collection of many subfields. Consider as just one example of the lack of connection between and among sectors of IR the following observations about research on the causes of war (Gat 2009: 571; see also Haas 2017: 41 on fragmentation in general): (a) the causes of war remain a strangely obscure subject in IR, (b) studies dedicated to the question are scarce, and (c) available studies tend to focus on conditions that affect the likelihood and frequency of war. The preceding assertions reflect the long-standing and harmful divide involving qualitative and quantitative methods—a "flawed dichotomy" in one prominent exposition (Brecher 1999). A vast range of books and articles focus on the causes of war per se, not just its likelihood and frequency. Quantitative studies, however, tend to appear in outlets such as *International Interactions, Conflict Management and Peace Science, Journal of*

Conflict Resolution, and *Journal of Peace Research*. Without monitoring these publications, it would be easy to believe that very little is being done explicitly in IR on the causes of war.

Synthesis of existing paradigms as an approach to deal simultaneously with lack of communication and ongoing disagreement, under current conditions, therefore seems unrealistic in light of accumulating bonding capital and relatively limited bridging capital in the community of IR. Intense interparadigmatic strife is the rule rather than the exception under these conditions. Any effort toward synthesis would seem most likely to create yet another axis of conflict, with adherents of respective paradigms fighting over degrees of incorporation within any proposed combination.

Toward Constructive Engagement

Shy of synthesis and perhaps more realistic regarding implementation is the idea that theories and methods previously isolated from each other, due to perceptions of incompatibility based on paradigmatic thinking, could be linked together in a mutually beneficial way. This would not need to take the form of an overly ambitious attempt at synthesis, but rather would be best carried out through an increased level of conversation among approaches (Barkin and Sjoberg 2019: 18). For example, a review of classical realist theory reveals that it is compatible with constructivist epistemology (Barkin 2010: 3). Realism is not inherently about only the material world; it also can focus on ideational aspects of power politics. Thus Barkin (2010), through a meticulous and insightful effort, is able to develop realist constructivism. Insights otherwise unavailable may be obtained through exploring previously neglected points of intersection.[21]

The preceding arguments against synthesis, but in favor of cooperation between and among theories and methods that previously have been separate from each other, lead naturally into analytic eclecticism as a more promising approach for IR. A summary statement is available from Sil (2009: 649; see also Sil and Katzenstein 2010b: 415, 417):

Analytic eclecticism is a problem-driven approach featuring the extraction, adaptation, and integration (but *not* synthesis) of discrete concepts, mechanisms,

---

[21] The preceding combination makes sense only if constructivism is understood as an approach—more akin to a *method* rather than a paradigm. Otherwise, in principle, constructivism could be made compatible with anything that turns up. For example, assumptions associated with traditional power politics, such as the concept of the national interest as objective in character and universal, simply are rewritten. Among the convincing arguments that designate constructivism as an approach are Barkin (2003: 336; 2010), Walker (2018: 196), and Barkin and Sjoberg (2019: 44).

logical principles, and interpretive moves normally embedded in emergent research traditions, each identified with distinct styles of research reflecting distinct combinations of ontological and epistemological principles.

Analytic eclecticism is gaining traction within the field of IR as adversarial communication and attendant disappointment with results from strict paradigmatic adherence become the norm. In seeking to transcend confrontation in IR, Cornut (2015: 3) observes that analytic eclecticism "is the most established and respected kind of problem-driven pragmatism." With its emphasis on relevance to problems in the real world of policy, analytic eclecticism represents a middle ground of "epistemological agnosticism" (Sil 2000b: 650; see also Katzenstein and Sil 2008: 111; Sil and Katzenstein 2010b: 417, 2010c: 113; Lake 2011: 471).[22] The exposition from *Beyond Paradigms* (Sil and Katzenstein 2010a), which stands as the magnum opus for analytic eclecticism, will be used to organize discussion about a way forward for IR.

Three markers of eclectic scholarship—(1) an open-ended approach to problem formulation, (2) middle-range causal arguments, and (3) an emphasis on practical application—are identified by Sil and Katzenstein (2010d: 19). Analytic eclecticism includes "a pragmatic ethos, manifested concretely in the search for middle-range theoretical arguments that potentially speak to concrete issues of policy and practice," and "addresses problems of wide scope" that "incorporate more of the complexity and messiness of particular real-world situations" (Sil and Katzenstein 2010b: 412). Analytic eclecticism thereby generates causal accounts that encompass "interactions among different types of causal mechanisms normally analyzed in isolation from each other within separate research traditions" (Sil and Katzenstein 2010b: 412). For all of the preceding reasons, analytic eclecticism represents a major departure from paradigm-driven research.

Given its pragmatic character and inherent skepticism of any pretensions to dominance for a particular school of thought, analytic eclecticism notably pursues theories of the middle range. These theories transcend "individual causal mechanisms" and focus on "how *combinations* of mechanisms interact in specified and often recurrent scope conditions or contexts to produce outcomes— whether these contexts are defined as kinds of states or other units, specific periods of time or areas of social space, or recurrent problems around which research traditions have formed, such as 'civil war,' 'democratic transitions,' or 'imperialism'" (Bennett 2013: 470). Some see the efforts of such "bridge builders" as quite successful already (Checkel 2010: 5). All of this seeks to go, as revealed

---

[22] Analytic eclecticism also goes against the trend in philosophy of science against claiming to inform practice. For a more extended treatment of such issues, see Gunnell (2011: 1454).

in the title of the prominent book-length exposition, *Beyond Paradigms* (Sil and Katzenstein 2010a).

Analytic Eclecticism in Practice

Analytic eclecticism is introduced more specifically in tandem with illustrations from a prominent classical realist text from IR, *A World Restored* (Kissinger 1957). Kissinger's study focuses on processes of settlement for the Napoleonic Wars, which included the Congress of Vienna as well as other lesser-known but nevertheless important events. *A World Restored* is selected among many possibilities because its author, Henry Kissinger, is one of the most significant practitioners in the history of international relations. Kissinger served as national security advisor and secretary of state for the United States during the Nixon and Ford administrations. He continues to be active as a pundit and seeks influence over foreign policy through editorials, books, and other platforms.

A World Restored is fundamentally realist in terms of paradigmatic allegiance, yet also incorporates ideas from elsewhere. Kissinger's intellectual formation, as described in an authoritative review of realpolitik as a concept, "bore the imprint of an eclectic range of influences and experiences" (Bew 2016: 257). This is not an uncommon assessment with regard to major scholars and publications from classical realism. Consider, for instance, the most prominent among the classical realist scholars of modern times, Morgenthau, who produced *Scientific Man and Power Politics* (1946), *Politics among Nations* (1959 [1948]), and other lasting works. Rosecrance and Steiner (2010: 342) sum up Morgenthau's perspective on international relations, which is revealed to have some diverse features from a theoretical point of view, as "ecumenical realism." Despite their state-centrism and emphasis on military security, classical realists such as Morgenthau have "depended on a transnational society of accomplished diplomats to produce the moderation they expect from a balance-of-power system" (Rosecrance and Steiner 2010). While power politics are front and center for classical realism, its theorizing also entails ideas from beyond paradigmatic boundaries.

Given the desire to introduce analytic eclecticism in a clear and accessible way, *A World Restored*, a major work within classical realism, is a suitable choice to illustrate its properties. These markers, as introduced above, are as follows: (1) open-ended assessment regarding formulation of problems, (2) development of a middle-range causal account that transcends paradigmatic boundaries, and (3) emphasis on practical relevance to foreign policy. Discussion of analytic eclecticism then turns to (a) priorities, (b) value added, (c) its connection to criteria regarding results for progress identified in Chapter 2, (d) what the approach does not entail, and (e) the need for a method of implementation.

Analytic eclecticism's first marker is an open-ended approach to problem formulation. This process should encompass the "complexity of phenomena" and is "not intended to advance or fill gaps in paradigm-bound scholarship" (Sil and Katzenstein 2011: 19; see also Sil and Katzenstein 2010b: 415). Thus, programs of research should draw on ideas from a range of theories in a focused effort to confront the intricate nature of real-world phenomena. Complexity is not held up as valuable for its own sake, but rather as a reaction to the fact that human societies indeed are multifaceted. Only by embracing that intricacy can scholars link theory with reality.

For example, *A World Restored* is identified with the realist paradigm, but its contents turn out to be eclectic, in an interdisciplinary sense, when put under the figurative microscope. Kissinger did not represent any specific theory of international relations and thus "perhaps evaded some of the theoretical grooves associated with these" (Bew 2016: 257). Factors emphasized by Kissinger (1957) originate within different disciplinary matrices—history and philosophy, among others—but all are found to matter with respect to how the settlement of the Napoleonic Wars played out from 1812 to 1822. For example, Kissinger's philosophy of history plays the same role for him as belief about human nature did for other classical realists (Smith 1986: 194).

Consider, specifically, the in-depth, *philosophical* assessment by Kissinger of Prince Klemens Wenzel von Metternich's worldview (Kissinger 1957: 191–213). The conservative principles of Austria's star diplomat are explored at length and used to account for his series of manipulations in search of a stable equilibrium for the European system. In a more general sense, the *historical* character of Kissinger's exposition comes through most directly in its chronological presentation of coalition formation against France, the Napoleonic Wars' denouement, and efforts toward settlement. Protracted negotiations included the well-remembered Congress of Vienna but also other lesser-known but still significant events and actions such as the Congress of Aix-la-Chapelle, Carlsbad Decrees, Congress of Troppau, and Congress of Laibach. Thus problem formulation and analysis in *A World Restored* transcend the boundaries of a given discipline or theories within it; solutions are to be gathered from wherever insight may be gleaned.

Second among the markers for analytic eclecticism is development of a "middle-range causal account" that incorporates "complex interactions among multiple mechanisms and logics drawn from more than one paradigm" (Sil and Katzenstein 2010d: 19; see also George and Bennett 2005; Sil and Katzenstein 2010b: 420; Freyberg-Inan 2017a). Sil and Katzenstein (2010b: 419) regard the concept of a mechanism as "a key feature in causal stories cast at the level of the middle range." Moreover, a focus on causal mechanisms and middle-range theories may reduce destructive infighting associated with research based on paradigms (Lake 2013: 568). Those theories could incorporate both hypotheses associated with respective paradigms and other hypotheses beyond such boundaries to zero in most effectively on a given empirical problem.

Sil and Katzenstein (2010a: 22) advocate development of middle-range theories that "shed light on specific sets of empirical phenomena" and "do not aspire to offer a general model or universal theory that can be readily adapted to investigate other kinds of phenomena." In that context, consider the mutual presence in *A World Restored* of (i) biographical chapters that zero in on the psychological makeup of key diplomats; and (ii) implicit applications of principles from rational choice. On the one hand, Kissinger explores the life experiences and mindsets of Lord Castlereagh (Robert Stewart, Second Marquess of Londonderry) and Metternich to account for their conduct of diplomacy in the complex and even confusing interactions in the late stages and aftermath of the Napoleonic Wars. On the other hand, *A World Restored* discusses the formation and breakup of wartime coalitions and thereby anticipates ideas presented more systematically in the pathbreaking rationalist exposition from Riker (1962) just a few years later. The presence of both types of analysis bridges the ongoing gap between political psychology and rational choice through an inclusive approach toward IR.

From the standpoint of analytic eclecticism, incorporation of factors taken from such diverse paradigmatic backgrounds is not only acceptable but worth pursuing. Middle-range theorizing for a given set of dependent variables may work best with diverse explanatory factors that transgress paradigmatic boundaries. The burden of proof, moreover, falls on critics of analytic eclecticism, who need to show why efforts to combine propositions from different theories and even paradigms should *not* be pursued. All of that is reinforced in a prominent exposition by Lake (2011), which went so far as to say that "isms"—meaning paradigms—can be "evil" because of the extremism and intellectual closure that they sometimes induce in adherents. While "evil" seems too strong a few years onward, "pernicious" might work instead with regard to some aspects of paradigmatic life.

Third among the markers of analytic eclecticism is an emphasis on practical relevance—a connection with concerns of policymakers, among those playfully designated as serfs in the extension of the medieval metaphor from Barkin (2010). An important goal of analytic eclecticism is to obtain findings that "pragmatically engage both academic debates and the practical dilemmas of policymakers" (Sil and Katzenstein 2010: 19; see also Wight 2017: 32). This marker works well for *A World Restored*, which includes a full chapter on the nature of statesmanship (Kissinger 1957: 312–332). One practical insight offered is that the "acid test" for a policy is "its ability to obtain domestic support" (Kissinger 1957: 326). This direct affirmation of the importance of domestic politics for policy implementation—and far from the only one in a primarily realist exposition—once again highlights the analytic eclecticism of *A World Restored*. It even harks back to Morgenthau (1959 [1948]), who assessed domestic politics as both (a) a detriment to policymaking via moralistic intervention from the mass public; and (b) an asset when national morale, expressed through pride, enhances overall power and efficacy.

What, then, are the *priorities* of analytic eclecticism? The approach "trains its sights on the connections and interactions among a wide range of causal forces normally analyzed in isolation" (Sil and Katzenstein 2010a: 12). This priority is manifested in *A World Restored* through a panoramic mode of operation that incorporates personalities, domestic politics, and geography, among other factors. (All of these considerations, it should be noted, are taken up in Morgenthau (1959 [1948]) as well.) Some of the most entertaining moments from Kissinger's exposition, for instance, pertain to Metternich's view of Tsar Alexander I of Russia, described as "too weak for true ambition, but too strong for pure vanity" (Kissinger 1957: 90). *A World Restored* also contains references to the impact of location on national interests, strategy, and tactics: "That Austria should seek stability was inherent in its geographic position and domestic structure" (Kissinger 1957: 325). Kissinger's exposition is primarily realist but secondarily many other things; it is both material and ideational in approach. In that way, *A World Restored* foreshadows Barkin's call (2010) to consider the potential for a realist version of constructivism.

Analytic eclecticism attends carefully to processes that "cut across different levels of analysis and transcend the divide presumed to exist between observable material factors and unobservable cognitive or ideational ones" (Sil and Katzenstein 2010a: 21).[23] With its combination of philosophical reflections on the worldviews of diplomats and assessment of relative capabilities among states and coalitions, *A World Restored* incorporates both ideational and material analyses in a state-centric and power-oriented way. It might be added that, when *A World Restored* focuses on individuals, these are top-level decision-makers. In that sense, Kissinger's analysis remains state-centric even at its ideational points of reflection.

Analytic eclecticism encourages theorizing that generates "'pragmatic engagement' with the social conditions within which prevailing ideas about world politics have emerged" (Sil and Katzenstein 2010a: 22). Thus, analytic eclecticism

---

[23] According to Sil and Katzenstein (2010a: 14–15), incommensurability of paradigms is not insurmountable: (1) differences are "less constraining when it comes to integrating elements from these theories"; and (2) "theories concerning substantive questions must ultimately rely on empirical referents to operationalize concepts, variables, and mechanisms." Moreover, multiple theories within paradigms and variation in how terms are defined and used point in the direction of feasibility (Sil and Katzenstein 2010a: 15, 31).

is rooted in the "real world" and derives its agenda from a desire to better link the abstractions of theory to complex outcomes that populate the international system. Implicit is a sense that paradigm-based research, by contrast, will prove self-limiting and perhaps even barren with respect to policy-related application.

The "Balance Sheet"

What is the *value added* of analytic eclecticism for IR? Sil and Katzenstein (2010a: 20; see also Sil and Katzenstein 2010c: 111) emphasize expanding the complexity and scope of questions to "facilitate a more open-ended analysis that can incorporate the insights of different paradigm-bound theories and relate them to the concerns of policymakers and ordinary actors"; the approach brings "attention to the multiplicity, heterogeneity, and interaction of causal mechanisms and processes that generate phenomena of interest to scholars and practitioners." Analytic eclecticism provides an agenda for developing frameworks by directing scholars to engage theory across paradigmatic boundaries with how actors comprehend the world and act upon their perceptions. Analytic eclecticism therefore provides a guide for IR scholars—the producers of research—to think about the relationship between theories and concepts and a foundation for developing causal mechanisms that emphasize grounding in the real world of politics. All of this is expected to work out to the advantage of those designated as consumers of research—both leadership and the lay public.

Analytic eclecticism connects well with the criteria regarding results for progress identified in Chapter 2: range of explanation, predictive value, and public exchange of views. Range of explanation is enhanced via the inclusive approach that is at the center of analytic eclecticism. With a wider range of ideas brought into the fold, theorizing from analytic eclecticism also possesses positive implications for predictive value. As a general rule, forecasting models get better as they incorporate a greater quantity and range of variables. Finally, analytic eclecticism promotes public exchange of views in terms of the diversity of those involved in the discussion. By definition, interparadigmatic dialogue is more inclusive than its intraparadigmatic equivalent.

Sil and Katzenstein (2010a: 23) sum up analytic eclecticism as follows:

> Our conceptualization of eclectic scholarship is distinctive in that it seeks to bridge *all* of these concerns, linking a pragmatist orientation towards the production of useful knowledge to problem-driven research aimed at better understanding of real-world phenomena and to mid-range causal accounts that draw upon mechanisms and processes normally analyzed in isolation within separate paradigms.

Eclectic work "accommodates and encourages efforts, alongside paradigm-bound research, that aim at translation, comparison, and dialogue within and beyond academic circles" (Sil and Katzenstein 2010d: 21). Haas (2010a: 5) adds that analytic eclecticism "is a work of art in the sense that it helps us see the world in new ways and to appreciate multiple perspectives, as is the goal of all good art." This praise, however, indirectly draws attention to what is lacking so far in the review of analytic eclecticism: a sense of its relationship to standards for *scientific* inquiry.

Given the inclusive story told above about how to study international relations, a natural question to ask is this one: "With its encompassing nature, what does analytic eclecticism *not* include?" "Analytic eclecticism," Sil and Katzenstein (2010a: 16; see also Sil and Katzenstein 2010c: 111) are careful to note, "does not imply that 'anything goes.'" A need for logical consistency among diverse causal mechanisms is implicit. Otherwise, internal contradictions would take analytic eclecticism down the path to scientific irrelevance identified by Vasquez (1983, 1998; see also Legro and Moravcsik 1999) with regard to realism.[24]

Analytic eclecticism is neither (a) "theoretical synthesis" that calls for dismantling of established research traditions nor (b) "coterminous with multi-method research or methodological triangulation" (Sil and Katzenstein 2010a: 17, 18). The first assertion makes immediate sense because of the effective impossibility of synthesizing diverse paradigms into one; the result would be a Frankenstein monster of self-contradiction. Instead, Sil and Katzenstein's unstated but virtually certain intention is to combine logically consistent axioms *across* paradigms to derive previously unavailable and possibly interesting propositions for subsequent evaluation. The second claim made just above opens the door to the question of how method *does* come into play for Sil and Katzenstein (2010a, 2010b). How is analytic eclecticism to be implemented? The very nature of the approach argues against orthodoxy, so it is not obvious how to proceed.

Via examples of research throughout IR—on security studies, political economy, and order and governance—Sil and Katzenstein (2010a) show analytic eclecticism in action. These illustrations, which are compelling, suggest that knowledge consistent with analytic eclecticism already is plentiful. Yet the discussion in Sil and Katzenstein (2010a) concludes with a sense that an "invisible hand" is at work. Research projects do not *intend* to pursue an eclectic approach, but if applied creatively, good things can and do happen.

Take, for example, the territorial and border-related explanation of war, already noted above (Huth 1998; Senese and Vasquez 2008; Gibler 2012). It developed outside of both the liberal and the realist paradigms. The territorial account

---

[24] This point will re-emerge during Chapter 6 on the role of methods within the metatheory of progress.

Table 4.1 Analytic Eclecticism and Implementation

Numeral	Statement
I	"The specific contours of this strategy depend on the relevant intellectual context.... In the context of contemporary international relations, analytic eclecticism is minimally operationalized as analysis that extricates and combines elements of theories embedded in the three major paradigms—realism, liberalism, and constructivism—in the process of building complex middle-range causal stories that bear on important matters of policy and practice."
II	Quotation from T. V. Paul: "We need to know how these different variables (often drawn from different paradigms) are connected, and how they affect or cause the outcome—alone or in conjunction with others—that we are trying to explain."
III	What makes an eclectic approach rigorous is not the incorporation of each and every imaginable factor, but judicious attention to how a set of clearly defined causal mechanisms normally posited in different paradigms interact with each other and combine to generate interesting outcomes.
IV	It is not possible to construct a definitive "model" or "guide" for conducting eclectic scholarship.

Source: Sil and Katzenstein (2010a: 37, 89, 100, 205).

for war started out, to some extent, as a critique of realism's penchant for treating all substantive issues as existing in the same way under the umbrella of power politics. The territory-based line of research then went on to focus upon peaceful borders and served as a rallying point for criticism of liberal concentration on regime type, notably democracy, as the explanation for pacific interstate dyads. The territorial account for war and peace presently exists outside of paradigmatic boundaries, although of course it could be absorbed by one or more such entities already in existence. The significant point here is that research on territorial issues and borders already has achieved a great deal without paradigmatic guidance.

Table 4.1 conveys a few selected statements (numbered I to IV) from Sil and Katzenstein (2010a) that pertain to implementation of analytic eclecticism. Statement I asserts that intellectual context should be taken into account. Elements from major paradigms—today most commonly but inappropriately identified as liberalism, realism, and constructivism—should be used to build complex middle-range theories that maintain relevance to the real world.[25] From

---

[25] Left aside once again is the question of whether constructivism should be included as one of

Statement II comes the admonition that it is essential to know how variables from across paradigms are connected. Statement III calls for judicious attention to how interparadigmatic causal mechanisms interact and combine to form a more convincing whole. Statement IV warns against attempting to develop a model or guide for eclecticism—a point that would seem in line, perhaps, with the very nature of the approach itself. All of these items make sense individually, but the engagement of Statements II and III with IV is troubling. How can variables from across paradigms be connected logically and coherently without a method to guide the process?

Interesting to ponder in response to the preceding question is the tendency of analytic eclecticism to occur in a natural way. In a review of the approach, Ba (2010: 14) asserts that those carrying out a certain kind of project "*had* to become analytically eclectic to be true—that is, their empirical problems 'made them do it' even against their social science trained inclinations and desire for parsimony." This probably accurate assessment of analytic eclecticism in practice identifies an essential problem: in the effort to evade paradigmatic parochialism, the pendulum of research could swing toward a maze of studies with individual value but collective self-contradiction. "While supporting analytic eclecticism," observes Lake (2011: 472; see also Checkel 2010: 24), "the only real alternative to the status quo, I nonetheless fear an intellectual tower of Babel." From a scientific point of view, that is not a desirable state of affairs.

Exponents of analytic eclecticism are aware of the risk that confusion might end up as the replacement for the long-standing silo-like predominance of paradigms. Sil and Katzenstein (2010b: 414) acknowledge the "danger of theoretical incoherence linked to the problem of incommensurability across traditions." Others express this concern in reaction to the trend away from research based explicitly on a given school of thought: "While I am not advocating a return to the 'good old days' of isms, I do worry that IR theory has swung too far in the other direction" (Checkel 2016: 5). Parsons (2015: 30) adds that electicist literature "gives strikingly little attention to competing accounts. These scholars justify engagement almost entirely in combinatory rather than competitive terms." At the same time, Sil and Katzenstein (2010b: 425) remind critics that incommensurability, in principle, can "exist across theories *within* research traditions as well as across applications of the same theory in different contexts." Intense debates within realism over offensive versus defensive variants reinforce that point; at times, it can sound like participants are talking past each other. Realists, as Brooks (1997: 473;

---

the paradigms for IR. Alternatively, it would seem more accurate to regard it as a vision of units and methods, with ideas given status along with material factors in seeking to explain the world. Thus it would be possible to imagine constructivist theorizing within the boundaries of any given paradigm, as pursued by Barkin (2010) with regard to realism.

see also Schmidt 2007) observes, lack "a unified set of assumptions about state behavior." This in all likelihood explains why some debates never seem to end, within realism and elsewhere—arguments keep returning to axioms and thus possess no natural point of termination. In sum, an impasse exists for the moment: understanding of, but not actions about, the deleterious side effects of eclectic theorizing in the absence of guidelines for implementation.

Additional concerns about analytic eclecticism derive from its tendency, at least so far, toward qualitative rather than quantitative research. Depth therefore is privileged over breadth of explanation (Grieco 2019). More specifically, Grieco (2019) draws attention to a resulting inability, with a small number of observations, to take into account variables in the form of interaction terms. This suggests that analytic eclecticism, upon implementation, would be better off with a process of research in which qualitative and quantitative methods are combined through alternation with each other. Such an approach would avert the problem posed by the need to take into account interaction terms and perhaps others associated with a current self-imposed restriction to qualitative rather than quantitative methods.

Analytic eclecticism will be in a position to contribute even more to progress in IR if it can be linked to a *method* that preserves its appealing traits while creating the potential for more effective implementation. Standards for good research, according to Ba (2010: 15; see also Sil and Katzenstein 2010c: 111), do not permit "an "everything goes" approach." Eclecticism should encourage problem-driven rather than random activity—in sum, a pluralist but nonetheless organized approach. As Cornut (2015: 51) observes, scholars so far "neither sufficiently clarify the internal consistency of an eclectic analysis, nor establish convincing criteria for which theories were to be included or excluded in analyses." Thus there still is no escape from the need for a method to accompany analytic eclecticism.

Among those well disposed toward analytic eclecticism, some reflections on method already exist. Sil and Katzenstein (2010b: 415) assert that analytic eclecticism "may utilize but is not synonymous with methodological triangulation or multi-method research." Bennett (2010: 7) observes that paradigms had value because of an ability to combine theories about causal mechanisms "in ways that have proved memorable and easy to convey," so the onus is on any alternative approach to accomplish that but "without creating new constraints on theorizing and research." Paul (2010: 18) adds that "willingness to work through the causal mechanisms and pathways rather than simply narrating variables" is essential to a productive eclectic approach. Thus the principal challenge to analytic eclecticism is to maintain its inclusive character while also coping with tendencies toward chaos in the absence of some overarching principles for linking together diverse approaches.

Given existing conditions, it is appropriate to turn to a model of cognition—essential to processing the results of the expansive research agenda that follows on from increasing adoption of analytic eclecticism in IR. The forthcoming model of cognition produces the conclusion that a *graphic* turn is essential for IR at this stage of its development. In Chapter 6 on methods, it will be argued that systemism, which emphasizes visual representation of causes and effects, provides the technique that IR needs. This is true especially with regard to research carried out under the auspices of analytic eclecticism. Systemism, moreover, offers analytic eclecticism a method that is anything but a Procrustean bed. The graphic approach instead provides a valuable means toward reconciliation of diverse theorizing with the need for logical consistency. Visual presentation of causal mechanisms facilitates detection of errors of omission and commission within an eclectic framework assembled from inside, across, and even beyond paradigms.

What about analytic eclecticism in an overall sense? On the positive side of the balance sheet, the approach offers flexibility and a welcome break from interparadigmatic rivalry. Analytic eclecticism encourages combination of diverse insights into empirical problems and also emphasizes pursuit of research that is relevant to policy. Potential chaos occupies the negative side of the balance sheet for analytic eclecticism. What if its ecumenical approach just leads to confusion rather than progress? A potential solution to this problem is identified and pursued in the section that follows, which introduces a model of cognition.

A Model of Cognition (X)

This section pursues four goals. First, the vastness of IR is identified as a challenge to the discipline with regard to maintaining coherence and thereby staying on the path toward scientific progress. The second goal is to introduce the concept of metacognition, which is essential to developing a model of the mind that will be helpful to IR. Third, cognitive load theory is used to identify priorities for that model. Fourth and finally, the model calls for a graphic turn, along with implementation of techniques for relational reasoning that will help with combining pictures and words into more compelling explanations for IR.

Too Much Information?

While precise estimates of its pace and quantity may vary, there is no doubt concerning the rapid accumulation of academic research over the last century. Based on three indicators—PhDs granted, patents issued, and papers published—Gastfriend (2015) estimates that 90% of all scientists who ever have lived are active now. Obviously from the standpoint of a discipline like IR, patents are not directly relevant, but the other two metrics point toward massive expansion of the field. The precise calculation of 90% for scientific activity today does not have to obtain for the review from Gastfriend (2015) to provide a foundation for the argument that will proceed within this section on cognition. The same conclusion would be reached even with a lower estimate because accumulation of theorizing and research findings over the course of decades so obviously is extensive.

There is no question that patterns of development and discretionary income, along with population growth, have resulted in a rapid expansion of the number of scholars producing research over the last century. This increase fanned out from contributions initially made by scientists in a few especially wealthy and advanced states to include more diverse locations over time. The world of today is one in which vast amounts of research have accumulated and therefore need to be processed in some way by continuing participants, along with new entrants, in any given field of study. Discussion naturally ensues in the context of IR.

While various creation stories might be told about IR, a sociological one is most relevant for present purposes.[26] Intense curiosity about the causes and prevention of major war accounts for the origin of IR. From a sociological standpoint, the beginning of IR as a discipline can be traced to the first academic unit in its name. Immediately after the Great War, now known as World War I, IR came into existence. Academics and diplomats in search of lasting peace created the discipline of IR toward that end (Guzzini 1998: 15; Knutsen 2016: 8, 52). Founded in 1919, the Department of International Relations at Aberystwyth University is the first entity known to have brought together scholars in an organized and sustained way to study the subject matter of IR (Porter 1972; see also Guzzini 1998: 9).

Today, a century later, IR is vast and features high internal complexity. For example, as compared to 2,300 members of the International Studies Association (ISA) in 1988, there were over 7,000 in 2017. For 1980 versus 2017, the respective numbers in parentheses with regard to ISA sections (8, 29), caucuses (0, 4), and journals (1, 7) tell the tale (Saideman 2018). The sociology of knowledge for IR continues to become more intricate with time.

IR also is highly diverse in terms of viewpoints and quite interdisciplinary. Ideas associated with the Global South challenge points of consensus and even

---

[26] Chernoff (2014: 8–9; see also Knutsen 2017: 52) cites one example of what, depending on how it is defined, may be the earliest instance of explanation within IR: "Around 430 BCE Sun Tzu developed a set of principles based on observations of multiple cases, from which he derived regularities in the decisions of military leaders." The exposition from Sun Tzu and others in ancient times provided the basis for what evolved into realism today.

complacency in the Global North (Acharya 2014). New cognate fields continue to arise and make significant contributions to IR (Yetiv and James 2016). The increasing number of social scientists and resulting quantity and diversity of research produced becomes relevant across the board. To cite just a few prominent instances, innovations from various disciplines are impacting foreign policy analysis and the study of conflict processes.[27] Moreover, this type of interdisciplinary borrowing also tends to move IR in the direction of analytic eclecticism, as concepts and methods are imported from other disciplines to address longstanding empirical problems. In some instances, incorporation of ideas from another discipline can produce a vast literature in and of itself, such as the expected utility theory of conflict, with origins in economics (Bueno de Mesquita 1981; James and Jones 2018).

What, then, can be said in an overall sense about IR as a result of such developments? The discipline has expanded enormously in terms of both sheer content and internal complexity. Knowledge lags behind because the challenges of integrating the vast amount of information, increasingly segmented among specialized areas of research, remain to be met.

Metacognition

How, then, does all of that matter with regard to a metatheory for IR? An answer to that question entails discussion of metacognition, which "literally means cognition about cognition, or more informally, thinking about thinking" (Baker 2016). To begin, learning is a process rather than a product and involves "*change in knowledge, beliefs, behaviors, or attitudes*" (Ambrose et al. 2010: 3). Change in knowledge derives from experience (Mayer 2010: 14). Ambrose et al. (2010: 4) observe that organization of knowledge influences learning and application of what is learned. It is best for the organization of what is known to feature rich connections that occur in meaningful rather than superficial ways (Ambrose et al. 2010: 46). Knowledge obviously means something beyond retaining information through memory. Links and cross-referencing distinguish knowledge organization by an expert, who in turn can draw upon such material more effectively (Ambrose et al. 2010: 51). An authority in IR, for example, would know that a subject such as trade plays different roles throughout the infrastructure of the discipline. It will tend to be an independent variable in quantitative scholarship about conflict processes. By contrast, international political economy more

---

[27] Examples would include neuropolitics in relation to how trust, cooperation, and strife connect with each other in relation to foreign policy (Kugler and Zak 2017), along with technology studies (Fritsch 2017) and gender studies (Basu and Eichler 2017) as linked to conflict processes.

often will treat trade as a dependent variable—along with investment and a few other entities—among the preeminent items identified for explanation.

Paradigms thus represent a double-edged sword for IR. These schemes of organization provide links and cross-referencing through a network of concepts. Consider, for example, the role of international society in moderating power politics that is central to the English School as a paradigm (Bull 1977; see also Ruane and James 2008, 2012). The same could be said of liberalism, which sees international and domestic politics as intertwined. Liberal theory entails a bottom-up view of politics and therefore sees research into domestic preference formation as essential (Moravcsik 1997: 517, 544).

However, what if a paradigm begins to inhibit processing of unwelcome data that contradicts its propositions? For example, what if English school or liberal adherents ignored or dismissed, for instance, evidence that supported power politics *writ large*? This type of reaction certainly can occur among adherents of an ideology (Homer-Dixon et al. 2013: 352). Loyalty to a paradigm might reach that level of intensity as well—one that blocks rational updating of beliefs in a Bayesian sense when new information creates discomfort. The ongoing possibility of this type of bias for any paradigm constitutes yet another argument in favor of a visual turn for IR. Graphic representation and consensus on causal mechanisms for a theory within a paradigm enhances the likelihood of scientifically motivated processing of discordant information.

Although a scientifically grounded literature exists on metacognition, educational practices tend to reflect views with a philosophical basis (Shuell 2016). Pashler et al. (2009: 116; see also Rohrer and Pashler 2012: 635 and Bleiker 2018b: 11) sum up insights from empirical research with regard to learning:

> The optimal instructional method is likely to vary across disciplines. For instance, the optimal curriculum for a writing course probably includes a heavy verbal emphasis, whereas the most efficient and effective method of teaching geometry obviously requires visual-spatial materials. Of course, identifying the optimal approach for each discipline is an empirical question, and we espouse research using strong research methods to identify the optimal approach for each kind of subject matter.[28]

---

[28] Pashler et al. (2009: 106; see also Rohrer and Pashler 2012: 634) acknowledge the existence of a range of self-stated preferences with regard to learning style, that is, individuals' belief that a given approach toward instruction will be better for them. While available research acknowledges that study preferences exist, it does *not* support the reality of individual learning styles. In other words, people sometimes hold faulty beliefs about what works best for them, which can cause problems and lead to suboptimal choices regarding instruction (Pashler et al. 2009: 108, 111, 116–117).

Rohrer and Pashler (2012: 635) add that the best ways to present particular bodies of content "often involve combining different forms of instruction, such as diagrams and words, in mutually reinforcing ways." This process can facilitate development of a schema, "an organizing structure that connects knowledge elements into a coherent mental representation" (Mayer 2010: 29).[29] Consider also the Multimedia Principle (Danielson and Sinatra 2017: 56–57), which

> posits that verbal and graphical information are processed in different cognitive subsystems, which leads the reader to construct two mental models, one for the text and one for the graphic. These two are then mapped on to one another. Thus, the additive effect of presenting information in two forms provides a potential learning advantage over the singular mode of presentation.

In sum, psychologists of learning have identified a priority for IR, along with other disciplines: a graphic turn. IR and other social sciences tend toward verbal over visual communications, and a more balanced approach is in order.

Observations about best practices with regard to learning are interesting to ponder in the context of IR. Among its many scholars, most pursue research that is communicated only in words, while others use equations, diagrams, and still further means to understand and explain. Regardless of format, however, theory and research in IR resemble work in other disciplines in terms of the sheer quantity of words accumulating over time. Thus, in turn, it becomes more challenging to sum up and synthesize insights into a body of knowledge.

Over two decades ago, Walt (1998: 29) called for more theory to help with the problem of a fast-paced world:

> We need theories to make sense of the blizzard of information that bombards us daily. Even policymakers who are contemptuous of "theory" must rely on their own (often unstated) ideas about how the world works in order to decide what to do.

In the new millennium, however, IR is past the point in its evolution where even major sectors of scholarship can be reviewed and synthesized effectively if efforts are restricted to words alone. "IR is today, if anything," observe Snidal and Wendt (2009: 4), "over-supplied with theories of every conceivable variety." IR theory continues "to evolve at an almost bewildering pace, which can be interpreted as evidence either of wondrous vitality in the field (as I prefer) or of intellectual fragmentation to the point of absurdity—or perhaps of something in between"

---

[29] Analysis of schema in IR began with the pathbreaking study by Axelrod (1973). Cognitive maps for decision-makers have continued to develop within the domain of foreign policy analysis.

(Ferguson 2015: 3). The truth probably lies somewhere in the middle, as Ferguson implies, but the direction of movement is cause for concern. Ferguson (2015: 8) adds that "the more we seem to know the more it is apparent how much we still do *not* know and the daunting complexity of the countless puzzles that remain." Expansion of the research community is resulting, to use an audial analogy, in "less of a symphony and more of a cacophony" (Harrison, Freyberg-Inan, and James 2016: 1). "The chief problem of this study," observes the author of a comprehensive history of IR theory, "is not that there are too few sources, but that there are too many" (Knutsen 2016: 5). This assessment only becomes more accurate with time.

All of this applies to realism in particular. Both advocates and critics draw attention to vast bodies of theorizing. From inside realism, one observer—and over two decades ago—described the hypotheses about causes of war as "large but unuseful" (Van Evera 1999: 2). Critics, meanwhile, identify extensive and expanding lists of realist propositions (Wayman and Diehl 1994a: 10–12). These collections of hypotheses lack the integrated character that would seem essential to facilitate a compelling explanation for war, the most important empirical problem that realism addresses.

Consider, as a parallel development in the real world of international relations, the dynamic tension in the intelligence community with regard to collection versus processing (Lowenthal 2017). On the one hand, there is more information than ever to collect. On the other hand, what if the budget for processing is so limited that much of what is collected gets processed slowly, badly, or not at all? This is yet another manifestation of the problem of information overload in the 21st century—an example from the reality of world politics that can inform IR as a discipline.

Assertions about expansiveness and intricacy of accumulated research, and a later recommendation about how to respond to challenges posed by the vast body of work compiled in IR, follow logically from cognitive load theory. Well established in the discipline of psychology, cognitive load theory "can provide guidelines to assist in the presentation of information in a manner that encourages learner activities that optimize intellectual performance" (Kirschner, Kirschner, and Paas 2016). The theory identifies types of memory and asserts that learning occurs most effectively when burdens are managed effectively through proper communication.

Consider, to begin, working memory. This capability is used when people engage in activities such as reading. With short duration and relatively small capacity, working memory's format is organized (Mayer 2010: 36). This type of memory "is limited to about seven new items or elements of information at any one time when the information merely has to be remembered" (Kirschner, Kirschner, and Paas 2016; see also Mayer 2010: 35). According to Kirschner, Kirschner, and Paas

(2016), when material obtained through reading (or other means) used for analytical purposes also is applied "to organize, contrast, compare or work on, only two or three items of information can be processed simultaneously." This is because the duration of working memory is short and its capacity is small (Mayer 2010: 36). Thus even greater limits occur when analysis is pursued—just two or three rather than seven new items can be dealt with at a time.[30]

Within the era of self-consciously scientific research on IR, introduction of multiple concepts and manipulation of more than two at once turns out to be the norm rather than the exception. So-called traditional critics of the scientific (and at times even scientistic) turn in IR during the era of high behaviorism in the 1960s may have been right about some things but perhaps for reasons other than those stated at the time.

Take, for example, certain aspects of the debate involving Kaplan (1966) and Bull (1966), mentioned earlier, over the utility of importing techniques from the sciences into IR. Among many arguments back and forth between advocates of "old and new research methods" (Knutsen 2016: 62; see also Guzzini 1998: 32), the debate between Bull and Kaplan remains representative and even iconic. Bull (1966: 364) begins his critique by saying that some reasons for opposing science-oriented approaches are of limited importance or even irrelevant, such as "tortuous and inelegant writing." He then moves on to defense of a classical approach, which emphasizes the role of accumulated "wisdom" and eschews the narrow constraints of so-called scientific research (Bull 1966: 366). For Bull (1966: 366), the classical pathway, with its emphasis on history and philosophy, is the only one that will lead to lasting insights about international relations with relevance to the real world.

Ironically, the barb concerning bad communication on the part of IR scholars who favor a scientific approach—dismissed by Bull with a figurative wave of the hand—ultimately may turn out to be more relevant than points of criticism he regarded as compelling. This conclusion is a product of the insights regarding cognition summarized above. When multiple concepts are introduced and manipulated simultaneously—and Kaplan (1957), singled out by Bull (1966) for its infelicities of style, contains a vast array of new formulations—overwhelming cognitive obstacles can ensue.[31] This problem

---

[30] Analysis means connection between and among items, which can entail both those that are direct and those of a higher order. Thus the complexity of analysis rises at a greater pace than the mere linear addition of items because of the combinations involved. For example, consider the shift from three to four items. Possible combinations of items rise from four to 11.

[31] Inspired by general systems theory, Kaplan (1957) introduced simultaneously a wealth of concepts from across respective disciplines, with terminology adopted from the early years of computer science and related fields. Game theory, along with cybernetic and system-based analysis, came together to produce a demanding exposition on international politics.

becomes even more likely as the innovative concepts are manipulated within complex frameworks. While Kaplan (1957) stands as an extreme example, it is not difficult to cite many other studies that introduce multiple concepts simultaneously and engage in densely worded manipulation of them, which in turn is likely to produce limited comprehension and even hostility from readers.

Many years later, another prominent controversy can be traced, at least in part, to proliferating concepts and limitations in the ability to grasp their meaning and connections to each other. This refers to devastating critiques from Vasquez (1983, 1998, 2003a) directed toward realism. While many more instances are available, those that follow are sufficient to make the point. Vasquez (2003a: 32) expresses exasperation with the rapidly changing character of realism. Why, he asks, is balance-of-threat theory from Walt (1987, 1990) a "refinement" rather than an "unexpected anomalous finding" for realism? Balance-of-threat theory, after all, is not in realist tracts prior to Walt (1987, 1990), who used that concept to account for the origins of alliances. In addition, Vasquez (2003a: 34) is troubled by Schweller's finding that bandwagoning is more common than balancing. This finding, he asserts, poses difficulty for every type of realist. How can realism ever be falsified, Vasquez (2003a: 34) asks, if both balancing and bandwagoning are accepted as confirming evidence? Many other questions about aspects of the scientific viability of realism have been posed as well.

Vasquez (Elman and Vasquez 2003: 291) sums up the process leading to such conundrums: "Part of the reason for the protean nature of realist explanations of balancing undoubtedly has to do with the ease with which the ambiguity and multiple referents of balancing of power lends itself to shifting the evidentiary base of the theory in light of discrepant evidence." At least some variation of realism is likely to be consistent with *any* future event, but that is a function of its self-contradictory, as opposed to compelling, nature. Under such conditions, realism forfeits scientific status.

All of this leads back, predictably, to problems of cognition. In this case, the reference is not to the critic, Vasquez, but to the purveyors of concepts that do not fit together. That is, at least some exponents of realism have not realized the importance of logical consistency to maintaining scientific status. The way to achieve such congruity is further reflection on how proliferating concepts fit together—or, importantly, are at odds with each other and require rethinking. What Vasquez describes is conceptual expansion in the absence of diagrammatic monitoring, for want of a more elegant expression, to facilitate clear communication and prevent the persistence of contradictions. A graphic turn therefore is needed to begin sorting things out.

Cognitive Load Theory

This is a good point at which to offer further specifics regarding cognitive load theory and its relevance to a graphic turn for IR. Three types of cognitive load are identified (Kirschner, Kirschner, and Paas 2016):

- Intrinsic cognitive load is a direct function of performing the task, in particular, of the number of elements that must be simultaneously processed in working memory.
- Germane cognitive load is related to processes that directly contribute to learning.
- Extraneous cognitive load is the extra load beyond the intrinsic cognitive load, mainly resulting from poorly designed instruction. For instance, if learners must search in their instructional materials for the information they need to perform a learned task, that creates extraneous cognitive load.

When these three loads are added together, learning can take place only if the sum does not exceed the capacity of working memory (Kirschner, Kirschner, and Paas 2016). It becomes a priority to limit cognitive load to whatever degree possible while still communicating essential information.

Consider contemporary IR in the context of cognitive load, most notably the extraneous type. While various studies include diagrams, these appear without widely accepted guidelines for their creation. Through poor design, these figures create what Tufte (2006: 121) labeled hyperactive optical clutter—an obvious form of extraneous cognitive load. Put differently, current diagrammatic expositions do not combine to advance the field and may even be aggravating communication problems in IR.

Better graphics can help to manage cognitive load in IR. In addition, four types of relational reasoning are available to help in processing text and graphic material in tandem with each other: analogy, anomaly, antinomy, and antithesis (Danielson and Sinatra 2017).[32] Each type is introduced at this point and applied at various locations in later chapters that present realist theories about the causes of war.

---

[32] Experimental evidence from Danielson and Sinatra (2017: 68) supports the idea that visual and verbal expositions, coupled with a stimulant toward relational reasoning, work effectively together: "The best performing group was that of those students who read the refutation text paired with the standard graphic showing the potential *additive effect* of graphics paired with refutation text." Danielson and Sinatra (2017: 68) observe that the strongest performance condition corresponded to the "'kitchen sink' version which paired all three": refutation text, graphic, antinomy.

Analogies represent "essentially a mapping process by which the conceptual properties of one domain are mapped onto the conceptual properties of another" (Danielson and Sinatra 2017: 58). A long-standing example of an analogy in international relations concerns the balance of power. If an equal amount of weight is placed on the two sides of a scale, it is in balance. The international system is said to show a balance of power if the states lined up in opposing coalitions possess approximately the same level of capabilities. This is just one of many variations on application of the balance-of-power concept to international relations by way of analogy (Zinnes 1967).

Anomalies refer to "events, data, or occurrences that are unusual or do not fit with our expectations" (Danielson and Sinatra 2017: 59). Anomalies can help to stimulate creative thinking. Danielson and Sinatra (2017: 60) contend that "surprising information works to promote conceptual change" because anomalous data "prompts individuals to reconsider their prior position to resolve the discrepancy with the information." In making this point, Danielson and Sinatra (2017: 61) refer to a classic case from the history of science: the Broad Street cholera outbreak in London in 1854. Only after answering the questions posed by anomalies that became apparent through assessing graphic data could John Snow, a physician, "determine the cause of the epidemic—a tainted water pump. Once the handle was removed, the epidemic ceased." Snow inferred from the data that water rather than air had conveyed the contaminants producing serious illness. Anomalies therefore can play a very positive role in stimulating creative thinking about causal mechanisms.

One example in the context of realism—and not easily resolved—is the anomalous existence of various cooperative arrangements in contemporary Europe that seem to violate the assumption of a state-centric world. Thus the existence of the European Union (EU) should give pause to those who see anarchy as something that plays a determining role in how states interact with each other. One realist response is to say that such institutions are epiphenomenal and that, in turn, concerns about relative gains will impede cooperation. Interstate war therefore cannot be regarded as an anachronism (Mearsheimer 1994–95: 7, 8, 19). So far, at least, the EU continues to exist and play a significant role in shaping the policies of its member states. The realist claim about limitations on institutions such as the EU, however, seems more credible in light of multiple recent events. These include the Brexit vote in 2016, the British election of 2019 that ensured departure from the EU on 31 January 2020, and performance beyond expectations of various Euroskeptical politicians in elections elsewhere. To this list of political events could be added the fallout from the Covid-19 pandemic, which at this time of writing remains unknown but almost certainly in opposition to transnationalism and open borders. In short, the jury remains out on the magnitude of the EU as an anomaly for realism and debate continues.

Antinomy is a form of reasoning that refers to understanding what something is by focusing on what it is *not* (Danielson and Sinatra 2017: 61).[33] "As a pedagogical tool," so Danielson and Sinatra (2017: 64) observe, "antinomies can be extremely useful to illustrate precisely what *not* to do as a citizen, statistician, or graphic designer." In some instances, drawing attention to a point of contrast could be essential in communicating a concept with multiple dimensions.

One instance from IR is the definition of a great power. Consider, as an antimony, Switzerland. It is very advanced in terms of technology and possesses great wealth. However, this state lacks size of population and, except in regard to civil defense, military prowess. Switzerland also does not exhibit the expansiveness of interests that is associated with great power status and even is recognized as a neutral state. To this can be added the relative insulation of Switzerland as a result of its geographic setting—not a state with any obvious pathway toward expansion. These points of opposition help in identifying essential dimensions of great power status, which span capabilities and dispositions.

When two representations are in an "oppositional relation to one another," this is referred to as an antithesis (Danielson and Sinatra 2017: 66). Consider the borders of North America a thousand years in the past versus those of today. Nothing resembling a modern state existed a millennium ago; borders as understood in the Westphalian era simply did not exist. The boundaries of the three states in North America today include some tensions with regard to movement back and forth, but the *location* in each instance—the United States with Canada and Mexico, respectively—is well understood.

Some of the insights derived from research stimulated by cognitive load theory in particular and educational psychology in general already are in place with regard to teaching and research, as a matter of course, for IR and for academic disciplines in general. For example, intrinsic cognitive load can be managed through communication that begins with the easiest tasks and builds up to those that are increasingly challenging, while extraneous cognitive load can be limited by providing guidance and support at the outset of the learning process (Kirschner, Kirschner, and Paas 2016). This type of presentation, with ascending level of difficulty, is the norm in teaching and research for IR. An introduction to game-theoretic analysis, for instance, is likely to begin with models that are within the vernacular, such as Chicken in relation to deterrence, and advance to more complex forms that include varying information conditions among players

---

[33] Perhaps the most famous antinomy is Schrödinger's paradox: "a thought experiment illustrates how by extending the predictions of quantum mechanics, we can reach a point at which two realities can be said to exist simultaneously—a cat being both alive and dead—until one *observes* reality, at which point multiple realities converge into a singular state (the cat is *either* alive or dead)" (Danielson and Sinatra 2017: 63). This visualization helps to explain the quantum perspective in terms of its dramatic departure from classical Newtonian physics.

and a range of equilibrium concepts (see Morrow 1994). Yet it is possible and essential to do more than recognize ascending degrees of sophistication in the order of presenting material, given the vast and still expanding size of IR.

All of this builds toward an urgent message, accompanied by an implicit recommendation, for IR. Consider the observation of Knutsen (2017: 67): "There is theoretical overload. Post-Cold War IR has acquired so many diversities and subdivisions that it is hard to make sense of them." IR, in a word, is incoherent. This is a result of its sheer size and range of content in the absence of effective organizing principles and practices. As advocates of cognitive load theory observe, it is essential to enhance comprehension rather than take its presence for granted; instructional design therefore should integrate "graphical and textual information, thus reducing the need for the learner to do this" (Kirschner, Kirschner, and Paas 2016). Cognitive burdens otherwise virtually guarantee proliferation of miscommunication and misunderstanding. The short exercise in academic forensics presented previously, which offered a reinterpretation of certain aspects of the debate between Bull (1966) and Kaplan (1966), serves as a case in point.

Realism thus serves as the "canary in the coal mine" for IR. Other paradigms, trailing behind in sheer size but expanding, can be expected to encounter the same problem of incoherence over time. Analytic eclecticism, on its own, is not the answer to the question of how to transform information into knowledge under these conditions. An eclectic approach, accompanied by implementation of a visual technique to convey cause and effect, is the most promising way forward under these circumstances. Greater use of each form of relational reasoning—analogy, anomaly, antinomy, and antithesis—also should facilitate communication about causal mechanisms.

Principles from the science of learning reinforce the conclusion reached about the need for clear communication on the part of both realism in particular and IR in general. People are not "tape recorders that take in and record vast amounts of material"; instead, processing capacity is limited (Mayer 2010: 30). Moreover, Mayer (2010: 30) confirms the existence of dual channels—separate ways of processing verbal and visual materials. Perhaps most important of all, in making the case for a visual turn for IR, is the "*picture superiority effect*: an item is better remembered if it is presented as a picture rather than a word" (Mayer 2010: 31).[34] Visualization helps in dealing with complexity (van Gelder 2015: 186). IR today and beyond, in a word, is complex.

---

[34] This insight goes back to the prehistoric world. One example is the Lascaux Cave in the Dordogne region of southwestern France; its walls and ceilings include nearly 1,500 engravings that date back to 15,000 BCE. These graphics show a considerable range of complexity—from straight lines to entire collections of animals (Leroi-Gourhan 1982: 104, 107, 112).

Interesting to note in the preceding context, over the last few decades in particular, is enhanced interest in graphics among *mathematicians* (Celucci 2019: 583). Diagrams, as Celucci (2019: 594) observes, play a significant role in facilitating both discovery and understanding. Graphic constructions can trigger hypotheses through a process that is not rigorously deductive but valuable nonetheless with regard to solving problems (Celucci 2019: 598, 599). Yet most studies in IR still do not complement words with graphic reiteration. Thus it is credible to claim that enhanced visualizations could improve the discipline's prospects for discovery of interesting ideas, along with the level of mutual understanding and potential for cooperation.

Toward a Graphic Turn

Given the evolving state of IR in conjunction with insights from cognitive load theory, the time has come to implement a *visual* turn for IR. Innovative attempts at teaching in IR—for example, on the subject of conflict analysis—profitably include visual materials such as documentaries and media sites (Ayres 2016: 41, 43). A vast range of examples is available from the Active Learning in International Affairs Section (ALIAS) (2019) of the ISA, and articles about visualization and pedagogy in IR continue to accumulate, most notably in journals such as *International Studies Perspectives* and *Journal of Political Science Education*.

Consider also the expanding use of research posters as a means for presentation at conferences in disciplines beyond the natural sciences (Hobbs 2016: 3). Major academic organizations that include scholars from IR, such as the American Political Science Association, International Studies Association, and Peace Science Society, feature poster sessions at their conferences. From the standpoint of communication, a great advantage of the poster format is that it requires setting of priorities and encourages succinctness (Hobbs 2016: 4). Increases in poster sessions among academic organizations reflect, at least in part, largely unstated intuition in support of a graphic turn for IR.

Further illustrations of rising consciousness regarding the need for a graphic turn focus on methods. One example, in the context of formal modeling, is the shift to extensive form game theory (see also Brams 1993 on the matrix form), in which diagrams show player types, information conditions, and moves in sequence. Another instance is movement toward graphic presentation of results from regression-style analyses, notably with regard to statistical significance. A visual turn also comes to mind with the advent of directed acyclic graphs in the social sciences (Morgan and Winship 2015) and the rise of network analysis in peace science (Maoz 2012). Note specifically, as well, creation of a "Best Visualization Award" by the *Journal of Peace Research*.

Perhaps most notable among developments that point toward a graphic turn is the extraordinary work of Branch (2014) on the cartographic state. This study reveals how map use led to "a long-term change in society-wide normative structures and mentality" that culminated in emergence of the modern state (Branch 2014: 12). Important developments in cartography during the 15th century altered ideas in a direction that favored "discrete boundaries" (Branch 2014: 13–14). For present purposes, within which an argument for a graphic turn plays an essential role, the following observation from Branch (2014: 12–15) is of special importance: "The resulting changes in cognitive frameworks were slow and unintended and may have had effects beyond what actors themselves were aware of." More accurate maps, in other words, impacted ways of thinking significantly in the real world of international politics. This observation reinforces the idea that a *lack* of visual representation may be holding back communication about theories in the discipline of IR in particular and perhaps the academic world in general.[35]

All of the preceding developments can be explained to some degree in other ways, but each is significant and includes a shift toward graphic representation of theory, evidence, or both. Arguments in favor of visualization go well beyond the examples just presented. In addition, reviews of literature in this volume will be truncated, with sustained use of a tabular format to aid in retaining the most important details. When systemism is introduced in Chapter 6 on methods, implementation of a graphic approach to communicate cause and effect will be covered in detail. For now, it is enough to observe that systemism encourages completeness and logical consistency in theorizing.

Interesting to observe, as a point affirming the model of cognition, is how well it works in tandem with criteria for research anticipated to produce progress enumerated in Table 2.1 in Chapter 2. Characteristics and results associated with research progress are covered in turn.

Consider characteristics linked with conduct of theorizing: causal mechanisms, rigor and falsifiability, and comprehensiveness. Visualization helps with causal mechanisms because of greater ability to recognize and recall such "If x, then y with greater likelihood than otherwise" statements as opposed to rendering them only in words. Putting an argument into graphic form, moreover, reduces the ability to "hide" in prose, within which vagueness is easier

---

[35] This argument is reinforced by arguments encountered even within the quite distant perspective of reflexivity; for example, Aradau and Huysmans (2014: 613) assert that "methodological debates are about the substantive worlds enacted through the method and the potential rupture that its enactment creates. This understanding invites eclectic and experimental processes of connecting and assembling."

to preserve. Even a simple diagram, with boxes and arrows and no specific instructions for how to interpret them, offers the potential to enhance rigor and falsifiability. Finally, the model of cognition is consistent with efforts toward comprehensiveness. As a theory becomes more expansive, a turn toward visual presentation is essential in order to manage resulting cognitive burdens. Greater use of relational reasoning is expected to help as well.

With regard to criteria for results, the model of cognition works just as well. A visual turn will help to promote range of explanation and predictive value by improving comprehension. In addition, a graphic approach can assist with public exchange of views.

Perhaps more than any other school of thought in IR, given its long history and vast range of expositions, realism needs graphic representation to help find its way. As Part IV of this volume will confirm, many entities claim status as realist theories, and the terminology associated with this infrastructure can become overwhelming. While a visual turn cannot solve all of the problems that have resulted from the size and internal complexity of realism, it is one reasonable way forward in light of evidence from educational psychology.

Summing Up

Knowledge as a component of the metatheory of IR contains three elements: scientific realism, analytic eclecticism, and a model of cognition. Scientific realism is a perspective based on a combination of belief in objective reality (i.e., world-mind dualism) and the existence of unobservables (i.e., transfactualism). Objective reality exists, but a scientific approach also must recognize the essential role played by unobservables in the process of explanation. Analytic eclecticism is an inclusive means toward development of problem-solving, middle-range explanations that go beyond paradigmatic boundaries and possess significance for policy. Key elements of analytic eclecticism include an emphasis on middle-range theory, a problem-solving orientation, and pursuit of policy relevance. Finally, the outlook on knowledge includes a model of cognition that points toward a visual turn for IR. The simple reason behind the call for such a shift is the vastness of research on international relations and challenges associated with transforming that accumulating information into knowledge. Implementation of the model also relies upon relational reasoning in the forms of analogy, anomaly, antinomy, and antithesis. Each preceding element of the knowledge component for the metatheory is compatible with the others.

Chapter 5, which focuses upon units, is the natural follow-up to the now-completed enumeration of elements for the knowledge component of the

KNOWLEDGE 123

metatheory for IR. Two units are introduced in Chapter 5. One unit of the metatheory consists of individuals who act on the basis of instrumental rationality. The other unit consists of the system of explanation, which conveys a given school of thought on the basis of both (a) inductive and sociological and (b) deductive and rationalist criteria.

5
Units

Units as a Component of the Metatheory of Progress

Ontology refers to units of observation. Enumeration of units must be consistent with the components of knowledge—scientific realism, analytic eclecticism and a model of cognition that favors visualization—laid out in Chapter 4. Thus the present chapter focuses on units within the proposed metatheory of progress that are well suited to work in tandem with scientific realism, analytic eclecticism, and a graphic turn for IR. And all of this work builds toward development of a realist research enterprise that is better suited than ever before for creation of scientific knowledge.

Two elements are included within this chapter's specification of units. One element consists of individuals who act on the basis of instrumental rationality, that is, in their perceived self-interest under conditions of constraints on time and information. The other element is the research enterprise, a system of explanation that is put forward as an improvement over previous incarnations such as methodology of falsificationism (Popper 2002 [1959]), paradigm (Kuhn 1970 [1962]), research program (Lakatos 1970), and research tradition (Laudan 1977). A research enterprise uses both inductive and deductive logic to obtain a more comprehensive and convincing sense of any given body of research.

Consistent with scientific realism in particular, the elements within the unit component—rational choice and research enterprise—encompass observables in conjunction with unobservables to provide a full treatment of units. Rational individuals and systems of explanation appeared at the micro level of the academic world as a system in Figure 3.1, which in Chapter 3 depicted the elements of a metatheory of progress. Each of the elements from the unit component of that metatheory will be put forward in this chapter with illustrations from IR. These elements will be combined with the others, for knowledge (Chapter 4) and methods (Chapter 6), into a metatheory that takes the form of a working system (Chapter 7).

This chapter unfolds in three additional sections. The second section covers the concept of rationality, which is implemented as the vision of individual choice and behavior. The intended overall contribution is establishment of *ordinal* rationality, a concept intended to be more in line with the way choices are made in the practice of international relations. The third section focuses on systems of explanation, with the concept of a research enterprise put forward as a point of culmination for the philosophy of inquiry as applied to IR. A research enterprise is distinguished by incorporation of both inductive and deductive logic in identifying a body of research. The fourth section sums up the accomplishments of the chapter, which moves closer to Chapter 7, within which the metatheory is assembled into graphic form on the basis of respective elements contained in its components—knowledge, units and methods.

Instrumental Rationality (β)

This section pursues three goals. One is identification of a baseline position on behavior. Second comes an assessment of how realist theory and rational choice relate to each other. The third and final goal is to make the case for ordinal rationality, a variant that seems more in touch than others with the way choices are made in world politics.

A Baseline Position on Behavior

What is the nature of actors within the metatheory of progress for IR? Instrumental rationality provides the basic answer to that question. Rather than judging what individuals want by a moral standard, the focus of research from the standpoint of instrumental rationality is on how they go about getting it. At the level of the individual, pursuit of self-defined interests is regarded as the foundation for action.

Thus actors are deemed rational in the instrumental sense. Means, rather than ends, are evaluated. It is assumed that people normally can define their goals and put them in order of priority (Freyberg-Inan 2016). Rationality is equated with the "best means to achieve a given end" (Mercer 2005: 79; see also Freyberg-Inan 2016; Haas 2017: 107) under conditions of constraint. As Coleman (1990: 18) observes, "Much of what is ordinarily described as nonrational or irrational is merely so because the observers have not discovered the point of view of the actor, from which the action *is* rational." This point resonates with IR, within which the beliefs of leaders and the general public sometimes can be challenging to comprehend.

Alluded to briefly already, one major point of confusion concerns distinguishing instrumental from normative rationality. This is an ongoing problem in IR (Freyberg-Inan 2016a). For example, from a realist standpoint, Morgenthau (1959: 7) observed that democratic control "cannot fail to impair the rationality of foreign policy itself." This assertion is normative, with rationality meant in the sense of assessing the goals to be pursued. It further is important to "distinguish between a rationalist thinking style and the substantive belief that the power of reason is capable of solving social ills and remaking all politics for the better, both domestic and international" (Rathbun 2019: 45). Rational choice is not incorporated that way within the metatheory of progress; the focus in this context is on means rather than ends.[1] Rather than any given set of preferences, rationality refers to decision-making with utility functions that could include virtually any ordering.[2]

Rational actions are assumed to have a few basic characteristics that combine to form a baseline for expectations.[3] Individuals pursue outcomes based on perceived self-interest. Potential benefits and costs are weighed to obtain an ordering over outcomes (Haas 2017: 107). Is war preferred to negotiation? Should a trade deal be signed or not? All such outcome-related questions about international relations can be answered, from the standpoint of rational choice, on the basis of costs and benefits as weighted by leaders.

Orderings for preferences also are complete and transitive; if outcome A is preferred to B, and B to C, then A must be preferred to C (Kydd 2008: 429; Quackenbush 2015: 48; Hafner-Burton et al. 2017: S6). Preferences correspond to "subjective rank-ordering of the terminal nodes or outcomes of the strategic interaction" (Hafner-Burton et al. 2017: S6). Preferences over outcomes are presumed to be stable for the foreseeable future (Kydd 2008: 426). While an order of preference can change, it is stable and transitive across the options available at any given time.

All of that is in line with classic expositions from Arrow (1951a), Downs (1957), Black (1958), Buchanan and Tullock (1962), Riker (1962), and Olson (1965) that applied rationality models with intellectual origins in economics to the study of politics.[4] Along with others, these pathbreaking studies provided the

---

[1] Debates about rationality are beyond the scope of this investigation and already may be supraoptimal in terms of yielding practical insights. Sil (2000: 353), for example, refers to "acerbic" arguments between rationalists on one side and structuralist or culturalist critics on the other. Note further that such quarrels tend to take place in words alone rather than in conjunction with graphics.

[2] Some expositions stress the process of decision-making as well in defining rational choice; for example, see Rathbun and Stein (2020).

[3] Instrumental rationality, rational choice, rational action, and rationality are terms that will be used interchangeably throughout this study.

[4] While others could be listed, these are the encompassing studies that remain most influential in the study of politics; subject matter includes social choice, coalitions, and the logic of collective action. The classic introductory text for rationality models in political science and IR is Riker and Ordeshook (1973), with respective editions of Mueller (1979, 1989, 2003) identifying significant progress in use of economic principles to explain nonmarket decision-making. A vast range of applications of rational choice models throughout the social sciences, which include political science and IR, have appeared over the course of decades (e.g., Booth, James, and Meadwell 1993). Models based on instrumental rationality continue to accumulate in the journals of IR and political science, along with outlets that cross over into other disciplines, such as *Journal of Theoretical Politics* and *Public Choice*.

foundation for increasingly sophisticated models grounded in rational choice over subsequent decades. Based on the assumption of instrumental rationality, these expositions gradually covered a wide range of substantive domains beyond a point of origin in economics, such as burden-sharing within alliances (Olson and Zeckhauser 1966). The basic properties just enumerated for instrumental rationality underlie a vast literature that can be quite inaccessible, however, once it turns to a more mathematical style of expression borrowed from economics. Rationality as adopted in the metatheory for IR therefore entails only the instrumentalism and clarity of what has been presented here, as opposed to any particular approach toward communication. Words, diagrams, and equations all have a place in sustaining contact among the widest possible range of scholars.[5]

Rationality is the baseline position on behavior. People are assumed to pursue interests from their point of view. Goals are inferred from actions. What does that mean, however, in operational terms?

From the standpoint of the rationalist approach to IR, individuals achieve their best feasible results "by determining the payoffs attached to all possible outcomes, assessing their probabilities, updating information on those probabilities, and choosing the strategy with the highest expected return" (Hafner-Burton et al., 2017: S6). More precisely, people are assumed to be Bayesians. Bayes' theorem contains a specific set of rules for how to update beliefs about the probability of some event in reaction to information provided.[6] In other words, the theorem focuses on how and why people change their mind as events unfold. Confidence in a point estimate, along with the margin of error around it, can increase or decrease as new information becomes available.

Imagine, for example, someone was a member of the US team at the Olympics in Tokyo during the summer of 2021. What if you had to guess whether that person participated in basketball versus another sport? An initial probability

---

[5] For a compelling case in favor of a pragmatic approach to typologies in particular and communication in general, see Maradi (1990: 154).

[6] See Kydd (2008: 42 n. 3) on Bayes' theorem and instrumental rationality in IR at a more general level. Bayes' theorem contains a specific formula for how to adjust a probability estimate in the optimal way based on any new piece of information. Let "i" and "j" be events, with the probability of j being greater than zero. The equation for Bayesian inference takes the form

$$p(i|j) = \frac{p(j|i)p(i)}{p(j)}$$

p(i), p(j) = probabilities of events i and j without regard to each other;
p(i | j) = probability that i is true given that j is true;
p(j | i) = probability that j is true given that is i is true.
The basic point of the equation is to provide a Weberian ideal type of updating for beliefs in response to new information.

estimate could be based on the fraction of US Olympians on the two basketball teams. Once given further information—about the person's height, to cite a relevant additional datum—you are asked to guess again about team membership. The probability estimate for basketball team membership would be adjusted upward or downward accordingly. Some sports would assume an effective probability of zero or close to it as a result of new information. The degree of confidence about the margin of error for the estimate of team membership also would be affected. This is an example of Bayesian reasoning: updated beliefs on the basis of relevant data as it becomes available.

Realism and Rationality

While Chapter 8 will look into this issue in more depth when axioms are identified, IR realism displays a surreal engagement with the concept of rationality. Every imaginable opinion is available among the academic community of realists. Morgenthau (1964: 107, 108), amusingly, tried to sit on the fence but ended up falling off and landing in the rationalist backyard:

> As long as man believed that the relations among nations were beyond human control, beyond reform by the human will, there was no place in the intellectual scheme of things for a theory of international relations.... There is a rational element in political action which makes politics susceptible to theoretical analysis, but there is also a contingent element in politics which obviates the possibility of theoretical understanding.

While the second statement equivocates on rationality, the first describes it as a de facto necessary condition for any relevant theorizing about IR.

Overall, from the time of its origins long ago, realism has seemed intertwined with rational choice. Along those lines, Smith (1986: 11; see also Freyberg-Inan 2006: 254) offers a compelling assessment of Machiavelli and Thucydides that attributes to them a rationalist point of view: "The key to understanding state behavior is the calculation of power, interest, and consequences." Legro and Moravcsik (1999: 22) offer similar observations about great figures from realism in more recent times: "Morgenthau emphasizes power itself as a goal, by which he may have meant a generalized desire to expand. Waltz speaks of survival as the ultimate goal of states, but allows that states may seek anything between minimal survival and world domination." In each instance the description corresponds to goal-seeking behavior, regardless of specific objectives at hand. With reference to realism in general, Wohlforth (2008: 133, note 6) identifies rationality as a frequently identified premise. In the most basic sense, if realists of various stripes focus on the role of power in diverse types of goal-seeking behavior, this suggests a natural affinity with instrumental rationality.

Among various clarifications that might be made regarding instrumental rationality, Kahler (1998), Sil (2000a), and Mercer (2005) identify and respond to those of particular importance. Their observations are sufficient to establish how rational choice is understood at present among exponents in IR. This review also sets the stage for refinement of the rationality postulate for more effective incorporation in realism.

Sil (2000a: 356–357) offers a compelling summation of rational choice that works well for IR:

> Rational-choice theorists typically assert that all social phenomena—including the formation of rules, institutions, communities, and norms—ultimately can be reduced to the instrumental behavior of strategic individual actors. The notion of instrumental action, in turn, is predicated on the existence of self-conscious, deliberate individuals who are able to define a hierarchically ordered set of preferences and who can make quasi-mathematical calculations to determine the ideal strategies for realizing those preferences based on their estimates of other actors' behaviors in a given situation.

Rationality thus lines up with scientific realism: "The instrumental decision-making of the individual agent may not be observable, but this is not problematic since the resulting behavior and the gains from that behavior (money, property, consumption, etc.) are observable proxies for the former" (Sil 2000: 369). In other words, rational choice is confirmed via empirical research and gains credibility as a key unobservable within IR. One example is with regard to the study of deterrence, within which rationality models have become more elaborate and substantive from the point of origin with Schelling (1960) onward.

Rational choice, according to Kahler (1998), is not incompatible with influence from norms or culture on decision-making. Such a fundamentally incorrect inference results from "an unfortunate conflation of methodology and substance" (Kahler 1998: 933). It is quite possible and even likely that a rational actor will take into account factors such as a cultural context or normative prohibitions in deciding upon how to act. Instead, rationalists "challenge cultural analysis by insisting that shared norms and values are only relevant for depicting the choice situation for a given course of action" (Sil 2000: 359). To disregard such information could reduce the likelihood of success, so of course it is taken into account to some degree.

Consider, for instance, the presence of embedded journalists alongside US military personnel during the invasion of Iraq in 2003. The Bush administration hoped that such direct media access would undermine potential accusations about military misconduct that otherwise might go unchallenged and impact negatively upon public opinion. Loss of support at home, in turn, could affect the ability to continue prosecution of the war and ultimately did during the Obama administration. In contrast to such instrumental rationality, norm-driven behavior is not oriented toward outcomes (Kahler 1998: 937). In sum, subjective entities such as norms can impact the calculation of costs and benefits for rational actors.

Rationality models, contrary to intuition, are not separate from psychological theory—a point made effectively by Mercer (2005) and increasingly accepted across the board as findings from neuroscience accumulate. Instead, rationality models "are not distinct from, but rather depend on, psychological assumptions" (Mercer 2005: 79; see also Kertzer 2017: 86). "Friedman's famous 'as if' assumption," Mercer (2005: 84) observes, "gave economists license to stop worrying about psychology and learn to love aggregate data." However, research in neuroscience reveals that emotion, in particular, is essential for rationality (Mercer 2005: 93). With no concern whatsoever for a choice—something akin to robotic or randomized decision-making—instrumental rationality is not anticipated. Lack of even minimal interest in an outcome causes concentration to dissipate to the point of possibly no attention at all. For example, poker played without betting causes players to tune out rather quickly. Without real interest in consequences from action, demands that rationality puts on human behavior are quite unlikely to be met (Mercer 2005: 93, 94; Rathbun 2019). Given the issues entailed by foreign policy, which range from seeking enhanced prosperity to national survival, lack of interest among leaders is not an obstacle to application of rational choice models.

The Case for Ordinal Rationality

People engage in Bayesian updating as stimuli are experienced and processed. This means that beliefs about other actors, including their capabilities and possible actions, are adjusted on the basis of updated information. Irrationality therefore is defined as disregarding or distorting information with implications for existing beliefs. In the preceding example about the Olympics, imagine learning that the athlete in question had a height of six feet, ten inches. While precise mechanics of calculations might not be carried out perfectly in line with new information, the estimate of membership on one of the basketball teams must move upward. Put differently, it is easy to label as irrational an *unchanged or downward* revision of the probability estimate for being a member of one of the basketball teams.

One way to think about this position on rationality is in connection with levels of measurement. The options are nominal, ordinal, interval, and ratio. Critics of rational choice models appear to adopt a *ratio* level of exactitude in assessing performance. In other words, when provided with information, Bayesians ought to update their beliefs in a precise way. Yet common sense alone shows that will happen rarely. Among others, Grieco (2019) questions the relevance of models that assume people act with "high levels of rationality." Instead, *ordinal* measurement makes more sense when the mechanism is human rather than machine calculation. This point is made implicitly by Yarhi-Milo (2013: 13): "The concept of Bayesian updating suggests that disconfirming data will always lead to some belief *change, or at least to lowered confidence*" (emphasis added). In other words, rather than anticipating a precise revision of beliefs based upon calculations, expecting that existing views will be updated in one *direction* or another is more in line with the cognitive capabilities that people possess and use. Take, for example, the assertion of Waltz (2002: 66)—normally identified as a critic of rational choice as a concept—about World War I as an event "prompted less by considerations of present security and more by worries about how the balance might change later." This proposition clearly refers to the direction of change in the military balance anticipated by leaders, as opposed to highly precise and unlikely calculations that would be based on something like the COW index of national capabilities.

Important to note for purposes of application to international politics is that updating of prior beliefs possesses two basic dimensions: central tendency and dispersion (Imai 2017; Graham 2017). Additional information, as per the example above, could increase the confidence in both estimates. In other words, what is the best point estimate and the margin of error around it? Three basic possibilities exist regarding the relationship to each other of estimates before and after: (a) uninformative estimate before → estimate after determined by data, (b) informative estimate before → estimate after combines the estimate from before plus data, and (c) highly informative estimate before → more data is required to alter beliefs because the estimate from before is highly influential over the one from after (Imai 2017). Each of these scenarios will be illustrated in turn with an example from IR.

Scenario (a), with an uninformative prior estimate leaving the one from after to be determined by data, can be illustrated through aspects of the aerial battles from World War I. While balloons had been used for battlefield management and surveillance for a long time, highly mobile aircraft with attack capacity had not been deployed on a large scale before the Great War. (Use of airplanes in wartime began with the Italo-Turkish War in 1911 and the First Balkan War of 1912, with some bombing in each instance.) Who, therefore, knew with much confidence what to expect when adversaries met in the skies for combat? German deployments took the form of squadrons—initially frowned upon by French and British adversaries as lacking in derring-do. However, given the greater effectiveness of the German style, the British and French began to imitate it rather quickly (Ruane and James 2012). Thus data caused change in the playing out of a situation with a limited sense of what would happen under wartime conditions.

Scenario (b), with an informative estimate beforehand and updating through that belief and new information, corresponds to analysis based on the highly regarded International Terrorism: Attributes of Terrorist Events (ITERATE) data (Mickolus 2006). Time series analysis of this data reveals patterns for terrorist events (Sandler and Enders 2004). Projections from this research can be updated as new data are collected in order to improve estimates—already quite good as inferred from existing statistics—over time.

Scenario (c) is one in which a highly informative estimate from beforehand will change only in response to a great deal of new data. The fall of the Berlin Wall and collapse of the German Democratic Republic (GDR) reside in this category. After many decades of oppression, the Soviet-controlled GDR shockingly, and almost unwittingly, no longer blocked passage in and out of East Berlin (Sarotte 2011, 2014). Events happened quickly indeed toward the end of the process and defied belief in many quarters, causing a prominent book on the subject to be entitled *The Collapse* (Sarotte 2014).

Instrumental rationality not only is consistent with existence of error and failure—these frequently observed features of life are *implied* by it. Resources, especially time, are limited. Thus it is entirely possible that pursuit of self-interest will lead to failure because of missing or incorrect information. When information is lacking or wrong, even rational choice will not always lead to success (Frankel 1996c). Time constraints are quite germane for IR in particular. If a decision-maker had infinite time to process all information, then perfection might be expected in terms of results achieved. The real world of politics, however, does not work like that. At least so far in history, people, not computers, make the decisions at the highest levels of government.

Crisis situations, for example, require response to threat within a finite time and under conditions of increased likelihood for military hostilities. A crisis therefore can produce varying (and sometimes awful) results for one or more parties to that conflict (Brecher and Wilkenfeld 1997, 2000). Thus perfect Bayesian updating of beliefs cannot be expected in reality because of limitations in cognitive ability that are exacerbated by time pressure. This point applies quite directly to decisions that leaders must make about war. "Technically," as Levy (2008: 21) points out, "most of these decisions take place not under conditions of risk (where probabilities of outcomes are known) but rather under conditions of uncertainty (where probabilities are not known), which are more difficult to analyze." Thus rational processing of information and acting upon it becomes the baseline position, with departures from that to be expected because of time pressure, bias, and other factors.

Deviations from instrumental rationality, held to an ordinal standard, are anticipated only when very strong contaminating conditions are in place. Consider the Japanese surprise attack against Pearl Harbor that occurred on 7 December 1941. US leadership in both the army and navy disregarded warning signals of an imminent attack. For example, the US military had access to radar, but some in important positions of leadership did not trust this technology, which existed only in rudimentary form. Thus Japanese planes, which had been detected by radar coming from the *west*, were interpreted as American aircraft returning from the mainland. The idea of a Japanese attack did not make sense to those in command, so even a very strong signal did not alter existing beliefs. US military leaders put their aircraft very close together on the ground in order to make it more difficult for saboteurs to inflict damage upon them, which made the unexpected attack from the air more successful. Even a Japanese submarine detected within the exclusion zone also did not prove sufficient to produce a high level of alert from US officers on duty when dawn came that Sunday for Pearl Harbor (Prange 1982). In sum, bias against belief in a Japanese attack caused vital pieces of intelligence to be disregarded, and thus the surprise attack succeeded, in at least a tactical sense. Errors of this magnitude, with devastating consequences, become memorable precisely because they are rare.

What, then, can be said in summing up rational choice? "Instrumentally rational players," according to Quackenbush (2015: 48), "are those who *always* make choices they believe are consistent with their interests and objectives *as they define them*. In other words, instrumentally rational players are purposeful players." In line with human capabilities, instrumental rationality is taken to mean that updating is direction-based rather than exact—in a word, ordinal. A given belief becomes more or less credible in light of new information, which represents a pragmatic movement away from the false precision of rational choice in an ideal, Bayesian sense. All things considered, rational choice means acting on the logic of consequences from action.[7]

Ordinal rationality, in sum, is put forward as an element of the unit component within the metatheory of progress. This is regarded as a realistic vision of how people make choices; options are reordered in response to relevant new information. Ordinal rationality is in line with the model of cognition, which acknowledges limitations that exist in practice with regard to accessing and processing information as decisions are made. This is *not* a rejection of rational choice, but instead a modification of the strongly mathematical and normative variant that does not describe very well what is going on in the human mind. The

---

[7] This contrasts with the logic of appropriateness, which would emphasize normative thinking at the point of decision—rule-driven behavior (March and Olsen 2011). These types of reasoning play varying roles in respective schools of thought about IR, with the logic of consequences being central to realism and various others (Sending 2002).

ordinal conception also fits well with analytic eclecticism because it incorporates insights from outside of the conventional rationalist frame of reference, exemplified in game-theoretic models, about how choices are made in practice.

Interesting to revisit at this point is the tendency of some realists to reject rational choice while at the same time seeming to rely upon it. Take, for example, Waltz (1979), the foundational text on structural realism. "Waltz's decision to eschew the rational actor assumption," observes Mearsheimer (2009: 242; see also Brown 2012: 860), "is an important matter to which scholars have paid little attention." Waltz does not assume that states act strategically because "he sees too much evidence of suboptimal behavior" (Mearsheimer 2009: 246). This inference is revealing in a further way. Is it possible that Waltz and other antirationalists within the realist camp are rejecting it on grounds of *false precision*? This is not just possible, but even probable, when we review the many passages from Waltz (1979) and other realist works that allude to goal-seeking behavior.

Ordinal rationality also is in line with the analysis from Rathbun (2019: 5) that emphasizes the essential nature of corresponding thought processes. Put simply, instrumental rationality requires procedural rationality; emotions play a role in that process as the "raw material of intuitions" (Rathbun 2019: 15, 30). Individuals vary in the degree to which they rely upon thinking that is quick, intuitive, and automatic as opposed to slow, conscious, and effortful (Rathbun 2019: 7). All of that is in line with bounded rationality, with some degree of variation among those observed, as the reasonable expectation for decision-making (Rathbun 2019: 34). Ordinal rationality fits quite well with this pragmatic vision of how choices are made in practice.

Systems of Explanation (Σ)

Two tasks are carried out in this section. One is to review systems of explanation that seek to organize an academic discipline such as IR, with deductive and inductive reasoning as the main point of division between available options. The other task is to develop a new approach, the research enterprise, which combines inductive and deductive logic to obtain a more compelling scheme of organization for IR in particular and academic disciplines in general.

Approaches to Organizing a Field

From a scientific realist point of view, unobservables are not only likely but even certain to play a role as theory advances. Concepts such as ideology, equality, power, and many others begin as fully abstract and obtain operational meaning through observation of political decision-making and behavior. (The time line, of course, will vary from one instance to another.) Concepts, in turn, are used to aggregate knowledge into a system of explanation. This type of system is defined as a network of concepts that collectively organize and present knowledge within a substantive domain of research. A prominent example of a system of explanation is the paradigm (Kuhn 1962, 1970), a designation to be presented momentarily in more detail. The network of concepts that Kuhn united under the heading of a paradigm include, among others, normal and revolutionary science. These ideas continue to influence dialogue over the meaning of, and path toward, progress in IR and many other fields.

Diverse approaches exist for organizing a field of study in order to assess its progress as a whole. These frameworks go by various names and contain sets of metatheoretical assumptions (Wight 1996: 299; see also Haas 2017: 24). While many expositions could be included, the forthcoming review focuses on essential features from systems of explanation that are intended to be brought together into a more effective synthesis for the study of IR. These systems are, respectively, the prominent creations from Popper, Kuhn, Lakatos, and Laudan. Each is quite familiar within the philosophy of inquiry itself and in IR through application, so only vital aspects are described in turn. The final product of this review is a synthesis that leads to the concept of a *research enterprise*. As it develops below, the research enterprise is best suited for evaluation of realism and also amenable to a graphic turn that will increase and improve communication for IR scholars in general.

Table 5.1 displays in chronological order the four systems of explanation that have gained significant support, at one time or another, within IR. The concept of a research enterprise, a new system of explanation, also appears in the table. Columns of the table show the name of each system of explanation, along with its inductive or deductive character, a summary statement, and principal exposition. The systems in the table have been swinging back and forth between a deductive versus inductive orientation. A reasonable response to this pendular history is a quest for something in the middle—a system of explanation that incorporates the positive and complementary traits of what came before. This pragmatic approach also is in line with analytic eclecticism.

Among systems of explanation, the initial full-fledged effort is credited to Popper (2002 [1959]) and represents "a watershed between the old and the new views of the philosophy of science" (Blaug 1980: 2). Prior to Popperian thinking, a relatively simple sense of the "facts speaking for themselves" predominated—a fully inductive way of conducting research. Popper brought forward the "methodology of falsificationism," in which "good science offers bold conjectures, which are then subjected to rigorous scrutiny; the conjectural theory is retained so long as it continues to pass rigorous tests" (Chernoff 2014: 17, 30; see also

Table 5.1 Systems of Explanation

Name of System	Inductive or Deductive Character	Summary Statement	Principal Exposition
Methodology of falsificationism	Deductive	A hypothesis is put forward for purposes of refutation; falsification, rather than confirmation of a hypothesis, is the purpose of research.	Popper (2002 [1959])
Paradigm	Inductive	A community of scholars share beliefs about the agenda for research and how to carry it out; this frame of reference is incommensurable with others and persists until supplanted through an all-out and even sudden shift among adherents.	Kuhn ([1970] 1962)
Research program	Deductive	A series of theories exist within a given area of research; falsification occurs when one entity with superior empirical content replaces another either in a research program or from beyond its boundaries.	Lakatos (1970)
Research tradition	Inductive	The focus is on solving empirical problems rather than expanding content.	Laudan (1977)
Research enterprise	Inductive and deductive	A series of theories is identified and assessed on performance in solving empirical problems.	James (this volume)

Guzzini 1998: 33).[8] This is a counterintuitive idea but ultimately quite appealing: trying to *falsify* rather than confirm a hypothesis as the essential pathway to progress. Rather than a futile quest for inductively derived empirical confirmation, scientists instead are advised to put forward bold conjectures and seek their refutation. In fact, *Conjectures and Refutations* (Popper 2002 [1963])

---

[8] It is reasonable to ask whether something labeled as a "methodology"' also can be regarded as a system (Freyberg-Inan 2020). Rather than attempting to sort this out, the original name from Popper (2002 [1959]) is preserved in order to avoid creation of additional terminology.

is the title of a classic exposition on the methodology of falsificationism. Many philosophers and scientists find falsificationism compelling "because of its fidelity to the goal of avoiding induction, which it does by depicting theories as having the capacity to be conclusively refuted but not the capacity to be conclusively proved true" (Chernoff 2014: 17). The logic is Darwinian; only propositions that survive the harshest possible tests deserve continuing attention.

Hypotheses contradicted by empirical observation, under a strict implementation of falsificationist logic, are to be discarded. Commensurability is a key assumption behind that modus operandi for the methodology of falsificationism. For the process of competition to unfold, scientists must be able to agree on what constitutes a valid test for a given proposition that exists within some larger theoretical edifice. This is what commensurability means in practice. Thus the Popperian system consists of hypotheses put forward, tested, and either discarded or, if they survive a given round of empirical research, tentatively retained for further assessment.

Potential complications with the vision of progress from Popper opened the door to the sociological and also quite influential exposition put forward by Kuhn (1970 [1962]). With an intended focus on the natural sciences, the apparatus from Kuhn became famous because of many reactions throughout the social sciences to his inductive conception of progress. Kuhn identified a weakness within Popper's set of rules, namely, poor performance for a given hypothesis usually does *not*, in practice, lead to abandonment of the larger frame of reference within which it is embedded. At a deeper level, Kuhn undermined "naïve falsificationism" or the idea that facts can "falsify or confute" theories (Ball 1976: 159; see also Vasquez 1998: 29). Instead, communities of research exist and are more durable than a strict falsificationist mindset ever would imagine.

One of many such examples for IR is survival of the Malthusian point of view about the causes of international conflict in spite of various instances of refutation. The "crowding and combat" hypothesis, to put it in a pithy way, sees interstate war as more likely when high population density drives a government toward aggression that is intended to yield badly needed resources from beyond its borders. However, this basic Malthusian linkage between population density and war—at least for data analysis based on the experiences of European states— does not hold true (Bremer, Singer, and Luterbacher 1973). While the crowding-and-combat proposition failed to perform in various tests, research that can be traced back to the influence of Malthus continues on about connections, to some extent indirect, which involve resource limitations and conflict processes.

Central to the Kuhnian (1970 [1962]) system—both a successor and competitor to that of Popper—is the concept of a paradigm. "Kuhn," as Walker (2018: 195; see also Guzzini 1998: 12 and Sil 2000b) observes, "argued that efficient productivity of a scientific community requires a single, authoritative paradigm or theoretical framework." A paradigm identifies fundamental assumptions about the world (Vasquez 1998: 22–23). Paradigms even identify those deemed competent in forming a community (Guzzini 1998: 12). Adherents of a paradigm, understood in general as a consensus on basic concepts and methods in a field of research, combine to produce what is known as "normal science." This work refers to "problem-solving activity in the context of an orthodox theoretical framework" (Blaug 1980: 29; see also Guzzini 1998: 4; Sil 2000b). Normal science is routine in the sense that progress is obtained in an incremental way that does not challenge assumptions underlying the paradigm. At any given time, under ordinary conditions, only one paradigm is in place. Within its boundaries, however, multiple theories can coexist (Vasquez 1998: 24). For Kuhn, a paradigm stands as "a set of models of scientific explanation, exemplary experiments, background assumptions about the world, and the like, in the context of which researchers formulate specific research problems" (Wight 1996: 291). Thus Kuhn "demonstrates that knowledge is to a certain extent conventional" (Guzzini 1998: 4). A paradigm provides coherence to an academic discipline through a narrative about what knowledge is being pursued and why.

Take, for example, the easily recognized wave of studies associated with the liberal paradigm that became identified as the democratic peace. This research from the late 1980s onward is traced to the observation that democracies do not go to war with each other. Attention built in response to the emphasis from Doyle on this finding (1986; see also Babst 1972). Research quickly converged in terms of the modal unit of analysis and method: interstate dyad-years and statistical testing (Maoz and Abdolali 1989). Maoz and Russett (1993) offered normative and institutional explanations for the sustained finding that democracies do not fight wars with each other. Common values, along with tendencies toward greater deliberation in decision-making, combine against escalation of interdemocratic conflict. Research also revealed that democracies, on a pairwise basis, had a lower probability of other types of conflict as well. In addition, auxiliary propositions, such as the likelihood of democracies winning wars they fought with other states, found confirmation (Lake 1992).

Research then expanded into what became known as neo-Kantianism—a sense that democracy, membership in international organizations, and economic interdependence represented the pathway to peace (Oneal and Russett 1997; Russett and Oneal 2001). Even critics have engaged the neo-Kantian program of research largely on its own terms, with additional variables and statistical techniques playing a central role in the dialogue (Choi and James 2005; Gartzke 2007; Mousseau 2013). Overall, the pathway of neo-Kantianism is one of *convergence*—a paradigmatic success story.

Revolutionary science in Kuhn's world occurs, by contrast, in relatively rare instances when a paradigm is in the process of being challenged by a potential replacement. Anomalous findings accumulate and stimulate fundamental questions about the paradigmatic status quo. Kuhn (1970 [1962]; see also Blaug 1980: 29) sees change in an "all or nothing" way; opposition to the paradigm in place increases to the point where something like a switch flips, metaphorically speaking, and allegiance shifts. How exactly this change occurs is not spelled out directly by Kuhn. Mechanisms with the potential to decide between paradigms, such as a "crucial case" (Eckstein 1975), remain controversial at best. The framework from Kuhn, however, does serve as a reminder that science is dynamic and not simply cumulative in an incremental way (Ball 1976: 158).

These points are relevant to the democratic peace as described above. While it experienced great success along the way, research that concentrated overwhelmingly on one type of linkage—state-to-state pairings—eventually encountered significant limitations. Critics began to mobilize on the issue of restrictions in regard to level of analysis even with the democratic peace still in its heyday (Thompson 1996; James, Solberg, and Wolfson 1999). Eventually, the neo-Kantian program on interstate dyad-years ran its course, and research moved on to other levels of analysis, along with a wider range of causal mechanisms regarding processes observed within interstate dyads (Harrison and Mitchell 2014; Mousseau 2013).

Paradigms are deemed incommensurable with each other, within the Kuhnian frame of reference, due to inherently different terminology and practices. (Kuhn (1970) later adjusted the concept somewhat and relabeled it as a "disciplinary matrix," with partial rather than full incommensurability (Chernoff 2014: 29; see also Ball 1976: 157).) To serve as a paradigm, "a set of theories must involve not merely common assumptions and orientations but *shared incommensurable content* with respect to some other paradigm" (Jackson and Nexon 2009: 907). A scientific revolution therefore entails a change in control over the profession—assessed through criteria such as faculty positions and journal editorships—as opposed to a process of rational argument across paradigms. Thus the story told by Kuhn ([1970] 1962) about progress is inherently psychological, inductive, and sociological (Jackson and Nexon 2009: 909). The account also is anti-scientific realist (Chakravartty 2011: 8); incommensurability is the norm regarding communication if attempted across paradigmatic boundaries. This situation is a product of divergent languages used to put forward paradigms, with the ability to translate back and forth seen as extremely circumscribed.

Consider in the context of language the outcome of debate regarding the legacy of the Great War, later known as World War I. The basic story is the triumph of realism, which won a one-sided great debate against what became labeled as idealism and subsequently reigned over IR for many years. Yet the story emerges as more nuanced upon further inspection. Adversaries of realists in the years immediately following the Great War, to begin, did not refer to themselves as *idealists*. A more accurate designation for these opponents of realists would be classical liberals—a precursor to neo-Kantians in more contemporary IR (Oneal and Russett 1997; Ruane and James 2012). The story of realism's ascendancy shows how language matters, in that the winners of debates—like those of wars in the real world—generally are able to tell the story and thereby define the losers. Reference to their adversaries as "idealists" enabled realists to associate a liberal orientation with starry-eyed dreaming. All of this tends to support Kuhn's basic point regarding a sociological element within the practice of research as it is observed rather than imagined.

While Kuhn ([1970] 1962) had focused on the natural sciences, his emphasis on a sociopolitical aspect to the rise and fall of a given school of thought resonates with the experience of IR as well. In fact, Kuhn's analysis of paradigm change and normal science is "uncannily reminiscent of the world of politics" (Guilhot 2016: 17). As Bennett (2010: 6) points out, Kuhn argued that "the sociological process of achieving support among scientists" had importance to the outcome of scientific revolutions. "If IR theorists found so much to like in Kuhn," Guilhot (2016: 22) asserts, "it is because rather than pressing scientific concepts onto politics, he did exactly the contrary and brought politics into science." Within IR, for instance, Walker (2018: 205) draws attention to the existence of intense competition for limited resources that range from career promotion to journal publications. The Kuhnian vision of paradigmatic change, quite obviously, invoked a process of agenda control that is inherently political.

While acknowledging its descriptive accuracy for research carried out in any number of academic disciplines, critics identify several problems with Kuhn's paradigmatic frame of reference. With the falsificationist Popper among the most prominent, skeptics long have noted "how the drift toward one dominant theoretical framework tends to impoverish inquiry by limiting both scholarly vision and problem-solving skills" (Walker and Morton 2005: 342; see also Guzzini 1998: 12; Sil and Katzenstein 2011: 483; Lake 2013: 573; Bew 2016: 298). Paradigmatic research, in other words, always is at risk of self-perpetuation.

What does the debate over paradigmatic research mean for IR as a discipline? Chernoff (2014) provides both sides of what seems like an indeterminate argument over the feasibility of applying Kuhn's sociological analysis to IR. Nickles (2014: 2; see also Walker 2018: 206) regards the framework from Kuhn as something that "requires possibly unrealistic strong senses of incommensurability and theory-ladenness." Incommensurability is not such a great problem because (a) possibilities exist for "translation and redefinition" and (b) theories seeking to answer research questions "ultimately rely on empirical referents to operationalize various concepts, variables, and mechanisms" (Sil and Katzenstein 2010b: 414–415). Wight (1996: 311, 318) adds that observation is theory laden, but not necessarily "theory-determined," and throws down the gauntlet regarding the necessity for different schools of thought to exist apart from each other: "If paradigms are truly incommensurable, how do proponents of differing paradigms 'know' that they differ?" Moreover, the sociological model from Kuhn does not provide a place for rationality within the account of persistence and change for paradigms (Nickles 2014: 2). For such reasons, the Kuhnian system of explanation is in need of elaboration.

Paradigms in IR tend to accumulate rather than replace each other in sequence (Ruane and James 2012). IR and at least some other fields do not see "a clear sequence of normal and revolutionary science as Kuhn envisioned, nor any evidence that the progressive character of a research program [from Lakatos] will be recognized as such by any but its own adherents" (Sil and Katzenstein 2010b: 426). In addition, "Not even the most popular approaches in these fields have enjoyed the staying power of those dominant paradigms considered exemplary by Kuhn (for example, Newtonian physics, which spanned centuries)" (Sil and Katzenstein 2010b: 426). Thus the concept of a paradigm as articulated initially by Kuhn needs revision, at the very least, as a would-be designation of how research unfolds within a discipline such as IR.[9]

Kuhn's emphasis on the sociology of science and paradigm choice stimulated criticism, led by Lakatos (1970), that the concept of a paradigm "had portrayed judgments on scientific progress as more subjective and relativistic than they actually are" (Bennett 2013: 464; see also Bennett 2010: 6). Thus swinging back toward a deductive approach is the system of explanation from Lakatos (1970)—known as the scientific research program—perhaps the most heavily referenced in IR among this type of concept.[10] On the one hand, according to Chernoff (2014: 31), Lakatos resembles Popper at many points, notably in his view that advancements in science proceed in a plausible manner, while also moving away from the hypothesis as the focal point for assessing progress. On the other hand, the framework developed by Lakatos (1970) had some common traits with the vision from Kuhn but also offered a direct challenge to the idea of paradigm-based research. Harrison, Freyberg-Inan, and James (2017: 10) further observe that Lakatos "offers a way around the problems of Popper's falsificationism while avoiding the perils associated with Kuhn's relativism." This threading of the needle is accomplished through articulation of the scientific research program, a

---

[9] In fairness to Kuhn ([1970] 1962), it is important to point out once again that he did not intend his framework to be applied to a discipline concerned with the social world—especially one that includes expositions that he likely would have regarded as prescientific in nature (Lake 2011: 466; Walker 2018: 196). With greater attention to science and associated methods in IR, "The concept of the paradigm became the key to reading international relations" (Molloy 2003: 720). Thus the present critique does not focus on the articulation from Kuhn but instead on application of the concept of a paradigm in IR.

[10] The terms "research program" and "scientific research program" will be used interchangeably throughout this exposition.

system of explanation that includes more internal structure than Kuhn's idea of a paradigm.

Given the relatively dense exposition from Lakatos (1970), there are advantages to introducing the concept of a research program through secondary sources. Presented in summary form by Nickles (2014: 2; see also Lakatos 1970 and Blaug 1980), a research program consists of the following elements: (a) a hard core, which enumerates "features of the theories that are essential for membership in the research programme"; (b) a protective belt, or "the features that may be altered"; (c) a negative heuristic, that is, "an injunction not to change the hard core"; and (d) a positive heuristic or "a plan for modifying the protective belt." In effect, a research program can be summed up as "an ideal-typical specification of how a series of theories relate to one another; its utility is in the evaluation of that series, not in directing the series as it evolves" (Jackson and Nexon 2009: 914). The concept of a research program is inherently deductive and rationalist in character.

While definitely a primarily deductive rather than inductive frame of reference, Lakatos's network of concepts is not entirely unrelated to those put forward in a relatively terse way by Kuhn. For example, scholars will be found pursuing normal science within a paradigm as described by Kuhn, while under the regime from Lakatos, participants in a research program seek to expand the positive heuristic while not challenging the hard core. The hard core of a scientific research program as per Lakatos, therefore, "consists not merely of substantive claims, but also contains *commitments to particular kinds of observational theory*: ideas about how measurement works, how terms are to be defined, and how auxiliary hypotheses derived from the theory's hard core are to be evaluated" (Jackson and Nexon 2009: 913). Thus parallels do exist between the concepts of paradigm and research program.

Consider, for instance, the English school. In the language of a research program, state-centrism and international society exist within the hard core. The protective belt of hypotheses would be tested via qualitative research that focuses on diplomacy and related subject matter. This would be labeled, in paradigmatic terms, as normal science. A revolution for the English school thus would occur only if, in some gestalt manner, its exponents began to openly reassess the utility of international society and state-centrism as a foundation for research.

Paradigms and research programs, in spite of their respectively inductive and deductive identities, reveal some of the same things about any given area of research. However, at least in the abstract, important differences are apparent as well. For Lakatos, but not Kuhn, explicit (albeit abstract) rules exist for one scientific research program being replaced by another. Lakatos thereby stands in proximity to a rationalist rather than sociological vision of persistence and change for research.

Progress, for Lakatos, refers to a particular kind of change within the protective belt. Any problem that arises—an anomaly, meaning something that might challenge the hard core—must be dealt with in a way that offers at least one novel prediction and some initial level of support for it. (Novel predictions encompass "phenomena that may have been observed before the time of the prediction but which were not among the problems which the alteration was designed to solve" [Nickles 2014: 2; see also Elman and Elman 2003a: 81].) Progress means expansion of empirical content through incorporation of novel facts but without altering the hard core of the research program.

With its serial approach toward assessing performance, this regime from Lakatos (1970) gets around the "all or nothing" approach of Popper regarding falsification of a hypothesis through a failed test. Instead of focusing on a hypothesis, a series of theories is to be developed, with each one falsifying its predecessor via expanding empirical content created through novel predictions and some degree of tentative support. The best theories from rival research programs, in turn, compete with each other. The conceptual apparatus from Lakatos also averts the troubling subjectivity embedded within Kuhn's sociological vision and offers a rational model of how allegiance should shift from one set of theories to another. A paradigm shift, translating Kuhn's terminology into Lakatos's frame of reference, comes about when a progressive research program supersedes one that is degenerating. Scientific research programs compete by producing theories, in turn, which either gain more adherents through empirical success or lose support as a result of failure. These trends are labeled, depending on the direction, as positive and negative problem-shifts.

Critiques of this system of explanation zero in on challenges that arise from efforts to apply the methodology of scientific research programs. How, Vasquez (2003b: 97) asks, is a degenerating trend to be distinguished from the legitimate domain of a hypothesis? Mearsheimer and Walt (2013: 446) add that it is easy to generate novel results "when the relevant variables are defined in different ways, data quality is poor, and the hypotheses being tested are loosely tied to theory." Nickles (2014: 3) furthermore asserts that "Lakatos does not provide us with details concerning ways to measure degeneracy, nor does he locate the point at which degeneracy can prove fatal to a research programme." From the standpoint of IR as a discipline, Walt (2002: 201; 2003: 60; see also James 2002b) views the idea of empirical content as especially problematic. How is it to be measured? Is it possible to know whether one theory possesses more empirical content than another? These questions still lack convincing answers.

Both the idea of a paradigm shift on the one hand and a problem shift for a research program on the other would seem inherently retrospective (Jackson and Nexon 2009: 913, 914). Thus one critique that seems applicable to both Kuhn and

Lakatos is related to time of application. Is it possible to recognize progress at a given time or only later on?

Realists question whether the framework from Lakatos, exported by Vasquez from the philosophy of science into IR, is relevant to that discipline. For example, Wohlforth (2003: 259, 261) asserts that the assumption of Lakatosian research programs "might not only be empirically false but actually damaging to scholarly inquiry" and that perhaps other "rationalist approaches to theory appraisal" might look better instead. Waltz (2003a: xi) also sees problems with Lakatos at an operational level; the shift to a series of theories is not deemed helpful for various reasons: (a) an original theory might be good, but successors make it weak and defective; (b) the problem of evaluating a theory endures, whether alone or in a series; (c) and what counts as a novel fact is not obvious. Among these three critiques, the first two seem less serious than the third. Point (a) simply describes a process of degeneration for a series of theories. Including this assertion, curiously, tends to weaken Waltz's overall position that Lakatos's framework is unworkable. Put differently, if it is possible to see that the first in a series of theories is the best, then some means of assessment *does* exist. Point (b) is just a restatement of skepticism about the idea of evaluating a theory in the first place.

Most challenging is assertion (c) from Waltz (2003a) regarding what is meant by a novel fact. This critique brings out directly, yet again, the principal difficulty with application of major concepts from Lakatos to IR. Much of his apparatus is more worthwhile in terms of reinforcing values for good practices as opposed to identifying such actions by sight. This assertion is true especially of the concept of a novel fact. On the one hand, who would be against discovery of new data? On the other hand, does discovery of a novel fact mean just any piece of information not encountered before, reconceptualization of an existing datum, both, or neither? While the answer is not obvious, it matters a great deal in practice. How otherwise is a research program to be designated as progressive and worthy of further attention or degenerating and in need of abandonment?

While impressive in its scope, the Lakatos-inspired volume from Elman and Elman (2003b) also tells a cautionary tale regarding implementation. Six research programs from IR are identified and evaluated: institutions, neoclassical realism, liberalism, operational code, power transition, and the democratic peace. In each instance the research program is deemed to be at least tentatively progressive. This set of results raises an obvious question: what would it take for a research program *not* to meet the standard for progressiveness? The answer is not obvious, although at least some adherents of realism might smirk and say, "Everyone is progressive but us."

Even after the large-scale implementation of the framework from Lakatos via Elman and Elman (2003b), it is fair to say that its operational rendering still leaves much to desire. Since ideas from Lakatos frequently are invoked to say that variations of realism represent degenerating programs of research, this point should be kept in mind for later. It is appropriate to cite established but conflicting positions on the applicability of Lakatos's conceptual apparatus as further evidence in favor of a visual turn for IR. In the absence of graphic representation, words will not be enough to settle the generally abstract and persistent points of disagreement.

With the goal of moving past some of the difficulties inherent in operational use of the scientific research program as articulated by Lakatos, Laudan (1977) introduced the concept of a research tradition. Thus the pendulum swings back in an inductive direction as a result of concerns about practical application. As Sil and Katzenstein (2010b: 413) observe, "Laudan emphasizes the significance of shared, enduring, foundational commitments to the conduct and evaluation of normal scientific research." Unlike a research program, a research tradition is not equated with a series of theories. Instead, the focus of a research tradition is on identifying and solving conceptual and empirical problems (Laudan 1977). For Laudan, the value of a theory depends "more on its ability to solve problems than on its contribution to the cumulation of knowledge" (Sil and Katzenstein 2010d: 21). The research tradition is an idea that therefore reflects a pragmatic point of view and seems in line with the spirit of analytic eclecticism.

Attention thus turns to performance of rival theories within and across research traditions. This type of competition is a "prerequisite for Laudan's standard of progress" (Park 1998: 3). Theories are compared in terms of (1) overall performance and (2) pace maintained with regard to solving empirical problems. Research traditions as articulated by Laudan "can coexist and compete for long periods of time, generating substantive claims that may overlap with those produced in other traditions" (Sil and Katzenstein 2010b: 413). Sequences of paradigms, which rise and fall consecutively, fit more directly into the history of natural rather than social sciences (Sil and Katzenstein 2010b: 426). The story told by Laudan about simultaneous existence and competition between and among paradigms—or, for that matter, research programs—looks a lot more like the track record of IR in general and realism in particular.

Rather than replace one another, paradigms are more likely to simply accumulate in IR, at least over the course of its initial century of existence. Paradigms, over time, branch off into new incarnations. It is quite easy to see that world system theory descends from Marxism and carries its vision of class struggle into a globalized setting. The same could be said for so-called idealism, seemingly moribund for decades but then resurrected through the neo-Kantian phase of research that reached a high level of intensity around the time of the new millennium. Other examples would not be difficult to locate.

With its shift toward problem-solving, Laudan's system of explanation makes sense because of the brick wall that rises up whenever efforts are made to assess empirical content for a given theory as compared to others. Empirical content sounds good in principle, but is quite unwieldy in practice. As Nickles (2014: 2) points out, from the standpoint of Laudan, it is appropriate to "*accept* the research tradition that has solved the most problems and *pursue* the tradition that is currently solving problems at the greatest rate." For Laudan, the basic purpose of problem-solving is to create theories that increasingly are *reliable*, defined in terms of a capability "to stand up to increasingly robust and probative empirical tests" (Park 1998: 2–3). In a field like IR, it seems more realistic to identify empirical problems rather than estimate empirical content.

One long-standing example of an empirical problem is the causes of interstate war (James 2002b). Competing causal mechanisms regarding war, moreover, can be depicted easily in visual form as box-and-arrow diagrams of one sort or another. The same cannot be said for empirical content of a theory. Would containers of different shapes and sizes be used to show competing theories? It is not obvious how visualization would take place in this context—an obstacle to commensurability in any debate over which theory is better than another.

None of this is to say that application of the research tradition as a system of explanation is without its challenges. While empirical problem-solving is easier to envision than empirical content, other issues remain in place. "Laudan," as Nickles (2014: 2) observes, "downplays the sociological and pedagogical elements" from Kuhn ([1970] 1962). Bennett (2013: 464) adds that Laudan "provides little structure to his concept of research traditions and he is frustratingly vague on the issues of theoretical progress and theory choice." Nickles (2014: 2) asks, "How do we determine which research tradition has solved the most problems?" The same question could be asked about rate of performance. No general answer is obvious in either instance. Instead, assessment is likely to be highly context-dependent, that is, varying from one discipline to another. Even when principles are agreed upon, existing approaches to *measurement* of progress are difficult to apply in practice (Nickles 2014: 4). To sum up, the concept of a research tradition is most valuable for its emphasis on solving empirical problems, but still faces challenges when attention turns to operational renderings.

A New Approach

Positive and compatible aspects of the preceding series of frameworks from the philosophy of inquiry—methodology of falsificationism, paradigm, research program, and research tradition—are combined to form the system of explanation known as a *research enterprise*. Creation of this new system therefore is an exercise in analytic eclecticism (Sil and Katzenstein 2010a, 2010b, 2010c, 2010d, 2011) and sociable pluralism (Freyberg-Inan 2016a). This approach is pragmatic as well because it recognizes the fact that, in practice, none of the four familiar systems of explanation from Table 5.1 is fully up to the task of implementation. This is because each option constitutes either a fundamentally deductive or inductive approach. A union of inductive and deductive reasoning is much more likely to identify something that is both acceptable to adherents of a school of thought and recognized by its critics as scientifically viable.

Combination of inductive and deductive approaches to specify a system of explanation also helps to counteract problems not yet discussed. Some might argue that a strictly inductive and sociological approach tends to create centers of power and even coercion in an academic discipline. If a system of explanation is flawed but in a reigning position, its adherents might be able to perpetuate existence of their favored approach regardless of what evidence turns up. Thus a deductive element in identifying and assessing the identity of a school of thought is essential to counteract self-reinforcing tendencies that otherwise might develop. At the same time, a purely deductive and rationalist approach is problematic because its designations may be regarded as unrealistic by participants who have created a body of research. At least some degree of inductive logic and sociological analysis therefore becomes necessary to avert rejection of a scientific research enterprise by the community it seeks to identify.

Rules for identification of axioms for a research enterprise, to continue, will have multiple (a) sociological and inductive and (b) rationalist and deductive stages, thereby combining insights from Kuhn ([1970] 1962) and Laudan (1977) on the one hand and Popper (2002 [1959]) and Lakatos (1970) on the other hand. This is in line with the convincing defense offered via Blagden (2016) for the role of inductive reasoning in such processes: "One does not simply sit down of an afternoon and decide to theorize without at least some prior inference about theory-worthy (ir)regularities in international politics." Wight (2019: 78) adds that, to someone outside of a research community, "it is often difficult to identify what the participants do that makes them operate as a whole."[11] At the same time, consider this observation from Levine and Barder (2014: 867): "The work of a body of theory is not reducible to the conscious intentions or desires of the theorist." Thus it makes sense to adopt a comprehensive approach; for example, begin by identifying research communities through inductive reasoning and then apply deductively derived criteria regarding viability for carrying out the work.

Put forward in detail in Chapter 6 on methods, implementation of rules starts with a subjective sense of a research enterprise from those who self-designate within and beyond its boundaries, respectively. Assumptions are gathered

---

[11] For a dissenting view that associates a sociological and inductive specification of research problems with less advanced sciences, see Nurmi (1974: 11).

together for review from the academic literature, with an emphasis on identification of content from sources both within and beyond the boundaries of a putative research enterprise. Additional rules, with a rationalist foundation, continue the process of identifying assumptions for inclusion. One example is a requirement for logical consistency among would-be axioms. A final stage, once again sociological in nature, assesses whether a significant faction among self-designated adherents of a research enterprise object to one or more of the surviving axioms and thereby justify its elimination. In this way a set of axioms, from which theories can be derived, is identified as the foundation for a research enterprise.

From Lakatos (1970) is adopted the idea of a system of explanation that encompasses a series of theories. Thus a research enterprise consists of an axiomatic basis and theories that build upon it. To be crystal clear, research does not focus on *axioms*. Theories become more elaborate through auxiliary assumptions. Testing of such frameworks leads to refinement and further assessment of those that perform well. A prominent example from IR is the series that begins with the expected utility theory of war (Bueno de Mesquita 1981). The initial theory focused on comparative statics and performed well in statistical analysis of interstate war in the post-Napoleonic era. Support expanded into the domain of crisis escalation in the era after World War II (James 1988). A refinement of the theory to include dynamics—expressed through a game-theoretic model with incomplete information and player types—produced further confirmation through aggregate data analysis based on Militarized Interstate Disputes (MIDs) (Bueno de Mesquita and Lalman 1992). Theory and testing based on expected utility models continues to thrive, with a wide range of applications to war in particular and conflict processes in general.

Taking a page from Laudan (1977), note that empirical problems, rather than content, will provide the focus for theorizing and research within a research enterprise. An empirical problem is one of cause and effect to be solved through identification and testing of explanatory propositions. Why, for instance, do interstate wars occur? What causes a trade agreement to be signed (or not)? These are examples of empirical problems. They do not focus on any one occurrence, but instead on the causal mechanisms for a set of events.

Consider interstate war, for example, as an event around which any number of empirical problems can be identified. The study of war initially might be divided into empirical problems that focus on its causes, processes, and consequences. Long- and short-term causes and consequences could be explored. With regard to processes, one example among many of interest would be the question of whether states follow the laws of war (Morrow 2007). In a review of the vast academic literature on the causes of war, it would be possible to subdivide into a number of more specific empirical problems cast at different levels of aggregation. At the system level, the frequency and intensity of war could be studied in aggregate form. At the state level, involvement in war as either an initiator or target could be assessed. It is easy to imagine many other ways in which empirical problems linked to war could be designated within a realist research enterprise or elsewhere. The same could be said for other forms of international conflict, such as foreign policy crises (Brecher and Wilkenfeld 1997, 2000).

Even a cursory discussion of the causes of interstate war as a multifaceted empirical problem is sufficient to demonstrate an advantage for Laudan's conceptualization over that of Lakatos. The idea of empirical content is very difficult to put into operational terms in the manner above. To begin, empirical content suggests some kind of metaphor with a receptacle that is being filled up with research, analogous to liquid being poured into a glass. But what is the size of that glass? How can it be said with confidence that the containers corresponding to respective theories have the same size and shape, whatever that might mean, in the context of the empirical world? Thus the idea of empirical content, while quite appealing on the basis of intuition, is very difficult to apply in practical terms. The concept of an empirical problem, by contrast, seems more likely to be of practical use if the goal is to assess relative performance among theories.

Within the set of systems of explanation, the research enterprise is put forward as a hybrid option that combines the best features of its predecessors in Table 5.1. First, the research enterprise includes inductive and deductive stages of identification for axioms, which takes into account insights from Kuhn and Popper, respectively, with regard to construction of theory. Second, from Lakatos is borrowed the idea that a series of theories, rather than one entity in particular, should be the focal point for evaluation. Essential to preserve among the contributions from Lakatos is the insight that nothing will be accomplished through debate over assumptions rather than payoffs from a theory (Ball 1976: 164). Third, and finally, a shift from the vain quest for measurement of empirical content to more tractable assessment of performance in solving empirical problems is adopted from Laudan. Taken together, the preceding characteristics of the research enterprise enhance its ability to serve as an organizing principle for schools of thought within IR.

Amalgamation of frameworks looks, perhaps, even better after further reflection. It certainly is in line with analytical eclecticism. Taking the best ideas from different approaches creates the potential for a structured pluralism that facilitates "intelligible discourse and cumulative progress" (Bennett 2013: 461). Consider from the standpoint of intellectual viability the reflections from Chernoff (2013: 354): "If someone advances an IR argument that relies on methods consistent with a range of philosophers, such as Kuhn, Lakatos, Popper and Quine (i.e., any of those philosophers or their followers will accept the starting point), it will be less vulnerable and thus more persuasive than an argument that requires a stronger, or more specific, set of premises, for example, that

Kuhn is right and the others wrong." In other words, it is more difficult for an opponent "to disprove (a disjunction of) a wide range of foundational doctrines than to disprove a specific one" (Chernoff 2013: 357). The research enterprise, which brings together ideas from several systems of explanation with prior application to IR, therefore stands on especially firm ground with regard to its philosophical range.

Two concepts must be defined more explicitly in order to operationalize a system of explanation. One is "theory" and the other is "empirical problem."

What is a theory? Some might see the question as a dead end. Ward (2018: 554, 564) asserts that "the word 'theory' is used in so many different ways in international relations that it has become meaningless" and that "we still have no single, intersubjectively shared idea of what theory in international relations might be." What, then, about simply doing away with the concept of a theory? An authoritative response in favor of theory is available from Mearsheimer and Walt (2013). Theory is valuable to IR because it can provide an overarching framework, revolutionize thinking, facilitate prediction and retrodiction, assist in diagnosing problems of policy and evaluating potential responses, guide activity when information is sparse, and provide structure for testing of hypotheses (Mearsheimer and Walt 2013: 435–437). In short, a world without theory becomes one that lacks explanation on a scientific basis and relevance to policy-related issues. Thus it is worth the effort to reassess concept formation about theory to obtain a meaning with value for practical application that includes a graphic approach.

Among many expositions in the social sciences that focus on the subject of theory, it is possible to glean some degree of convergence toward the purpose of *explanation* (Mearsheimer and Walt 2013: 431–432; Özdemir 2015: 5; Knutsen 2016; Shuell 2016; Walker 2018). A theory should not be equated with an individual hypothesis; instead, it must identify causal mechanisms that explain recurring behavior (Mearsheimer and Walt 2013: 429, 430). In turn, a theory therefore offers a vision that simplifies the world (Walker 2018: 197). This requires a set of axioms and propositions derived from them. To be worthwhile, a theory must specify "an entire chain of action in a way that is consistent in its assumptions" (Lake 2013: 574; see also Ward 2018: 558). All of this points in the direction of more comparative analysis for causal mechanisms put forward by different theories in IR (Mearsheimer and Walt 2013: 448). For realism, such an approach is long overdue.

Within the metatheory of progress advanced here, theory will be defined as follows: a theory consists of a set of axioms that are logically consistent with each other and used, in conjunction with additional assumptions, to generate propositions that admit to testing on an empirical basis. The axioms are analogous to first-ranking, core concepts within an ideology; interplay among them is essential to development (Freeden 2013). Put differently, explanation based on a combination of axioms emerges in response to empirical problems identified as priorities for the research enterprise.

Propositions, also labeled as hypotheses, designate empirical problems to be solved through research. Empirical problems include unobservables that come into focus as research accumulates over time. As in the context of an ideology, a given theory will have second-ranking concepts that are important but not essential (Freeden 2013). In the language of social science this refers to auxiliary assumptions, which must be articulated for any theory within an overall system of explanation. (Note that auxiliary assumptions must not contradict the axioms.) All of this is in line with a scientific realist point of view.

Both in designated and solved incarnations, empirical problems are the metric of progress for a research enterprise. An empirical problem takes the form of an event for which causal mechanisms are to be identified. Time frame and level of analysis provide a starting point, in terms of dimensions, for a more comprehensive sense of meaning with regard to the idea of an empirical problem. Figure 5.1 conveys a typology of war as an empirical problem in an overall sense, which includes many specific manifestations. The typology's dimensions, time and level of analysis combine to produce four categories.[12] The first stage is designation of time frame. Is the research question synchronic (i.e., at one time) or diachronic (i.e., unfolding over time)? This creates two branches in the figure. The second stage focuses on level of aggregation. Is the research question about the system or the state? These queries combine to create four possibilities, arrayed along the bottom row of the figure, each of which is covered in turn. The respective queries are variants on the most basic one posed by IR from its outset: what causes warlikeness? In each instance, a sample answer is provided in overview form. This exercise is intended to convey something other than an abstract meaning for the concept of an empirical problem.

First, consider the combination of a synchronic time frame with the system as the level of aggregation. A sample answer for warlikeness in this context is provided via the debate over stability and polarity. The polarity of the system refers, in common parlance, to its number of great powers. Stability is taken to mean the absence of warfare. Debate initially focused on bipolar versus multipolar systems, that is, those with two versus a higher number of great powers (Waltz 1964; Deutsch and Singer 1964). In later years, Schweller (1998: 44) identified properties of tripolarity that made it possibly the worst option of all. Unipolarity as an option joined the fray, with Monteiro (2011–12: 11), for instance, noting that, unexpectedly, it had persisted since the 1990s and that theorizing about its

---

[12] Introduced at greater length in Chapter 9, a typology consists of ideal types, and the order in which dimensions are considered is irrelevant (Doty and Glick 1994: 243; Maradi 1990: 143).

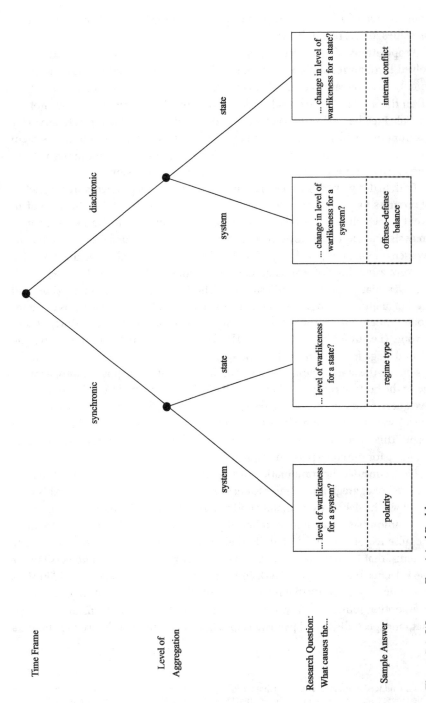

Figure 5.1 War as an Empirical Problem

conflict-related properties had been lacking. Debate over polarity and war continues to this day.

Second comes the profile that includes a synchronic time frame and state level of aggregation. A sustained effort to answer the question of warlikeness for a given state focuses on regime type and is known widely as the democratic peace phenomenon. The idea of peace between democracies as an observed regularity goes back to Babst (1972) and produced a substantial body of research on interstate dyads (Russett and Oneal 2000). More controversy exists, however, over the research question directly at hand, namely, the warlikeness of an *individual* state. Arguments persist about whether regime type—autocratic versus democratic and even divisions within each—can assist in figuring out a state's propensity toward war and other forms of interstate conflict. Attention recently turned to unpacking the two basic categories, with one line of research offering a taxonomy of autocracies (Weeks 2014). Elaboration of regime type as a category creates a wide range of possible associations with warlikeness that significantly transcend the original research questions that focused on expectations for democracy versus autocracy.

Third is the combination of a diachronic time frame with a system level of aggregation. An idea with good intuition behind it, regarding dynamics at the level of the system, is the offense-defense balance. At a given time in history, is the advantage to the attacker or the defender? If the former, the system should be more warlike; if the latter, the reverse is expected. The basic reason is that the level of opportunity for war will differ under these respective conditions. If the advantage is with the offense, there is a greater temptation for a state to strike first (Glaser 2010: 117; see also Glaser 2003: 269). An authoritative historical study supports the idea that the profile of weapons, notably the offense-defense balance, in a given era will have important effects on the playing out of international politics in terms of the degree of warlikeness observed (McNeill 1982).

Finally, consider the combination of a diachronic time frame with a state level of aggregation. A long-standing attempt to answer the resulting question about warlikeness is the diversionary theory of war (Levy 1989). The basic idea is that internal conflict will be projected outward by the leadership of a state in an effort to divert attention away from mounting problems at home, such as unrest as a byproduct of bad economic news. A potential foreign adversary is targeted as a scapegoat, with war as the most intense possible result of the effort to restore cohesion at home through conflict abroad (Coser 1956; James 1987, 1988). With a great deal of research compiled already, it is fair to say that diversionary theory continues to stimulate debate over its mechanisms and boundaries, with highly sophisticated research designs as the norm within the attendant literature (Fordham 2005; Pickering and Kisangani 2010).

With the research questions and tentative answers specified, an initial step toward operationalization is in place for warlikeness as an empirical problem. A few additional points about progress and priorities are worth adding at this juncture.

Graphic presentation of warlikeness as an empirical problem helps with a long-standing point of disagreement over causal mechanisms, noted by Sil and Katzenstein (2010b: 420): scholars "differ over whether mechanisms must necessarily exist at a level of generality that transcends singular spatio-temporal contexts." A glance at Figure 5.1 is sufficient to render this disagreement moot. Research questions that vary across time and level of aggregation cannot possibly be answered by a single model with causal mechanisms that apply in all instances. Why, for instance, would it automatically make sense to explain the warlikeness of a given state at a particular time in the same way as the evolution of that property at the system level? Instead, it is virtually certain to expect that aspects of a general explanation will shift in importance—and perhaps even come in and out of play—in different contexts.

Furthermore, empirical problems can vary along additional dimensions over and above those portrayed in Figure 5.1. Ripsman, Talaiferro, and Lobell (2016: 109) observe that a dependent variable can be charted along an additional time-related axis: short versus long. For the causes of war as an empirical problem, the time frame clearly tilts toward the short end. This is an antithesis to creation of grand strategy, for example. Grand strategy is about "harmonizing of means and ends, in peace as well as war," to serve the national interest (Brawley 2009: 3). Deliberations about grand strategy can cover decades.

Interesting to consider as well is the matter of empirical content. This is a concept that provokes intense debate about meaning. Lack of consensus about operational rendering, when empirical content is invoked as a criterion for scientific progress, tends to cause a stalemate when any specific theory is at issue. One way to move past this problem, in line with scientific realism, is to put forward a straightforward proposition: empirical content is unobservable, but inferred to be an increasing function of fully, or even partially, solved empirical problems. While assertion is not proof, it is difficult to imagine an argument for the *opposite* connection.

Finally, warlikeness, in and of itself, is just one empirical problem among many with regard to conflict processes. Correlates of War (COW) Project theory and research, for instance, identify a range of dimensions for interstate war; intensity, magnitude, and other aspects, over and above sheer frequency, have been the subjects of extensive study. It also is possible to identify other forms of conflict, such as international crises (Brecher and Wilkenfeld 1997, 2000), which have been designated as empirical problems and explored across multiple dimensions in the same way. Still further beyond warlikeness or crisis activity is the set of empirical problems that could be identified for international *cooperation* rather than conflict. Why do states join international organizations? What explains compliance with international law? It would be easy to list many other cooperation-centered empirical problems and produce graphics analogous to Figure 5.1 to accompany them.

With all pieces in place, it is time to assemble the concept of a research enterprise. When combined, the methodology of falsificationism and paradigm concepts teach the lesson that both (a) deductive and rationalist and (b) inductive and sociological criteria are essential means toward the end of identifying axioms. Rigor and a gestalt sense of recognition are essential in designating assumptions in order to "get the nod," respectively, from those from inside and outside of a school of thought. With a focus on a series of theories, the concept of a research enterprise incorporates a positive trait from the apparatus associated with a research program. Finally, work on empirical problems is taken from the concept of a research tradition.

Figuratively speaking, the research enterprise is a concept that draws the best cards from the "deck" of systems of explanation. At the same time, there are "discards"; the research enterprise eschews undesirable traits from previous entities. Naive falsification and hyper-inductivism are rejected in favor of a middle ground. The idea of empirical content is put aside because, for the foreseeable future, it is metaphorical and normative rather than operational and relevant. False precision is inherent in the criterion of favoring theories that are solving empirical problems at the fastest rate. In practical terms, it is just not going to be obvious, except perhaps with hindsight, what theory is maintaining the best pace in terms of solutions. Thus this aspect of a research tradition, like the preceding unhelpful characteristics of other systems of explanation, is excluded from the apparatus of a research enterprise.

Figure 3.1, which conveys the elements within a metatheory of scientific progress, attempts to thread the needle on the difficult issue of paradigmatic affiliation—so divisive within the field. Theories, as Walker (2018: 206) observes, "should be a source of puzzles for scholars to investigate, not the source of scholarly identity or tribal affiliation." With a similar interest in moving forward in a constructive way, Wight (2019: 76) asks how IR might be restructured to enhance communication at the level of theory. Toward such ends, the metatheory of IR in Figure 3.1 includes the concept of a research enterprise along with analytic eclecticism. Paradigmatic entities can serve as rallying points for research, but must maintain logical consistency in engaging with ideas taken from outside that naturally include auxiliary assumptions. Thus the concept of a research enterprise maintains the value associated with previous systems of explanation while moving forward in a way intended to improve communication and ultimately progress.

Summing Up the Units

Two elements make up the units of the metatheory for progress in IR: (1) individuals who act on instrumental rationality and (2) systems of explanation for research. Rational choice in this context refers to decision-making about means and does not pass judgment on the ends pursued. The vision of instrumental rationality is ordinal, meaning that people are anticipated to update their preferences in a direction compatible with new information. Rationality therefore does not assume that precise calculations take place in the process of decision. A system of explanation is a scheme of organization, such as a research tradition or paradigm. Unlike these and other prior options, however, the research enterprise synthesizes the best characteristics of familiar efforts that are primarily inductive and deductive. The concept of a research enterprise is based upon both (a) deductive and rationalist and (b) inductive and sociological reasoning about what can be implemented to best advantage. For a research enterprise, the focus is on performance of a series of theories in solving empirical problems. The properties of a research enterprise, moreover, should facilitate its ability to work in tandem with a graphic approach toward dialogue.

Rational individuals and systems of explanation are in line with elements from the knowledge component presented in Chapter 4: (a) scientific realism, (b) analytic eclecticism, and (c) a model of cognition that favors a visual turn. This assertion about compatibility is backed up systematically in Chapter 7, when elements of the knowledge, units, and methods components are assembled into the metatheory of progress. Attention now turns in Chapter 6 to specifics about elements within methods, the remaining component from the metatheory not yet covered in detail.

6
Methods

Methods as a Component of the Metatheory of Progress

Knowledge and units have been specified for the metatheory of progress, which sets the stage for designation of methods. Established in Chapter 4, commitments to scientific realism, analytic eclecticism, and a model of cognition that favors a visual turn for IR are elements of the knowledge component. Covered in Chapter 5, individuals who act on the basis of instrumental rationality, along with the research enterprise (a new type of system of explanation or organizing principle for an academic discipline) are the elements that comprise the metatheory's unit component. It is important to bear in mind that, throughout the process of assembling the metatheory, the ultimate goal is application to realism in a manner that promotes scientific progress.

Attention thus turns to methods, last among the metatheory's components. How are the knowledge and unit components of the metatheory to be integrated with each other and applied to the substance of IR? This chapter identifies two elements within the methods component of a metatheory for progress in IR. One element is identification of axioms for a research enterprise. The other is systemism, a technique that implements the recommended visual turn for IR. These elements reside at the micro level in Figure 3.1, which depicted the seven elements of the metatheory of progress but stopped short of an explanation of it as a working system.

This chapter unfolds in three additional sections. The second section focuses on identification of axioms for a research enterprise. Both (i) inductive and sociological and (ii) deductive and rationalist steps are included in that process in order to achieve rigor in designating a research enterprise while also keeping it viable in the eyes of its exponents. The third section presents systemism and includes a sample application, namely, to neoclassical realism. This choice of illustration is appropriate because neoclassical realist theories are developing quickly and attracting greater interest with time. Systemism implements the graphic turn for IR in a manner intended to facilitate progress. The fourth and final section sums up the methods introduced and provides a transition into Chapter 7, in which elements from respective components in Chapters 4–6 are assembled into a metatheory of scientific progress that is conveyed graphically as a working system.

Identification of Axioms for a Research Enterprise (↑)

This section carries out six tasks. The first is a plan of work for designation of axioms, which unfolds in four stages. The second through fifth tasks are to present in greater detail the respective stages for selection of axioms that combine to create the foundation of a research enterprise. These are Stages I and IV (i.e., inductive and sociological) and II and III (i.e., deductive and rationalist). The sixth and final goal of the section is to sum up the conditions as a process of identification for axioms that provide the foundation for a research enterprise.

Plan of Work

From the standpoint of progress for IR, the last few decades have been quite impressive in terms of evaluation of theories. For example, quantitative analysis has climbed to a very high level of sophistication. Over the last two decades, Barkin and Sjoberg (2019: 125) observe, statistical work in IR has become exponentially more refined, following innovations that mostly appeared in economics and then political science. Advancements in statistical testing, along with the revolution in thinking about case studies stimulated by King, Keohane, and Verba (1994; see also Brady and Collier 2004), are quite obvious in their effects. Sophisticated debates about case selection and causal inference transcend any narrowly focused sense of conflict over quantitative versus qualitative methods (Gerring 2007). At the same time, Blagden (2016) observes that, "while literature on the methodology of theory testing has proliferated exponentially in the last two decades, theory *building* remains something of a black art." Ongoing disagreements about the meaning of theory itself explain why. For that reason, efforts to identify a research enterprise begin from the ground up. The starting point is to designate an axiomatic basis and build upon it. What follows is a set of rules for doing so that are feasible with respect to implementation—notably with regard to a vast domain such as realism in the field of IR.

Given the foundational nature of what follows, it makes sense to carry out the process in multiple stages that incorporate views from inside and outside whatever is to be designated as a research enterprise. Thus some conditions used to identify axioms are sociological and inductive, while others are rationalist and deductive. This combination of criteria is intended to enhance validity and reliability of the set of assumptions ultimately identified for a research enterprise. While the focus in this volume is on realism, the approach developed can be applied in principle to any body of research.

One basic question should be answered before going ahead with the task at hand: why bother with something that simply should be obvious and occur by default? Names already exist for various schools of thought, so a critic might wonder whether the work really is needed. The answer to the preceding question is that identification of criteria to designate a school of thought rigorously is long overdue rather than lacking in purpose. The status quo is *not* one that includes consensus on the meaning of realism or, for that matter, other schools of thought. Different studies use the same word in ways that vary significantly from each other and the range of content is increasing with time. Levine and Barder (2014: 879) point toward "staleness" in debates over grand theory that consist of "a series of scholarly and intellectual performances" that seem likely to continue on in the same way. Under these conditions, rigorous designation of criteria for the axiomatic basis of a research enterprise becomes a priority rather than a tangential exercise.

Table 6.1 displays the conditions for the axiomatic basis of a research enterprise. Four stages, designated as I to IV in the first column, correspond to implementation of deductive or inductive criteria. Nine conditions, of two types—(1) sociological and inductive, and (2) rationalist and deductive—appear in the first column of the table. These conditions are labeled with the letters (a) through (i). A condition's type and meaning appear in the second and third columns of the table. Order of implementation is in the fourth and final column.

Work begins at Stage I, in line with Kuhn ([1970] 1962) and Laudan (1977), on the basis of an inductive and sociological approach that entails two criteria, labeled (a) and (b). Potential status as an axiom requires some degree of identification from within and beyond the research enterprise. This is followed by implementation in Stages II and III of five deductively derived and rationalist criteria, (c) through (g), which are intended to maximize the potential of the axioms to account for cause and effect. There are two deductive and rationalist stages because conditions (c) through (e) are implemented on an individual basis, while criteria (f) and (g) involve comparison of axioms to each other. Two further criteria of a sociological nature, (h) and (i), then are imposed to complete the process in Stage IV. These final two conditions are intended to ensure that adherents of the research enterprise, generally speaking, would not object to the set of axioms that emerges after the five prior rationalist criteria have been applied to optimize its potential for the purpose of explanation. Each of the preceding conditions will be explained in further detail.

Sociological and Inductive Stage I

Two initial conditions are sociological and inductive in nature. Any candidate axiom must be (a) included among at least two expositions from inside and (b) at least one source from outside the boundaries of a research enterprise.

Table 6.1 Conditions for the Axiomatic Basis of a Research Enterprise: Stages of Identification

Stage and Condition	Type	Meaning	Ordering
I—(a) Internal designation	Sociological and inductive	A candidate axiom must be included among two or more sources coming from inside the research enterprise.	Prior to (b)
I—(b) External identification	Sociological and inductive	A candidate axiom must be included in least one source from outside the research enterprise.	After (a)
II—(c) Primitive Statement	Rationalist and deductive	A candidate axiom must be a primitive statement—simple and declarative.	After (a) and (b)
II—(d) Universal statement	Rationalist and deductive	A candidate axiom must be a universal statement—it applies regardless of context.	After (c), before or after (e)
II—(e) Abstract statement	Rationalist and deductive	A candidate axiom must be abstract—not a brute fact.	After (c), before or after (d)
III—(f) Logical consistency	Rationalist and deductive	A candidate axiom must be logically consistent with other axioms.	After (c), (d) and (e), before (g)
III—(g) Economy of exposition	Rationalist and deductive	A candidate axiom must not be redundant with others.	After (f), before (h)
IV—(h) Distinctiveness	Sociological and inductive	A set of candidate axioms, collectively speaking, must be distinguished readily from other collectivities.	After (g), before (i)
IV—(i) Internal acceptability	Sociological and inductive	A candidate axiom must not be unacceptable to a critical mass of dissenters within the research enterprise.	After (h)

The reasoning here is straightforward and attempts to operationalize Kuhnian thinking about valid designation for a research community in a way that also takes into account the need for reliable identification. A research community is identified as a whole that is greater than the sum of its parts, which then enables implementation of the series of steps, inductive and deductive, required to designate its axiomatic basis. "For the most part," as Sil and Katzenstein

(2010b: 412) observe, "social scientific research is still organized around particular research traditions or scholarly communities, each marked by its own epistemic commitments, its own theoretical vocabulary, its own standards, and its own conception of 'progress.'" The process that follows in this chapter also is consistent with the exposition by Jackson (2016a) that puts great emphasis on the *public* nature of science as carried out in practice. Science is a "systematic, worldly inquiry subject to public criticism intended to improve results" (Jackson 2017: 17). As will become apparent, criteria (a) and (b) from Table 6.1 reflect the ongoing presence of these well-verified conditions.

Criterion (a), labeled as internal designation, follows intuition; how can an axiom be incorporated unless at least two of those who identify with the research enterprise include it on their list? Arguments could go back and forth, of course, about whether a majority, supermajority, or even unanimity should be required for an axiom to pass this particular test. Imposition of a highly exclusive rule could eliminate virtually all of the candidate axioms. In surveying a vast and complex literature such as realism, it is quite possible that a candidate assumption could be deemed implicit on various lists. At the other extreme, there is no internal validation for an axiom mentioned just one time among the many sources included. Condition (a), which requires appearance in expositions among two or more of those identified within the research enterprise, seems most in line with Kuhn's inclusive and subjective sense of a research community.

Consider condition (a) in the context of debate over the nature of realism that ensued after Legro and Moravcsik (1999), clearly outside its frame of reference, put forward would-be defining criteria. From the standpoint of Legro and Moravcsik (1999), realism had evolved into an amorphous entity that seemed to combine anarchy and rational choice with other concepts that collectively made the school of thought difficult to distinguish from liberalism or any number of other approaches. Walt (2002: 200 n. 7), in a searing response, vigorously rejects the core preferences of realism as described by Legro and Moravcsik (1999): "Few scholars working in the realist tradition would endorse it." Schweller ([Feaver et al.] 2000: 174) is even more emphatic in responding to Legro and Moravcsik: "The moral of the story is (and I mean this in a purely professional, not personal, way): *Never let your enemies define you*." Schweller ([Feaver et al.] 2000: 174) adds more specifically that "Legro and Moravcsik mischaracterized realism as a paradigm based solely on the objective, material capabilities of states." Perhaps the most negative reply of all comes from Wohlforth ([Feaver et al.] 2000: 184): "One can defend the necessity of debating the merits of real schools of international relations scholarship. It is hard to see what value would be added by a new debate over imaginary ones." Taken together, these preceding instances of rejecting a purely external designation are sufficient to establish the need for internal criteria in the process of identifying axioms with regard to any research enterprise. It is virtually impossible to imagine constructive engagement involving advocates and critics otherwise.

With implementation of sociological criteria for identifying axioms, a question posed by Legro and Moravcsik (Feaver et al. [Legro and Moravcsik] 1999: 189) in the heat of an intense debate over realism now can be revisited more effectively: "Should scholars employ intellectual history, rather than adherence to core assumptions, as the measure of paradigmatic fidelity?" The best answer is to say that it is not a matter of adopting one criterion or the other. Instead, valid identification of axioms for a system of explanation—methodology of falsificationism, paradigm, research program, research tradition, or the preferred type here, research enterprise—must include both inductive and deductive criteria. To exclude intellectual history, as Legro and Moravcsik would prefer, risks perception of irrelevance among the community that is (1) being addressed and (2) encouraged to place greater emphasis on various aspects of scientific inquiry.

Condition (b), external identification, also is inductive and sociological. The requirement reflects the need for validation of an assumption by those outside of a research enterprise. If no external confirmation exists, this suggests that the axiom may lack clarity and be intelligible only within a sector of a particular research community. Condition (b) effectively checks for existence of commensurability regarding assumptions that serve as the foundation for a given research enterprise. If at least one source from outside picks up on the existence of an axiom, it serves as confirmation, independent from perceptions of advocates, of what appears in the research enterprise's foundation. This point indirectly reinforces the importance of a graphic turn for IR because presenting a theory in that way facilitates comprehension of its axioms. This is because causal mechanisms, when depicted in visual form, represent inferences based on assumptions combined together.

Once again, debates could occur over the specific decision rule here. Why should just one external validation be deemed sufficient? From a pragmatic point of view, this can be answered in terms of a claim about whether a research enterprise exists or not. If even one person from beyond the figurative walls of a research enterprise can recognize a given axiom that also is claimed by adherents, then that is good enough. In addition, external validation will tend to come from numerous sources with the passing of time as the identity of a research enterprise solidifies in practice.[1]

Conditions (a) and (b) each perform an essential service vis-à-vis measurement. Condition (a), which takes into account the views of participants within

---

[1] The likelihood of validation building with time is high because of the way in which a research enterprise will come to resemble an ideology. Freeden (2013: 125) points out that identifying "the conceptual morphology of an ideology assists in assessing its staying power—its longevity or ephemerality—and its claim to social validation." A research enterprise such as realism, as time goes by, therefore will solidify in place and become recognized in the same way as an ideology.

the research enterprise, constitutes an assessment of validity. An axiom should not be included without recognition from those who supposedly rely upon it. Reliability, another essential aspect of measurement, is assessed on the basis of condition (b). This criterion is implemented through external validation of an assumption; it must be visible to those who do not identify with the research enterprise. Thus an initial set of candidate axioms is designated for further revision in a rationalist and deductive context.

Note so far the word *candidate* is in use regarding assumptions that would meet requirements (a) and (b). These are necessary conditions for presence in the axiomatic basis of a research enterprise. Further criteria, when collectively met, then become sufficient for an axiom to be included in a research enterprise's foundation: (c) primitive statement, (d) universal statement, (e) abstract statement, (f) logical consistency within a system, (g) economy of exposition, (h) distinctiveness, and (i) acceptability not questioned by a critical mass from within. Conditions (c) through (g), collectively speaking, are not sociological like (a) and (b). Instead, these deductively derived and rationalist criteria are intended to enhance prospects for the research enterprise to succeed in explaining the subject matter of IR. Requirements (c) through (g) reflect concerns expressed by Vasquez (1983, 1998), Legro and Moravcsik (1999), and various other critics of realism in particular and problems associated with loosely stated frameworks of analysis in general. The final two conditions, (h) and (i), refer to sociological designation after essential criteria for rigor and falsifiability have been imposed via conditions (c) through (g).

Rationalist and Deductive Stages II and III

Before moving ahead to describe each of the rationalist and deductively derived conditions in further detail, it is essential to explain the order of implementation. Conditions (c) through (e) are applied on an individual basis in Stage II. The requirement for primitive statement (c) naturally goes first. All candidate axioms must be stated in this way to facilitate further assessment. Universal and abstract statement, conditions (d) and (e), can be implemented in either order without impacting the ultimate result.

Since conditions (f) and (g) involve comparison of potential axioms with each other, their order of implementation in Stage III can prove to be important. On the basis of the Arrow Impossibility Theorem it is known that seemingly innocent properties of a collective decision-making rule, such as the order in which alternatives are put forward, can alter the final result (Arrow 1951a). For this reason, the individual requirements are applied first and the comparative ones second. Within the subset of the two comparative conditions—(f) logical consistency and (g) economy of exposition—it makes sense to resolve contradictions before moving on to Occam's razor. Put differently, intuition strongly supports the idea that removing disagreements from a set of axioms should take precedence over putting them forward in the most compact way, even while it is acknowledged that both things matter.

Condition (c), primitive statement, rules out compound assertions. Each axiom must be primitive in the sense of making a simple, declarative affirmation. Both conjunctive (i.e., the logical "and") and disjunctive (i.e., the logical "or") statements must be reduced to a primitive form in order to be enumerated as axioms. Statements such as "X and Y are true" and "X or Y is true" must be simplified to "X is true" and "Y is true." This point might seem self-evident, but it is violated in practice and causes confusion. The problem is analogous to a double-barreled question in survey research. Asking something like "Do you approve of the president's foreign policy and economic plan—yes or no?" is badly worded because, logically speaking, four possible answers exist, not just two. A respondent could approve of both, neither, or one or the other. An axiom should not have ambiguity—of this sort or others—built into it. This is the essence of condition (c).

Condition (d) requires that each assumption is universal. In other words, criterion (d) means that the assertion must be deemed true regardless of context. If epistemic conditions are required, then the would-be axiom really takes the form of a proposition instead. In other words, if it is true in some circumstances and not others, the would-be axiom becomes ineligible for inclusion. When Mearsheimer (1994–95: 11) began to develop offensive realism, for example, he properly enumerated a set of axioms (e.g., rationality) and inferred multiple patterns of behavior from them. Resulting offensive realist inferences about states in the international system include the assertions that (i) they will fear each other, (ii) aim to guarantee their own survival, and (iii) maximize relative power over others. These inferences are viable for testing as long as the axioms hold true (Mearsheimer 1994–95).

Abstract statement, condition (e), is in place to prevent the axiomatic basis from being overrun with assumptions that every research enterprise must adopt a priori. The concept of "brute or natural facts" (Guzzini 2000; see also Wight 2007: 381 n. 12) is helpful here. These are overwhelmingly confirmed elements of the empirical world that are not contested in terms of interpretation. For example, Canadian Confederation in 1867 is a natural or brute fact. It is assumed to be true. While the deeper meaning or significance of such an event could be debated endlessly, its occurrence is not. Thus it is superfluous to include such facts among the axioms of a paradigm, which instead should be abstract and distinctive.

Prior to implementation of the comparative conditions (f) and (g), one principle is identified as essential and concerns the manner of elimination for candidate conditions. This process will adopt the Anti-Brutus Criterion (ABC). The rule is based on an adage that dates back to a play by Shakespeare: "Brutus does not get to be Caesar." In the play, Brutus is involved in the assassination of Caesar, which in turn rules him out as a successor. In the present context, ABC means that no candidate assumption can be eliminated by another if the latter does not end up, itself, in the final set of surviving axioms. Put differently, no ultimately irrelevant axiom can be used to knock out another along the way.[2]

Logical consistency, condition (f), obviously is necessary because a set of assumptions that contains "X" and its negation, "~X" (i.e., not X), is consistent with anything that is observed. The research enterprise thus becomes functionally useless without condition (f) (Legro and Moravcsik 1999: 9). Condition (f), surprisingly, is at times disputed during discussions of theorizing in IR. Along those lines, Legro and Moravcsik ([Feaver et al.] 2000: 193) call explicitly for "a defensible set of core realist assumptions" and an explanation of "precisely which midrange hypotheses they include and exclude." These critics of realism show exasperation about those points when asking two further questions: "Wouldn't anyone see this as desirable? Shouldn't everyone care?" (Legro and Moravcsik [Feaver et al.] 2000: 193). In sum, logical consistency is essential to scientific viability.

Condition (g), economy of exposition, involves a process of comparison that includes style to some degree. Thus, in application, condition (g) becomes less absolute than something like (f). When candidate axioms are compared to each other, some may take the form of derivations. Any assumption that can be derived from others, but does not exhibit this power itself, is eliminated on grounds of economy of explanation. It is important to note that condition (g) becomes problematic if not embedded in a larger set of criteria. If pursued in a single-minded way, economy of exposition may result in theorizing that is very narrow in scope and ultimately dissatisfying.

For example, this problem is the foundation for many critiques of the structural variant of realism in IR. The structural realist framework in Waltz (1979) is so austere and holistic that it can produce just a few hypotheses and even then only about aggregate processes: (i) power balancing and warfare will recur in the international system and (ii) bipolarity is more stable than multipolarity. Thus a framework is not necessarily superior because it is compact; a more intricate

---

[2] The ABC resembles independence of irrelevant alternatives, a condition that appears in the Arrow Impossibility Theorem (Snidal 2018). This condition asserts that whether someone prefers option "x" to "y," or vice versa, should not be influenced by the presence or absence of option "z" (Arrow 1951a: 26–28). In formal terms, the ABC requires that if axiom "i" is used to eliminate axiom "j," then "i" must be among the set that survives the entire process of selection.

alternative, if it is able to show greater breadth and depth in terms of resulting propositions and performance under testing, would be preferred.

Sociological and Inductive Stage IV

Condition (h), distinctiveness, returns to inductive and sociological concerns. It is appropriate to establish whether the research enterprise possesses a distinct identity before moving on to condition (i), assessment of whether advocates find its description acceptable. The opposite ordering, upon reflection, would make no sense. How could exponents of a research enterprise decide on its acceptability without agreeing that something distinct has been identified?

Condition (h) focuses on whether the set of axioms can be recognized as representing something unique. Freeden (2013) draws attention to the importance of "conceptual morphology" in identifying an ideology; the argument works in this theory-oriented context just as well. A belief system becomes associated with a network of concepts that interact with each other to produce an identity. Thus ideologies such as Marxism become understood to exist over time and entail certain collections of concepts, such as socioeconomic class. In the world of explanatory theory, axioms become fused together in much the same way and provide an identity for a school of thought. A significant test to pass, therefore, is recognition as a research enterprise rather than as a combination of assumptions that possesses no obvious identity.

Debates over the merits of realism already reveal awareness of the importance of condition (h) among those in the field of IR. Legro and Moravcsik (1999: 12) see this as a matter of survival for realism, which otherwise risks being hopelessly confused with various competitors, such as institutionalism and liberalism. Systematic use of ideas associated with another research enterprise, such as perceptions and beliefs, threaten realism's continuing relevance (Legro and Moravcsik 1999: 39, 54). Guzzini (2004: 536) adds that many assumptions regarded as unique to realism are not, and that prominently includes "the microassumption of self-interest (and hence, disclaimers notwithstanding, instrumental rationality) and the macro-assumption of anarchy, both widely shared among non-realists." Thus realism must feature a unique *combination* of axioms, even if it almost certainly includes at least some assumptions also held by another research enterprise.

Condition (i) also represents a sociological and inductive approach to identification of axioms. This final stage examines the surviving axioms, after implementation of requirements (a) through (h), to see whether one or more is deemed unacceptable to adherents of the research enterprise. Significant and compelling opposition to an assumption—normally taken to mean a majority of adherents—must be exhibited from within the research enterprise in order to consider its removal. Arguments for removal of an axiom must be connected to the identity of the research enterprise itself. Thus it makes sense to begin identification of a research enterprise with an effort to designate it in the gestalt sense of things. For example, what in a basic, one-word way is meant by realism? Once this question is answered, critiques of axioms, if any, can be evaluated for their significance via condition (i).

Two possible outcomes can be imagined for implementation of condition (i). One is that miscommunication is identified and the candidate axiom is retained. In other words, those who call for rejection of a potential assumption have not understood its content. This is deemed the more likely result because of a dynamic already noted many times, namely, confusion arising from the sheer size of the field and its proliferation of terminology. Less likely is the outcome of rejection. This result would lead to designation of a competing research enterprise that includes the former candidate axiom.

Summing Up

With all of the details in place about the nine conditions that identify axioms for a research enterprise, a summary seems appropriate. Four stages of identification for assumptions—two that are sociological and inductive (I, IV) and two that are rationalist and deductive (II, III)—have been enumerated. Among the nine conditions from Table 6.1, the first two, (a) and (b), reflect a sociological and inductive viewpoint about identification of assumptions that provide the foundation for a research enterprise. These conditions put together views from inside and outside of the research enterprise with regard to its axiomatic basis. Requirements (a) and (b) combine in Stage I to offer tests of validity and reliability, respectively. The next five conditions, (c) through (g), are implemented in Stages II and III to maximize prospects for the research enterprise to succeed at explaining international relations. These deductively derived, rationalist requirements enhance the ability of the research enterprise to address and solve empirical problems. The research enterprise thereby provides a solid foundation for scientific inquiry. Conditions (h) and (i) return to a sociological approach in Stage IV to check whether conditions (c) through (g) in Stages II and III have caused difficulties in terms of identity for the research enterprise. Condition (h) focuses on whether the axioms that have survived the deductive and rationalist criteria possess an identity that can be distinguished readily from other collections of assumptions that might be thrown together. Finally, condition (i) assesses whether one or more axioms that remain in place have generated serious opposition from adherents to the research enterprise.

When considered as a whole, the nine conditions affirm the call from Blagden (2016) for recognition that successful theorizing naturally combines inductive and deductive reasoning. Conditions (a), (b), (h), and (i) represent the former and (c) through (g) the latter at a metatheoretical level. Taken together, the nine criteria incorporate insights from inductive (Kuhn and Laudan) and deductive (Popper and Lakatos) frameworks that designate schools of thought. The process of identifying axioms, in an overall sense, represents a combination of insider "understanding" and outsider "explaining" to obtain knowledge (Jackson 2016: 31). Put more concretely, designation of a research enterprise entails empirical identification of a like-minded community of scholars, along with a rigorous presentation of foundations for its research.

One objection that might be raised, after introduction of the nine conditions above, is that the degree of complexity involved is not necessary. Why bother with all of these stages when intuition might be enough? The admittedly detailed series of steps is essential because of the greater goal of deriving and identifying causal mechanisms that can be assembled into coherent sets and conveyed in visual form. The negative consequences of relying on intuition to identify the axiomatic basis of realism, with variation permitted from one study to the next, have been established overwhelmingly within the classic expositions by Vasquez (1983, 1998).

What just concluded is a process that previously did not take place in IR. Conditions (a) through (i) are the first fully specified set of rules to designate the axiomatic basis for a system of explanation. Put differently, identification of paradigms, research programs, or other such entities previously took an impressionistic form. Proliferation of meaning and confusion naturally ensued and have contributed mightily to dissatisfaction with realism in particular and paradigmatic entities in general. Whatever improvements it may need, the process of designation implemented here, which includes both (i) sociological and inductive and (ii) rationalist and deductive steps, provides a starting point. Value is expected to accrue from that forthcoming process when used to identify realism in Chapter 8 and, subsequently and beyond this volume, other collectivities in IR. Prospects for productive debate within and across more clearly designated boundaries for schools of thought almost certainly would be enhanced.

Systemism (∫)

This section accomplishes six goals. One is to give an account of how system-oriented theorizing evolved prior to the advent of systemism. The second goal is to make the case for systemism as the best option among available graphic methods. The third objective is to show how systemism, causation, and complexity are linked to each other. Fourth, systemist graphics and notation, which are essential to the later exposition of realist theories, are explained. The fifth goal is to use a significant work on neoclassical realism to illustrate systemism and show value added from its implementation. Sixth, and finally, Systemist International Relations (SIR) is introduced as a perspective that warrants further attention from a discipline that needs unifying principles in pursuit of advancement.

Evolution of System-Oriented Theorizing

Systemism answers the question raised in Chapter 4 about how to proceed with a visual turn for IR. With a rigorous approach toward representing theories through causal mechanisms, systemism relies upon diagrams rather than words alone to enhance the potential for effective understanding and dialogue. This graphic shift is the key to unlocking progress for IR as a discipline at its present stage and beyond. It is anticipated to have a salutary effect for realism in particular. The evolution of system-oriented theorizing will be recounted to provide context, followed by an exegesis of systemism.

Given its centrality in the study of politics at one time, it is appropriate to begin the review with Easton's version of systems analysis (1953, 1965a, 1965b).[3] General systems theory began in engineering and focused on analyzing operational requirements and efficient allocation of resources in a system and, in turn, greatly influenced the thinking of Easton and others who followed him in political science and IR (Luard 1992: 516).[4] The approach Easton introduced, with the look and feel of the behavioral revolution strongly imprinted upon it, generated considerable reaction for over a decade. Systemism, which relies upon a diagrammatic exposition to convey cause and effect, is therefore by no means the first conceptual framework of its kind in the study of politics.

This is neither the time nor place to review the works concerned in detail, but system-level theorizing about politics to this day tends to favor interdisciplinary borrowing rather than ideas drawn more directly from within either IR or political science.[5] Since systems analysis fell out of favor in the 1970s, there is no need

---

[3] Although the description and analysis that follows relies on Easton (1965a), it just as easily could proceed on the basis of his other two works noted, which also convey essential concept formation and arguments from systems analysis. For excellent summaries of Easton's exposition on systems analysis, see Green (1985: 131–132) and Fisher (2011: 73–74).

[4] In a comprehensive assessment, Leslie (1972: 155) confirmed Easton's systems analysis as occupying a leading place in the study of politics during the 1950s and 1960s. The most memorable example in IR probably remains Kaplan (1957), which identifies types of systems, operations, and prospects for equilibrium. Systems analysis as pursued by Kaplan (1957), as will become apparent, is quite distant from systemism's agenda, which focuses on visual presentation of theories through their causal mechanisms.

[5] In a prominent review of system-level theorizing, Young (1968: 37) observes that Easton created "one of the few systemic frameworks originally developed by a political scientist rather than adapted for political analysis from some other discipline."

to focus in any detail on alternative strands of research within IR. Systemism's similarities with, and differences from, Easton's conceptual apparatus will highlight progress in thinking about sociopolitical systems since the 1960s. General systems theory, in an overall sense, can be applied as an antinomy—to give a sense of what systemism *is* by explaining what it is *not*.

For Easton (1965a: x, 23), the point of departure is to view politics as a system of behavior. He designates systems analysis of political behavior as an intellectual movement in academe (Easton 1965a: 4). The behavioral turn in IR included, during the 1960s and 1970s, an implicitly Easton-inspired emphasis on flowchart-style diagrams in conveying cause and effect. Four components are identified in systems analysis (Easton 1965a: 24–25; see also Fisher 2011: 71, 73): a system made up of political behavior, an environment that can be distinguished from the system at issue, the members' response to stress within the system's operation, and feedback to actors and decision-makers that is (or is not) sufficient for the system's persistence. The overall focus of Easton's (1965a: 84; see also Haas 2017: 85) analysis is on the ability of a system to continue in the face of stress and return to a state of equilibrium. Stress can induce change through adaptation to new circumstances. While at one time the paradigm based on systems had pretensions to subsume all others, it never fulfilled that promise (Haas 2017: 86).

Easton (1990: 4) revisited his theorizing and pointed out that, decades after its heyday, the emphasis of the system-oriented approach in the 1950s and 1960s on political behavior had caused neglect of the "broad context" of activity. He argued that more attention therefore needed to be paid to the "overarching structure of the whole political system in shaping all its major parts" (Easton 1990: 6). This would not mean "throwing the baby out with the bathwater," in that a focus on individual action needs to be sustained. Theorizing would continue to be individualistic in terms of social behavior being "reducible to the activities of persons and their empirically traceable connections with each other" (Easton 1990: 257). However, Easton (1990: 257) added soon after that emergent properties "may be accessible only if dealt with at the collective level." Individual actions matter, but constraints imposed by overarching structures "are very real, even though they are invisible and seldom identified and recognized for what they do" (Easton 1990: 280). Easton's exposition, from the standpoint of a systems approach as it might be applied today, anticipates the need to combine levels of action into a single frame of reference. The final quotation in this paragraph also sounds a lot like scientific realism in its inclusion of overarching structures as significant unobservables.

Offered three decades ago, Green's assessment of systems analysis as Easton had put it forward rings true today: systems theory is "nearly friendless among political scientists" (1985: 127; see also Haas 2017: 86; Braumoller and Campbell

2018: 444).[6] On the one hand, Jervis (1998) makes an impressive case for a system orientation by showing how unintended consequences from actions are an important part of what is observed at the international level. His work takes the form of a critique of holist approaches such as structural realism, and the point of view conveyed about social theory is quite consistent with systemism. On the other hand, in spite of Jervis's positive views (1998), systems thinking continues to be marginalized even after publication of his thoughtful and convincing book (Monteiro 2012; see also Haas 2017: 86).

Declining interest in systems analysis can be traced to characteristics that systemism, as will become apparent, seeks to avoid. Quite recently, Fisher (2011: 74; see also Özdemir 2015: 7 on related points) produced a valuable review that sums up the multifaceted criticism of systems analysis that caused it to go out of favor: methodological weakness (i.e., how to incorporate events into a comprehensive model), difficulty in specifying boundaries and variables in a system, and problems with the operational meaning of equilibrium. Systemism seeks to go beyond these limitations.

Making the Case for Systemism

While on the surface it might seem justified simply to do away with systems analysis, this would not be the right decision. Such a verdict effectively disregards important lessons learned from the history of social theory. While events occasionally reflect a straightforward summation of individual behavior, emergent properties at the level of the system cannot be ignored (Coleman 1990: 2, 5). In a prominent exposition on the foundations of social theory, Coleman (1990: 9) observed that Weber and any number of subsequent theorists had not specified *how* actions of individuals would be aggregated into outcomes at the level of the system. Thus even the wave of impressive studies that explain conflict processes in international relations through a focus on interstate dyad-years would be unable to say anything about properties of the system as a whole. Solving such problems of aggregation is no easy matter—the stunning breakthrough by Olson (1965), which demonstrated how the logic of collective action would tend to inhibit anything that looked like a proletarian revolution—solved a puzzle confronting Marxists for over a century. The challenges facing actor-based theories about international relations, when it comes to saying anything interesting about the level of the system, are no less daunting today.

---

[6] Exceptions are rare; see (i) Vancouver (1996) for application of modeling from organizational behavior to the study of foreign policy, (ii) Jervis (1998) on complexity, (iii) the ICB project on data analysis that incorporates both the system and state levels (Brecher and Wilkenfeld 1997, 2000); and (iv) Viterale (2019) on science, technology, and innovation.

Consider also the assessment by Pickel (2007: 392): "Abandoning conceptions of systems has imposed a high price on the social sciences: a lack of ontologies and methodologies that are both philosophically profound and scientifically defensible."[7] Monteiro (2012: 361; see also Viterale 2019: 5) adds that "we should not abstain from studying politically important phenomena just because of the complications introduced by system effects." Given acceleration of events and increasingly complex relationships in international relations that challenge formulation and implementation of policy, a systems perspective is essential to prevent "a higher likelihood of breaking or damaging one thing while trying to fix or improve another" (Fisunoğlu 2019: 232). A focus on any one level of analysis, for instance, is likely to prove misleading.

Without a system orientation, a mechanismic account cannot be achieved; instead, research becomes an exercise in increasingly sophisticated empiricism that is unable to depict cause and effect directly.[8] Thus the key concern becomes successfully identifying and explaining *mechanismic causation*, defined as an explanation for change in one variable as a product of a shift in one or more others.[9]

Correlation does not equate with causation, and that is the point of departure for systemism as it seeks to incorporate mechanisms—a goal consistent with scientific realism. Consider the adage about storks and birth rates as a simple illustration of what is at issue here. The correlation might exist, but not because storks, as parents might tell their young children, are bringing the babies. Instead, a causal mechanism involving rural areas is at work. The degree to which an area is rural versus urban will explain both the frequency of storks and the birth rate. Something more IR-related to consider might be a fanciful (or perhaps even observed) connection involving the number of letters in a state's name and the frequency of its involvement in Cold War conflict. This could be a simple artifact of the prominence of the United States of America and the Union of Soviet Socialist Republics, two states with long names, in the Cold War. The underlying causal mechanism is that the superpowers became that way through federation—voluntary or otherwise—and thus also had relatively long names as a byproduct of their history. In sum, systemism does not focus on obtaining ever-larger coefficients from regression-style research or accumulation of case

---

[7] General systems theory, front and center in the behavioral era of the 1960s, had been dormant for decades by the time of that observation. Reasons for its demise are covered by James and James (2017; see also Haas 2017: 86).

[8] For an effort to integrate individualism (i.e., reductionism) and holism with each other, derived from a perspective built upon studies from philosophy, see List and Spiekermann (2013).

[9] Authoritative treatments of mechanisms and explanation, nested within the philosophy of inquiry, appear in Bunge (1997, 2004). It is important to recognize that within the various expositions from Bunge (1996, 1997, 2004) on systemism, graphic presentation of arguments plays a less central and developed role than in the present study and others related to it (e.g., James 2019a, 2019b).

studies that show association between variables. Instead, systemism goes beyond debates over qualitative or quantitative methods to focus explicitly on explanation.

For causal mechanisms to be identified more effectively, a return to system-oriented thinking becomes essential. The ontology and method of systems analysis open up new vistas to research. With respect to being and existence, a system orientation reminds us that causal effects often may be nonlinear or disproportionate. With regard to method, such thinking calls attention to the fact that causal relationships "cannot be inferred from linear correlations" (Pickel 2007: 394). Furthermore, systems analysis offers a way beyond the increasingly tedious debate over material versus ideational analysis in IR. Social systems, as Pickel (2007: 404) asserts, cannot be observed directly and therefore any exposition that is thorough must include composition, structure, environment, and causal mechanisms. For such reasons, an ensuing argument about whether idea-based or material explanations are paramount is rendered irrelevant.[10]

Nearly lost in the mists of academic time, Easton's vision of system-oriented theorizing from the era of the behavioral revolution creates a context within which to introduce and evaluate systemism. To what extent is systemism similar to Easton's formulation? How is it different? Does systemism represent an improvement over what Easton proposed long ago? And most germane of all, does this improvement result in theoretical and explanatory power that can enhance ability to account for world politics?

Systemism, Causation, and Complexity

Systemism's creator, Bunge (1996: 264; see also 1998), puts it forward as a way to think about life in general: "The world is a system of systems rather than either a solid block or an aggregate of individuals" (Bunge 2003: 286). These systems can be explained and understood most effectively through incorporation of a graphic approach. In principle, systemism can be applied to any aspect of social life to obtain a better sense of cause and effect (Bunge 1996: 264):

> The alternative to both individualism and holism is systemism, since it accounts for both individual and system, and for individual agency and social structure. Indeed, systemism postulates that everything is a system or a component of one. And it models every system as a triple (composition, environment,

---

[10] This conclusion is anticipated in the philosophical exposition from Collingwood (1946) on historical processes.

structure), or CES for short, so it encompasses the valid features of its rivals [individualism and holism].

To convey explicitly the contribution made by the diagrams entailed by systemism, Pickel (2007; see also Bunge 2004) adds causal mechanisms to the CES apparatus. This elaboration results in what this study will refer to as CESCM. Each aspect of CESCM will be introduced in turn.

Composition refers to participants—who may be individuals, social groups, or those speaking for government institutions—and the interactions between and among them. In the world of international relations, the state is central to composition of the system (Singer 1961). Additional participants, such as multinational corporations, interstate organizations, transnational social movements, individuals, and others, have been theorized into existence over decades of research in IR (Vernon 1971; Keohane and Nye 1977; Rosenau 1991; Keck and Sikkink 1998).

Beyond the boundaries of the system lies the *environment*. It may have an influence on the system and vice versa, and clarification of such boundaries would seem long overdue (Buzan and Little 2003: 432). Consider, from Figure 1.1, the example of Latin America in relation to the United States in particular. Well established over time is the role of the United States as one of the essential actors from outside of Latin America. There is an inductive element to designation of geographic boundaries in some instances. Where certain entities might go, in terms of system versus environment, may depend on context. A challenging example is Turkey. A study of the global system would not have to make a decision about its location, but what about Turkey's place in regional designations of one sort or another? A pragmatic approach would be to designate Turkey, and other liminal states, as being in or out of a region based on density of interaction. Thus for Europe and Asia Minor, Turkey would be a system member, while for the Middle East it would be significant but designated as within the environment. Other examples that come to mind, such as Mexico relative to Latin America, the Caribbean, North America, or other regions, can be handled in the same pragmatic way. Deductive and inductive reasoning come together to provide answers with regard to designation of system versus environment.

Structure refers to the rules that govern interactions among participants. For international relations in a realist context, structure refers to the distribution of capabilities among states. It is easy to imagine many ways to assess structure in these terms, especially if both states and coalitions among them are included (James 2002b). Consider, for example, combinations of polarity and polarization as these terms conventionally have been applied in realist IR. Polarity refers to the number of great powers, while polarization is about the tightness of interstate coalitions. The world at the outset of World War I provides a memorable illustration of one combination among various possibilities: multipolarity coupled with high polarization. The great powers of Europe eventually joined opposing coalitions—the Triple Alliance and Triple Entente. Polarization could be detected easily on the basis of high and low levels of communication within and across coalitions, respectively. Escalation to war ensued, as multiple great powers in a polarized setting could not prevent it (Holsti 1972).

Finally, a *causal mechanism* is a link through communication or material action involving variables within the system.[11] This concept plays an essential role in social science and is highlighted, for example, in expositions on analytic eclecticism (Sil and Katzenstein 2010b: 419). In other words, a causal mechanism is a statement of the form "If x is true, then y is more likely than otherwise" accompanied by an explanation for why "x" is expected to impact "y." Visual representation of a causal mechanism is "x → y."

Causation does not equate with correlation, which instead ought to be understood as an indicator of its possible existence. Valuable in reinforcing that point is the typology in Haas (2017: 187–188), which identifies eight alternative renderings for a correlation. In the context of social science, one possibility—a probabilistic relationship for variables with each other, where X → Y in a high percentage of cases—is most relevant.[12] This type of association, accompanied by a convincing account for *why* X leads to Y on a regular basis, is the essence of a causal mechanism. As an everyday example of how both aspects matter, consider the case of aspirin. All the way back to antiquity, people used willow bark to treat headaches. This went on for a very long time before the process of cause and effect became understood in the era of modern medicine (Jeffreys 2005).

Cause and effect are essential and linked concepts in the quest to explain international relations. In the early years of IR as a discipline, conceptions of causation stayed largely implicit and remained underdeveloped (Kurki 2002: 13). Table 6.2 is a collection of ideas expressed about cause and effect. The idea of a causal mechanism is pervasive in the discipline of IR. Cause and effect can be understood through an analogy with vectors; a resultant can be expected from the sum of forces. The idea is to understand what resides within causal arrows that are depicted in either verbal or visual form. For a causal process leading to any outcome, a point of origin must be designated. Taken together, the contents of

---

[11] Pickel (2007: 397) provides a more detailed account of how systems and mechanisms relate to each other. Causal mechanisms vary with system ontology—ideational or material.
[12] The alternative renderings for a correlation are as follows: sufficient relationship (X → Y); intervening relationship (X → T → Y); endogenous relationship (T → X and T → Y); probabilistic relationship (X → Y in a high percentage of cases); reverse relationship (Y → X); inverse relationship (−Y → −Z); recursive or simultaneous relationship (X → Y → X) (Haas 2017: 187–188).

Table 6.2 Ideas about Cause and Effect

Idea	Source
Causation should be seen in terms of forces that can be counteracted rather than as laws.	Kurki (2002: 32)
An event or change of state is *the* cause of another event if and only if *c* is sufficient for that of *e*.	Bunge (2003: 38)
Definition of a mechanism: All entities—whether individual actions or choices, social relations or networks, environmental or institutional characteristics, specific events or contextual factors, individual cognitive dispositions, or collectively shared ideas and worldviews—that generate immediate effects through processes that may or may not recur across contexts and that may be, but often are not, directly observable.	Sil and Katzenstein (2010b: 421)
"*To explain an outcome causally,* which is one instance of *explaining* in general, is to impart an understanding of the outcome's *sources and emergence*.... When we formulate a causal account, what constitutes the beginning point, and what features of it are highlighted, is a choice we make, and this choice has potentially quite significant political implications—just as much as what we focus our attention on as the end result to be explained is a matter of decision, again with perhaps quite important political consequences."	Kurki and Suganami (2012: 403, 408)
Extant paradigms and research programs have implicitly relied on causal mechanisms all along and can be mapped onto an approach that focuses on explanatory mechanisms without reifying them into grand schools of thought.	Bennett (2013: 476)
"Good" theory thus links the entire chain of action in a way that is consistent in its assumptions. The full chain is often left implicit, as implied in the call for greater attention to microfoundations or causal mechanisms.	Lake (2013: 574)
"The most important aspect of theorizing mechanisms in the system's understanding is therefore capturing explicitly what is *inside causal arrows*, making explicit the causal logic whereby the activities of one part of a mechanism link it to the next part, attempting to formulate an overall mechanism with 'productive continuity' between the cause (or set of causes) and an outcome.... A missing arrow or the inability to specify an activity connecting one part to the next leaves an explanatory gap in the productive continuity of the mechanism."	Beach (2016: 17, 18)

the table convey long-standing interest in cause and effect and a range of overlapping viewpoints about how to identify it.

Causal mechanisms play a central role in system-based analysis. The correlation of a cause with its effect is implicit, but what really matters is a compelling explanation for why one thing leads to another. It is essential to discover what is inside would-be causal arrows. The focus on causal mechanisms, moreover, is foundational to analytic eclecticism (Sil and Katzenstein 2010b: 419). A comprehensive sense of cause and effect, which can be traced all the way back to Aristotle, is offered in Kurki (2002): efficient (movers), material (passive potentiality of matter), formal (defining shapes or relations), and final (purposes that guide change). This complete specification of cause and effect is in line with the principles of systemism as well.

Consider, as an illustration of the framework of Kurki (2002) in action, an explanation for the outbreak of a war. In the US Civil War, the efficient cause is the Confederate artillery-based attack on Fort Sumter. The material cause is that the Confederate states had built up significant military capabilities independent of those in the Union. Background conditions, most notably the sectional conflict between North and South and weak responses from US presidents, constituted the formal cause. The final cause would be the motive that secessionism provided to attack the federal military installation (Kaufman 2017).

How, then, does a system operate in terms of cause and effect? From the standpoint of systemism (Bunge 1998: 65), the choice between unit and system is a flawed dichotomy, and that point is well recognized already in IR (Brecher 1999; James 2002a, 2002b). All theories must be expected to deal with both systems and units—that is, the macro and micro levels—in some way. A system, as designated by Bunge (2003: 282), is an entity "every part or component of which is related to at least one other component." Schweller (1998: 7, 8) reinforces this point in outlining the nature of complex systems in the context of international relations:

- The behavior and outcomes of such systems are determined by the interplay among the units and the structural environment within which they are embedded; therefore, the dynamics of complex systems cannot be inferred through study of unit or structural attributes alone.
- Straightforward purposive action within a complex system often produces unintended consequences.
- Consequential transformations in system dynamics do not occur in a linear manner.
- Relationships are nonadditive and noncommutative—cannot simply add effects from each variable.
- The order in which elements are taken matters.

Homer-Dixon et al. (2013: 342) combine the preceding set of properties into an effective summary of a complex system: "A system is categorized as complex if it exhibits behavioral properties such as emergence, nonlinearity (disproportionality of cause and effect), path dependency, and multiple equilibria." Thus complex systems can be expected to have "dense and recursive causal connections" that include "positive and negative feedback loops" (Homer-Dixon et al. 2013: 342). One example—and important to acknowledge in light of research designs that have become conventional—is that interstate dyads are not independent of each other (Ward 2018: 559; see also Jervis 1998 and James 2002b).

Based on the preceding observations, the international system certainly qualifies as complex. Unintended consequences are anything but surprising. It is easy to come up with examples of foreign policy intended to achieve one thing and instead leading to another, with unanticipated effects coming about in a step-level rather than incremental way. One important instance is the Six Day War, which Arab leaders entered into as a result of policies that unintentionally produced strategic disaster (Barnett 2003: 245).

Consider a historical example from the simpler but nevertheless challenging international system of the past—when rising German power posed a threat to equilibrium in Europe at the outset of the 20th century. German building of dreadnoughts, in conjunction with what became labeled as "gunboat diplomacy," pushed Britain toward an entente with France and Russia—exactly the opposite result from that intended by those policies. (Germany had hoped to encourage Britain into some kind of modus vivendi, but that did not happen.) Entry of the United States into the war on the side of the Triple Entente—France, Russia, and Britain—constituted a further problem arising from Whitehall's decision at the brink of war to side with the enemies of Germany. These results stand as unintended, sudden, and disastrous consequences of German policies that had altogether different objectives.

For a complex system, INUS causation—sets of conditions that individually are not necessary, but collectively are sufficient to bring about a certain result—represent the expected norm (Mahoney and Barrenchea 2016). This profile is very likely at the international level because multiple pathways can be expected toward the same outcome.[13] Consider, for example, power cycle (Doran 1971, 1991) and power transition (Organski 1958; Organski and Kugler 1980; Lemke 2002; Tammen and Kugler 2020a), two theories about the dynamics of capability that can lead to great power war. Power cycle focuses on critical points of change along a pathway of evolving capability, while power transition concentrates on the balance between a leading state and challenger. A war could come about through the process identified by either theory—coinciding critical points among great powers, as per power cycle, and evenly matched capabilities, as

---

[13] In more formal terms, ~X → ~Y, but Y can come about through a different pathway. This means that X is not a necessary condition for Y. In addition, while A and B together are sufficient for C; A and B are not necessary for C (Mahoney and Barrenchea 2016: 39, 40).

emphasized by power transition. There is no single route on the way to war, but instead multiple possibilities identified by respective theories.

Pause now to look back at the apparatus from Kurki (2002) to provide a complete account for cause and effect: efficient (movers), material (passive potentiality of matter), formal (defining shapes or relations), and final (purposes that guide change). Causal mechanisms from systemist figures can be understood as fitting within these respective categories and combining to provide an overall explanation for whatever outcome is depicted. The foundation from Kurki (2002) will provide structure for analysis of cause and effect for realist theories about war in Chapters 11 through 18.

Systemism's value is apparent in looking back on the discussion of ideas from *A World Restored* (Kissinger 1957), which accompanied the review of analytic eclecticism in Chapter 4. *A World Restored* offers a convincing analysis of the grand bargain that brought an end to the Napoleonic Wars. Macro and micro levels in that context influenced each other and did not operate in isolation within Europe as a system (Hayes 2009; Hayes and James 2016; see Archer 1996: xxi on social theory in general). Instead, the power structure and foreign policy impacted each other to produce the observed outcomes. Thus the question is how best to put together a theory that takes this complexity, recounted so effectively by Kissinger in *A World Restored*, into consideration. And all of this remains viable even when noting, with a touch of irony, that a classical realist scholar and practitioner such as Kissinger would seem likely to dismiss systemism as academic obscurantism.

Denials of systemism tend to include self-contradiction. Consider the following assertions (Waltz 1988: 39, 42) about creation of IR theory:

- A theory is a depiction of the organization of a domain and of the connections among its parts. A theory indicates that some factors are more important than others and specifies relations among them. In reality, everything is related to everything else, and one domain cannot be separated from others. But theory isolates one realm from all others in order to deal with it intellectually.
- If an approach allows the consideration of both unit-level and structural-level causes, then it can cope with both the changes and the continuities that occur in a system.
- With both systems-level and unit-level forces in play, how can one construct a theory of international politics without simultaneously constructing a theory of foreign policy? An international-political theory does not imply or require a theory of foreign policy any more than a market theory implies or requires a theory of the firm.

Two of these three sets of statements imply a course of action that is rejected by the third. The first assertion affirms the need for completeness in theorizing as put forward by systemism, namely, incorporation of micro- and macro-level causal forces. This vision of cause and effect then is affirmed by the second statement in the context of foreign policy (micro) and international politics (macro). Yet the conclusion in the third statement favors separation of the two—micro from macro. This result goes back to Waltz's (1988: 39; see also Kaarbo 2015: 194) vision of a theory, which "isolates one realm from all others in order to deal with it intellectually." While perhaps convincing when envisioned in abstract terms, this will not work out well in practice. The reason is that putative causal mechanisms will be altered via forces that intrude from outside the subset of linkages—at either macro or micro levels—considered in isolation. Misleading conclusions about cause and effect easily can ensue.

For example, consider the familiar Waltzian (1964, 1979, 1988) proposition—a signature item in structural realism—that bipolarity is more stable than multipolarity. Forces intruding from the micro level are capable of altering such a macro-level relationship in respective contexts. This is not a retreat into reductionism but rather an argument, based on systemism, against the misleading "comfort zone" created by implementation of one or more ceteris paribus clauses. Put simply, when theorizing about a given level of analysis, it is untenable to claim that all other things have been held constant.

For a theory of relations among aggregates to have value, "It is necessary that they be defined in a manner derived from the theory of individual behavior" (Arrow 1951: 134). However, after many more years of social science, Kertzer (2017: 82) notes in the IR context "a surprising lack of specificity about what microfoundations are, or why we should use them." A microfoundation can be defined as "an analytic strategy where one explains outcomes at the aggregate level via dynamics at a lower level" (Kertzer 2017: 83).[14] Contrary to Waltz (1979)above, an analogue to the theory of the firm from economics *is* essential if IR is to make sense of aggregate patterns.

Systemism conceives of systems as entities nested within one another as subsystems, systems, and supersystems (Bunge 1996: 270). Thus work begins with identification of boundaries. Within IR, for example, the usual focus is upon levels of analysis, with international, state, and individual as near universal in usage after the highly influential treatment by Waltz (1959). However, as will be demonstrated through later application of systemism, the Waltzian language can produce confusion when efforts are made toward the all-important objective of integration vis-à-vis explanations. Put differently, the terminology developed

---

[14] The exposition from Kertzer (2017: 84) shows a systemist-type of figure, although its contents are not explored at length.

below provides more rigorous boundaries for classifying variables in one category or another and thereby creates a better platform for articulating comprehensive explanations.

What is meant by an international system? The usual approach involves geographic designation and regular interaction—an inductive method.[15] Intuition suggests that the boundaries of an international system—say, a given region—should be identified on the basis of a greater amount of interaction *within* as opposed to *beyond* its borders. Data-based studies, such as those founded upon the Correlates of War (COW) Project and International Crisis Behavior (ICB) Project collections, have identified regions in this way for many years (Small and Singer 1982; Brecher and Wilkenfeld 1997, 2000; Lemke 2002; Brecher 2018). Variation is a natural product of the inductive element present in designating regional boundaries, which are porous and permeable (Tammen and Kugler 2020b: 15).

However, scholars with a more qualitative and interpretive bent find the approaches favored by COW, ICB, and others unconvincing. Buzan and Little (2003: 404) assert that the term "international system" possesses "no generally accepted meaning" and that "within the framework of what it might reasonably be taken to encompass, plausible empirical referents for it can be found right back to the dawn of urban civilization." In particular, critics do not like the presumably Eurocentric foundation underlying conventional designation of units and systems and call for "a clearer idea of how to put boundaries around international systems other than global ones" (Buzan and Little 2003: 424). These concerns are addressed during implementation of systemism in explicating and assessing theories from within the realist research enterprise in Part IV of this volume.

Systemism goes beyond holism and reductionism through inclusion of all basic connections that are required to make up a theory.[16] This is in line with calls already in place from within IR to study the causes of war across levels of analysis (Gat 2009: 593). While structural realism will receive a detailed critique in Chapter 12, one point is germane at the moment. Structural realism as put forward by Waltz (1979) is holistic. As pointed out by Feaver (Feaver et al. [Feaver] 2000: 167), the "key realist causal mechanism of 'system constraints' or 'system

---

[15] Definitions for the international system are plentiful; a detailed list appears in Ripsman, Taliaferro, and Lobell (2016: 35 n. 3).

[16] The diagrammatic exposition that follows in the context of IR builds upon James (2019a, 2019b) and Pfonner and James (2020); see also James (2012a, b) and the generic version from Bunge (1996). Alternative graphic approaches, such as cognitive-affective maps (Homer-Dixon et al. 2013) and argument mapping (van Gelder 2015), are assessed in Pfonner and James (2020) as valuable in many ways but unable to substitute for systemism as an easily grasped means for conveyance of cause and effect. The Unified Modeling Language (Lucidchart 2022), with origins in the natural science, is diagrammatic but entails much greater barriers to entry.

punishment' is undertheorized and has yet to be satisfactorily operationalized." Such a connection would drop down from the system level to the unit level—a step ruled out by Waltz (1979). In addition, Kahler (1998: 939) points out that the "issue of appropriate aggregation or modification in order to preserve assumptions drawn from the individual level has seldom been broached explicitly." Thus both micro-macro and macro-micro—the hybrid causal mechanisms from systemism that go up and down between levels—are in need of much more attention as theorizing moves forward.[17]

Systemist Graphics and Notation

Systemism requires a commitment to "understanding a system in terms of a comprehensive set of functional relationships" (James 2002a: 131). Figure 6.1 depicts functional relations in a social system from a systemist point of view in the context of the international system and any designated region within it. Variables operate at macro (X, Y) and micro (x, y) levels. (The specific shapes that appear for respective variables are explained at a later point.) Conventional in IR, as included in the figure, are designation of processes in the region as macro and the state as micro (Singer 1961). Outside of the region is the environment—the greater international system—within which variable "E" resides. The environment can be expected to provide inputs into, and experience outputs from, the system. A system in international relations, put simply, is a region, with the world beyond its boundaries as the environment. The role of the individual is not ignored within this frame of reference, but instead classified by location. An individual might even act at a global level, beyond the region, but this is likely to be quite rare. One example is the series of telegrams sent by the prominent philosopher Bertrand Russell to key leaders during the Cuban Missile Crisis. Acting as a private citizen, Russell urged President John F. Kennedy and others to de-escalate and resolve the crisis without nuclear war.

Within a regional system as depicted by Figure 6.1, four basic types of linkages are possible: macro-macro ($X \rightarrow Y$), macro-micro ($X \rightarrow x$), micro-macro ($y \rightarrow Y$), and micro-micro ($x \rightarrow y$).[18] In addition, effects may go back and forth with

---

[17] None of what appears at this point should be interpreted as creating a systemist bias in favor of complexity. Systemism calls for recognition that cause and effect can operate through a range of possible types, with no special status accorded to any one of them (e.g., macro-macro). While every type of connection should be considered, a given theory may contain more of one variety than another. Testing of a theory's logic, along with empirical assessment of its purported set of connections, may result in respecification as something more or less complex than an initial variant.

[18] In a compelling exposition on how to convey theorizing in visual form, Tufte (2006: 79) opposes the use of boxes to contain variables. While this argument normally holds when looking at figures that display cause and effect—the boxes tend to be uninformative and even distracting—an exception

the environment, such as E → X or y → E. In this generic figure, upper- and lower case characters correspond to macro- and micro-level variables, respectively. It is difficult to specify in advance how causal mechanisms operate within and beyond a system, so all possible types are displayed. The nature of cause and effect depends on specification of mechanisms, which are identified by scholars addressing particular systems—global or regional.

Adoption of systemism entails specificity with regard to causal mechanisms. *How* are any two variables connected to each other? Assessment of "Y" as a function of "X," by intuition, begins with an incremental or linear relationship. More complex specifications are added as necessary. For example, some linkages may be incremental, such as water cooling down or heating up by degrees, and then step-level, with temperatures of 0 and 100 Celsius resulting in freezing and boiling, respectively. Functional form also is important in strengthening the falsifiability of a theory by increasing the specificity of its causal mechanisms.

Examples from international relations will be used to convey the respective stages of assembly for Figure 6.1. Use of sub-figures to highlight specific contents is consistent with advice from the model of cognition that appeared in Chapter 4.

Figure 6.1a shows a region and the international system, which serves as its environment. Figure 6.1b adds the causal linkages in the region as a system—Europe, Southeast Asia, or whatever—with designation of macro and micro levels in state-centric terms as a starting point. Regions are designated via consensus about boundaries that become standardized as research accumulates over time. An example would be West Asia, which encompasses the states that are conventional in lists from major research projects.[19] The four generic connections in Figure 6.1b are introduced in turn.

Figure 6.1b shows a macro-macro linkage (X → Y). This linkage operates strictly at the international level. An example is the connection of a system's degree of polarization with its propensity for war. The archetypal example of a dangerously polarized region is Europe at the outbreak of World War I (Albertini 1953).

Figure 6.1b also incorporates a micro-micro linkage—a connection that is purely intrastate (x → y). A classic example is development of a garrison state as a result of militarization (Lasswell 1941; Friedberg 1992). As the leaders of a state engage in militarization, freedom is likely to be eroded. When the process is carried to an extreme, such as the Soviet Union in the 1930s, the result resembles

---

is made here. The reason is that the shape of boxes will be used to distinguish types of variables from each other. This feature, implemented at the stage of application for systemism to respective theories, is expected to increase overall comprehension of the visual display.

[19] For example, the ICB project designates Turkey, Armenia, Azerbaijan, Georgia, and Cyprus as the states included in West Asia (Brecher et al. 2017).

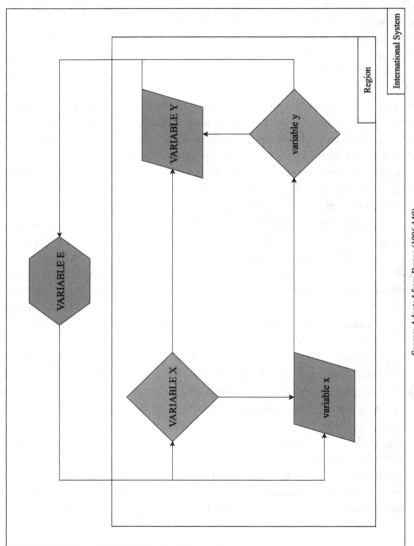

Source: Adapted from Bunge (1996:149).

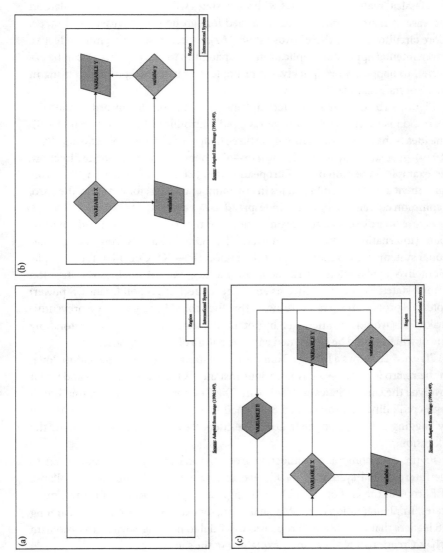

Figure 6.1 International System and Region

an armed camp. The essence of the garrison state concept is loss of freedom and autonomy for its citizens.

Figure 6.1b further incorporates a micro-macro connection—from the state up to the system level (y → Y). Take, for example, this proposed connection from neoclassical realism: "Countries with weak states will take longer to translate an increase in material power into expanded foreign policy activity or will take a more circuitous route there" (Rose 1998: 167). By contrast, with a more effective governmental apparatus, application of capabilities to activity abroad can be expected to happen more quickly. An example is France, exceptionally strong in terms of state relative to society.

Figure 6.1b adds a macro-micro linkage (X → x). This downward connection corresponds to the "second image reversed" introduced by Gourevitch (1978). The idea is that the second among the three images of cause and effect from Waltz (1959)—the state impacting the system—also operates in the opposite direction. An example is creation of the European Union (EU) at Maastricht in 1993. This agreement affected member states in any number of ways; for example, the euro, a common currency, came into widespread use as a result.

Figure 6.1c displays a set of connections for the region (system) and environment (international system) with each other. One linkage is from the international system to the macro level of the region (E → X). Consider, for example, Monteiro's explanation (2012: 360) for the low rate of nuclear proliferation among states. This is described as an indirect effect of preponderant US power; potential proliferating states are aware that they could be targeted by a preventive strike. This would be anticipated by potential nuclear weapons proliferators, any one of which would be concerned with the nature of a US response.

Figure 6.1c shows a linkage from the international system to the region down to the micro level (E → x). A notorious instance is the wiretapping scandal that involved the United States and Germany. The German government claimed, with high credibility, that the United States had spied on Chancellor Angela Merkel by bugging of her telephone in 2013. President Barack Obama did not deny the allegation.

Figure 6.1c conveys a connection from the macro level of a region out to the international system (Y → E). A dramatic example is the virtual collapse of Europe at the end of World War II, impacting grand strategy for the United States. Implementation of the Marshall Plan, for example, reflected belief among US leaders that rebuilding Europe was essential to holding Soviet expansionism at bay. Creation of NATO can be explained in the same way.

Figure 6.1c finishes up with a connection from the micro level of the region outward to the international system (y → E). Consider, for example, the financial crises that coincided for several members of the EU—Greece, Italy, Ireland, Portugal, and Spain—in 2008–9. This shock within a subset of European states impacted international financial markets, along with global institutions such as the World Bank and International Monetary Fund.

Analysis could continue with designation of functional form for each connection in Figure 6.1. The default position is an incremental or linear process. Consider the example of the European financial crisis of 2008–9, just noted. For decades, the states at the center of the crisis—Greece, Ireland, Italy, Portugal and Spain—fell further into deficit. This incremental process gave way to a step-level change. Suddenly, all of Europe worried about default as the financial situation in each of these states went from bad to worse.

Functional form tends to be implicitly incremental in IR theories. For systemist graphics, that will be the default position for each linkage. Any nonlinear connections within a theory will be noted directly. This will take place in the text rather than in figures to prevent these visualizations from becoming difficult to read.[20]

Systemism is of great practical value for articulation of theories to facilitate their comparison to each other. Causal mechanisms are put forward explicitly. This approach helps with a major problem identified by Cornut (2015: 51): the inability to construct explanations in the absence of "contrastive questions." If a query is put forward as "Why is outcome A observed?" it is difficult to answer. Instead, it makes more sense to ask, "Why is outcome A observed instead of outcome B?" This approach provides context; an explanation always responds to a contrastive question (Cornut 2015: 2). So an answer may take the form "A is observed rather than B because of factors X1, X2, X3 and so on" (Cornut 2015: 54, 57). Contrastive questions should become a priority for realism in light of critiques that focus on what appears to be a reluctance to test propositions against those of nonrealist theories (Legro and Moravcsik 1999: 47; see also Fozouni 1995: 487).

Systemism is ideal for putting forward causal mechanisms in a way that facilitates responses to contrastive questions. Thus the method increases clarity of exposition for theories, which in turn facilitates comparison and resolution of differences regarding causal mechanisms. Systemism thereby enhances prospects for integration of theorizing and results from testing with regard to designated empirical problems.

Balance-of-power theory comes to mind when we think about the need for a focus on contrastive questions and conveyance of answers on a visual basis. While a central concept in various forms of realism, balance of power also is perhaps an exemplar when it comes to the problem of incoherence. Zinnes (1967) identified a range of meaning for balance of power. At times it appears in

---

[20] This type of problem for graphic presentation, discussed emphatically by Tufte (2006), is addressed systematically a bit later in the chapter.

multiple forms even within the same realist exposition. Realists include balance of power in their theories, but do not agree on its meaning (Guzzini 1998: 45). "Morgenthau," as Park (1998: 4) observes, "uses four distinct meanings of the term balance of power in his work: 1) as a policy aimed at a certain state of affairs; 2) as an actual state of affairs; 3) as an approximately equal distribution of power; and 4) as a distribution of power." When, however, should one meaning or another be used within an overarching statement of realism? No definite answer exists. Thus it becomes difficult to apply balance of power to an empirical problem such as the occurrence of war.

Systemism puts axioms into action. Assumptions are combined to produce theorems (Priest 2017: 35)—propositions about cause and effect. Systemism provides a way to translate these statements into a visual representation of causal mechanisms. Figure 6.1 shows an ideal system. There is a cycle of cause and effect, with precisely one of each type from among the eight potential linkages. Note that there is no sense of time lags or other empirically oriented details—just the causal possibilities. Realist and other stories about cause and effect can be told through more complex versions of this figure, with an emphasis on identifying missing types of connection or contradictions in expositions based on words alone. An obvious reference would be balance of power, which continues to occupy an important yet problematic status within the realist school of thought.

One example of how systemism can help to review what is known more effectively concerns the nearly hegemonic status of regression-based techniques among statistical analysis of conflict processes. The commanding position occupied by such models is an obvious product of path dependency that nevertheless defies the fact that very few processes are linear (Fisunoğlu 2019: 233, 234).

Systemism entails an intuitively obvious critique with regard to this development over several decades. Since the publication of Bremer (1992), approximately speaking, regression models based on the state and (especially) dyad-year (e.g., United States–Costa Rica, 1995) have become the norm in the study of international strife. From a systemist point of view, this convergence of approach comes at some cost with respect to accurately portraying would-be causal mechanisms about escalation of conflict. The rigorous and compelling study from Buhaug (2005), which offers an advanced statistical reassessment of the classic work by Bremer (1992), will serve as the example here. The dependent variable in the model is war onset (or its absence) within an interstate dyad-year. The list of independent variables includes geographic proximity, degree of power difference, regime type, development, and militarization. These variables are coded for each interstate dyad on an annual basis.

Reflection upon the above-noted set of variables, from a systemist point of view, suggests a different configuration with respect to causal mechanisms. Rather than arranging all of the (presumably) independent variables together and instituting a time lag regarding the dependent variable, it makes sense to explore potential linkages between and among them. Consider geographic proximity. This variable is an anchor in the sense that nothing else in the system will cause it to change.[21] Proximity, however, will impact other variables in the system; by intuition, this must include prospects for being allied, along with additional traits from above such as regime type and development. Type of regime and level of development, furthermore, can be anticipated to affect each other. It also seems obvious that regime type will have implications for militarization and vice versa. Militarization, in turn, can impact power difference between states, which might lead—directly or otherwise—into the dependent variable, onset of war.

These connections—just the most obvious ones to consider within the set of designated independent variables—are sufficient to reveal that implementation of regression as a statistical method restricts theorizing. A linear regression model "yields incorrect results when the relationship among the key variables is non-linear, conjunctural, or reciprocal" (Mearsheimer and Walt 2013: 440). Perhaps other statistical techniques, which allow for multiple stages of causation, should become a priority in re-examining even the most successful regression-based models of conflict processes. This recommendation follows from a systemist-inspired reassessment of the regression-based approach that is modal within the study of international conflict processes.[22] Structural equation modeling (Schumacker and Lomax 2010), which maintains a long-standing presence in other disciplines but less so in IR, comes to mind. This type of data analysis seems particularly relevant to networks of cause and effect as conveyed by systemist graphics.

Implementation of systemism within IR is relatively new, so it is appropriate to include a methodological appendix that conveys the steps taken to convert words into a diagrammatic exposition. Appendix 6.A includes instructions on how to create figures that communicate causal mechanisms within a given study. Figures that depict realist theories in Part IV of this book have been created by reading respective texts and following the instructions from Appendix 6.A. The appendix also summarizes the types of causal connection that can exist between variables.

---

[21] Exceptions will occur in the rare instances of a state's exit from the international system or alteration of its borders. Even allowing for such occasional developments, proximity will remain relevant for a research design that focuses on a short-term matter such as escalation of conflict.

[22] Another issue to consider with regard to the trustworthiness of regression results concerns dramatic differences among individual cases with respect to impact on overall results (Aronow and Samii 2015: 258). For example, in reanalysis of one model, the 14 least impactful states contributed "less than 0.05% of the weight used to construct the effect estimate," and the top 32 states accounted for 90% of the weight (Aronow and Samii 2015: 258).

Table 6.3 Systemist Notation

Initial variable	(oval)	The starting point of a series of relationships
Generic variable	(rectangle)	A step in the process being depicted
Divergent variable	(diamond)	Multiple pathways created from a single linkage
Convergent variable	(parallelogram)	A single pathway created from multiple linkages
Nodal variable	(hexagon)	Multiple pathways created from multiple linkages
Co-constitutive variable	(double rectangle)	Two variables that are mutually contingent upon each other
Terminal variable	(octagon)	The end point of a series of relationships
Connection stated in study	⟶	A linkage explicitly made by the author
Connection crossing over	⟶⌒⟶	Two separate linkages that do not interact
Connection inferred from study	----▶	A linkage inferred by the reader but not made explicit by the author
Interaction effect	⟵⟶	Two variables that depend upon the effect of each other

Each systemist figure depicts a region and the international system as its environment. The macro and micro levels in each figure correspond to regional system and state. Variables at these levels are designated, respectively, with upper- and lowercase characters. Uppercase characters also are used for variables in the international system. Table 6.3 displays systemist notation for respective boxes and arrows. Each is summarized in turn.[23]

---

[23] While not possible for this volume, other publications based on systemism (e.g., James 2019a, 2019b; Pfonner and James 2020) also include color to distinguish variables from each other. The expanded notation is as follows: initial variable (green oval), terminal variable (red octagon), divergent

An initial variable is represented with an oval. This type of variable is one with an arrow pointing out but nothing coming back in from other variables in the system. A generic variable, with a single arrow pointing in and out, is depicted with a plain rectangular box. A diamond signifies a divergent variable—one that initiates multiple pathways from what had been a single route. A convergent variable—one in which multiple pathways come together into a single route—appears as a parallelogram. A hexagon indicates a nodal variable—one that is both divergent and convergent. Pathways come together and then separate once again.

Co-constitutive variables share a rectangular box. This type of connection enables the approach to depict constructivist arguments, within which the concept of co-constitution is essential (Barkin 2010: 156; see also Brown 2012: 862):

> Constructivism as a specific logic of the study of international relations is about the social, which is to say the intersubjective, construction of international politics. From this definition follows the focus on the co-constitution of agent and structure, because only through a recognition of co-constitution can the research address both the social aspect (existent norms and discourses matter) and the constructed aspect (it is agency, rather than, say, system structure or biology that create those norms and discourses).

Co-constitution differs from positing an endogenous relation of cause and effect (i.e., labeled Types II and III in Appendix 6.A), within which variables take turns in the independent and dependent roles or combine to form an interaction term. Freyberg-Inan (2016: 78) adds that "purely constitutive" is taken to mean that "cause and effect are co-emergent out of one and the same set of properties." An example of a co-constitutive or purely constitutive statement is "This is a free country by virtue of being a democracy" (Freyberg-Inan 2016a: 78).

Last among the types that appear in Table 6.3, an octagon indicates a terminal variable, with connections coming in and nothing pointing out.

Table 6.3 also shows arrows that depict a range of connections. Arrows that appear in normal type signify a connection articulated within a study. When one link crosses over another, a small curve is put into it to indicate a nonrelation between these connections. A broken arrow indicates a linkage that is inferred from a study rather than stated within it. Finally, a double-headed arrow depicts an interaction effect.

variable (orange diamond), convergent variable (blue parallelogram), and nodal variable (purple hexagon). Note that the green, red, and orange colors correspond to those used for traffic lights to assist with memory and recognition.

According to the National Eye Institute (2019), approximately 8% of men and 0.5% of women are colorblind. While unable to rely on colors to distinguish the role of a given variable, the shapes remain available to those who are colorblind.

With notation in place, a natural question arises: Is all of this going to be worthwhile? Is there any assurance that a systemist figure will produce an accurate representation for a given work of scholarship? What if disagreement ensues with an author versus an exponent of systemism, with the latter creating a visual representation to which the former objects (even if only at an initial point of contact)? This possible, even likely, scenario reveals a *positive* trait of systemism. It brings out, into the open, ambiguity in arguments that can be quite difficult to identify in words alone. Misunderstandings about the nature of causal mechanisms put forward in a given work can be cleared up as well. Graphic representation through systemism will be especially valuable in pointing out contradictions and missing steps in causal arguments, thereby promoting more productive dialogue. While not a proven point, intuition suggests that many debates could have been resolved if conducted in a manner that included a *common* graphic depiction of arguments about causal linkages.

More dialogue—and especially the constructive kind—is needed to counteract research communities' isolation from each other. Diverse theoretical collectivities in IR "are not engaging each other in ways that could be mutually productive" (Snidal and Wendt 2009: 4–5). "In a rather anti-climactic way," Lake (2013: 571) observes, "the various schools of thought, positivist and reflectivist alike, have simply retreated to their own corners of a multi-sided boxing ring, occasionally tossing a punch in one or the other direction but more often talking among themselves and complaining of not being taken seriously by others." For example, articles in *International Security* and *Journal of Conflict Resolution* rarely acknowledge scholarship in the other—even when the topic is the same (Sil and Katzenstein 2010c: 117, cited from Bennett, Barth, and Rutherford 2003). These journals publish work, respectively, that tends to be based on qualitative and quantitative methods. This silo-based existence is by no means exceptional within IR.

Further advantages, as enumerated within learning theory, accrue from application of systemism. As a visual means of communication, systemism can help with both interpretation and explanation. Interpreting can involve "converting words to words (e.g., paraphrasing), pictures to words, words to pictures, numbers to words, words to numbers, musical notes to tones, and the like" (Anderson et al. 2001: 70). Systemism is intended to facilitate such processes, with words converted into pictures and then back again through debate over correspondence of graphic representation with the exposition in a book or article. The approach also is well disposed toward mixed methods, which might further enhance the ability to transit back and forth between words and pictures.

Favorable also is the connection of systemism with explanation, which means to "construct and use a cause-and-effect model of a system" (Anderson et al. 2001: 76). Thus systemism offers a very effective answer to the most basic problem identified via the model of cognition in Chapter 4. A comprehensive investigation of causality asserts that diagrams "offer an alternative language for combining data with causal information" (Pearl 2009: 96). Thus implementation of systemist graphics can go a long way in managing the challenges posed to comprehension by the sheer volume of information available about realism in particular and IR in general. This positive result is anticipated because systemism is well suited to promotion of a back-and-forth process regarding causal mechanisms represented, respectively, in words and diagrams.

Aspects of learning are promoted through this approach, with positive implications for making progress in IR. The concept of "transfer" refers to "the effect of prior learning on new learning" (Mayer 2010: 20). Thus the ability to express an explanation in words might be enhanced through replication in a visual format and vice versa. A graphic turn therefore might accelerate the process of converging on explanations that are convincing. For example, the process of writing could be facilitated via creation of a graphic outline.

Two likely critiques should be addressed before moving forward with an illustration of systemism in action: first, what if the proposed graphic turn makes everything *worse* for IR by adding further terminology and methods to an already crowded field but without commensurate value? This is deemed unlikely because the systemist approach can be picked up in an autodidactic way over the course of a few hours. Systemism entails very limited barriers to entry, as confirmed in Appendix 6.A, and might even be described as postmethodological in that it can be used in tandem with any other technique from the social sciences. This is a key point in favor of systemism in comparison to other visual approaches, such as formal modeling, which require a great deal of training to implement at anything beyond a rudimentary level. The simplicity of the graphics keeps systemism away from the problem that Tufte (2006: 62; see also Cleveland 1985: 8, 57 on graphing data) labeled "hyperactive optical clutter." Thus the visualizations provided via systemism simplify rather than complicate material and thereby increase comprehension and communication. These graphics therefore also are suited to assess the "logical soundness" of a theory (Mearsheimer and Walt 2013: 434). A second critique, with a point of departure different from the first, concerns oversimplification: should the graphics from systemism be permitted to substitute for a well-reasoned analysis? The answer is no; instead, systemist graphics are implemented to probe for logical consistency and completeness in a given argument. Systemist graphics are entirely consistent with the admonition from Galileo that the language of the universe is written in mathematical characters.

An Illustration from Neoclassical Realism

Systemism, so far, is put forward in a primarily abstract manner as a possible solution to the problems posed by cognitive limitations in conjunction with vast and rapidly accumulating information about the theory and practice of international politics. To complement the case made so far, an application to realist theory will be provided to breathe life into the assertions in favor of systemism. Given its rising prominence, neoclassical realism is a salient choice for graphic presentation.[24]

What is neoclassical realism? It is appropriate to begin with a designation from Rose (1998: 11; quoted in Parent and Baron 2011: 205), who created the term:

> It explicitly incorporates both external and internal variables, updating and systematizing certain insights drawn from classical realist thought. Its adherents argue that the scope and ambition of a country's foreign policy is driven first and foremost by its place in the international system and specifically by its relative material power capabilities. This is why they are realist. They argue further, however, that the impact of such power capabilities on foreign policy is indirect and complex, because systemic pressures must be translated through intervening variables at the unit level. This is why they are neoclassical.

Neoclassical realism developed significantly as an area of research over the last two decades. "We should understand neoclassical realism not as a distinct variety of realism," according to Rathbun (2008: 296; see also Ripsman, Taliaferro, and Lobell 2016: 31), "but rather as the next generation of structural realism and reflective of a common and coherent logic." Rather than a single neoclassical theory of foreign policy, there exist "a diversity of neoclassical realist *theories*" that cover a long list of topics (Taliaferro, Lobell, and Ripsman 2009: 10, 8, 9). The rise of neoclassical realism is connected directly to unpacking the state, within a realist context, while continuing to grant pride of place to the international system vis-à-vis cause and effect.

From a neoclassical realist point of view, the state is "epitomized by a national security executive, comprised of the head of government and the ministers and officials charged with making foreign security policy" (Taliaferro, Lobell, and Ripsman 2009: 25). Neoclassical realism, as Taliaferro, Lobell and Ripsman (2009: 28) observe, "identifies elite calculations and perceptions of

---

[24] Neoclassical realist theories occupy a significant place and continue to expand in IR. Ripsman, Taliaferro, and Lobell (2016: 183) provide an authoritative list of topical areas covered already; examples include state extractive capacity (Taliaferro 2006) and political economy and grand strategy (Brawley 2009).

relative power and domestic constraints as intervening variables between international pressures and states' foreign policies." Taken together, the efforts of neoclassical realists represent a revitalized connection of domestic politics with power politics (Glenn 2009: 526). In the language of systemism, neoclassical realism includes causal connections from the micro to the macro level—previously excluded explicitly from the holistic world of structural realism in particular.

Table 6.4 conveys some ideas about the basic nature of neoclassical realism. The anarchical international system is of primary importance, even as previously excluded state-level and state-to-system processes are incorporated. The role of domestic politics in shaping foreign policy is acknowledged and included within the theoretical edifice. Unit-level diversity among states helps to explain revisionist versus status quo preferences. Objective reality exists for neoclassical realism, but not to the exclusion of a role for (mis)perception between and among leaders in shaping outcomes at the international level. The approach calls back to classical realism, which focused on foreign policy to a much greater extent than approaches oriented toward structure that held sway after the advent of neorealism with Waltz (1979).

Figure 6.2 shows a model of international outcomes from a major neoclassical realist exposition, *Neoclassical Realist Theory of International Politics* (Ripsman, Taliaferro, and Lobell 2016).[25] Neoclassical realist theory, according to Ripsman, Taliaferro, and Lobell (2016: 1), "can explain political phenomena ranging from short-term crisis decision-making, foreign policy behavior, and patterns of grand strategic adjustment of individual states, to systemic outcomes, and ultimately to the evolution of the structure of the international system itself." Rathbun (2008: 311) adds that neoclassical realism "is not a separate variety of realism nor is it degenerative. In fact, it is a natural and progressive next step." The diagrammatic version of that argument differs from the Weberian ideal type conveyed by Figure 6.1 in significant ways. For instance, Figure 6.2 includes a variety of pathways, as opposed to a generic cycle of cause and effect, within which each type of connection had appeared exactly once.

Figure 6.2 and other systemist diagrams that follow are in line with criteria from Tufte (2006) for creation of effective graphics. One feature is that variables in respective figures include names rather than letter codes such as "X" or "Y" (Tufte 2006: 43). To return momentarily to cognitive load theory, use of abbreviations

---

[25] Figure 6.2 is a reconstruction of Figure 2.1 from Ripsman, Taliaferro, and Lobell (2016: 34). Consultations with Steven E. Lobell and Norrin M. Ripsman resulted in minor adjustments of an initial graphic version that are incorporated into Figure 6.2.

Table 6.4 Neoclassical Realism at a Glance

Source	Ideas
Sterling-Folker (1997: 20)	The proposition that domestic actors operate under a dual pressure from both the anarchic environment and their own domestic processes goes a long way in explaining why the international choices domestic actors make often appear to be objectively inefficient.
Legro and Moravcsik (1999: 28)	Most neoclassical realists seek to incorporate in one form or another variation between states with underlying status quo and revisionist preferences.
Walt (2002: 211)	Neoclassical realist theory asserts that, because there is no overarching authority to control what states do, unit-level forces within states can affect the choices they make.
Taliaferro (2006: 482)	There is no deductive reason why neoclassical realism cannot incorporate unit-level variables while maintaining the causal primacy of structural variables.
Rathbun (2008: 315)	Neoclassical realism puts limits on its use of ideas. It problematizes perception but not the objective nature of reality.
Ripsman, Taliaferro, and Lobell (2009: 281)	Neoclassical realism is a useful approach for understanding foreign policy.
Taliaferro, Lobell, and Ripsman (2009: 21)	Neoclassical realism seeks to explain variation in the foreign policies of the same state over time or across different states facing similar external constraints.
Brawley (2009: 2)	"Neoclassical realism positions the state at the nexus between the two levels, as the bridge between two political realms.... It introduces domestic factors very differently than 'analytical liberalism,' which emphasizes an approach from the bottom up."
Parent and Baron (2011: 205)	Neoclassical realists take the spare versatile foundation of neorealist thought and add domestic factors to explain foreign policy.
Yoo (2012: 323)	Neoclassical realism sees system forces as independent variables and domestic attributes as intervening variables.
Melbauer (2019: 23)	Neoclassical realism differs from other realisms primarily in the degree to which the translation of systemic conditions into state behavior is explicitly analyzed rather than either simply assumed or treated as a conceptually distinct sphere of inquiry.

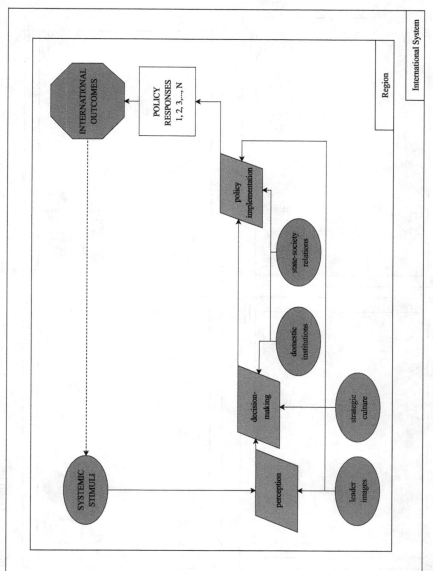

Figure 6.2 Neoclassical Realist Model of International Outcomes

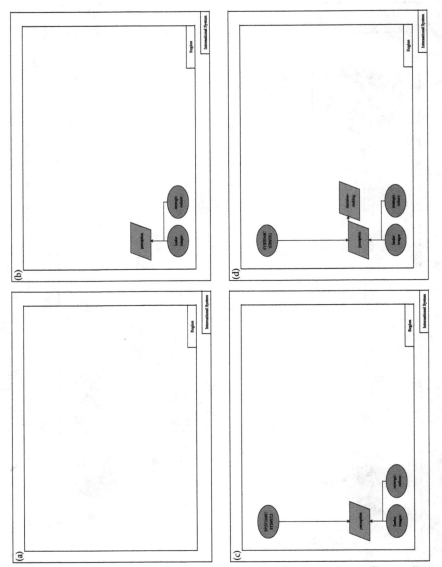

Figure 6.2 Continued

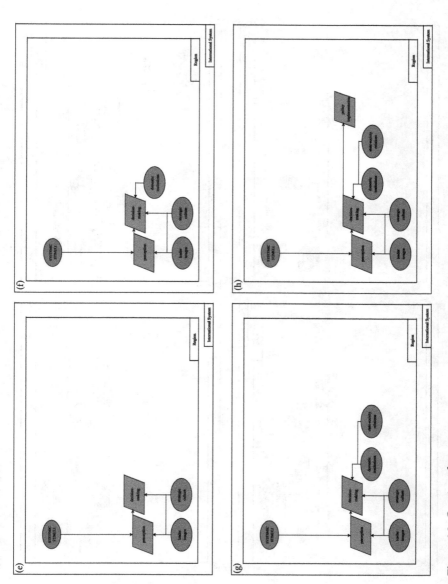

Figure 6.2 Continued

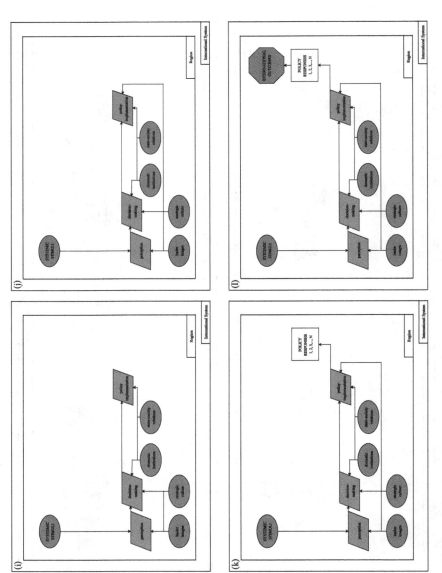

Figure 6.2 Continued

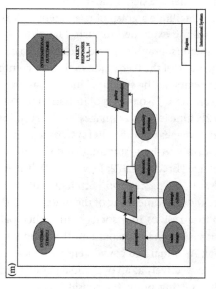

Figure 6.2 Continued

creates unnecessary burdens upon someone trying to understand a diagram.[26] The systemist figures also zealously avoid something noted already—what Tufte (2006: 62) calls hyperactive optical clutter. As observed in Chapter 3, a notorious instance of this is the "death by PowerPoint" slide, in which content is densely packed and formatted so badly that the viewer is turned off.

Note the high number of starting points in Figure 6.2; five ovals exist and four reside at the state level. This is a point to be revisited later because neoclassical theory tends to emphasize the international system with regard to causation (Ripsman, Taliaferro, and Lobell 2016: 34). For now it is worth noting that the diagram possesses an intuitive quality because, in particular, international outcomes can come about through multiple pathways and that the point of origin might be at either the system or the state level.

Figures 6.2a–m build the neoclassical model of international outcomes, one step (or a few) at a time, to facilitate a grasp of its contents. The contents of each alphabetized sub-figure will be explained in turn. Figure 6.2 is relatively intricate and challenging as systemist graphics go, so the ability to convey its contents clearly is a compelling example of the technique's value for communication.

Figure 6.2a depicts the region as the system of interest, along with the international system as its environment. Two points of initiation follow on at the micro or state level in Figure 6.2b. One is "leader images" → "perception." Marked with an oval in the figure, leader images refer to belief systems among those at the apex of decision-making for a state. A long-standing tradition of research supports the operation of this linkage (Brecher 1972; Jervis 1976). The other point of initiation is "strategic culture" → "perception." Strategic culture refers to beliefs, norms, and assumptions about the meaning of the material world in the domain of security. Strategic culture resides in a society; an archetypal instance is the martial nature of Spartan society in the account by Thucydides (1972 [431 BCE]) of the Peloponnesian War. As initial and convergent variables, "strategic culture" and "perception" appear respectively as an oval and a parallelogram.

Figure 6.2c shows the starting point for causal linkages at the level of the region: "SYSTEMIC STIMULI" → "perception." Note that "SYSTEMIC STIMULI" appears as an oval, which indicates a point of origin for a causal pathway. Aspects of the system that can impact perceptions at the state level, developed in detail within Ripsman, Taliaferro, and Lobell (2016), are structure and interaction capacity. Thus leaders obtain a sense of their position and possibilities from what sits around them at the international level. For example, polarization in Europe leading up to August 1914 induced concerns about safety for Belgium, given its position between France and Germany. The next link in this pathway,

---

[26] Figure 6.1 would appear to violate that rule, but it is a special case. It is a fully abstract introduction to systemist graphics and thus includes letters rather than variable names.

added in Figure 6.2d, is "perception → decision-making," which is a nod to the collective contribution of many studies from political psychology. A parallelogram is used for "decision-making" to designate the multiple pathways leading into it. One example, in the aftermath of a summit meeting at Vienna in 1961, is Premier Nikita Khrushchev's perception of President John F. Kennedy as a weak leader, which contributed to decision-making that resulted in deployment of nuclear missiles to Cuba.

Another point of initiation appears at the state level with strategic culture, marked with an oval in Figure 6.2e. The linkage is "strategic culture" → "decision making." Thus strategic culture, from society as a whole, resembles leader images in that it can affect how decisions are made. One example is pervasive belief during the Cold War in mutually assured destruction (MAD). A nightmare scenario, within which MAD leads to World War III, is portrayed in the dark comedy *Dr. Strangelove* from 1961. A strategic culture of suspicion and readiness to act results in Armageddon when a stray US aircraft triggers a doomsday device secretly constructed by the USSR.

Added in Figure 6.2f, a new point of origin is "domestic institutions" → "decision making." As an initial variable, "domestic institutions" appears as an oval. This connection is straightforward because, for example, the institutional setting creates (in)formal limits on what leaders can do. In the United States, to offer one illustration, the president is given leeway in deciding on foreign policy, but Congress controls spending. A substantial literature on civil-military relations contains a wide range of propositions and evidence about how institutions impact foreign policy decision-making.[27]

Figure 6.2g depicts the last micro-level pathway, starting with "state-society relations" → "decision-making." As an initial variable, "state-society relations" takes the form of an oval. This branch takes into account some degree of input from the domestic level into foreign policy—acknowledged while also condemned by classical realists for its often distorting effects on pursuit of national interests. The basic point of variation concerns the strength of the state apparatus relative to the power of society to impact decision-making. A point of contrast, along those lines, is the more insular French and more open US state structures.

Depicted in Figure 6.2h, a natural following step is "decision making" → "policy implementation." Policy implementation, a convergent variable, also appears as a parallelogram. The classic study from Allison (1971) on the Cuban Missile Crisis reveals the range of possibilities that exist for implementation of decisions presumably "dictated" by the top leadership.

---

[27] Among the journals that convey important insights about civil-military relations are *Armed Forces and Society* and *Journal of Military Sociology*.

One other route, added in Figure 6.2i, starts with "state-society relations" → "policy implementation." This link recognizes that how policy is implemented will be impacted by processes not entirely within the state itself. Actions from society may affect directly state (in)action.

Another pathway begins in Figure 6.2i with "domestic institutions" → "policy implementation." This link brings to mind the many stories, backed up by research, about how the structure of government affects whether policy gets made. For example, some governments include veto points that can permit implementation or block it.

With "leader images" → policy implementation, another route continues in Figure 6.2j. This proffers the possibility of an independent impact for leader images upon the carrying out of policy. A prominent historical example is the sense of personal responsibility that Lyndon Johnson accepted for the tactical level of the Vietnam War, which caused him to engage in what later would be called micromanagement.

Figure 6.2j conveys another micro-level connection: "strategic culture" → "policy implementation." As an illustration, consider the unwillingness of German generals to move tank units to meet the Allied landings on D-Day. This occurred as a product of extreme hierarchy under Adolf Hitler; without his approval, the panzer units remained distant from the battlefront and facilitated Allied success.

Once policy is in place at the state level, it can be moved forward to the regional system. Thus the next link, in Figure 6.2k, is "policy implementation → "POLICY RESPONSES 1, 2, 3, ... , N." The final connection in the pathway, added at the macro level in Figure 6.2l, is "POLICY RESPONSES 1, 2, 3, ... , N" → "INTERNATIONAL OUTCOMES." The terminal variable, "INTERNATIONAL OUTCOMES," is marked with an octagon.

One other connection appears in Figure 6.2m: "INTERNATIONAL OUTCOMES" → "SYSTEMIC STIMULI." This recognizes a cycle of cause and effect that goes beyond any specific outcome. While the system sets the context for action, the outcomes that result from interactions of states have an effect as well. Stimuli from the region to its constituent states will evolve or even change dramatically as a result of international outcomes. This connection, added to the argument from Ripsman, Taliaferro, and Lobell (2016), appears as a broken line. The series of sub-figures now is complete and thus identical to Figure 6.2.

After this extended process, what is the value added from assembling Figure 6.2? There are multiple payoffs from the effort expended here because properties of neoclassical realism will come through that might not be so easily identified with a presentation restricted to words alone. Four observations can be made about the communication of neoclassical realism via systemist figures based on Ripsman, Taliaferro, and Lobell (2016).

First, note the range of connections that appear in the figure. Neoclassical realism is neither holist nor reductionist. It includes linkages within and across the state and system levels. Thus neoclassical realism is immune, from the outset, to attacks made on other varieties of realism that have been associated with one basic type of connection. For example, structural realism tends to be criticized for its overwhelming focus on macro-level processes. By contrast, neoclassical realism includes all four basic connections: macro-macro, macro-micro, micro-macro, and micro-micro. Neoclassical realism, however, does remain incomplete with regard to the full set of possible linkages; so far, it does not include any explicit connections for a region with the surrounding international system.

Second, it is clear to see a great deal of contingency in neoclassical realism. This point comes through in graphic form through the presence of multiple points of convergence, which appear as three parallelograms in the figure. In addition, five ovals are available as respective starting points for cause and effect in the figure. This is an interesting feature because neoclassical realism grants causal priority to the macro level. Yet all but one pathway begins at the micro level in the figure. Thus elaboration of the macro level emerges as a priority for neoclassical realism. This is a point about neoclassical realism as an exposition on cause and effect that, without a systemist format, might not be identified so readily.

Third, note the detail provided in terms of cause and effect as a process. The pathways in the figure, understood in the context of Kurki (2002) on aspects of causation—formal, material, final, and efficient—unite to tell a convincing story. Ten variables appear in this network of cause and effect. Material and ideational factors are combined to explain how international outcomes are reached through multiple convergent pathways that encompass macro and micro levels.

Fourth, and finally, visualization of cause and effect should assist with policy analysis and relevance. It is possible to zero in on each step in the process through the series of sub-figures. Greater policy relevance is a priority for analytic eclecticism, and the graphic portrayal of neoclassical realism points in the right direction. Note that perception, decision-making, and policy implementation—all high in real-world relevance—are convergent variables within the system.

One obvious critique comes to mind when looking at Figure 6.2: in a long and complex exposition such as *Neoclassical Realist Theory of International Politics*, would it not be possible to draw an *alternative* picture of cause and effect, different from what appears in the figure? Yes, and that potential once again emerges as a key point in *favor* of systemism as a method that promotes mutually intelligible dialogue. An exposition in words alone is much more forgiving than visual representation when it comes to vagueness and contradictions in an argument. Systemism is quite strict along those lines—and that is a good thing. If the level of analysis is unclear, for instance, that will come out into the open right away in a systemist-inspired figure but can "hide" more easily in any text beyond a few pages. Consider also self-contradiction through the presence and negation of the same causal mechanism. This is clear for all to see in a systemist-inspired figure but comparatively hard to detect in a parallel (and especially an extended) written exposition.

Figure 6.2 therefore represents a new means toward more effective argumentation about cause and effect for IR in general and realism in particular. Authors and readers can reach convergence on what has been said, and what it means, much more effectively through figures inspired by systemism as opposed to exchanging words unaccompanied by visualization. The same point obtains regarding the suboptimal nature of figures created without rules such as those imposed by systemism. The risk of incommensurability increases without protocols in place to facilitate comparison of graphic representations of cause and effect.

What, then, about formal modeling as a salient alternative to systemism? Its presentations are literally mathematical and therefore already more precise than mere words. Systemism should be looked at as an essential partner, rather than replacement, for formal modeling. Mathematical models, unaided by visualization for cause and effect, entail high barriers to entry.[28] Even after decades of formal theorizing, only a relatively small fraction of the research community in IR is engaged in such work. A technique such as systemism, which conveys cause and effect in graphic form, can help to convey the value of formal models in a way that goes beyond the increasingly sophisticated yet also daunting mathematics involved in that research.[29]

Systemist International Relations

Systemist International Relations (SIR) is the designation given for the graphic approach to theory developed in this chapter. SIR emphasizes completeness and logical consistency vis-à-vis explanation. Regardless of specific agenda, all theories about international relations should include at least one link from each of the four basic types within the system, along with some connection back and forth with the environment. SIR's graphic format enhances the ability to see gaps in existing explanations and also envision ways in which partially specified theories could be combined with each other. SIR also assists in identifying and eliminating contradictions within a theory, which cannot possibly coexist in a visual format.

---

[28] Formal modeling often is accompanied by visual aids such as game trees and Edgeworth Boxes. However, these techniques do not convey cause and effect in the matter of systemism as per below.

[29] For assessment of a wider range of alternatives, see Pfonner and James (2020), which concludes that only systemism is (a) easy to learn and (b) able to convey causal arguments in diagrams that also enhance intelligibility.

SIR also is compatible with ideas based on analytic eclecticism that encourage contact between and among sectors of the discipline that do not currently communicate much with each other. For example, Grieco (2019) calls for collaboration in which adherents of different schools of thought would consult on, and implement, tests for each other's understanding of world politics. A shift toward SIR would facilitate the obviously challenging communication involved in such efforts. To facilitate such exchanges, an archive of graphic representations for works of scholarship is available under the auspices of the Visual International Relations Project (VIRP). The VIRP archive contains graphic summaries of a wide range of books, articles, and book chapters. The contents of the figures can be used, in line with insights from educational psychology, to aid memory of existing material and facilitate comprehension of newly encountered items. From the standpoint of pedagogy, it is easy to imagine any number of uses for items from the VIRP archive, such as instructors refreshing their memory during preparation or review of lectures.

With regard to SIR's application of graphics to research and teaching purposes, two basic possibilities can be identified. One is *systematic synthesis* and the other is *bricolagic bridging*.[30]

Systematic synthesis refers to carrying out a standard literature review that focuses on graphic representations of the items included. Thus the VIRP archive might be accessed in tandem with an authoritative source of references—perhaps the Oxford Bibliographies in International Relations (2019). An example of systematic synthesis that includes a graphic element is James (2019a: 8), which focuses on the research question of crisis escalation to war and assembles causal connections from 14 studies that appeared from 1999 to 2017 into an overall representation.[31] This activity is in line with an emphasis on the logic of confirmation. Systematic synthesis also could be carried out in other ways. For example, even prior to testing, graphics for multiple theories could be combined to produce a potentially superior account for cause and effect.

Bricolagic bridging is the other basic possibility for use of material from the archive in research.[32] Bricolage is a practice "based on notions of eclecticism, emergent design, flexibility and plurality" (Rogers 2012: 1). It is in line with the pragmatic account of research from analytic eclecticism (Sil and Katzenstein 2010c: 114) and can be implemented to counteract the harmful "identity politics"

---

[30] Applications of systematic synthesis and bricolagic bridging have appeared in a special issue of *Canadian Foreign Policy Journal* on systemism; see Gansen and James (2021).

[31] See also James and James (2017), which implemented a still-developing variant of systemist graphics to summarize arguments about foreign policy analysis from textbooks.

[32] This application is inspired by the discussion of bricolage in Onuf (1989: 104–105 n. 10). To the extent that bricolage is underway in an academic setting, its presence remains restricted to critical social theory. A review of such bricolage, with favorable implications for a wide range of uses, appears in Rogers (2012); see also Aradau and Huysmans (2014: 607) on application to IR.

of IR (Jackson and Nexon 2009: 920; see also Lake 2013: 580). An antinomy can help to introduce bricolagic bridging in a more operational way. Bricolage can be understood as an enterprise quite different from engineering. An engineer works with a plan and a designated set of tools and materials; by contrast, a bricoleur assembles something out of whatever is available (Rogers 2012: 1). Bricolagic bridging is an academic version of that latter activity, where graphics are introduced—perhaps even taken at random from the Visual International Relations Project (VIRP) archive (www.visualinternationalrelationsproject.com)—into engagement with each other to break down barriers and produce insights that otherwise might not be obtained.

Bricolage can be carried out in any number of ways. One method, pursued in James (2019b) and Pfonner and James (2020), consists of assembling key variables from across a range of studies that otherwise would be unlikely to engage with each other. This activity would be in line with the logic of discovery—possibly stimulating new propositions or even full-fledged theories.

While systematic synthesis offers a graphic augmentation to a literature review—a conventional academic exercise—why carry out bricolagic bridging? The answer is that the two activities complement each other in important ways and can combine to move the discipline forward.

Systematic synthesis counteracts tendencies toward chaos. This problem becomes more acute under conditions of increasingly diverse research in terms of both paradigmatic studies and investigations fitting the description of analytic eclecticism. As one type of assessment, systematic synthesis already is well established at least when carried out in words alone; for example, one of the ISA journals, *International Studies Review*, is mandated to publish review essays.

By contrast, bricolagic bridging is all but unknown in IR. Bricolagic bridging encourages integrative thinking within IR—valuable under conditions in which hardening of academic "silos" stand as an ongoing challenge to discipline-wide communication. Put differently, bricolagic building provides one rigorous means toward operationalization of analytic eclecticism by offering a method for combining diverse variables into a potentially coherent account of cause and effect.

Summing Up on Methods

Two elements of the methods component for a metatheory of progress have been identified in this chapter. One element is identification of axioms for a research enterprise, the type of system of explanation to be incorporated in the metatheory. Candidate axioms are identified through a process of elimination that combines inductive and deductive stages to produce a result that resonates with those inside a school of thought while also taking into account the need for rigorous specification.

The other element is systemism, which offers a visual representation of causal mechanisms derived from analysis conveyed in words. Systemism is intended to enhance dialogue about cause and effect with regard to empirical problems. Neoclassical realism in its generic form is used to show the nature and value of systemism in application to theories about international politics. The resulting approach, SIR, is to be implemented via graphic portrayal of individual studies, along with systematic synthesis and bricolagic bridging between and among works of scholarship. Chapter 7 will bring together the now fully identified components of the metatheory—knowledge, units, and methods—into a working system.

Appendix 6.A
Implementation of Systemism

Implementation of systemism begins with identifying the type of exposition to be represented in terms of causal mechanisms. Three types exist, based on whether (and if so, how) a study includes graphic display of causal mechanisms. A further question concerns qualitative versus quantitative methods.

One type is a presentation already based upon systemism itself. Implementation in this context takes the form of an assessment of reliability. A reading of the exposition in words is appropriate to check for degree of correspondence with its visual presentation. Does the author's graphic representation of causal mechanisms correspond to what appears in the accompanying analysis from the text? Points of difference then can produce efforts toward reconciliation or even launch competing variations of a theory.

Another type of exposition is one that includes diagrams that depict causal mechanisms, but without following the rules from systemism. Work thus begins with a reading of the text and finishes with redrawing the figure(s) in accordance with systemism's rules for presentation. For example, James and James (2017) employ systemism to redraw diagrams from major textbooks on foreign policy analysis to enhance clarity and facilitate further evaluation.

Most common is the third type of exposition—one that consists purely of words. In this instance, the text can be reviewed for declarative statements of the "If X, then Y with a higher likelihood than otherwise" variety. Put differently, hypotheses are gleaned from the words that appear and then are assembled into a network of cause and effect.

Qualitative and quantitative studies create different pathways to visual representation of cause and effect. In a quantitative study, explicit hypotheses normally are included. Even if not, such studies will include, in effect, a summary regarding cause and effect in the form of a regression-like table of results. This will be true even if explicit propositions do not appear. The table will isolate one variable as dependent and others as independent, with coefficients attached to them. A table of this kind can be deconstructed by looking at how the presumed independent variables might relate to each other, along with the dependent variable.[33]

---

[33] Visual representation could be restricted to linkages with statistical significance if the purpose is a meta-analysis of results from a set of studies with the same dependent variable. An example that focuses on quantitative research designs for crisis escalation to war appears in James (2019a).

For a qualitative study, no numerical table of results will exist. The focus in that context is on identifying statements that include causal inference from within the text—either fully stated hypotheses or "if, then" assertions of the type noted already.

Validity can be assessed via consultation with authors. In other words, does the figure represent their intended set of arguments about cause and effect?[34] Assessment of reliability would involve critiques of the diagram from additional readers. When the contents of a given study are agreed upon, it can be entered into the archive of the Visual International Relations Project (VIRP) and made available to the community of scholars in the ISA.

Figure 6.A displays the four basic kinds of causal assertions that appear in figures created via systemism. In each instance lowercase characters are used, which indicates a micro-micro connection (i.e., the first half of this dyadic connection refers to x and the second half to y). Each also could appear in either macro-macro (i.e., all uppercase) or a mixture of upper- and lowercase if the connection is either macro-micro or micro-macro.

Type I is a unidirectional causal connection, from variable x to y. This is the simplest and modal kind of causal assertion encountered in the social sciences. An example is the macro-macro connection put forward by Waltz (1964, 1979) for polarity with stability: "A bipolar system will be more stable than a multipolar system." In other words, an international system with two rather than three or more great powers is expected to be less conflict prone, especially in terms of interstate war.

With Type II, cause and effect is bidirectional. Variable x is a cause of y and vice versa. An example is the endogenous relationship proposed for regime type and conflict: "Democracy facilitates peace and vice versa" (Thompson 1996; James, Solberg, and Wolfson 1999). The connection is envisioned as going back and forth between the two variables—a virtuous cycle in this context. These are hybrid linkages because democracy and (interstate) peace are micro- and macro-level variables, respectively. Hence "democracy → PEACE" is micro-macro and "PEACE → democracy" is macro-micro.

Type III depicts synergistic causation. Variables x and y act simultaneously upon each other, rather than in sequence (Tufte 2006: 67).[35] An example of this type of interaction involves hyperinflation and panic buying, which reinforce each other to spiral out of control. Germany, for example, experienced this malady during the 1920s as a byproduct of reparations imposed after World War I.

Finally, Type IV depicts an omitted linkage through use of a broken rather than solid line. This is a connection derived from an author's argument but excluded from the presentation in words. Bueno de Mesquita (1980), for example, points out the need to consider risk propensity among leaders in putting forward propositions about international conflict processes. This is an important gap that causes respective sides in one or more debates, such as stability in relation to polarity, to remain unconvincing (Bueno de Mesquita 1980). Common in practice will be the need to insert connections for feedback. This is because of the modal tendency of quantitative studies to use the regression format, within which recursive modeling is possible but uncommon. For example, generations of

---

[34] For authors who are deceased or choose not to participate, possible substitutes include both former students and scholars who have specialized on their work. These options are pursued for various realist theories in Chapters 10, 12–13, and 15.

[35] This graphic will help in counteracting a problem Grieco (2019) identifies with regard to analytic eclecticism, namely, its tendency to rely on qualitative methods, which in turn are not well suited to incorporation of interaction terms.

METHODS 211

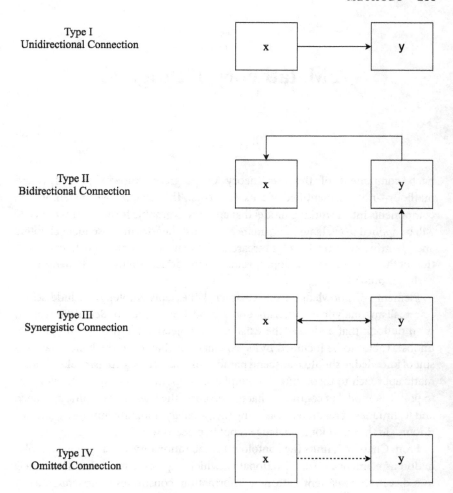

Figure 6.A Types of Causal Connections

research based on COW data treat war versus some other outcome as the terminal point in statistical analysis.

Shapes also provide information about the properties of variables within the system. This notation is covered in Table 6.3.

Figures in this volume have been created with www.diagrams.net. A tutorial that shows how that software program can be used to create these systemist figures is available upon request from the VIRP.

7
A Metatheory of Progress

Overview

Each component of the metatheory of progress—knowledge, units, and methods—now is identified via its elements. This chapter will assemble the components into a working model that appears in graphic form. The metatheory will be applied to evaluate performance of realist theories in subsequent chapters and identify new directions for research. Before moving forward with construction of the metatheory, it is appropriate to reintroduce briefly the elements from each component.

Elements of knowledge from Chapter 4 (i.e., epistemology) include scientific realism, analytic eclecticism, and a model of cognition. Scientific realism is an outlook that endorses the existence of objective knowledge and permits unobservables to be included in its explanations. Based on the belief that pursuit of knowledge should transcend paradigms, analytic eclecticism takes a pragmatic approach to theorizing that emphasizes solving problems with relevance to policy. A model of cognition that underscores the value of a graphic approach and techniques of relational reasoning (i.e., analogy, anomaly, antithesis, and antinomy) in the quest for knowledge is put in place as well.

From Chapter 5, units (i.e., ontology) entail rationality and a system of explanation as elements. Ordinal rationality, which expects actors to update beliefs in a direction consistent with new information, constitutes a movement away from requirements for data processing associated with intellectually challenging models. Among available systems of explanation, the research enterprise is selected for inclusion in the metatheory. A research enterprise moves beyond prior deductive and inductive systems of explanation to include both types of reasoning in identifying a body of research for assessment.

Covered in Chapter 6, elements from the method (i.e., methodology) component include rules for identifying axioms of a research enterprise and systemism. A series of inductive and deductive conditions are enumerated for identifying the assumptions of a research enterprise. Systemism is an overarching frame of reference on theorizing that includes a visual technique for conveying causal mechanisms.

This chapter will combine the components of knowledge, units, and method, via their elements, into a working system that culminates in scientific progress.

A METATHEORY OF PROGRESS 213

This work is in line with a pragmatism as a philosophical foundation for IR. The chapter unfolds in three further sections. The second section presents the metatheory as a working system. The third section focuses on essential characteristics of the metatheory, which include logical consistency between its elements and efficient operation. The fourth section reflects on the accomplishments of this chapter and turns toward application of the metatheory to realism and its respective theories about war in Parts III through V of this volume.

The Metatheory as a Working System

Figure 3.1 from Chapter 3 conveys a metatheory of progress for International Relations as a potential working system. Its contents include variables corresponding to (a) the seven elements from the knowledge, units, and methods components described in Chapters 4–6 and (b) scientific progress. Recall that Figure 3.1 depicts the variables and their positions, but not the dynamics between and among them. Figure 7.1 shows the working system in complete form. In particular, addition of arrows, along with shapes for certain variables in the system, breathes life into the vision of progress.[1]

The figure's presentation is systemist, with notation following Table 6.3 from the exposition on systemism. At this point, the purpose is to go beyond the summary in Chapter 3 to explain how elements within it are presumed to impact each other and, collectively speaking, produce scientific progress.

The appearance of the metatheory and the way it operates is consistent with principles associated with its elements. In terms of the logic of discovery, note the presence of reflexivity at this point.[2] A few knowledge-related examples should be sufficient to establish that point. First, the figure is conveyed in a manner that is self-consciously in line with an essential element of the metatheory, namely, systemism. The arrows that appear indicate cause-and-effect relations, and it is understood that it is somewhat provocative to present the elements of the metatheory in this way. Second, unobservables such as the scientific research enterprise are central to the metatheory. This trait is consistent with scientific realism. Third and finally, the metatheory connects processes in the academic world to the public domain. This feature reflects the priority analytic eclecticism grants to policy relevance.

Consider, in a bit more detail, the metatheory from a systemist point of view. Systemism demands that every type of connection—environment-system,

---

[1] See Tufte (2006: 66) on the specific features of visual formats that promote their value in terms of communication.
[2] For an effective argument in favor of such reflexivity, see Branch (2018: 112).

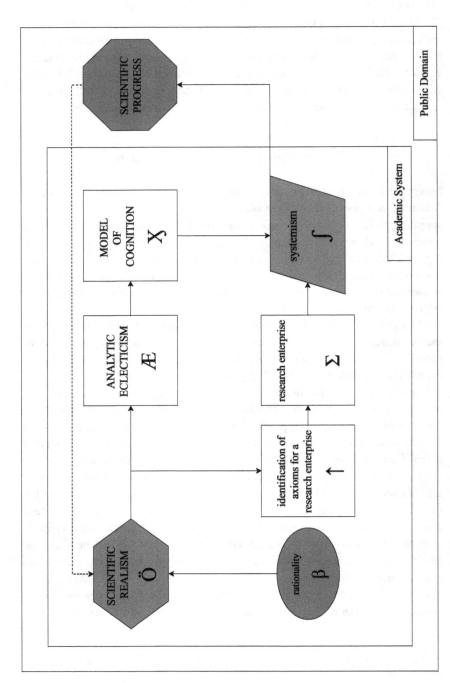

Figure 7.1 The Metatheory as a Working System

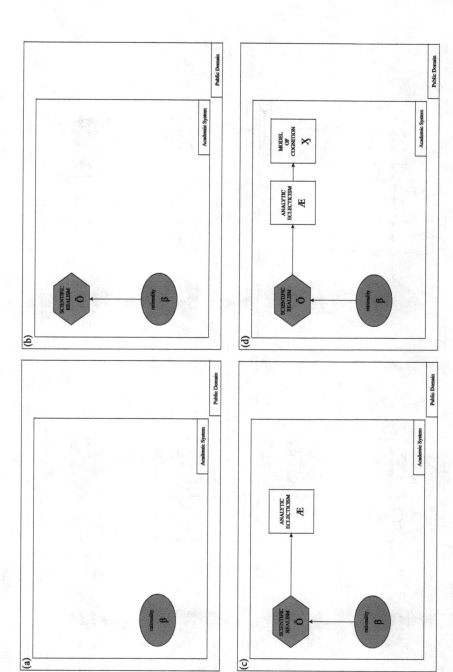

Figure 7.1 Continued

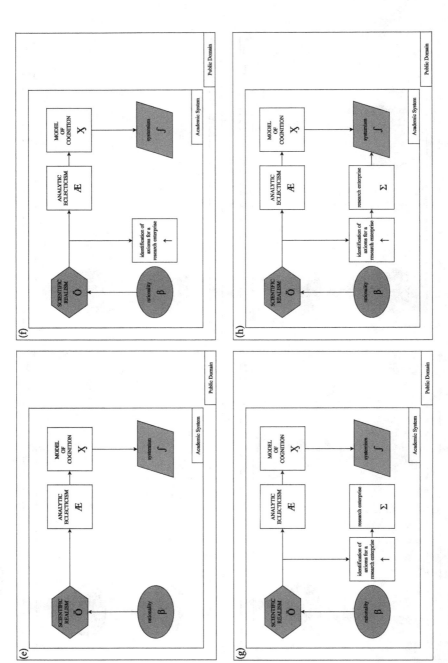

Figure 7.1 Continued

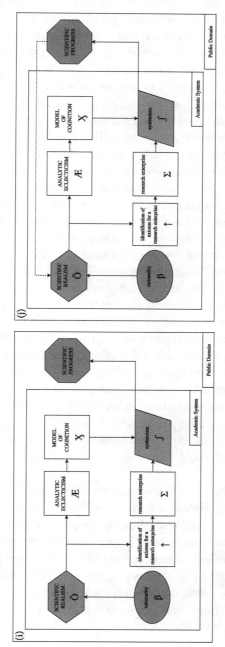

Figure 7.1 Continued

macro-macro, micro-macro, macro-micro, micro-micro, and system-environment—be represented in some way for a model to be regarded as complete. The first and last links in the preceding list—environment to system, along with system to environment—require a bit more explanation at the outset. The first on the list is a link from the environment to the *macro* level of the system, whereas the final item is from the *micro* level of the system to the environment. Thus at least one connection comes in and out of the system, even if *all* logically possible pathways in either direction—(a) environment to macro *or* micro and (b) macro *or* micro to environment—are not depicted. In sum, no ceteris paribus clause is entailed for any one type of linkage. Thus Figure 7.1 meets the requirement that at least one type of connection goes in and out of the system.

Figure 7.1 depicts the academic world as a system, along with its environment, the public domain. Items at the macro and micro levels appear in Figure 7.1 with upper- and lowercase letters, respectively. The macro level corresponds to scholars in a collective sense, identified as an academic discipline such as IR. At the micro level are found individual scholars who carry out research.

Knowledge-related elements—scientific realism (Ö), analytic eclecticism (Æ), and a model of cognition (X)—occupy the macro level within the academic system. These elements exist at a collective level among minds within the discipline.

Unit- and method-related elements are depicted at the academic world's micro level. Rationality (β) and research enterprise (Σ) are the unit-level elements, with identification of axioms ($\uparrow$) and systemism ($\int$) as the elements representing methods. These are micro-level entities that exist for an individual carrying out research. For example, a scholar is anticipated to act out of perceived self-interest in building a career. Ordinal rationality is the anticipated norm for decision-making; individuals adjust their views about a given hypothesis in the direction suggested by new evidence. Note that a poor performance for a proposition under testing may not lead to its abandonment, as per strict falsificationism. Instead, a lower level of *confidence* in a hypothesis could result, with redoubled efforts to collect evidence as the result.

Outside the boundaries of the academic world as a system—drawn as a box containing the preceding elements at the macro and micro levels—is scientific progress, which exists in the public domain. Scientific progress is depicted as a macro entity in uppercase letters; it reflects public engagement of the research community, a point of consensus regarding advancement emphasized in Chapter 2.

Presentation of Figure 7.1 in stages will enhance ability to follow its pathways. Figure 7.1a depicts the public domain and academic world—environment and system, respectively. Within the process that begins in Figure 7.1a, "rationality" is the anchor.[3] It appears at the micro level and is exogenous relative to other

---

[3] Starting with designation of units also is a metamethodological guideline of scientific realism. See Wight (2007: 388) and Gunnell (2011: 1469) on this point.

elements. Rationality takes the form of an oval, the designated shape for an initial variable. Note that rationality is ordinal; in the academic world (and elsewhere, for that matter), encounters with evidence shift beliefs (and confidence about them) in a given direction. Social scientists, in a word, are rational in the sense developed here.

First among the connections is "rationality" → "SCIENTIFIC REALISM," conveyed in Figure 7.1b. Instrumental rationality naturally points toward a scientific realist view of subject matter, whether IR or otherwise. The reason is that a scientific realist approach, with its acknowledgment of incompleteness of explanation, is the most convincing and effective position about the meaning of knowledge among the options enumerated in Chapter 2.[4] Thus the choice of scientific realism is regarded in line with the philosophical pragmatism that underlies the entire project.

Adherence to neopositivism, by contrast, would stand as quite optimistic in light of limitations upon all research. Unlike neopositivism, scientific realism quite pragmatically recognizes the essential role of unobservables in theorizing. Scientific realism also is preferred to either analyticism or reflexivity—the other two possibilities regarding overall perspectives introduced in Chapter 2 (Jackson 2011, 2016a, 2016b)—because these options entail subjectivity (i.e., world-mind dualism) and thus do not recognize the existence of objective reality. Analyticism and reflexivity thus are ruled out of hand because neither includes an anchor in objective knowledge to enable what Lakatos (1970) named in a famous book title, *Criticism and the Growth of Knowledge*. The value of studies based in analyticism or reflexivity lies in the potential for discovery rather than confirmation of ideas about international relations.

For such reasons, scientific realism is assessed as optimal among overarching outlooks on the philosophy of inquiry. It is a viable option for the logics of both discovery and confirmation. Unobservables come into being through the logic of discovery and take hold if effective with regard to the logic of confirmation. An example of success in both areas, consecutively, is the concept of an "attitudinal prism" within the foreign policy system of decision and implementation for a state (Brecher 1972). The idea of an attitudinal prism came into being through intensive study of Israel and the legacy of founding Prime Minister David Ben-Gurion—not a representative case but certainly an important one for international relations. The concept formation and elaboration in an initial, single-state study provided the foundation for a perception-based program of research on foreign policy crises, through which explanations have been derived for any

---

[4] For a contrary view, which sees the choice of an epistemology and particular philosophy of science as necessarily "made in reference to standards that are more social than universal," see MacDonald (2003: 563).

number of empirical problems over a sustained period (Brecher and Wilkenfeld 1997, 2000). One example is identification of crisis-related characteristics associated with escalation to war (James 2019a).

Scientific realism, then, is part of diverging and converging pathways in the network of variables. This is why, as a nodal variable, it is designated with a hexagon. The story continues at the macro level. The ensuing connection, which appears in Figure 7.1c, is "SCIENTIFIC REALISM" → "ANALYTIC ECLECTICISM." Perhaps the most effective way to grasp the compatibility of scientific realism with analytic eclecticism is to consider the opposite connection: what about allegiance to a single research enterprise? This position would imply a belief that all of reality could be comprehended within the boundaries of that one entity.

However, in addition to other previous arguments in favor of analytic eclecticism, consider the role of events that have not as yet occurred. It is possible that even a research enterprise performing at a very high level would require elaboration, possibly including concepts from outside of its current boundaries, in order to continuing moving forward in response to new events and especially technological change. Consider, for example, how the politics of images have accelerated for a world in which mobile phones are pervasive (Blieker 2018b: 5). An event at one location "happens" virtually everywhere else at once, which means that theorizing must take into account the potentially rapid and global impact from anything that can make its way onto a social media platform.

Previous arguments, notably based on Gödel's theorem about incompleteness in the domain of mathematics, also become relevant to the way in which scientific realism implies analytic eclecticism. If there are truths that elude any particular enumeration of axioms, then logically that problem would be exacerbated by permanent fidelity to a given research enterprise and its consequently narrowing effects. Consider, for example, what became known as Richardson (1960) process models of arms races. These models focused on how rival states would adjust military spending in response to each other. The Richardson approach also included a coefficient for fatigue from sustained allocations. The ensuing models of arms races could be characterized as material and objective in character (Kecskemeti 1960: 1931). Subsequent studies, notably of political psychology (Brecher 1972; Jervis 1976), gradually revealed that decision-making about security issues transcended purely material conditions. Thus models such as those of Richardson, while valuable stimulants to further research, provided an incomplete basis for explaining security policies such as allocations to military spending.

Analytic eclecticism and scientific realism also function well with each other in a more positive sense, over and beyond the former's incompatibility with strict adherence to one paradigm. Middle-range theory—a concept going back to

Merton (1957)—is favored explicitly by analytic eclecticism and strongly implied within a scientific realist framework. A middle-range theory starts with empirical observation and generalizes from it to create encompassing statements that can be assessed through testing. Specific hypotheses are assessed on the basis of empirical evidence (Merton 1957; Boudon 1991). This approach is *not* due to any sense of defeatism—the impossibility, perhaps, of obtaining a single comprehensive theory. The overall objective is to consolidate collections of theories with each other to achieve progress in a unifying way (Merton 1957).[5]

For analytic eclecticism, the natural starting point in IR is realism, not only because of longevity but also because of the time and energy already devoted to its evaluation. From a pragmatic point of view, realism becomes a target for elaboration, with its axioms complemented by other assumptions to build theories of the middle range that address a diverse set of empirical problems. All of this must proceed, of course, in a logically consistent way.

Realist theorizing, specifically, should put a priority on a more convincing treatment of leadership at the state level. Foreign policy analysis contains a wealth of ideas that could be accessed toward that end (Kaarbo 2015: 190; see also Tellis 1996: 91). Covered in further detail in subsequent chapters on realist theories are issues such as risk propensity, which sometimes play hidden but important and even determining roles within explanations of war.

One other macro-macro connection, added in Figure 7.1d, is "ANALYTIC ECLECTICISM" → "MODEL OF COGNITION." This link follows directly from the most basic property of analytic eclecticism, which calls for combining ideas from across and even outside of paradigms. Middle-range theories of various kinds are anticipated to result. These frameworks, moreover, will become diverse over time and thus, collectively speaking, pose greater demands in cognitive terms. The model of cognition therefore calls for a combined presentation of theorizing—in both words and *visual* form—to enhance comprehension and protect logical consistency.

Realism within IR is plagued by problems that ensue from analytic eclecticism in the absence of a model of cognition. Perhaps instead that should be stated in the plural: realism*s* abound, and their collective contribution is uncertain vis-à-vis explanation. A scheme of organization for realist theories will be developed at length in Chapter 9, but for now it is enough to say that many variants exist and some are at odds with each other. A prominent example includes defensive versus offensive realism, with opposing beliefs about what states, and especially great powers, seek through foreign policy. Defensive realism asserts that leaders pursue security, while offense realism instead emphasizes pursuit of power.

---

[5] For a convincing version of this argument in the context of IR, see Donnelly (2000: 197–198).

Next in the sequence comes a macro-micro linkage in Figure 7.1e: "MODEL OF COGNITION" → "systemism." Note that systemism appears as a parallelogram because it is a point of convergence. The model of cognition calls for some means of visualization to accompany presentation of cause and effect in words. Systemism is the best available choice. It includes explicit and easily intelligible rules for graphic representation of causal mechanisms. Systemism, in particular, guards against the risk of simultaneous incorporation of contradictory statements, for example, "x → y" and "x → ~y" through its process of visual representation for causal linkages. These statements, respectively, are read as "If x occurs, then y is more likely than otherwise" and "If x occurs, then the negation of y is more likely than otherwise." A systemist exposition would demand, for any x and y, explicit theorizing of scope conditions. For example, "x → y" if "z" is present and "x → ~y" if "z" is absent would be acceptable for a theory within a given research enterprise.[6]

Scope conditions are identified as a significant need for theorizing about international relations in general and especially in the domain of realism. Lack of consistency is endemic within realism; a standard example is balance-of-power theory (Levy 2004: 44–45). Contradictions persist. Thus causal mechanisms from realism "are likely to obtain under certain scope conditions and unlikely to obtain when those scope conditions are not present" (Feaver [Feaver et al.] 2000: 168 n. 3; see also Schweller 1997: 929). Even an enthusiastic exponent of realism acknowledges that, for the post–Cold War world, exact forecasts will differ because a range of theories are invoked that "employ different parameter values when analyzing contemporary events" (Walt 2002: 219). Wivel (2005: 364) calls for building a bridge between offensive and defensive realism: "Instead of debating whether states tend to pursue offensive or defensive strategies, [contingent realists] ask when and how states pursue which strategies." Systemism can facilitate exactly this kind of investigation.

For ease of presentation, it makes sense to return to the other pathway in the figure, which also later leads into systemism. A macro-micro connection, "SCIENTIFIC REALISM" → "identification of axioms for a research enterprise," appears as Figure 7.1f. Axioms are unobservables that provide the foundation for empirical research. Note that axioms *inherently* are unobservables, which scientific realism regards as a natural aspect of the research process. Take, for example, the concept of utility, which refers in a general way to the level of satisfaction perceived by an individual, in various models from rational choice. The utility function for an individual, or how experiences are aggregated into an overall sense of things, is neither visible nor comparable to that of any other person (Mueller

---

[6] This type of relationship also could be put forward in probabilistic terms: "x → y" with probability (p) if "z" is present and probability ($1 - p$) if "z" is absent ($0 \leq p \leq 1$).

1979, 1989, 2003). Scientific realism, furthermore, calls for *systematic* identification of axioms rather than assuming consensus about what is included. Realism alone is a sufficient example to justify explicit designation of the unobservable foundations for a research enterprise.

Figure 7.1g continues the pathway with "identification of axioms for a research enterprise" → "research enterprise," a micro-micro connection. The set of axioms provides the foundation for a system of explanation, with the concept of a research enterprise deemed the most advanced version of this concept and thus adopted here. A research enterprise consists of a logically congruent set of assumptions. Axioms produce theorems for testing—labeled as hypotheses or propositions and intended for empirical assessment—and both the complexity and potential contribution of the research enterprise build in that way. Potential causal mechanisms are identified and evaluated on the basis of evidence about empirical problems.

Once a research enterprise exists in words, the next stage is to depict its causal mechanisms in a graphic manner: "research enterprise" → "systemism" naturally follows on and is added in Figure 7.1h. Systemism, as described already, depicts causal mechanisms. This graphic presentation facilitates comprehension of a research enterprise, along with its comparison to competing formulations. The visual representation of cause and effect becomes even more essential with time because the *velocity* of international relations is increasing. Velocity, rather than speed, is the appropriate word because both pace and direction are changing. To cite just the most obvious example, what Rosenau (1990) labeled the "microrevolution" in world politics has come to fruition via the internet. Events happen almost simultaneously around the world, and anyone with access to the internet can be an actor or recipient much more rapidly than even a few years ago. This effect on communication is intensifying as Moore's Law continues to hold—computing power steadily increases and the velocity of interpersonal contact goes up with it.

Each pathway now converges toward an output from the micro level of the system into the environment: "systemism" → "SCIENTIFIC PROGRESS," added in Figure 7.1i. To emphasize this as the ultimate destination for the process of research, an octagon appears. Expositions based on systemism, created by individuals or teams of scholars, develop knowledge via comparison and competition facilitated by a common graphic presentation of causal mechanisms.

What about functional form? With one exception, what appears in Figure 7.1 is a product of deductive inference. Connections have been inferred from each other along the way. Depicted in Figure 7.1i, "systemism" → "SCIENTIFIC PROGRESS" is empirical in nature. It is anticipated to exhibit various functional forms—incremental but also step-level—as research falls into place.

Enhanced clarity from graphic representation of ideas is extremely important in preventing distortion of scientific knowledge that can harm society when implemented within a political agenda. An egregious example of that process is social Darwinism as a contributing factor to World War I. All of the participating states tended to see their own fighting ability as superior to that of the others. For example, opinion in France favored the idea of *élan vital*—the notion that weapons mattered less than the fighting spirit of the soldiers using them. Technologies such as artillery, barbed wire, and the machine gun disproved that doctrine, along with comparable versions that held sway in other European states, quite decisively.

Last within the cycle of cause and effect is a linkage from the environment back into the macro level of the system: "SCIENTIFIC PROGRESS" → "SCIENTIFIC REALISM." This is conveyed in Figure 7.1j as a broken line because it is not within the metatheory prior to implementation. Instead, the connection is anticipated positively. As knowledge accumulates, it should generate both empirical findings and new unobservables to include in further theorizing. These expectations follow from reasoning that parallels Gödel's theorem within mathematics, which points toward incompleteness from theorizing based on any given set of assumptions. Alternative outcomes would reduce the credibility of, and even potentially falsify, scientific realism. Such results would include (a) realization of a fully empirical system of knowledge, which instead would affirm neopositivism; or (b) failure of knowledge to accumulate as described—thus a confirmation of pessimism among antirealists across the board.

What would falsification of the metatheory mean in the context of IR? Refutation would tend to support the intuition of scholars who have eschewed social science for one reason or another. Lack of success for the metatheory also could give credence to the position of Feyerabend (1975), who prominently opposed any such approach in a book with the title *Against Method*, which summed up his worldview.[7] He proposed instead methodological anarchism, which stands as the antithesis for the metatheory and its application to IR.

Essential Characteristics of the Metatheory

Elements from the components of the metatheory—knowledge, units, and methods—have been combined together into a working system. Before moving forward, it is worth reflecting on an underlying question: will creation of a metatheory possibly result in more trouble than it is worth? Skepticism abounds regarding a focus on metatheory in the context of IR. As Wight (2016: 34) points

---

[7] The metatheory also could "fail" if, at some point, all empirical problems have been solved, signaling the triumph instead of neopositivism. See Ward (2018: 555) for a skeptical and convincing argument about the elusiveness of a fundamental answer to the question "Why?"

out, it is "a widely held view that debates surrounding the philosophy of science in IR are getting nowhere." Chernoff (2014: 23), quite involved in such debates as played out in IR, asks, "How much metatheory and methodology is enough?" and some would argue that a pragmatic approach would eschew such arguments altogether (Sil and Katzenstein 2010c: 111).

One response is to agree that debate shows no sign of reaching a conclusion, but to observe as well that arguments back and forth about metatheory have taken place overwhelmingly in *words*. A shift to visualization enhances prospects for (a) debate with a reduced level of misunderstanding and (b) possibly even consensus. A more direct reply to an argument against metatheory on practical grounds is to say that some point of departure for research always exists even if it is not acknowledged in any conscious way. Put differently, vagueness is not a virtue in this context or any other. Ambiguity is a basic reason debates never end. Thus the present study focuses on creation of a metatheory that is inclusive while also rigorous and in line with principles for scientific investigation with demonstrated worth. IR deserves nothing less.

Consider a more specific concern about the metatheory's contents: Are the seven elements—scientific realism, analytic eclecticism, a model of cognition, rationality, identification of axioms for a research enterprise, research enterprise, and systemism—logically consistent with each other? Some imply the presence of others directly, as represented in the connections depicted in Figure 7.1. If not directly linked through logical inference and therefore illustrated by an arrow in the figure, a given pair of items still exhibits independence rather than contradiction.

For example, consider the model of cognition and identification of axioms for a research enterprise. One element focuses on coping with potential cognitive overload through visual representation, while the other is a method for enumerating assumptions. Existence of one neither implies nor contradicts the other. Systemism, moreover, is compatible with analytic eclecticism's emphasis on building mid-level theory (Kesgin 2011: 337). A review of all other pairings does not suggest any issue with logical consistency.

Often parsimony and generalizability, in the wake of Waltz (1979), are put forward in IR scholarship as primary virtues for a theory (Bladgen 2016). The metatheory, however, takes more than those traits into account. The emphasis instead is on performance of a theory relative to its degree of complexity.[8] Rather than one dimension, two exist and form a ratio. The numerator is how much can be explained—assessed in terms of empirical problems either partially or

---

[8] Among the studies that favor this position, Taliaferro, Lobell, and Ripsman (2009: 23) argue in a neoclassical realist context that explanatory power, not just parsimony, must be taken into account when assessing a theory.

fully solved. The denominator is the degree of complexity required to achieve those accounts—represented by the axiomatic basis. Thus the Performance Ratio is introduced as a new concept that can guide assessment of a theory in a pragmatic way:

$$\text{Performance Ratio} = \frac{\text{fully and partially solved empirical problems}}{\text{complexity of axiomatic basic}}$$

Given this trade-off, it is not guaranteed that the simpler model always is best—only that it is preferred over one more complex if the Performance Ratio favors it. On the one hand, paradigms can be parsimonious, "But as a consequence they are highly indeterminate" (Bennett 2013: 467). Structural realist theory, within the realist school of thought, is a standard example of that limitation in practice.[9] On the other hand, "The scientific need to find evidence-based explanations for particular phenomena is stifled if nonparadigmatic and ad hoc" (Haas 2017: 46).

More specifically, a theory of the middle range is at risk of being overdetermined because it can be difficult to assess the causal significance of any specific variable (Checkel 2010: 24; Grieco 2019). Consider, for instance, neoclassical realism. To succeed, this innovation "would need to describe or explain a wider variation of outcomes than structural realism (or other approaches), without adding too much complexity to the argument" (Brawley 2009: 5). Advocates of neoclassical realism assert that "inclusion of unit-level variables, provided it is done in a careful, scientific manner, can add significantly to our ability to explain past events and predict future behavior" (Ripsman, Taliaferro, and Lobell 2016: 178).

Thus the shift to analytic eclecticism and its emphasis on theories of the middle range is functional only if a method is developed to cope with potential overspecification. The recommended method is systemism, which provides a graphic representation that facilitates assessment of a theory's Performance Ratio. In other words, how does it look, literally speaking, as a vision of cause and effect?

Multiple considerations exist for assessment of a model in light of evidence about it. The most straightforward means of evaluation for an "ideal-typical procedure" is to monitor its insight into the world of observation (Jackson and Nexon 2009: 926). This is consistent with the viewpoint of analytic eclecticism, which emphasizes the overall value of scholarship to theory and policy, as opposed to a single-minded focus on parsimony (Sil and Katzenstein 2010c: 111). Put differently, the Performance Ratio is impacted by the magnitude of both its numerator and its denominator.

---

[9] For an extended and encompassing critique on that basis, see Fozouni (1995: 500). Arguments in favor of elaborating structural realism appear in James (2002b) and Glaser (2003).

With seven elements, the metatheory has been constructed with the Performance Ratio in mind. The metatheory includes essential elements from within its three components of knowledge, units, and methods. Performance of the metatheory in application to IR will stimulate its simplification, preservation, elaboration, or elimination. Thus the metatheory is to be assessed in the same way as a specific IR theory within a research enterprise. The bottom line is this one: is the metatheory leading to scientific progress or not?

Given some of the previous difficulties in application to IR, it is appropriate to point out that the metatheory offers "addition by subtraction." It jettisons the effectively nonoperational criterion of expanding empirical content. This must remain an unobservable—and no longer a pernicious one because it is not put forward as a would-be measurement of success. Another concept that is eliminated from the framework, also associated with empirical content, is the idea of a novel fact. This is another extremely contested term that tends to hinder rather than help in assessing performance for a series of theories tasked with explanation.

What about the Performance Ratio in that same context? To what extent is it significantly more operational than empirical content?

Consider first, in response, the denominator. With a method in place to identify axioms for a research enterprise, a specific number should be available for any given theory within its boundaries.

Second, with regard to the numerator of the Performance Ratio, a method is in place to assess how well a set of studies is performing, collectively speaking, with regard to an empirical problem. This technique—one form of implementation for systematic synthesis—involves combination of theorizing from a number of studies into one graphic summary. Among the linkages portrayed in such a diagram, those that receive empirical support are preserved in a reduced form. Through a series of such figures, updated on the basis of further research findings, the *direction* of movement for theorizing could be identified. In other words, is the numerator of the Performance Ratio increasing or decreasing for respective empirical problems?

In addition, bricolagic bridging can be carried out to identify new empirical problems for consideration. Engagement with scholarship outside of the research enterprise thereby could increase the Performance Ratio, if the trade-off for expansion in the numerator and denominator is favorable.

Summing Up and Moving Forward

Part II of this book now is complete. A metatheory of scientific progress for IR is depicted as a working system. The working system consists of seven elements, all told, from within three components. The knowledge component includes scientific realism (Ö), analytic eclecticism (Æ), and a model of cognition (X) as its elements. The elements for the unit component consist of rationality (β) and system of explanation, with the research enterprise as the favored variant (Σ). Finally, systemism (ʃ) and identification of axioms for a research enterprise (↑) are the elements from the methods component.

Figure 7.1 shows the dynamics of the metatheory as a working system. The metatheory therefore stands ready for application to IR. This process begins in Part III of the book, which turns to identification of realism as a research enterprise and categorization of its attendant theories about the causes of war. When carried out, these tasks set the stage for Part IV, in which a graphic-led reassessment of realist theories will unfold.

PART III
IDENTIFYING REALISM

Part III of the volume identifies realism in terms developed via the metatheory. Chapters 8–10 compose this part of the book.

Realism at a gestalt level appears in Chapter 8, along with critiques of its viability. This chapter also uses the process described in Chapter 6, which includes both (a) inductive and sociological and (b) deductive and rationalist criteria, to designate the axiomatic basis of realism as a research enterprise. Assumptions are gleaned from the vast literature of realism and assembled in a manner that emphasizes completeness and eschews contradiction. When the process is completed, four axioms are identified for realism as a research enterprise: anarchy, state-centrism, pursuit of power, and rationality. These assumptions are used to distinguish realism from other schools of thought that depart from at least one item on the preceding list. Thus realism emerges from Chapter 8 with a logically consistent axiomatic basis that also establishes it as a unique presence within IR.

Chapter 9 develops a scheme of organization for existing realist theories, which facilitates their evaluation and comparison to each other. The purpose of Chapter 9 is to classify realist theories of war in a way that will facilitate later comparative analysis and ultimately scientific progress. This chapter begins by defining typologies and taxonomies that, respectively, are deductive and inductive means of classification. Prior efforts to create typologies and taxonomies are reviewed to obtain insights about how best to organize realist theories on the causes of war. A combined approach, both typological and taxonomic, is applied to the realist theories of war; in chronological order, these are identified as classical, power cycle, structural, balance of threat, balance of interests, defensive, dynamic differentials, offensive, and predation. In some instances, more than one variant exists. Types of theory are identified on the basis of two dimensions: (i) dynamic or static specification and (ii) system- or state-level emphasis. With each type of realist theory, a taxonomy is developed through identification of a characteristic that is anticipated to be most useful in the process of evaluation.[1] The trait that stands out is the capability-base metric that is emphasized by a given theory.[2]

Chapter 10 focuses on classical realism. The modern variant of classical realism dates back to *The Twenty Years' Crisis* (Carr 1964 [1939]), which appeared at the outset of World War II and foreshadowed many such expositions in its aftermath.[3] It is intriguing to reflect on classical realist ideas about why wars occur because, strictly speaking, adherents explored international relations from the standpoint of philosophy or history more than social science. The study of cause and effect in a systematic way did not motivate this phase of realism. Instead, exponents reflected upon human nature and prospects for a more peaceful world. The most memorable expositions along those lines are credited to Morgenthau (1946, 1959 [1948]), who influenced both realist thought and IR as a discipline in a central way for decades. The dark sense of the world from Morgenthau and other classical realists—one in which human nature is immutable and disposed to seek dominance—made sense in light of its timing from the decades following World War II, a conflict so destructive that it exceeded even World War I. Other significant realists who produced expositions that can be depicted in visual form as theories about the causes of war include Wight (1978 [1946]), Kissinger (1957), Wolfers (1962), and Aron (1966). In this process of transferring verbal to visual expositions, it is important to bear in mind the largely pre-social scientific mandate of the classical approach. Thus respective accounts from classical realism for why wars occur are more challenging, but not impossible, to reproduce in graphic form. Visualizations of classical realism identify it as the foundation for social scientific theories of war to come.

---

[1] Prominent omissions from the set of theories designated as realist, such as power transition theory (Organski 1958), are explained in Chapter 9.

[2] Use of just two dimensions for the typology and one characteristic for the taxonomy is a by-product of the relatively limited number of realist theories about the causes of international war.

[3] This time frame is a matter of consensus in the field; see, for example, Elman and Jensen (2014: 3).

8
The Nature of Realism

Overview

This chapter explores the nature of realism and identifies its axiomatic basis as a research enterprise within IR. Parts I and II of this volume have set the stage for a review of realism, which initiates the process of identifying its foundations and reorienting the research enterprise in the direction of scientific progress. Part I established the meaning of such progress for IR: growth of knowledge guided by a scientific realist position adopted from the philosophy of inquiry. Part II developed a metatheory of scientific progress, with knowledge, units, and methods as its components. Elements from those components, assembled into a working system, set the stage for tasks to be carried out in the rest of this volume.

One trait that sets the present analysis apart is that it takes on, from *within* a realist frame of reference, the question of meeting scientific standards from first principles onward. The resulting agenda includes identifying realism as a research enterprise from the ground up. Deductive and inductive logic will combine with each other as this chapter identifies a foundation for realism with potential to produce scientific knowledge more effectively.

Before the discussion moves ahead, a question from Chapter 1 returns to prominence: Why devote all of this time and attention to realism? The importance of realism is recognized from the earliest days of International Relations onward. Realists can boast of many accomplishments; just a few examples from recent decades include analysis of the sources of military doctrine (Posen 1984), prevalence of overexpansion (Snyder 1991), great power intervention in the periphery (Taliaferro 2004), grand strategy of the United States (Layne 2006), and the politics of European integration (Rosato 2011). In sum, it is reasonable to argue that realism continues to be indispensable to development of the field.[1]

Advocates see the tradition of realism as "the single most important approach for understanding international politics" (Walt 2002: 198), and realist accounts "often set scholars' baseline expectations" (Elman and Jensen 2014: 12). As Taliaferro (2000–2001: 131) observes, "Regardless of whether realism is the

---

[1] This assertion leaves aside, for the moment, which items might be above the bar for inclusion once deductive and rationalist criteria are applied along with an inductive and sociological sense of boundaries for realism.

dominant theoretical approach in international relations, it remains the bête noir of every nonrealist approach." While realism had seemed to fall out of favor for a while, Elman and Jensen (2014: 1) see it as "again in contention as a leading tradition in the international relations sub-field." The sheer amount of criticism leveled against realism ends up reinforcing these points. As Williams (2005: 1) observes:

> Whatever stance one takes, there is little doubt that despite continual declarations of its irrelevance or imminent demise, Realism remains at the heart of theoretical and political dispute in world politics, constituting a continuing reference point against which competing positions consistently defend themselves and a conceptual and rhetorical fulcrum around which both analytic and political debates revolve.

Even discussions of theoretical diversity in the discipline usually begin with reference to some variety of realism (Walker 2018: 200; see also Schmidt 2004: 428–429). However, what if the critics are right? Should the focus be on enhancing the value of alternative paradigmatic entities, such as liberalism, instead of realism?

Reasons over and above its age and pervasiveness justify a concentration on realism. It is worthwhile to challenge liberalism, the most prominent alternative to realism at present. The US debacle in Vietnam and oil shocks in the 1970s created interest in viewpoints at some distance from realism; over the course of subsequent decades, various liberal-inspired theories gained traction in IR. The advent of Keohane and Nye (1977; see also Young 1969 and Keohane and Nye 1971), with its emphasis on *interdependence* in addition to power, stands out as a symbol of sustained movement in the field toward liberal thinking. *Power and Interdependence* stimulated areas of research beyond security studies, which collectively became known as international political economy. Descended from Keohane and Nye (1977), liberal theorizing departed significantly from realist assumptions, such as a fully state-centered world. International political economy took seriously, for example, the role of nonstate actors such as multinational corporations in building explanations for diverse policy outcomes across issue areas.

Liberal thinking, however, only challenges rather than supplants ideas from realism and includes problem areas of its own. In particular, the liberal idea that certain forms of government inherently are more peaceful than others is in need of further assessment, and a stimulating literature is building on that subject (Oneal and Russett 1997; Gartzke 1998; Mousseau 2005, 2013). This point is even more relevant to the institutional explanation of the democratic peace—an important item within the liberal collection. Democratic publics can be prone to jingoism; consider the Crimean and Spanish-American Wars as just two examples.[2] It is interesting to ponder, in the context of public sentiments in democratic states concerning various wars, warnings from prominent classical realists such as Morgenthau and Kennan about crusading, even messianic, foreign policies.[3]

Every research enterprise in existence is subject to some criticism about its ability to explain international relations, and some of the concerns about liberalism are ongoing and serious. Other options for a point of departure, such as the English school and its emphasis on international society, possess limited support in comparison to realism or liberalism. Thus it would be incongruous to pass over realism and concentrate on more recently articulated schools of thought that, collectively speaking, have not demonstrated their superiority.

Realism thus emerges as the natural starting point for application of the metatheory of progress developed in Part II. It also is worth returning to the point that realism, in terms of challenges resulting from sheer size, is the literature in IR that serves as the "canary in the coal mine." As will become apparent in chapters that follow, realism is at the leading edge among schools of thought that can benefit from a visual turn. Others are trailing along behind realism, inexorably, as theorizing and research findings accumulate. Problems associated with expansiveness, such as proliferation of competing and contradictory variants among would-be adherents to a research enterprise, can be expected across the board. There is no immunity based on substantive content. No research enterprise exists at this time for which theories are depicted in the manner of systemism. In addition, respective schools of thought, within which theories are housed, have not been identified through axioms based on any process that resembles what is described in Chapter 6.

This chapter's purpose is to use the metatheory of progress to identify realism in a way that enhances its potential scientific value. Specifically, this means enumerating the axiomatic basis of realism. The process will follow the steps described in Chapter 6, with (i) deductive and rationalist and (ii) inductive and sociological criteria combined to designate realism as a research enterprise.

Work proceeds in four additional sections. The second section reviews efforts to articulate the realist worldview. Critiques of realism writ large appear in the third section. It is established that problems attributed to realism, collectively speaking, reflect analytic eclecticism in the absence of systemism or another analogous technique to rein in logical inconsistency. The fourth section identifies

---

[2] For a set of case studies that claim to contradict the causal mechanisms of the democratic peace, see Elman (1997). Ray (1995) explores would-be anomalies for the democratic peace and concludes that apparent exceptions, collectively speaking, pose no significant threat in terms of either theory or evidence.

[3] For a contemporary polemic against liberal internationalism in foreign policy, see Mearsheimer (2018).

the axiomatic foundation of realism on the basis of the nine criteria assembled in Chapter 6. Both inductively and deductively derived conditions are included, to enhance the fidelity of the axiomatic basis to those identifying with realism, on the one hand, and preserve its rigor, on the other hand. The fifth and final section reflects on the meaning of realism. This review leads into Chapter 9, which offers a scheme of organization for existing realist theories in order to facilitate assessment and revisions that move in the direction of scientific progress. All of this sets the stage for comparative analysis of realist theories about the causes of war in Part IV.

The Realist Worldview

One way to move forward is from generalities to specifics with regard to the meaning(s) of realism. It is essential to the later process of designating axioms that realism be identified in a gestalt sense—as a whole greater than the sum of its parts. In other words, what is the basic nature of realism, in a few words or less? This question must be answered to apply a sociological standard, at multiple stages, during the process of enumerating axioms. Inductive aspects of the process for identifying assumptions make it necessary to distinguish points of view expressed inside and outside realism from each other. Axioms then can be designated to establish realism as a research enterprise.

Realism, to begin, may be better thought of as a worldview than as a "conventional theory or explanation" (Smith 1986: 226). It is used within the vernacular in many overlapping ways, such as references to "Machiavellianism" or "Might makes right." These usages are more in line with a worldview or philosophy than with rigorous, social scientific theory. This initial observation is not surprising given the long existence of realism and the many contexts within which it is invoked.

Table 8.1 displays respective efforts to sum up the meaning of realism. The contents of the table are a mixture of one-sentence statements of the gestalt variety and paragraph-long summaries of realism. While many more sources could be added, with nuances resulting from that inclusion, basic traits identified at this point through sources from the post–World War II era would seem unlikely to change.

Realism is identified as political thought, a philosophical disposition and state of mind. It entails a pessimistic view of human life; the world today is the same as yesterday and tomorrow, with interstate conflict as the norm. Anarchy and human nature, with each receiving more or less attention depending on the realist exposition in question, combine to ensure a world of strife. The substantive focus of realism at the level of foreign policy therefore is on power and coping with insecurity. Self-help is the basic story of international affairs because each

Table 8.1 The Realist Worldview

Source	Summary Statement
Herz (1951: 18)	"Realism characterizes that type of political thought which in one form or another, sometimes not fully and at other times in an exaggerated manner, recognizes and takes into consideration the implications for political life of those security and power factors which, as outlined above, ... are inherent in human society."
Morgenthau (1959: 9)	Realism considers prudence—the weighing of the consequences of alternative political actions—to be the supreme virtue in politics.
Gilpin (1984: 289–290)	"I believe that political realism must be seen as a philosophical disposition and a set of assumptions about the world rather than as in any strict sense a 'scientific' theory."
Smith (1986: 1)	"In its most basic outline, the realist picture of the world begins with a pessimistic view of human nature. Evil is inevitably a part of all of us which no social arrangement can eradicate: men and women are not perfectible. The struggle for power—which defines politics—is a permanent feature of social life and is especially prominent in the relations between states."
Mearsheimer (1994–95: 9)	International relations is not a constant state of war, but it is a state of relentless security competition, with the possibility of war always in the background.
Frankel (1996b: xiii)	"A key element of realism ... is the assumption that there are significant things out there which exist independently of our thoughts and experience."
Tellis (1996: 3)	Realist approaches thus perceive politics primarily as a conflictual interaction.
Donnelly (2000: 6, 9)	"Realism is not a theory defined by an explicit set of assumptions and propositions. Rather, as many commentators have noted, it is a general orientation.... Realism emphasizes the constraints on politics imposed by human nature and the absence of international government. Together, they make international relations largely a realm of power and interest."
Schweller and Wohlforth (2000: 69, 99)	"People cannot transcend conflict via progressive power of reason to discover a science of peace; politics are not a product of ethics and morality is the result of power and material interests; and necessity and reason of state trumps ethics and morality when there is disagreement.... We simply claim that power is more important than the causes and causal mechanisms central to competing theories in international relations, such as changing ideational preferences and domestic democratization (liberalism), norms and identities (constructivism) and structures of information (institutionalism)."

(continued)

Table 8.1 Continued

Source	Summary Statement
Walt (2002: 200)	The central conclusion of all realist theories—what might be termed the realist *problematique*—is that *the existence of several states in anarchy renders the security of each one problematic and encourages them to compete with each other for power or security*. Realist theories see the insecurity of states (or groups) as the central problem in international relations, and they portray international politics as a self-help system where states must provide security for themselves because no one else will. Thus, the realist tradition places power at the center of political life: it sees the acquisition and management of power as the main issue that political actors face. It also takes a fairly pessimistic view of the human condition, emphasizing the recurring elements of tragedy rather than hard-won instances of progress.
Barkin (2003: 329)	Power is the core, and common, element of realist theory.
Guzzini (2004: 546, 552)	"I define realism in IR as a scholarly tradition characterized by the repeated, and for its basic indeterminacy repeatedly failed, attempt to translate the practical rules or maxims of European diplomacy into the scientific laws of a US social science.... Realists are there to remind us about the fearful, cruel side of world politics."
Rothstein (2005: 411)	"The more subtle contention that Realists share an awareness that full security is beyond attainment and that compromise and adjustment of interests are necessary, is more helpful. It implies that Realism involves a state of mind with which to approach problems, rather than the possession of a few characteristics or attachment to the permanent significance of a single operating principle."
Freyberg-Inan (2006: 256)	Political realism in IR generally addresses two basic questions: why does conflict occur? And what can be done about it?
O'Loughlin (2008: 100)	Realists share a common political philosophy.
Wohlforth (2008: 131)	Realism is not now and never has been a single theory.
Jackson and Nexon (2009: 92).	Realism as a polar point on two debates: Can power be tamed? (no) and Is anarchy a parametric constraint? (yes).
Taliaferro, Lobell, and Ripsman (2009: 14)	"Realism, like Marxism and liberalism, is first and foremost a philosophical position, not a single theory subject to empirical confirmation or disconfirmation.... All realists share a pessimistic view of human condition and prospects for change in behavior; rejection of teleological conceptions of politics or end of history; skepticism about schemes for international order; and recognition that morality and ethics are products of power and material interests, not the other way around."
Kirshner (2010: 55)	Realists see states, pursuing interests, in an anarchic setting where the real possibility of war, and with it the prospect of subjugation or annihilation, must be accounted for. Realists see humans as actors with political instincts, who organize into groups that are discriminatory and typically conflictual.

Table 8.1 Continued

Source	Summary Statement
Lizée (2011: 22)	Universal application of realist point of view means the rational use of instrumental violence—force at the service of political ends—will be morally defensible because it protects the political community from its internal and external enemies, and that community is essential to morality itself.
Parent and Baron (2011: 208)	What makes a realist a realist is superlative emphasis on the power of external circumstances, and this trait has been as impressively (or depressively) uniform over time as the prevalent patterns they have always explained.
Brown (2012: 857)	Realism: the international order and the foreign policies of states are, at a fundamental level, shaped by considerations of power and interest.
David (2015: 10, 9)	"In its simplest form, realism is an approach or theory that purports to describe the way in which the world behaves. Central to realism is the belief that the world today is the way it has always been and will always be.... Realism paints a very bleak picture of world politics where states struggle over power with the constant threat of war lurking in the background."
Elman and Jensen (2014: 2)	Most realists take a pessimistic and prudential view of international relations.
James (2016)	From a realist point of view, a state's primary goal is to maintain independence, understood in terms of sovereignty, based on security.

state must seek power, obtain security, and maintain sovereignty for itself. And at no point is that effort ever enough—danger persists, albeit at a reduced level, even for the most capable states. Taken together, the contents of Table 8.1—assembled mostly from advocates—reinforce the important conclusion from Vasquez (1983, 1998) about the lack of integration within realist thought.

For purposes of illustration, *Scientific Man versus Power Politics* (Morgenthau 1946) works well with regard to obtaining a basic sense of realist thinking as it emerged in the period after World War II. The title tells the basic story of confrontation between an idealistic sense of the world, in which humanity learns to control its baser urges and experiences advancement, versus the perspective of realism, in which power politics is the norm. Morgenthau (1946) argued that liberal notions of progress do not apply to power politics. The realist vision is philosophical, with a focus on continuities in human life and the study of history. From the standpoint of Morgenthau (1946), power and insecurity promise to be with humanity for a long time to come. Words from the title of the book noted at the outset of this paragraph sum up the realist vision: even a scientific humanity cannot expect to overcome power politics.

Classical realists, with Niebuhr (2010 [1952]) as a prime example, put forward a pessimistic position on the subject of human progress in the aftermath of World War II. In particular, within the context of US leadership and overseas conflict, realists such as Niebuhr advocated limits on intervention. War should occur only when absolutely necessary and well justified. Cozette (2008: 678) adds some important nuances about the realist worldview:

> Pessimism however is not to be equated with nihilism or despair; while realism warns against ideological prophecies, it does not necessarily teach resignation to the existing *status quo*. On the contrary, for Morgenthau and Aron, politics, while being a struggle for power or survival, is also to be regarded as part of man's never ended attempt to implement what he regards as ethically right, even though this attempt is bound to fall short of the ethical ideal from which it arises.

Prudence, rather than a liberal focus on use of power for humanitarian intervention, is central to realist thinking.

While the reflections on realism from Table 8.1 are thoughtful and informative, there is considerable diversity. In particular, the contents of the table collectively fall short of offering an *operational* sense of realism. Thus a turn to critics of realism and responses to them is appropriate to obtain further insight.

Critiques of Realism and Responses

Critiques of realism focus on both general issues and specific points of difference. The review that follows emphasizes more encompassing disagreements about the viability of realism as a scientific approach to IR.[4]

Basic critiques of realism tend to focus on its chaotic character and invoke principles from the philosophy of science—especially allusions to Kuhn (1962, 1970) and paradigms or Lakatos (1970) and research programs—as debate unfolds. Legro and Moravcsik (1999: 55) assert that it would be helpful if realists would "observe greater precision in stating and applying its premises." Vasquez (2003a: 27) throws down the gauntlet against realism:

> It will be argued that what some see as theoretical enrichment of the realist program is actually a proliferation of emendations that prevent it from being falsified. It will be shown that the realist paradigm has exhibited (1) a protean

---

[4] Among the many other points of controversy about realism, beyond the scope of this chapter, are debates over whether the approach is obsolete (Smith 1986: 234; Rothstein 2005: 409, 418), accuracy of assumptions (Miller 2004: 37; Brawley 2009: 139), (in)ability to account for change (Ashley 1984: 257; Schweller and Wohlforth 2000: 78; Schroeder 2003: 125; Guzzini 2004: 548; Özdemir 2015: 7), the meaning of balance of power (Levy 2003: 138; Vasquez 2003b: 92, 107), the role of alliances (Maoz 2003: 214), and explanation of major events such as the end of the Cold War (Schweller and Wohlforth 2000). Aspects of these debates and others will be reviewed in Part IV when attention turns to specific variants of realism.

character in its theoretical development; which plays into (2) an unwillingness to specify what form(s) of the theory constitutes the true theory, which if falsified would lead to a rejection of the paradigm; as well as (3) a continual and persistent adoption of auxiliary propositions to explain away empirical and theoretical flaws that greatly exceed the ability of researchers to test the propositions, and (4) a general dearth of strong empirical findings. Each of these four characteristics can be seen as "the facts" that need to be established or denied to make a decision about whether a given research program is degenerating.

At the foundation of realism's problematic character, according to Vasquez, is a lack of compliance with standards for scientific inquiry. In practical terms, since realism cannot be falsified, what scientific purpose does it serve?

Efforts to defend realism from refutation end up creating a new problem: lack of distinctiveness: "If we can no longer say what causal processes the realist paradigm excludes, we cannot say what it includes. In sum, realists confront a fundamental tension: Define realism broadly and one subsumes all rationalist theories; define it precisely and one excludes much recent scholarship" (Feaver et al. [Legro and Moravcsik] 2000: 185). Thus realism begins to lose its identity and becomes equated with IR as a whole. Realism grows to a vast size and ends up with incoherence as its basic trait. "Increasingly," as Legro and Moravcsik (1999: 22) observe, "realist research invokes factors extraneous, even contradictory, to the three core realist assumptions, but consistent with core assumptions of existing nonrealist paradigms." A related critique of realism raises the issue of vagueness: "If defined just in terms of self-help under anarchy," observes Guzzini (2004: 536), "definitions of realism are too encompassing, collapsing realism with the early self-definition of IR." If realism is everything, then it ends up being nothing.

What about synthesis as a response from realism to its critics? It is a complex family of theories, to be sure, but perhaps realism still could be compelling in summation. Critics see this idea as a further illustration of what is wrong with realism from a scientific point of view. Legro and Moravcsik (Feaver et al. [Legro and Moravcsik] 2000: 189) take realists to task "for labeling the resulting synthesis as a progressive confirmation or extension of realist theory rather than as a demonstration of its limitations or as an evaluation of the relative weight of two theories." Vasquez (2003a: 35; see also Fozouni 1995: 492) describes the pernicious dynamic in operational terms: "In fact, the protean character of realism prevents the paradigm from being falsified because as soon as one theoretical variant is discarded, another variant pops up to replace it as the "true realism" or the "new realism."" According to the critics, the many existing versions of realism simply do not add up. From their point of view, realism evades falsification via incoherent proliferation.

Interesting to ponder, in the context of uncertainty regarding the identity of realism, is the review conducted by David (2015) of foreign policy during the Obama administration. The point of departure for David (2015: 9) is the sense of Obama, among critics, as "weak, indecisive, naïve, afraid to lead and fearful of using force." The president, however, might instead be regarded as a misperceived practitioner of realism.[5] The pivot to Asia, according to David (2015: 15), clearly demonstrates the Obama administration's realist inclinations. Asia's rise is the explanation: "From a realist perspective, it is easy to see why Asia needs to be the primary focus of the United States" (David 2015: 16). Six of the ten largest armies in the world are in Asia, so focusing instead on "intractable Middle East disputes" does not make sense for Washington (David 2015: 16, 17). Moreover, policies implemented by Obama that dampened down potentially more intense involvement in the Middle East became quite visible: attempting to reduce the likelihood of an Israeli attack on a nuclear-capable Iran; recognizing, at least implicitly, Ukraine as a vital interest for Russia; limiting allocation of resources to Afghanistan; considerable restraint in reacting to President Abdel-Fattah el-Sisi's arrest of the former president, Mohamed Morsi, and a crackdown on the Muslim Brotherhood in Egypt (David 2015: 19, 21, 27). In sum, David (2015: 41) sees the foreign policies pursued in the Obama years as in line with realism.[6]

Quite troubling, from a scientific standpoint, is that virtually all of the assertions attributed to realism in the last paragraph could be *reversed* and also seen as in line with one variation or another. Each statement in its present form is both consistent, and at odds, with some variant of realism. If Obama had not been reluctant to use force, then that would be more in line with intuition from offensive realism about expansive great powers (Mearsheimer 2014 [2001]). Yet the restrained approach toward distant military deployments looks just fine from the standpoint of another realist argument, namely, offshore balancing (Layne 2006). One or more variants of neoclassical realism could be used to explain, via public opinion in the United States, the drawing down of forces from the Middle East (Lobell, Taliaferro, and Ripsman 2009). At the same time, withdrawal might be seen by structural realism as a failure to balance (Waltz 1979). The pivot toward Asia, meanwhile, looks to be in line with defensive realism, but does evolution of policy in specific terms, which turned out to be quite restrained under

---

[5] Perception of Obama as a realist went beyond the academic world. For example, the German weekly *Der Spiegel* ran an article in May 2012 claiming that Obama stood as the "unlikely heir to Kissinger's realpolitik" and quoted the editor of the *National Interest* to the effect that he "may even start speaking about foreign affairs with a German accent" (quoted in Bew 2016: 3–4).

[6] David (2015: 28, 30) is careful to point out that at least some significant policies during the Obama administration are out of sorts with realism; he cites the Libyan operation and Syrian red line remark as examples.

the Obama administration, not violate offensive realism? If it is not in line with offensive realism, then why? Contradictions such as those listed above are not difficult to find with regard to any application of realism because another exposition based on power politics, somewhere, virtually is guaranteed to point policy in a different direction.

Rather than a flaw identified through application of principles from philosophy of science, defenders of realism see its diversity as a positive trait. Adherents of realism "reach surprisingly dissimilar conclusions on a wide range of issues"—and more often than would be assumed (Smith 1986: 2; see also Walt 2003: 61). According to advocates, this feature is misinterpreted by cognoscenti; since various strands of realism offer diverging predictions and explanations, critics recently have asserted that "realism is a failing research program" (Glaser 2003: 266). "Most importantly," Walt (2002: 221) adds, "disagreements between different realist theories are an important source of theoretical progress, just as they are for other approaches to international relations." When realist theories produce predictions that diverge from each other, "It is more properly seen as a sign of theoretical vigor than evidence of degeneration" (Walt 2002: 221; see also Snyder and Lieber [Snyder] 2008: 184). Schweller (2003b: 78; see also Schweller 1997: 927) concurs, with a further admonition against critics who see realism as a Tower of Babel: "When proper attention is paid to the scope conditions of our theories, much of what appears to be contradictory and discrepant proves consistent and complementary." Thus, from an inside view, realism admittedly is intricate but not necessarily incoherent.

These responses from the realist side are not convincing. The essential problem is that scope conditions rarely are identified in realist studies. When does offensive versus defensive realism apply? Why might states seek expansion versus security? How do neoclassical variants, with incorporation of domestic factors, fit into the panoply of realism? Answers to these queries are not easily forthcoming. This is because *realism reflects analytic eclecticism in the absence of systemism or a related graphic technique to preserve coherence*. Realism takes the form of a vast and highly diverse literature, largely unaided by visual representation of cause and effect. Later chapters, which depict realist theories in a commensurable way through implementation of systemism, will seek to enhance coherence and facilitate comparison.

One response to Vasquez (2003a), by Walt (2003: 63), emphasizes the limited scope of its observations: "Viewed as a whole, Vasquez's essay is a classic illustration of the hazards of small sample size." Walt observes specifically that Vasquez (1983, 1998, 2003a) relies on one modern work on the history and philosophy of science and five contemporary realist works. This riposte, however, is not convincing in relation to at least one prominent criticism by Vasquez, namely, lack of internal consistency among realist expositions. Adding more studies in the continuing absence of an organizing principle simply would *increase* the amount of self-contradiction for realist theorizing in the aggregate.

One other line of response by Walt (2003), regarding the framework conventionally applied to realism, leads to a more encompassing reflection. Consider the conventional status of Lakatos (1970) as a means toward evaluation in light of the metatheory for progress developed in Part II of this book. The usual line of attack against realism is based on its seemingly dismal performance when viewed as a research program in the manner of Lakatos (1970). While that concept is valuable in drawing attention to falsification as something to be pursued at the level of a series of theories rather than an individual hypothesis, the frame of reference in Lakatos (1970) is found wanting in ways already discussed.

What is meant, in particular, when Lakatos (1970) refers to the empirical content of one theory versus another (or in general)? Taken from the concept of a research program and frequently applied in a rhetorical way, empirical content remains far from any operational form. Realist respondents therefore are justified in asking that more than one system of explanation be applied to assess their collection of theories before a decision is reached to pursue alternatives once and for all.

Consider, for example, the research enterprise as a system of explanation, developed in Chapter 5 as a combination of features from existing approaches applied to IR—methodology of falsificationism, paradigm, research program, and research tradition. Perhaps a focus on solving empirical problems, which is central to the research enterprise as a system of explanation, could produce new and more positive ideas about the future of realism. On a more critical note, implementation of an alternative system, such as the research enterprise, still would have to deal with the well-established problem of contradictions within realism. Thus attention turns to identifying assumptions for realism in a way that will facilitate its ability to generate scientific explanations for interstate war and other empirical problems.

The Axiomatic Basis of Realism

This section will accomplish six goals. One is to locate candidate axioms for the axiomatic basis of realism within the academic literature. The second through fifth objectives are application of inductive and sociological (Stages I and IV) and deductive and rationalist (Stages II and III) selection criteria. The sixth and final goal is to summarize the axioms that have been selected to form the axiomatic basis of realism.

Location of Candidate Axioms

Work begins with a compilation of axioms taken from academic literature on realism. A survey of books and articles took place in multiple stages.[7] Each potential assumption then is put through a process of elimination, with multiple stages that include both inductive and deductive logic.

Why bother, however, with such an extended process? Realism, it might be said, already is known to possess a set of assumptions that provide the basis for a variety of theories (Mastanduno 1997: 50). The method that follows will reveal that, while many lists of axioms have been assembled, the degree of overlap between and among them is weak. A systematic approach is required to derive for realism a set of assumptions that is valid and reliable.

Outlined in Chapter 6, the procedure for exclusion of candidate axioms will consist of multiple stages that go back and forth between inductive and deductive methods. The steps below are carried out in the order that complies with criteria from Chapter 6. Two inductive and sociological stages are bookends for two deductive and rationalist stages that take place in the middle. Stage I, which is sociological and inductive, includes conditions that focus on whether those inside and outside the research enterprise are able to agree on inclusion of an axiom. Deductive and rationalist evaluation in Stage II includes three conditions that are applied on an individual basis, for example, confirming that an axiom constitutes a universal statement. Stage III of rationalist and deductive assessment incorporates two comparative conditions; one instance concerns whether an assumption is redundant. Stage IV includes two inductive and sociological conditions—as one example, does the axiom run into objections from a critical mass of those associated with the research enterprise?[8]

Table 8.2, with contents taken from a wide range of academic sources, conveys candidates for the axiomatic basis of realism.[9] Possible axioms are arranged in

---

[7] Studies deemed relevant included original works on realist theory and review essays intended to evaluate those contributions. Both books and articles have been incorporated in the review. This is an inherently inductive process and can continue as further publications accumulate. For reasons offered below, however, identification of axioms is expected to have converged already for realism because of the nature of the process involved. In other words, as sources accumulate, the process developed in this chapter makes it *less* likely that a shift will take place within the set of axioms associated with a given research enterprise such as realism.

[8] The process that follows also complies with the Anti-Brutus Condition imposed in Chapter 6. This means that no axiom that itself ultimately is eliminated can be used at an earlier stage to prevent inclusion of another candidate assumption.

[9] The table might have missed some studies that listed axioms and, obviously, items published afterward are excluded out of hand. Such omissions are not expected to pose a problem, however, given that a significant number of studies already are in place. This is because it becomes increasingly unlikely that a new study will be sufficient to cause a change in membership for the final set of axioms. The basic reason is that only a highly specific *combination* of studies—very unlikely to appear in light of the nine conditions imposed—could lead to addition or subtraction of an axiom. The stability of

Table 8.2 Candidates for the Axiomatic Basis of Realism

Source	Human Nature Always Tends toward Conflict	States as Principal Actors	States as Unitary and Rational	States Focus on Power	States Inherently Possess Some Offensive Military Capability	Utility of Force	Meaning of Power Can Vary with Time	States Focus on Security	States Focus on Survival	States Predisposed toward Conflict	States Uncertain about Each Other's Intentions
Morgenthau (1959: 4, 5, 7, 8, 9, 10)	✓		✓[a]				✓				
Wolfers (1962: 82)		✓		✓						✓	
Gilpin (1984: 290)		✓[b]		✓				✓		✓	
Smith (1986: 219–221)	✓[c]	✓	✓	✓							
Grieco (1988: 488)[d]		✓		✓				✓	✓		
Mearsheimer (1994–95: 10)[e]			✓[f]		✓				✓	✓	✓
Frankel (1996: xiv, xv, xviii)		✓	✓[g]	✓	✓		✓	✓			
Mastanduno (1997: 50)		✓	✓	✓							
Schweller and Priess (1997: 6)	✓	✓[h]		✓							
Van Evera (1999: 7)[i]		✓	✓	✓							

Schweller and Wohlforth (2000: 69, 71)		√[j]	√		√
Schweller (2003b: 74–75)	√	√[k]	√		√
Walt (2003: 61)		√	√		
Layne (2006: 15)		√	√[l]		
O'Loughlin (2008: 101)		√	√		
Taliaffero, Lobell and Rispman (2009: 14–15)		√[m]	√		
Glaser (2010: 29–32)		√	√		
Ripsman, Taliaferro and Lobell (2016: 179)	√			√	√
Holsti (1995: 36–37)		√	√		
Legro and Moravcsik (1999: 12, 13, 16)		√	√		
Barkin (2003: 327)		√	√[n]	√	
Vasquez (2003b: 108)		√	√	√	
Ryan (2004: 5, 11, 14, 23, 35)		√	√	√[o]	√

(continued)

Table 8.2 Continued

Source	State Not Influenced by Domestic Characteristics or Traits of Leaders for Those States	Anarchy	System Structure Consists of Material Capabilities	Institutions as Epiphenomenal	Demarcation of International and Domestic Politics	Autonomy of Political Sphere	Universal Moral Principles Cannot Be Applied to State Action	Morality of a Particular State Cannot Be Identified with Universal Moral Laws
Morgenthau (1959: 4, 5, 7, 8, 9, 10)						✓	✓	✓
Wolfers (1962: 82)								
Gilpin (1984: 290)								
Smith (1986: 219–221)								
Grieco (1988: 488)		✓		✓				
Mearsheimer (1994–95: 10)		✓						
Frankel (1996b: xiv, xv, xviii)		✓	✓ᵖ					
Mastanduno (1997: 50)		✓						
Schweller and Priess (1997: 6)		✓						

Van Evera (1999: 7)	✓[q]				
Schweller and Wohlforth (2000: 69, 71)					
Schweller (2003b: 74–75)	✓				
Walt (2003: 61)	✓				
Layne (2006: 13)	✓				
O'Loughlin (2008: 101)					
Taliaferro, Lobell, and Ripsman (2009: 14–15)			✓		
Glaser (2010: 29–32)	✓	✓			
Ripsman, Taliaferro and Lobell (2016: 179)	✓				
Holsti (1995: 36–37)	✓			✓	
Legro and Moravcsik (1999: 12, 13, 16)	✓			✓	
Barkin (2003: 327)	✓				

(continued)

Table 8.2 Continued

Source	State Not Influenced by Domestic Characteristics or Traits of Leaders for Those States	Anarchy	System Structure Consists of Material Capabilities	Institutions as Epiphenomenal	Demarcation of International and Domestic Politics	Autonomy of Political Sphere	Universal Moral Principles Cannot Be Applied to State Action	Morality of a Particular State Cannot Be Identified with Universal Moral Laws
Vasquez (2003b: 108)					✓			
Miller (2004: 5, 11, 14, 23, 35)		✓		✓				

a The analogy of a set of billiard balls or chess pieces is mentioned in conjunction with state sovereignty and acting with a single mind and will.
b This is stated as the essence of social reality being the group.
c This is put forward as an assumption of an ineradicable tendency to evil.
d This list, along with those of Mearsheimer (1994–95), Schweller (2003b), and Vasquez (2003b), contains further items that take the form of propositions.
e The list of assumptions is preserved in the second edition of this book (Mearsheimer 2014 [2001]: 29–31).
f This assumption is presented as states thinking strategically about how to survive within the international system.
g This assumption takes the form of instrumental rationality.
h This assumption mentions the group rather than the state explicitly.
i This list is assembled by the author from other sources.
j This assumption is put forward as conflict groups being the key actors in world politics.
k This assumption is presented in the broader form of humans facing each other primarily as groups, not individuals.
l The assumption is about seeking power advantages over rivals (Layne 2006: 15).
m The specific reference is to membership in larger groups (Taliaferro, Lobell, and Ripsman 2009: 14).
n Only rationality is mentioned explicitly.
o This assumption refers to states acting in order to protect vital interests.
p This takes the specific form of asserting that the international system, consisting of the distribution of capabilities and power trends, is mostly responsible for state conduct.
q Foreign policies are influenced heavily by the environment, taken to mean anarchy.

the table approximately along a spectrum, starting with what is believed about individuals, states, and the international system, respectively. Material is assembled here from (i) those who either identify as realists (insiders) or seem positively disposed with their work and (ii) others who fit the description of critics (outsiders). The breakpoint in the table is with Ripsman, Taliaferro, and Lobell (2016); those up to and including that source are enumerating the assumptions of realism from an internal point of view, while after that point the perspectives are external.[10]

Noteworthy from the outset is the sheer number, 19, of axioms mentioned by at least one source in the table. The range across sources is a minimum of three and a maximum of eight assumptions, with the frequency appearing in parentheses for each instance: 8 (2), 6 (1), 5 (2), 4 (9), and 3 (8). Note that the count is skewed downward, with 17 of the studies enumerating three or four axioms and just five studies identifying five axioms or more.

All of this confirms the amorphous character of realism as envisioned with regard to assumptions. No obvious pattern of expansion or contraction is apparent when the sources are scanned over time. The numerous collection of assumptions reflects the Kuhnian (1970 [1962]: 197) vision of a paradigm as something that must be identified, at least to some degree, in sociological terms. With a number such as 19, implementation of any deductively derived criteria would be certain to remove at least some candidate axioms due to the anticipated effect from mutual contradiction alone.

Inclusion in the table of axioms from both insiders and outsiders, of course, reflects an analytic eclecticist point of view that calls for at least some input that is obtained at a distance from a given framework. Significant value is expected from taking into account visions from within and beyond realism. While insiders represent the most obvious source for sociological identification of a research enterprise, outsiders temper this view and offer a check on the impact of perceptions. Such validation reflects a less subjective sense of meaning while still remaining sociological in character. As described via the method of identification for axioms in Chapter 6, insiders and outsiders, respectively, are used to assess validity and reliability.

---

the set of axioms identified would become even greater if the table included *citations* of existing lists, such as Barkin (2010: 21) and Cristol (2017), which currently do not appear.

[10] It turns out to be relatively simple in practice to designate insiders and outsiders. Insiders self-identify with realism and do so accurately in relation to the gestalt meaning gleaned toward the outset of this chapter. Outsiders who devote time and effort to enumerating assumptions tend to identify explicitly as critics or at the very least self-designate as working beyond what are understood as conventional boundaries for realism.

Sociological and Inductive Conditions: Stage I

Initial conditions for identification are as follows: An axiom must appear at least (a) twice among insiders and (b) once among outsiders. Given conditions (a) and (b), the following axioms are in contention, with the number of appearances on internal and external lists in parentheses:

- Human nature always tends toward conflict (2, 1)
- States as principal actors (11, 4)
- States as unitary and rational (6, 4)
- States focus on power (12, 4)
- States focus on security (3, 1)
- States focus on survival (2, 2)
- States predisposed toward conflict (5, 2)
- The international system is one of anarchy (10, 2)

The preceding eight axioms now remain from among the initial 19.

Rationalist and Deductive Conditions: Stage II

Stage II, which applies criteria (c) through (e), will reduce further the list of eight candidate axioms for realism as a research enterprise.[11] Conditions (c) through (e) are those applied on an individual basis.

Based on condition (c), primitive statement, the assumption of states as unitary and rational actors, must be divided in two. Recall that the requirement of primitive statement rules out compound clauses.

What about condition (d), universal statement, meaning that the axiom must apply at all times and places? Consider in this context the candidate assumptions that states focus on security and survival. These axioms violate the condition regarding universal statement because both refer to *objectives* rather than *processes*. No two goals that differ even slightly can be given priority over each other at all

---

[11] Table 8.2 is based on an extensive reading of literature produced by realists and their critics, but obviously the list could expand if other sources produced additional axioms. Further research will explore this point, but conditions (c) through (g) are certain to restrict expansion. (Conditions (h) and (i) also are deemed likely to play a major role in limiting the extent of the axiomatic basis.) While the list of candidate assumptions could continue to increase in length, those ultimately included in the foundation of realism are *very* unlikely to expand beyond what emerges by the end of this chapter. The likelihood of rejection increases for a potential axiom as a simple function of what already is in place via recognition from both inside and outside of the research enterprise. By contrast, assumptions added on to designate specific, competing realist theories would not have to command support from all of those within the research enterprise and beyond its boundaries.

times. This is a contradiction in terms. Thus epistemic conditions must be added to these assertions to specify when each would take priority. Consider, by contrast, power seeking. States focusing on power is the assumption that wins out here. This is because security is an end state and power is not. Security refers to a specific goal—in ultimate sense, full safety against an attack from other states. Under conditions of anarchy, only the polar point of an overwhelming world state—the Great Leviathan, in line with Hobbes from long ago—could guarantee security. This is because, by definition, external threats no longer exist. Aside from this likely irrelevant case—the equivalent in mathematics of dividing by zero and coming up with infinity as the answer—multiple states will persist for a long time to come. Power can be applied to obtain security or any other goal the leadership of a state might pursue (Layne 2006: 17). Thus the objectives of security seeking and survival are eliminated on the basis of the universal condition.

All of the candidate axioms are in compliance with condition (e), abstract statement—put simply, no proper nouns are permitted. None refers to any spatiotemporal domain or specific actors or events.

Rationalist and Deductive Conditions: Stage III

Attention now turns to requirements (f) and (g), which involve comparison of axioms with each other. In the context of condition (f), logical consistency, consider the assumption that human nature always tends toward conflict. A war of all against all—which rules out even temporary cooperation required to achieve statehood—would be the expectation from the above-noted assumption regarding human nature. This inference, however, contradicts the axiom that states are principal actors. This is because the emergence of a state requires some degree of cooperation among its eventual citizens—a minimal agreement, at least initially, to live together within a political system that possesses sovereignty. Individuals "transfer their egotism and power impulses to the state" (Barnoschi 2017; see also Hobbes 1982 [1651]; Lake 2009: 1; Lizée 2011: 29; Hall and Ross 2014). It becomes clear that the axiomatic basis must exclude either the assumption about human nature or state-centrism. This difference will be resolved at a later point in the process.

Logical consistency, condition (f), eliminates either the unitary or rational actor assumptions. These axioms cannot coexist and, in fact, are not logically consistent with each other. A rational decision-maker will not simply pursue the national interest beyond the water's edge while treating events inside the state as irrelevant to that process. Outcomes that seem puzzling can be explained by a leader's need to balance multiple interests simultaneously (Sterling-Folker 1997: 20; see also Rosecrance and Steiner 2010: 341). The assumption of instrumental rationality demands that the leader treat all interactions in the same way, namely, as opportunities for advancement of interests.

From a sociological standpoint, this might seem to violate realism as an intellectual tradition. What about the idea that international and domestic politics are separate? (This potential axiom appears in Table 8.2 but did not pass the threshold for further assessment.) Oddly enough, to separate these domains requires a decision-maker to be a realist in carrying out foreign policy but not when doing other things. If that separation is deemed part of the realist tradition, then the enterprise is inherently self-contradictory. Instead, it makes more sense to accept rationality as an axiom in need of further review and jettison the state as a *unitary* actor.

Consider next the axiom regarding predisposition of states toward conflict. It can be derived from others in the remaining list of contenders, but not the reverse. Thus it is eliminated on the basis of requirement (g), economy of exposition. For example, the assumption that states are the principal actors, in league with other axioms, could be used to infer that these political units are predisposed toward strife. If anarchy and a focus on power are assumed, then it is easy to derive the statement that states are amenable to conflict. There is no Leviathan, as Hobbes would have put it, so the contest for power naturally moves in that direction. Given this reasoning, economy of explanation dictates that predisposition of states toward conflict is eliminated from contention regarding axiomatic status.

Four contenders remain from among the initial set of 19 candidate axioms: states as principal actors, states as rational actors, states focus on power, and anarchy.[12]

All four of the remaining conditions—states as principal actors, states as rational actors, states focus on power, and anarchy—are primitive, universal, and abstract statements. Are the remaining candidate axioms logically consistent with each other? Dividing the pie in terms of macro and micro levels may be helpful here. In other words, are the subsets of assumptions about the units and their system coherent? States as rational and power-seeking actors—the micro-level vision—contains no contradiction. Power is a resource that can be applied to any desired end state; efforts by states to obtain it to the best of their ability therefore make sense by intuition. (The idea goes back to Dahl [1957] and the concept of relational power, which can be exercised as a function of resources available.) The macro level is just as straightforward. The system is made up of states as its principal units under conditions of anarchy, which offers no contradiction. If these statements are put together across levels, the vision remains

---

[12] The designation of states as rational actors is meant in the following way: rational leaders are representing states.

logically consistent: states, as rational actors, seek power under conditions of anarchy.

Economy of explanation, condition (g), also is satisfied by this set of axioms. None of the four can be derived by any combination of the other three. Appendix 8.A establishes this point.

Sociological and Inductive Conditions: Stage IV

Conditions (h) and (i) are applied in this stage to complete the process. Distinctiveness, criterion (h), refers to whether a research enterprise can be understood as representing something truly separate from other approaches. Figure 8.1 displays realism as the point of origin for theorizing about IR. Macro and micro designations correspond to the system and state levels, respectively. The lower-right box in the figure represents the possible departures from realism at the *micro* level, with dimensions that correspond to degrees of power seeking and rationality among leaders. Realism, at the origin, assumes both rationality and power seeking. The upper-left box in the figure shows possible movements away from realism at the *macro* level, with axes that display degrees of state-centrism and a continuum from anarchy to hierarchy. At the origin, realism adopts both anarchy and state-centrism.

Any given research enterprise can be identified through its departures, at either the macro level, micro level, or both, from the profile of realism in terms of its axioms. Four instances are provided in Figure 8.1.[13] (The exact position of each research enterprise along an axis is arbitrary—halfway, just to make things easier to see.) Examples at the macro and micro levels are provided in turn.

Power transition theory and neo-Kantianism represent departures from realism at the macro level. Neo-Kantianism departs from the axiom of state-centrism because it reserves a role for institutions in the famous triad, which also includes interdependence and democratic regime type (Russett and Oneal 2001). Power transition theory focuses on the leading state in the system and its principal challenger, with danger in the system expected when a process of overtaking gets underway. As a vision of international politics, power transition theory is at some distance from the assumption of anarchy. The leading state in the system creates an order that reflects its interests, with other states expected to fall into line (Tammen, Kugler, and Lemke 2017: 83). Thus some degree of hierarchy not only exists but is essential to cause and effect because war may come

---

[13] It also should be noted that, aside from realism, each research enterprise in the figure is represented here in gestalt terms. A rigorous approach to identification would require use of the nine conditions, designated as (a) through (i), which combine (1) inductive and sociological and (2) deductive and rationalist reasoning to designate the axiomatic basis for a research enterprise.

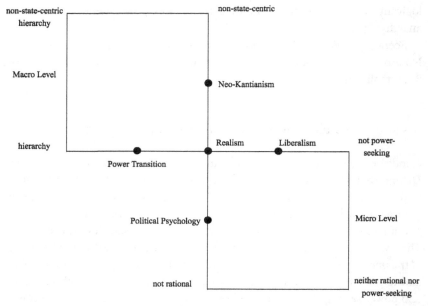

Figure 8.1 Realism as the Point of Origin for International Relations Theory: Anarchy, State-Centrism, Rationality, and Power Seeking

as a result of the challenging state's mounting dissatisfaction with the status quo that favors the leader.[14]

Political psychology and liberalism depart from realism at the micro level. The rationale for political psychology is a belief that deviations from instrumental rationality are sufficient to justify an entire program of research. Political psychologists study any number of mechanisms that impact he processes and outcomes of foreign policy decision-making. For example, groupthink and polythink refer to ways in which collective decisions are impaired as a result of supraoptimal and suboptimal degrees of consensus, respectively (Mintz and DeRouen 2010). Movement away from realism on the part of liberalism, to a significant degree, is based on skepticism about power seeking. Cooperation is not ruled out under conditions of anarchy (Keohane 1984). From a liberal point of view, states pursue absolute rather than relative gains. Debate over this subject occupied a decade or more and did not produce a consensus (Baldwin 1993; see also Grieco 1988; Powell 1991; Snidal 1991).

---

[14] Essential works on power transition theory include Organski (1958), Organski and Kugler (1980), Kugler and Lemke (1996), Tammen et al. (2000), and Lemke (2002). For an effective overview of the program of research on power transition and conflict processes, see Tammen, Kugler and Lemke (2017).

Valuable here is the designation from Legro and Moravcsik (1999: 12) of competing research enterprises (labeled by them as paradigms): liberal, epistemic, and institutionalist. Examination of each, in turn, reveals that none of the four remaining candidate axioms for realism is found across the board in another research enterprise. The assumption about states as principal actors is rejected by institutionalist and epistemic paradigms. A rational state is an idea at odds with epistemic theorizing, which focuses on ideas and norms and eschews Homo economicus. Adherents of the liberal and institutionalist paradigms reject the power-seeking assumption for states. While scholars from within the epistemic paradigm focus on anarchy, it is not an assumption but instead a concept that is subject to considerable debate.

Figure 8.1 could be expanded to include many other approaches. The present version, however, is sufficient to make the point that realism, once defined rigorously, is *not* all-encompassing. Note that approaches that depart even more significantly from realism—at *both* macro and micro levels—could not be displayed in the current figure. Instead, a third dimension would be needed to depict simultaneous movement, in both directions, away from realism at the point of origin.[15] Thus requirement (h), distinctiveness, is in place as well.

Interesting to consider in the context of distinctiveness is the degree to which a process of designating axioms is not entirely separate from well-accepted ideas regarding identification of an ideology. This is not to say that a research enterprise should be regarded as an ideology, but instead that it serves at least one parallel purpose. The axiomatic basis of a research enterprise, like the set of assumptions that possess fundamental status in an ideology, is designed to halt a certain kind of competition "by opting for one conceptual structure rather than another" (Freeden 2013: 120). A belief system does that, as Freeden (2013: 120) observes, "with clusters of concepts, whose mutual ordering creates further morphological variations, conferring specific meanings on each concept in an ideology's domain." In other words, a set of axioms develops a collective identity and provides the basis for competition to obtain adherents. An ideology provides an antimony with a research enterprise in a very important sense. These entities resemble each other in competing for adherents on the basis of a crystallized meaning, but a key point of difference is that, unlike an ideology, a research enterprise must fulfill a set of deductive and rationalist conditions regarding its foundation.

One more criterion, of a sociological variety, is imposed to identify a final list of axioms. Condition (i) asserts that any axiom is disqualified if there is a critical

---

[15] Each alternative position in the figure appears on a line for purposes of simplicity in presenting some of the prominent frameworks that diverge from at least one of the four axioms for realism. Interior positions within the boxes also could be occupied, but identifying such theories is a matter beyond the scope of the present exposition.

mass of inside opinion that it should *not* be included for a research enterprise. Among the surviving candidate assumptions, only rationality inspires notable debate along such lines. "At the time of its entry into American intellectual life," observes Kahler (1998: 920), realism and rationalism in politics had a relationship "more confrontational than complementary." This uneasy engagement dates back to *Scientific Man versus Power Politics*, in which Morgenthau (1946) cited the calamity of World War II as overwhelming evidence against liberal notions of rationality (Kahler 1998: 920). The polemics of classical realists against liberalism, however, focused more on the sense of rationality vis-à-vis learning among humanity that eventually could eradicate war. This form of rejection did not necessarily rule out *instrumental rationality in terms of self-interest*. The pursuit of power, for example, could be viewed as rational along those lines.

More controversial are efforts among outsiders to reduce realism to an axiomatic basis that includes rationality and little else. "By reducing realist core assumptions to anarchy and rationality," Legro and Moravcsik (1999: 6–7) claim, "minimal realism broadens realism so far that it is now consistent with *any* influence on rational state behavior"—even factors that once had been "uniformly disparaged by realists." The axiomatic base identified for realism here, however, goes beyond just those two items.

Realist opposition to emphasis on, and even inclusion of, rationality as an axiom is significant but in all likelihood a matter of terminological confusion. In a high-profile symposium in response to Legro and Moravcsik, Taliaferro (Feaver et al. 2000: 179–180) does not accept rationality as "a core assumption of classical realism." Schweller and Wohlforth (2000: 70) assert that although "some realist theories make strong assumptions about rationality, such assumptions are not essential to realism." Just as adamant is Schweller (2003a: 324), who observes that realism's "hard core of assumptions do not—contrary to conventional wisdom—include rationality" and that both Morgenthau and Waltz rejected it. Haslam (2010: 328) adds that insistence on assumed rationality "goes entirely against the grain of realism as traditionally understood." In a sharply worded critique of offensive realism, Haslam (2010: 340) points out that "a key assumption is the rationality of decision-making; an assumption realists have always abjured. And for good reason: insistence on assumed rationality defies common sense and accumulated experience." In sum, a number of adherents (and even critics) of realism are doubtful about a role for rationality.

While the views expressed are intense, other realists and those beyond the boundaries see things differently. In terms of the sociology of knowledge, some self-identified realists *insist* on inclusion of rationality. For example, Brooks (1997: 462) observes that, since power is regarded as a mechanism rather than an end in itself, "states are expected to pursue power subject to cost-benefit calculations." Countless realist expositions, moreover, refer to pursuit of foreign policy objectives that imply self-interest and eschew a sense of the world as one that results from random action.

Table 8.2 reveals the presence of rationality as an axiom in a wide range of expositions among insiders. Moreover, most of those who dismiss the assumption almost certainly are thinking of rationality in *normative* rather than instrumental terms and thus, like Morgenthau (1946), understandably see that conception as being at odds with a world of power politics. This is likely to be the case, for example, with Taliaferro, Lobell, and Ripsman (2009: 22), who disagree with rationality as a "core assumption of realism." Elsewhere in their exposition on realism, however, perceptions and calculations of leaders are included in the analysis—a clear connection with instrumental rationality (Taliaferro, Lobell, and Ripsman 2009: 28). The same could be said for any number of other studies that identify with realism.

One other point argues positively regarding instrumental rationality within the axiomatic basis of realism. Recall from Chapter 5 that rational choice is taken to be *ordinal* in character; in other words, when beliefs are confronted with new information, it is assumed that the *direction* of change can be anticipated. This is opposed to a stricter sense of Bayesian updating, in which beliefs are altered to a more precise degree in light of new information. Adherents of realism, on average, have tended to be skeptical of exact calculations, such as those of game theory or statistical analysis, when applied to international relations. Thus the pragmatic shift to ordinal rationality, developed in Chapter 5, also is more consistent with the realist tradition.

Rationality therefore will be preserved within the axiomatic basis of realism. Of course, a *rival* research enterprise could begin with a different set of axioms—perhaps excluding rationality in particular—but that is a separate matter.

Summarizing the Realist Axioms

Realism as a system of explanation includes four axioms: anarchy and state-centrism at the system level, along with rationality and power seeking at the actor level. Each axiom is summarized in turn.

Anarchy means the absence of hierarchy. Nothing is entailed in this axiom about how it came about. Anarchy in international relations simply means the denial of hierarchy, which at its extreme would mean a world government with full control over all of its citizens. Nothing close to that exists today or is likely in the foreseeable future. It would be naive to say that no hierarchy of any kind can be found in international politics; this clearly is false (Lake 2009). Adoption of anarchy instead is meant to maximize what can be explained in comparison to the complexity of what is used to account for it—in line with the Performance Ratio from Chapter 6.

State-centrism means that sovereign states are taken as the basic units of international politics. States have "unique status as authoritative actors" (Lake 2008: 44). This means formal equality but, of course, the existence of exceptions. Part of the title from a prominent book works well here; states are engaged in "organized hypocrisy" (Krasner 1999). From the realist standpoint, states remain the principal actors. Even surface violations of this assertion end up confirming it in a deeper sense. Take, for example, the (possibly) moribund ISIS, along with other nonstate actors that perpetrate significant violence and challenge a state, a region, or even the international system itself. The name of ISIS, Islamic State in Iraq and Syria, tells the tale. It refers to a *state*, not a transnational entity. ISIS and other significant nonstate actors, from a realist point of view, seek to join the international system of states, although possibly with the goal of its ultimate overthrow.

Instrumental, not normative, rationality is assumed by realism. Self-interest is an assumption common to realist approaches (Freyberg-Inan 2004: 86). Advice from Snidal (1985: 594) is worth heeding here: there is "a need to broaden the realist notion of rationality beyond the simple pursuit of immediate self-interest. States are better characterized by strategic rationality, which takes into account the likely reactions of other states as well as the pursuit of interests across a wide range of issues and through time." Strategic rationality as just described is clear to see in at least some realist theories already.

Consider, for example, balance of threat (Walt 1987, 1990). According to this theory, leaders are concerned not so much with power endowments directly as with how much a given state may pose a threat to them. Thus both capabilities and intentions factor into calculations about foreign policy for such leaders. Balance-of-*interests* theory (Schweller 2006), also from realism, establishes a link with instrumental rationality through its very name.

Finally, realists believe that states seek power. Material capabilities are finite within the biosphere, so competition is to be expected. Power therefore is not desired either primarily or exclusively in and of itself; instead, it can be used to improve prospects for achievement of goals across the board (Donnelly 2000: 50). "The goals that might be pursued by nations in their foreign policy," Morgenthau (1959: 7) observed, "can run the whole gamut of objectives any nation has ever pursued or might possibly pursue." Thus a realist focus on power in terms of resources that can be put to work in order to obtain desired outcomes inherently means conflict will occur. In the language of game theory, strategic interactions involving power seeking are zero- rather than positive-sum. This point is essential to separating realism from liberal theories that focus on absolute rather than relative gains.

Designation of axioms, of course, is the beginning of the story for theory building within the realist research enterprise. Further axioms will create diversity and stimulate both cooperation and competition among realist theories in putting forward potential solutions to empirical problems. It is reasonable to expect that a variety of secondary axioms, which complement those designated as primary, can and will generate predictions that conflict with each other (Donnelly 2000: 75). Analytic eclecticism can ensue in this form, but with the promise that additional axioms must be logically consistent with (1) those already in place and (2) each other for any given theory. This process unfolds in Part IV, which follows the effort in Chapter 9 to classify realist theories and graphic presentation of them in Chapters 10–18.

Axioms are unobservables that become understood more thoroughly as research moves forward. Note also that these axioms transcend a purely material sense of the world. In particular, there is no requirement among the assumptions that capabilities take a strictly material form. Barkin (2003: 329) sees that ongoing emphasis as a byproduct of the behavioral and rationalist turns, as opposed to "an expression of a core realist idea." Thus it is permissible and even desirable to build upon the assumptions of realism through inclusion of both material and ideational variables.

Summing Up and Moving Forward

This chapter began with a focus on the nature of realism in gestalt terms. Essential traits of realism include existence as a philosophy as opposed to a social scientific framework, belief that human nature and anarchy combine to guarantee continuing international conflict, an associated pessimistic view of human life, and a focus on power and (in)security in the study of foreign policy.

Attention then shifted to the central critique of realism, which sees it as protean and undeserving of scientific status and even further attention. While this assessment is accurate today to some degree, realism possesses the potential to meet the standards of science through a specific kind of reformulation. This is because its current woes reflect analytic eclecticism in the absence of systemism (or an analogous visual technique) to rein in incoherence resulting from unbridled expansion. The sizable number of assumptions mentioned at least once among efforts to define realism speak with one voice on that point.

Reformulation began in this chapter with identification of axioms for realism as a research enterprise: anarchy, state-centrism, rationality, and power seeking. This combination of assumptions resulted from a multistage process that incorporated both (i) inductive and sociological and (ii) deductive and rationalist criteria for selection. Identification of axioms in this manner responds to variegated concerns from those inside and outside the research enterprise.

Chapter 9 will focus on mapping realist theories. Classification will facilitate efforts toward revision of realist theories in a manner that promotes clear, falsifiable statement and subsequent competition both within the research enterprise and beyond its boundaries. This work sets the stage for more detailed presentation and assessment of realist theories in Part IV.

Appendix 8.A
Independent and Essential Axioms

Can any one of the final set of axioms—power seeking, rationality, state-centrism, and anarchy—be derived from the others? Each possibility is considered in turn.

Consider power seeking as potentially derived from a combination of anarchy, state-centrism, and rationality. This is ruled out because cooperation, rather than competition, could take place even in the presence of the other three conditions. While rational states under anarchy might end up seeking power, less myopic thinking could take hold. Taylor (1976) provides a valuable formal analysis in this context. A study of cooperation under anarchy reveals that it is possible, albeit difficult to achieve, for rational actors when faced with conditions of strategic interaction. Once society forms beyond a state of nature, overarching authority provides order. Its removal virtually guarantees disorder, with *The Lord of the Flies* as a touchstone in the world of literature.[16] However, the key point is that cooperation is feasible, just difficult to achieve, under anarchy.

Could anarchy, state-centrism, and power seeking combine to produce rationality? This would seem certain not to occur at least some of the time. Consider in this context insights from political psychology. It would be possible for some, if not all, states to pursue power in a monomaniacal way. While some might engage in trade-offs between "guns and butter" induced through rational choice, others might simply seek power until one among them achieved world domination or each fell victim to overextension or exhaustion.

What about state-centrism as a product of anarchy, rationality, and power seeking? It is possible to envision rationality and seeking of power under anarchy leading to either diverse units or empire. To cite one example, the Roman Empire ruled for centuries over the Mediterranean region, along with significant territories elsewhere. While one possible result from rational seeking of power under conditions of anarchy is a system of states, significant periods of empire also can occur. A highly state-centric world is something familiar today, so it is natural to make the error of expecting it to be the norm throughout history.

Finally, could anarchy be derived from the combination of state-centrism, rationality, and power seeking? Both history and logic say no. Consider, as a counterexample, the East Asian tributary system from centuries ago. While resembling the Western world in some ways, East Asia for centuries existed as a hierarchical system led by China (Kang 2012). Respective polities, such as Japan and Korea, existed independently in medieval times. However, payment of tribute to China took place for centuries and is sufficient to infer that something other than a state of anarchy existed in the region.

---

[16] The story by Golding (1954) focuses on schoolboys marooned, in the absence of adults, on an island after an airplane crash. Degeneration into cruelty and violence is the essence of what happens in terms of an emerging order among these children who are isolated from prior experience with the authority and rules of society.

9
Classifying Realist Theories of War

Overview

This chapter asks and tentatively answers a basic question: what types of realism can be identified? Classification of realist theories about the causes of war emerges as the highest priority in setting the stage for graphic portrayal and evaluation. A scheme of organization will enable more effective comparison of realist theories in the overall pursuit of knowledge about international politics. Chapter 8 prepared the way for this work because it derived an axiomatic basis for realism. The realist research enterprise entails four assumptions: anarchy and state-centrism at the level of the system, along with rationality and power seeking at the level of the state. Thus to be classified as realist, a theory must be in line with this set of axioms.

It is fair to say, at the outset, that a consensus is lacking about any definitive list of realist theories fitting into a set of well-understood categories. One point of agreement is the diversity of realist theorizing about war and other subjects. To momentarily revisit Chapter 8, a wide range of definitions and designations exist for realism as a whole (Donnelly 2000: 7–8; see also Pashakhanlou 2013). Glaser (2003: 266) identifies a "variety of strands of the realist family," Snyder (2002: 149) calls attention to splinter groups that wave "an identifying adjective to herald some new variant or emphasis," and O'Loughlin (2008: 100) refers to a "broad church," with no single theory uniting its members. The range of ideas connected in some way to an overarching concept of realism is, in a word, daunting. Varieties of realism, in turn, provide the foundation for many realized and potential theories about a range of subject matter.

Consider, for example, disagreements over classical realism—just one variant among many. Controversy exists over reconstruction of beliefs attributed to classical realism. Recall that classical realism is associated with a fatalistic sense of human nature as disposed to strife. This is the standard account of the classical realist vision of war (Copeland 2000: 256; Elman and Jensen 2014: 3). Parent and Baron (2011: 198) are able to create lists of classical realists who endorse anarchy (Herz, Niebuhr) and structure (Spykman, Carr, Meinecke, Taylor) as conditioning factors. Rereading its principal texts makes it obvious that there is more to classical realism than purely philosophical reflections on human nature. "The structure of anarchy," assert Parent and Baron (2011: 198), "leads to the same consequences for the same reasons in classical and neorealism." Moreover, classical realists frequently observed that "in an anarchic environment states tend to imitate each other" (Parent and Baron (2011: 199). While the *animus dominandi* attributed to classical explanations is present, pursuit of power "represents less an end in itself than a means to security" (Parent and Baron 2011: 200). In sum, the classical variant, most long-standing among those associated with realism in the era after World War II, is able to stimulate arguments about its character well into the 21st century.

After the process carried out in Chapter 8, axioms identified for realism as a research enterprise combine to set boundaries for what can be included in any catalog of theories. It is interesting to explore existing efforts to organize realism to see the degree to which that research is based, in an implicit way, on anarchy, state-centrism, rationality, and power seeking as axioms. Along with an introduction to typologies and taxonomies in a general way, this chapter will pursue the task of classifying realist theories.

Work unfolds in five further sections. The second section focuses on typologies and taxonomies, the means available for classifying theories. These instruments of organization, respectively, are deductive and inductive in character. The third and fourth sections review existing efforts to sort realist theories into categories based on typologies and taxonomies. The fifth section identifies realist theories that pertain to the causes of war. These theories are placed in respective typologies and taxonomies that will facilitate comparative analysis. A sixth and final section sums up the classification of realist theories and sets the agenda for the next chapter.

Typology and Taxonomy

Classification schemes are essential to facilitate research, which naturally includes comparative analysis. Thus categories are created to place phenomena into mutually exclusive and exhaustive sets on the basis of clear decision rules (Doty and Glick 1994: 232). Two basic types of classification exist: typology and taxonomy (Smith 2002: 381). The essential trait of a typology is that "its dimensions represent concepts rather than empirical cases" (Smith 2002: 381). A taxonomy, in contrast, is developed on the basis of observation. Thus typology and taxonomy, respectively, are deductively and inductively derived. Implementation of both approaches in this chapter is consistent with the established practice of obtaining insights from both (i) inductive and sociological and (ii) deductive and rationalist modes of reasoning.

Type, as a concept, is descended from the Greek term *typos*. The word refers to a cast or model (Maradi 1990: 134). With a conceptual basis to its categories, a typology consists of "interrelated sets of ideal types" (Doty and Glick 1994: 232, 243; see also Smith 2002: 381). A typology therefore is a product of deductive reasoning. In a typology, classification along the set of dimensions takes place simultaneously. Order of consideration, in other words, is irrelevant (Maradi 1990: 143).

When a complete set of types is in place—mutually exclusive and exhaustive—a typology exists (Maradi 1990: 134, 143). "Within an ideal type," observe Doty and Glick (1994: 244), the configuration of constructs "is hypothesized to have a synergistic rather than an additive effect." Typologies therefore enable researchers to go beyond limitations from the current world of observation (Doty and Glick 1994: 245). Assessment of cause and effect is facilitated with a typology in place.

Challenges arise in terms of the composition of a typology in relation to its purpose. "As the number of descriptive dimensions is increased," observe Doty and Glick (1994: 245), "it becomes more difficult to ensure that only those dimensions that are causally related to the dependent variable are included in the typology." Thus the Performance Ratio, which assesses the explanations obtained from a theory in comparison to its founding assumptions, comes back to mind at this point. A typology should not be so complex in its composition that intelligibility becomes a problem and thus the Performance Ratio is affected adversely.[1]

Guidelines exist for creation of a typology that is optimal within given circumstances. First, at the time a typology is created, a theorist should introduce "grand theoretical assertion(s)" and present explicitly "assumptions about the theoretical importance of each construct used to describe the ideal types" (Doty and Glick 1994: 246, 247). Second, the resulting typology must define fully the set of ideal types (Doty and Glick 1994: 246). Required, therefore, is an exhaustive description that is based on the same dimensions (Doty and Glick 1994: 246). It almost goes without saying that, for practical purposes, the number of dimensions must be kept small. This is all the more true if the items to be classified are relatively limited in number.

Consider, as one possibility, a typology of superpower involvement as actors in international crises. Assume that a definition for a superpower is in place—something along the lines of a preeminent state within the international system. The rationale for the typology would be that the degree of superpower involvement in a crisis should help to explain any number of aspects, such as management and resolution, which are of both academic and policy-related interest. If "present" and "absent" as a crisis actor are taken to be basic categories, this creates a typology with 2^N categories, where "N" is the number of superpowers. To

---

[1] While this item is not directly in the denominator of the Performance Ratio, which contains the number of assumptions, it is taken to be a cognate indicator.

simplify matters, assume that the period of interest is the Cold War and that the US and USSR are the superpowers, so N = 2. Using the standard data provided by the ICB Project (Brecher et al. 2017), the superpower involvement variables for the United States and USSR combine to create four categories: both present, both absent, USSR present and United States absent, and United States present and USSR absent. Such a typology could be used to test any number of propositions. For example, is the type of superpower involvement associated with more pacific crisis management and outcomes or vice versa?

Taxonomies differ from typologies. A taxonomy is obtained from an inductive process. In a taxonomy, items are classified "on the basis of empirically observable and measurable characteristics" (Smith 2002: 381).[2] In addition, ordering matters; for a taxonomy, "*fundamenta* are considered in succession" (Maradi 1990: 143, 146). Consider, for example, a collection of blocks that vary by size (large, medium, and small), shape (sphere, cube, pyramid), and color (red, green, and blue). It is easy to see that the choice of size, shape, and color as first, second, or third among the criteria will make a difference in group composition. Supposed that color is first. Then green, red, and blue groups will appear, with membership further structured consecutively in terms of shape and size. Results are analogous for beginning with shape or size and following on with the other fundamental traits.

Within the context of IR, consider a taxonomy that focuses on branches of the military to organize the study of resource allocation or some other topic. One obvious dimension to consider would be area of operation. The categories might start with land and sea and then expand to include air and space. The US, with recent creation of a new branch of the military, would have this coding: land (army, Marine Corps), sea (Coast Guard, Marine Corps, navy), air (air force, navy), space (Space Force).[3] (Further traits would be required to eliminate the multiple appearances for the Marine Corps and Navy.) States with either lower capabilities or interests (or both) might have a more restricted number of entries. At the other extreme, consider Costa Rica, which depends entirely on the United States for national defense. Note also that technological change, such as air travel, can cause the number of categories and entrants to expand.

With an emphasis on applying both deductive and inductive reasoning in the process of identifying realism, both typologies and taxonomies are of interest. The approach parallels that of Chapter 8, which identified assumptions that

---

[2] The literature on taxonomies takes on any number of technical issues that are beyond the scope of application here. See, for example, Law, Wong, and Mobley (1998) on multidimensional constructs.

[3] Space Force is the most recent addition to the list, with precursors in other branches of the military that have included missions at Vandenberg Air Force Base and portable launch platforms for nuclear weapons.

combine to form the basis of a realist research enterprise. Thus realist theories of war, recognized through a taxonomy, are combined with categories corresponding to a typology that are intended to facilitate comparative analysis.

Both taxonomies and typologies possess value for an effort to create a template within which realism can be assessed more effectively and well beyond the scope of the present investigation. In line with the modus operandi throughout this volume, the approaches offer complementary insights. These are obtained from (a) deductive and rationalist logic, with regard to a typology; and (b) inductive and sociological thinking, in the case of a taxonomy. A few points should be kept in mind as respective efforts toward typology and taxonomy are reviewed. One is that these expositions have focused on power politics in general, not realist theories of war in particular. Thus any number of variants identified for realism will not warrant further consideration in this volume. Note also that the ensuing typologies and taxonomies emerge from a myriad of combinations with regard to axioms, explicit or otherwise. Thus a uniform set of categories for either taxonomies or typologies is not to be expected. Work remains to be done.

Typologies of Realism

Eight typologies have been located. Table 9.1 lists the typologies in chronological order. Each classifies realist theories based on cause and effect.[4] Columns include the point of origin for a typology, along with the types of realism it identifies. The dimensions used to classify realist theories, plus corresponding categories, appear in the table as well. Finally, the table notes whether the typology is complete or not with regard to status of application. A complete typology is one that places all theories into a category, while a partial one is able to do this in some, but not all, cases. The typologies are introduced in turn, followed by comparison between and among them. Several theories appear in preexisting typologies and taxonomies of realism but are not included from this point onward. Rather than identifying theories directly for further assessment, the purpose is to learn from what has been done already in terms of typology. In particular, it is deemed likely that very little in the way of consensus will emerge, which is informative in its own way.

Units of analysis and locus of causation provide the dimensions for the typology from Tellis (1996: 98). Classical realism in Morgenthau and Waltz's structural variant are used as counterpoints to each other in those terms. For

---

[4] Table 9.1 does not include the many passing references that are made to categories of realist theories. Only an explicit enumeration of types, with a deductively derived explanation, is included in the table. The same approach, but with an inductive foundation, underlies Table 9.2.

Table 9.1 Typologies of Realism

Origin of Typology	Types of Realism	Dimensions	Categories	Status of Application
Tellis (1996)[a]	Classical realism; structural realism	Locus of causation Units of analysis	States; state and system of states individual; state; system of states	Partial
Rose (1998)	Offensive realism; defensive realism; neoclassical realism[b]	Locus of causation Nature of security[c]	System of states; system primary, state and individual secondary; system balanced with state and individual scarce; plentiful	Complete
Van Evera (1999)	Classical realism; structural realism; fine-grained structural realism; misperceptive fine-grained structural realism	Locus of causation Prime goal of states Granularity of capabilities Perception-based	Human nature; anarchy power; security coarse; fine absent; present	Complete
Copeland (2000)	Classical realism; neorealism; hegemonic stability; dynamic differentials	Locus of causation Role of change	State; system of states static; dynamic	Complete
Donnelly (2000)[d]	Structural realism; biological realism; radical realism; strong realism; hedged realism	Emphasis on core propositions of egoism and anarchy Stringency of commitment to rigorous and exclusively realist analysis	Both; just one present; absent	Complete
Taliaferro (2000–2001)	Structural realism;[e] dynamic differentials; hegemonic stability; power transition;[f] balance of interests; offensive realism;[g] balance of threat; domestic mobilization; offense-defense; state-centered; war aims; hegemonic theory of foreign policy	Phenomena to be explained Assumptions about what anarchy induces	System patterns; foreign policy offensive; defensive	Complete
Tang (2008)[h]	Offensive; nonoffensive	Intention to do harm	offensive; nonoffensive	Partial

Table 9.1 Continued

Origin of Typology	Types of Realism	Dimensions	Categories	Status of Application
Elman and Jensen (2014)	Classical realism, balance of power theory; neorealism; defensive structural realism; offensive structural realism; rise and fall realism; and neoclassical realism.	Core assumptions Logic	Sources of state preference	Complete

[a] This typology is developed through comparison of Morgenthau (1948) with Waltz (1979).

[b] This cannot be identified and is classified as a null set.

[c] This dimension separates offensive from defensive realism.

[d] Some variants discussed go back to before 1945. Radical realists adopt extreme versions of anarchy, egoism and power politics, while strong realists accept the premises to the point of virtually excluding nonrealist concerns. "The arguments advanced by the Athenian envoys at Melos," observes Donnelly (2000: 23), "are so rigorously realist that they provide one of the few examples of a sustained, consistently radical realism." Strong realism is grounded in Chapter 13 from Hobbes, *Leviathan* (Donnelly 2000: 13–14).

[e] This is labeled as balance of power.

[f] Power transition theory, as per assessment in Chapter 8, is not included within realism.

[g] This is labeled as great power politics.

[h] Tang (2008: 466) offers a critique of Taliaferro (2000–2001), who had classified dynamic differentials as defensive realism. Tang instead sees Copeland (2000) as putting forward a variant of offensive realism. This is because the theory of dynamic differentials entails no possibility that states will remain benign "when they are capable of doing harm."

Morgenthau, the focus is on "both individuals and states with no generative mechanism linking the former to the latter." Egoistic states seeking power are "prime movers" in the classical realism of Morgenthau (Tellis 1996: 98). Things look different for Waltz, according to Tellis (1996: 100), with regard to units of analysis and locus of causation: the primary focus of structural realism is "on how the international political system constrains states." In terms of cause and effect, the state and system therefore "share the status of 'prime mover'" (Tellis 1996: 100; see also Bennett 2013: 463). Structural realism envisions an international system of anarchy and power balancing between and among states. Comparison of Waltz and Morgenthau in this way points in the direction of a full-fledged typology but does not complete it.

Several types of realism are identified by Rose (1998), with locus of causation and nature of security as the dimensions distinguishing one type from another. Rose (1998: 154) identifies defensive and offensive realism, plus neoclassical, as types of realism.

According to Rose (1998: 146), offensive realism (sometimes referred to as "aggressive" realism) essentially reverses the *Innenpolitik* logic and asserts that system-level factors are preeminent. Offensive realism crystallized as a theory of war with the exposition in Mearsheimer (2014 [2001]), which makes a system-level argument in favor of great power disposition toward conquest, but with a twist. Offensive realism brings to mind the classical vision because of its pessimism with regard to changing the commitment of great powers in particular to making gains relative to each other. Security is scarce, so states maximize power (Hamilton and Rathbun 2013: 441).

For defensive realism, by contrast, anarchy's implications are variable, units are highly differentiated, and either external or internal factors can produce foreign policy. Defensive realism, taking a softer line, argues that in practice factors from the system level "drive some kinds of state behavior but not others" (Rose 1998: 146). The base assumption for defensive realism, according to Zakaria (1992: 191), is that rational states expand only to seek security. The operation of the international system, according to defensive realism, ensures that a state can obtain security through "limited external interests, small armies, and carefully restrained foreign policies" (Zakaria 1992: 192). From the standpoint of defensive realists, the default position of the international system's structure is to discourage aggression (Leiber 2008: 192). Defensive realism "assumes that international anarchy is often more benign—that is, that security is often plentiful rather than scarce—and that normal states can understand this or learn it over time from experience" (Rose 1998: 149). A basic reason for belief in this relatively favorable situation is that states are expected to balance against aggressive powers (Walt 2002: 205).

Neoclassical realism offers a balance; it incorporates explicitly "both external and internal variables, updating and systematizing certain insights drawn from classical realist thought" (Rose 1998: 146). Rose (1998: 153) asks, "Why use the title 'neoclassical'?" and answers, "Unfortunately there *is* no simple, straightforward classical realism." Neoclassical realism sees anarchy as murky, with units as differentiated. Cause and effect for neoclassical realism may be summed up as follows: system-level incentives (independent variable) → internal factors (intervening variables) → foreign policy (dependent variable) (Rose 1998: 154). Thus Rose (1998) identifies three types of realism and continues to be recognized for designation of neoclassical realism as a departure from reigning approaches that emphasized structure.

Two schools of realism are designated by Van Evera (1999: 7): classical and neorealist (or structural) realism. According to Van Evera (1999: 7), these schools "differ on two main issues: (1) What causes conflict: human nature (Classical Realists) or the anarchic nature of the international system (Neorealists)? (2) What is the prime goal of states: power (Classical Realism) or security

(Neorealists)?" After further analysis, Van Evera (1999: 10–11) identifies four types of realism:

- I—(formerly Classical Realism), power seeking by states as a product of human nature;
- II—(formerly Neorealism or Structural Realism), A = Waltz on polarity and B = other realists who emphasize effects from other power structures (e.g., preponderance versus parity);
- III—(fine-grained Structural Realism), causes of war located in offense-defense balance, size of first-move advantages, size and frequency of power fluctuations, and cumulativity of resources;
- IV—(misperceptive fine-grained Structural Realism), national misperceptions of fine-grained indicators cause war.

Van Evera (1999) identifies four dimensions, with the idea of granularity as quite innovative in distinguishing one theory from another. Expressed as dichotomies, the dimensions are human nature and anarchy, power and security, coarse and fine-grained capabilities, and perception-based or not.

Based on the nature of cause and effect on the one hand and the role of change on the other, Copeland (2000) identifies several types of theory: classical realism, neorealism, hegemonic stability, and dynamic differentials. Classical realism, observes Copeland (2000: 110), asserts that major war becomes "likely when one state is preponderant and unlikely when great powers are relatively equal." The causal mechanism for war is at the unit level, as per arguments from Morgenthau: "The preponderant state initiates war for unit-level reasons—for greed, glory, or . . . its 'lust for power' manifested in 'nationalistic universalism'" (Copeland 2000: 11). Implications for the system level are straightforward from a classical realist point of view; superior states become more likely to attack, so multipolarity is expected to be more stable than bipolarity (Copeland 2000: 11). For neorealism, cause and effect operates in the opposite way—bipolarity is more stable than multipolarity—for three main reasons: "In bipolarity, great powers avoid being chain-ganged into major war by crises over small powers; they also stand firm, however, to prevent losses on the periphery, thus enhancing deterrence; and finally, the great powers are less inclined to neglect internal military spending that might allow a superior military power to arise" (Copeland 2000: 120).

According to Copeland (2000: 13), another realist perspective on major power war, hegemonic stability theory, can be traced to Gilpin and Organski: "Major war is the result of a growing equality of power between the two most powerful states in any system." Hegemonic stability theorists "argue that although equality between individual great powers may not be associated with major war, relative equality between their *alliance blocs* is" (Copeland 2000: 14). Finally, Copeland (2000: 15) introduces dynamic differentials theory as an account for major war: "The core causal or independent variable of the argument is the dynamic differential: the simultaneous interaction of the differentials of relative military power between great powers and the expected trend of those differentials; distinguishing between the effects of power changes in bipolarity versus multipolarity." Note that within this typology, the role of change is an innovation; previous systems of classification had taken a static approach when identifying dimensions.

Two dimensions combine to form the typology of realists from Donnelly (2000: 11): "the relative emphasis they give to the core propositions of egoism and anarchy and the stringency of their commitment to a rigorous and exclusively realist analysis." Several types emerge as a result (Donnelly 2000: 11–12):

- Structural realists emphasize international anarchy.
- Biological realists stress the importance of a fixed human nature.
- Radical realists adopt extreme versions of anarchy, egoism, and power politics.
- Strong realists accept the premises to the point of virtually excluding nonrealist concerns.
- Hedged realists accept anarchy and egoism as defining the problem to be studied, but show "varying degrees of discomfort" with power politics as a solution.

Structural realism would correspond to Waltz (1979)—a quite holistic sense of things. Anarchy is given pride of place in explaining how the international system works. Biological realists would include those from the classical era, such as Morgenthau (Donnelly 2000: 47), but perhaps also a new generation that might arise in response to findings from neuroscience. Radical realists exist at an extreme point along the dimensions of egoism and anarchy—pure power politics. Not surprisingly, hedged realism merges gradually into views that fundamentally represent something else (Donnelly 2000: 13). This type, in all likelihood, is at the foundation of the intense critique put forward by Legro and Moravcsik (1999), which questioned whether anyone still truly espoused realism.

Taliaferro (2000–2001: 132, 135) identifies "crosscutting divisions within contemporary realism" that result from combining the dimensions of (1) phenomena to be explained and (2) assumptions about anarchy. The divisions consist of offensive versus defensive realism on the one hand and neorealism versus neoclassical realism on the other: "neorealism seeks to explain international outcomes, such as the likelihood of major war, the prospects for international cooperation, and aggregate alliance patterns among states. Neoclassical realism, on the other hand, seeks to explain the foreign policy strategy of individual states"

(Taliaferro 2000–2001: 132). Neorealism is unable to anticipate foreign policy among states, while neoclassical realism attempts to explain "why different states or even the same state at different times pursues particular strategies in the international arena" (Taliaferro 2000–2001: 133).[5]

For Tang (2008), the most enlightening point of division is offensive versus nonoffensive realist theories. Nonoffensive realist theories can be summarized through the following equation (Tang 2008: 454):

Probability that a state poses a threat to you = Function of (state's offensive capabilities x resolve to do harm x intention to do harm).

For offensive realism, intention to do harm simply takes a value of "1," so the probability of threat always exists. Realist theories aside from the offensive variant would allow for the possibility of intention taking a value of zero.

Finally, Elman and Jensen (2014: 2) offer a "mid-level typology" that averts the "one-size-fits-all generalities" among critics of realism. Seven research approaches are identified. The variants of realism "largely share the view that the character of relations among states has not altered" and that any change that does occur is anticipated to follow "repetitive patterns" (Elman and Jensen 2014: 2). In Elman and Jensen's typology, fundamental constitutive and heuristic assumptions shared by respective realist theories differentiate groupings. One example is sources for state preferences, notably the mixture of a human quest for power and/or the need to obtain security in a world of self-help.

Quite a few dimensions are implemented among the typologies—11 are mentioned at least once. This is an expected consequence of the many candidate axioms for realism across the studies surveyed in Table 8.2. Some of these dimensions are likely to prove more useful than others for the purpose of classifying realist theories about war in order to compare and assess cause and effect. A scheme of organization is needed to evaluate the potential value of so many options. A natural approach is to combine the dimensions under more general headings to reduce their number and then connect these collectivities with the already identified axiomatic basis of realism: (a) at the macro level, anarchy and state-centrism and (b) at the micro level, rationality and power seeking.

Two groupings are relevant to anarchy and state-centrism, the macro-level axioms: (1) locus of causation and (2) units of analysis. Locus of causation appears

---

[5] Theories corresponding to respective profiles are enumerated by Taliaferro (2000–2001) with sample authors: (1) neorealism x defensive: balance of power (Waltz); dynamic differentials (Copeland); (2) neorealism x offensive: hegemonic theory of war (Gilpin); power transition (Organski and Kugler); balance of interests (Schweller); great power politics (Mearsheimer); (3) neoclassical x defensive: balance of threat (Walt); domestic mobilization (Christensen); offense-defense (Van Evera); and (4) neoclassical x offensive: state-centered realism (Zakaria); theory of war aims (Labs); hegemonic theory of foreign policy (Wohlforth).

in four typologies. Two other dimensions—(i) emphasis on core propositions of system and anarchy and (ii) assumptions about what anarchy includes—are deemed appropriate to be relabeled under locus of causation as a more general heading. Units of analysis subsume "phenomena to be explained" in terms of foreign policy versus system patterns.

For the micro-level assumptions, rationality and power seeking, three dimensions are identified: (1) state goals, (2) nature of capabilities, and (3) static or dynamic specification. State goals serve as an umbrella that covers prime goals of states, intention to do harm, core assumptions (sources of state preference), and nature of security.[6]

Taxonomies of Realism

Table 9.2 displays four taxonomies of realism in chronological order. The origin of each taxonomy, along with the varieties of realism it identifies and their characteristics, is listed.[7] Note that like typologies, taxonomies of realism began to emerge in the 1990s. This in all likelihood is a byproduct of the debate involving neorealism versus neoliberalism, with at least some of the arguments being about how to identify schools of thought.[8] Snyder (2002: 149–150) provides a list of theories as well, but this enumeration is excluded because there is no detail provided for classification. The lists in the table include varieties of structural realism (Waltz and the English school), three kinds of offensive realism, several types of defensive realism, plus neoclassical, contingent (associated with Glaser), and specific and generalist (identified by Rosecrance). Note also that the English school, which emphasizes the role of an international society in moderating power politics, is included here.

Offered by Wohlforth (1993: 11), a compelling description of diverse theorizing under the umbrella of realism serves as an effective point of departure for a review of taxonomies:

> Numerous incompatible formulations and propositions coexist under the "realist" rubric. Many differences are methodological or epistemological: classical versus neorealist, quantitative versus rational-choice realist, and so on.

---

[6] Two dimensions on the list lie outside of the agenda for this volume. One is use of logic and the other is stringency of commitment to rigorous and exclusively realist analysis.

[7] Status of application always is complete at any given time for a taxonomy. Whether additional categories will emerge is a function of multiple factors. For instance, change in technology could expand a taxonomy of weapons through invention of new ones.

[8] The point of culmination for this debate usually is identified with Baldwin (1993).

Table 9.2 Taxonomies of Realism

Origin of Taxonomy	Varieties of Realism	Characteristics
Schweller and Priess (1997)	traditional realism; structural realism[a]	Borrowing from sociology and history; borrowing from microeconomics Power as an end in and of itself; security as highest end Power and interests of states drive behavior; anarchy and distribution of capabilities as paramount Capabilities of specific states or coalitions; system wide distribution of capabilities or polarity of system Theory of foreign policy; theory of international politics Inclusion of processes in defining system; inclusion of only structure
Wohlforth (2008)	defensive realism; offensive realism; neoclassical realism[b]	Difficulty of conquest is relevant under anarchy; anarchy is conflict-generating in and of itself Focus on general (system patterns) versus particular (foreign policy)
Brown (2012)	offensive realism; defensive realism; neoclassical realism	Focus on international system; focus on international system and foreign policy
Quinn (2013)	Structural realism; neoclassical realism	System as supreme; unit-level proliferation

[a] This is referred to as "neorealism" in Schweller and Priess (1997).

[b] Wohlforth (2008) also refers to subschools and theories, which consist of security dilemma, offense-defense, hegemonic stability and power transition.

Many disputes concern interests; whether states seek security, for example, or also seek power for its own sake, for glory, or for control over the states system. And some differences are more apparent than real, reflecting the ubiquitous scholarly tendency to use the same terms to discuss different things or different terms to discuss the same things.

Summarized by an exponent of realism, these features make it challenging to describe this school of thought in an intelligible way. It is especially notable, in light of prior references in this volume to rising incoherence in realism, that terminology is identified as a significant aggravating factor. This observation further reinforces the position in favor of a graphic turn for communication about realism.

First among the entries in Table 9.2, Schweller and Priess (1997: 6, 7) identify six major differences that separate traditional realists and neorealists and see this as the "major division":[9]

- Traditional realism reflects sociology and history, while neorealism borrows primarily from microeconomics.
- Traditional realists view power as an end in itself, while neorealists believe security is the highest end.
- Traditional realism sees power and interests of states as driving behavior, while neorealists focus on only anarchy and the distribution of capabilities.
- Traditional realism focuses on capabilities of specific states or coalitions; neorealism concentrates on systemwide distribution of capabilities or polarity of system.
- Traditional realism is a theory of foreign policy, while neorealism is a theory of international politics.
- Traditional realism includes processes in defining a system, while neorealism incorporates only structure.

Intellectual identity is the most fundamental characteristic that differs for the traditional and neorealist schools. Aspects of cause and effect, such as goals valued by states and explanation for how these are pursued, also exhibit variation. In addition, a different research agenda is entailed within neoclassical and neorealist varieties.

Realist research, from the standpoint of Wohlforth (2008: 136), always has been highly diverse. Three theoretical subschools coexist. For the defensive variant, as conquest becomes more difficult, all states can be more secure (Wohlforth 2008: 139). Offensive realists, by contrast, are "more persuaded by the conflict-generating, structural potential of anarchy itself" (Wohlforth 2008: 139). Given such uncertainty, Wohlforth (2008: 139) observes, states rarely can be confident about security and always must be suspicious of increases in power for other states. Finally, neoclassical realism tries to rectify the imbalance between the general and particular (Wohlforth 2008: 140). This takes the form of a return to classical realism's focus on foreign policy.

Even the preceding theoretical subschools, however, are not sufficient to capture the full diversity of realism (Wohlforth 2008: 141, 143). Several *theories* also can be identified. Perhaps the best known among theoretical propositions about international relations, according to Wohlforth (2008: 141), "is *balance-of-power theory*." Another option, balance-of-threat theory, anticipates that states

---

[9] Schweller (2003a: 330) elaborates on some of the characteristics that follow.

will try to balance against threats (Wohlforth 2008: 141). The list in Wohlforth (2008: 142) also includes security-dilemma theory, offense-defense theory, hegemonic stability theory, and power transition theory.

Offensive, defensive, and neoclassical realism are the available options according to the taxonomy in Brown (2012). Offensive realism sees states as certain to attempt maximization of relative power and thereby create strife "even though such conflict is unwanted—this is the 'tragedy of Great Power politics' to which the title of his [Mearsheimer's] most influential book refers" (Brown 2012: 860). Defensive realism, by contrast, adopts the position that "circumstances may favour a defensive stance towards other powers" (Brown 2012: 860). Finally, neoclassical realists "accept the broad contours of the anarchy problematic but believe that foreign policy considerations cannot be disregarded, because some states may not simply seek security"; this, in effect reintroduces the long-standing realist notion of differentiation "between 'status quo' and 'revisionist' powers, hence the 'neo-classical' tag" (Brown 2012: 860–861).

Finally, Quinn's (2013: 160) taxonomy identifies neoclassical and structural realism as options.[10] Neoclassical realism has emerged as a "thriving theoretical sub-field in the United States" (Quinn 2013: 163). Under the neoclassical worldview, the distribution of material resources remains the primary causal driver, but variables identified at the unit (that is, state) level mediate its translation into foreign policy (Quinn 2013: 163). Structural realism is epitomized by Waltz (1979), "the first, and arguably still the purest, advocate of the supremacy of the system" (Quinn 2013: 165). "If we return to the original source material of Waltz's structural theory," Quinn (2013: 177) asserts, "it is apparent that he viewed his contribution as a reaction against precisely the sort of unit-level proliferation and fine-grained historical case-study in which NCR [neoclassical realism] finds both its *raison d' être* and much of its *joie de vivre*."

Eight characteristics appear at least once in Table 9.2. Only one of these traits is listed in more than one taxonomy—a focus on the international system versus foreign policy. This characteristic, which appears three times, is not enough to point toward more of a consensus for taxonomies than among typologies. Leaving aside for now the question of how each realist theory might be defined, five appear at least once in the table: traditional, structural, defensive, offensive, and neoclassical.

---

[10] References to contemporary realism include two basic categories: structural (also commonly referred to as neorealism) and neoclassical (Elman 2003: 5; Wivel 2005: 356; Brawley 2009: 1, 2).

A System of Classification for Realism

Looking forward to a system of classification, what can we say when reflecting upon typologies and taxonomies developed so far? While some dimensions are noted multiple times across typologies, none is pervasive. The same can be said of characteristics among the taxonomies. The resulting overall verdict regarding typologies and taxonomies is the same: divergence rather than convergence is the norm. Suboptimal from a scientific point of view, this outcome is not a reflection on the academic quality of the individual efforts toward classification of realism. Given the lack of consensus on axioms for realism—a basic conclusion from the multifaceted review carried out in Chapter 8—lack of agreement on either dimensions or characteristics virtually had to ensue.

What, then, should be done about classification? With regard to a typology, intuition favors an emphasis on the most basic dimensions: time and space. Each of these can be operationalized in a way that is in line with the assumptions of realism as a research enterprise. These axioms, derived at length in Chapter 8, are anarchy, state-centrism, rationality, and pursuit of power. Compliance with that set of assumptions reduces the set of realist theories about the causes of war to eight. This is quite good for purposes of comparison, but the current relatively limited number rules out a typology with many dimensions.

Two dimensions, deemed most fundamental, are used to classify the realist theories of war. With respect to time, the point of division is whether the theory's account focuses on statics or dynamics. Do its key variables focus on the situation as it exists at a given time (i.e., static) or how it is changing (i.e., dynamic)? For realist theories, this question is answered with whether *capability-based* variables are assessed in static or dynamic terms. Polarity is an example of a static indicator, while a focus on change in the distribution of capabilities qualifies as dynamic. The spatial dimension is about system versus state as a point of emphasis in constructing explanations. Figure 9.1 uses these dimensions to produce a genealogy for realist theories of war.[11] Time and space, the stages of identification, are irrelevant in terms of ordering. This is a property of all typologies.

---

[11] It is beyond the scope of this study to offer detailed reasons for exclusion of some theories categorized as realist in respective typologies and taxonomies. The examples, covered briefly, are (a) Niou, Ordeshook, and Rose (1989); and (b) G. Snyder (1991) and Zakaria (1998). For a further discussion of liminal theories regarding realism, see Freyberg-Inan (2006: 263).

While consistent with realism in other ways, the system-level theory in Niou, Ordeshook, and Rose (1989) includes a key component that is directly at odds with realism. As pointed out in G. Snyder (1991: 135), a state under certain circumstances is expected to transfer, voluntarily, resources to another state that threatens it, with the goal being to put the latter on the brink of preponderance. This directly contradicts the assumption of power seeking.

State-centered realism is excluded because Zakaria (1998: 35–41) focuses exclusively on the United States and overwhelmingly on the topic of how its foreign policy activities expanded from the 19th into the 20th centuries. The theory's distance from the axiom of power seeking places it more

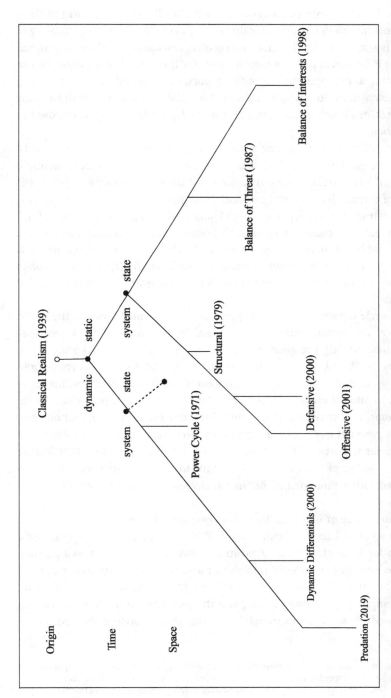

Figure 9.1 Genealogy for Realist Theories of War

Classical realism is the point of origin for the family tree, with Carr (1939) as the exemplar for modern classical realism—not an oxymoron because this way of thinking is ancient as well. The node for classical realism is a blank circle to signal that there is no direct point of continuation for this school of thought. Rather than existing as one rigorously specified theory, classical realism incorporates a range of expositions that largely antedate the social scientific turn with IR. Thus classical realism is valued more in terms of the logic of *discovery* as opposed to *confirmation*.

With a range in age from half a century to just a few years in existence, 14 realist theories seek to explain war. Four of the theories feature multiple versions: (i) structural realism—structural realism and hegemonic stability; (ii) balance of threat—balance of threat and revolution; (iii) balance of interests—additive, extremely incoherent states, and polarized democratic models; and (iv) defensive realism—stability, windows, and offense-defense models. Each theory is introduced briefly in chronological order. The choice for date of appearance is linked to publication of a magnum opus—a book-length exposition. Theories about both war in general and those that focus on the great powers in particular are included.

Power cycle theory is the first to appear in the dynamic branch of the realist family tree. This system-oriented theory focuses on dynamics of relative capability, notably among the great powers (Doran 1971). Power cycles are set in motion by absolute growth rate differentials across states in the system (Doran 2012: 76; see also Doran 1971). The likelihood of major war among leading states is related to "abrupt changes in power and projected foreign policy role *at the critical points on the relative power curve*" (Doran 1989a: 375). Rapid onset of change in power at a critical point on the cycle causes adjustment problems for a great power with regard to its foreign policy role (Doran 1989a: 377). Rather than continuation of a linear trend, leadership in proximity to a critical point is confronted with a fundamental shift in velocity with regard to the distribution of capabilities.

Structural realism is the initial system-oriented theory in the static branch of Figure 9.1. It is launched with Waltz (1979), which argued strongly in favor of system-level theorizing. This exposition stands, as least in part, as a polemic against reductionist theories of one sort or another that opposed an emphasis on the international system. Waltz (1979) rejected summarily classical realism, with its emphasis on human nature and the unit level, in favor of theorizing that focused on aggregate patterns. This neorealism therefore focused on the

---

properly within another research enterprise. Zakaria's theorizing also pertains to state expansion per se and would not be adapted easily to present purposes, which focus more directly on conflict escalation to war. The same can be said for the three theories of overexpansion in Snyder (1991).

distribution of capabilities among great powers and its implications, collectively representing structure, for properties of the level of the international system. Another prominent structural realist theory emerged soon after (Gilpin 1981), with a focus on stability in the system achieved through quasi-hegemonic leadership under conditions of anarchy.[12]

Balance-of-threat theory, a static and state-oriented entity, came into being with Walt (1987). The story gets underway with an external threat to a state, which is magnified with greater proximity and capabilities. The target state can be expected to form an alliance against its potential adversary in war. For subsequent cause and effect, much depends on whether the target is regarded as essentially weak or strong. War remains a possible outcome, but further iterations can be expected for a strong state when faced with a threat. An alliance formed by a weak state can be anticipated to disintegrate and lead to bandwagoning with the threatening state. By contrast, a strong state is in a better position to pursue balancing. While further iterations can be expected, interstate war is the ultimate outcome (Walt 1987).

For balance of interests, an additional state-focused and static theory, the story begins with a state that is unitary and motivated to expand (Schweller 1998). A state identified as the defender then perceives an external threat. This is expected to impact the defender—perhaps leading to fragmentation that weakens the ability to stand up to the threat. A lack of resolve may produce underbalancing by the defender and thereby increase the likelihood of interstate war (Schweller 1998).

Defensive realism is a static and system-focused theory of war put forward in Van Evera (1999).[13] The theory focuses on communication between and among adversaries, most notably from the standpoint of strategic interaction. The starting point is first-mover advantage at the level of the international system, which can set in motion a number of pernicious pathways toward war. The danger of either an opportunistic or preemptive first strike is high under such conditions. Perceptions among leaders, which easily can include fear and overreaction to accidents, along with hasty and unproductive efforts toward diplomacy, make the situation even more difficult. Interstate war becomes a very likely result (Van Evera 2000).

Dynamic differentials, as its name suggests, is a kinetic and also system-oriented theory of war. This theory focuses on pathways toward outbreak of major war (Copeland 2000). The basic danger to system stability is the existence

---

[12] Structural realism is the only theory in which one of the set is different from the initial version in terms of authorship, so both Waltz (1979) and Gilpin (1981) are mentioned here.

[13] Note that defensive realism is identified as a variety of theorizing well before Van Evera (1999). This study, however, is given pride of place because it contains the first fully specified defensive realist theory in a book-length exposition on *war*.

of a state with aggressive motives and a declining share of capabilities. The road to war is quite complex, so only a few aspects of the theory are highlighted here. With regard to military technology, intuition supports the idea that dominance of the offense creates greater danger of mobilization. In addition, with preeminence for offense, overcommitment of reputation can be expected, which in turn reinforces unhelpful tendencies toward confrontation. The ultimate result is major power war (Copeland 2000).

Offensive realism is a system-oriented and static account of war. Induced by anarchy, security competition begins the story of cause and effect for the theory of offensive realism (Mearsheimer 2014 [2001]). Most dangerous among the possible structural conditions is unbalanced multipolarity, which contains the most potential conflict dyads. Subsequent fear and miscalculation can lead to war involving minor powers. This strife, in turn, increases the likelihood of major power war. Escalation may take place within a given region and even beyond. One factor from the international system—the stopping power of water—is expected to play a mitigating role with regard to war among great powers. Although not in all scenarios, at least some of the time the profile of capabilities will limit pursuit of conquest to within a given region rather than beyond its boundaries (Mearsheimer 2000).

Finally, predation is a system-oriented and dynamic realist theory. Predation focuses on change in relative capabilities—notably significant decline for one of the great powers—as a menace to system stability (Shifrinson 2019a). Rather than ordinal rankings, Shifrinson (2019a: 14) argues that insecurity is driven by expansion of a power gap. Rising great powers observe such changes and can react in various ways to peers in relative decline. How this process is managed—perhaps akin to handling dynamite—will be essential to management of attendant conflict on the one hand or escalation of war on the other hand (Shifrinson 2019a).

With a basic introduction to each realist theory of war in place, a few traits of the genealogy are worth noting. At least so far, no realist theory is both dynamic and state oriented—hence the broken line in the figure. This long-standing gap undoubtedly reflects the sharp turn away from classical realism, which had been state-centered and identified with the descriptive study of foreign policy as opposed to analysis that would encompass dynamics of the international system. From the standpoint of systemism, this constitutes a shortcoming for the corpus of realist theories in the era of social scientifically motivated efforts toward explanation.

Note also the gap along the pathway that contains theories that are both dynamic and system oriented. Power cycle theory, first put forward in Doran (1971), existed alone in its class for about a decade. Dynamic differentials (Copeland 2000) and predation (Shifrinson 2019a) came along later.

Along the other branch of the figure are theories of war that focus on statics, with either a system or state orientation. Waltz (1979) developed structural realism, which arguably occupied the dominant position among realist theories for approximately two decades. Later theories that focus on the statics of the system are defensive realism (Van Evera 1999) and offensive realism (Mearsheimer 2000). Finally, the static and state-oriented branch gets underway with balance of threat (Walt 1987), followed on by balance of interests (1998). These two theories, which focus on national traits, reveal the influence of neoclassical thinking in response to the holistic mindset of structural realism and hegemonic stability.

Perhaps the most noteworthy overall traits of the figure concern the limited number of theories that appear, along with the relatively long gaps that exist along the branches. A total of 14 theories—as noted already, counting variants within the basic designations (e.g., balance of threat includes two variants)—does not sound like many, but given the restrictions imposed through the process of identification for realism in Chapter 8, those present are diverse and interesting. The 14 theories possess the potential to play either complementary or competing roles, once more thoroughly laid out in Chapters 11-18. In addition, just one realist theory appears in the last two decades, and that is within the dynamic and system-oriented profile.

Table 9.3 displays the realist theories of war. The columns correspond to dimensions, identified by the typology, and characteristics, designated within the taxonomy. As in the case of the typology, the taxonomy does not emerge out of a consensus. Thus it makes sense in this context, as well, to look at the axioms of realism for ideas about classification.

One dimension focuses on the system—anarchy and state-centrism—or causes at the aggregate level. The other dimension pertains to states—rational and power seeking—or causes at the unit level. Thus the typology identifies four possible profiles—dynamic and system oriented, static and system oriented, static and state oriented, and dynamic and state oriented—with the first three of these in existence.

With 14 theories to put in categories (i.e., counting multiple variations for some), one characteristic is salient for creation of a theory: key variables related to pursuit of power. These metrics can be taken at either the system or state level and are covered at length as respective theories are introduced in Chapters 11-18. Among the set of key variables, those for three theories—power cycles, dynamic differentials, and predation—refer to shifts in the distribution of capabilities at the system level. The first among those theories identifies points of rapid change in dispersion among great powers, while the latter two theories focus specifically on how great power decline impacts system dynamics. Among the static and system-focused theories, structural realism and offensive realism zero in on aspects of polarity, while defensive realism concentrates on perceived

Table 9.3 Classifying Realist Theories of War

Theory	Typology Based on Dimensions in Time and Space	Taxonomy Based on Content of Key Variable(s) Related to Seeking Power
Power cycle	Dynamic and system	Proximity to critical point(s) of great powers
Structural realism (structural realism and hegemonic stability theory)	Static and system	Polarity, i.e., number of great powers in the international system
Balance of threat (balance of threat and revolution)	Static and state	Magnitude of external threat perceived by a state
Balance of interests (additive, extremely incoherent states, and polarized democratic)	Static and state	Degree of internal cohesion for a defender faced with an external threat
Dynamic Differentials	Dynamic and system	Aggressive state with declining capabilities
Defensive realism (stability, windows, offense-defense)	Static and system	Danger of first strike based on perceived geostrategic conditions consisting of first-mover advantage, offense dominance and impending shifts in power
Offensive realism	Static and system	Unbalanced multipolarity
Predation	Dynamic and system	Significant decline for a great power

geostrategic conditions. Note that defensive realism is the only system-oriented theory to incorporate perceptions directly in its key variables.[14] For the two state-focused theories, the key variable in each instance is the magnitude of a perceived threat and internal coherence, respectively.

More will be said about the power-based metrics when the theories are discussed collectively in Chapter 19. For now, it is enough to say that the typology and taxonomy derived in this chapter are sufficient to classify realist theories about war—both those that exist now and others that may come into being in the future.

---

[14] It might be argued that defensive realism really is about dynamics, since it refers to impending shifts in power. However, this is about perception, rather than a realized event, which contrasts with theories such as predation that focus on observed shifts in capabilities.

Summing Up

Realism today incorporates a vast range of ideas. To proceed effectively with a social scientific reassessment of realist theories about war, classification becomes a priority. In line with the metatheory of progress, both (i) deductive and rationalist and (ii) inductive and sociological criteria are brought to bear on developing a scheme of organization. Prior efforts toward typology and taxonomy are reviewed, and consensus turns out to be lacking in each instance. This is a natural product of proliferating ideas about realism as a school of thought in the prior absence of an agreed-upon set of axioms.

With four assumptions now in place—anarchy, state-centrism, rationality, and pursuit of power—a logically consistent foundation exists for classification of realist theories about war. A total of 14 theories, with some representing multiple variations (e.g., structural realism and hegemonic stability), are found to comply with the preceding four axioms. A typology with two dimensions, space and time, produces four categories: system and dynamic, system and static, state and dynamic, and state and static. A taxonomy also is developed, with the capability-related variable(s) from the theories being used to create categories.

Chapter 10 will review classical realist theories about war, placed into systemist graphics, to identify the foundation of what subsequently can be identified as a research enterprise. This work sets the stage for Chapters 11–18 in Part IV, where realist theories about war are converted to systemist visualizations in order to promote dialogue and scientific progress. Classification will pay further dividends in Part V, when Chapters 19 and 20 will carry out comparative analysis of various kinds for the realist theories.

10
Classical Realism

Overview

Classical realism is an outlook on international politics that originated in ancient times. Its foundations are in philosophical tracts from around the world that date back to antiquity. Classical realism is associated most closely with a view of human nature as immanent and disposed toward conflict. Power politics, as a result, can be expected to persist even as knowledge advances. Given the vastness of classical realism, this chapter will focus on the modern era. Realism became resurgent after World War II, and analysis covers that modern classical period, which includes a sufficient number and range of expositions to give a compelling sense of this school of thought.

Classical realism, in and of itself, is not a theory about war. The term instead refers to a loosely associated school of thought that emerged in the early years of the Cold War (Freyberg-Inan 2004: 67). Its principal exponents, who reflected on the human condition in the years following World War II, did so with the belief that violent conflict would be likely to recur. Leading realists, most notably in the United States, conveyed "a discourse of restraint and responsibility, skeptical of adventurism, formed under the shadow of potential nuclear war" (Bew 2016: 190). Classical realism therefore centered on the interests and capabilities of the great powers (Schweller 1998: 15).

Classical realism's view of the world reflected a conclusion about the immutability of human nature—doomed to war because of a relentless quest for power. At the same time, classical realists believed that states could make the best of this bad situation through pragmatic policies. Thus classical realism emerges not as a social scientific framework of explanation, but instead as a way of thinking that is philosophical and policy oriented. Its exponents, with practitioners included among them, searched for ways to manage foreign policy to best advantage in a world where states are in danger and on their own in dealing with it.

Recall Figure 9.1, which placed classical realism at the point of origin for subsequent realist theories about the causes of war. The purpose of this chapter is to assess classical realism in that context to obtain a sense of its foundation for realist theories that developed subsequently.[1] Thus the chapter is more about the

---

[1] In an intense critique of structural realism in particular, Ashley (1984: 275) calls for a review of classical realism "as part of the explanation within a theory of modern international political

logic of discovery than about confirmation: What are realist ideas about war? Can propositions be identified about how events escalate to war? These questions are posed and answered for the body of work identified with classical realism in the modern era.

Work in this chapter unfolds in seven additional sections. The second section begins with an inductive and sociological approach to identifying classical realism as a school of thought. In line with a deductive and rationalist perspective, assumptions of classical realism also are enumerated. The third section conveys classical realist ideas about war. This is carried out most appropriately on the basis of major texts that reflect on the character of world politics. The fourth section covers critiques of classical realism and responses that are deemed relevant to a process of updating its contents to permit visualization in terms of cause and effect. The fifth section places classical realist theorizing about the causes of interstate war into figures based on systemism. Sixth, the collective character and overall contribution of the classical realist theories are assessed. The seventh section outlines the approach to be used in Part IV for presenting theories that have descended from modern classical realism. The eighth and final section sums up the accomplishments of this chapter, which focuses on the initial variants of realism in the post–World War II era as a foundation for work that continues to this day.

What Is Classical Realism?

Classical realism is introduced most easily as a philosophical position that emphasizes the pervasiveness and durability of conflict. The basic reason for this outlook is belief that human nature creates a quest for dominance in the international sphere (Scheuerman 2007: 525). With ideas from Thucydides as the point of departure, Smith (1986) provides an effective summary of classical realist thought from time immemorial up to the modern world. In *The Peloponnesian War*, an epic history of rivalry involving coalitions led by the city-states of Athens and Sparta, Thucydides (1972 [431 BCE]) provided the basis for realism today in three ways. First, he focused on the structure of the international system and the observation that states "define their interests in terms of power and fear for their security" no matter what their type. Second, a reading of Thucydides reveals his suspicion of moralizing. Third, and finally, Thucydides rejected ideas about a benign or perfectible human nature (Smith 1986: 9–10). As a historian, Thucydides stayed away from "explicit generalizations" and "propositions" that would be

practice." This recommendation, from a viewpoint that is reflexive, also supports the review of classical realism, even if not in the form this chapter will pursue.

identified in the context of today's social science (Hoffmann 1977: 41). All of the preceding traits from Thucydides are front and center in classical realism during the period following World War II.

Among others, Machiavelli and Hobbes are additional and essential antecedents to classical realism as it developed from 1945 onward. For Machiavelli, a memorable thinker from Renaissance Italy, "The state must take precedence," and thus interstate conflict is expected to be intense and even agonistic (Smith 1986: 12). In *The Prince*, Machiavelli (2003 [1502]) created a guidebook for leadership firmly grounded in realism and influenced by the complexities of ensuring security for his home city of Florence. Realist readings of *The Prince*, into the modern era, took inspiration from its emphasis on pursuit of power through whatever means necessary. Against the backdrop of the highly destructive English Civil War, Hobbes produced *Leviathan*, a work "less concerned with states *per se* than with individuals, for whom life in the state of nature is, in his unforgettable phrase, 'solitary, poor, nasty, brutish, and short'" (Smith 1986: 13). Modern realists adopt, in various ways, two essential ideas from Hobbes: (a) description of the international state of nature as one of war; and (b) radical skepticism about moral behavior under such conditions (Smith 1986: 14).

Although others certainly could be mentioned, Thucydides, Machiavelli, and Hobbes are sufficient to give a sense of thinking among precursors to modern realism (Freyberg-Inan 2004). After World War I, what are now recognized collectively as modern classical realists built upon the ideas from centuries past in opposition to what they viewed as liberal idealism. The vision in Angell (1911), which emphasized economic interdependence in prevention of war, serves as an antithesis to the classical realist view. Classical realists saw this conclusion as fundamentally out of touch with the awful ensuing realities of World War I. After World War II, the classical realists became more explicitly recognized as a school of thought that claimed to be *realistic*, as opposed to idealistic, and therefore relevant to policy. Realists saw the almost immediate slide into the Cold War as confirmation that confrontation would continue in the international system and not be overturned by collective reason (Kahler 1998: 920).

Table 10.1 contains a set of reflections about classical realism that converge toward a gestalt sense of its identity as a school of thought about international politics.[2] Classical realism, at least to some degree, possesses an inductive character; it is an attempt to create a general sense of world politics on the basis of European history and especially its experience of recurrent warfare. The classical variant of realism focuses on the quest for power, which is regarded as a constant feature of

---

[2] Table 10.1 does not include material from the classical realists featured in this book. The table thereby represents a wider range of views about classical realism in an overall sense.

Table 10.1 Classical Realism at a Glance

Source	Summary Statement
Guzzini (1998: 11)	Realism is understood here as the attempt to translate the rules of the diplomatic practice in the 19th century into scientific rules of social science that developed mainly in the United States.
Walt (1998: 31)	According to classical realists, states, like human beings, had an innate desire to dominate others, which led them to fight wars.
Van Evera (1999: 7)	The focus of classical realism is on the quest for power.
Rothstein (2005: 409)	Realism involved commitment to a set of propositions about international politics which were essentially extrapolations from the diplomatic history of 19th-century Europe.
Taliaferro (2009b: 205)	"For classical realists, the balance of power is a system or pattern of relations created consciously and maintained by the great powers.... Rules for balance of power systems include fluidity of alliances, respect for other great powers' vital areas of interest, postwar settlements that do not eliminate the defeated great power, and territorial compensation."
Kirshner (2010: 69)	A classical realist would have preferred to live in a world where Weimar thrived, and was reintegrated into the international economy, and, however a bitter pill this might be to swallow, to re-emerge with some respect of its power and interests.
Brown (2012: 858)	The older generation of realists addressed their arguments to foreign policy practitioners, and to what they hoped to turn into an informed public opinion.
Elman and Jensen (2014: 3)	Since the desire for more power is rooted in the flawed nature of humanity, states are continuously engaged in a struggle to increase their capabilities.
David (2015: 10)	Classical realism is identified with inherent and permanent flaws in human nature.
Özdemir (2015: 7)	Carr and subsequent realists argued that since there was no peaceful mechanism of change, wars erupt between states, and that this is the nature of international politics.

life in the international system because the aspects of human nature that produce it are not expected to change. Foreign policy, in both an abstract and applied sense, is of central interest to classical realism. While difficult to define precisely, the concept of the balance of power, as imported from the European experience, plays a significant role. Finally, a link to the practice of international relations, to accompany its place in IR as a way of thinking, is essential to the agenda of classical realism.

Effective as an overview, the words of Taliaferro, Lobell, and Ripsman (2009: 16; see also Ripsman, Taliaferro, and Lobell 2016: 169) point to a need for caution in labeling classical realism:

> What we now call classical realism was never a coherent research program, but rather a vast repository of texts written by different authors for different purposes and in different contexts over the course of 2,500 years. Most classical realists were not social scientists; even the twentieth-century classical realists never adhered to what are now widely accepted standards of social science methodology.

Classical realists focused on "the primacy of power and conceived of politics—both domestic and international—as an endless struggle by self-interested actors coping with scarcity and uncertainty" (Ripsman, Taliaferro, and Lobell 2016: 169). Ideas about how to deal with a world that always would be in conflict more naturally came from philosophy and history as opposed to social sciences.

Who is a classical realist in modern times, meaning post–World War II, and why? Various lists might be put together because of the very nature of this school. Status as a classical realist would not depend on conscious adoption of a set of axioms and commitment to producing hypotheses on that basis. Thus the issue of "Who is in and who is out?"—a matter more suited for intellectual history—is elided here.[3]

With regard to assumptions, classical realism clearly is in line with at least three of the four designated for realism as a research enterprise. It is relentlessly realist in emphasis upon anarchy and centrality of states in the international system. At the level of the state, seeking of power is clear to see in all classical realist expositions.

Classical realism does put forward a dark view of human nature, so what place does it offer to rationality, the fourth and final axiom in the foundation of the research enterprise? The two concepts do not pose a problem for each other. State behavior, from a classical realist standpoint, "can be understood as having rational microfoundations" (Elman and Jensen 2014: 3). Power as a resource is pursued by states in order to achieve various goals, and within classical realism the drive is quite strong as a result of human nature itself. Rationality as it plays out in the classical realist context possesses a Darwinian character—survival of the fittest in a world of self-help. Given the tendency of classical realists to reject

---

[3] Ripsman, Taliaferro, and Lobell (2016: 169) provide a list of names that includes Morgenthau, Niebuhr, Herz, Kissinger, Aron, Carr, Lippmann, Kennan, Spykman, Taylor, and Wolfers, among others. Additional lists, which largely intersect but always incorporate the scholars covered in this chapter, include Wayman and Diehl (1994a: 6), Freyberg-Inan (2004: 175–176), Barkin (2010: 5 n. 11), and Elman and Jensen (2014: 3).

behavioral science, an ordinal sense of rationality—as opposed to something based on complex calculations—also fits in well.

Classical Realist Ideas about the Causes of War

Accounting for war is the basic mission of classical realism. Rather than full-fledged theories, classical realists offer ideas that can be assembled into frameworks that account for war. In other words, classical realism is closer to understanding than explanation in the contemporary sense of IR. Its expositions are inspired by history and philosophy more than any other disciplines. Thus the present chapter, to some degree, is an exercise in translation of classical realism into the context of explanatory theory that also seeks to remain true to the ideas of the tradition.

Interesting to ponder are the reflections of Morgenthau (1964: 106) on why, until shortly before his time of writing, "nobody even considered the possibility of writing a theory of international relations." The answer Morgenthau (1964: 108) offered—that a persistent "negative orientation toward the nature of international relations and foreign policy" made it "impossible to deal in a theoretical, that is, an objective, systematic manner, with problems of international relations"—is persuasive. Thus the contents on offer from classical realism vis-à-vis the *causes* of war are not put forward in ways that are recognized easily through the eyes of the 21st century. The basic classical realist story is about aggressive leaders or political systems that provide the opportunity to pursue "self-serving expansionist foreign policies" (Elman and Jensen 2014: 3). Classical realism did not unfold in the contemporary social scientific "article culture," with Kuhnian normal science driving a steady stream of publications. Instead, insights from classical realism about cause and effect are derived primarily from major books.

Volumes of central importance within classical realism are relatively easy to identify on the basis of references that survive all the way through to contemporary IR. What follows is not intended to be a population of those books but instead a sample that is substantial enough to identify the classical realist vision of war. This is meant in both literal and figurative terms. The items included are Wight (1978 [1946]), Morgenthau (1959 [1948]), Kissinger (1957), Wolfers (1962), and Aron (1966). To return momentarily to Appendix 6.A, which described methods for creation of systemist figures, it not surprisingly turns out that classical realist ideas about the causes of war must be translated from expositions put forward almost exclusively in words. In a few instances, such as Morgenthau (1959 [1948]), it is possible to use an existing figure taken from a more recent study as a starting point (Guzzini 1998). Across the board, however, what appears in this chapter will be a translation of largely philosophical reflections into a 21st-century graphic format. The expositions differ in length, it should be noted, because the five studies offer varying degrees of detail about the potential causes of war.

One question to answer before moving forward concerns the subset of five works included as opposed to others. Why not, for instance, reference Claude (1962) on great power competition or a range of other possibilities? While it would be interesting to place all of the major classical realist studies into a graphic format, for present purposes that would produce diminishing returns and prove overwhelming. The five items included in the forthcoming review are sufficient to introduce the concepts, such as the balance of power, identified with classical realism. One study from just before World War II is deemed essential, however, to introduce classical realism as a whole.

The Twenty Years Crisis (Carr 1964 [1939] is a major study that antedates, by a few years, the time frame designated for this study. This book very often is identified as the starting point for the modern variant of classical realism (Elman and Jensen 2014: 3).[4] Realism, according to Carr (1964 [1939]: 10), "is liable to assume a critical and somewhat cynical aspect." Military power is essential to the state and "becomes not only an instrument, but an end in itself" (Carr (1964 [1939]: 111). "The most serious wars," Carr (1964 [1939]: 111) asserts, "are fought in order to make one's own country militarily stronger or, more often, to prevent another country from becoming militarily stronger." This is not, however, the end of the story: "Wars, begun for motives of security, quickly become wars of aggression and self-seeking" (Carr 1964 [1939]: 112). For Carr and realists who followed in his footsteps, a lack of means toward peaceful change guaranteed that wars would continue to take place (Özdemir 2015: 7). And all of the preceding ideas became standard fare within classical realism after World War II.

War obviously matters as both an academic subject and a policy concern. Interesting to note is that Wight (1978 [1946]: 141) identifies a statistical regularity with regard to war outcomes: "Since the American Declaration of Independence in 1776, every war between great powers, with three exceptions and those before 1860, has led to revolution on the losing side." Thus at least one major exposition from classical realism included an assessment of possible reverberations from interstate war in domestic conflict.

---

[4] Given his influence, why did Morgenthau, rather than Carr, emerge as the recognized founder of classical realism in its resurrected form after World War II? Guzzini (1998: 23) provides a convincing answer: "Carr's stance was too ambiguous and his style too polemic to found a school of thought, to provide an emerging discipline with a paradigmatic example. But he prepared the ground." Furthermore, an edition of Carr right after World War II featured revisions that made it more explicitly realist than the initial version had been.

With a book entitled *Power Politics*, Wight (1978 [1946]) gave classical realism its principal synonym from that point onward. He saw war as being within the realm of possible explanation because, while every belligerent might have multiple reasons for taking action, "A predominant motive is generally not beyond the power of historians to arrive at agreement about" (Wight 1978 [1946]: 138). At the same time, in trying to account for war, it is easy to "fall into twin errors, exaggerating the freedom or exaggerating the necessity" (Wight 1978 [1946]: 136). This position is borne out in decades of social scientific research that identifies both deterministic and contingent aspects along the road to war. In the realist context, anarchy and power seeking combine to produce contingency—situations that contain the risk of war. As for whether war occurs and how things will turn out if it does, more specific factors must be probed.

Politics among Nations, Morgenthau's magnum opus (1959 [1948]), served as the defining text for IR over many years. In spite of that centrality, Williams (2005: 82) observes, for several decades Morgenthau may have been "more often cited than read" and "reduced by both his supporters and his critics primarily to an implacable opponent of liberalism and an advocate of power politics." This is a simplification of a very long and complex book that, if anything, might be critiqued more accurately for its range of possible interpretations.

For example, ambiguities with the realist conception of power raised the ire of any number of critics (Schmidt 2007). This uncertainty is important because *Politics among Nations* offers balance of power as a basic tool in accounting for international politics. Balance of power, according to Morgenthau (1959 [1948]: 179), is not just one single system—it frequently includes subsystems with balances of power of their own. Local balances, moreover, differ in their degree of connection to the dominant one (Morgenthau 1959 [1948]: 180–181). "When Morgenthau views the balance of power as a universal phenomenon," Little (2007: 139) observes, "he assumes that statesmen have always been acutely conscious of their own power base and the power possessed by their neighbours." The magnitude of any possible miscalculation at the time cannot be known, so Morgenthau asserts that leaders therefore must attempt to maximize the power of their state (Little 2007: 139). Tellis (1996: 43) sums up Morgenthau's view: *Politics among Nations* is "the summation of the inductivist construction of the realist paradigm because it is such a detailed inventory of the complex and often divergent behaviors that are manifested in international politics" (Tellis 1996: 47). Morgenthau's most famous book stands out in opposition to calls for deductive rigor that became louder as the behavioral revolution gained momentum, with Kaplan (1957) as an early example.

What, then, about the causes of interstate war from a balance-of-power standpoint? "Three types of wars," Morgenthau (1959 [1948]: 190) claims, "are intimately connected with the mechanics of the balance of power: preventive war, already referred to, where normally both sides pursue imperialistic aims, anti-imperialistic war, and imperialistic war itself." Great wars have been fought "for real stakes, not for imaginary ones," and "the more thoroughly one understands the other side's position, character, and intentions, the more inevitable the conflict often appears to be" (Morgenthau 1959 [1948]: 491). The path to war, from the standpoint of Morgenthau, is summarized by Scheuerman (2007: 513):

> Morgenthau meant that our basic biologically rooted (though socially variable) need for food, shelter, and security represents an elementary source of social conflict. Second, the *animus dominandi*, or lust for power, constitutes an additional feature of human nature. We not only seek the satisfaction of our basic needs, but we are always necessarily preoccupied with our relative position in relation to others even after our survival has been guaranteed.

The quest for power works out better for some states than others. Differences ensue and lead to danger. For example, Morgenthau (1959 [1948]: 190) drew attention to different increases in power for status quo states (France, Britain) and imperialistic states (Germany) prior to World War II. By September 1939, war became the only choice; otherwise, status quo states would be absorbed "into the power orbit of the imperialistic nation" (Morgenthau 1959 [1948]: 190). Efforts toward collective security, from the standpoint of Morgenthau (1959 [1948]: 393), would not have worked out favorably either then or later. Instead, due to obligations, war simply would spread beyond any initial pair of states.

Fortunately, a thorough effort to translate the causal links from Morgenthau into a graphic format already exists. Guzzini (1998: 25) provides a causal map and accompanying discussion of its contents. Morgenthau argued that at the national level, the central state could "control the struggle for power—but not eradicate it" (Guzzini 1998: 26). At the international level, "Morgenthau identified "three different mechanisms, in rising order of actual impact: ethics, including mores and law; then world public opinion; and finally, international law" and inferred that, if these fail, "the system will always fall back on the brute clash of national forces" (Guzzini 1998: 29).

While Morgenthau did focus on human nature, he also drew upon the other images famously introduced in Waltz (1959) (Guzzini 1998: 30):

> He argued that the typical war of the gruesome twentieth century was a result of the democratization and hence nationalization of international politics. This was how he called the shift to mass societies whose rulers have to respond to large constituencies. This is a form of a second image explanation. And finally, although it is true that politics is about the struggle for power based on human nature, the specificity of the international system, what he called multiplicity,

explains why the warlike struggle for power, while tamed at the domestic level, is endemic to the international level.

To sum up, international war, for Morgenthau, represented a natural result of state-based aggression—a byproduct of human nature in operation under conditions of anarchy.

A World Restored is the book that launched the career of Henry Kissinger, initially a professor of political science but also one of the most long-standing and influential practitioners of international relations. "If Machiavelli is commonly understood to be the father of *Realpolitik*," Bew (2016: 2) observes, "Kissinger himself is assumed to be its most prominent torchbearer in the modern era." His career included service as national security advisor and secretary of state for the United States. Kissinger, as both a scholar and practitioner, routinely is cited as an iconic figure among realists.

A World Restored focuses on the complex series of negotiations, punctuated by continuing warfare, that brought Europe out of the Napoleonic Wars and into what is sometimes described as a long peace or, at least, a century with limited violence compared to what would occur before and after. The main characters in the story are Viscount Castlereagh, the British foreign secretary, and Klemens Wenzel von Metternich, foreign minister of Austria. The machinations and intrigue among diplomats recounted by Kissinger (1957) are fascinating; the analysis of coalitions in *A World Restored* set the standard at the time, and, as will become apparent, its primarily realist but also eclectic content foreshadowed diverse ideas associated with other perspectives on IR.

Long-standing is the influence from *Discord and Collaboration*, an insightful study by Wolfers (1962) about cooperation and conflict at the international level.[5] Anarchy creates insecurity among states (Wolfers 1962: 84). "In its pure form," observed Wolfers (1962: 82), realism is founded on the proposition that "states seek to enhance their power." States are the principal and sovereign actors in the international system, and "their goal is to enhance if not to maximize their power" (Wolfers 1962: 82). "The degree to which power is available or attainable frequently affects the choice of ends," and "goals of foreign policy as they refer to the national 'self' can be classified under the three headings of goals of national self-extension, goals of national self-preservation, and goals of national self-abnegation" (Wolfers 1962: 90, 91).[6] The traits of leaders themselves are

---

[5] Interesting to note is that Wolfers (1962: 99) did not self-identify purely as a realist. However, it is fair to say that his lasting reputation is as a member of that school of thought.

[6] According to Wolfers (1962: 95), "Idealist pressures at home in favor of self-denying policies may persist and either delay or reduce the effort to enhance defensive national power." The view of public opinion as an impediment to effective foreign policy is common among classical realists.

acknowledged as significant by Wolfers (1962: 42) and can help to explain variations in foreign policy among states.

What, then, leads to war? Self-extension "almost invariably calls for additional power," so states that seek it "tend to be the initiators of power competition and the resort to violence" (Wolfers 1962: 96). This is not, however, the only reason for war. Concern with self-preservation also comes into play. "The resort to violence," according to Wolfers (1962: 96; see also Elman and Jensen 2014: 8), "may be the preventive act of a nation that believes itself to be menaced by an attack on its own values or those of its friends." Thus the vision of war that emerges from Wolfers (1962) is contingent; it may be a product of either offensive or defensive motives.

Peace and War is the magnum opus from Aron (1966). According to Aron, three goals set states in opposition to each other. The initial element is animosity; belligerent action is second; and the third element is that "war is a political action" and "rises out of a political situation and results from a political motive" (Aron 1966: 22–23). Consider each element in turn. First, eternal objectives—human nature and will to survive—are at the foundation of conflict (Aron 1966: 72). Aron (1966: 341) asserts that human beings, among animals, are relatively combative. Maximization of resources does not, in turn, ensure security; there is a search for power and glory among leaders to consider as well (Aron 1966: 73–74). Second, historical objectives—over space—must be recognized (Aron 1966: 77). Third, and finally, are offensive and defensive considerations that influence the ability and disposition to attack (Aron 1966: 82). With all of these considerations in place, war possesses "roots that are simultaneously biological, psychological and social" (Aron 1966: 355).

What can be said, in an overall sense, about the preceding visions from classical realism about the causes of war? Several points can be made about the character of the classical approach.

First, aggressive unit-level motives for expansion produce the events that lead to major wars (Copeland 2000: 55). Copeland (2000: 55) observes that, for classical realism, when one state possesses a preponderance of power, events that raise the risk of inadvertent wars are more likely to ensue. A corollary is that such events are not expected "when there is a balance of power between individual states or between alliance blocs" (Copeland 2000: 55). Prospects for war and peace reside in the distribution of capabilities because the will to dominate is an ever-present aspect of human nature.

Second, classical realism emphasizes relevance to foreign policy. This goal influences the associated methods, which consist of reflections upon historical cases, notably pertaining to war. The approach is inductive rather than deductive in character and does not proceed according to any research design as that would be understood by contemporary social science.

Third, and finally, the classical realist theories are in compliance with the axioms of the realist research enterprise: anarchy, state-centrism, power seeking, and rationality. Given the tendency of classical realist expositions to reference philosophy and history, lists of assumptions, such as the one above, will not be found in their pages. However, it is easy to see that, collectively speaking, classical realists conducted analysis in line with the preceding four axioms. Anarchy, not the rule of law, is anticipated to shape international relations. The world is one of states, with transnational actors given no space at all. Seeking power is inherent in human nature, and rationality is expressed through pursuit of the national interests from the standpoint of respective leaders.

Critiques and Responses

Three decades into the period of realist predominance, Hoffmann (1977: 51) asked this question about IR: "Can one point to any great breakthroughs?" Rather than sensing progress, Hoffmann (1977: 51) is "more struck by the dead ends than by the breakthroughs" and "contradictions that have rent its community of scholars, than by its harmony." IR did move away from what became known as classical realism, if not only for reasons that Hoffmann (1977) had emphasized. Over four decades later, is it possible that classical realism might have something of value to offer the world of today? Does it still have something to say about war in particular?

Classical realism can be described as self-limiting because of its Eurocentrism. A search through classical realist works confirms a tendency to rely upon the history of Europe, especially in the post-Westphalian era, for both generation and assessment of ideas. Guzzini (1998: 3), speaking for any number of critics, observes that "the evolution of realist thought in International Relations can be fruitfully understood as the attempt, repeated and repeatedly failed, to translate the maxims of nineteenth century's European diplomatic practice into more general laws of an American social science." Thus the international system as a whole does not factor into classical realist expositions on war in the same way that it might in more recent times, during which greater consciousness about other regional systems is on the rise.

Critics from inside the research enterprise have identified classical realism as "primarily inductive" (Waltz 1995: 68). Among empirical IR scholars, if not others, *Scientific Man and Power Politics* is regarded as "too philosophical" (Scheuerman 2007: 527). "Morgenthau's classical realism," Park (1998: 19) observes, "insightfully grapples with critical concepts, issues, and assumptions, but fails to develop a theory of international politics." For example, the frame of reference lacks what later would be referred to as causal mechanisms: if, as Morgenthau claims, "the quest for power is rooted in human nature, *why* is it there and why is its significance so overwhelming, if indeed it is?" (Gat 2009: 572). Ripsman, Taliaferro, and Lobell (2016: 16) add that "human nature theories could not explain why states with different political systems behave similarly in similar circumstances." A further question comes to mind: "If human nature explains war and conflict, what accounts for peace and cooperation?" (Holsti 1995: 38).

Another line of criticism focuses on a lack of correspondence between classical realism and observed foreign policy. From a classical realist standpoint, capabilities shape intentions (Zakaria 1998: 35). However, Zakaria (1998: 32) points out that history includes many instances in which a rising state did not extend its interests, politically speaking, overseas. Copeland (2000: 12) adds that classical realism "cannot explain how multipolar systems with tight alliances against the potential hegemon, such as the one that existed before 1914, can still fall into major war." Classical realism never solved that puzzle in particular.

Classical realism gradually lost adherents as a product of its pessimistic character and incommensurability with the wave of modern social science that took hold with the behavioral revolution in the 1960s. However, one line of defense in favor of classical realism concerns its purpose. Among classical realists and notably Morgenthau, Schmidt (2007) observes, international politics existed as "more of an art than a science." A hard turn away from the classical variant among those identifying as realists therefore entailed a certain kind of cost. While there are advantages to the parsimony of neorealism, "the breadth and detail of classical realism" possesses value as well (Parent and Baron 2011: 197). Classical realism is more in line with analytic eclecticism than at least some other options because of its emphasis upon searching for insights relevant to foreign policy.

Unfair in relation to *Politics among Nations*, according to Little (2007: 137), is the prevailing tendency to "ransack the text, looking for quotations that expose a reductionist view of politics." Instead, when looking at the balance of power as "a universal phenomenon," Morgenthau had assumed that leaders are conscious of both their own base of power and that of their neighbors (Little 2007: 139). "Since the size of any potential miscalculation cannot be known, at the time," Little (2007: 139) observes, "Morgenthau insists that statesmen have no alternative, as a consequence, but to attempt to maximize their power position." This would stand as a first image sense of the balance of power. At the same time, however, for many years critics have noted that the balance of power possesses many possible meanings across the field of classical realists (Zinnes 1967). The location of balance of power in terms of level of analysis remains an uncertain aspect of classical realism to this day (Kessler and Steele 2018: 62).

While classical realism might seem deeply flawed from the standpoint of 21st-century social science, it did not pursue the same goals. In the language of IR today, classical realism emphasized understanding over explanation. It therefore should be appreciated for its contributions to the logic of discovery more than the logic of confirmation. Classical realism serves as the foundation for realist theories that aim toward explanation through logically interconnected propositions. Concepts such as power politics, the security dilemma, and balance of power originate with the largely philosophical expositions from classical realism and thereby become available for incorporation in later social scientific theories.

Graphic Representations

This section conveys in graphic form the ideas about war from leading classical realists. The visual representations that follow are taken from the magnum opus of each scholar under review.[7] Included on the list of great books are Wight (1978 [1946]), Morgenthau (1948), Kissinger (1957), Wolfers (1962), and Aron (1966). Given its focus on one specific historical case, the study by Kissinger (1957) is pursued in somewhat greater detail for purposes of illustration. Once each classical realist study is converted to graphic form, comparative analysis will ensue. An overall sense of classical realism's contribution to the logic of discovery will be given as well.

Before moving on to the theories that depict respective visions of cause and effect, a few reminders are in order. Each figure depicts processes within a region and possibly connections involving the international system as well. The boxes and arrows along the top row of a region portrayed within a figure represent macro-macro linkages, in this context meaning interstate relations. The contents of the boxes appear in uppercase to emphasize that point, as in Figure 6.2, which showed a systemist representation of cause and effect in generic form for neoclassical realism. Boxes and arrows along the bottom row show micro-micro linkages, meaning here processes at the level of the state. Lowercase is used for the contents of these boxes, once again paralleling Figure 6.2. Vertical arrows convey macro-micro and micro-macro connections. Variables that play different roles are depicted with a range of shapes. A generic variable in the system appears as a plain rectangle. An oval signifies a starting point for cause and effect. A diamond and parallelogram represent, respectively, points of divergence and convergence for pathways. A point of simultaneous divergence and convergence appears as a hexagon. Finally, an octagon represents a stopping point.

---

[7] Carr (1939) is excluded from the graphic stage. While it is essential to understanding how realism developed in later years, this study falls outside of the timeline from after World War II.

Figure 10.1 puts forward in graphic form the ideas of Martin Wight, from his magnum opus, *Power Politics* (1978 [1946]), about the causes of war.[8] As with other examples from classical realism, the exposition used to generate the visual representation is purely in words. Classical realists such as Wight came at the problem of international war from a primarily philosophical, as opposed to social scientific, point of view. Thus their studies feature neither explicit hypotheses that could be combined together into a theoretical edifice nor any diagrammatic expositions that might be applied to that same purpose. Figures 10.1a–d will assemble the arguments from Wight into an overall sense of why wars occur.

Figure 10.1a depicts boundaries for the region and its environment, the international system. Within Figure 10.1b, the story of cause and effect begins with "ANARCHY," which as the starting point is designated with an oval. This point of departure is interesting to observe because of an ongoing tendency to equate classical realism with reductionism to the state level. The first connection, "ANARCHY" → "Hobbesian fear," is from the macro to micro level. This portrays an intense concern for survival that results from lack of global governance. Note that Hobbesian fear takes the shape of a diamond because of the multiple pathways that emerge from it. Each of the three micro-micro linkages that follows will be considered in turn.

One state-level connection, added in Figure 10.1c, is "Hobbesian fear" → "blundering." This makes sense on the basis of intuition and even foreshadows the vast body of research in political psychology about how error follows on from intense emotion. Another micro-micro pathway, which also appears in Figure 10.1c, is "Hobbesian fear" → "seeking gain." This is more of a purely rationalist vision of how events might unfold in the minds of national leaders. Rather than bad judgment, existential fear might induce more of a cold sense of calculation that focuses on the opportunity to gain advantage. Third and last among this set of micro-micro connections in Figure 10.1c is "Hobbesian fear" → "promoting doctrine." This linkage takes into account the role of ideology, or in a more inclusive sense, belief systems.

Next comes movement upward from the state to the system level. One branch is depicted through Figure 10.1d as "blundering" → "INTERSTATE WAR." Since war is the focal point regarding outcome, this terminal variable appears

---

[8] The passages used to generate Figure 10.1 are as follows: Wight (1978 [1946]: 102) asserted that "wars are fought for many different causes; some are blundered into through a maze of mixed policies, as historians have usually seen the Crimean War; some are coldly willed and planned by a single power, as Hitler undoubtedly willed the Second World War. But all particular causes of war operate within the context of international anarchy and Hobbesian fear." In addition, Wight (1978 [1946]: 138) observed that many kinds of wars exist: "aggressive wars and preventive, prestige wars and wars of security, idealistic wars and perhaps even just wars. But it is convenient to classify them under three chief motives: wars of gain, wars of fear, and wars of doctrine." The content of Figure 10.1 has benefited from a consultation with Ewan Harrison, an expert on IR theory, along the way to completion.

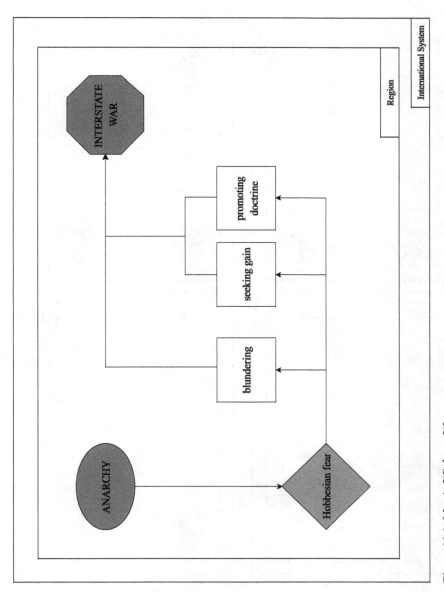

Figure 10.1 Martin Wight on War

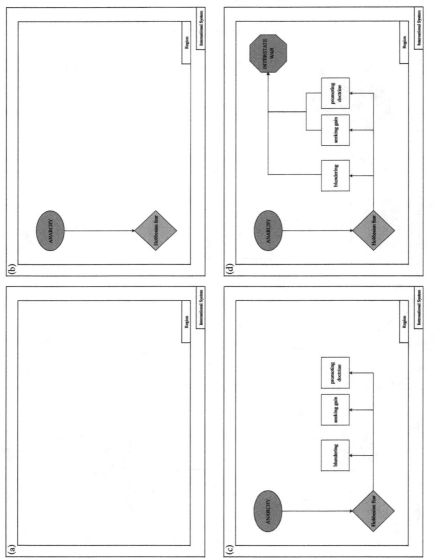

Figure 10.1 Continued

as an octagon. Note that, in Figure 10.1d, two other branches come together and lead up to interstate war: "seeking gain; promoting doctrine" → "INTERSTATE WAR." This is because promoting doctrine and seeking gain easily can come together along the road to war. Consider, for example, the intertwined nature of these goals for National Socialist Germany under the rule of Adolf Hitler. Ideology in this context explicitly included the idea of Lebensraum, or living space—the assumption that a state must expand its territory in order to survive.

Figure 10.2 puts the ideas of Morgenthau's *Politics among Nations* (1959 [1948]) about the causes of war into graphic form.[9] The story begins with Figure 10.2a, which depicts the region and international system as its environment.

Figure 10.2b shows "ANARCHY" → "STRUGGLE FOR POWER," the initial connection at the level of the system. Note that "ANARCHY" appears within an oval because of its role as a starting point. This origin is interesting already because a conscientious interpretation from Guzzini (1998) begins at the *system* level, which goes against stereotypes of *Politics among Nations* as reductionist in character. Given that it is a point at which multiple arrows converge and diverge, "STRUGGLE FOR POWER," as a nodal variable, is shown as a hexagon. Another pathway at the state level is set in motion with Figure 10.2c, which adds "will of domination" → "power seeking." Like anarchy, the will of domination initiates a pathway and therefore appears as an oval. The pathway continues upward in Figure 10.2d to the level of the system with "power seeking" → "STRUGGLE FOR POWER."

More than one pathway emerges from the initial hexagon in the figure. One connection, added in Figure 10.2e, is "STRUGGLE FOR POWER" → "BALANCE OF POWER."

Depicted in Figure 10.2f, the story continues with "BALANCE OF POWER" → "WORLD PUBLIC OPINION, NORMS, INTERNATIONAL MORALITY."

Figure 10.2g shows the next step, which is "WORLD PUBLIC OPINION, NORMS, INTERNATIONAL MORALITY" → "INTERNATIONAL LAW." From the realist standpoint, this acknowledges the reality of international institutions, norms, and the apparatus later identified with a liberal frame of reference. However, international institutions are seen as at best temporarily able to stave off conflict in a world of power politics. The League of Nations, which came into existence after World War I, ultimately ran aground as a result of perceived self-interest and power politics among states. World War II ensued.

Figure 10.2h shows a feedback loop: "INTERNATIONAL LAW" → "BALANCE OF POWER." While international institutions are active, nothing

---

[9] The description that follows is based on Guzzini (1998: 24–30) and a review of Morgenthau 1959 [1948]). Particular emphasis is placed on Figure 2.1 in Guzzini (1998: 25), which attempts to summarize the international system as articulated in Morgenthau (1959 [1948]). This figure also has benefited from a consultation with Stefano Guzzini, a recognized authority on Morgenthau.

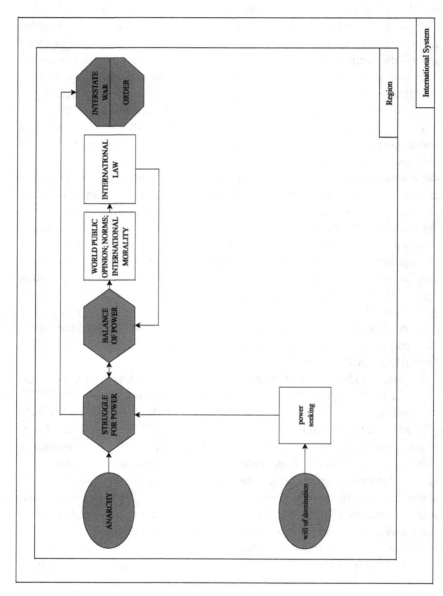

Figure 10.2 Hans Morgenthau on War

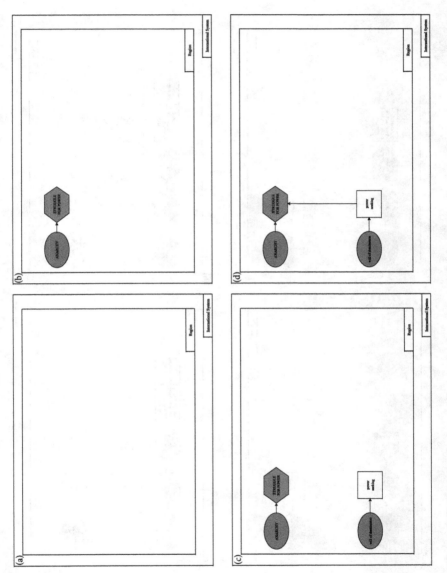

Figure 10.2 Continued

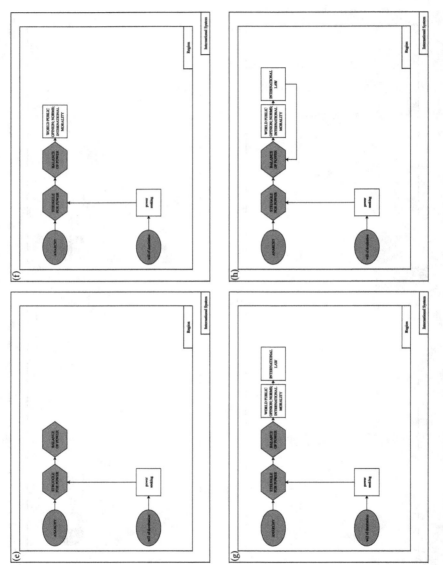

Figure 10.2 Continued

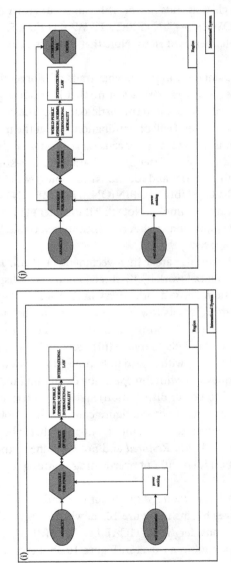

Figure 10.2 Continued

within such forums can overturn the balance of power. Next comes an interaction effect, as revealed in Figure 10.2i with "BALANCE OF POWER" → "STRUGGLE FOR POWER." This symbiosis of cause and effect, in a realist world, can only be temporary. Eventually the balance of power will give way, once again, to a struggle that ends in war. This can occur either directly, as with "STRUGGLE FOR POWER" → "INTERSTATE WAR | ORDER" in Figure 10.2j, or after a more complex series of steps. Note that the latter, a terminal variable, also is coconstitutive.

With a graphic presentation in place, what traits of Morgenthau's vision are noteworthy? Multiple pathways exist, a feature that is at odds with a tendency to think of classical realism as a deterministic outlook. The starting points in Figure 10.2, "ANARCHY" and "will of domination," are at the macro and micro levels, respectively. Thus the treatment of cause and effect is neither reductionist nor holist, but instead closer to systemist in character. Interesting to note also is the presence of both material and ideational variables, with "BALANCE OF POWER" and "WORLD PUBLIC OPINION, NORMS, INTERNATIONAL MORALITY" as respective examples. Note that the cluster of ideational variables is present but deemed epiphenomenal. A coconstitutive variable, "INTERSTATE WAR | ORDER," also appears.

From the years prior to his career in government, *A World Restored* (1957) stands as the most influential work by Kissinger. Figure 10.3 displays the vision of an international system derived inductively in *A World Restored* via a review of the world-transforming events toward the end, and in the aftermath, of the Napoleonic Wars.[10] The interior border identifies the European system. Note that the environment does not play a role in this vision of international relations; there are no inputs or outputs with regard to Europe. This obviously is a product of the time period in question, with Europe as the dominant (and relatively self-contained, with regard to power distribution) system in international relations in the 19th century. Elaboration of the figure could include colonialism as an output and wealth from overseas as an input, but all of that is beyond the scope of the exposition from *A World Restored* and not germane to the task at hand. These linkages could be added without overturning anything that appears in the figure now.

What, then, does *A World Restored* say about war and peace? The European-based story by Kissinger begins in Figure 10.3a, which depicts Europe and the international system. Consider "POLITICAL EQUILIBRIUM," a starting point that accordingly is depicted as an oval in Figure 10.3b. Peace, conceived of as

---

[10] The connections conveyed in Figure 10.3 are taken primarily from Kissinger (1957: 1, 2, 13, 30, 31, 70, 315), with further affirmations of those linkages found elsewhere in the text from that book. Figure 10.3 also benefited from a consultation with Harvey Starr, an expert on the scholarship of Kissinger (Starr 1984).

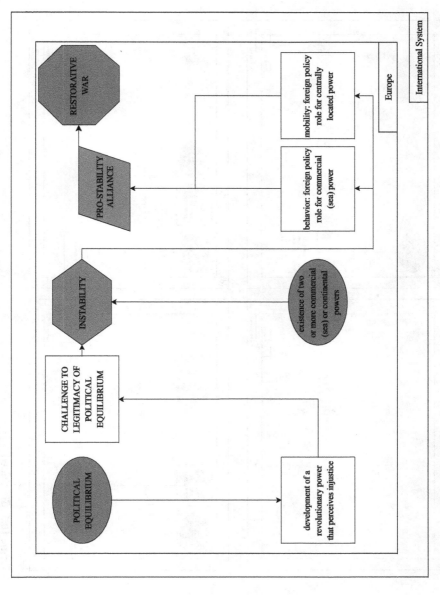

Figure 10.3 Henry Kissinger on War

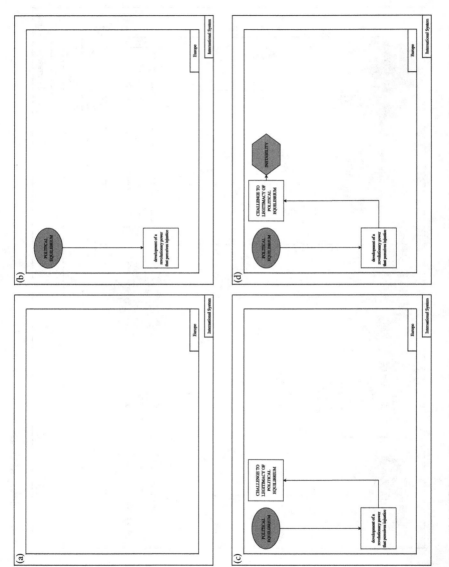

Figure 10.3 Continued

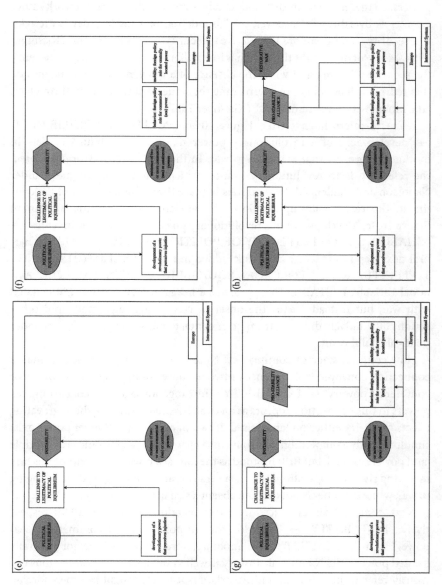

Figure 10.3 Continued

the absence of interstate war, exists at the outset (Kissinger 1957: 1). In terms of concept formation, the realist nature of peace as an equilibrium, from the standpoint of Kissinger (1957: 5), is quite apparent: "an order accepted by all the major powers, so that henceforth they sought adjustment within its framework rather than in its overthrow." Moreover, the "foundation of a stable order is the *relative* security—and therefore the *relative* insecurity—of its members" (Kissinger 1957: 145). Put differently, the system is in equilibrium when all states experience the security dilemma, but with "the absence of a grievance of such magnitude that redress will be sought in overturning the settlement rather than through an adjustment within its framework" (Kissinger 1957: 145).

A macro-micro linkage from Figure 10.3b, "POLITICAL EQUILIBRIUM" → "development of a revolutionary power that perceives injustice," sets in motion the process that may lead to war. In the context of *A World Restored*, the reference is to revolutionary France, which engaged in conquest under Napoleon and challenged the dynasties in place throughout the rest of the continent. This reverberates upward in a micro-macro connection that appears in Figure 10.3c, "development of a revolutionary power that perceives injustice" → "CHALLENGE TO LEGITIMACY OF POLITICAL EQUILIBRIUM." The natural next step is a macro-macro link, added in Figure 10.3d as "CHALLENGE TO LEGITIMACY OF POLITICAL EQUILIBRIUM" → "INSTABILITY." As a nodal variable, INSTABILITY appears as a hexagon. Instability is not equated with war, but instead means the onset of crisis-laden diplomacy and other actions qualitatively different from prior contact among the great powers under political equilibrium.

Now comes a stage of contingency. Note in Figure 10.3e the micro-macro connection conveyed by "existence of two or more commercial (sea) powers or continental powers" → "INSTABILITY." The exogenous variable concerning sea powers in this connection appears as an oval. Kissinger warns of the aggravating effects of rivalry either on land or sea. If two of either type of great power exist simultaneously, competition will come into play. In the Napoleonic era, multiple land powers existed, but Britain stood as the lone sea power. One part of this link involving rivalry is operational (Russia versus France on land) and encouraging to war, while the other is not (Britain absent a seafaring rival).

Next come a pair of macro-micro connections in Figure 10.3f, respectively: "INSTABILITY" → "behavior: foreign policy role for commercial (sea) power" and "INSTABILITY" → "mobility: foreign policy role for centrally located power." The Napoleonic history is well known, so these connections obviously refer to how Britain and Austria, respectively, might see their foreign policy priorities in light of growing instability caused by projection of rapidly rising French power. On the one hand, Britain, with its great navy and more limited ground forces, would seek to tilt the balance against any state attempting to gain control of Europe. On the other hand, Austria, positioned at the center of the continent, would have every interest in keeping its options open as the best path toward survival.

Two micro-macro connections, added in Figure 10.3g, reveal the expected courses of action from the key states of Britain and Austria: "behavior: foreign policy role for commercial (sea) power" → "PRO-STABILITY ALLIANCE" and "mobility foreign policy role for centrally located power" → "PRO-STABILITY ALLIANCE." These are the natural responses for the featured states in the story, Britain and Austria. As Europe became more unstable in the wake of Napoleon's conquests, a four-power alliance with overwhelming power—Russia, Britain, Prussia, and Austria—developed in response. The story Kissinger tells about Austria is especially interesting; it did not, in an automaton-like way, engage in balancing at all times. Instead, judiciously chosen neutrality and elements of bandwagoning are part of the complex foreign policy that Metternich pursued in the late stages of the Napoleonic era and its aftermath. As a convergent variable, "PRO-STABILITY ALLIANCE," is depicted as a parallelogram.

Figure 10.3h completes the story with "PRO-STABILITY ALLIANCE" → "RESTORATIVE WAR." Note that, as a terminal variable, "RESTORATIVE WAR" appears as an octagon.

Several traits of the account from Kissinger are interesting to ponder. With multiple pathways present, this vision of cause and effect is not deterministic. The starting point is "POLITICAL EQUILIBRIUM," a macro-level variable. This argues once again against a sense of classical realist theories as collectively reductionist in character. Note the presence of material as well as ideational factors, with "existence of two or more commercial (sea) or continental powers" and "CHALLENGE TO LEGITIMACY OF POLITICAL EQUILIBRIUM" as respective illustrations.

Given the contents of Figure 10.3, intuition already points toward analytic eclecticism as an important element in the world according to *A World Restored*. The realist character of the figure is undeniable, but quite striking is the range of other ideas present, some of which today normally are regarded as beyond realism per se. A few examples will be sufficient to make the point: (a) the meaning of power, (b) analysis of coalitions from a rationalist point of view, and (c) connections with, of all things, general systems theory.

Kissinger (1957) brings together material and ideational elements in his treatment of power as conveyed by Metternich, which implicitly is endorsed in *A World Restored*: "The power of states, Metternich argued, depends on two factors, their material strength and the personality of their rulers" (Kissinger 1957: 79). The "acid test" for a policy, Kissinger (1957: 326) further observes, "is its ability to obtain domestic support." *A World Restored* contains numerous instances of power-based analysis that brings in both material and ideational elements that reflect the preceding observations. Austria, for example, had to rely overwhelmingly on the diplomatic ability of Metternich due to its difficult geographic position and limited capabilities in comparison to Russia and France.

With regard to coalitions, elements of thinking associated with rational choice appear at various places in *A World Restored*. Here are a few observations (Kissinger 1957: 89, 94, 109):

- (A) "Metternich was watching Napoleon with one eye and the Tsar and Poland with the other."
- (B) "The total defeat of the enemy removes, if nothing else, a weight in the balance and confronts the status quo power with the alternative of surrender or a war with an erstwhile ally whose relative position has improved with the enemy's defeat."
- (C) "When the enemy has been so weakened that each ally has the power to achieve its aims alone, a coalition is at the mercy of its most determined member."

Consider these assertions in the context of the size principle from Riker (1962), which greatly impacts the study of coalitions to this day. Kissinger's observations are in line with Riker's size principle, which sees natural movement away from a supramajority and toward a minimum winning coalition (i.e., 50% plus one) as a result of an inclination to redistribute gains among the smallest feasible subset. Metternich, as described by *A World Restored*, anticipated elements of Riker's basic idea about coalitions. As the overwhelming four-state coalition against Napoleon moved inexorably toward victory, a vulnerable member such as Austria might start worrying about what will come next (A). The logic of the size principle and natural movement toward a minimum winning coalition appears implicitly in (B) and (C). If Russia could get away with it somehow, feathering its nest at the expense of current allies would be the order of the day after becoming the preeminent land power via final defeat of Napoleonic France.

While clearly and accurately associated with realism, *A World Restored* (Kissinger 1957) turns out to be a product of its times in more than one way. The dominance of historical and philosophical approaches from the time of *A World Restored* is apparent throughout its contents. However, general systems theory, which originated with Easton (1953 and see also 1965a, 1965b, 1990), also exerted great influence among political scientists and is latent within *A World Restored*. Easton's theorizing, summarized in Chapter 6, most importantly emphasized the concept of equilibrium and how a political system might be studied from the point of view of challenges to its current state and attempts to restore stability.

While Easton's work is not cited in *A World Restored*, implicit connections frame much of the discussion. One chapter of *A World Restored*, for instance, is entitled "Metternich and the Definition of the Political Equilibrium" (Kissinger 1957: 41–61). The goal of Metternich, perhaps the single most important character in Kissinger's story of the European grand bargain after Napoleon, is not conquest. Instead, Metternich sounds like an Easton-inspired advocate of homeostasis—the return to a system's steady state in its prior equilibrium. Along those lines, consider how often the word "repose" appears in *A World Restored* (e.g., Kissinger 1957: 270), especially in relation to the goals of Austrian foreign policy. Metternich did not seek aggrandizement for Austria but instead to return things on the continent, to whatever extent possible, to what they looked like before the French Revolution and Napoleonic Wars. And why would Austria's interests be "identical with those of European repose" (Kissinger 1957: 321)? The answer lies *inside* its borders. Austria joined the grand coalition against Napoleon with the goal of restoring political equilibrium because its leadership quite rationally feared disintegration as a byproduct of revolution and interstate war. The incoherent and increasingly dysfunctional Austrian empire faced many problems, not least the rise of nationalism, as the 19th century moved forward. Thus Austria's foreign policy via Metternich had a homeostatic, not Homeric, quality.

Taken together, the preceding observations establish *A World Restored* as a primarily realist exposition, but with important elements of analytic eclecticism throughout its pages. One of the reasons why Figure 10.3 seems convincing is that it represents anything but a narrow exegesis of the international system in relation to the central problem of war and its causes. From a systemist point of view, the figure falls just short of passing a basic test: it contains three of the four basic types of linkage—macro-macro, macro-micro, and micro-macro—but excludes micro-micro. Moreover, Figure 10.3 easily could be elaborated to include cause and effect in relation to the environment. Imperialist rivalry, for example, could be added as a force destabilizing the European system as the 19th century wore on.

Perhaps most important, again from a systemist point of view, is the apparent lack of contradiction in the set of causal mechanisms from the figure. While doing so is beyond the scope of the present exposition, the respective linkages could be unpacked to see if any entail axioms that contradict each other. If not, the influence of Kissinger's (1957) study may now be explained in a different way than before: it tells a story about war and its aftermath that brings together ideas from across schools of thought and even disciplines but not in a way that collapses upon itself due to contradiction.

Figure 10.4 conveys the ideas about why wars occur in *Discord and Collaboration* (Wolfers 1962).[11] Figure 10.4a depicts a region and surrounding

---

[11] Figure 10.4 is based upon Wolfers (1962: 82, 84, 90, 91, 96) and a consultation with Annette Freyberg-Inan (2004, 2006), a recognized expert on realism.

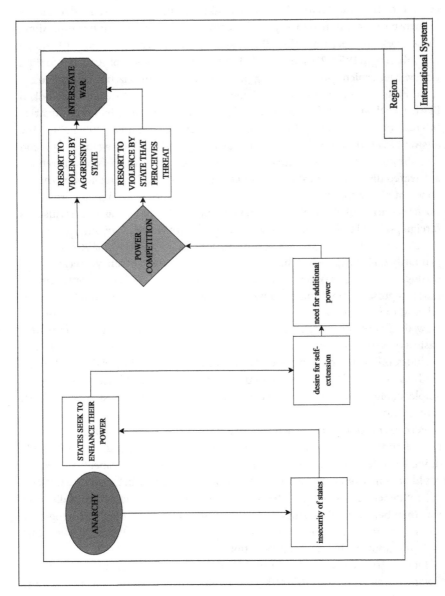

Figure 10.4 Arnold Wolfers on War

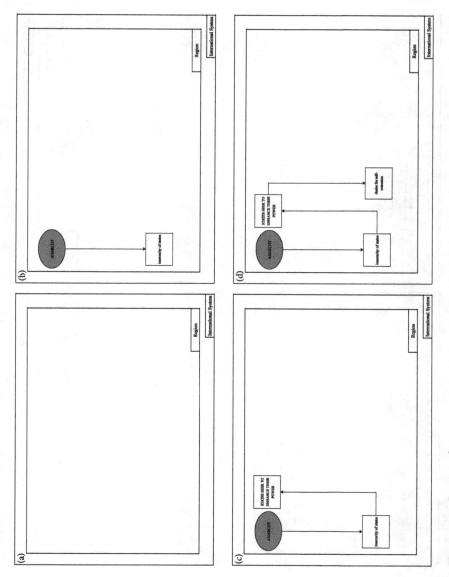

Figure 10.4 Continued

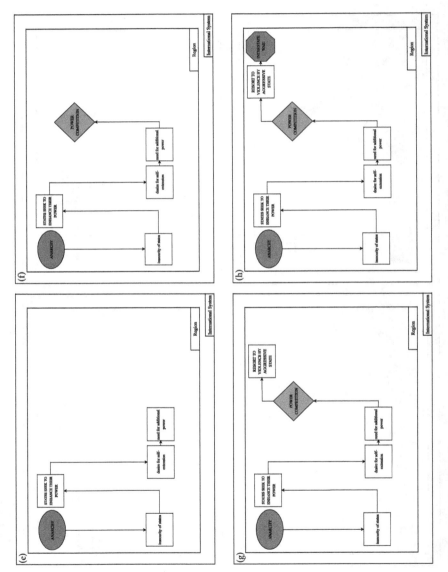

Figure 10.4 Continued

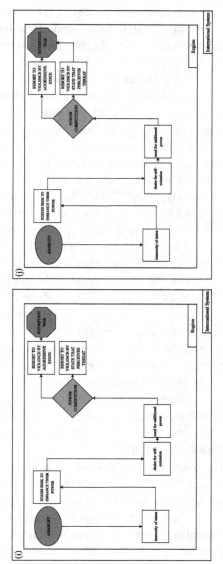

Figure 10.4 Continued

international system, with the macro and micro levels in the region corresponding to the system and state levels. The vision of cause and effect gets underway in Figure 10.4b with an initial linkage, namely, "ANARCHY" → "insecurity of states." An oval is used to show "ANARCHY" as the point of departure. Figure 10.4c adds "insecurity of states" → "STATES SEEK TO ENHANCE THEIR POWER," a connection up from the state to the level of the system. In Figure 10.4d, movement from the system down to the state level ensues with "STATES SEEK TO ENHANCE THEIR POWER" → "desire for self-extension." A further linkage at the state level, added in Figure 10.4e, is "desire for self-extension" → "need for additional power." Movement upward ensues in Figure 10.4f, which includes "need for additional power" → "POWER COMPETITION." This stands out as a vicious circle that is very basic to realism. As a point of divergence for pathways, "POWER COMPETITION" is designated with a diamond.

One pathway continues in Figure 10.4g with "POWER COMPETITION" → "RESORT TO VIOLENCE BY AGGRESSIVE STATE." A termination point is reached when Figure 10.4h adds "RESORT TO VIOLENCE BY AGGRESSIVE STATE" → "INTERSTATE WAR." As the final part of the story, "INTERSTATE WAR" is designated with an octagon. Another pathway moves forward in Figure 10.4i with "POWER COMPETITION" → "RESORT TO VIOLENCE BY STATE THAT PERCEIVES THREAT." This route is completed in Figure 10.4j with "RESORT TO VIOLENCE BY STATE THAT PERCEIVES THREAT" → "INTERSTATE WAR." Thus war can be initiated by a state on either the offensive or defensive.

Several features stand out in the graphic presentation of Wolfers's vision of the causes of war. Note the presence of multiple pathways, yet again arguing against a sense of classical realism as a deterministic and even simplistic school of thought. The starting point in Figure 10.4 is "ANARCHY," a macro-level variable, which points away from the reputation of classical realism as reductionist in its vision of cause and effect. Finally, both ideational and material variables appear in the network of effects. Examples, respectively, are "insecurity of states" and "RESORT TO VIOLENCE BY AGGRESSIVE STATE."

Figure 10.5 shows the road to war as envisioned in *Peace and War* (Aron 1966).[12] The story begins in Figure 10.5a, which depicts the international system and a region with it. Once again, the macro and micro levels in the region are the system and states within it, respectively. An initial connection, "human nature and will to survive" → "combative humans," appears in Figure 10.5b. Since it is the starting point, "human nature and will to survive" is designated with an oval, while "combative humans," a divergent variable, is depicted with a diamond.

---

[12] Figure 10.5 is based on Aron (1966: 22–23, 72, 73–74, 77, 341, 355) and a consultation with Annette Freyberg-Inan (2004, 2006), a recognized expert on realism.

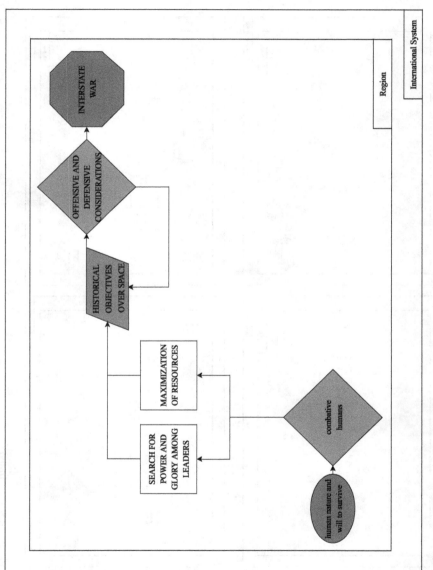

Figure 10.5 Raymond Aron on War

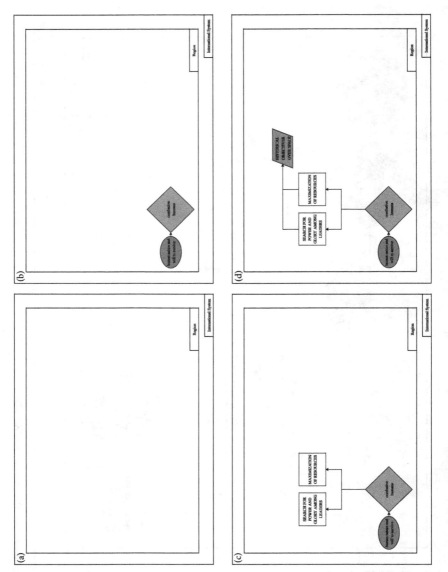

Figure 10.5 Continued

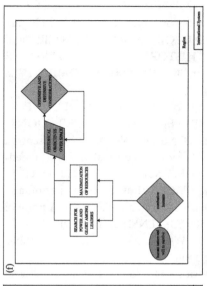
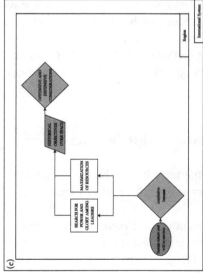
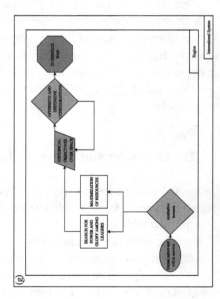

Figure 10.5 Continued

Figure 10.5c continues along one of two upward pathways with "combative humans" → "SEARCH FOR POWER AND GLORY AMONG LEADERS." Since the latter is taken to be pervasive in the system, it is properly designated as a macro-level variable. The other pathway moves forward in Figure 10.5c with "combative humans" → "MAXIMIZATION OF RESOURCES." This is a fundamental expectation within realism. A point of convergence is reached in Figure 10.5d with "SEARCH FOR POWER AND GLORY AMONG LEADERS" and "MAXIMIZATION OF RESOURCES" → "HISTORICAL OBJECTIVES OVER SPACE." Since pathways come together in it, "HISTORICAL OBJECTIVES OVER SPACE" appears as a parallelogram.

Depicted in Figure 10.5e, the next step is "HISTORICAL OBJECTIVES OVER SPACE" → "OFFENSIVE AND DEFENSIVE CONSIDERATIONS." Since "OFFENSIVE AND DEFENSIVE CONSIDERATIONS" represents a point of divergence, it takes the form of a diamond. Figure 10.5f shows a feedback, loop, involving "OFFENSIVE AND DEFENSIVE CONSIDERATIONS" and "HISTORICAL OBJECTIVES OVER SPACE." Thus the feasibility of, and disposition toward, conquest can impact each other in a cyclical way. A point of termination is reached in Figure 10.5g with "OFFENSIVE AND DEFENSIVE CONSIDERATIONS" → "INTERSTATE WAR." As a terminal variable, "INTERSTATE WAR" is depicted as an octagon.

What stands out from the graphic exposition of Aron on the causes of war? Note once again the presence of multiple pathways to war. This is the only classical realist theory among the five surveyed here that begins at the micro level alone, with "human nature and the will to survive." Present along the way are both material and ideational variables, with "MAXIMIZATION OF RESOURCES" and "SEARCH FOR POWER AND GLORY AMONG LEADERS" as examples, respectively.

The Character and Value of Classical Realist Theories of War

Table 10.2 summarizes the properties of the great books that have been converted to graphic form in this chapter. Several specific patterns emerge from scanning the table.

First, the works emerge as relatively straightforward visions of cause and effect. The range of variables across this set of classic realist studies is from six up to nine—a fairly limited range and also not a huge number in any instance. All of the graphics feature at least one initial variable and terminal variable, so there are no cycles of causation.

Second, the classical realist vision of war is contingent rather than deterministic. Every image features at least one divergent, convergent, or nodal variable. With three such variables, Aron is at the maximum within this group.

Table 10.2 Properties of Variables in the Great Books

Magnum Opus	Overall Number	Initial	Generic	Divergent	Convergent	Nodal	Coconstitutive	Terminal	Interaction Effect	Feedback	Missing Links[a]
Wight (1946)	6	1	3	1	0	0	0	1	0	0	M→m S→E E→S
Morgenthau (1946)	8	2	3	0	0	2	1	1	1	1	M→m S→E E→S
Kissinger (1957)	9	2	4	0	1	1	0	1	0	1	m→m S→E E→S
Wolfers (1962)	9	1	6	1	0	0	0	1	0	0	S→E E→S
Aron (1966)	7	1	2	2	1	0	0	1	0	1	M→m S→E E→S

[a] The notation is as follows: Macro (M), micro (m), System (S) and Environment (E).

Third, the exposition from Morgenthau stands out for the range of variable types that it incorporates. It is the only diagram with more than one nodal variable, which appears in the form of a hexagon. The two nodes in the Morgenthau graphic are both at the macro level: "STRUGGLE FOR POWER" and "BALANCE OF POWER." These variables also exhibit an interaction effect, indicated with a double-headed arrow. In addition, the figure includes a coconstitutive variable—"INTERSTATE WAR | ORDER"—that appears in a bifurcated form. This is striking because it antedates the rise of constructivism, which usually is associated with such variables, by several decades. The presence of a coconstitutive variable reinforces the idea that ideational analysis dates back far beyond the tendency to see it as a product of constructivism (Bobrow 1996).

Fourth, the classical realist studies fall short of specifying the full range of connections required by systemism. All of these theories leave out explicit effects back and forth for the region and environment. This reflects the origins of classical realism, which emerged through observation of great power politics in Europe. Until the rise of Japan and the United States from the late 19th century onward, power politics had been restricted to major players on the European continent. With regard to connections within a system, only Wolfers includes all four types.

What can be said, in a more general sense, about the classical realist studies now that the task of graphic portrayal and identification of specific patterns is complete? Several observations are in order.

While not intended for assembly into a would-be scientific theory of war, the realist theories are valuable as stimuli for identifying key variables and conjectures. Evaluation of classical realist propositions, based largely and ironically on quantitative data, took place for decades in isolation from primarily qualitative expositions about the causes of war. This activity took the form of what Zinnes (1976) referred to as testing of ad hoc hypotheses, many of which focused on the interstate distribution of capabilities in connection with conflict processes.

Classical realist expositions incorporate, interestingly enough, material and ideational variables. The tendency to associate realism of any stripe with material factors alone emerged from the above-noted testing regime, which focused on indicators such as population and GNP to assess capabilities. Claude (1962: 64), a prominent classical realist, observed that mistrust is not directed "against power *per se*, but against particular holders of power." In more recent times, Wivel (2005) encourages realists to think about how ideational and material factors interact with each other in accounting for foreign policy. Rathbun (2008: 300) adds that all approaches to international relations have access to ideas. Realism is no exception.

Echoes of the past are easy to hear in the realism of today. If classical realism is viewed through the lens of the logic of discovery rather than confirmation, it looks productive. As a few examples from just the studies covered here, consider (a) Wight on seeking gain, (b) Morgenthau regarding balance of power, (c) Kissinger vis-à-vis alliances, (d) Wolfers with respect to aggressive and threat-perceiving states, and (e) Aron about offensive and defensive considerations. Classical realism, in sum, provides a foundation for theorizing that could add rigor to its demonstrated creativity.

Assessing the Descendants of Classical Realism

With a review of classical realism in place as a foundation, attention turns to how subsequent theories about war, exhibited in Figure 9.1, will be reviewed in Part IV of this book. These realist theories will appear in chronological order from Chapters 11 through 18. Classification, as per Chapter 9, is along two dimensions: (a) dynamic versus static; and (b) system or state in orientation.

Each chapter about a theory in Part IV will start with answers to basic questions. What is its point of origin in a magnum opus? In addition, does the theory comply with the axioms of realism as a research enterprise? Furthermore, what other assumptions are entailed? A sense of the theory as a whole greater than the sum of its parts then is identified, along with its connection to classical realism. Expositions on the causes of war and critiques follow on.

With the preceding tasks completed, graphic representation of realist theories about war can get underway. In creating these visualizations, the standard practice of the metatheory—seeking knowledge through both (i) deductive and rationalist and (ii) inductive and sociological means—continues to be applied. Diagrams are drafted in compliance with instructions from Appendix 6.A. The figures then receive clarification from respective author(s) or appropriate substitutes when unavailable. This process, with its obviously deductive and inductive components, is intended to promote validity and reliability with regard to the diagrammatic exposition.

Each theory is profiled in terms of the variable types and connections that it includes. The format of the diagram is the same in every instance; a region is designated as the system, with the international system as its environment. The micro and macro levels in the region correspond to processes, respectively, involving states and collectivities of them. All of this will prove demanding enough that other aspects of importance to systemism in particular and graphic communication in general are not as yet implemented. One omission is functional form for connections between and among variables—linear versus more complex linkages. Also beyond the scope of this initial process of transforming realist theories into graphic form is representation of the time scale for cause and effect (Tufte 2006: 45). The arrows that connect one variable to another are not in proportion to any time lag. This is because the diagrams representing realist theories will be sufficiently complex to prevent insertion of a time element; to do so would mar comprehension in an overall sense.

Cause and effect are assessed in line with the components adopted from Kurki (2002). The efficient cause is the mover that occurs in close proximity to the effect. Material causes refer to the passive potentiality of matter—analogous to opportunity within the framework from Most and Starr (2015 [1989]) that is familiar in IR. Final causes are purposes that guide change—motivation to act that parallels willingness from Most and Starr (2015 [1989]). There also are background conditions that serve as defining shapes or relations. Once all of these categories are covered, an account for cause and effect is deemed to be in place.

Graphic portrayal of each theory will facilitate responses to critiques already noted. Concepts developed in the metatheory, such as the Performance Ratio, will be referenced along the way. This should confirm an expected payoff from implementation of systemism, namely, an enhanced ability to identify and resolve points of misunderstanding. Deemed valuable in its own right to enhance rigor, the work involved in graphic portrayal of realist theories also sets the stage for their engagement with each other and nonrealist expositions in Chapters 19 and 20.

Classical Realism in Retrospect

Classical realism serves as a foundation for expositions on power politics up to this day. A graphic reassessment reveals that, through the mists of time, classical realist theories of war have become at least somewhat misunderstood. The set of theories reviewed here, derived from great books that did not have a mission in line with contemporary social science, emerge as neither simplistic nor deterministic in character. Moreover, the five theories include both material and ideational variables—once again at odds with how such work tends to be remembered. At the same time, classical realism offers an incomplete and prescientific vision of world politics. Part IV will apply the metatheory of scientific progress to evaluate the theories about war that have descended from classical realism.

PART IV
REALIST THEORIES OF WAR

Assessment of realism takes place in Part IV, which consists of Chapters 11–18. The focus is on how well realist theories have performed in solving the most basic and important empirical problem in IR: *the causes of war*. Theories are expressed in visual form, using the method of systemism, to facilitate understanding and constructive criticism leading to effective revision when that seems in order. The theories depicted in Chapters 11 through 18 are conveyed in chronological order with regard to time of origin.

Chapter 11 focuses on power cycle theory. It theorizes about operation of the international system as a whole and constitutes the initial significant departure from classical realism in research that can be identified with power politics. The theory of power cycles puts forward the idea that great powers in the system pass through waves of increase and decrease in their standing relative to each other (Doran 1971; Doran and Parsons 1980; Doran 1991). These cycles of capability feature turning points, where either the direction or pace of movement shifts and creates high uncertainty. A great power's sense of its foreign policy role will lag behind these objective conditions with regard to change in relative capabilities. As a result, either a surplus or deficit of capacity to act will pose a challenge to the leadership in coping with the international system. At such times, according to power cycle theory, the likelihood of great power war reaches its maximum. This is true especially when more than one great power is in proximity to a critical point along its power cycle.

Chapter 12 conveys structural realism. Like power cycle theory, structural realism shifted away from the classical emphasis upon the nature of human beings in relation to inevitability of conflict. Traced to Waltz (1979), structural realism focuses on how the distribution of capabilities at the level of the international system impacts its propensity for conflict. States face a situation of self-help and can be expected to engage in power balancing for their own protection. The principal idea about war put forward by structural realism is that bipolarity is better than multipolarity. A system with two leading states, as opposed to three or more, will be less prone to break down into highly destructive conflict. Under bipolarity, the two leading states can be expected to match and monitor the efforts of each other. Thus war becomes less likely than in the relatively more chaotic world of multipolarity. Two structural realist theories are identified: an initial version (Waltz 1979) and one that focuses on hegemonic stability (Gilpin 1981).

Balance of threat is the subject of Chapter 13. This theory departs from structural realism in that, while it also emphasizes balancing, the focus is on identifying and coping with threat. In a word, the leadership of a given state is anticipated to identify the most serious threat it faces and pursue appropriate policies in response. Perception of threat is a function of aggregate power, geographic proximity, offensive power, and aggressive intentions (Walt 1987, 1990, 1996). A key contribution of balance-of-threat theory is identification of a range of foreign policy options available to states under anarchy. While balancing is the anticipated norm, bandwagoning also can be expected to occur under certain circumstances. As opposed to balancing against a threatening state, bandwagoning refers to joining in with the would-be aggressor in the hope of either benefiting directly from conquest or at least averting losses. Balance-of-threat theory also contributes to the diversity of realism by integrating perceptions, as opposed to more purely material considerations, into theorizing about what states can be expected to do. Two theories are identified within balance of threat: a generic version, along with one that focuses on effects from revolution.

Chapter 14 conveys balance-of-interests theory. This theory, which emphasizes variation among goals pursued by states, emerged from a critique directed toward balance of threat. In order for threats to exist in the international system, at least some aggressive states must exist (Schweller 1994, 1998, 2004, 2006). Interests pursued by states in foreign policy are explained, at least in part, through processes unfolding at the domestic level. This is not, however, a rejection of realism's state-centric outlook on the world. Instead, balance-of-interests theory elaborates on power politics through identification of different kinds of states. While power as a resource is the goal at a strategic level, the tactics observed in the international system are not simply one variety of balancing or another. Thus balance-of-interests theory claims to be more realistic in its expectation of diverse foreign policies among states and pathways to war. Balance-of-interests theory exists in three variants: additive, extremely incoherent states, and polarized democratic.

Chapter 15 is about defensive realism. Exponents of this theory see the international system as one that, in general, does not facilitate expansionism. The specific form that the quest for power takes under such circumstances is pursuit of security (Van Evera 1999). Three theories about the causes of war, each with an overlapping set of contributing factors, fit within defensive realism. The first theory emphasizes first-mover advantage as a property of the international system that can set in motion processes that threaten its stability. A second theory focuses on windows of opportunity, which aggressor states, figuratively speaking, may jump through in pursuit of gains at the expense of others. Third, and finally, the offense-defense balance possesses potential to destabilize a system. The dangerous situation is one in which the offense is at an advantage, whereas dominance for defense is less likely to encourage efforts toward conquest.

Dynamic differentials, a theory that emphasizes the impact of change in the distribution of capabilities, is covered in Chapter 16. Major war becomes more likely when a great power experiences significant decline (Copeland 2000). While at any given time some states will have aggressive leadership at the helm, escalation to high levels of violence will not necessarily ensue. A key development in bringing about major war is noteworthy decline for a great power. Once its leadership becomes aware of this trend, hard-line policies are likely to follow soon after. This shift threatens the stability of the international system as a whole. Dynamic differentials take the form of a deductive argument about the probability of major war in relation to shifting capabilities among states and how these changes feed into their interplay at the apex of the international system (Copeland 2000). Multiple pathways to war are identified along the way.

Offensive realism is the subject of Chapter 17. This theory envisions great powers as disposed toward expansion (Mearsheimer 2014 [2001]). Under conditions of anarchy, intentions do not matter because the existence of capabilities, in and of itself, creates a threatening situation between states. Thus a rational response for a great power to this predicament is to go on the offensive. The more power that can be accumulated, all other things being equal, the higher the level of security that results. Security, however, proves elusive because all of the great powers are thinking the same way. The result is that great power war can be expected to recur within the international system. This feature accounts for the title of the book by Mearsheimer (2014 [2001]) that puts forward the theory, namely, *The Tragedy of Great Power Politics*.

Chapter 18 introduces predation theory, the most recent among realist expositions on the causes of war. Shifrinson (2019a) puts forward an explanation for war that focuses on the dynamics of relative capability among the great powers. Predation theory begins with the insight that "rising states differ wildly in their approaches to declining great powers" (Shifrinson 2019a: 2). Predation theory assumes, with justification, that leaders rarely possess fully accurate information about the distribution of power (Shifrinson 2019a: 3). Policies among rising states therefore will vary by context; there is no deterministic pathway to either peace or war under conditions of strategically significant change in relative capabilities. Predation theory seeks to "understand and account for a rising state's predatory or supportive policies toward its declining peers" (Shifrinson 2019a: 3). The focus is on the politics associated with power shifts. In a major study, *Rising Titans, Falling Giants*, Shifrinson (2019a: 6) puts forward predation theory as an explanation for the degree of conflict observed during times of significant change in relative capabilities. War becomes more likely under such circumstances.

11
Power Cycles

Overview

Power cycle theory focuses on how the dynamics of great power capabilities impact the stability of the international system. Shifts in direction of movement for power shares among the leading states pose challenges for foreign policy leadership, which must cope with new and probably dangerous realities. The onset of major change, in turn, creates tension and greater than usual potential for escalation of conflict. Decades of testing confirm the value of power cycle theory as an explanation for war involving major powers.

Power cycle theory occupies an interesting place in the lexicon of realism. While it turns out to be in compliance with realist principles, the power cycle normally is not included when theories from that school of thought are enumerated. This instance of exclusion reinforces the practice of the present study, which takes into account rationalist and deductive, as well as sociological and inductive, aspects when identifying membership for a theory in one research enterprise or another. Power cycle theory is a member of the realist family, it might be said, which deserves an invitation to its events. The likely reasons for its exclusion from intrarealist dialogues will be explored later in the chapter.

This chapter unfolds in five additional sections. The second section focuses on the meaning of power cycle theory in a gestalt sense and conveys its axiomatic basis. The third section focuses on power cycle theory as an explanation for war. The fourth section concentrates on critiques regarding the theory. The fifth focuses on a visual representation of power cycle theory that conveys cause and effect. The graphic version also is implemented to respond to critiques. The sixth and final section reflects on the contributions of power cycle theory to explanation of why great power war occurs.

What Is Power Cycle Theory?

Power cycle theory focuses on the experiences of the subset of great powers as they eye each other suspiciously within, figuratively speaking, the stratosphere of the international system. Yoon (2003: 9) and many others agree in tracing the origins of power cycle theory to *The Politics of Assimilation* (Doran 1971).

The theory is based on the insight that it is important to "integrate the cyclical and evolutionary aspects of historical change into a unified analytic framework" (Doran 1971: 59). Both relative and absolute changes are essential to understanding conflict processes. The focus is on leading states in the international system. In particular, "Intra-actor organic changes are vital to the potential rise of hegemonies, to their eventual emergence as a major systemic threat, and to the success or failure of their reintegration into the system" (Doran 1971: 60). The process of assimilation is a success, Doran (171: 191) asserts, if a former would-be hegemon does not again threaten its peers and sustains a position as a viable member of the interstate system.

Consider, for example, Germany after World Wars I and II. As a principal result of the harsh Versailles Treaty that followed World War I, anger in German society set the stage for a war of revenge. After World War II, the victorious Allies divided Germany into two states, with the much more capable one in the Western camp and not at all inclined toward further warfare. Political realism as practiced among European leaders focused on recovery from war and making the best of a challenging geostrategic position between the superpowers.

Rather than absolute levels, power cycle theory is concerned with the rhythm of *relative* capabilities among great powers. Research reveals that, over a long period of history, the share of capabilities for each great power moves along a pathway that resembles a sine wave. These cycles of relative power vary in height and length from one leading state to the next, but always possess the same basic shape. Declining states recede from the great power subset over time and are replaced by rising states that begin to take on major roles in the central system (Doran 1989b: 87). According to Doran (1989b: 85), at least a dozen major states have gone through segments of their power cycle from the sixteenth century onward. Among the six major systems transformations since the modern state system started, only the collapse of the USSR ended peacefully (Doran 2012: 78). War in proximity to critical points during power cycles is the anticipated means toward change at the systems level, but, Doran asks, what is the causal direction of structural change and the proximate warfare?

Along the power cycle, critical points occur at four locations. At such critical points, "Change suddenly counters the linear trend," and inverted expectations about force become probable during an abnormal interval along the power cycle (Doran 1989b: 90, 109). The two simple points are the minimum and maximum along the curve. In the former instance, increase replaces decrease, and in the latter instance, vice versa. Two points midway along each side of the curve, called inflections, correspond to when the rate of change itself reverses. The first point of inflection occurs when the rate of increase begins to slow down, eventually reaching the maximum of the curve. The second point of inflection takes place when the rate of decrease begins to slow down, culminating in the minimum of the curve.

Does power cycle theory qualify as realist? To answer that question, recall the basic assumptions of realism as a research enterprise: anarchy, state-centrism, rationality, and power seeking. Power cycle theory clearly is in line with this set of beliefs. Doran (1991: 14) asserts that hegemonic dominance neither devises nor maintains "the mechanics of world order." Anarchy is sustained in the international system. Theorizing about power cycles focuses on the experiences of great powers—an obvious nod to state-centrism. Doran (1991: 25) adds that decision-making about foreign policy "involves rational choice on the part of government concerning the ends and means of foreign policy." Given limitations on time and resources, this is in line with an ordinal sense of rationality. In other words, decision-makers are anticipated to respond, although not all at once, in a manner that is consistent with the direction of the changes that are observed.

Perhaps most obviously in light of its emphasis on the dynamics of relative capability, actors in the world of the power cycle are assumed to engage in power seeking. In reference to great powers, Doran (1991: 55) observes that "the leading players compare themselves to each other as a set, rather than to the system as a whole." Thus power as a resource is pursued; the quest is to obtain a preferred position even among the elite of the international system. There is no reason to believe, moreover, that power cycle theory would not extend this assumption to states in general. While a minor power would not assess its standing in relation to great powers around the globe, it could be expected to show concern with developments in relative capabilities within its immediate neighborhood.

Many other statements of the four axioms from realism appear throughout the corpus of work on power cycles and conflict processes. However, what about other assumptions? Does power cycle theory include further axioms that should be specified? The need to answer that question makes this an ideal time to introduce a claim from Schweller and Wohlforth (2000: 76) on behalf of realism in general: "The primary causal mechanism of international change is the law of uneven growth of power among states, which continually redistributes power in the system and thereby undermines the international status quo." This is designated as the Realist Law of Uneven Growth (Schweller and Wohlforth 2000: 76). In power cycle theory, this law is an axiom. The rule is applied to derive a particular functional form for the shifts in relative capabilities among the great powers. Cycles of change that resemble sine waves thereby create the dynamics of power and, in turn, stimulate changes in foreign policy that in some instances lead to war when the system is just overloaded with uncertainty and becomes unmanageable.

Taken together, the assumptions of power cycle theory are in compliance with the realist research enterprise. This theory endorses anarchy and state-centrism at the system level, along with rationality and power seeking among states as actors. With its emphasis on dynamics, power cycle theory also includes the Realist

Law of Uneven Growth as an axiom. Cause and effect about war and peace, for this theory, depend upon change in the distribution of capabilities among great powers.

Table 11.1 provides a basic sense of power cycle theory. From its perspective, foreign policy in place for a great power is a function of position along the power cycle. The power cycle corresponds to rhythmic change in the proportion of capabilities for each member of the great power subset. The focus is on system-level regularities to gain insights about continuity and change in policies pursued by major powers. Critical points along power cycles are those that significantly alter or even reverse a trend in place regarding change in the distribution of capabilities held among the great powers. Proximity to critical points challenges the ability of leaders to manage sudden change and greatly increases the risk of war involving major powers.

Despite its plainly realist character, power cycle theory is nowhere to be found in the typologies and taxonomies of Chapter 9. This omission, in its own odd way, vindicates use of both (i) inductive and sociological and (ii) deductive and rational approaches to distinguish realism from other schools of thought. In this context, the first approach alone would not be sufficient to identify a full set of realist theories about war. The second way is required to situate power cycle theory within realism.

Why, then, is power cycle theory excluded from ongoing realist exchanges about international relations? Self-identified realists either perceive power cycle theory as being outside their domain or remain unaware of it. This outcome likely is the result of certain properties discussed during identification of axioms for a research enterprise in Chapter 8. Recall that some realists reject the concept of rationality because of its association with highly mathematical expositions associated with game theory in particular and formal modeling in general. Rational choice in this context therefore is regarded as out of touch with reality. This point extends to quantitative methods per se, which have provided the overwhelming amount of evidence in support of power cycle theory. These observations combine to solve the mystery about power cycle being left out of conversations among self-identified realists.

Power cycle theory, as will become apparent, relies upon mathematical formulas and lends itself quite easily to testing with statistical data. Yet the theory clearly resides within the canon of realism and will be explored as an explanation for war in that context. Note that the emphasis on foreign policy role creates a connection with the overall agenda of classical realism. In particular, this point of view can be associated with Wight (1978 [1946]) on seeking gain, Kissinger (1957) with regard to alliances, and Wolfers (1962) about aggressive and threat-perceiving states.

Table 11.1 Power Cycles at a Glance

Source	Summary Statement
Doran (1971: 2, 192–4)	[by] observing the cyclical patterns of relative war-potential variation between states, the political analyst may overcome the limitations of the balance-of-power theory as it is traditionally conceived.... This is necessary because the evolution of real systemic novelty is largely dependent upon patterns of long-term change in relative war potential. [2] ... Based on historical intuition and fragmentary data, we already have some notion as to where ... on the cyclical path of relative individual war potential variation ... the various hegemonies of the past have occurred, although the curves have never been drawn. Such analyses deny [balance-of-power stances that] automatically equate hegemonic activity with excessive maximized power [Figure 4, p. 193].
Doran (1980: 36)	Analysis of the mode [the political substance] of systems transformation is critical to a determination of how far-reaching systems change will become.
Doran and Parsons (1980: 947)	Relative nation-state capability follows a generalized nonlinear pattern over long periods.... Specific changes [turning points, inflection points] in a state's relative capability dynamics increase its propensity to initiate extensive war.
Gilpin (1981: 95)	The differential growth of power among groups and states is very important to an understanding of the dynamic of international relations (see especially Doran,1971; 1980).
Doran (1983: 427)	... power cycle theory emphasizes that the causes and consequences of major war are inseparable from the international political system which actor and process define and within which alone they can have meaning.
Levy (1985: 352)	The nature of a state's foreign policy is a function of its position on its power cycle.
Doran (1989a: 371)	Confronting widespread ambiguities in concept and research design, this article ...1) dissects the cycle of relative power and role to elucidate the concept of general equilibrium, depicting graphically the trauma of role adjustment that accompanies critical changes in relative power; (2) compares the empirical results for transitions and critical points using the same set of data; (3) shows mathematically that the inversion in the trend of slope can approximate critical intervals; and (4) demonstrates via diagrams of each state's critical change why the disequilibrated system 1885–1914 succumbed to massive world war. Empirical research ... must incorporate both strategic power-balancing and power-role equilibrium fir states in the central system in a broader concept like general equilibrium.

(*continued*)

Table 11.1 Continued

Source	Summary Statement
Doran (1991: 93, 98, 104–106)	There is a time when the tides of history change.... This existential interval is the critical point on the state power cycle. [93] ... The essence of critical change is an inversion from the prior trend of the curve, taking the state farther and farther away from past expectations. [98] ... *Lower turning point: birth throes of a major power.... First inflection point: trauma of constrained ascendancy.* [104] ... *Upper turning point: trauma of expectations foregone... Second inflection point: hopes and illusions of the second wind.* [105] ... *Lower turning point [ending the cycle]: throes of demise as a major power.* [106]
Jervis (1992: 861)	The international system is prone to wars at particular points in the rise and fall of great powers.
Doran (2003: 21; 28)	The principles of the power cycle reveal the unique perspective of statecraft in the expectations, and unexpected non-linearities, of relative power change in contrast to the perspective of absolute trends.... Together, the relative power changes on these component power cycles map the *changing structure of the system*.... Over time, the changing systems structure reflects each state's rise and decline in systemic share. [21] ... The principles of the power cycle, and their predictions, are quite in contrast to those of other structural theories. [28]
Inoguchi (2003: 167)	Power cycle theory is a robust framework seeking to account for the foreign policy behaviors of national actors placed in competitive situations.
Yoon (2003: 5)	Power cycle theory is an outgrowth of this tradition of searching for regularities in international history and attempting to draw practical implications for the policymakers of contemporary international politics.
Doran (2012: 77)	Change usually takes place on a flat chessboard; it becomes twisted and distorted around critical points.

Expositions on the Causes of War

Power cycle theory, as a way of looking at war, concentrates on aspects associated with realism: the number of great powers, their relative capability and roles within the international system. Studies two decades apart share the status of a magnum opus with regard to power cycle theory: *The Politics of Assimilation* (Doran 1971) and *Systems in Crisis* (Doran 1991). Power cycle theory, as per its placement in Figure 9.1, is classified as a dynamic and system-oriented theory and this point seems well recognized in the field. Cashman (2013), for example, sums up the power cycle as a theory that focuses on change in the international system. A key element for recognition as a theory about systems is the central role designated for unanticipated effects. Put differently, it is not obvious what will ensue from a specific shift in power shares when encountered at a critical point in the cycle. Thus properties of the international system cannot be inferred in a strictly additive way on the basis of individual actions. Put differently, power cycle theory leans inherently toward systemism.

Growth in capabilities, which serves as the foundation of structure, takes the form of a logistical curve. This reflects "nonlinear growth in the context of limited resources" and thus relative power focuses on distribution of capabilities among major powers (Doran 1991: 9).[1] This emphasis on material capabilities is in line with realist theories in general, which tend to emphasize resources that states might use to influence each other (Wohlforth 1993: 4). Within a competitive international system, relative capability among great powers therefore follows a dynamic that is cyclical (Doran and Parsons 1980: 949). The resulting pattern for any given state takes the form of a sinusoidal wave, except that displacement and duration will vary from one state to the next.

Power cycle theory asserts that, at each of the four critical points on the cycle, role change is most traumatic for state leaders. The trend within the dynamic of power inverts abruptly (Doran and Parsons 1980: 949). In other words, foreign policy role is stable for a long time, but at critical points, perceptions of it lag behind changes in power (Doran 1989a: 377). Thus the great powers, when confronted with a critical point, realize suddenly that prior thinking about relative power is "radically mistaken" (Cashman 2013). These critical points challenge the ability of leaders to manage their portfolio of interests.

Power cycle theory asserts that the dynamics of state capability and role create fundamental reasons for major war, which is high in intensity (battlefield deaths), magnitude, and duration (Doran 1989a: 374, 1991: 95). At critical points on the cycle, change in power is abrupt and nonlinear. This interferes with role projection; perception lags behind reality. Disagreements about such fundamental matters therefore can lead to "initiation of major war (not just the weaker claims of incidence and association)" (Doran 1991: 9; see also Doran 1989a: 375). Accelerating events can create cognitive overload that overwhelms the ability of ordinal rationality to locate and implement agreements that are viable alternatives to war.

Appendix 11.A includes Figure 1 from Doran and Parsons (1980: 949), depicted as Figure 11.A, to facilitate presentation of the theory. The two inflection

---

[1] Doran (1991: 7) enumerates standard measures of material power: size (iron and steel production, population, and size of armed forces) and development (energy use [coal production] and urbanization). For the period after World War II, size of armed forces and urbanization are replaced with defense spending and GNP per capita. On the complexities facing assessment of power in the new millennium, see Rosecrance and Steiner (2010: 363).

points are *b* and *d*, and the two turning points are *a* and *c*. At these critical points, leaders of a state are "most vulnerable to overreaction, misperception or aggravated use of force which may generate massive war" (Doran and Parsons 1980: 949). Each critical point violates monotonicity and linearity with regard to relative capabilities. These inevitable shifts in relative capability concern velocity and acceleration (Doran and Parsons 1980: 951). Figure 11.A conveys the equations underlying the power cycle theory of war.

Uncertainty suddenly becomes monumental in and around a critical point. Sustained knowledge about the power structure is out of date abruptly and *risks no longer can be estimated properly* (Doran 1991: 28). For a great power, this new situation produces a desire to resolve ambiguity. How should the leadership adjust in terms of foreign policy role? The challenge of answering this question, in turn, causes the pace of events to increase.

According to Doran (1991: 33), severe foreign policy threat stems from

(1) the shock of abrupt, unanticipated change in relative power; (2) the nature and ineluctability of the associated change in the projection of role; (3) the high stakes involved; (4) the increase in uncertainty associated with decision making; (5) the raw military strength at the disposal of major rivals, and (6) the presence of power-role gaps now suddenly the focus of foreign policy attention. When several states undergo such critical changes on their power curves at about the same time, the level of threat in the system becomes excessive.

When multiple states face severe power-role surplus or deficits that demand adjustment, the international system experiences a shift out of equilibrium. The probability of world war rises to a maximum level (Doran 1989: 380; see also Doran 1989: 375, 1991: 40). This occurs because leaders, who are expected to live up to the standard of ordinal rationality, will not respond immediately and perfectly to movement away from equilibrium. Coping will lag behind challenging events.

Each critical point entails more specific types of challenge to the stability of the international system. Points *a* through *d* are considered in turn.

When the cycle gets underway at point *a*, the minimum along the curve, "Recent entrants into the system reveal expansionist proclivity and heady nationalism" (Doran and Parsons 1980: 951). Impatience in foreign policy is likely to follow on from such preferences. War, if it occurs around this point, is likely to be intense. Serious danger exists because of a looming threat to the territorial status quo. The Russo-Japanese War, which occurred in 1905, is a case in point.

For points *b* (first inflection) and *c* (maximum), decline in the rate and level of relative capability, respectively, is inevitable. At point *b*, linear projections suddenly exceed actual growth. The shock is even greater at point *c*, when relative

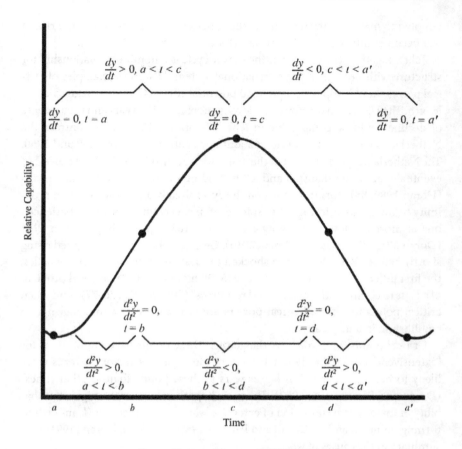

Source: Doran and Parsons (1980: 949, Figure 1).

Figure 11.A Power Cycle Theory

capability abruptly goes into decline. Dealing with these unpleasant surprises can produce defensiveness out of insecurity and attendant aggressiveness in trying to maintain a long-standing foreign policy role (Doran and Parsons 1980: 951–952).

Also challenging is the situation at point *d*, the second inflection (Doran and Parsons 1980: 952). A great power passing through point *d* faces cross-pressures. On the one hand, it increasingly depends on alliance partnerships with more powerful states to secure existing interests. On the other hand, the great power could seek to reverse the process of decline—for which it may not be prepared at all. The onset of a reduced *rate* of decline at point *d* therefore could trigger "foreign policy over-reaction and misperception." Since other great powers could be tempted to make significant gains at the expense of this great power, the risk of war becomes much higher than usual (Doran and Parsons 1980: 952).

Taken together, the essence of the power cycle is a nonlinear relationship for structure with process in the international system. Historical examples of critical points should help to comprehend potential effects. Cycles, to begin, vary in length. The US rise on the power cycle took more than 175 years and thus a phase of decline could be comparable in length (Doran 2012: 75). By contrast, the Netherlands completed its cycle in about one century, between 1650 and 1750. The Netherlands paid for most of the major wars against Louis XIV of France, but eventually became exhausted and fell behind new and rising industrial powers (Doran 1989: 85). Turning points on the cycle already are known to be in proximity to major historical junctures; for example, each great power experienced one or more of these challenging events from 1880 up the Great War in 1914 (Doran 2012: 78; see also Cashman 2013). German relative power stopped rising shortly before World War I and shocked the system. In the era after Versailles, the first inflection point for Japan in 1935–39 highlighted a "perceived problem of access to commodities and natural resources" (Doran 2012: 76, 77). And when critical points for multiple great powers are near each other, the challenge to equilibrium is at its greatest.

Critical points, in a word, are dangerous. These points have implications for "extensiveness of war initiation and use of force," and "A major power is more likely to become involved in *bigger* wars at these points than at other times" (Doran and Parsons 1980: 952). The basic hypothesis is that the highest probability of major power initiation of extensive war is near inflection (b and d) and turning points (a and c) (Doran and Parsons 1980: 952–953). Doran (1991: 115) summarizes the causes of war:

> At least three sources of instability are at work within the critical interval. First, suddenly discovered nonlinearity at a critical point on the state power cycle creates a foreign policy disjuncture which the state finds difficult to accept and to cope with in policy terms. Second, fissures long in the making between power and role come to the surface during a critical interval because the clash of interests both internal to the polity and external to it tear away the delusion that has half-concealed these clefts in the past. Third, war results from the inversion of force expectations inside the critical interval.

These sources of instability reinforce each other and greatly increase the likelihood of major war at or around critical points for the great powers (Doran 1991: 116).

Encouraging to see in power cycle theory are ongoing assertions that show awareness of the need for comprehensive theorizing as per systemism. To cite just a few instances, changes in "interacting state units and changing systemic structure are inseparable (albeit different) aspects of a single structural dynamic" (Doran 1991: 117) and power cycle theory reasons "from the evolution of individual state foreign policy to the international system and then, given that perspective, from the international system to the foreign policy behavior of the individual state" (Doran 1989b: 83). Yoon (2003: 5) adds that power cycle theory theorizes about both the structure of the system and decisions among its actors. These properties, from a systemist point of view, are desirable for any theory.

Data analysis offers consistent support to power cycles, so just a few examples of war-related findings are summarized here. One study focuses on 77 cases of war initiation by a major power—coded by magnitude, severity, and duration. The hypothesis about proximity to critical points is confirmed by that data (Doran and Parsons 1980: 957, 960). Another research design includes 28 states and 36 dyads during test periods that also encompass power transitions for the years from 1816 to 1975. It turns out that only transitions "occurring at a critical point (high, low, first inflection, or second inflection) are likely to lead to major war" (Doran 1989a: 382, 388; see also Doran 1991).

Through testing of a basic hypothesis that links critical points to likelihood of alliance formation, Chiu (2003: 130) produces support for power cycle theory. Chiu (2003: 130) focuses on critical points from 1814 to 1985 and relies on alliances and interstate wars from the usual sources (e.g., COW). Data analysis associates critical points, but not alliance formation, with the incidence of war (Chiu 2003: 134). This finding is important to power cycle theory because alliances appear epiphenomenal by comparison to critical points in accounting for war.

Case studies on war also support power cycle theory. One example concerns Iraq—noteworthy because it provides evidence from beyond the strictly great power subset. Wars involving Iraq with Iran and a US-led coalition occurred in proximity to critical points (Parasiliti 2003). Iraq, for example, "peaked in relative power prior to the Gulf War" and experienced "acute relative decline at the time it invaded Kuwait" (Parasiliti 2003: 160). Thus Parasiliti (2003: 160) accounts for Saddam Hussein's decision in favor of war as a failed adjustment to significant shifts in the strategic environment. Iraq went into relative decline after the war with Iran from 1980 to 1988. The subsequent attack on Kuwait in 1990 reflected concerns about "loss of regional power," such as the share of oil production in comparison to Kuwait, Saudi Arabia, and the UAE (Parasiliti 2003: 160).

What can be said in an overall sense about results from testing power cycle theory? Studies from Yoon (2003), Inoguchi (2003), and various others support the idea and associated evidence from Doran (1989, 1991) that proximity to critical points in the power cycle is associated with conflict processes.[2] Cashman (2013), in particular, observes that studies from Doran have been replicated many times. Inoguchi (2003: 172; see also Doran 2012: 80) observes that the power cycle, given complex and fundamental changes in Asia, will retain significance in the new millennium. Furthermore, a study with results that contradict the association of critical points with war among great powers has yet to appear.

Critiques

Interesting to consider is the relatively light criticism of power cycle theory. This may be a product of its successful explanation for war, but also a place outside the intense debates associated with theories explicitly designated as realist. Discussion will focus primarily on reactions to the two major books associated with the power cycle: *The Politics of Assimilation* (1971) and *Systems in Crisis* (1992). Critiques, to be reviewed in turn, so far have focused on (a) potential for falsification, (b) statement of hypotheses and the role of surprise, (c) exclusion of domestic politics, and (d) measurement of capabilities.

With relevance to falsification criteria, consider the following summary statement by (Doran 1991: 2):

> At a minimum, structure involves the number of actors within the central or great power system, their relative power, their systemic roles, the extent of polarization (ideological as well as structural), the nature and extent of alliance association, and the nature of the norms and codes of governing behavior constituting the prevailing international regime.

With this enumeration of structure, can the hypotheses of power cycle theory be refuted? Its sense of structure would appear to go beyond the boundaries of the realist research enterprise and thereby create potential "escape clauses" for propositions that are not supported by testing.

While taking a positive view of the theory in an overall sense, Mansbach (1992: 839), raises issues about statement of hypotheses, noting "tension between the claim that shifts are perceived and the central role played by surprise in the analysis." Moreover, according to Mansbach (1992: 840), "The process by which perception takes place remains nebulous." Jervis (1992: 861) also challenges the theorizing, but in a more fundamental way, expressing skepticism that either the power cycle (or any other single) theory can explain all wars. In particular,

---

[2] Hebron, James, and Rudy (2007) produce evidence that links foreign policy crises and MIDs with proximity to critical points.

observes Jervis (1992: 863), the element of surprise is emphasized by Doran (1991), but is "not always associated with high tensions and wars." Disintegration of the USSR can be cited as just one example of how major war is not inevitable in the wake of rapid and unanticipated change at the level of the international system (Jervis 1992: 863).

One criticism pointed toward the theory—its lack of a role for domestic politics (Jervis 1992: 863)—is a byproduct of a structural emphasis. While power cycle theory is not exclusively about system-level processes, its treatment of foreign policy decision-making could benefit from elaboration. Insights from the study of crisis management, for instance, could be accessed to obtain a more complete story about major power war.

What about the measurement of capability upon which the power cycle relies? Specifically, Rosecrance (1974: 860, 861) takes issue with the attempt to "reach conclusions by means of estimates of crude power." The goal instead should be to inquire into how power is exercised in order to obtain "the key to war" (Rosecrance 1974: 861). In a more general sense, the power cycle is typical of realist theories in its emphasis on material aspects of power. Perhaps the theory, to sustain relevance in the new millennium, would benefit from a review of conceptualization and measurement for capabilities.

Graphic Representation

Figure 11.1 offers a graphic account of how power cycle theory explains major power war.[3] The story begins in Figure 11.1a with designation of the great power subset as the system and the international system as its surrounding environment. Figure 11.1b conveys the initial macro-micro connection: "ANARCHY" → "foreign policy role." As the point of origin for cause and effect, "ANARCHY" is designated with an oval. An essential element in power cycle theory is the way in which leaders conceive of their role within the system. This refers to both expansiveness and content of action. While seeking power is paramount, rational leaders are anticipated to keep their aspirations and associated foreign policies in line with what is feasible. This is expected for states across the board—even great powers. The principal decision at the national level is spending on capacity to act abroad. While military capability on land and sea and in the air would be most basic, other aspects matter as well. Additional considerations include degree of international economic involvement and range of diplomatic activity.

---

[3] This visual representation is based upon Doran and Parsons (1980: 948–953), Doran (1989: 374–388), and Doran (1991: 9–14, 33–55, 98–117). An informative consultation with Charles F. Doran produced the final version of Figure 11.1.

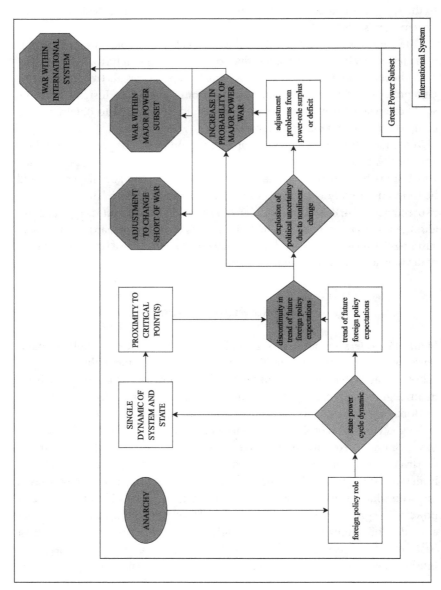

Figure 11.1 Power Cycle Theory

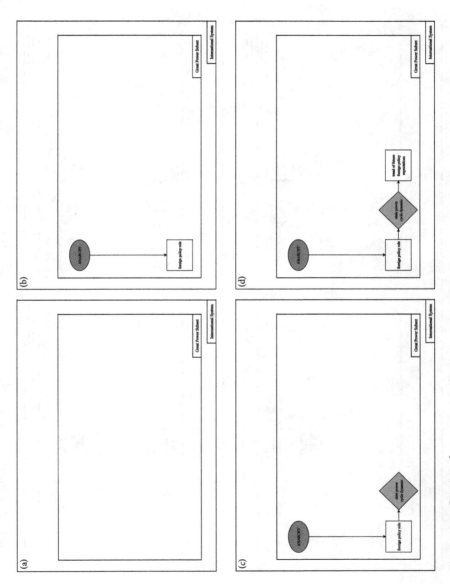

Figure 11.1 Continued

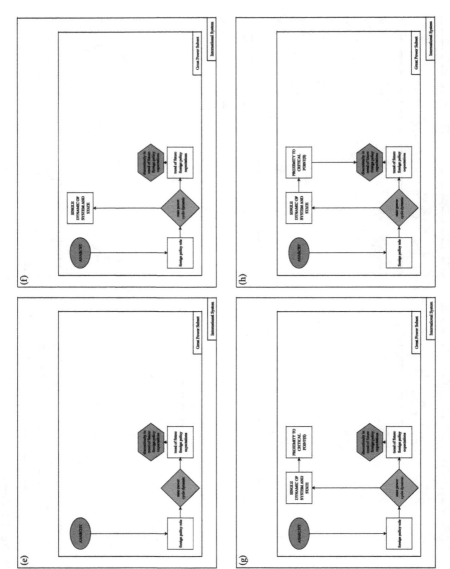

Figure 11.1 Continued

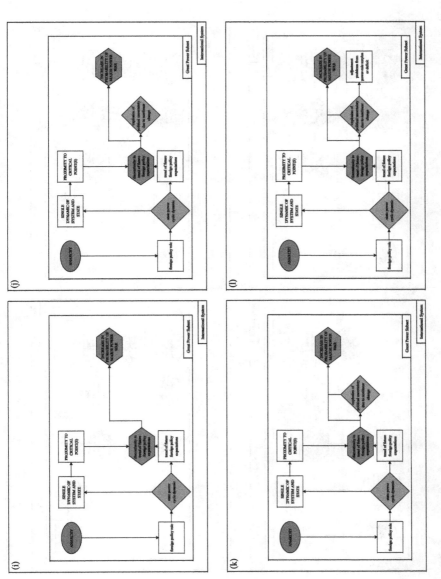

Figure 11.1 Continued

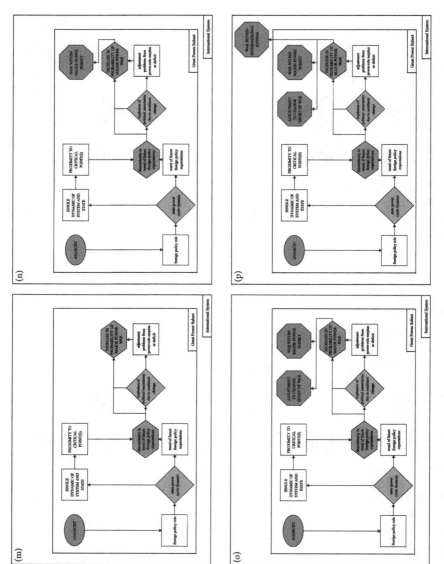

Figure 11.1 Continued

Figure 11.1c displays a micro-micro connection: "foreign policy role" → "state power cycle dynamic." Note that "state power cycle dynamic," a divergent variable, is depicted as a diamond. The linkage refers to the rhythmic movement along the power cycle that is shaped by allocation of resources to "guns and butter" respectively. For example, a highly demanding foreign policy role can impact the height and length of the power cycle because resources are deployed to short-term, security-related purposes; in turn, this reduces what is available for investment in the long-term.[4]

Figure 11.d adds the following connection along one of the pathways for the divergent variable: "state power cycle dynamic" → "trend of future foreign policy expectations." Leaders will anticipate a linear progression in terms of capability in connection with foreign policy actions. Role expectations, in other words, become entrenched. This is in line with the staying power of the status quo. As identified by Samuelson and Zeckhauser (1988), bias toward processing information will tilt toward the status quo, in this context meaning a sense of linearity in expectations about the future.

Micro-level convergence moves forward in Figure 11.1e with "trend of future foreign policy expectations" → "discontinuity in trend of future foreign policy expectations." Note that the latter, a nodal variable, appears as a hexagon. Introspection among leadership is to be anticipated at this point in terms of foreign policy role. For example, intense reflection on the burdens of a vast empire took place in Great Britain at the outset of the 20th century. The title of an authoritative work on the subject, *The Weary Titan*, provides a sense of what that involved for Whitehall (Friedberg 1988).

Figure 11.1f depicts movement from the micro to the macro level, namely, "state power cycle dynamic" → "SINGLE DYNAMIC OF SYSTEM AND STATE." For each member of the great power subset, it is possible to identify a cycle in its proportion of capabilities. This takes the form of a sinusoidal wave without fully uniform length and height. In other words, the cycles for any two great powers would be unlikely to feature the same duration or range with regard to share of capabilities. These waves unfold over decades and combine to form an overarching trait of the international system. Added in Figure 11.1g, the next linkage is "SINGLE DYNAMIC OF SYSTEM AND STATE" → "PROXIMITY TO CRITICAL POINT(S)." Turning points for (i) rate of change and (ii) acceleration are built into the mathematical formulas that trace out each power cycle. There are four critical points, as per above, for each great power. Given variation

---

[4] For insightful treatments of issues related to trade-offs in foreign policy and international relations, which identify a range of possibilities for allocation of resources to security versus other purposes, see Powell (1999) and Hughes and Hillebrand (2006).

in height and length, it is possible for the critical points of great powers to be either at some distance or close in proximity to each other.

When one or more great powers is near a critical point, a connection points downward from the system to the state level. This linkage, added in Figure 11.1h, is "PROXIMITY TO CRITICAL POINT(S)" → "discontinuity in trend of future foreign policy expectations." This connection is most dramatically visible at the minimum and maximum points of the cycle, but also deemed significant at points of inflection, where the rate of change begins to increase or decrease. Previous trends either are reversed or change qualitatively with regard to pacing at a critical point. Thus a rising or declining great power that experiences a reversal is much like a person seated on a roller coaster who, at a comparable point on their ride, suddenly is looking upward or downward instead of the reverse. The points of inflection are more subtle but also important in producing a realization that capabilities and role are evolving away from each other. At the first inflection point, halfway up the curve, comes awareness that the positive trend now is slowing down. At the second inflection point, the opposite occurs, with the downward trend diminishing. At the preceding points, leaders must reflect upon whether the foreign policy role, in terms of expansiveness and even content, is either (a) too ambitious or (b) missing out on opportunities.

One branch from the nodal variable moves up to the macro level in Figure 11.1i: "discontinuity in trends of future foreign policy expectations" → "INCREASE IN PROBABILITY OF MAJOR POWER WAR." As a nodal variable, the latter appears as a hexagon. Rapid and complex developments overwhelm information processing via ordinal rationality. As an analogy, consider the role played by the clock in a chess match; its purpose is to limit the time available for moves by each player. At a critical point in the power cycle, time is compressed and can create errors among foreign policy leadership that compare to those of an otherwise competent chess player who simply cannot process the situation on the board within the limits in place. In the real world and the chess game alike, the result can be a blunder and subsequent undesirable outcome.

Awareness of a fundamental change in trend leads to movement along another branch from the nodal variable, added in Figure 11.1j, which is "discontinuity in trend of future foreign policy expectations" → "explosion of political uncertainty due to nonlinear change." As a divergent variable, the latter is depicted as a diamond. These stresses and strains quite naturally can produce foreign policy crises, any one of which might lead into major power war. Note that, at this stage, adjustment problems could produce more limited wars within a given region. Consider, for example, the Balkan Wars that took place just a few years before World War I. Great powers did not participate directly in these conflicts, which featured a range of smaller states on each side, and the violence reflected uncertainty and volatility that increasingly came to characterize Europe as a whole leading up to August 1914.

Figure 11.1k shows a micro-macro connection: "explosion of political uncertainty due to nonlinear change" → "INCREASE IN PROBABILITY OF MAJOR POWER WAR." As a nodal variable, the latter appears as a hexagon. War becomes more likely as cognitive overload takes hold among leaders confronted with accelerating and menacing developments.

Another route from the divergent variable, added in Figure 11.1l, moves along the micro level: "explosion of political uncertainty due to nonlinear change" → "adjustment problems for power-role surplus or deficit." Errors among great powers in assessing their relative capabilities ensue in a way, it should be noted, that is entirely consistent with ordinal rational choice. Time pressure under crisis conditions can lead to escalation and ultimately produce a war neither planned nor desired by some of its participants.

Figure 11.1m conveys a micro-macro connection: "adjustment problems for power-role surplus or deficit" → "INCREASE IN PROBABILITY OF MAJOR POWER WAR." Recall the model of cognition from the metatheory of progress, which points toward overload as an ongoing challenge to information processing. Anticipated at this stage is the onset of crisis. Time pressure under such conditions induces errors that accumulate and pave the way to war.

Movement continues along a pathway depicted in Figure 11.1n: "INCREASE IN PROBABILITY OF MAJOR POWER WAR" → "WAR WITHIN MAJOR POWER SUBSET." The latter, as a terminal variable, appears as an octagon. This connection focuses on the escalation of crisis to war, which is the expected outcome under conditions that resemble the playing of Russian roulette.

Figure 11.1o shows another path to conclusion: "INCREASE IN PROBABILITY OF MAJOR POWER WAR" → "ADJUSTMENT TO CHANGE SHORT OF WAR." As a terminal variable, the latter appears as an octagon. This outcome is a product of successful crisis management, which remains possible even at the brink of war.

Last comes Figure 11.1p, which connects the macro level to the international system: "INCREASE IN PROBABILITY OF MAJOR POWER WAR" → "WAR WITHIN INTERNATIONAL SYSTEM." As a terminal variable, "WAR WITHIN INTERNATIONAL SYSTEM" is depicted as an octagon. This represents an escalation from regional warfare to strife among great powers in the international system. Note that power cycle theory, with many contingencies along the way, sees a range of possible outcomes, from successful crisis management all the way along to a general war in the international system.

With a graphic exposition in place, what can be said about the types of variables and connections exhibited by power cycle theory? There are 13 variables in the network of cause and effect depicted within Figure 11.1. The diagram features significant contingency—two divergent and two nodal variables. The account of cause and effect is missing just one type of connection, from the international environment back into the great power subset.

Consider the graphic exposition from Figure 11.1 in relation to the range of causes from Kurki (2002): formal, material, final, and efficient. Each is considered in turn, leading up to the three outcomes. One point about the style of presentation should be made that also pertains to what appears for each subsequent theory, all the way through to Chapter 18. While material and final conditions are covered in sequence, the variables that are included under each heading can be mixed together in a given account of cause and effect. This does not occur for power cycle theory, but does take place in later chapters.

Formal causes are background conditions—defining shapes or relations. Anarchy and foreign policy role fit that description for power cycle theory. Great powers under anarchy seek power and compete for control over outcomes. A foreign policy role evolves into place and comes to reflect the staying power of the status quo (Samuelson and Zekhauser 1988).

What about material causes—the passive potentiality of matter, or opportunity to act, in the language of Most and Starr (2015 [1989])? State power cycle dynamic, single dynamic of state and system, and proximity to critical points combine to tell this part of the story. The distribution of material capabilities among great powers, as it nears one or more critical points, creates the potential for rapid change that can culminate in war.

Final causes are the purposes that guide change—or the willingness to act (Most and Starr 2015 [1989]). The ideational components here are trend of future foreign policy expectations, discontinuity in trend of future foreign policy expectations, and an explosion of political uncertainty due to nonlinear change. A felt need to act, with preemptive war as a salient possibility, is one likely product of the preceding set of beliefs and perceptions.

What are the efficient causes, or movers in proximity to outcome, for power cycle theory? This concerns movement that begins with (i) adjustment problems from a power-role surplus or deficit, through to (ii) an increase in probability of major power war, to (iii) an outcome. If crisis management succeeds, the outcome is something other than war. If adjustments fail, the result is either war among members of the regional major power subset or more extensively in the international system.

With the graphic presentation and review of cause and effect in place, it is time to return to the critiques of power cycle theory from earlier in this chapter.

What about the expansive sense of structure? This problem does not intrude into the explanation for war from the power cycle. While structure as put forward in Doran (1991) includes items that fall outside of realism—referring in particular to norms and codes of governing behavior—this does not turn out to be an issue in practice. These aspects of structure do not take on a putative causal role in power cycle theory as applied to war. A nonrealist version of the power cycle could incorporate such variables, but in so doing would spill over into the logic of appropriateness and an associated agenda for research with a normative emphasis.

Consider two other critiques in tandem: the role of surprise and the question of whether the power cycle can stand as an explanation for all wars. It might be more accurate to claim that the power cycle is valuable in tracking the risk of war at the system level, notably among major powers. It even could be associated with other types of destabilizing events, such as crises, but research remains at a very early stage. The graphic exposition in Figure 11.1 highlights the need for elaboration at the micro level. On the one hand, power cycle theory incorporates a foreign policy role in its account of war. On the other hand, further theorizing about how different kinds of states might handle passage through critical points could strengthen explanations for great power war on an individual and collective basis.

What about measurement of power? Power cycle theory relies upon a set of indicators that possess face validity and also find application elsewhere in assessment of capabilities. At the same time, additional measurements might be considered in light of technological changes from the new millennium.

Consider power cycle theory in the context of the Performance Ratio. The theory relies on five assumptions and performs well in testing based on aggregate data about major power war. Thus the power cycle theory looks good with regard to solving empirical problems in terms of breadth. It therefore would be worthwhile to elaborate the power cycle theory, in connection with other versions of realism with more of a state orientation, to obtain greater depth of explanation. The ideas put forward here will be pursued in Chapter 19.

Reflections on Power Cycle Theory

Power cycle theory offers a compelling, realist explanation for great power war. It is linked to classical realism through a focus on foreign policy, notably how leaders of great powers cope with rapidly changing material conditions at a critical point in their cycle. Difficulties in adjustment follow on and endanger peace in the international system. Great power war becomes much more likely than otherwise. It is interesting to note, in spite of its realist character, the general absence of power cycle theory from dialogues among those who identify with that tradition. Engagement of power cycle theory with theories from realism and beyond, later on in Chapters 19 and 20, therefore should be especially worthwhile.

Appendix 11.A
The Power Cycle

Figure 11.1A is taken from Doran and Parsons (1980: 949, Figure 1). It depicts the four critical points, *a* through *d*, when a change in either pace or acceleration occurs with regard to relative capability for a great power. Calculus appears in the figure to give a precise meaning to critical points and pathways that connect them. For the interval from *a* to *b*, the first and second derivatives for relative capability are positive. Gains are being made throughout and more rapidly with time. At point *b*, the second derivative shifts from positive to negative; an analogy is with a vehicle that continues to move faster but at a lower rate of acceleration. Thus from *b* to *c*, the first derivative is positive and the second is negative. Gains continue in each time interval, but at a lower magnitude than the one preceding. At point *c*, relative capabilities begin to diminish. From points *c* to *d*, both derivatives are negative. In the analogy, the car now is slowing down more rapidly. Once at point *d*, losses continue but at a diminishing rate until point *a'*. The first derivatives is negative and the second is positive. The cycle is completed at point *a'*.

12
Structural Realism

Overview

This chapter focuses on structural realism, the theory that has generated the most debate since the modern classical era. The essential idea is to move away from the individual to the system level for an explanation, based on power politics, of conflict as an immanent reality. States seek a balance of power, but war occurs when they are unable to achieve it. World politics resembles an oligopoly from the realm of economics, with the great powers in the role of major corporations that control a market. Structural realism focuses on patterns at the level of the international system as opposed to the details of foreign policy for individual states.

Also known as neorealism, the structural variant obtained that designation because, when put forward by Waltz (1979), it stood as a significant and systematic departure from the classical tradition. As opposed to an emphasis on human nature as the foundation for a world of conflict, structural realism takes its cue from the discipline of economics. Neorealism, according to Waltz (1995: 68), breaks with classical theories in multiple and significant ways: conceptualization of international politics as a system, assessment of cause and effect, interpretation of power, and treatment of the unit level.

Along with subsequent expositions, Waltz (1979) features a metaphor with microeconomics. With the great powers at the center of events, international politics is taken to resemble an oligopolistic market. A few major players control the dynamics of supply and demand—analogous to the leading companies in the oil industry, for example. The focal point of neorealist theorizing therefore is the structure of the international system, understood in terms of the number of great powers. The size of the great power subset is regarded as essential for explaining the degree of stability in an international system, most notably its war proneness.

Work unfolds in five subsequent sections. The second section identifies structural realism in an overall sense and enumerates its axioms. The third section presents structural realist theories about war. The two variants are structural realism in its original form and hegemonic stability theory. The fourth focuses on critiques with regard to structural realist theories. The fifth section offers a graphic representation of structural realism and hegemonic stability as theories about the causes of war. This visualization also is applied in response to points raised by critics. The sixth and final section reflects on the accomplishments and future prospects of structural realism.

What Is Structural Realism?

Two variants exist—structural realism and hegemonic stability theory. As per the classification in Figure 9.1, both variants are system oriented and focus on comparative statics. Each is introduced in turn.

Structural Realism

How does structural realism fit within the set of theories from Table 9.3? It is system oriented and focuses on comparative statics. The theory is the product of a magnum opus, *Theory of International Politics* (Waltz 1979), recognized as the founding work by advocates and critics alike (Freyberg-Inan 2004: 73). Classical realist theories had taken an inductive form and emphasized gleaning of insights from history and philosophy, while neorealism stood in contrast as "heavily deductive" and influenced by microeconomics (Waltz 1995: 68). Along those lines, one observer sees neorealism as the advent of something that claimed to be "founded on scientific truth" (Bew 2016: 221). Structural realism took its inspiration from social scientific concepts available for transportation out of economics and into the study of politics—at the time, a great departure from the philosophical and historical foundations of the classical approach.

Analysis based on the concept of a working international system is the essence of structural realism. "The idea that international politics can be thought of as a system with a precisely defined structure," Waltz (1995: 68) observed, "is neorealism's fundamental departure from traditional realism." Structural realism emphasizes that cause-and-effect relations run not only from states to structure but also in the reverse direction (Waltz 1995: 68; see also Waltz 2003b: 52). The balance of power therefore can be explained as something that results from the nature of an anarchical international system, as opposed to the mere machinations of states. Thus there is more to IR than the study of foreign policy through either proliferating case studies or statistical analysis. Sterling-Folker (1997: 17) adds that system-based theorizing sees anarchy as a situation in which actions are "unregulated and unsupervised," so war can break out at any time.

Table 12.1 conveys structural realism in an overall sense. Embedded within neorealism is an endorsement of deductive theory, inspired by economics, as the pathway to scientific advancement. Anarchy in the international system is

Table 12.1 Structural Realism at a Glance

a. Structural Realism

Source	Summary Statement
Ashley (1984: 230)	Neorealists claim to offer a progressive scientific redemption of classical realist scholarship.
Schroeder (1994: 113, 114)	"All states are guided by structural constraints and imperatives of anarchy, self-help, and balance of power, and must be if they hope to survive and prosper.... States are not functionally differentiated within the structure of international politics."
Brooks (1997: 467)	It would be a caricature, however, to say that neorealists regard international cooperation as impossible—they merely view it as greatly constrained.
Walt (2002: 202)	Waltz's most fundamental contribution was his emphasis on the international system as an active and autonomous causal force.
Schmidt (2007)	All structural realists insist that systemic forces explain why international politics is necessarily a continuous struggle for power.
Parent and Baron (2011: 203)	Neorealism affords a number of advantages. It updated the theoretical foundations of realism. It sharpened how concepts like agent and structure were delimited; it is an extraordinarily parsimonious and elegant option that scholars may use as something of a standard base model, and it provides enduring stimulus for thought and debate.
Elman and Jensen (2014: 6)	The international outcomes that Waltz predicts include that multipolar systems will be less stable than bipolar systems; that interdependence will be lower in bipolarity than multipolarity; and that, regardless of unit behavior, hegemony by any single state is unlikely or even impossible.
Ripsman, Taliaferro, and Lobell (2016: 17)	For Waltz and other structural realists, differential growth rates, which over time change the relative distribution of capabilities between states, are the driving forces of international politics.

b. Hegemonic Stability

Source	Summary Statement
Booth (1982: 507)	Robert Gilpin's world is that of Thucydides with telephones and ICBMs.
Lake (1982: 950)	By combining the sociological approach and the economic (or rational-choice) approach, Gilpin attempts to derive a theory of international change that applies equally well to the fourth century BC and the 20th century AD.

(*continued*)

Table 12.1 Continued

b. Hegemonic Stability	
Fox (1982–83: 684)	The book is notable for use of the concepts of microeconomics and rational choice theory to account for the behavior of great states and their challengers and use of the methods of historical sociology to put our contemporary states system in a genuinely comparative context.
Levy (1985: 351)	A hegemonic war arises because of an increasing disequilibrium between the governance of the system and the actual distribution of power, determined largely by the law of uneven development.
Yoon (2003: 8)	The main cause of global wars is a discrepancy between the existing governance of the international system and the changing distribution of power.

the driving force behind the theory's expectations about the struggle for power. Self-help is the rule for states under anarchy. The distribution of capabilities will shape interactions among states, which are the functionally undifferentiated units in the system. Bipolarity is more stable than multipolarity, within which the balance of power is less likely to preserve the peace.

What about the beliefs of structural realism? Are its assumptions in compliance with realism? Various answers put forward about the axioms of neorealism combine to tell an interesting story. Waltz (1979: 88) draws attention to three dimensions that, taken together, identify the structure of the international system. The first dimension is the ordering principle, which at the international level is anarchy (Waltz 1979: 89, 100). Second among the dimensions is differentiation of units and specification of their functions (Waltz 1979: 88). For the international system, the units are functionally undifferentiated states that seek survival (Waltz 1979: 88, 91, 97, 101; see also Schroeder 1994: 114). The third and last dimension is the distribution of capabilities among units, which for the international system refers to states (Waltz 1979: 88, 101). Taken together, these assertions match well with three of the axioms identified for the basis of realism as a research enterprise: anarchy, state-centrism, and power seeking. Whether states seek to maximize security or power "has become the basis of an important debate among structural realists" (Schmidt 2007). However, security as a desired *end state* is not at odds with power seeking as a *means* toward that objective. Power possesses value in pursuit of any national objective, so foreign policy cannot be anticipated accurately without knowing its purpose (Feaver et al. [Schweller] 2000: 177). The foundation of a state's security is its power, so the two are intertwined (Layne 2006: 17).

Various efforts to enumerate the assumptions of structural realism ensued after Waltz (1979) and, with one issue as an exception, do not stimulate controversy. According to Glaser (1996: 127), structural realism is founded upon a few axioms: "that states can be viewed as essentially rational unitary actors; that states give priority to insuring their security; and that states confront an international environment that is characterized most importantly by anarchy." Bueno de Mesquita (2003: 168) enumerates four central assumptions for neorealism: (1) international politics is characterized by anarchy; (2) states, as rational unitary entities, are the central actors in international politics; (3) states seek to maximize their security above all else, considering other factors only when security is assured; and (4) states try to increase their power if doing so does not put their security at risk. Like various others that could be added, these lists of axioms include rational choice, and that is where disagreement is found.

Quite explicitly, Waltz (1979) denied the presence of rational choice as an assumption of neorealism. Yet James (2002b) observes that the theory *needs* the assumption of rationality in order to explain the processes it claims would exist under conditions of anarchy. Furthermore, O'Loughlin (2008: 114) asserts that the state as a rational actor is central to neorealism. Ripsman, Taliaferro, and Lobell (2016: 22), among others, describe rationality as implicit within neorealism. Controversy seemingly never ends with regard to the presence of rationality among the axioms of structural realism.

From one point of view, Waltz (1979) had just *one* assumption: "States seek to ensure their survival" (Wæver 2009: 210). Schweller (1996: 109), at an earlier time, said the same thing in an implicit way, namely, that the "core tenet is that states under anarchy fear for their survival as sovereign actors." Those who claimed to recognize or even advocate structural realism, by contrast, thought about assumptions in a different way (Wæver 2009: 210):

> Fundamentally different is to list assumptions that are not part of one integrated concept, but separately meant to be "reasonably accurate." This leads to a computational logic of factors that interact. This approaches the if-then format of propositions dominant in IR. The pictorial approach, in contrast, organises around one core idea.

It is revealing that close readings of Waltz (1979) could produce such different views of something so basic, namely, the foundations of structural realism as a theory.

Essential to answer before exploring its vision of war is the question of whether the structural variant indeed qualifies as a realist theory. A review of the axioms from realism as a research enterprise reveals points of ambiguity that, in the end, can be resolved in a satisfactory way. Anarchy and state-centrism are affirmed at various points in Waltz (1979: 95). While security is identified as the principal goal of states, Waltz (1979: 91–92) adds that "the aims of states may be endlessly varied." This assertion is quite important in sorting out the situation regarding goals versus means toward them. The international system, according to Waltz (1979: 91), is "structurally similar to a market economy." Thus seeking power as a *resource* is a logical entailment; it plays a role analogous to money within a market. In the end, the axiom of seeking power is consistent with the rest of the framework developed by Waltz (1979).

Finally, and covered in some detail already, comes the assumption of rationality. The engagement with this concept is a true oddity within the Waltzian world. For example, states are assumed to imitate success. Why, however, would that occur in the absence of instrumental rationality? Rejection by Waltz and some other realists of rationality as an assumption, in all likelihood, is in reaction to its association with highly technical expositions. Every page of Waltz (1979) and subsequent structural realist studies, however, is consistent with *ordinal* rationality. Waltzians, in a touch of irony, may be reacting in line with classical realism as expressed in *Scientific Man and Power Politics* (Morgenthau 1946). Rationality in that work is linked to the idea of human perfectibility—completely out of bounds for realism of all kinds. In addition, rationality models, which even four decades ago tended to include complex diagrams and mathematics, look quite off-putting to the majority of realists, who tilt toward qualitative methods.

One other assumption is embedded within structural realism. Consider its basic hypothesis about the effects of polarity. An additional axiom is clear to see—a threshold effect from two to three among the set of great powers in the international system. The presence of potential coalitions is what underlies Waltzian concerns about the pernicious effects of a more complex system. In a word, it is better to operate under risk, where probabilities can be assigned to possible outcomes, than uncertainty, when that is not possible. None of this is at odds with the four axioms of realism as a research enterprise.

While Waltz (1979) put forward structural realism in opposition to the classical approach, his theory is not without its roots in that tradition. Obvious references are Morgenthau (1959 [1948]) on balance of power and Kissinger (1957) with regard to the role of alliances. The greatest departure from the classics is an approach to theory that is deductive and inspired by economic analysis.

Hegemonic Stability Theory

One other theory, hegemonic stability, is classified as structural realist in nature. It resides at the system level and takes a static form as a theory of war. The theory comes out in the form of a magnum opus, *War and Change in World Politics*

(Gilpin 1981), which followed soon after the advent of structural realism with Waltz (1979). Positive reviews recognized the exposition in Gilpin (1981) as a welcome shift from the "ephemeral micro-analysis" that some perceived as prevailing at the time (Booth 1982: 507). Like structural realism, hegemonic stability borrows significantly from concepts in economics.

With a focus on the structure of the international system, hegemonic stability theory fits in the category of structural realism. Its emphasis is on the standing of the leading state in particular, as opposed to the number of great powers that exist. In a compelling review of realist schools of thought, Taliaferro, Lobell, and Ripsman (2009: 17) reach the same conclusion: hegemonic stability is a structural realist theory. Ripsman, Taliaferro, and Lobell (2016: 18) add that Gilpin would expect a unipolar system "to be the most stable, as none could anticipate a successful war against the unipole, which thus has unfettered power to create a stable order." At the same time, as a realist theory, hegemonic stability sees unipolarity as a temporary condition due to natural forces exerted via competition under anarchy.

Table 12.1b conveys a basic sense of hegemonic stability theory. It is a grand theory about history, war, and system-level change. Hegemonic stability emphasizes the concept of equilibrium based on processes understood through rational choice as well as sociology. War is a product of disequilibrium—uneven development leads to a mismatch between how the system is run and newly rearranged capability shares.

Hegemonic stability theory quite explicitly adopts the four axioms from the realist research enterprise. Gilpin (1981: 7) summarizes international relations as "a recurring struggle for wealth and power among independent actors in a state of anarchy." Thus anarchy and power seeking come together explicitly. Instrumental rationality is incorporated within the analysis and the state is described as the "principal actor in the international system" (Gilpin 1981: x, 17).

Hegemonic stability theory features one additional assumption.[1] The Realist Law of Uneven Growth from Schweller and Wohlforth (2000) clearly is present. Lake (1982: 951) notes the existence of an S-shaped curve for development in the model from Gilpin (1981), during which powers rise but eventually experience

---

[1] While Gilpin (1981: 10–11) enumerates five additional assumptions, each of these really takes the form of a *proposition*. For example: "An international system is stable (i.e., in a state of equilibrium) if no state believes it is profitable to attempt to change the system" (Gilpin 1981: 10). This is not really an axiom but instead an assertion of what will happen under a certain profile of beliefs among states. The status quo is likely to be reinforced under some conditions and challenged under others. Brief reflection on the matter is sufficient to reveal that the additional explicit assumptions from Gilpin (1981: 10–11) instead serve as hypotheses that are expected to hold under respective scope conditions.

diminishing returns, and thus a full-fledged Leviathan never emerges in world politics.

Hegemonic stability theory is connected to classical realism in various ways. The theory is linked to Wight (1978 [1946]) on seeking gain and Wolfers (1962) with regard to aggressive and threat-perceiving states. In addition, Booth (1982: 507) praises hegemonic stability theory for combining insights from multiple disciplines, in an impressive manner, with inspiration from history as worth noting in connection to classical realism.

Expositions on the Causes of War

What does structural realism have to say about the causes of war? The theories from Waltz (1979) and Gilpin (1981) are reviewed in turn.

Structural Realism

Structural realism offers a vision of war as an ongoing feature of international relations under anarchy. For example, Waltz (1988: 44) asserts that the structure of the international system can explain recurrence of war. Thus a central question for structural theory is this one: "How do changes of the system affect the expected frequency of war?" (Waltz 1988: 44). A key consideration is whether the international system features two or more great powers. On the one hand, under bipolarity "a loss for one is easily taken to be a gain for the other" and the leading states therefore "promptly respond to unsettling events" (Waltz 1988: 46). On the other hand, Waltz (1988: 46) observes that, in a multipolar world, "dangers are diffused, responsibilities unclear, and definitions of vital interests easily obscured." Thus potential escalation of conflict under multipolarity is more about miscalculation than overreaction: miscalculation poses greater danger "because it is more likely to permit an unfolding of events that finally threatens the status quo and brings the powers to war" (Waltz 1988: 47). From a structural realist point of view, multipolarity therefore is undesirable across the board (Waltz 1988: 48):

> Interdependence of parties, diffusion of dangers, confusion of responses: These are the characteristics of great-power politics in a multipolar world. Self-dependence of parties, clarity of dangers, certainty about who has to face them: These are the characteristics of great-power politics in a bipolar world.

The hypothesis that bipolarity will be more stable than multipolarity is emphasized by Waltz (1979) and others (e.g., Bueno de Mesquita 2003: 169) as central to structural realism. Two rivals keeping track of each other are preferred to a more complicated situation featuring three or more great powers. War, therefore, is deemed more likely under multipolarity than bipolarity.

Evidence from Waltz (1979: 165–170) focuses on the experiences of the great powers, primarily located in Europe, over the course of two centuries. The story of multipolarity is one of complicated alliance systems that form and break down, with attendant uncertainties that make it more difficult to manage conflict and prevent war. With the advent of bipolarity after World War II, major powers no longer fought wars with each other. From the standpoint of Waltz (1979: 170), precisely because the two leading states eye each other like scorpions in a bottle, their leaders are able to avert a major war because the system is much simpler to manage. This is most notably true with regard to alliance politics.

Hegemonic Stability Theory

Hegemonic stability theory is put forward as an explanation for war in Gilpin (1981). A system is in equilibrium if no state believes that an attempt at change would be "profitable" (Gilpin 1981: 10). Change is pursued through "territorial, political and economic expansion" until marginal costs exceed marginal benefits (Gilpin 1981: 10). According to Gilpin (1981: 11; see also Lake 1982: 951), the status quo is expensive to maintain; economic cost tends to rise faster than economic capacity to support it. This weighs upon the ability and willingness of the leading state to manage the international system. Differential growth rates and technological change can cause costs to exceed benefits, which in turn can encourage efforts to change the status quo (Gilpin 1981: 14). Copeland (2000: 55) adds that, when two most powerful states in the system are roughly equal and one is overtaking the other, there is a higher risk of inadvertent major war. Thus war emerges as a means toward basic change in the international system and also restoration of equilibrium (Gilpin 1981: 15).

Once again, the insightful study of a great power in decline by Friedberg (1988) provides a valuable illustration within the context of a realist theory. At the end of the 19th century, Great Britain sagged under the burdens of empire. It faced a pressing need for consolidation in the face of a rising Germany that, as France had in centuries past, threatened to unite the European continent and thereby endanger even the British home territory itself. German development of a blue water navy caused British concerns about the security of its empire. From the standpoint of Germany, Pax Britannica looked obsolete in the wake of a major shift in relative power. This account of the lead-up to the Great War might even be regarded as the archetypal case for hegemonic stability theory.

Critiques

Each of the structural realist theories continues to exert significant influence on the study of international relations. Critiques of structural realism and hegemonic stability theory are reviewed in turn.

Structural Realism

Over four decades later, *Theory of International Politics* (Waltz 1979) stands as one of the most controversial works in the history of the discipline. For example, Tellis (1996: 89) observes that "the best available general realist theory today, that of Waltz, still remains internally deficient and externally incomplete." Vasquez (1998: 212) points out that neorealism does not perform well under testing. Some critics simply reject structural realism outright as intellectually uninteresting (Fozouni 1995: 499). Yet structural realism endures.

Various lines of criticism and responses are well established in IR. What follows is not intended as a comprehensive coverage of arguments back and forth but instead a survey that will draw attention to the main issues that impact structural realist explanations for war. Critiques begin with abstract matters and move on to more operational concerns.

Debates about structural realism may be categorized as follows: (a) effects from a high level of parsimony; (b) the role of rationality, along with security and power as goals; (c) an inability to account for system-level change; (d) lack of graphic communication; (e) observation of balancing versus other behaviors; and (f) relevance to foreign policy. Each point of criticism is considered in turn.

Although advocates see it positively, various critics have noted effects that follow on from the parsimonious nature of structural realism. Structural realism, as assessed by Bew (2016: 278–279), depends on a "selective and overly mechanized view of the international system." This line of criticism brings to mind the Performance Ratio, which focuses on the degree of success for a research enterprise in solving empirical problems as compared to complexity. Near the outset of the theory's existence, Ashley (1984: 233; see also Fozouni 1995: 499) described as holistic the arguments put forward by structural realism and noted its lack of a role for agency. In the language of systemism, it excludes actor-based causal mechanisms.

Structural realism defines power "in terms of resources" that also are "highly fungible" (Schmidt 2007). This overwhelmingly material assessment of the distribution of capabilities, however, is not enough to say much about what world politics will look like in practice. The international system, in and of itself, "does not always present clear signals about threats and opportunities" (Ripsman,

Taliaferro, and Lobell 2016: 21). Thus the role of uncertainty must enter into structural realism in some way if it is going to explain why states seeking security would not be expected to cooperate with each other (Glaser 2010: 47). How otherwise are power balancing and episodic warfare to be explained? In sum, to improve its Performance Ratio through relevance to a wider range of empirical problems, structural realism must be elaborated.

Based on a wide range of critiques, structural realism would seem to fall short of the standards imposed by systemism for theoretical completeness. Accusations of structural determinism are common, along with admonitions to include theorizing at the micro-level (Fozouni 1995: 501; Fiammenghi 2011: 154). Waltz (1995: 68), however, tended to dismiss such criticism: "Ambiguity cannot be resolved since structures affect units even as units affect structures." This seems defeatist and not at all compelling in light of what systemism offers in terms of graphic representation of theorizing that spans levels of analysis.

All of that leads naturally into critiques related to the role of rationality, along with pursuit of power versus security, among states. Consider the observation by Brooks (1997: 448) that, within a neorealist context, "rational states adopt a worst-case focus because this is the only way to ensure against being caught off guard." Brooks (1997: 449) adds that the preceding assumption "performs the bulk of the explanatory work in the Waltzian neorealist framework." In sum, internal coherence for neorealism depends significantly on the assumption that, generally speaking, actors are quite fearful (Brooks 1997: 449).

Others are uncertain about rationality as an assumption of structural realism but never seem to rule it out. Kahler (1998: 925), for instance, draws attention to the ambiguous role of reason within neorealism. Given "tight structural constraints of international competition and selection," rationality might not seem to be required (Kahler 1998: 925). Waltz, however, does not demonstrate that structures create such consistent and therefore predictable effects (Kahler 1998: 925). The neorealist argument instead is that the international system socializes and "selects in such a way that any state response that is not in line must be anomalous, subject to punishment, and liable to be selected out over time" (Quinn 2013: 178). In the end, however, does this not look suspiciously like instrumental rational choice under different terminology? An answer is available, in another context, from Ripsman, Taliaferro, and Lobell (2016: 22 n. 27): "While Waltz argues that balance-of-power theory does not require an assumption of rationality, most structural realists do make rationality a core assumption of structural realism." If states are not rational, how can threats and opportunities from the system level explain international politics? Taken together, the effects neorealism expects to see in the international system require rational responses by states to external stimuli based on the distribution of capabilities.

Another frequent point of criticism aimed toward structural realism is its lack of ability to account for change (Ashley 1984: 257; Holsti 1995: 40). While neorealism tells a story about what goes on within a given structure—bipolar versus multipolar—how do these entities come and go? An analogy with the market once again comes into play. Supply and demand create a market without any formal process of assembly; an international power structure is inferred to come into being in much the same way.

Perhaps most germane to the present study is the critique put forward about method: a lack of visual aids in the exposition by Waltz (1979). Wæver 2009: 211) observes that *Theory of International Politics* "contains strikingly few diagrams." This is deemed odd because structural realism would seem to be "basically a picture of an arrangement," and thus "one should expect to see it—depicted." The critique would seem justified when looking over the graphics in Waltz (1979) and even later with regard to the level of detail provided. For example, Figure 3.1 in Waltz (200b3: 52), which shows international structure in the top box and interacting units in the bottom box, with arrows in each direction, is very sparse. Hidden, in particular, is the lack of any arrow pointing from the system downward to the state, which puts structural realism at least somewhat out of line with systemism.

Another issue concerns the balance of power, a basic expectation for structural realism. Schroeder (1994: 124), an emphatic critic, claims that neorealist "generalizations about the repetitiveness of strategy and the prevalence of balancing in international politics do not withstand historical scrutiny." Puzzling exceptions, for instance, are failure to balance against the hegemonic ambitions of Louis XIV in the 17th century and Anglo-French domination at the time of the Crimean War (Schroeder 1994: 134, 122). To this could be added Pax Americana in decades following the end of the Cold War. Elman (2003: 13) observes that "it is simply unclear how widespread Waltz believes balancing behavior to be"; moreover, Vasquez (2003b: 98; see also 1998: 284) notes that research has not been very successful in identifying a domain in which the balancing proposition holds.

Neorealism's account of balancing, according to Schroeder (2003: 118), "ignores too much historical evidence." Schroeder (2003: 119) offers the following summary assessment of balancing:

> Balancing has historically been more often a fall-back position than a first choice; states that perceive real threats usually try to handle them, if they can, not by balancing but by other means. The range of alternative responses and strategies, moreover, is not limited to the usual IR categories—bandwagoning, hiding, and buck-passing. One further strategy is what I have called *transcending*, i.e., trying to deal with the dangers both of concentrations of power and of concrete

threats by taking the problem to a higher level, establishing norms of a legal, religious, moral, or procedural nature to govern international practice, with these norms to be somehow maintained and enforced by the international community or by a particular segment of it.

Many instances exist when states perceive a threat but make no effort to balance against it since resistance is regarded as futile and even counterproductive (Schroeder 2003: 121). Rather than acting as a balancer, any number of different roles can be designated for states. Consider the roles observed during one extended period, the first half of the 19th century in Europe: Russia as guardian of the monarchical order; the Papal State functioning as political base for the pope as an independent political actor, and so on (Schroeder 1994: 126). Other approaches adopted by states, past and present, include hiding (e.g., pursuing neutrality or seeking to avoid a threat in some other way), transcending (e.g., trying institutional arrangements), and bandwagoning (Schroeder 1994: 117). Note that transcending in particular lies beyond the boundaries of realism in general.

Numerous critics draw attention, at a more general level, to actions exhibited frequently by states as opposed to a fixed policy of balancing. For instance, Wivel (2005: 357) observes that structural realism "cannot explain why states behave differently when subject to the same structural pressure." Taliaferro (2006: 466) follows up with a more specific question about "why and how states choose among different types of 'internal' balancing strategies, such as emulation, innovation, or the continuation of existing strategies." In sum, the critics are convincing with regard to a need for elaboration of structural realism to account for diverse actions witnessed in the international system.

Critics of structural realism also see it as detached from foreign policy. According to Tellis (1996: 83), the basic internal problem with Waltz's approach "lies in his failure to explain how anarchy in international politics forces states to behave in certain determinate ways which can be explained simply and parsimoniously." There is a missing link from structure to action. Joseph (2007: 348) adds that "the neorealist conception of structure is based on stable patterns of aggregate behaviour ultimately traceable to micro-level behavioural patterns," and Bennett (2013: 473) notes the absence of a social mechanism from agent to structure. Along those lines, Brawley (2009: 1) observes that structural realism is positioned poorly to distinguish when a state would either look for allies that possibly face similar threats or attempt to deploy domestic resources in a more effective way.

Various critiques about a lack of connection to foreign policy are summed up effectively by Ripsman, Taliaferro, and Lobell (2016: 21): "If leader perceptions of systemic constraints diverge from reality and differ from leader to leader, systemic theories of foreign policy and international politics would be, at best, incomplete, as the sources of a state's behavior may lie less in the external environment than in its leaders' psychological make-up." Aggregate patterns anticipated by neorealism could obtain, but not always, or perhaps even often, according to a uniform process among states.

Hegemonic Stability Theory

Critiques of hegemonic stability theory pose an important question without an answer: What about foreign policy? "An encompassing theory of major war," Doran (1989b: 101) observes, "should probe the significance of the remaining segments of the power curve for major war." Shifrinson (2019a: 7) adds that hegemonic stability theory provides "few clues as to why rising states pursue a revisionist or status quo policy." At no point does Gilpin (1981) develop a "formal action and reaction theory" (Lake 1982: 951). Furthermore, hegemonic stability theory focuses in a nearly exclusively way on "competition between a dominant state and a rising challenger, thereby missing the fact that great powers face different incentives for cooperation and competition when more than two great powers are present" (Shifrinson 2019a: 7).

Another critique, with a turn toward measurement, focuses on a threshold effect that is central to the theory. What constitutes a *significant* change in the distribution of power? This is the stimulus for a response from the international system, which is said to be out of equilibrium. A more specific sense of what is meant by change in kind, as opposed to degree, is needed. Otherwise, hegemonic stability theory would not be subject to falsification (Sheetz and Mastanduno [Mastanduno] 1997–98: 173).

Graphic Representation

Structural Realism

Figure 12.1 conveys structural realism in visual form. This graphic is derived from the text of the magnum opus in structural realism, *Theory of International Politics* (Waltz 1979), along with a few diagrammatic expositions available in other sources.[2] Figure 12.1a identifies a region as the system and the

---

[2] This author is deceased and therefore could not be contacted directly to assess the accuracy of the diagram. Figure 12.1 therefore is a composite of several sources. One is Waltz (1979: 102–128, 161–193) with regard to anarchic orders and balances of power, on the one hand, and structural causes and military effects, on the other hand. Additional sources that present structural realism

international system as its surrounding environment. A linkage from the system to the state level appears in Figure 12.1b with "ANARCHY →self-help." As the starting point for cause and effect, "ANARCHY" is designated with an oval.[3] Note that, while at various points Waltz (1979: 91, 105–107, 111, 118) refers explicitly to self-help, a claim is maintained throughout the exposition that theorizing is strictly system-level. This cannot be sustained in light of the key role played by self-help in accounting for the principal cause put forward by Waltz at the system level. Depicted in Figure 12.1c, this micro-macro connection is "self-help" → "DISTRIBUTION OF CAPABILITIES." As a divergent variable, "DISTRIBUTION OF CAPABILITIES" is depicted as a diamond. Two pathways ensue from that point.

Within the two pathways, the first gets underway in Figure 12.1d with "DISTRIBUTION OF CAPABILITIES" → "BIPOLARITY." As a convergent variable, "BIPOLARITY" appears as a parallelogram. A system with two principal powers is one profile that can emerge from any number of processes that unfold over time. This is the preferred structure from the standpoint of Waltz because of the pathway that ensues—better system management in the presence of two main rivals. Thus the connection that follows in Figure 12.1e is "BIPOLARITY" → "great power vigilance." Each of the leading states will be quite keen to keep up with the other. Moreover, because these states are preeminent, it is their dyad that determines how things will work out for the system as a whole. These points account for the next linkage, which appears in Figure 12.1f: "great power vigilance" → "BALANCING." The two leading states will end up in a balanced situation, vis-à-vis each other, and no other state is at a level high enough to alter that situation. Thus a circuit within the figure is completed in Figure 12.1g with "BALANCING" → "BIPOLARITY."

Second is the pathway that gets underway in Figure 12.1h with "DISTRIBUTION OF CAPABILITIES" → "MULTIPOLARITY." A multipolar system features three or more great powers. From a structural realist standpoint, multipolarity is more dangerous than bipolarity and no circuit that entails stability can be expected this time. The next linkage, from the system to the state level in Figure 12.1i, is "MULTIPOLARITY" → "free riding mindset." As a divergent variable, "free riding mindset" is designated as a diamond. With more great powers comes the possibility that at least some will be disposed to act either too slowly, or not at all, when one or more among them shows aggressive tendencies.

(also labeled as neorealism) in visual form are used to complement reading of the original text: (a) Figure 1 from Schroeder (1994: 109); (b) Figure 7.1 from Taliaferro (2009b: 208); and (c) correspondence (Kaufman 2017). Figure 12.1 also reflects a consultation with Jeffrey Taliaferro, an expert on realism and notably classification of its theories.

[3] It should be noted that anarchy, referred to as a variable, is an assumption for Waltz and other realists. In other words, the variable corresponding to basic system structure—anarchy versus hierarchy—is a constant in realist expositions.

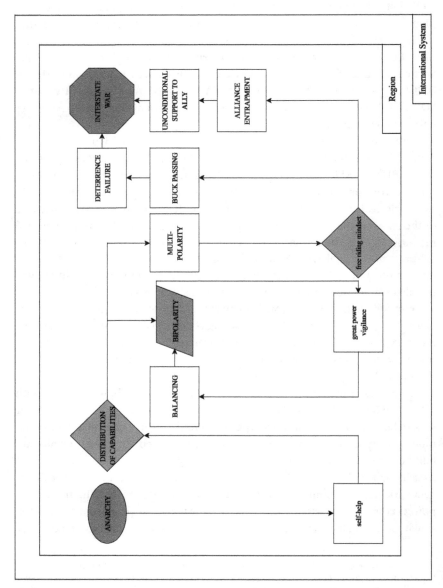

Figure 12.1 Structural Realism

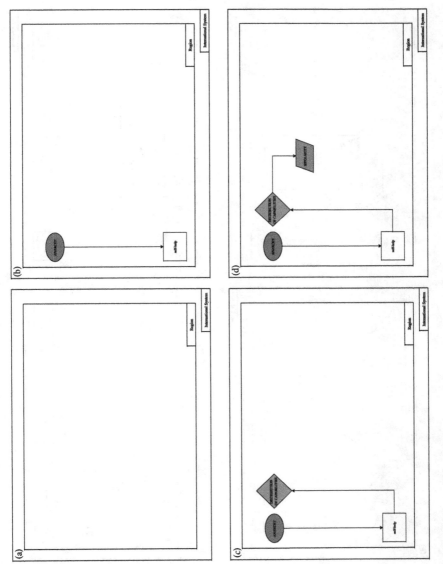

Figure 12.1 Continued

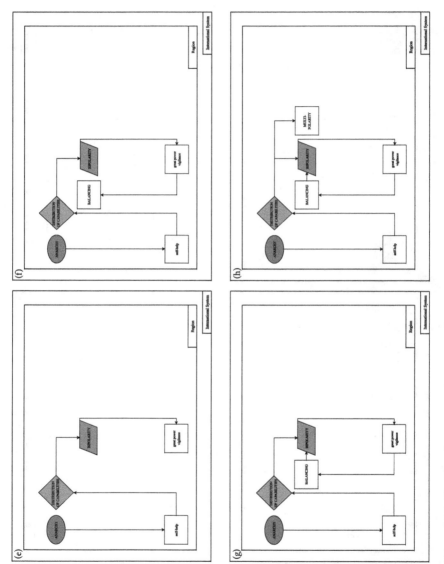

Figure 12.1 Continued

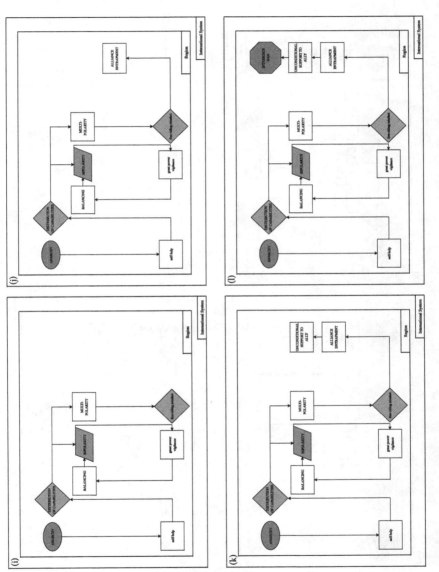

Figure 12.1 Continued

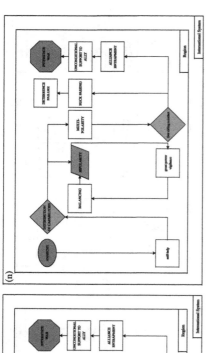
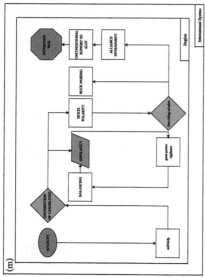
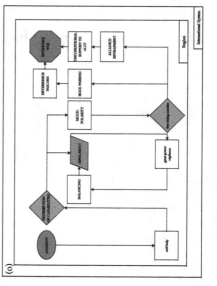

Figure 12.1 Continued

This inclination is referred to as free riding, i.e., "Let someone else absorb the cost of dealing with it." The "it" in this context is something quite dangerous to system stability, namely, self-aggrandizing foreign policy.

Figure 12.1j conveys a micro-macro connection: "free riding mindset" → "ALLIANCE ENTRAPMENT." This brings to mind the archetypal case of World War I, in which the irresponsible and provocative actions of lesser allies come back to haunt great powers. Leading states had to intervene on behalf of clients and ultimately ended up in a general war.

Movement along the macro level ensues with "ALLIANCE ENTRAPMENT" → "UNCONDITIONAL SUPPORT TO ALLY" in Figure 12.1k. In this context, it is interesting to ponder the concept of "frenemies"—troublesome lesser allies that pose challenges for great power patrons—as explored by Taliaferro (2019). One serious risk is that defending these sometimes nettlesome allies will go too far and, at the very least, end up being perceived as unconditional backing.

Figure 12.1l continues along the macro-level route: "UNCONDITIONAL SUPPORT TO ALLY" → "INTERSTATE WAR." As a terminal variable, "INTERSTATE WAR" is depicted as an octagon. The quintessential instance of this occurs at the threshold of the Great War, when Germany issued its "blank check" to the Austro-Hungarian Empire. This gave the empire a free hand in dealing with Serbian defiance in the aftermath of a high-profile assassination and greatly accelerated events along the road to war (Albertini 1953).

Leading back from the state to the system level in Figure 12.1m is another pathway: "free riding mindset" → "BUCK PASSING." The disposition not to balance will result in efforts among great powers to pass the buck. If this type of foreign policy is pervasive, the system becomes fraught with danger. The linkage that follows in Figure 12.1n is "BUCK PASSING" → "DETERRENCE FAILURE." An aggressor state, if not balanced, can be expected to continue along the same course until it reaches a point of no return for the system. Belated efforts to balance are anticipated to fail and thereby produce the final linkage in Figure 12.1o, which is "DETERRENCE FAILURE" → "INTERSTATE WAR."

Table 12.2 displays the variable types and connections for the respective realist theories. With 13 variables in its network of cause and effect, structural realism appears more intricate than might have been expected from its reputation for extreme parsimony. The theory includes some contingencies, with one convergent variable and two divergent variables, but no variable is nodal. The international system is, in fact, the region of interest for structural realism, so missing links back and forth are not surprising. The diagram contains a feedback loop; bipolarity can forestall war.

Also expected is the lack of any observed connection purely at the micro level. While not systemist, structural realism is not strictly holist, either. It goes beyond purely macro level connections. The figure brings out situational pursuit

Table 12.2 Variable Types and Connections for Structural Realist Theories

Theory	Overall Number	Initial	Generic	Divergent	Convergent	Nodal	Coconstitutive	Terminal	Interaction Effect	Loops	Missing Links[a]
Structural Realism	13	1	8	2	1	0	0	1	0	1	E→S S→E m→m
Hegemonic Stability Theory	9	1	4	2	0	0	0	2	0	0	E→S S→E m→m

[a] The notation is as follows: Macro (M), micro (m), System (S), and Environment (E).

of self-interest via balancing, buck-passing, and unconditional support for an ally. Structural realism does not contain effects back and forth for the system and environment.

Consider the structural realist version of cause and effect in relation to the components from Kurki (2002). Formal, material, final, and efficient conditions are identified in turn.

For structural realism, formal conditions—background shapes or relations—are twofold. Taken directly from the axiomatic basis of realism is anarchy. Self-help follows on from that condition, and thus the possibility of war always lurks in the background.

Material conditions—passive potentiality of matter, coterminous with opportunity in Most and Starr (2015 [1989])—are represented through the distribution of capabilities. This dispersion develops into either multipolar or bipolar forms. Bipolarity leads into a presumably self-reinforcing loop of power balancing. An analogy with chemical compounds is useful in summing things up here. Multipolarity is inherently more volatile and even explosive than bipolarity.

Formal causes—purposes that guide change or willingness as articulated in Most and Starr (2015 [1989])—take two forms: (i) great power vigilance or (ii) a free-riding mindset. Under bipolarity, great power vigilance is the anticipated norm. This property reinforces stability in the system, as two predominant rivals keep a careful eye on each other. Multipolarity, by contrast, encourages a free-riding mindset. States therefore become more willing to initiate war in what is perceived to be a permissive setting.

Finally, consider efficient causes or movers. Two of these processes appear in the diagram. One is buck-passing that in turn produces deterrence failure and war. The other process involves alliance entrapment—unconditional support for an ally facilitates aggression and brings on war.

With the graphic version of structural realism in place, it is time to circle back to the critics. Each point from earlier on in the chapter is considered in turn.

What about the issue of excessive parsimony? A visual presentation of structural realism suggests a softening of that point. The graphic version contains 13 variables, and its connections go beyond purely macro-level hypotheses about balance of power and recurrence of war. On the one hand, the familiar hypothesis about greater stability for bipolarity over multipolarity is present. On the other hand, multiple pathways to war also appear and are relevant today. Consider, for instance, how a confrontational North Korea complicates matters for the People's Republic of China, which at least so far is reluctant to offer unconditional support for Pyongyang's sometimes erratic behavior.

Rational choice is clear to see as structural realism unfolds in diagrammatic form. More specifically, the pathways are consistent with ordinal rationality.

Leaders respond to the direction of change. Under bipolarity, great power vigilance is consistent with ordinal rationality. Balancing ensues and stabilizes the international system. Multipolarity is more complex and creates opportunities for free riding (Olson 1965). Problems accumulate in the absence of sufficient balancing, which in turn leads to destabilization and war.

What about the inability of structural realism to account for system-level change? Implicit is the idea that war produces system-level transformation, but the rest is speculation. This question will be addressed via extension of structural realism when the theories undergo that process in Chapter 19.

One critique, interestingly enough, focuses on how structural realism lacks graphic communication. The systemist presentation rectifies that problem because it brings out neglected aspects of structural realism. While the theory tends to be perceived as macroscopic, it incorporates a wider range of variables than expected. In addition to its familiar macro-macro connections, structural realism also includes macro-micro and micro-macro links. One way forward would be to theorize at the state level beyond a generic sense of self-help—perhaps taking a closer look at power seeking in this context.

Another point of criticism concerns observation of balancing versus other forms of behavior among states. This seems more like a matter of orthodoxy versus reality. Even observers with a positive disposition toward neorealism see it as consistent with policies beyond balancing, notably bandwagoning and even others (Elman and Elman 2003a: 83). Wohlforth (2003: 251) adds a clarification of what structural realism means in this context: "Rather than saying that the theory predicts a 'tendency toward balance' it might be more accurate to say that it predicts a tendency against hegemony." Figure 12.1 includes, for instance, a free-riding mindset. Buck-passing and alliance entrapment are possible in a neorealist world. There is no pathway to war otherwise—even for a multipolar world.

Is structural realism relevant to foreign policy? Rather than responding to critics on this, Waltz (1988: 43) tended to see foreign policy as a concern for theorizing at the national level. This is not so much a reply to critics as an implicit endorsement of holism. The position creates a ceteris paribus clause with regard to processes at the micro level. In adopting that position, structural realism is inherently incomplete and requires elaboration. Once again, it makes sense to expand upon the role of the state—a priority during engagement with other realist theories in Chapter 19.

Elaboration of structural realism seems worthwhile in terms of its standing vis-à-vis the Performance Ratio. With five axioms and 13 variables, the theory is able to generate insights about the collective experiences of great powers and patterns in the international system related to war. This breadth of contribution should be accompanied by pursuit of greater depth in the explanation.

Hegemonic Stability Theory

Figure 12.2 depicts hegemonic stability in Gilpin (1981) as a theory of war.[4] A region as the system, along with the international system as its surrounding environment, appears in Figure 12.2a. Movement gets underway at the macro level in Figure 12.2b with "STATE IN SYSTEM OF EQUILIBRIUM" → "DIFFERENTIAL GROWTH OF POWER." As an initial variable, "STATE IN SYSTEM OF EQUILIBRIUM" appears as an oval.

Figure 12.2c continues along a macro-level pathway: "DIFFERENTIAL GROWTH OF POWER" → "SIGNIFICANT REDISTRIBUTION OF POWER IN SYSTEM." This is a clear instance of the Realist Law of Uneven Growth in action. Figure 12.2d displays a connection from the macro to the micro level: "SIGNIFICANT REDISTRIBUTION OF POWER IN SYSTEM" → "demands from states for change." Figure 12.2e moves up from the micro to macro level: "demands from states for change" → "SYSTEM IN DISEQUILIBRIUM." Note that "SYSTEM IN DISEQUILIBRIUM," a divergent variable, appears as a diamond. Thus hegemonic stability is a theory consistent with multiple pathways that can result from foreign policy demands directed against the status quo.

Added in Figure 12.2f, a final connection at the macro level is "SYSTEM IN DISEQUILIBRIUM" → "INTERSTATE WAR." As a terminal variable, "INTERSTATE WAR" appears as an octagon. Once out of equilibrium, the system inherently tilts toward war. This is in line with a probabilistic sense of things, in which war comes about through sheer repetition of its possibility—sometimes referred to as an "urn" model (Bremer and Cusack 1980).

Another branch moves downward in Figure 12.2g with "SYSTEM IN DISEQUILIBRIUM" → "non-war bargaining outcomes." This route moves from the state back up to the system level with "non-war bargaining outcomes" → "RESOLUTION OF SYSTEMIC CRISIS" in Figure 12.2h. As a divergent variable, "RESOLUTION OF SYSTEMIC CRISIS" appears as a diamond. The pathways merge in Figure 12.2i, which depicts "RESOLUTION OF SYSTEMIC CRISIS" → "INTERSTATE WAR." For example, the Japanese attack on Pearl Harbor instantly transformed years of confrontation with the United States and its allies in the Pacific into full-scale war (Prange 1982). The final connection appears in Figure 12.2j: "RESOLUTION OF SYSTEMIC CRISIS" → "NON-WAR BARGAINING OUTCOME." The latter, as a terminal variable, is depicted as an octagon. An example is the outcome of a confrontation that took place at Fashoda, along the Nile, in 1898. An intense crisis for France and Britain almost

---

[4] Figure 12.2 is based on Gilpin (1981: 11–15) and most directly Figure 1, "Diagram of International Political Change" (Gilpin 1981: 12). The accuracy of this figure has benefited from a consultation with Arie Kacowicz, a recognized expert on the work of Robert Gilpin.

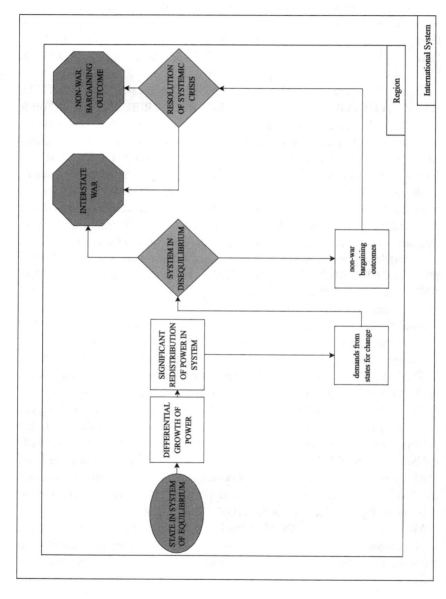

Figure 12.2 Hegemonic Stability

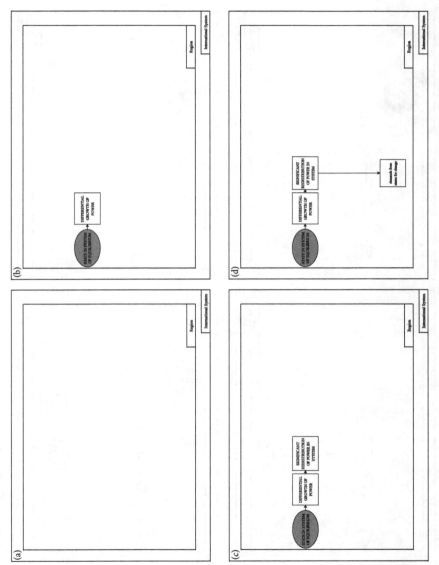

Figure 12.2 Continued

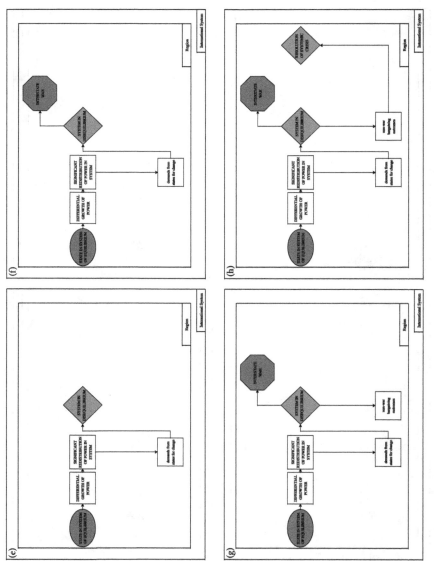

Figure 12.2 Continued

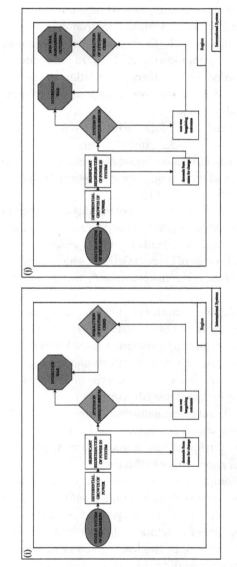

Figure 12.2 Continued

resulted in war, with access to the Sudan as the center of disagreement. A negotiated settlement, favorable to the British, resolved the crisis.

With nine variables, hegemonic stability includes the lowest number among realist theories of war reviewed in this volume. The theory entails two divergent variables, so there is some contingency. At the same time, several links are not included—micro-micro, along with the environment to the system and vice versa. From the standpoint of the Performance Ratio, hegemonic stability stands out as a candidate for elaboration directed toward greater depth of explanation.

Consider hegemonic stability theory in relation to cause and effect as enumerated by Kurki (2002). Respective conditions—formal, material, final, and efficient—are considered in turn.

What about formal conditions, with reference to defining shapes or relations—that exist in the background? Existence of a state in a system of equilibrium defines the situation at the outset of events. Under anarchy, disturbances always are possible, and there is no automatic return to equilibrium. War always sits in the background as a possibility.

Two material conditions—passive potentiality of matter, or opportunity, as designated by Most and Starr (2015 [1989])—can be identified. One is differential growth of power, and the other is significant redistribution of capabilities in the system. The Realist Law of Uneven Growth, which gained that name at a later point in evolution of the research enterprise (Schweller and Wohlforth 2000), is in operation here.

Two formal conditions—referring to purposes that guide change, or willingness, in the terms of Most and Starr (2015 [1989])—are identified: (i) demands from states for change; and (ii) a system in disequilibrium. Revisionism jostles the system as one or more rising powers demand change. A contemporary example is the South China Sea. China is most prominent as a revisionist power in this locale, poised against multiple adversaries.

Last comes the efficient cause, namely, resolution of the systemic crisis. This is decided for or against war on the basis of cost-benefit calculations.

With the graphic version of hegemonic stability in place, it is appropriate to respond to critiques noted earlier in this chapter.

What about incompleteness as a basic problem for the theory? Various critiques focus upon how not much is said about foreign policy, such as why a state might pursue a revisionist or status quo policy. As a specific example of the indeterminate nature of structural realism, consider the bipolarity-balancing loop in Figure 12.1. How do the two leading states exit from this? With a lack of agency built into its account of world politics, structural realism cannot answer that question. Thus elaboration is needed at the micro level to tell a more complete story about the causes of war.

Related observations pertain to an exclusive focus on the leading and challenging states, along with lack of specification for processes of action and reaction, for hegemonic stability theory. Figure 12.2 reinforces this sense of "something missing," most notably at the brink of war. Note that the diagram lacks any micro-micro connection. The outcome, one way or the other, is a product of cost-benefit analysis, but not much else is said beyond that assertion. The preceding points of criticism collectively encourage further contact for hegemonic stability theory with more state-centered versions of realism. The door is open to elaboration at the micro level, which will be pursued in Chapter 19.

Another line of questioning focuses upon measurement: what is meant by a *significant*, as opposed to routine, shift in capabilities? The theory cannot be falsified unless some type of threshold is identified. Once again, contact with other realist theories can lead toward a worthwhile answer to this question. Both the components of power and specifications for major versus minor change already exist within realism and will be accessed in Chapter 19.

Reflections on Structural Realism

Structural realism stands as a significant attempt within realism to move beyond a long-standing emphasis on human nature in accounting for international politics. It departs from classical realism in multiple ways. Structural realists borrow ideas from economics, as opposed to philosophy, which had been the foundation for the classical approach. The structure of the international system is emphasized as a basic cause of the processes observed within it. Each variant—structural realism and hegemonic stability theory—focuses on aspects of the distribution of capabilities among great powers in an effort to account for war in the international system. While structural realism focuses on the number of great powers, hegemonic stability theory concentrates on the standing of the leading state. These structural realist theories are alike in that progress depends on elaboration to provide depth to complement existing breadth of explanation.

13
Balance of Threat

Overview

Balance-of-threat theory goes beyond power to consider a range of factors that shape security policy and potential pathways to war. Balance of threat is an indirect descendant of time-honored ideas from classical realism about the balance of power. The theory is offered as a potential solution to the well-confirmed observation that, in a significant number of instances, states do not balance against power alone. Instead of power, what about the idea that states more naturally would focus on responding to *threat*? The level of threat perceived by leaders would reflect more than just the capabilities that other states possessed. Balance-of-threat theory builds in intentions and other factors that purport to give a more complete explanation for the range of behavior observed among states that is not in line with seeking a balance of power. The theory emphasizes the role of alliances as a means toward self-help in a realist world. In sum, when a war occurs, that outcome reflects how threat perception plays out within the overall story of power politics.

This chapter unfolds in five additional sections. The second section provides a *gestalt* sense of the theory and enumerates axioms for both variants—balance of threat and revolution—which are consistent with the realist research enterprise. The third section explains why, from the standpoint of balance of threat and revolution, wars occur. The fourth examines critiques of the two versions of the theory. The fifth section conveys balance of threat and revolution as theories about war in graphic terms. These visualizations also are accessed in response to criticism of the theory. The sixth section reflects upon the contributions and prospects of balance-of-threat theory.

What Is Balance-of-Threat Theory?

Balance of Threat

Balance of threat, as per classification in Figure 9.1, is static and state oriented. The magnum opuses for respective variants of the theory are *The Origins of Alliances* (Walt 1987, 1990) and *Revolution and War* (Walt 1996). These theories are well received in the field. *The Origins of Alliances* is described as a "major contribution to the theory of international politics" (Benson 1988: 132) and an "impressive start" on a subject, alliance politics, which had yet to receive sufficient attention, while *Revolution and War* is summarized as a "provocative analysis that demonstrates the limitations of realism and the importance of beliefs and ideology in accounting for revolutionary wars" (Larson 1997: 492).

Balance of threat focuses on the overall strategic situation, as opposed to the distribution of capabilities alone, in assessing how leaders are likely to respond through policy to perceived danger. Perceptions of threat are based on three components: aggregate power, degree of hostile intent, and the offense-defense balance (Walt 1987, 1990; see also Rose and van Dusen 2002: 7–8).

Essential concepts for balance-of-threat theory include alliances and balancing behavior. Walt (1990: 10) defines an alliance "as a formal or informal relationship of security cooperation between two or more sovereign states." Balancing refers to "allying with others against the prevailing threat," while *bandwagoning* means "alignment with the source of danger" (Walt 1990: 17). A straightforward benefit from balancing is that joining the weaker side in an alliance means greater influence within it (Walt 1990: 18–19). Bandwagoning and balancing, Walt (1990: 21) observes, usually are considered strictly in terms of capabilities. This limitation equates with the world of structural realism, which provides a point of departure for balance of threat as a potentially more complete and effective theory. Structural realism serves in this context as an antinomy for balance of threat because of its exclusive focus on material conditions. Balance of threat, by contrast, includes an essential ideational component: *perception* of danger.

Advocates of balance of threat see it as an advancement for realist theory. For instance, Walt (1987, 1990: 5, 264) asserts that balance-of-threat theory is better than balance-of-power theory and even subsumes it. "It is more accurate," according to Walt (1990: 21), "to say that states tend to ally with or against the foreign power that poses the greatest threat." Intention rather than power alone is crucial in shaping foreign policy (Walt 1990: 26). Various factors, which include "aggregate power, geographic proximity, offensive power, and aggressive intentions," impact the threat posed by a state (Walt 1990: 22; see also Snyder 1991: 126; Rose and Van Dusen 2002: 7; Chernoff 2014: 147–148; Bock, Henneberg, and Plank 2015: 104). Two worlds come to exist: "In a balancing world, policies that convey restraint and benevolence are best," while, by contrast, a bandwagoning world "is much more competitive" (Walt 1990: 27). Rational leaders will respond in each instance to the type of threat that exists.

With its focus on perceptions, balance-of-threat theory connects with the call from Barkin (2010: 169) for realist thinking that sees power politics as (i) relational rather than structural; and (ii) connected to foreign policy. Balancing against threat is the default position. This is because "it is safer to balance against potential threats than to rely on the hope that a state will remain benevolently disposed" (Walt 1990: 29). Bandwagoning, by contrast, should be expected "to occur only under certain identifiable conditions," and fear of it normally is "fanciful" (Walt 1990: 28, 283). Consider, for example, attempts to achieve hegemony in Europe; all such efforts, across centuries, ultimately have been stopped by defensive coalitions (Walt 1990: 28-29). Bandwagoning, by contrast, emerges as a localized and mostly temporary practice throughout the history of international relations.

Conditions that encourage bandwagoning are uncommon. A weak state will consider this option only when it is most vulnerable. For example, even Ireland, which faced a very difficult strategic situation during World War II, eschewed bandwagoning throughout the conflict (O'Loughlin 2008: 112-113). Bandwagoning can be expected when a weak state, which cannot add much to a balancing coalition, is in close proximity to a threatening state (Walt 1990: 29-30). The situation is aggravated when allies are not obviously available as an alternative (Walt 1990: 30-31). For example, to cite an extreme case, Belarus has bandwagoned with Russia virtually by default since the end of the USSR.

Bandwagoning also should be expected when the outcome of a war becomes clear (Walt 1990: 31-32). An archetypal case is the rapid expansion of the allied forces, known as the United Nations, once the outcome of World War II became certain. Consider, for example, how Turkey handled that situation. The preceding Ottoman Empire had been a German ally in World War I. Turkey maintained neutrality for almost all of World War II but joined the United Nations in February 1945.

Balance-of-threat theory evolved to include an emphasis on revolution as a potential cause of significant interstate conflict and even war (Walt 1996). This variant of balance-of-threat theory focuses on how a dramatic change in government can produce a greater risk of instability for the international system. Interstate war, in particular, becomes more likely under such conditions. Halliday (1997: 230) adds that Walt (1996) is able to demonstrate that all revolutions produce international tensions and increased competition for security.

Table 13.1 shows the balance-of-threat and revolution variants of the theory at a glance. Balance of threat incorporates both ideational and material factors in its vision of alliances and world politics. Anarchy is central to the rise and fall of alliances. The emphasis on structure in preceding theories, such as Waltz (1979) and Gilpin (1981), serves as an antinomy. Balance of threat emphasizes coalitions in foreign policy, which in turn elaborates upon how self-help operates in practice. Revolution, as a theory, focuses on threat and warfare in the wake of regime change. Revolutionary states create uncertainty and thus can produce miscalculation leading to war. A state experiencing revolution also can be

Table 13.1 Balance of Threat at a Glance

Source	Summary Statement
Walt (1987: 21, 26)	"States tend to ally with or against the foreign power that poses the greatest threat.... Intention, not power, is crucial."
Benson (1988: 132)	Sovereign states form alliances primarily to balance threats.
Snyder (1991: 130)	System structure plays little role in his analysis.
Larson (1997: 491)	"Revolutionary state and foreign powers exaggerate each other's hostility, often leading to war.... States react to perceived threats rather than shifts in the balance of power."
Rengger (1998: 203)	Revolutions tend to produce situations in which the perceptions of threat, both on the part of the revolutionary state and on the part of its neighbors, are heightened, and thus, in the short term at least, this will often lead to war.
Rose and van Dusen (2002: 7)	Walt's original balance-of-threat theory presumes that states coexist in an anarchic environment in which no institution exists to protect them from each other.
Chernoff (2014: 148)	External threats are most frequent cause of international alliances.

a magnet for outside intervention—a likely path toward violence. In sum, the revolution-based variant of balance of threat develops the state or unit level in ways that go well beyond prior system-oriented realism.

How does balance-of-threat theory look in relation to the axioms associated with realism as a research enterprise? These assumptions, to reiterate, are anarchy and state-centrism at the level of the international system, along with rationality and seeking power at the level of the state.

Anarchy is evident within balance-of-threat theory because of its emphasis on self-help for states via balancing or bandwagoning. No place is reserved for international institutions; the focus is entirely on states. Power seeking also plays a central role; the story of cause and effect begins with external threat to a state. Finally, states try to optimize in the face of threat—a clear endorsement of rationality.

Three additional axioms inhere within balance-of-threat theory. One is that geographic proximity is assumed to impact policy choices under threat. Distance separating a weak state from potential allies and enemies is an essential explanation for foreign policy in response to a threatening state (Walt 1990: 32). Another assumption that is significant in accounting for how events play out is the profile of offensive capabilities and advantage (Walt 1996). In addition, perceptions, rather than purely material capabilities, are essential in summing up the threat that exists at any given time. This returns to the observation that realist theories can incorporate both material and ideational variables. Restrictions on ideas refer to those that inject normative content, over and above a commitment of leaders to the success of their state.

Numerous studies offer support to balance-of-threat theory, and a few examples are summarized. Case studies cover multiple regions and periods.

Based on results in the Middle East in the post–World War II era, a general hypothesis that "states choose allies in order to balance against the most serious threat" is a clear winner (Walt 1990: 263). In that region, balancing turned out to be much more prevalent than bandwagoning. Furthermore, even when pursued, bandwagoning almost always occurred with isolated and weak states. This foreign policy choice makes sense for that subset of highly vulnerable states, for whom balancing would not be a viable option.

Research from Mastanduno (1997: 51) reveals that balance-of-threat theory can account for the principal tendency observed in US foreign policy, namely, efforts to preserve a position "at the top of the international hierarchy by engaging and reassuring other major powers." The United States is the quintessential status quo power. Note that relatively greater attention by the United States to preserving its position is understandable in light of the diminishing marginal utility of further improvements. This makes sense for the leading power in any international system.

Balance-of-threat theory also is cited for its ability to account for both various historical cases and contemporary conflict involving Russia over the Ukraine (Bock, Henneberg, and Plank 2015: 102). Perception of threat, according to Bock, Henneberg, and Plank (2015: 103), resulted in balancing for both the Cuban Missile Crisis and more recent conflict over the Iranian nuclear program. In particular, sustained and fierce contemporary Russian resistance to the United States and its coalition can be accounted for most directly through balance of threat. The metaphor used by Bock, Henneberg, and Plank (2013) is a spring that will snap back when compressed. From the standpoint of the Russian leader, Vladimir Putin, for whom eastern expansion of NATO and associated developments appear quite threatening, this is how the situation looks. This perception provides the most straightforward explanation for highly intense reactions to anything that seems to threaten a sphere of influence that, while greatly contracted, still is believed by Russia to include the Ukraine (Bock, Henneberg, and Plank 2015). There is some irony and even tragedy in that the self-perception of democracies as being "good" is overtaken by the logic of realism.

Positively disposed, but with a twist, is a study that applies balance-of-threat theory to the Gulf states (Cooper 2003: 343):

> The six Gulf states were indeed threatened by Iran, but not in the manner that Walt's balance-of-threat theory would predict. The primary Iranian threat was

not to the Gulf states' territorial borders or political independence but to their internal security, a direct threat to the interests of the ruling monarchies.

Thus both external and internal threats to survival drove those states to affiliate more closely with each other through the Gulf Cooperation Council (Cooper 2003: 324). In turn, the Gulf Cooperation Council had, as its basic priority, not the pooling of military capabilities against external enemies, but instead efforts to reduce Iranian-inspired domestic threats to its member states (Cooper 2003: 343). Therefore, Cooper (2003) extends the concept of threat beyond an articulation that had focused on interests abroad.

What does balancing mean with regard to threat? Of what does it consist? Posed by Snyder (1991: 126), along with He and Feng (2010: 233), these questions are essential to answer for cases beyond the initial set considered by Walt (1987). He and Feng (2010: 246) incorporate prospect theory to build on Walt's balance-of-threat theory at the level of decision-making. Their model specifies "how states use alliances, that is, bilaterally or multilaterally, to cope with external threats based on states' prospects of future gains or losses" (He and Feng 2010: 246):

> By setting the level of threat as the reference point to determine the domain for states, we can infer the following general propositions: (1) if states face a high level of threat, then they are placed in a domain of losses and they are more likely to choose a multilateral alliance strategy with strong commitments to avoid further losses in security; and (2) if states face a low level of threat, then they are placed in a domain of gains and they are more likely to choose a bilateral alliance strategy with weak commitments to pursue gains in security.

Balance-of-threat theory thereby shows an ability to generate propositions with greater specificity about why choices are made (He and Feng 2010: 236).

Revolution

Essential to revolution as a threat-based theory is creation of uncertainty. When a state experiences a revolution, two developments are virtually certain. One is that the state will experience reduced capability in the aftermath of the upheaval, and the other is that it may be perceived by peers as more dangerous due to potentially new goals related to export of ideology (Walt 1996). For both reasons, a postrevolutionary state is a magnet for conflict. According to Walt (1996), such states are at great risk of escalating conflict due to bias toward offensive thinking in tandem with mutual suspicion. The postrevolutionary setting in a region may be summed up as zero-sum.

What about revolution as a theory in relation to realism? Revolution is in line with the four basic axioms of realism, along with the additional assumptions already enumerated for balance of threat: (i) geographic proximity, distance, and offensive capability and advantage impact policy choices under threat; and (ii) perceptions of threat affect policy choices. Forthcoming material from cases will be sufficient to establish those properties for the revolution variant of balance-of-threat theory.

Revolution entails one additional axiom: decisive entry and exit for a state in terms of regime type, via revolution, will increase uncertainty in its region. This does not incorporate effects from any specific kind of regime, but only the fact of turnover itself. If balance-of-threat theory accessed type of regime for its account of how revolution impacts international conflict processes, that would make it reside outside the boundaries of the realist research enterprise.[1] Instead, revolutions with vastly different content, such as France in the 18th century and Iran in the 20th century, are alike in destabilizing their respective regions as both initiators and targets of aggression.

Major wars, as Walt (1996) observes, followed on from revolutions in France, Russia, and Iran. In addition, the Maoist revolution in China served as one stimulant for the Korean War that took place soon after (Walt 1996). These cases serve as founding evidence in favor of revolution as a variant of balance-of-threat theory. In addition, Walt (1996) looks at a set of revolutions that did *not* produce a major war in the aftermath. The cases of Mexico, the United States, and Turkey—revolutions not followed by major war—help to identify the key factors that separate one outcome from another. In the cases where leaders eschewed war, several traits are identified as important in bringing about that result. Dominance of defense over offense, occurrence in a large state that is distant from Europe in its era as the central system of world politics, and a government that did not seek to export its ideology all are associated with pacific outcomes.

Additional research findings offer support to the revolution-based variant of balance-of-threat theory. Rose and van Dusen (2002: 43) apply the theory to Islamist revolutions in Sudan, a century apart, and find encouraging results: "The research supports Walt's premise that revolution causes security competition by means of two mechanisms: by altering perceived levels of threat between Sudan and its two neighbors, and by encouraging at least one of the sides to calculate that hostile actions could overcome the threat." In sum, the revolution-based variant of balance-of-threat theory performed well in cases widely separated in time (Rose and van Dusen 2002: 52).

---

[1] Rengger (1998: 204) notes the virtual absence of normative analysis with regard to revolution. This observation reinforces the status of revolution as a realist theory.

Both variants of balance-of-threat theory are linked to the tradition of classical realism. Most obvious in that sense are connections with Kissinger (1957) on alliances, Wolfers (1962) with regard to aggressive and threat-perceiving states, and Aron (1966) about offense versus defense. The balance-of-threat theories, like their classical ancestors, also seek insights about policy through the study of historical and contemporary case material.

Expositions on the Causes of War

Balance of Threat

Balance of threat, as a theory of war, highlights the role of coalitions along the road to one outcome or another. Covered in detail by Walt (1987: 58), one example is the Baghdad Pact in connection to outbreak of the Sinai War of 1956.

President Gamal Nasser of Egypt viewed the Baghdad Pact as a scheme by the Western great powers to make gains at the expense of Egypt (Walt 1987: 58). By contrast, he did not see the USSR—a distant state that had not bothered Egypt before—as a threat. Nasser had concerns about the emergence of Iraq as a potentially dominant power in the Middle East. Meanwhile, leaders in Israel felt threatened by an alignment of Egypt, Syria, and Saudi Arabia that came about in opposition to the Baghdad Pact (Walt 1987: 61). Nasser nationalized the Suez Canal in July 1956, which in turn threatened his "principal adversaries"—Britain, France, and Israel (Walt 1987: 63). In response, Anglo-French and Israeli military action ensued on 29 October 1956 (Walt 1987: 64). The Sinai War resulted from threat perceptions and efforts to balance via coalitions. A similar and convincing account of coalitions and escalation of conflict is provided for the Six Day War of 1967, along with other cases (Walt 1987, 1990).

Revolution

For the revolution variant of balance-of-threat theory, Walt (1996) draws upon several cases for evidence, with the French Revolution as a prominent instance. The French Revolution increased the likelihood of war because it shifted the balance of power significantly; the new regime looked weak to outside observers, notably Austria and Prussia (Walt 1996: 46). The revolution also affected intentions and perceptions among the European states and impacted upon French goals in foreign policy (Walt 1996: 46). Each side, as Walt (1996: 46) observes, came to believe that adversaries might be able to engage effectively in propaganda, subversion, or even a rapid military strike. Information shared among leaders on the continent deteriorated in accuracy, which in turn led to miscalculation about what others intended to do (Walt 1996: 47).

Opponents of the French had difficulty estimating the new state's power because it rested, to some degree, on previously unknown institutions and ideas (Walt 1996: 126). Lack of information, as Walt (1996: 127) observes, fueled a "spiral of suspicion between France and its adversaries." Diplomatic channels increasingly broke down and communication shifted to unreliable media; a resultant lack of accurate information perhaps explains why both sides "exaggerated the potential for both revolutionary contagion and counterrevolutionary subversion" (Walt 1996: 127). Biased processing of information, increasingly dependent on ideology, became the norm (Walt 1996: 127).

None of this, obviously, bodes well for controlling escalation of conflict. The objectives of the revolutionary government in France moved in a direction that caused foreign perceptions of threat to increase (Walt 1996: 120). War with Austria and Prussia ensued in 1792 and escalated in 1793 (Walt 1996: 121). The stories of war following other revolutions, as conveyed by Walt (1996), feature the same problems related to communication.

Critiques

Balance of Threat

Balance-of-threat theory is not without its critics, from inside and outside of the realist research enterprise. Points of controversy concern (a) a shortage of convincing theoretical arguments for the priority of balancing against threat; (b) lack of variation among states that is needed to produce the foreign policies attributed to states in the international system; and (c) selection of evidence and potential consistency with all that is observed.

Interesting to consider in light of the axiomatic basis for realism is the following observation from Barnett (2003: 245): "The resort to ideational variables to determine which state has aggressive intentions can be interpreted as an ad hoc emendation that is loosely connected, at best if at all, to neorealism's (or realism's) core propositions." Legro and Moravcsik (1999: 38) express concerns about "appropriation of nonrealist causal mechanisms." Vasquez (2003b: 99) adds that the theory "fails to derive a plausible explanation from the logic of realism of why states balance against threat rather than power." This observation about balance of threat might also be seen as a criticism directed against the use of text alone to convey arguments. It certainly is true about material variants of realism and will be revisited later in this chapter.

Another point of criticism, from within the realist research enterprise, focuses on the state level. Schweller (1994: 85) asserts that "balance-of-threat theory suffers from a problem that plagues all contemporary realist theory: it views the world solely through the lens of a satisfied, status-quo state." According to Schweller (1994: 88), a satisfied power "will join the status-quo coalition, even when it is the stronger side; dissatisfied powers, motivated by profit more than security, will bandwagon with an ascending revisionist state." These points combine to encourage balance-of-threat theory to allow for variation in states with regard to specific goals.

Critics from beyond realism dismiss balance-of-threat theory outright as something that cannot be falsified. Schroeder (2003: 121) adds that a proposition about states balancing against threats reduces to little more than states "do various things to counter things they do not like." If so, that does not add much in the way of explanation. "In effect," Wivel (2005: 367) observes, "balance of threat theory presents us with a grab bag argument. If one element in the theory does not explain state action, another probably will, but the exact conditions under which they apply as well as the relation between the variables remain unspecified." This calls for a greater a priori sense of how the components of threat combine to either rise above a threshold for war or fail to do so.

Revolution

Critiques of revolution focus on (i) employment of ideational variables; and (ii) causal inference and choice of cases. Each point is introduced in turn.

One objection focuses on the presence of ideational variables in the framework of revolution and war; Rengger (1998: 204) asserts that "there are times when Walt's thesis looks suspiciously like traditional neorealism with 'bolted on subjectivity.'" This critique is much the same as what has been directed toward the initial variant of the theory. To respond convincingly, balance-of-threat theorizing must develop arguments that establish its coherence.

Problems of causal inference are noted by Halliday (1997: 231): "The correlation of war with extreme revolution and no war with less extreme revolution also sits uneasily with cases Walt does not discuss. For example, Cuba, led by a radical revolutionary elite, did not become embroiled in all out war, but Ethiopia, run by nationalist military officers, did." Halliday (1997: 231) further observes that "revolutions are never unit-level, as international, social, economic, ideological, and political factors are inscribed in their very causation." Even in cases that seem to fit the theory in terms of timing, questions can arise about causal mechanisms. On the one hand, Larson (1997: 492) acknowledges that the Korean War had some connection to the PRC coming to power through revolution a year before.

On the other hand, she does not see the North Korean attack being caused by "a spiral of suspicion or exaggerated perceptions of hostility"—key components of the model based on revolution (Larson 1997: 492).

Graphic Representations

Balance of Threat

Balance of threat is presented in Walt (1987, 1990) through text, unaccompanied by diagrams, although some tables appear. Figure 13.1 is a graphic representation of balance-of-threat theory in relation to interstate war.[2] The story begins in Figure 13.1a with designation of a region and the international system as its surrounding environment. Figure 13.1b depicts a linkage at the macro level: "EXTERNAL THREAT" → "AGGREGATE POWER OF EXTERNAL THREAT." As initial and divergent variables, these are designated, respectively, as an oval and diamond. Thus the first component of threat in the system takes the form of overall material capability.

Another pathway begins in Figure 13.1c with a connection at the level of the system: "EXTERNAL THREAT" → "PROXIMITY OF EXTERNAL THREAT." Note that the latter variable also appears as a diamond. The second specific manifestation of threat therefore focuses on geostrategic position.

Figure 13.1d launches a third route at the system level: "EXTERNAL THREAT" → "OFFENSIVE CAPABILITIES OF EXTERNAL THREAT." As a divergent variable, the latter is depicted as a diamond. The third component of threat focuses on what resources are deemed ready for offensive deployment by the threatening state.

These pathways come together at the micro level in Figure 13.1e: "AGGREGATE POWER OF EXTERNAL THREAT"; "PROXIMITY OF EXTERNAL THREAT"; "OFFENSIVE CAPABILITIES OF EXTERNAL THREAT" → "strong target's perception of threat." As a convergent variable, the final one appears as a parallelogram. An analogous set of connections appears for a weak state in Figure 13.1f: "AGGREGATE POWER OF EXTERNAL THREAT"; "PROXIMITY OF EXTERNAL THREAT"; "OFFENSIVE CAPABILITIES OF EXTERNAL THREAT" → "weak target's perception of threat." As a convergent variable, "weak target's perception of threat" is depicted as a parallelogram.

Figure 13.1f also introduces a new macro-micro connection: "EXTERNAL THREAT" → "target's perceptions of aggressiveness in intentions for external

---

[2] This figure is based on Walt (1990: 17–49) and especially Walt (1990: 32–33), which conveys sets of hypotheses about balancing and bandwagoning.

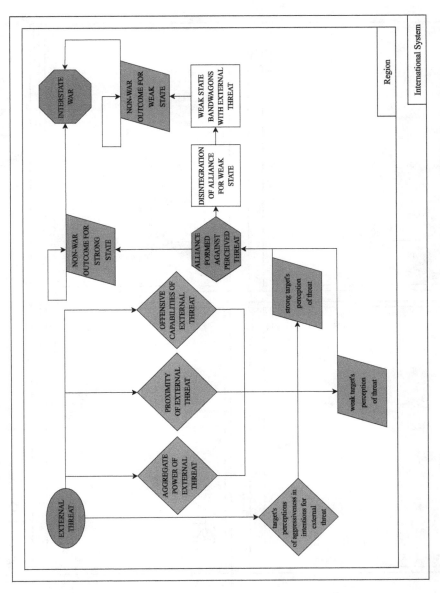

Figure 13.1 Balance of Threat

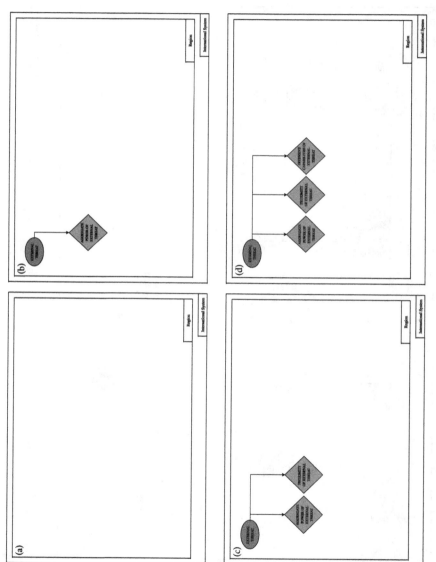

Figure 13.1 Continued

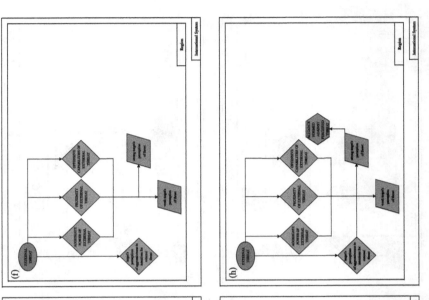
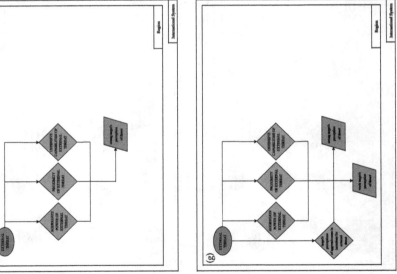

Figure 13.1 Continued

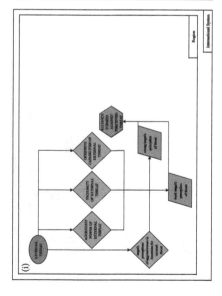
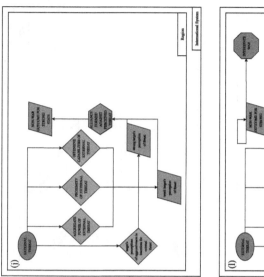
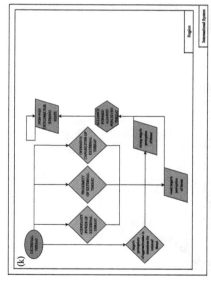
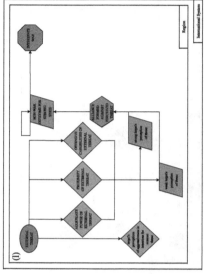

Figure 13.1 Continued

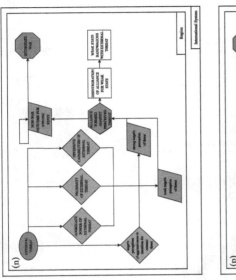
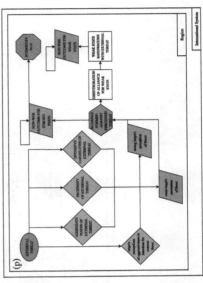
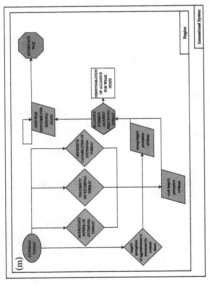
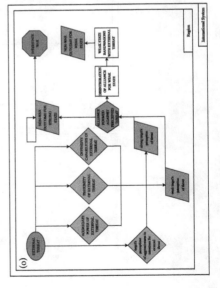

Figure 13.1 Continued

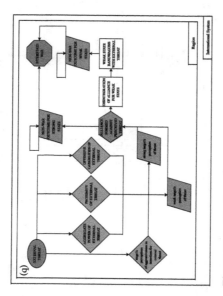

Figure 13.1 Continued

threat." Note the latter's appearance as a diamond—a divergent variable. All targets assess the degree of aggressive intent for an adversary. This can range from achievement of tactical goals all the way up to conquest at a strategic level. An example of a tactical issue would be conflict related to the city of Trieste, which developed into crises involving Yugoslavia and other states in 1945 and 1953. The quarrel focused on sovereignty over Trieste in the aftermath of World War II (Brecher and Wilkenfeld 1997).

Figure 13.1g shows two micro-level connections: "target's perception of aggressiveness in intentions for external threat" → "strong target's perception of threat"; "weak target's perception of threat." Perceptions for strong and weak targets about intentions are added to those in place about capabilities.

Depicted in Figures 13.1h and 13.1i, two pathways temporarily converge. Figure 13.1h shows one connection: "strong target's perception of threat" → "ALLIANCE FORMED AGAINST PERCEIVED THREAT." The other linkage, in Figure 13.1i, is "weak target's perception of threat" → "ALLIANCE FORMED AGAINST PERCEIVED THREAT." The latter variable appears as a hexagon because it is a node. One route leading out of the node continues in Figure 13.1j with "ALLIANCE FORMED AGAINST PERCEIVED THREAT" → "NON-WAR OUTCOME FOR STRONG STATE." As a convergent variable, the latter appears as a parallelogram.

Next along the strong state's pathway, added in Figure 13.1k, is a recursive step: "NON-WAR OUTCOME FOR STRONG STATE" feeds back into itself. This represents ongoing deterrence of the threat in place. The final step along this route, which appears in Figure 13.1l, is "NON-WAR OUTCOME FOR STRONG STATE" → "INTERSTATE WAR." As a terminal variable, "INTERSTATE WAR" appears as an octagon.

Another pathway, with a greater number of steps, maps out the experiences of a weak state. It moves forward in Figure 13.1m with "ALLIANCE FORMED AGAINST PERCEIVED THREAT" → "DISINTEGRATION OF ALLIANCE FOR WEAK STATE." Added in Figure 13.1n, the next step is "DISINTEGRATION OF ALLIANCE FOR WEAK STATE" → "WEAK STATE BANDWAGONS WITH EXTERNAL THREAT." Bandwagoning is a backup to balancing because the ceiling and floor for outcomes both are expected to be lower for this option, which is pursued out of perceived necessity. In other words, bandwagoning is inferior to balancing in terms of expected value and is more of a last resort than a genuine preference.

This connection is followed in Figure 13.1o with "WEAK STATE BANDWAGONS WITH EXTERNAL THREAT" → "NON-WAR OUTCOME FOR WEAK STATE." As a convergent variable, "NON-WAR OUTCOME FOR WEAK STATE" takes the form of a parallelogram. A recursive step, parallel to the one for the strong state, ensues with "NON-WAR OUTCOME FOR WEAK

STATE" feeding back into itself in Figure 13.1p. War is not inevitable and the policy could succeed, perhaps in the form of concessions passed along to the threatening state. However, the nonwar outcome may just be temporary, so a final step, depicted in Figure 13.1q, is "NON-WAR OUTCOME FOR WEAK STATE" → "INTERSTATE WAR."

Table 13.2 summarizes the variable types and connections exhibited by balance-of-threat theory. With 13 variables in its network of cause and effect, balance of threat is neither simplistic nor unwieldy. The initial and terminal variables appear at the macro level; in a word, balance of threat is not reductionist. The theory also is highly contingent rather than deterministic; note the presence of one nodal variable, along with four divergent and four convergent variables. Two feedback loops also appear. Missing are connections back and forth for the region with the environment.

What does cause and effect look like for balance of threat when translated into the terms of Kurki (2002)? Each type of condition from Kurki (2002)—formal, material, final, and efficient—is considered in turn.

Formal conditions focus on the background—defining shapes or relations. Two variables combine to play that role: (i) external threat and (ii) the target's perceptions of aggressive intentions. From a realist standpoint, such pairings always exist in a given region—analogous to "dangerous dyads" as identified by Bremer (1992) on the basis of a more extensive set of characteristics.

What about material conditions—the passive potentiality of matter or, in the words of Most and Starr (2015 [1989])—opportunity? Several variables come into play: (a) aggregate power, proximity, and offensive capabilities behind the threat; and (b) formation of an alliance against the threat. Thus the opportunity to carry out the threat is a function of how things stand with capabilities and coalitions.

Consider as well final causes, the purposes that guide change, which correspond collectively to willingness as put forward in Most and Starr (2015 [1989]). The relevant condition is a weak or strong state's perception of threat. Willingness for the target state refers to acting in self-defense to at least some degree.

What are the efficient conditions or movers in this context? For a weak state, disintegration of an alliance is followed by bandwagoning with the external threat. The result of this choice is either war or an alternative cycle of action that follows on from appeasement. For a strong state, movement occurs directly into war or some other situation that results from coercive bargaining.

With a graphic presentation and assessment of cause and effect in place, attention turns to critiques of balance of threat enumerated earlier in this chapter. Each is considered in turn.

Balance of threat is faulted for a lack of convincing arguments about what states should be expected to balance against. Why threat versus other concerns?

Table 13.2 Variable Types and Connections for Balance-of-Threat Theories

Theory	Overall Number	Initial	Generic	Divergent	Convergent	Nodal	Coconstitutive	Terminal Effect	Interaction	Loops	Missing Links[a]
Balance of threat	13	1	2	4	4	1	0	1	0	2	E → S S → E
Revolution	13	1	4	3	2	1	0	2	0	0	E → S S → E M → m

[a] The notation is as follows: Macro (M), micro (m), System (S), and Environment (E).

One response is to point out the comprehensiveness of threat assessment, which includes power, proximity, and offensive capabilities. This is in line with ordinal rationality; with limited resources, updating focuses on threat as an apex variable among aspects of security. At the same time, it is reasonable to ask, "How much is enough?" for each category of threat and whether categories can trade off with each other. This is a natural topic for when realist theories engage with each other in Chapter 19.

What about lack of variation in states to produce the range of foreign policies that is anticipated and observed? A focus on material conditions will help here. All states seek power, but levels of threat exerted and experienced are variables rather than constants. The opportunity to threaten depends on realized as well as potential capabilities, along with geostrategic position. Vulnerability matters. Long-standing Belgian neutrality, for example, reflected a status quo orientation virtually imposed by location and resources. In an overall sense, more needs to be said within balance-of-threat theory about types of states in order to account for the range of foreign policy behavior observed.

Consider next potential consistency with any and all evidence that might be encountered. Put differently, when would it be known that balance-of-threat theory is wrong? To achieve that purpose, it is essential to distinguish weak and strong states from each other a priori. The theory so far does not offer such a measurement and that is needed in at least a basic way to allow for potential refutation. Preceding questions about key variables and actors also must be answered for the theory to achieve the potential for refutation.

Revolution

Figure 13.2 displays revolution as a balance-of-threat-based theory of interstate war.[3] A region as a system and the international system as its surrounding environment appear in Figure 13.2a. Connections get underway in Figure 13.2b with "revolution" → "reduced capabilities." War is a possibility and administrative and governance-related challenges are a certainty in the aftermath of a revolution. As the point of origin for cause and effect, "revolution" appears as an oval. The story continues in Figure 13.2c from the micro to the macro level with "reduced capabilities" → "WINDOWS OF OPPORTUNITY." As an illustration, this is how Iraq in 1979 looked at Iran—a weakened state but also a dangerous neighbor determined to export its ideology (Walt 1996: 223–224). A macro-level connection

---

[3] This figure is based on the following sources: Walt (1996: 18–45) and especially Figure 1 (Walt 1996: 44), along with Figure 1 from Rose and Dusen (2002: 11), labeled "Walt's Theory of Revolution and Security Competition."

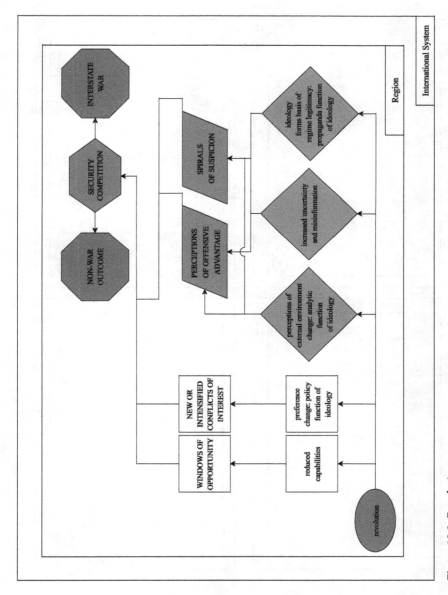

Figure 13.2 Revolution

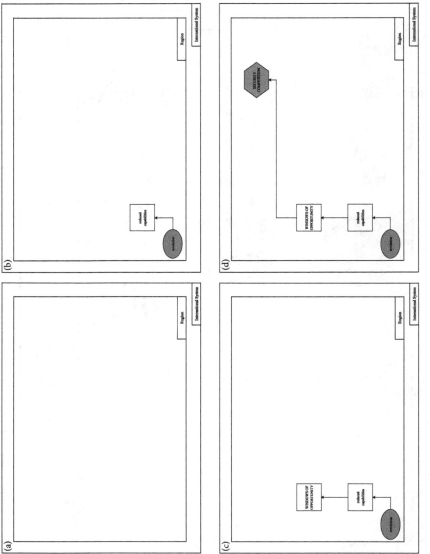

Figure 13.2 Continued

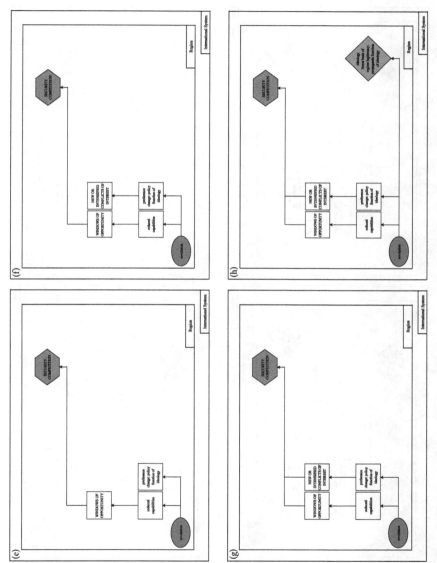

Figure 13.2 Continued

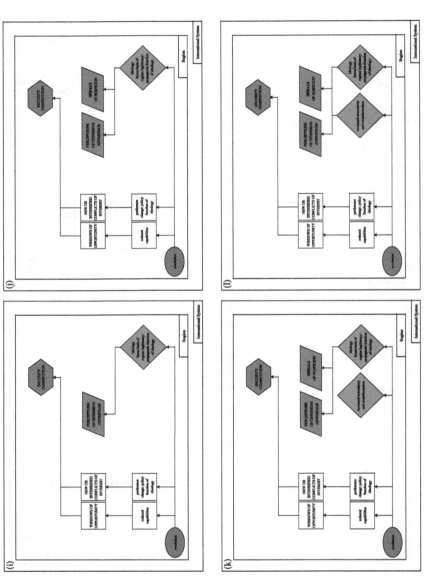

Figure 13.2 Continued

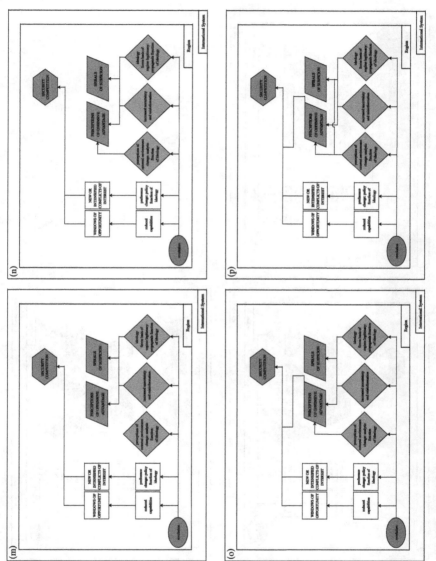

Figure 13.2 Continued

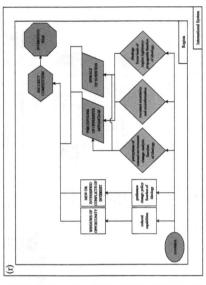
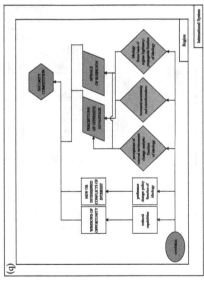
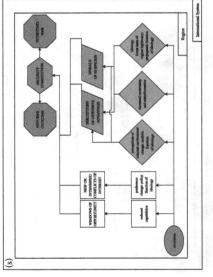

Figure 13.2 Continued

ensues in Figure 13.2d: "WINDOWS OF OPPORTUNITY" → "SECURITY COMPETITION." The latter—a nodal variable—appears as a hexagon. Iraq in the preceding time frame, for instance, would perceive Iran as a new and dangerous type of competitor (Walt 1996: 261).

Figure 13.2e initiates another pathway: "revolution" → "preference change: policy function of ideology." This route continues on to the macro level in Figure 13.2f with "preference change: policy function of ideology" → "NEW OR INTENSIFIED CONFLICTS OF INTEREST." To continue with the previous example, after Iran had its revolution in 1979, Iraqi concerns mounted with regard to a possible Shiite insurrection inspired by Teheran (Walt 1996: 260). The pathways join together in Figure 13.2g: "NEW OR INTENSIFIED CONFLICTS OF INTEREST" → "SECURITY COMPETITION."

Another pathway starts off in Figure 13.2h with "revolution" → "ideology forms basis of regime legitimacy: propaganda function of ideology." As a divergent variable, the latter appears as a diamond. The pathway continues in Figure 13.2i with "ideology forms the basis of regime legitimacy: propaganda function of ideology" → "PERCEPTIONS OF OFFENSIVE ADVANTAGE." As a convergent variable, the latter is depicted as a parallelogram. The belief system disposes the new regime toward a certain kind of response to stimuli—updating in favor of taking offensive action.

Another branch forms in Figure 13.2j: "ideology forms basis of regime legitimacy: propaganda feature of ideology" → "SPIRALS OF SUSPICION." As a convergent variable "SPIRALS OF SUSPICION" is depicted as a parallelogram. In the ongoing example of postrevolutionary Iran, leadership in Teheran and other capitals increasingly become suspicious about motives. Iran, for example, perceived the United States to "tilt toward Iraq" (Walt 1996: 255).

Yet another pathway from the point of origin gets underway in Figure 13.2k: "revolution" → "increased uncertainty and misinformation." The latter, a divergent variable, takes the form of a diamond. Point estimates and dispersion around them become worse with time; in the context of Iran versus Iraq in the 1980s, each side hoped vainly for an internal uprising in the other (Walt 1996: 261). In Figure 13.2l, the route continues in two ways up to the macro level: "increased uncertainty and misinformation" → "PERCEPTIONS OF OFFENSIVE ADVANTAGE"; "SPIRALS OF SUSPICION." This pathway, in an underlying sense, is driven by cognitive overload. Even the most prosaic actions obtain attention and are more likely to be regarded as provocations.

One more pathway comes out from the point of origin in Figure 13.2m: "revolution" → "perceptions of external environment change: analytic function of ideology." The latter, a divergent variable, appears as a diamond. Iran and its foreign adversaries in the postrevolutionary years, for example, "relied on stereotypes, worst-case scenarios, and the testimony of self-interested exiles and sleazy middlemen" (Walt 1996: 264). This route converges with others through the micro-macro connection in Figure 13.2n: "perceptions of external environment change: analytic function of ideology" → "PERCEPTIONS OF OFFENSIVE ADVANTAGE." While self-interest still operates, processing of new information is biased toward policies that offer potential satisfaction in an increasingly zero-sum setting. Put differently, while ordinal rationality remains in place, the magnitude of change in response to a negative (positive) action will be (over)(under)stated.

Movement continues at the macro level in Figure 13.2o with "PERCEPTIONS OF OFFENSIVE ADVANTAGE" → "SECURITY COMPETITION." At this stage, imperatives point overwhelmingly toward competition rather than cooperation.

Pathways join together with a micro-macro linkage in Figure 13.2p: "perceptions of external environment change: analytic function of ideology" → "SPIRALS OF SUSPICION." This route continues on at the macro level and joins together in Figure 13.2q with "SPIRALS OF SUSPICION" → "SECURITY COMPETITION." The final connection for that branch appears in Figure 13.2r: "SECURITY COMPETITION" → "INTERSTATE WAR." As a terminal variable, "INTERSTATE WAR" appears as an octagon.

Figure 13.2s shows a connection that completes the other branch: "SECURITY COMPETITION" → "NON-WAR OUTCOME." The latter, as a terminal variable, is depicted as an octagon. Take, for example, the aftermath of the American Revolution. Strife with Great Britain and France ensued, but stayed within manageable limits in the decades after the revolution occurred (Walt 1996: 270–277).

Table 13.2 displays the variable types and connections that appear for revolution as a variant of balance-of-threat theory. With 13 variables, revolution is in line with other realist theories about war. The revolution variant of balance of threat includes significant contingencies: one nodal variable, along with three divergent and two convergent variables. The missing links are back and forth for the system and environment, along with the absence of a macro-micro connection. Movement within Figure 13.2 is strictly lateral or upward.

With the graphic version of revolution and war in place, what does this theory say when translated into the terminology from Kurki (2002)? Each type of cause enumerated in Kurki (2002)—formal, material, final, and efficient—will be covered in turn.

Formal causes are defining shapes or relations—background conditions. Revolution plays this role within the network of cause and effect. Regime change creates greater uncertainty about both capabilities and dispositions. This effect operates for both the new regime and those in its neighborhood. The risk of war becomes greater than otherwise.

What about material conditions—the passive potentiality of matter or, as articulated in Most and Starr (2015 [1989]), opportunity to act? Four variables play a role here: (1) reduced capabilities, (2) preference change: policy function of ideology, (3) windows of opportunity, and (4) perceptions of offensive advantage. The potential target state is very likely to emerge from revolution as less capable than before, at least in the immediate aftermath of events. The new regime also might be less competent as a byproduct of information and decision-making that is influenced by ideology. Perceived time pressure and an advantage to being on the attack also contribute to a sense of war as an opportunity.

Final conditions focus upon purposes that guide change—willingness to act, in the language of Most and Starr (2015 [1989]). Several variables come into play for this aspect of cause and effect: (1) new or intensified conflicts of interest, (2) perceptions of external environment change: analytic function of ideology, (3) increased uncertainty and misinformation, and (4) ideology as the basis of regime legitimacy: propaganda function of ideology. Conflicts accumulate over an expanding range of issues. Beliefs, in turn, change in ways that make leaders more willing to consider war as an option.

What about the efficient cause or mover? Why in the end does war occur? The answer combines spirals of suspicion with security competition. A zero-sum mindset and lack of trust combine to produce—to call upon a standard analogy—a tinderbox that ignites war.

With a graphic presentation and review of cause and effect in place, it is appropriate to revisit critiques from earlier in this chapter.

One line of criticism focuses on subjective elements within the theory. Why are ideational variables welcome within a purportedly realist theory? This question has come up before and reflects misunderstanding of boundaries for realism as a research enterprise. Material and ideational variables both can be included, but with an important restriction. Ideational variables must be in line with the logic of consequences rather than appropriateness—not a problem for revolution as a variant of balance-of-threat theory.

What about cases that do not fit with revolution as a variant of balance of threat? This can be addressed through reference to omitted variables. Elaboration should focus on what distinguishes competition over security that does not escalate from interactions that end up in war. This matter is taken up during engagement with other realist theories in Chapter 19.

One further critique is a product of the graphic presentation of revolution as a variant of balance-of-threat theory. No connection exists downward from the macro to the micro level. As with some other points, this is a natural one to take up in Chapter 19.

Reflections on Balance of Threat

Balance of threat moves substantially beyond explanations that had appeared in either classical or structural realism. Rather than a purely material basis to account for international relations, with the emphasis on balancing against capabilities, the threat-based theories—balance of threat and revolution—include ideational components. States are anticipated to balance against threats, but the possibility of bandwagoning with an aggressor state exists and is expected under certain circumstances. Thus multiple pathways can lead to war. A variant of balance of threat features revolution as a point of departure along the road to war. Uncertainty about capabilities and motives put great cognitive burdens on, and can even overload, national leaders. Suspicions mount, beliefs increasingly favor taking aggressive action, and security competition intensifies. War can be the result. Through engagement with other realist theories, elaboration of balance of threat in Chapter 19 is expected to produce substantial benefits.

14
Balance of Interests

Overview

Balance of interests, more than anything else, is a realist theory identified through its recognition of variety in foreign policy. Despite unvarying imperatives from the international system, states act differently from each other on many occasions. Rather than make uniform efforts to balance against power, states pursue interests through a wide range of approaches. Power as a resource is essential to achievement of all such goals, along the way, but specific applications of it are not expected to be the same among states. Essential to comprehending action is a grasp of how the degrees of cohesion for a society and motivation on the part of its leadership impact what states can and will do. In that way, balance-of-interests theory can claim to offer a convincing account for the wide range of foreign policies seen in practice.

Work proceeds in five additional sections. The second section provides an overall sense of balance of interests as a theory and enumerates its axioms. The third section explores the balance of interests as a theory on the causes of war. Three models are put forward. The fourth section reviews critiques. The fifth section provides a graphic representation of the three models from balance of interests that seek to explain the causes of war. These visualizations also are applied in response to points of criticism. A sixth and final section reviews the accomplishments of balance of interests as a theory.

What Is Balance-of-Interests Theory?

Balance of interests is a neoclassical realist theory. It elaborates on the state to enhance explanation of foreign policy. While preceded to some degree by ideas in Schweller (1994), two books share the status of a magnum opus for balance-of-interests theory—*Deadly Imbalances* (Schweller 1998) and *Unanswered Threats* (Schweller 2006). Balance of interests, as expounded in these studies, is state-centered and static in orientation. The theory is well received—its respective major expositions are described variously as insightful, ambitious, superb, and valuable to the field (Banchoff 1999: 135, 467; Roth 2006: 488; Doran 2007; Resnick 2007: 417).

Schweller (1998: 25; see also 2003b: 78) characterizes the theory as a fundamental shift from structural realism. Balance of interests departs from the nearly exclusive emphasis on balancing in Waltz (1979): "Predictions are codetermined by the power and interests of the units and the structures within which they are embedded." While imperatives from an international system create some degree of conformity, not all foreign policies are alike in practice. Even a quick glance at the history of international relations, Schweller (2004: 160) points out, is enough to reveal numerous important instances of underbalancing. Yet balance of power, as a matter of course, is treated as a law of nature among many realists (Schweller 2004: 162). Balance of interests therefore moves away from a belief in uniformity and toward a research agenda that seeks an explanation for diverse foreign policies that are observed in the international system. In spite of its departure from an exclusive emphasis on balance of power, as will become apparent, the theory is grounded in the realist point of view.

Schweller (1994: 104) introduces balance-of-interests theory in summary form:

> At the systemic level, balance-of-interest theory suggests that the distribution of capabilities, by itself, does not determine the stability of the system. More important are the goals and means to which those capabilities or influence are put to use: whether power and influence is used to manage the system or destroy it; whether the means employed to further such goals threaten other states or make them feel more secure. In other words, the stability of the system depends on the balance of revisionist and conservative forces.

Amusingly, Schweller (1994: 168) claims to present a theory about "mistakes," if assessed "solely in terms of the international strategic setting." Balance-of-interests theory, in comparison to standard balance-of-power theory, offers a "more elaborate causal chain" for how changes in relative power bring about policy adjustments (Schweller 1994: 169). The emphasis on foreign policy identifies balance of interests with the neoclassical strain of realism.

States are distinguished from each other in terms of the principal interests that account for their foreign policy. Actors are diverse in regard to objectives and "the power-maximizing goals of revisionist states must be recognized along with the security-maximizing objectives of status-quo states" (Schweller 1996: 115). To achieve logical consistency and account for the issue of relative gains under anarchy, according to Schweller (1996: 120), realist theory therefore "must be based on the assumption that some states seek nonsecurity expansion or that there is good chance that they will become aggressive in the future." This is a firm rejection of structural realism on grounds of incomplete specification. Put differently, wars will not simply occur as a natural property of existence under anarchy.

Consider a continuum from status quo (satiated) states to revisionist (insatiable) states (Schweller 1994: 100). Each category is linked by analogy to an animal in order to enhance understanding of the associated actions: lions (self-preserving; balancing or buck-passing), lambs (self-abnegation; appeasement and wave-of-the-future bandwagoning; distancing), jackals (limited aims; jackal-style bandwagoning), and wolves (unlimited aims; risk-acceptant aggression). While all leaders seek power as a resource to further their aims, tactics pursued are diverse. Schweller (1998: 190) identifies 11 distinct forms of state behavior, over and beyond balancing: "buckpassing, distancing, engagement [peaceful revision by satisfied powers to accommodate rising, dissatisfied power], binding [allying with source of threat to try to control its policy], holding the balance [using advantage of position to make gains], and jackal and several other forms of bandwagoning." In principle, it would be possible for any given combination of aims, strategically speaking, to be coupled with one of the tactics.

While relatively complex in its expectations for foreign policy, balance-of-interests theory also seems in line with what is observed in practice. The different inhabitants in Schweller's (1998) "zoo," along with the categories of action available to them, create manifold possibilities. Consider a prominent historical example that on the surface seems out of line with realism per se: British appeasement at Munich. The point of departure for the realist analysis by Ripsman and Levy (2008: 175), however, is that the British choice of appeasement reflected "a bleak assessment of relative power." This makes sense in light of the following acceleration in British rearmament, with the Munich conference then interpreted as an instance of buying time (Ripsman and Levy 2008: 178). On the one hand, it is reasonable to argue that Germany made better use than its adversaries of the delay in outbreak of war, and thus appeasement should not be regarded as an optimal tactic (Ripsman and Levy 2008: 179, 180). On the other hand, British policy as observed fits with both ordinal rationality in particular and realism in general.

Table 14.1 offers balance-of-interests theory at a glance. Structure-unit interaction is anticipated to go beyond the limited range inherent in neorealism. States are expected to pursue a wide range of goals. Both capability and disposition will affect the likelihood of balancing in the system. A divided and weak society emerges as an aspect of power—this condition can impede foreign policy. It becomes possible and even likely under some circumstances that external threats will not be countered effectively.

Does balance of interests qualify as a realist theory? In regard to compliance with axioms, balance of interests is state-centric and sees the international system as one of anarchy rather than hierarchy. So it is in line with the realist vision of the macro level. The leaders in Schweller's world are pragmatic and

Table 14.1 Balance of Interests at a Glance

Source	Summary Statement
Schweller (1998: 7, 25)	"If international relations theory continues to be restricted to either structural or unit-level theories, opportunities for further advances in knowledge will be missed.... Unlike Waltz's theory, which is all structure and no units, the revised theory contains complex unit-structure interactions, such that predictions are codetermined by the power and interests of the units and the structures within which they are embedded."
Schweller (2003b: 78)	"Even if we conceded Waltz's point that survival is the sine qua non for the pursuit of other goals the question arises: When survival is assured, what does neorealism explain? Not enough, in my view; that is why I developed balance-of-interests theory."
Roth (2006: 486)	Variables found at the state level determine whether or not a threatened state will balance against accumulated power as predicted by neorealist theory.
Schweller (2006: 47, 67)	"Elite consensus and cohesion primarily affect the state's *willingness* to balance, while government/regime vulnerability and social cohesion affect the state's *ability* to extract resources for this task. The combination of these four variables determines the degree of *state coherence*.... Balancing is most likely with a stable regime, social cohesion and elite cohesion."
Resnick (2007: 417)	The study is motivated by the failure of many states throughout history to act in accordance with the cardinal prediction of structural realist theory that states will tend to balance against rising powers that threaten their survival, through the acquisition of arms and/or allies
Rosecrance (2007: 513)	One must look inside the state to "unpack" realism and find correlates that actually determine how a state will act.
Rathbun (2008: 313)	Governments presiding over fractured societies are weak and are unable to take the steps necessary to counter real threats.
Chernoff (2014: 157)	In Schweller's view there is no single political goal or concept of interest that all states pursue.

able to choose among policy options to achieve their goals. All of that is in line with ordinal rationality at the very least. In addition, none of the specific foreign policies enumerated poses a problem for the assumption of power seeking. Thus balance-of-interests theory is in line with the axioms of realism at the micro level as well.

What about insertion of domestic politics into balance of interests? The condition of the state and society with regard to degree of cohesion and motivation affects foreign policy. This is a fifth axiom for the theory. It does not, however, pose a problem for inclusion of balance of interests among realist theories. This is because the focus continues to be on states, not transnational actors, and the logic of consequences rather than appropriateness underlies the theory.

Balance of interests is connected in significant ways to the tradition of classical realism. Points of resemblance include Wight (1978 [1946]) on seeking gain, Kissinger (1957) on alliances, and Wolfers (1962) with respect to aggressive and threat-perceiving states. In a word, with these traits and its emphasis on foreign policy, balance-of-interests theory is neoclassical.

Expositions on the Causes of War

Three models are put forward to account for foreign policy, most notably instances of underbalancing (Schweller 2006: 62–64). Appendix 14.A depicts the models, in turn, which take the form of variables in sequence: (i) additive; (ii) extremely incoherent states; and (iii) polarized democratic. The exposition is quasi-diagrammatic; each connection from one variable to the next is depicted with an arrow. These models will be depicted in graphic form as explanations for interstate war.

Balance-of-power theory, from the standpoint of Schweller (1994: 200), erroneously assumes constant mobilization capacity and "ignores the trade-off between internal and external stability." In other words, the conventional vision of foreign policy requires elaboration if realism is to move forward in solving empirical problems such as "What causes war?" This provides an opening for balance-of-interests theory (Schweller 2006: 47, 48):

> Elite consensus and cohesion primarily affect the state's *willingness* to balance, while government/regime vulnerability and social cohesion affect the state's *ability* to extract resources for this task. The combination of these four variables determines the degree of *state coherence* . . . [A]ppeasement and other forms of underbalancing will tend to triumph in the absence of a determined and broad political consensus to balance simply because these policies represent the path of least domestic resistance and can appeal to a broad range of interests along the political spectrum.

Leaders, moreover, may be reluctant to mobilize hypernationalism because a large army can be used against them (Schweller 2006: 50).

Several causal schemes are put forward in theorizing about how states in the system will react to would-be aggression (Schweller 2006: 62–64). From where, however, does trouble emanate in the first place? "In addition to regime effectiveness and authority," observes Schweller (2006: 108), "aggressive expansion requires national unity of purpose, and not just any purpose." Yet, to date, realist theory "provides neither a theory of despotic power nor an ideology for whipping up nationalist sentiment to wage large-scale wars" (Schweller 2006: 115). This is because of ongoing reluctance to bring domestic political processes into realist explanations.

Four possible worlds result from combining state types in terms of cohesion and motivation: a potential expander that is (unitary and motivated *or* fragmented and unmotivated) x a defender that is (unitary and motivated *or* fragmented and unmotivated) (Schweller 2006: 126). The most dangerous and war-prone world is one in which the expander is unitary and motivated and the defender is fragmented and unmotivated. In standard realist accounts so far, however, both the expander and defender are assumed to be unitary and motivated (Schweller 2006: 126). The different types create the potential to explain foreign policies that previously could not be incorporated into a realist vision in which all states are deemed identical aside from power endowments. Put differently, balance-of-interests theory treats state-society relations as an element of capability.

Illustrations from the years leading up to World War II facilitate understanding of how the balance of interests is expected to influence world politics. For Britain during the interwar years, the way in which internal and external stability trade off with each other is essential to understanding foreign policy (Schweller 1994: 188). When Germany remilitarized the Rhineland in March 1936, Britain exhibited "an overwhelming consensus among elites and the public for appeasement" (Schweller 1994: 190). This is because Prime Minister Neville Chamberlain and the governing party feared that another war like 1914–18 would push the social order toward more control for the working class (Schweller 1994: 194). Schweller (1994: 194–196) identifies extreme fragmentation in France of the same era, which led to policies that incoherently and ineffectively brought together balancing on the one hand and buck-passing, bandwagoning, and appeasement on the other. All of this combined to encourage further German efforts to expand.

While Britain and France in the 1930s might be combined to form the most prominent example, other significant cases of underbalancing also can be identified in history. Brazil and Argentina before strife with Paraguay in 1864, along with France from the 1870s to 1898, reveal that underbalancing is far from unknown in foreign policy (Schweller 2006: see also Rosecrance 2007: 513). Threats against these divided states went unmet in spite of the resources that could have been applied in response (Rosecrance 2007: 513). Moreover, these cases include serious dangers that nonetheless produced underbalancing (Schweller 2006).

Critiques

Several points of criticism have been raised with regard to balance of interests. These arguments, in turn, focus on (a) whether the theory is realist or not, (b) lack of ethical content, and (c) how the theory has been constructed. The three models from Schweller (2006) can be equated with each other in this context; points (a) through (c) apply to all of them.

One critique focuses on the basic character of balance of interests. Legro and Moravacsik (1999: 30) assert that balance-of-interests theory "reverses the causal arrow of realism." Instead of arguing that the distribution of power affects the behavior of states even in the presence of varying preferences, Schweller "offers a compelling and creative account of how governments adjust their power to their preferences" (Legro and Moravcsik 1999: 30). In other words, is balance of interests really a set of reductionist arguments that does not fit within the lexicon of realism?

Balance of interests also is attacked for its lack of ethical content (Rosecrance 2007: 514). Aside from preservation of the state, the theory does not seem to have any normative element. A wide range of foreign policy outcomes are assessed only in terms of how things work out for the state in question.

Another critique, with *Unanswered Threats* cited as an example, concerns how theory is built. With its various actor types and categories of foreign policy action, balance of interests looks like an extreme swing of the pendulum away from deductive and toward inductive inference. Balance of interests therefore is criticized for being "cumbersome" (Resnick 2007: 418). It is summed up by Resnick (2007: 418) as a theory that may have "sacrificed too much theoretical parsimony in the pursuit of excess explanatory leverage." This critique bears on the Performance Ratio for balance of threat—is the denominator just too large relative to the numerator?

Graphic Representation

Figure 14.1 depicts the additive model, the first of three from balance of interests.[1] The model is referred to as "additive" because multiple factors, spanning state and society, combine against achievement of a unified and effective response to the external threat. A region and the international system as its environment appear in Figure 14.1a. A pathway begins in Figure 14.1b with "unitary

---

[1] The figure is based on Schweller (2006: 46–68) and especially "Causal Scheme 2: The Additive Model" (Schweller 2006: 63). The nature of the state labeled as an "expander" is taken from Schweller (2006: 126) and appears in Figures 14.1–14.3. Each of the preceding figures has benefited from a consultation with Randall Schweller.

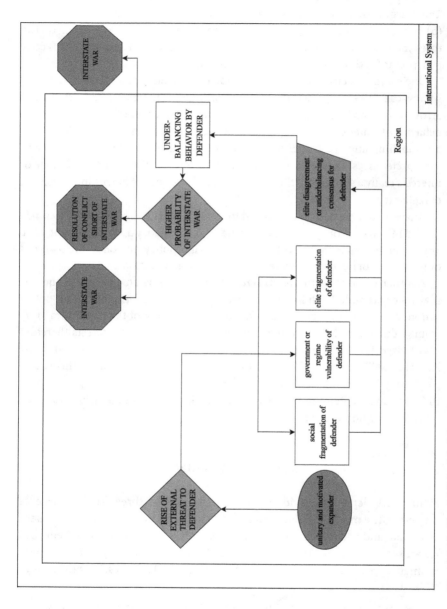

Figure 14.1 The Additive Model

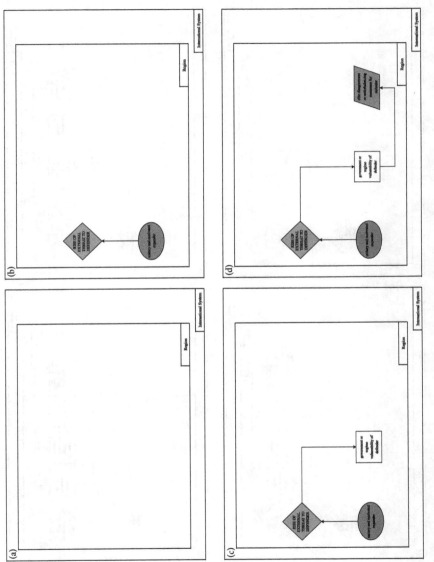

Figure 14.1 Continued

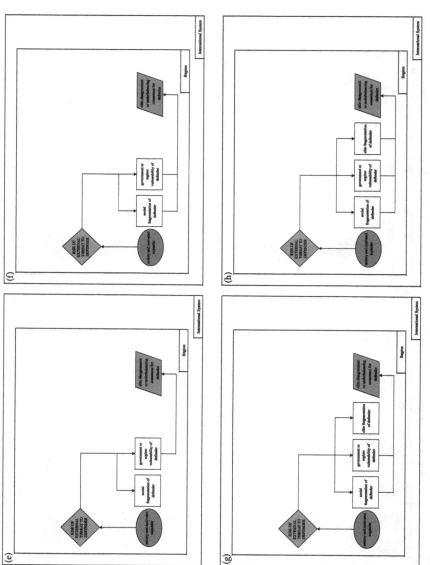

Figure 14.1 Continued

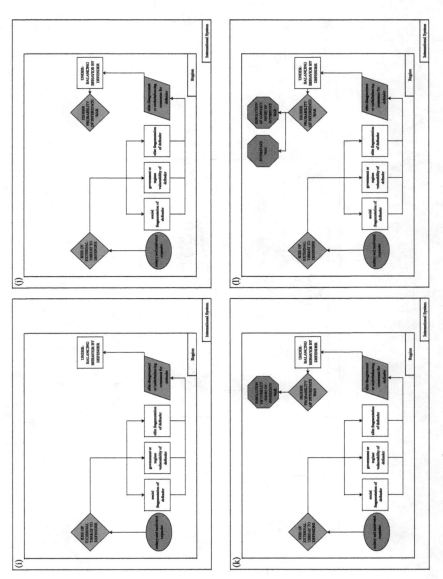

Figure 14.1 Continued

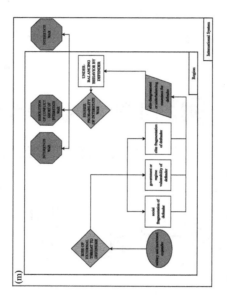

Figure 14.1 Continued

and motivated expander" → "RISE OF EXTERNAL THREAT TO DEFENDER." As the point of origin, "unitary and motivated expander" is depicted with an oval. The second variable, from which multiple pathways emerge, takes the shape of a diamond. Figure 14.1c shows one of the three routes that ensue: "RISE OF EXTERNAL THREAT TO DEFENDER" → "government or regime vulnerability of defender." This route continues at the micro level in Figure 14.1d with "government or regime vulnerability of defender" → "elite disagreement or underbalancing concerns for defender." As a convergent variable, the latter takes the form of a parallelogram. This connection may point toward a type of policy dialogue identified by Lowi (1969) as inherently divisive—redistributive politics. Contentions about how to divide an existing pie, to invoke an analogy, are intrinsically more difficult to manage through politics than those focusing on one that is expanding. If this is the ongoing reality of domestic politics for the would-be defender, the likelihood of reaching consensus in response to an external threat greatly is reduced.

Figure 14.1e puts forward another pathway: "RISE OF EXTERNAL THREAT TO DEFENDER" → "social fragmentation of defender." This route continues at the micro level in Figure 14.1f with "social fragmentation of defender" → "elite disagreement or underbalancing consensus for defender." This pernicious connection recalls the possibilities identified in a classic study of conflict and cohesion from Coser (1956). At very high levels of division, it becomes impossible to rally people behind a designated external threat to obtain renewed cohesion.

Another route appears in Figure 14.1g: "RISE OF EXTERNAL THREAT TO DEFENDER" → "elite fragmentation of defender." The elite, as well as society in general is stricken, with preexisting conflict. This pathway continues in Figure 14.1h with "elite fragmentation of defender" → "elite disagreement or underbalancing consensus for defender."

Movement from the micro to the macro level occurs in Figure 14.1i: "elite disagreement or underbalancing consensus for defender" → "UNDERBALANCING BEHAVIOR BY DEFENDER." A macro level connection ensues in Figure 14.1j with "UNDERBALANCING BEHAVIOR BY DEFENDER" → "HIGHER PROBABILITY OF INTERSTATE WAR." As a divergent variable, the latter appears as a diamond.

One of three end points is reached in Figure 14.1k: "HIGHER PROBABILITY OF INTERSTATE WAR" → "RESOLUTION OF CONFLICT SHORT OF INTERSTATE WAR." As a terminal variable, the latter takes the form of an octagon. Resolution short of war always is possible in light of the Coase Theorem (Coase 1960). Specifically, a bargain exists in which some resources that would have been lost in escalation of conflict can be used by one adversary to compensate the other (James 1988). The second end point is reached in Figure 14.1l: "HIGHER PROBABILITY OF INTERSTATE WAR" → "INTERSTATE

WAR." The existence of a potential bargain short of war does not, however, guarantee its resolution. As a terminal variable, the latter is depicted as an octagon.

Figure 14.1m shows movement from the region into the international system: "HIGHER PROBABILITY OF INTERSTATE WAR" → "INTERSTATE WAR." Balance of interests anticipates this type of escalation, geographically speaking, as additional actors come into the fray because of an expanding agenda of issues in conflict.

Table 14.2 conveys the variable types and connections for the additive model. With 11 variables, counting three points of termination, the causal network is neither simplistic nor ornate. There are three points of contingency—two divergent variables and one convergent variable. Among potential types of connection, only environment into the system is absent. No feedback loops are included.

How does the additive model look in relation to the conditions, implemented from Kurki (2002), with regard to cause and effect? Formal, material, final, and efficient causes are considered in turn.

Consider formal conditions, which are defining shapes or relations that serve as a background to the process. These are twofold: (a) a unitary and motivated expander and (ii) the rise of an external threat to the defender. This combination always lurks behind the next corner that a state will turn, figuratively speaking, in a realist world.

What about material conditions—the passive potentiality of matter or, in the words of Most and Starr (2015 [1989]), opportunity? The key elements in this context are (i) government or regime vulnerability of defender and (ii) social fragmentation of defender. A state seeking to make gains will process this information as an update that favors pressing forward more assertively.

Consider as well final conditions—purposes that guide change, corresponding to willingness from Most and Starr (2015 [1989]). In connection to a disposition to act, the following items are essential: (i) elite fragmentation of defender and (ii) elite disagreement or underbalancing concerns for defender. An expander will become more willing to move forward when faced with a divided and almost certainly indecisive adversary.

Efficient conditions or movers lead directly into an outcome. Underbalancing behavior by a defender is decisive at this stage. Lack of countervailing power leads either to war—at either the regional level or even beyond—or last-minute resolution that brings about de-escalation.

Figure 14.2 conveys the extremely incoherent states model.[2] A region and the international system as its environment are depicted in Figure 14.2a. The process gets underway in Figure 14.2b with "unitary and motivated expander" → "RISE

---

[2] The figure is based on Schweller (2006: 46–68), notably "Causal Scheme 3: Extremely Incoherent States Model" (Schweller 2006: 63).

Table 14.2 Variable Types and Connections for Balance-of-Interests Theories

Theory	Overall Number	Initial	Generic	Divergent	Convergent	Nodal	Coconstitutive	Terminal	Interaction Effect	Loops	Missing Links[a]
Additive	11	1	4	2	1	0	0	3	0	0	E→S
Extremely incoherent states	12	1	6	1	1	0	0	3	0	1	E→S
Polarized democratic	11	1	3	2	1	1	0	3	0	0	E→S

[a] The notation is as follows: System (S) and Environment (E).

OF EXTERNAL THREAT TO DEFENDER." As an initial variable, "unitary and motivated expander" appears as an oval. The next step, added in Figure 14.2c, is reverberation from the system to the state level with "RISE OF EXTERNAL THREAT TO DEFENDER" → "social fragmentation of defender." Stresses and strains within the state are exacerbated as a result of tensions beyond its borders.

Several developments ensue for the defender. Depicted in Figure 14.2d, the next step is "social fragmentation of defender" → "government or regime vulnerability of defender." Added in Figure 14.2e, the story continues with "government or regime vulnerability of defender" → "elite fragmentation of defender." The capacity to act decisively and effectively on foreign policy obviously is deteriorating as this process unfolds. What follows, added in Figure 14.2f, is "elite fragmentation of defender" → "elite disagreement about how to respond to threat or elite consensus not to balance for defender."

Added in Figure 14.2g, a further development at the state level is "elite disagreement about how to respond to threat or elite consensus not to balance for defender" → "further state disintegration of defender." The latter, a convergent variable, is shown as a parallelogram and initiates a feedback loop, added in Figure 14.2h, into itself. In other words, a vicious circle of incoherence takes hold. Think of this set of developments, perhaps, as building upon the standard "billiard table" analogy with international politics. Rather than identical and impenetrable, the billiard balls can begin to exhibit differences from each other, especially when struck hard enough. It even is possible for one or more of the billiard balls to fracture and no longer roll around in the same way as before.

Depicted in Figure 14.2i, a connection up to the system level ensues with "further state disintegration of defender" → "UNDERBALANCING BEHAVIOR BY DEFENDER." Intense conflict at home compromises the ability to act abroad. The process continues at the macro level in Figure 14.2j: "UNDERBALANCING BEHAVIOR BY DEFENDER" → "HIGHER PROBABILITY OF INTERSTATE WAR." As a divergent variable, the latter appears as a diamond.

One pathway is completed in Figure 14.2k with "HIGHER PROBABILITY OF INTERSTATE WAR" → "RESOLUTION OF CONFLICT SHORT OF INTERSTATE WAR." The latter, as a terminal variable, appears as an octagon. This process corresponds to appeasement in some form or another directed by that defender toward the expander. Another route is completed in Figure 14.2l: "HIGHER PROBABILITY OF INTERSTATE WAR" → "INTERSTATE WAR." Since it also is a terminal variable, "INTERSTATE WAR" takes the form of an octagon.

Among the pathways, the last is one that extends from the region into the international system. It is completed in Figure 14.2m: "HIGHER PROBABILITY OF INTERSTATE WAR" → "INTERSTATE WAR." Once again, the terminal variable in sequence appears as an octagon. The connection reflects the potential

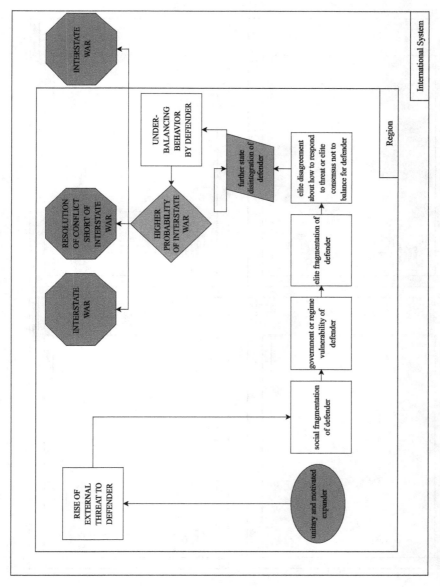

Figure 14.2 Extremely Incoherent States Model

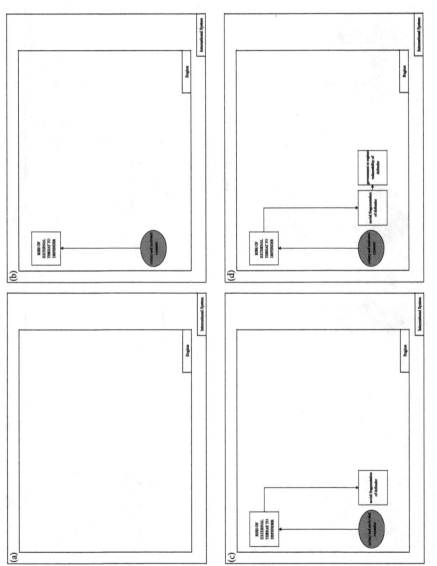

Figure 14.2 Continued

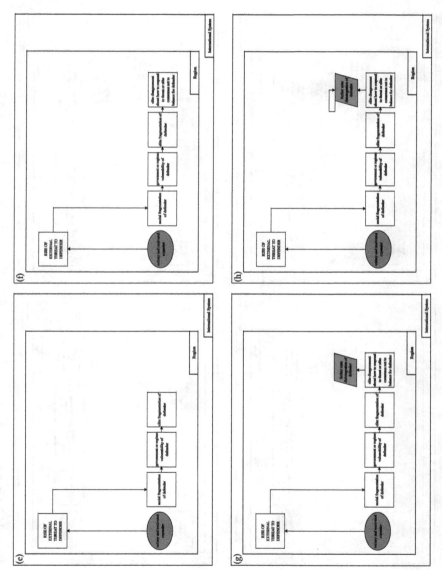

Figure 14.2 Continued

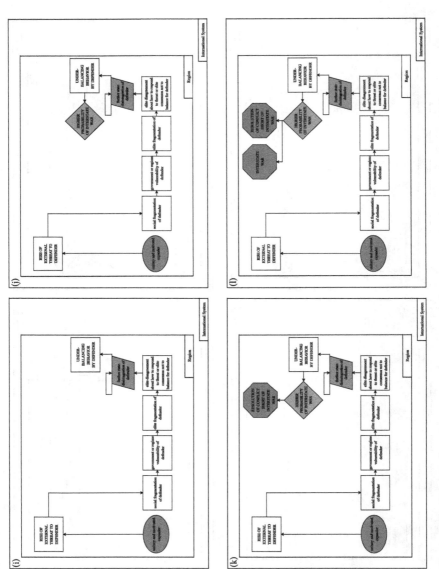

Figure 14.2 Continued

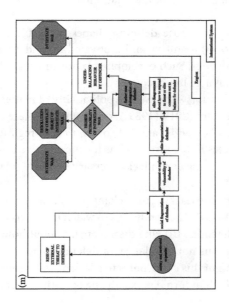

Figure 14.2 Continued

for a unitary and motivated state, as its demands accelerate and those affected expand in number and geographic expanse, to escalate in this way as well.

Variable types and connections are summarized for the extremely incoherent states version of balance of interests in Table 14.2. With a dozen variables, this model is neither simplistic nor overly difficult to follow. It possesses one convergent and one divergent variable, and there is no node in the system. The network includes a feedback loop, along with a connection from the macro level of the system into the environment. It lacks a connection for the international system into the region.

How does the extremely incoherent states model play out in relation to cause and effect in the framework adopted from Kurki (2002)? Each of the conditions identified by Kurki (2002)—formal, material, final, and efficient—will be covered in turn.

Consider formal causes—those defining shapes or relations in the background. These consist of (i) a unitary and motivated expander and (ii) the rise of external threat to defender. Such developments are anticipated to occur in a world of power politics as a matter of course.

What about material causes—the passive potentiality of matter or, in the terminology of Most and Starr (2015 [1989]), opportunity? These conditions are (i) social fragmentation of defender and (ii) government or regime vulnerability of defender. Each operates in the same way as for the additive model—creating conditions of indecision in the expander's adversary that facilitate an aggressive foreign policy.

Final causes are the purposes that guide change—willingness as articulated in Most and Starr (2015 [1989]). The conditions to watch in this context are (i) elite fragmentation of the defender, (ii) elite disagreement about how to respond to the threat or elite consensus not to balance for defender, and (iii) further disintegration of the state. All of this contributes to a lack of willingness to act on the part of the defender, which in turn has exactly the opposite effect for the would-be expander.

Efficient causes are the movers that bring about a result. The efficient cause is underbalancing behavior by the defender. The result is either war or a bargain of some kind short of all-out escalation.

Figure 14.3 shows the polarized democratic model.[3] A region and international system as its environment are depicted in Figure 14.3a. Events are set in motion with "unitary and motivated expander" → "RISE OF EXTERNAL THREAT TO DEFENDER" in Figure 14.3b. These initial and divergent variables

---

[3] Schweller (2006: 46–68) and in particular "Causal Scheme 4: Polarized Democratic Model" are used to create the figure.

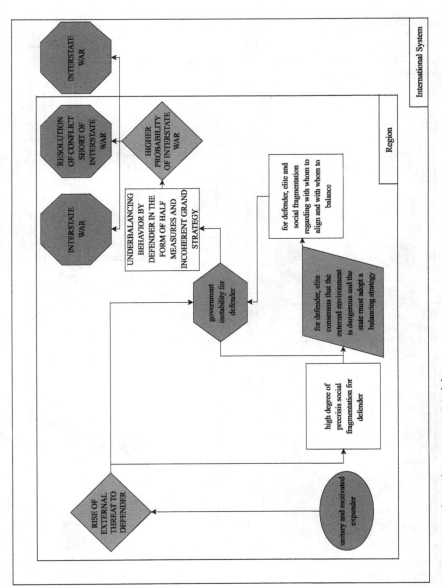

Figure 14.3 Polarized Democratic Model

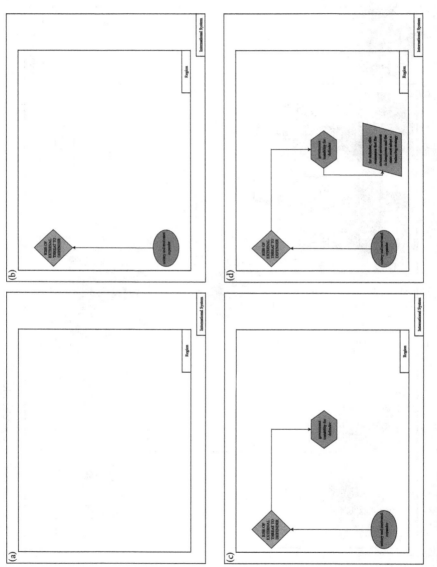

Figure 14.3 Continued

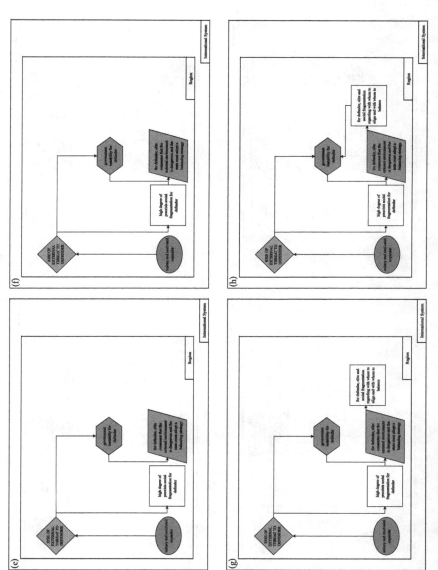

Figure 14.3 Continued

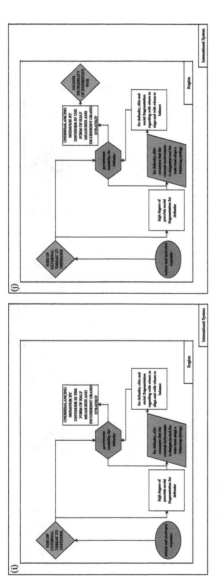
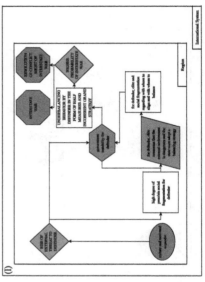
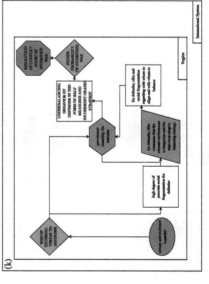

Figure 14.3 Continued

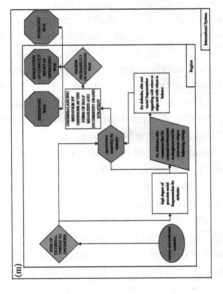

Figure 14.3 Continued

are represented, respectively, with an oval and diamond. Multiple pathways emerge and each is covered in turn.

More direct is the route that continues with "RISE OF EXTERNAL THREAT TO DEFENDER" → "government instability for defender" in Figure 14.3c. Instability of the defender's government is a nodal variable and therefore depicted with a hexagon. This connection reduces an essential aspect of capability for the state in question. One route leading from the hexagon, which appears in Figure 14.3d, is "government instability for defender" → "for defender, elite consensus that the external environment is dangerous and the state must adopt a balancing strategy." As a convergent variable, the latter appears as a parallelogram. This situation is different from the one reached for preceding models because balancing is more viable as an option. To return to the logic from Coser (1956), the connection suggests that the level of external threat is high, but not yet at a level that would prohibit an effective response in pursuit of internal cohesion.

Another branch emerges downward in Figure 14.3e: "RISE OF EXTERNAL THREAT TO DEFENDER" → "high degree of precrisis social fragmentation for defender." As confrontation builds, tensions at home are aggravated over how, if at all, to respond in light of the external threat. This route continues at the micro level in Figure 14.3f with "high degree of precrisis social fragmentation for defender" → "for defender, elite consensus that the external environment is dangerous and the state must adopt a balancing strategy." This once again corresponds to the logic behind pursuit of internal cohesion through confrontation with an external adversary. The pathway continues in Figure 14.3g with "for defender, elite consensus that the external environment is dangerous and the state must adopt a balancing policy" → "for defender, elite and social fragmentation regarding with whom to align and against whom to balance." Domestic divisions are highlighted when *specific* aspects of policy come into play.

Figure 14.3h shows a further micro-level connection, namely, "for defender, elite consensus that the external environment is dangerous and the state must adopt a balancing policy" → "government instability for defender." Time pressure plays a role in instigating conflict for a government seeking a response that meets foreign policy needs while also not upsetting a delicate balance at the level of domestic politics.

Movement from the micro to the macro level occurs in Figure 14.3i: "government instability for defender" → "UNDERBALANCING BY DEFENDER IN THE FORM OF HALF MEASURES AND INCOHERENT GRAND STRATEGY." Cross-pressures combine to produce this undesirable and probably ineffective set of policies. The route continues in Figure 14.3j with "UNDERBALANCING BY DEFENDER IN THE FORM OF HALF MEASURES AND INCOHERENT GRAND STRATEGY" → "HIGHER PROBABILITY OF INTERSTATE WAR." As a divergent variable, the latter is depicted as a diamond.

Via the operation of ordinal rationality, the deteriorating condition of the defender contributes to the expander's updated preference in favor of war.

One point of conclusion is reached in Figure 14.3k: "HIGHER PROBABILITY OF INTERSTATE WAR" → "RESOLUTION OF CONFLICT SHORT OF INTERSTATE WAR." Bargaining could lead to concessions from the defender to the expander that are sufficient to head off war, at least in the short term. As with the other two end points that follow, the terminal variable appears as an octagon. Figure 14.3l depicts an end point with "HIGHER PROBABILITY OF INTERSTATE WAR" → "INTERSTATE WAR." Last among the points of termination is one that extends into the international system in Figure 14.3m: "HIGHER PROBABILITY OF INTERSTATE WAR" → "INTERSTATE WAR." This connection allows for the expander's war aims increasing in scope during the process of escalation and even stretching beyond regional boundaries.

Table 14.2 summarizes the variable types and connections for Figure 14.3. With 11 variables, the polarized democratic model is neither simplistic nor unwieldy. It features several points of contingency, with two divergent, one convergent, and one nodal variable. Only one type of connection, from the environment into the system, is missing.

Consider the polarized democratic model in relation to the conditions for cause and effect adopted from Kurki (2002). Formal, material, final, and efficient causes as summarized in Kurki (2002) will be considered in turn.

What about formal conditions—defining shapes or relations in the background? Once again, two conditions are present: (i) a unitary and motivated expander and (ii) rise of an external threat to the defender. These are ongoing features of a realist world.

Consider as well material causes—the passive potentiality of matter, familiar as opportunity in the framework of Most and Starr (2015 [1989]). The condition to watch in this context is a high degree of precrisis social fragmentation for the defender, which signals probable indecisiveness under increasing pressure. This condition facilitates an aggressive foreign policy for the expander.

Final causes, or purposes that guide change, correspond to willingness as articulated in Most and Starr (2015 [1989]). Pertinent to this category, for the defender, are (a) elite and social fragmentation regarding with whom to align and with whom to balance; and (b) elite consensus that the external environment is dangerous and the state must adopt a balancing strategy. While the defender may be willing to respond, it is highly and visibly constrained—conditions that can be detected by an expander that then may press forward more assertively than otherwise in pursuit of gains.

What about efficient causes—the movers that bring about an outcome? The variable in this category is underbalancing behavior by the defender in the form of half measures and incoherent grand strategy. The expanding state, as a result, either will bargain for concessions or seek more decisive gains through warfare.

With a diagrammatic exposition and assessment of cause and effect in place for all of its models, what can be said in response to critics of balance-of-interests theory?

One critique focuses on the identity of balance of interests; in a word, is this theory realist? Another point of criticism focuses on its lack of normative content. A response to the former query can come through a reply to the latter. While balance of interests does include domestic politics, it incorporates neither transnational actors nor the logic of appropriateness. Thus it is realist and limited in the sense that all theories based on power politics are restricted. The emphasis of balance of interests, like other realist theories, is on the logic of consequences.

Is balance of interests so complicated that it is not worth the effort? This criticism, which bears upon the Performance Ratio, might be addressed through integration of the three models with each other. None of the three models, it should be observed, is more intricate than other realist theories about war included in this volume. At the same time, the graphic review brings out a high degree of overlap that might not have been apparent otherwise.

Visual representation also brings out the very limited nature of the analysis at the macro level. Put simply, how does underbalancing lead either to crisis de-escalation or war? Further development of balance of interests could help in answering, for example, persistent questions about the nature of Soviet foreign policy at the conclusion of the Cold War. Some ideas along such lines have been put forward already; for instance, Schweller and Wohlforth (2000: 89) make the following observation about Mikhail Gorbachev, general secretary of the Communist Party of the Soviet Union at the time: "A leader who promised to extricate the Soviet Union from its impasse while preserving the country's essential status as a superpower was sailing with the wind." Evaluation of balance of interests via engagement with other realist theories in Chapter 19 may point toward an answer.

Reflections on Balance of Interests

Balance of interests offers a convincing argument with regard to why, in spite of imperatives toward uniformity, it is not surprising to see diverse foreign policies pursued by states. The theory provides a series of models, constructed within a realist point of view, that account for how states in varying circumstances can end up at war with each other. The three models—additive, extremely incoherent states, and polarized democratic—bring out nuances about how threatening and defending states can be expected to interact with each other. Conflict management through balancing is made more or less likely as a byproduct of domestic conditions for a defending state. Unity, in a word, stands out as an element of state capability. The overall contribution of balance-of-interests theory is to elaborate, in a realist way, on the role of the state in foreign policy along the road to war.

Appendix 14.A
Models of Foreign Policy from Balance-of-Interests Theory

Model	Dynamics
Additive	Rise of external threat → social fragmentation (cohesion) + government or regime vulnerability (stability) + elite fragmentation (cohesion) → elite disagreement or nonbalancing consensus (elite balancing consensus) → underbalancing (balancing) behavior
Extremely incoherent states	Rise of an external threat → social fragmentation → government or regime vulnerability → elite fragmentation → elite disagreement about how to respond to threat or elite consensus not to balance → underbalancing behavior and very high probability of further state disintegration (e.g., civil war or revolution)
Polarized democratic	Rise of external threat(s) + high degree of precrisis social fragmentation and government instability → elite consensus that the external environment is dangerous and the state must adopt a balancing policy → elite and social fragmentation regarding with whom to align and against whom to balance → even greater government instability → underbalancing in the form of half measures and incoherent grand strategies

Source: Schweller (2006: 63–64).

15
Defensive Realism

Overview

Defensive realism, as theories within the research enterprise go, is perhaps the least pessimistic among them. While the balance between offensive and defensive capabilities under normal conditions does not rule out conquest, the disposition among states in the international system is believed to be against such action. This expectation is in place because the defense, on average, will be dominant over the offense. An aggressor therefore must be willing to accept a much higher level of losses, human and material, in the conduct of war. Thus interstate war is more the exception than the rule in world politics.

This chapter unfolds in five additional sections. The second section focuses on the basic meaning of defensive realism and conveys its axioms. The third section puts forward defensive realism as a theory about the causes of war. The fourth section offers critiques. The fifth section conveys defensive realist theories about the causes of war in graphic form. These versions are implemented to engage with critics of defensive realism as well. The sixth and final section sums up the contributions of defensive realism.

What Is Defensive Realism?

Defensive realism, by consensus, is descended from the exposition by Waltz (1979) (Hamilton and Rathbun 2013: 441; see also Posen 2002: 119). Like neorealism, defensive realism is system oriented and focuses on comparative statics. According to Montgomery (2014: 175), Snyder (1991) should be credited with initially distinguishing defensive and offensive realism from each other. (Offensive realism is covered in Chapter 17.) The magnum opus for defensive realism is Van Evera, *Causes of War* (1999). The theory in *Causes of War* has stimulated quite a bit of attention and even controversy (Mahnken 2000; Reiter 2000; Stam 2001; Gartzke 2002).

Defensive realists, Walt (2002: 205) observes, "assert that the offense-defense balance determines the *intensity* of security competition between states." The defensive realist viewpoint is summed up effectively by Leiber (2008: 191; see also Fiammenghi 2011: 126):

Defensive realists view most aggressive behavior as anomalous for a purely structural theory because the international system provides great powers with little motivation to seek additional increments of power. First, expansionism promotes efficient balancing by other great powers, which usually leaves a state worse off than if it had been willing to settle for the status quo ante. Second, defensive realists believe that the fine-grained structure of power—above all the offense-defense balance—is far more important than the gross distribution of aggregate capabilities.

Within a comprehensive review of realist thought, Elman and Jensen (2014: 7) identifies multiple important ways in which structural realism is distinguished from defensive realism as its progeny. One difference is that while neorealism would seem to allow for several possible microfoundations of state behavior, the defensive variant embraces rational choice openly. Defensive realism adds a key variable: the offense-defense balance (Elman and Jensen 2014: 7). Defensive realists, according to Elman and Jensen (2014: 7), "argue that prevailing technologies or geographical circumstances often favor defense, seized resources do not cumulate easily with those already possessed by the metropole, dominoes do not fall, and power is difficult to project at a distance." Given the presence of rationality and a strategic balance that discourages attack, defensive realism anticipates that states will seek to uphold the status quo much more often than not. Expansion rarely is mandated by structure and, in response to threatening concentrations of power, balancing stands as the appropriate choice (Elman and Jensen 2014: 7). Thus war appears less often than what might be gleaned from intuition derived about the exercise of power politics unaccompanied by consideration of geostrategic factors.

Table 15.1 conveys a set of observations that help to establish the meaning of defensive realism in an overall sense. Defensive realism combines ideational and material factors into an overall explanation for war. It is considered normal for the defense to have an advantage over the offense once all aspects are taken into account. Thus power balancing is expected to limit the outbreak of war. States do maximize power as a resource, but usually under significant constraint. Circumstances favoring the choice of war focus on the fine-grained aspects of power and how a situation is perceived by adversaries. Thus war is not the norm and all-out conquest is rare.

What are the assumptions of defensive realism? Anarchy and state-centrism, the system-level axioms within realism as a research enterprise, are affirmed resolutely within the defensive theory (Van Evera 1999: 7). The focus is on how states cope with insecurity under conditions of anarchy that could give way to war.

Rationality, one of two state-level axioms from the research enterprise, clearly is accepted as well. For example, defensive realists see states as responding

Table 15.1 Defensive Realism at a Glance

Source	Summary Statement
Frankel (1996b: xv)	"Defensive realists are more optimistic about the likelihood of avoiding war.... Attempts at hegemony/expansion are costly because they induce balancing and the defense usually has the advantage.... Thus states recognize that the best course is the pursuit of moderate aims and minimal security."
Mahnken (2000: 208)	War is more likely when conquest is easy—in other words, when the offense is at a marked advantage.
Reiter (2000: 1259)	The hypotheses are framed within the realist theoretical tradition, specifically allowing for states to misperceive the nature of power in the international system.
Stam (2001: 266)	"The major contribution lies in demonstration of the similarity of what heretofore have been presented as competing research paradigms: realism and constructivism.... Van Evera expands the explanatory and predictive power of realism by incorporating leaders' beliefs and misperceptions about 'fine-grained power' relations between states."
Taliaferro 2000–2001: 129)	Defensive realism holds that the international system provides incentives for expansion only under certain conditions.
Walt (2002: 207)	"Defensive realists argue that states should not try to maximize power (for fear of provoking a hostile coalition).... Defensive realists see balancing as the preferred tendency for most states."
Person (2017: 48)	Integral to the defensive realist school is the concept of power balancing.

systematically to specialized knowledge about capabilities. Seeking power, the other axiom from the level of the state, also is in place. However, pursuit of power operates under constraints imposed by the normally superior position of defense over offense in the international system. The fine-grained nature of power, manifested in traits such as first-move advantage or its absence, also is important in shaping foreign policy and creating a variety of outcomes that are more common than war (Van Evera 1999: 7–8). Perhaps the "calling card" of defensive realism is its consistency with the relatively rare occurrence of interstate war in world politics.

Defensive realism entails further axioms, given its emphasis on going beyond a strictly material sense of capability. Perceptions of geostrategic setting—first-move advantage, windows of opportunity, and offense-defense balance—are assumed to influence foreign policy actions. War is relatively rare because one or more of the preceding factors must be set up in a way to encourage it. Power seeking is a natural tendency, but pursuit of this up to and including war will be constrained.

Defensive realism is linked significantly to the tradition of classical realism. Connections are clear to see with Morgenthau (1959 [1948]) on the balance of power and Aron (1966) about defensive and offensive considerations. As will become apparent, defensive realists, also in line with the classical approach, seek insights that could have value in shaping policy.

Defensive Realist Theories of War

Among realists, one book-length exposition puts forward the defensive variant as a theory about why interstate war occurs. Thus *The Causes of War* (Van Evera 1999) is featured in this chapter. In an overall sense, Van Evera (1999: 11) advocates a theory that develops into what is designated as Misperceptive Fine-Grained Structural Realism. This theory incorporates perceptions about capabilities to account more effectively for when wars occur. The fine-grained approach refers to taking into account potential effects from both offensive and defensive capabilities. The net effect is to produce a defensive realist theory that integrates material and ideational factors into a more comprehensive explanation for war.

Van Evera (1999: 2, 9) seeks realist propositions about the causes of war that feasibly can be ameliorated by countermeasures and thus, in turn, yield practical ideas about policy. This pragmatic sense of things is in line with analytic eclecticism, which advocates pursuit of research that is relevant to policy. The defensive realist theories from Van Evera (1999: 4) focus on causes of war connected to the distribution and character of national power among states. According to Van Evera (1999: 5), the "master cause of other potent causes of war, raising all the risks they pose," is ease of conquest. Realist hypotheses, if recast to include intensified perceptions of danger, perform even better than purely material expressions in explaining the history of international conflict (Van Evera 1999: 6). For example, while the structure of power in and of itself causes few wars, perceptions of it often are "malignant" and able to explain "a good deal of war" (Van Evera 1999: 6). Belief in a forthcoming easy victory is worst of all in contributing to escalation.

Material considerations are not the only ones that matter for the variants of defensive realism addressed in this chapter. Van Evera (1999: 7) asserts that "the *fine-grained* structure of power" is of greater significance in accounting for the risk of war in comparison to "the *gross* structure of power." False optimism is caused by first-move advantage and offense dominance, which supports the idea of promoting transparency in order to prevent war (Van Evera 1999: 24, 34).

Under conditions of first-move advantage, observes Van Evera (1999: 47), states try to conceal military capabilities in order to maintain an ability for surprise attack. Thus the strongest dangers of all—concealment of grievances, capabilities, plans, and perceptions—have been overlooked so far in the quest to explain war (Van Evera 1999: 39).

According to Van Evera (1999: 42), there are three types of preemptive war: (i) generic, (ii) accidental, and (iii) resulting from reciprocal fear of surprise attack. The size of first-strike advantage is a function of four factors: feasibility of gaining surprise, effect of a surprise strike on the force ratio between two sides, offense-defense balance, and size of political penalty on first strikers (Van Evera 1999: 69–70). The problem of first-move advantage therefore resides less in reality than in perception, and it therefore becomes essential to address such beliefs (Van Evera 1999: 72).

Windows of opportunity also pose a danger to peace. According to Van Evera (1999: 103), two factors determine the number and size of windows: "the frequency and degree of fluctuations in the balance of power, and the offense-defense balance." A resource is described as "cumulative" if possession of it assists in protecting or acquiring other resources (Van Evera 1999: 105). While the historical trend is away from cumulativity, states have misread that and ended up in international conflict that could have been averted (Van Evera 1999: 116). Windows, in sum, cause war because they increase fear and, in turn, promote risk-taking and other pernicious developments (Souva 2018: 140–141).

False perceptions about the dominance of offense over defense raise many dangers (Van Evera 1999: 121). What, then causes either offensive or defensive dominance, respectively? "Military technology and doctrine, geography, national social structure, and diplomatic arrangements (specifically, defensive alliances and balancing behavior by offshore powers) all matter" and combine to determine the net offense-defense balance (Van Evera 1999: 122). The sheer range of such factors is sufficient to explain why miscalculations sometimes occur. Cognitive overload could overwhelm the ability of ordinal rationality to process updated information, especially under time pressure.

Secrecy produces any number of harmful effects: false optimism, greater first-move advantages, delayed reactions to others' military buildups, promotion of diplomatic faits accompli, deterrence failure, states triggering war unwittingly, promoting arms racing and inhibition of arms control agreements, and narrowing the circle of experts consulted on national policy (Van Evera 1999: 139–141). All of this might be summed up as a further obstacle to effective updating on the basis of ordinal rationality; put differently, a byproduct of secrecy is likely to be rampant misinformation among states as a result of the inability to shift beliefs in an accurate direction.

Van Evera (1999: 13) uses a medium "N" approach, with 30 wars used to assess the performance of defensive realism. With World War I as a featured example, evidence from cases supports offense-defense theory—one of three variants introduced—as an explanation of war (Van Evera 1999: 236, 185). In August 1914, "automatic military machinery" swept aside leaders and produced the Great War (Aron 1966: 43). This followed on from pervasive beliefs that favored offense over defense. Van Evera (1999) also references World War I to support theories about stability and windows.

Realism, in sum, becomes more convincing when it includes fine-grained structures and how these are perceived; however, Van Evera (1999: 236) observes that most of its advocates eschew these ideas. Note once again that incorporation of nonmaterial aspects of power does not violate the axioms of realism as identified in Chapter 8. Instead, the presence of perceptions in defensive realist theorizing transgresses boundaries imposed through long-standing belief about what should be "allowed," as opposed to any rigorous process of identification.

Critiques

Defensive realism is critiqued on various grounds. These include (i) a claim that it is too complicated, (ii) contamination of hypotheses with nonrealist reasons for going to war, (iii) a limited range of explanation, and (iv) evidence that is both in short supply and biased.

One difficulty, identified by Reiter (2000: 1260), concerns the sheer number of propositions within the theory. The three variants of defensive realism encompass many variables; it therefore becomes reasonable to ask about the trade-off from the standpoint of the Performance Ratio. At the same time, the variants offer only limited treatment of the state, notably with regard to foreign policy decision-making.

According to Zakaria (1992: 192), great power conduct in history is not explained all that well when it is assumed that "the system provides incentives for cautious behavior." Zakaria (1992: 196) claims that defensive realism accesses normative assumptions about state behavior and, as a result, assesses a lot of foreign policy as anomalous and then explains it by blaming guilty parties.

Another critique focuses on insertion of cognitive factors into the explanation for war. Is the theory, Gartzke (2002: 724) asks, still realist? Snyder and Lieber (2008: 184) add that "defensive realism introduces perceptual or domestic political factors to explain why states deviate from what structural logic would dictate, in particular why they often behave too aggressively for their own good, and offensive realists criticize defensive realists for taking this approach." Defensive realists claim that aggressors usually end up worse off because the structure of the international system tends to counteract and even punish aggression; thus the impetus to war frequently comes from domestic politics, and great powers "most often go to war for non-realist reasons" (Mearsheimer 2018: 221).

Among significant problems facing defensive realism, according to Elman and Jensen (2014: 7), one is being suited better to investigation of "structurally constrained responses to revisionism," as opposed to the origins of such expansionist behavior. Thus defensive realism needs either state-level factors or extreme dynamics based on the security dilemma to account for revisionist states.

Other issues concern the credibility of evidence for the theory. The introduction in Van Evera (1999) focuses overwhelmingly on World War I, and some of the same observations are used to derive and test the hypotheses (Reiter 2000: 1260; Stam 2001: 266). Mahnken (2000: 208) adds that the evidence seems selective; for example, Van Evera (1999) claims that a general belief exists about an offensive advantage, but does not check that out on any systematic basis. A lack of random sampling from the population of states that might go to war is a more general manifestation of that problem (Stam 2001: 266).

Graphic Representations

Theories from Van Evera (1999) are at the center of defensive realist explanations for war. The variants, which focus on perceptions about respective geostrategic factors, are (a) stability, (b) windows, and (c) offense-defense balance.

Stability

Figure 15.1 conveys stability in graphic form as a theory about the causes of war.[1] Figure 15.1a displays a region and the international system as its surrounding environment. The initial connection, which appears in Figure 15.1b, is "FIRST MOVER ADVANTAGE" → "INTERSTATE WAR." The point of origin, "FIRST MOVER ADVANTAGE," is indicated with an oval, while "INTERSTATE WAR," a terminal variable, appears as an octagon. An analogy comes to mind for this automatic connection, namely, with dueling. If someone can fire first, there is an inherent advantage; a good shot will decide matters favorably right away. Both sides know this, so a situation with advantage to a first mover probably will impact thinking in highly destabilizing ways.

---

[1] This figure is based on Van Evera (1999: 35–53) and especially Diagram 1, which depicts repaired stability theory (Van Evera 1999: 38).

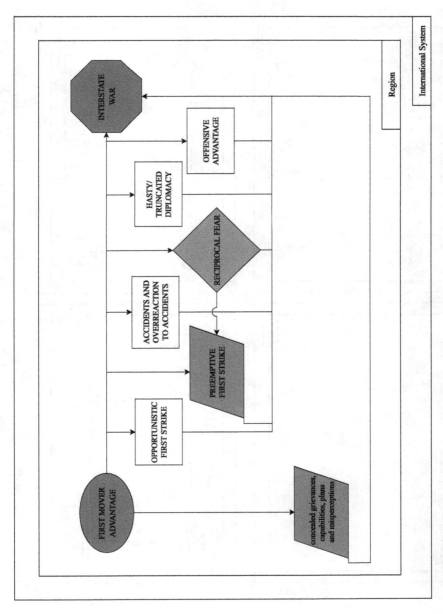

Figure 15.1 Stability

Figure 15.1 Continued

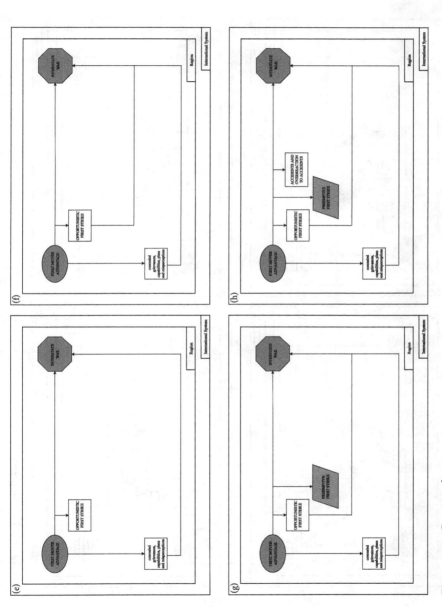

Figure 15.1 Continued

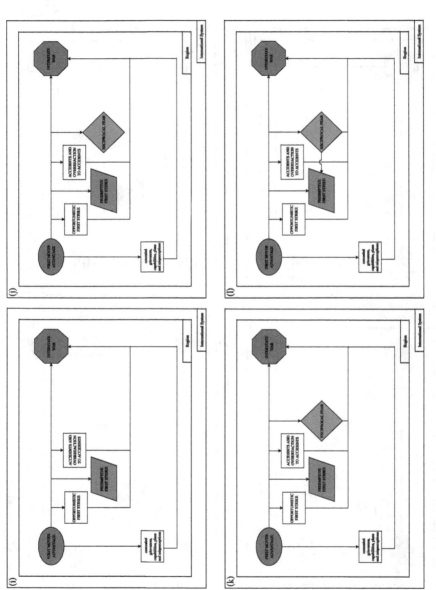

Figure 15.1 Continued

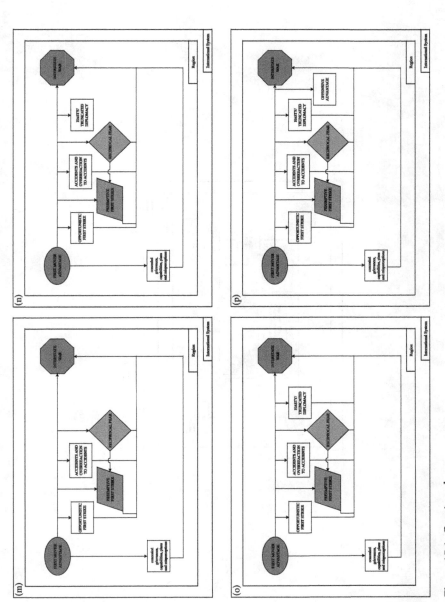

Figure 15.1 Continued

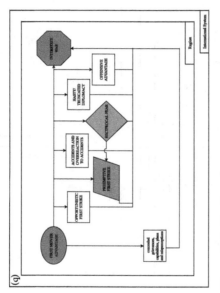

Figure 15.1 Continued

Figure 15.1c shows movement from the macro to the micro level: "FIRST MOVER ADVANTAGE" → "concealed grievances, capabilities, plans and misperceptions." Secrecy and attendant misperceptions on both sides are very likely to ensue in this "hair trigger" world. This brief pathway concludes in Figure 15.1d: "concealed grievances, capabilities, plans and misperceptions" → "INTERSTATE WAR." It is easy to imagine this collection of psychological maladies producing rapid escalation of conflict. War would be the point of culmination as the parties concerned become more eager to "act first and ask questions later."

Other pathways unfold in steps taken at the macro level. One connection, added in Figure 15.1e, is "FIRST MOVER ADVANTAGE" → "OPPORTUNISTIC FIRST STRIKE." It is very unlikely that the target state simply would accept this as the outcome. Instead, the next step, depicted in Figure 15.1f, would be "OPPORTUNISTIC FIRST STRIKE" → "INTERSTATE WAR." While perhaps it is at a disadvantage due the first strike, the high stakes involved guarantee that the target state will wage war in response.

Another route gets underway in Figure 15.1g with "FIRST MOVER ADVANTAGE" → "PREEMPTIVE FIRST STRIKE." As a convergent variable, the latter is depicted as a parallelogram. This strategic situation easily could produce a mindset in favor of preemption. Consider, for instance, controversies over missile defense and antisatellite technologies that focus on strategic vulnerability as a possible byproduct from deployment of such systems (Lowenthal 2017: 108).

Figure 15.1h sets another pathway in motion: "FIRST MOVER ADVANTAGE" → "ACCIDENTS AND OVERREACTION TO ACCIDENTS." This is a situation where, in game-theoretic terms, the information sets of participants are diverging over time. In other words, the degree of overlap regarding what is understood about events underway is declining and even menacingly so. Under such conditions, accidents become very likely, and, in addition, probably will be interpreted in the worst possible way. Overreaction to mishaps becomes one more element of danger as matters progress. This connection also makes sense because of the impulses toward preemption that would derive from experience with accidents increasingly misunderstood as acts of aggression. A preemptive first strike easily could occur as overreactions build and intensify. The route is completed in Figure 15.1i with "ACCIDENTS AND OVERREACTION TO ACCIDENTS" → "INTERSTATE WAR." This connection is credible because overreaction to accidents would be likely to transition quickly and easily from angry rhetoric into violence. Each side, interpreting mistakes of the other as intentional acts of aggression, would contribute to a spiral of escalation culminating in war.

Figure 15.1j initiates still another pathway: "FIRST MOVER ADVANTAGE" → "RECIPROCAL FEAR." This connection is obvious by intuition because of the concerns that inhere in a situation where getting caught off guard could prove disastrous. As a divergent variable, reciprocal fear takes the shape of a diamond and two routes emerge from it. One connection finishes a pathway in Figure 15.1k: "RECIPROCAL FEAR" → "INTERSTATE WAR." Another branch, depicted in Figure 15.1l, continues with "RECIPROCAL FEAR" → "PREEMPTIVE FIRST STRIKE." In this scenario, the leader of one state breaks ranks with the others and makes certain to get in a possibly decisive first shot at one or more adversaries. The completion of this loop appears in Figure 15.1m with "PREEMPTIVE FIRST STRIKE" → "INTERSTATE WAR."

Another pathway goes forward in Figure 15.1n with "FIRST MOVER ADVANTAGE" → "HASTY/TRUNCATED DIPLOMACY." Poorly conducted diplomacy is to be expected for adversaries who increasingly are secretive and at risk of misunderstanding even the most benign statements. This route finishes up in Figure 15.1o with "HASTY/TRUNCATED DIPLOMACY" → "INTERSTATE WAR." Instead of successful resolution of differences, diplomacy that is conducted under pressure and incomplete in its coverage of essential issues results in war.

Last among the pathways to be initiated is the one in Figure 15.1p: "FIRST MOVER ADVANTAGE" → "OFFENSIVE ADVANTAGE." An edge to the offense accrues from highly asymmetric information sets. Mutual understanding among adversaries decreases, and thus it makes more sense to act and take advantage of information that is held in secret from the enemy. Displayed in Figure 15.1q, the final step is "OFFENSIVE ADVANTAGE" → "INTERSTATE WAR." Force postures that emphasize offense will take hold throughout the system. This stimulates war as such capabilities accumulate and naturally come into use.

Table 15.2 displays the distribution of variable types and connections for stability as a defensive realist theory of war. The network of cause and effect includes nine variables—toward the low end among realist theories of war. There is one point of initiation and one for termination. The diagram also includes a single point of divergence and two of convergence. There is no nodal variable. The figure also does not include any connections back and forth for the system and its environment. With no macro-micro linkage in place, the route to war is either lateral or upward at all times. In addition, the pathways depicted are quite rapid—never more than three steps.

What can be said about cause and effect on the basis of the framework adopted from Kurki (2002)? Formal, material, final, and efficient causes are considered in turn.

Formal causes are the defining shapes and conditions that appear in the background to the story. Advantage to the first mover is significant in this context. When technology changes in either a general or localized way to produce that condition, everyone is less safe than before. The antithesis is the children's game of paper, rock, and scissors, in which moving second is a winning advantage.

Table 15.2 Variable Types and Connections for Defensive Realist Theories

Theory	Overall Number	Initial	Generic	Divergent	Convergent	Nodal	Coconstitutive	Terminal	Interaction Effect	Loops	Missing Links[a]
Stability	9	1	4	1	2	0	0	1	0	1	E→S S→E m→m
Windows	10	1	8	0	0	0	0	1	0	0	E→S S→E
Offense-Defense	12	1	10	0	0	0	0	1	0	0	E→S S→E m→m

[a] The notation is as follows: Macro (M), micro (m), System (S), and Environment (E).

What about material conditions, the passive potential of matter or, in the language of Most and Starr (2015 [1989]), opportunity? Offensive advantage is what matters here. An attack is more feasible than under defensive dominance, which is the normal and expected geostrategic setting. Starting a war emerges as an opportunity when high costs from mounting an attack, associated with dominance for the defense, no longer are anticipated.

Final conditions refer to the purposes that guide change, that is, willingness as articulated by Most and Starr (2015 [1989]). The factors playing that role include (i) concealed grievances, capabilities, plans, and misperceptions and (ii) reciprocal fear. The former set of conditions provides evidence about aggressive intentions, while the latter creates a highly unstable situation that increases willingness to attack because the alternative is to trust the other side not to do so.

Efficient conditions or movers complete the process of cause and effect. The movers are as follows: (i) opportunistic first strike, (ii) accidents and overreactions to accidents, (iii) hasty/truncated diplomacy, and (iv) preemptive first strike. All of these developments lead directly to war, which raises an issue about the layout of the theory that will be taken up later during critiques.

Windows

Figure 15.2 offers a visual representation of windows as a theory about the causes of war.[2] Figure 15.2a displays a region and the international system as its environment. The story begins in Figure 15.2b with a movement from the system to the state level: "IMPENDING SHIFTS IN RELATIVE POWER" → "motive for war among declining states." Note that the impending power shift—the point of origin for movement in the system—therefore appears as an oval. The expectation depicted in the figure is in line with any number of expositions that see a state losing ground as a candidate to take extreme measures, even warfare, to halt its slide. Next comes a linkage back up from the state to the system level, added in Figure 15.2c, "motive for war among declining states" → "BELLICOSE DIPLOMATIC TACTICS." Confrontation builds in the system as states seek to end or even reverse their decline through tactics that bring to mind "gunboat diplomacy" from the late 19th to the early 20th century. A more recent example would be Russian annexation of the Crimean Peninsula in February and March 2014.

What follows on in Figure 15.2d is a connection at the system level: "BELLICOSE DIPLOMATIC TACTICS" → "FEWER AND LESS STABLE

---

[2] This figure is based on Van Evera (1999: 73–87), most notably Diagram 2, which shows windows theory.

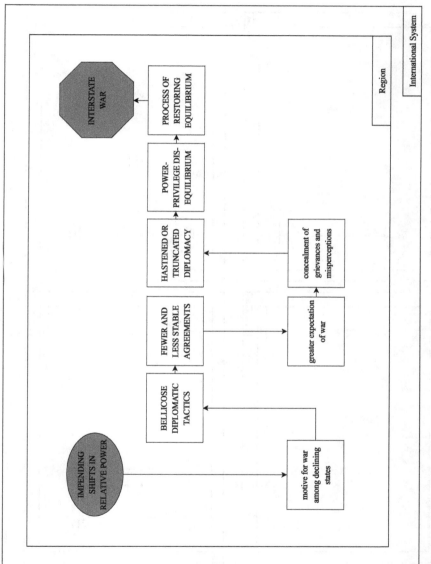

Figure 15.2 Windows

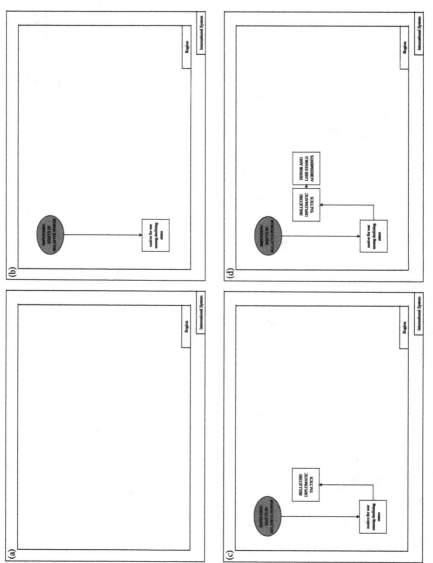

Figure 15.2 Continued

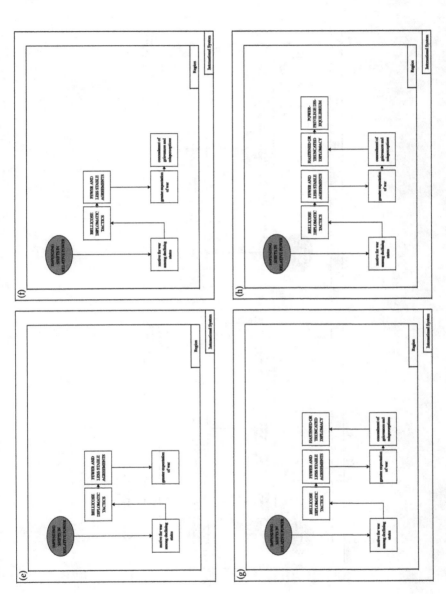

Figure 15.2 Continued

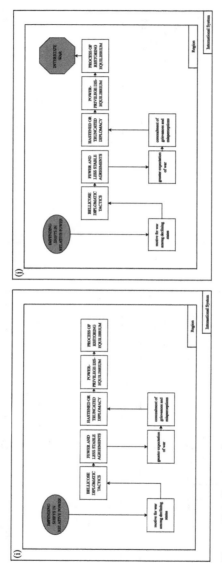

Figure 15.2 Continued

AGREEMENTS." Unpleasant dealings take their toll upon diplomacy. Conflict management is attenuated as it becomes increasingly difficult to resolve disagreements. The next linkage, added in Figure 15.2e, moves from the macro to micro level: "FEWER AND LESS STABLE AGREEMENTS" → "greater expectation of war." Leaders become pessimistic and perhaps even fatalistic about war breaking out as a result of mounting disappointment with diplomacy.

Depicted in Figure 15.2f, the next step is a change at the state level: "greater expectation of war" → "concealment of grievances and misperceptions." A growing trend toward secrecy results from building anticipation of war. This reflects the desire to gain advantage, at the strategic or the tactical level, if fighting should break out. A further linkage, added in Figure 15.2g, takes the story back to the system level: "concealment of grievances and misperceptions" → "HASTENED OR TRUNCATED DIPLOMACY." Secrecy impairs communications. Diplomacy increasingly takes place under time pressure and information conditions that vary significantly among participants. This does not bode well for the likely outcome.

Further steps take place at the macro level. The next linkage, which appears in Figure 15.2h, is "HASTENED OR TRUNCATED DIPLOMACY" → "POWER-PRIVILEGE DISEQUILIBRIUM." Diplomacy is conducted under time pressure and lacks comprehensiveness in terms of issues. The result is a widening of the gap between the position of a given state in terms of power and the privileges it enjoys. Some will be above what more objective power conditions would dictate and vice versa. What follows is "POWER-PRIVILEGE DISEQUILIBRIUM" → "PROCESS OF RESTORING EQUILIBRIUM" in Figure 15.2i. This stage inherently involves a reallocation of privileges to be more in line with changes in the distribution of capabilities. With a lack of common goals—some want redistribution of advantages while others support the status quo—confrontation builds to an even higher level. Thus the final step is taken in Figure 15.2j: "PROCESS OF RESTORING EQUILIBRIUM" → "INTERSTATE WAR." Interstate war, the terminal point in the figure, is indicated with an octagon.

Variable types and connections for windows as a defensive realist theory of war appear in Table 15.2. This network of cause and effect includes 10 variables. The distribution is striking in that it contains a single pathway from an initial variable through to a terminal variable. There are no convergent, divergent, or nodal variables. In addition, the diagram does not include connections back and forth for the region and environment.

How does windows theory look in terms of the framework for cause and effect in Kurki (2002)? Formal, material, final, and efficient conditions are enumerated in turn.

Defining shapes or relations, known as formal conditions, provide a background to the story. Consider, in this context, impending shifts in relative power.

In a world of power politics, this always is in play as a byproduct of leadership quality, technological change, economic performance, and any number of other possibilities in a world of states.

What about material causes, which correspond to passive potentiality of matter or, in a word, opportunity (Most and Starr 2015 [1989])? This category includes (i) bellicose diplomatic tactics, (ii) fewer and less stable agreements, (iii) greater expectation of war, and (iv) hastened or truncated diplomacy. All of these actions and beliefs facilitate escalation of conflict in intuitively obvious ways.

Final conditions are those that guide change—the concept of willingness in Most and Starr (2015 [1989]). These conditions consist of (a) a motive for war among declining states and (b) power-privilege disequilibrium. This combination of developments will set rising and declining actors against each other over revision versus preservation of the status quo.

Efficient conditions, or movers, are summed up in the process of restoring equilibrium. The theory does not offer specifics about what would unfold in this stage.

Offense-Defense

Figure 15.3 provides a graphic version of offense-defense as a theory that purports to explain why wars occur.[3] A region and the international system as its environment are depicted in Figure 15.3a. One route gets underway in Figure 15.3b with "OFFENSE DOMINANCE" → "expansionist mindset." The former of these two variables, as a point of origin, is depicted with an oval. Intuition is straightforward about this connection. Dominance of the offense creates possibilities for self-aggrandizement that will be noticed by leaders. The resulting mindset in favor of expansion takes hold and sets in motion a series of steps that can lead to interstate war.

From the state back up to the system is the next step in Figure 15.3c: "expansionist mindset" → "OPPORTUNISTIC OR DEFENSIVE EXPANSION." States will want to initiate revisions to the existing world map because such efforts are expected to happen anyway. Why wait and risk being caught short? On the one hand, a state seeing vulnerable borders can be expected to act in order to make gains. On the other hand, a state burdened with boundaries that are difficult to defend could seek expansion in order to improve its overall viability in light of offense dominance. Thus the initial move in an escalating conflict could result from either strategic defensive or offensive motivations. Precise conditions at the

---

[3] This figure is based on Van Evera (1999: 117–151) and especially the third and final version of Diagram 3, which gives a schematic history of offense-defense theory.

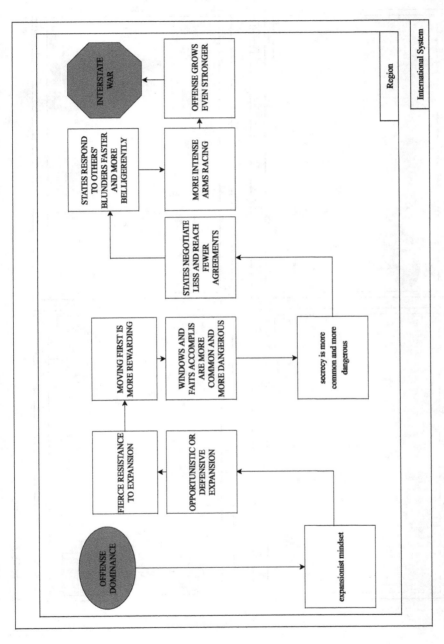

Figure 15.3 Offense-Defense

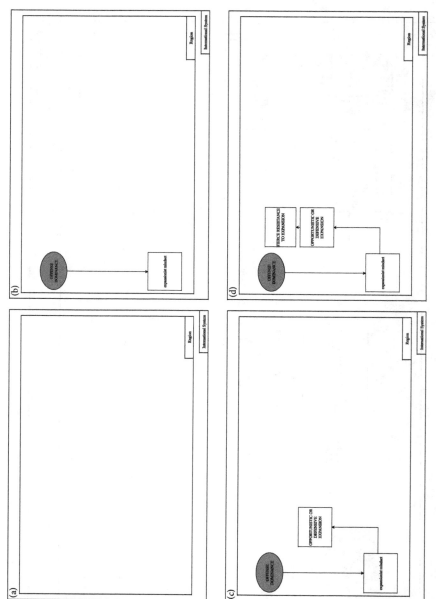

Figure 15.3 Continued

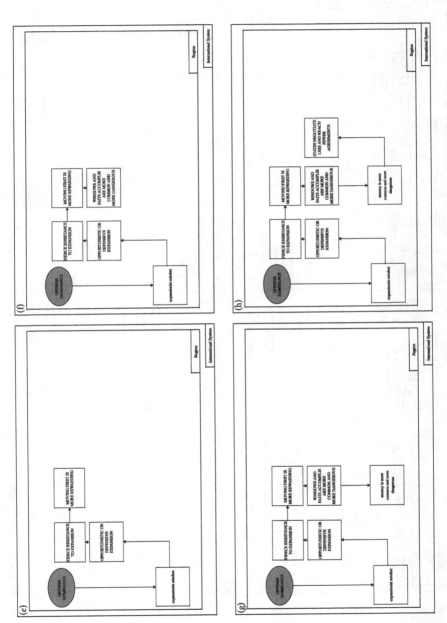

Figure 15.3 Continued

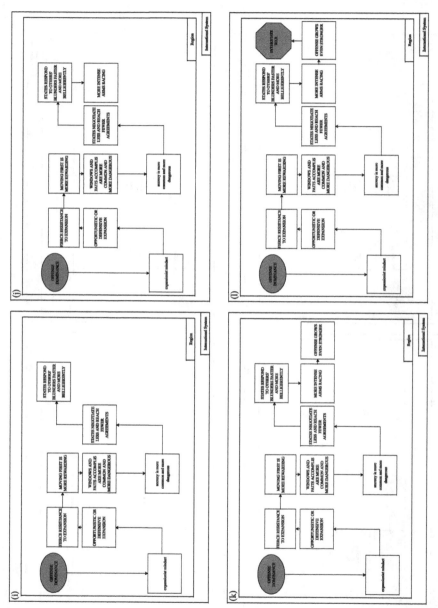

Figure 15.3 Continued

line of battle can vary greatly over and above sheer distance from a base of operations (Wohlstetter 1968).

Depicted in Figure 15.3d, next in line is "OPPORTUNISTIC OR DEFENSIVE EXPANSION" → "FIERCE RESISTANCE TO EXPANSION." In a setting with offense dominance, failure to stand up to even minor incursions, let alone major ones, rapidly could produce an untenable position. Thus fierce resistance to expansion, whatever its motives, is expected as a matter of course. States will fight back in any way that they can under arduous circumstances. Put simply, this is the logic of deterrence (Schelling 1960; Russett 1963).

Movement continues at the macro level in Figure 15.3e with "FIERCE RESISTANCE TO EXPANSION" → "MOVING FIRST IS MORE REWARDING." Consider, perhaps most infamously, development of railway schedules and military mobilization in Europe at the brink of war in August 1914. Efforts to mobilize ahead of rival states resulted from inherent rigidity built into war plans across the board.

Figure 15.3f shows a macro-level connection: "MOVING FIRST IS MORE REWARDING" → "WINDOWS AND FAITS ACCOMPLIS ARE MORE COMMON AND MORE DANGEROUS." Dominance of the offense opens windows wider than otherwise because differences that exist in national capabilities are magnified. Moreover, from the standpoint of a declining state, an attempt at a fait accompli becomes very tempting. Action without warning is more attractive when offense is dominant. Both the opening of windows and carrying out of faits accomplis are more dangerous because of ongoing concerns about possibly decisive effects resulting from accumulation of even small setbacks.

Revealed in Figure 15.3g, the next linkage is "WINDOWS AND FAITS ACCOMPLIS ARE MORE COMMON AND MORE DANGEROUS" → "secrecy is more common and more dangerous." The menacing nature of windows and faits accomplis carries over into communications for each state. Leaders will guard more jealously than ever their military secrets and other information that might be useful to a potential adversary contemplating an attack. Concealment of intentions and even capabilities will become the norm and serve as an aggravating factor for conflict management. Virtually any nuclear-equipped rivalry, with India and Pakistan as an obvious example, features this element of danger.

Figure 15.3h shows the process moving back up to the system level: "secrecy is more common and more dangerous" → "STATES NEGOTIATE LESS AND REACH FEWER AGREEMENTS." With a penchant for concealment, states are not inclined to speak with each other and take the risk of giving away information that would increase vulnerability to attack. Under such conditions, the likelihood of reaching significant agreements also goes into decline.

Next comes a linkage at the level of the system in Figure 15.3i: "STATES NEGOTIATE LESS AND REACH FEWER AGREEMENTS" → "STATES

RESPOND TO OTHERS' BLUNDERS FASTER AND MORE BELLIGERENTLY." With negotiations and agreements being scarce, an atmosphere of distrust takes over. Errors are likely to be misunderstood because the worst possible intentions are attributed to what is observed in a state that is trending toward enemy status. Rapid and belligerent responses will contribute to momentum toward all-out violent conflict.

Movement at the macro level continues in Figure 15.3j with "STATES RESPOND TO OTHERS' BLUNDERS FASTER AND MORE BELLIGERENTLY' → "MORE INTENSE ARMS RACING." As actions back and forth speed up and high levels of retaliation become the norm in response to perceived transgressions, rivalry expressed through acquisition of arms will gain traction. This can take the form of accumulating sheer numbers as well as competing to develop new weapons systems that might provide a decisive advantage if a war comes into being. What follows in Figure 15.3k is "MORE INTENSE ARMS RACING" → "OFFENSE GROWS EVEN STRONGER." As weapons accumulate, the advantage to the offense becomes even more pronounced.

Last among the linkages, denoted in Figure 15.3l, is "OFFENSE GROWS EVEN STRONGER" → "INTERSTATE WAR." As the terminal point in the figure, interstate war is designated with an octagon.

Table 15.2 shows the distribution of variable types and connections for offense-defense theory. There are 12 variables in the network of cause and effect. Note the presence of just one pathway—single initial and terminal variables—and no divergent, convergent, or nodal variables. Dominance for offense is highly determining for war as an outcome. There also is no purely micro-level connection or any links back and forth with the environment.

With a graphic representation in place, how does offense-defense theory look in relation to the framework for assessing cause and effect adopted from Kurki (2002)? Formal, material, final, and efficient causes are considered in turn.

Formal conditions refer to the background for events—defining shapes or relations. These are enumerated as (i) offense dominance, (ii) expansionist mindset, (iii) opportunistic or defensive expansion, and (iv) fierce resistance to expansion. Taken together, these features equate with the practice of power politics.

Material conditions—the passive potentiality of matter—represent opportunity (Most and Starr 2015 [1989]). The relevant factors are (i) states negotiate less and reach fewer agreements, (ii) secrecy is more common and dangerous, and (iii) windows and faits accomplis are more common and more dangerous. All of these features increase the opportunity for going to war.

Final conditions focus on what purposes guide change—willingness from Most and Starr (2015 [1989]). The key consideration in this context is the fact that moving first is more rewarding. States become more willing to engage in confrontational tactics because of an ongoing risk of falling behind the same actions available to rivals.

What about efficient conditions or movers? The list of factors for this category includes (i) states responding to others' blunders faster and more belligerently, (ii) more intense arms racing, and (iii) the offense grows even stronger. Taken together, this represents a vicious circle; events accelerate, and war ensues.

With a review of cause and effect in place, attention returns to the critiques offered earlier in this chapter. Each is considered in turn.

Defensive realism is criticized for its degree of intricacy. Consider, however, the contents of Table 15.2 in comparison to those for other realist theories. The theories include a range of nine to 12 variables. On an individual basis, this is not out of the ordinary for realist theories. At the same time, the theories exhibit considerable overlap and are ripe for assembly into an integrated framework. Figures 15.1–15.3 reinforce that point and also facilitate engagement with other theories in Chapter 19.

Graphic representation, to follow up on the previous point about intricacy, produces a mirror image critique—the presence of many ceteris paribus clauses and need for greater detail in some areas. Figure 15.1, for stability, includes just one micro variable and no connections at that level. In addition, no pathway includes more than three variables. For windows, Figure 15.2 lacks detail about the process of restoring equilibrium. The windows variant also is without any point of contingency. Finally, offense-defense, as portrayed in Figure 15.3, has no micro-level connection and also lacks any contingent variables.

What about the putative contamination of propositions about war with nonrealist factors? This claim returns once again to confusion about the eligibility of ideational variables to enter into realist frameworks. The nonmaterial factors included within defensive realism correspond to the logic of consequences, not appropriateness, so there is no resulting issue of compliance with the assumptions of the research enterprise.

One critique, concerning measurement, comes into bold relief after scanning the graphic presentation of defensive realist theories. For each key variable, such as first-mover advantage, what is the *threshold* for identification? This question must be answered in order for defensive realist theories to be subject, at least in principle, to falsification.

Finally, consider the critiques that focus on evidence. The diagrams reveal a number of connections that, generally speaking, could use more support from research. For example, when will belief in offensive dominance take hold and produce an expansionist mindset? Both additional case studies and aggregate data analysis would be of value. The value of defensive realist theorizing at this stage resides more in the logic of discovery than in confirmation.

Reflections on Defensive Realism

Defensive realism sees war as the exception rather than the rule in the international system. Three variants of the theory exist: stability, windows, and offense-defense. The basic insight behind defensive realism is that conditions for war are relatively demanding—either a first-mover advantage, an impending shift in relative power, offense dominance, or some combination of these factors must be in place. Defensive realism is an interesting candidate for combination with other realist theories in Chapter 19 in a more complete account of war.

16
Dynamic Differentials

Overview

Dynamic differentials is a theory that goes beyond comparative statics with regard to power politics and the causes of war. It focuses most directly on how a great power in relative decline impacts the stability of the international system. Dynamic differentials asks a question that, when answered, is certain to have implications for war: what can be expected, in a world of self-help, when one of the leading states is faced with a downward shift in its capacity to act? Various factors come into play as leaders from a state in that situation, most notably a great power, consider their options. While aspects such as the offense-defense balance are familiar within the lexicon of realism, the full set of connections put forward by dynamic differentials is highly original. The theory offers a sense of how preferences of states can evolve throughout a process of conflict and even contribute to its escalation.

This chapter moves forward in five additional sections. The second section looks at dynamic differentials in gestalt terms and also enumerates its assumptions. The third section provides a more detailed sense of what this realist theory says about why wars occur. The fourth section conveys critiques of dynamic differentials theory. The fifth section shows dynamic differentials in visual form as a theory about the causes of war. The graphic version of the theory also is applied in response to critics. A sixth and final section reflects upon the contributions of dynamic differentials theory.

What Are Dynamic Differentials?

Dynamic differentials theory focuses on shifts in power at the level of the international system. The magnum opus for this theory, *The Origins of Major Power War* (Copeland 2000), has received favorable reviews (Reed 2001; Schmidt 2001). Dynamic differentials theory lives up to its name and also is system oriented. The focus is on effects to be anticipated from redistribution of capabilities between and among states at the system's apex. Three categories of power—military, economic, and potential—are identified (Copeland 2000: 21). As dynamics of capabilities generate differences between and among states, the status quo may become unstable and even descend into major power war.

Most significant of all at the level of the system is the presence of a state that is experiencing relative decline in its capabilities. The model starts with a "decision-theoretical framework"; a state in decline is anticipated to act "on the basis of its estimates of various external conditions" (Copeland 2000: 37). The presence of one or more states motivated toward aggression is not enough for escalation, according to Copeland (2000: 22), because "even the most hostile leaders will be deterred from initiating major war unless power conditions make the bid for hegemony feasible." War is not automatic but instead depends on a specific profile of change at the level of the individual great power.

When decline for a state becomes deeper and seems inevitable, hard-line polices gain appeal and increase the likelihood of inadvertent war (Copeland 2000: 40). A resulting hypothesis is that leaders who perceive their state to be in decline are more likely to initiate events that increase the risk of inadvertent major war (Copeland 2000: 54). This undoubtedly is produced by an upward shift in risk propensity for leaders seeking to prevent or even reverse losses.

Table 16.1 includes some observations that help to provide a gestalt sense of dynamic differentials. The theory is deductive in nature and cast at the system level. Its key variables focus on change in capabilities and are limited in number. A decline in relative capability threatens existing interests and leads to foreign

Table 16.1 Dynamic Differentials at a Glance

Source	Summary Statement
Copeland (2000: 28)	Dynamic differentials theory is a deductive systemic argument modeled on microeconomic theory.
Reed (2001: 513)	"Dynamic differentials offers an explanation and some evidence for the relationship between power differentials and major power conflict.... The assumption that all declining states fear the future is at the heart of Copeland's theory."
Schmidt (2001: 409)	"Copeland's theory is consistent with neo-realism in that the argument is cast at the systemic level.... Major wars are initiated by states possessing superior military power but who fear deep-seated relative decline."
Thompson (2002: 334)	The dynamic differentials theory is parsimonious.
Souva (2018: 140–141)	Fear of deep decline, particularly in a bipolar system, is the primary explanation for major wars.

policy change for a great power, which, in turn, disrupts the international system. War can be the result.

What are the assumptions made by the theory of dynamic differentials, and how does it fit into realism? Copeland (2000) offers explicit lists at the unit and system levels. Each set of axioms is covered in turn and assessed in the context of the theory's status within realism.

For the unit level, six assumptions are designated: rationality ("actor calculates best means to desired ends, given information available"), ends (actor seeks security above all else), direction of ends (to self only), nature of actor (unitary), risk tolerance (neutral), cost tolerance (neutral) (Copeland 2000: 30). Consistent with realism as a research enterprise, instrumental rationality is one of the axioms. Two other assumptions describe the way in which rational choice is implemented. The theory is neutral regarding both risk and cost.

Actor goals include self-direction and security, but are not at odds with the assumptions of realism. It is clear that security is pursued in a conventional realist way, namely, power is the resource that matters. Leaders are expected to focus on their share of capabilities as a basic indicator of security. From a scientific realist point of view, capability share and security, respectively, are observable and unobservable variables.

Assumptions at the system level are threefold:[1] (1) degree of certainty regarding others' intentions (largely uncertain at present and fully uncertain for the future), (2) offense-defense balance (neutral), and (3) technological costs of war (moderate) (Copeland 2000: 30). Degrees of uncertainty are identified for updating about intentions and capabilities. All of this is expressed in state-centric terms. In practice, this sums up to anarchy rather than hierarchy. The additional assumptions about uncertainty regarding the capabilities of other states, neutrality of the offense/defense balance, and moderate costs of war elaborate rather than contradict realism.

How do the axioms combine to create an identity for the theory? Dynamic differentials stands out as a system-oriented theory about the dynamics of power. Its specification also is consistent with the assumptions of realism as a research enterprise.

Connections between dynamic differentials theory and the classical tradition is easy to see. Among the points of contact are Morgenthau (1959 [1948]) on balance of power, Wolfers (1962) on aggressive and threat-perceiving states, and Aron (1966) on offense versus defense.

---

[1] Other items listed under assumptions in Copeland (2000), such as the degree of certainty regarding one's past and present power levels, are not distinct from basic properties of rational choice and therefore not enumerated here.

Expositions on the Causes of War

Dynamic differentials is recognized as a significant contribution to realist theorizing about war. Its magnum opus, *The Origins of Major Wars* (Copeland 2000), is described as original, important, ambitious, and well informed through history (Ikenberry 2001: 167; Kaufman 2001: 181; Schmidt 2001: 409; Thompson 2002: 333–334).

Dynamic differentials theory seeks to explain high-intensity wars that involve all of the great powers and that might even eliminate members of that subset (Copeland 2000: 27). The key dependent variable, according to Copeland (2000: 33), is the probability of major power war. Copeland (2000: 15) conveys the essence of dynamic differentials theory on why such wars occur:

> The theory makes three main assertions. First, in any system, assuming states are rational security-seeking actors which remain uncertain about others' future intentions, it is the dominant but declining military great power that is most likely to begin a major war. Second, the constraints on the dominant state differ in bipolar versus multipolar systems.... Third, the probability of major war increases when decline is seen as both deep and inevitable.

Unlike most theories about the causes of war associated with realism, the exposition of dynamic differentials explicitly maps out pathways to war. Five such pathways are depicted in Copeland (2000) and later accessed to produce a systemist graphic presentation of the theory.[2]

When the dominant state in a bipolar world faces imminent decline, Copeland (1996: 51) observes, "The likelihood of major war is high, while in the multipolar situation the likelihood is low due to the restraining presence of the other equal great powers." When inequality is significant in either a bipolar or multipolar system, major war should be very likely in the presence of impending decline (Copeland 1996: 51). According to Copeland (2000: 20), a declining state is the one anticipated to initiate war regardless of system structure.

---

[2] From Figure 6 in Copeland (2000: 43), the pathways are as follows: (1) Systemic factors and trends in these factors → Preventive motives → Initiate major war; (2) Individual/domestic factors and trends in those factors → Aggressive motives → Initiate major war; (3) [Two branches converge at "Initiate crisis"] {Systemic factors and trends in those factors → Preventive motives; Individual/domestic factors and trends in those factors → Aggressive motives} → Initiate crisis → Initiate major war; (4) [Same as (3) up to "Initiate crisis"] → [Three sets of double-headed arrows: Accident ←→ Increased mobilization/heightened alert/tougher rhetoric; Accident ←→ Overcommitment of reputations; Increased mobilization/heightened alert/tougher rhetoric → Overcommitment of reputations] → Preemptive motives → Initiate major war; (5) Same as (4) but excluding "Preemptive motives" and finishing with Overcommitment of reputations → Initiate major war.

Overall, however, dynamic differentials theory sees bipolarity as more unstable (Copeland 1996: 51). An unanticipated war can take place within either bipolar or multipolar systems. Under bipolarity, a declining state, when nearly equal or preponderant in military power, is more likely to take actions that increase the risk of an inadvertent major war (Copeland 2000: 55). Copeland (2000: 54–55) observes that, in a multipolar system, a declining state that possesses noteworthy military superiority over other great powers on an individual basis is more likely to initiate events that make inadvertent war more likely. In a bipolar system, a declining state "can start major war when superior or only equal to the other great power" (Copeland 1996: 87). This argument effectively turns the one from Waltz (1979) on its head; a simple international structure can be more dangerous than a complex one.

Nuances exist with regard to dimensions of power (Copeland 1996: 55): "A state which is superior in military power but *inferior* in economic and especially potential power, however, is more likely to believe that, once it starts to decline in military power, decline will be inevitable and steep." In light of that assertion, consider an analogy with potential versus kinetic power in physics. Falling behind others in potential power is especially bad because it is the reservoir for the kinetic version. With kinetic power in relative decline, perception of pressure to act quickly to avert deterioration of established interests is likely to mount.

Evidence from Copeland (2000) for dynamic differentials takes the form of a set of case studies. These include an overview of the origins of major power wars from ancient times through the Napoleonic era, along with, specifically, World Wars I and II and the Cold War. Interesting to ponder, for instance, is the Second Punic War (Copeland 2000: 211–213). It follows a preventive logic. Carthage observed the rise of Rome as concomitant with its decline. Copeland (2000: 212) notes, for example, a shift in naval power that permitted Rome to project power "dangerously close to Carthage itself." Taken together, the story of the war supports the expectations of dynamic differentials theory for bipolarity. Faced with inferior potential power in the aftermath of the First Punic War, Carthage attacked Rome even without an advantage because its relative situation simply would get worse with time (Copeland 2000: 213). Three of the most prominent crises of the Cold War that had a realistic possibility of escalation to World War III—Berlin (1948, 1961) and the Cuban Missile Crisis (1962)—are considered in detail. In sum, a wide range of evidence produces significant support for dynamic differentials theory.

Critiques

Critiques of dynamic differentials theory focus on (a) excessive parsimony and incompleteness regarding levels of analysis, (b) lack of engagement with other theories, (c) incomplete and unconvincing evidence, and (d) potential obsolescence. Each is considered in turn.

One critique of dynamic differentials focuses on the theory being too parsimonious. Kaufman (2001: 210) claims that dynamic differentials theory "illustrates the consequences of the obsession with devising elegant theories that has plagued the study of international relations for two decades"; moreover, the profound insight among neorealist and related explanations with regard to the importance of structure and power "has ossified into a rigid mechanical formula that inhibits rather than clarifies our understanding." All of that reinforces the need for a theory that can integrate "all three levels of analysis when investigating the causes of war and the conditions of peace" (Kaufman 2001: 210).

Incorporation of insights from across levels of analysis therefore should become a priority. Kaufman (2001: 209) draws attention to gaps in respective explanations; for instance, the dynamic differentials theory leaves out "domestic and individual variables such as regime type, ideology, and the perceptions of key leaders." Consider, for example, how the "folly of appeasement" is explained. Unit-level variables play essential roles; consider, for instance, "structural difficulties liberal democracies face in taking strong preemptive action" and illusions among leaders "such as British prime minister Neville Chamberlain about the nature of Hitler's regime" (Kaufman 2001: 209). Thus dynamic differentials should be elaborated to say more about the individual level of analysis in particular.

Further critiques refer to interpretation of specific historical events. One example would be Kaufman (2001: 199) on the Truman administration military budget, which "hardly constitutes a preemptive initiation" of the Cold War as per Copeland (2000). Another instance is Thompson (2002: 335) on whether German perception of the Russians as their principal geopolitical rival is sufficient to "reduce World Wars I and II to German preventive action against the Russians." These points also connect to incompleteness; does dynamic differentials theory include a range of variables sufficient to account for decisions from states in the lead-up to major power war?

What about engagement with other theories? Reed (2001: 513–514) draws attention to "incomplete treatment of other theories of war that focus on how shifts in power may enhance the prospects for cooperation or conflict." A range of possibilities exist, such as greater contact for power transition theory with power cycle theory, along with individual propositions in place for some time (Zinnes 1976). Reed's (2001: 514) call for statistical testing of dynamic differentials is in line with the preceding suggestions because it could include a wider range of variables in the specification.

Given its focus on historical cases, it is possible to imagine that dynamic differentials is a theory more relevant to yesteryear because of changing circumstances in world politics. Ikenberry (2001: 167) wonders "whether strategic decline means the same thing today as it did in the past." In addition, can great powers be expected to engage in preventive war ever again (Ikenberry 2001: 167)? An answer to that query comes down to a debate about realism itself. The preceding points bring to mind more encompassing arguments about whether interstate war itself may be obsolete (Ray 2002).

Graphic Representation

Dynamic differentials theory is conveyed via text and nonsystemist diagrams. Figure 16.1 conveys dynamic differentials as a theory about major power war.[3] Figure 16.1a displays a region and the international system as its surrounding environment. Figure 16.1b gets one pathway started at the macro level: "DECLINING POWER SHARE FOR A STATE WITH DEADLOCK PREFERENCE" → "HIGH PROBABILITY OF MAJOR POWER WAR." As initial and nodal types, respectively, these variables appear as an oval and hexagon. A deadlock preference means that even a major war is preferred to continuation of the status quo. Thus a high level of confrontation is built into the system from the outset.

Another pathway emerges at the macro level in Figure 16.1c: "DECLINING POWER SHARE FOR A STATE WITH DEADLOCK PREFERENCE" → "CRISIS INITIATION." This connection is obvious by intuition; a state that prefers war to the status quo possesses ongoing potential to trigger crises for others in the system. As a nodal variable, "CRISIS INITIATION" is depicted as a hexagon.

Figure 16.1d shows a connection with routes already underway: "state with deadlock preference" → "CRISIS INITIATION"; "HIGH PROBABILITY OF MAJOR POWER WAR." As an initial variable, "state with deadlock preference" is depicted as an oval.

Figure 16.1e displays the same route with a different micro point of origin: "uncertainty about aggressive motives" → "CRISIS INITIATION"; "HIGH PROBABILITY OF MAJOR POWER WAR." The initial variable, "uncertainty about aggressive motives," appears as an oval. These pathways come together in Figure 16.1f with "CRISIS INITIATION" → "HIGH PROBABILITY OF MAJOR POWER WAR." A wide range of studies cover the myriad ways in which a crisis, once underway, can escalate to war (Brecher and Wilkenfeld 1997, 2000).

Movement downward from the macro to the micro level occurs in Figure 16.1g: "CRISIS INITIATION" → "stag hunt preference." As a divergent variable,

---

[3] The contents of Figure 16.1 are based on Copeland (2000: 42–46), most notably Figure 6 as described in the preceding note and a valuable consultation with Dale C. Copeland.

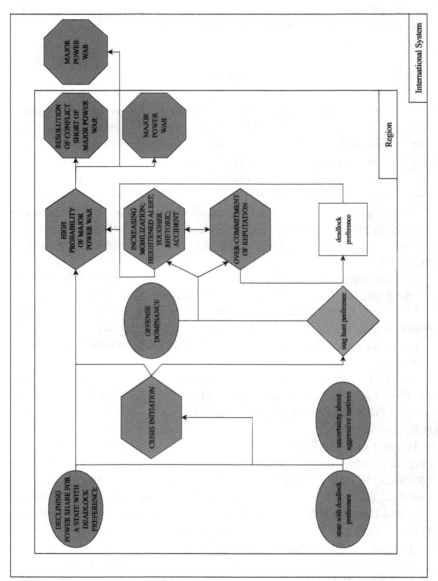

Figure 16.1 Dynamic Differentials

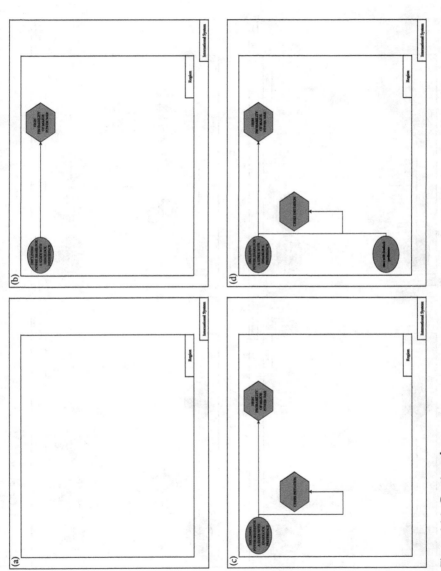

Figure 16.1 Continued

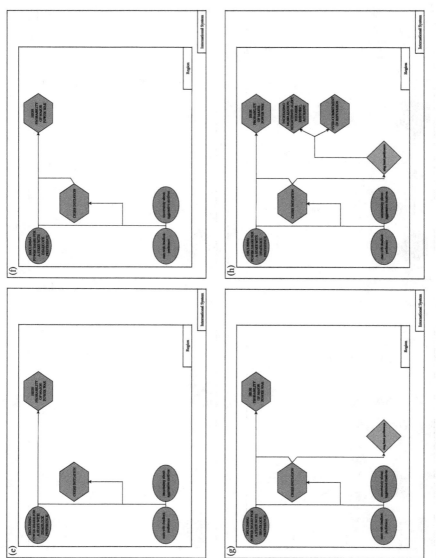

Figure 16.1 Continued

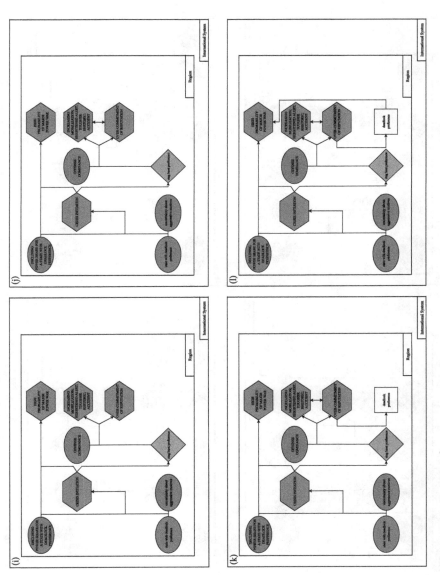

Figure 16.1 Continued

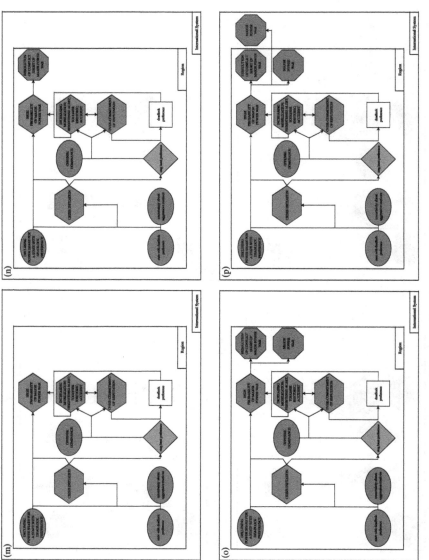

Figure 16.1 Continued

DYNAMIC DIFFERENTIALS 491

the latter appears as a diamond. Once in a crisis situation, a given state is expected to adopt the preference ordering identified with the famous example of the stag hunt from Rousseau. Peace is preferred to preemption, but the situation is quite difficult and escalation is a significant possibility.

Two branches emerge from the micro into the macro level in Figure 16.1h: "stag hunt preference" → "OVER-COMMITMENT OF REPUTATION"; "INCREASING MOBILIZATION, HEIGHTENED ALERT, TOUGHER RHETORIC; ACCIDENT." Note that the latter two variables are nodal and thus appear as hexagons. Even without a highly confrontational disposition, as in the case with the stag hunt preferences, a pair of pernicious factors comes into play under crisis conditions.[4] While peace is preferred to preemption, an overcommitment to protecting one's reputation is a natural byproduct of the tense situation in place. Along with that preference are witnessed actions, such a heightened state of alert, which inherently increase the likelihood of war.

Another pathway begins at the macro level in Figure 16.1i and joins in with other routes already in progress: "OFFENSE DOMINANCE" → "OVER-COMMITMENT OF REPUTATION"; "INCREASING MOBILIZATION, HEIGHTENED ALERT, TOUGHER RHETORIC; ACCIDENT." As an initial variable, "OFFENSE DOMINANCE" appears as an oval. Thus the geostrategic setting, in the form of offense dominance, emerges as a complicating factor.

With both the upper and lower branches underway, the next connection is synergistic and appears in Figure 16.1j: "INCREASING MOBILIZATION; HEIGHTENED ALERT; TOUGHER RHETORIC; ACCIDENT" ←→ "OVERCOMMITMENT OF REPUTATION." These factors exacerbate each other and make the situation more difficult than ever. Further pathways ensue.

Figure 16.1k shows movement from the macro to the micro level: "OVER-COMMITMENT OF REPUTATION" → "deadlock preference." Given the desperate urge to avert the appearance of weakness and reputational damage, the remaining flexibility in the situation is eliminated. The next step in this pathway moves back up to the macro level in Figure 16.1l: "deadlock preference" → "HIGH PROBABIITY OF MAJOR POWER WAR."

Pathways at the macro level converge in Figure 16.1m with "INCREASING MOBILIZATION; HEIGHTENED ALERT; TOUGHER RHETORIC; ACCIDENT" → "HIGH PROBABILITY OF MAJOR POWER WAR." A final connection for that route appears in Figure 16.n with "HIGH PROBABILITY OF MAJOR POWER WAR" → "RESOLUTION OF CONFLICT SHORT OF

---

[4] The four factors in the upper of the two hexagons added in Figure 16.1h could be disaggregated and modeled further in terms of cause and effect. Since the potential interplay within this collection of variables is not essential to the presentation of dynamic differentials, the subject is not explored further.

MAJOR POWER WAR." As a terminal variable, the latter appears as an octagon. Consider for example, what became known as the "War in Sight" crisis of 1875. Germany prohibited export of horses to France, which signaled an attempt to block rearmament. After a Russo-British protest against the move, Bismarck detected the danger of a two-front war and backed away from the confrontation. The other end point in the region is reached in Figure 16.1o: "HIGH PROBABILITY OF MAJOR POWER WAR" → "MAJOR POWER WAR." Once again, the terminal variable is depicted as an octagon.

One outcome extends from the macro level of the region into the international system in Figure 16.1p: "HIGH PROBABILITY OF MAJOR POWER WAR" → "MAJOR POWER WAR." This outcome would equate with escalation to general war, beyond issues and actors within the region. As a terminal variable, the one after the arrow appears as an octagon.

Dynamic differentials theory includes 13 variables in its network of cause and effect. Four are initial and three are terminal. There also are four nodal variables and one divergent variable. No variable is purely convergent. The network includes one synergistic relationship. Absent also are micro-micro connections, along with impact on the region from the international system.

With regard to cause and effect, what does the theory look like in relation to the framework adopted from Kurki (2002)? Formal, material, final, and efficient conditions are considered in turn.

Formal causes refer to defining shapes or relations, that is, background conditions. Relevant here are (a) declining power share for a state with deadlock preference, (b) a state with deadlock preference, and (c) uncertainty about aggressive motives. All of the foregoing conditions are associated with the usual practice of power politics.

What about material conditions—the passive potentiality of matter or, in the framework of Most and Starr (2015 [1989]), opportunity to act? Essential to this category are (i) crisis initiation and (ii) offense dominance. Conditions of crisis entail threat and time pressure, along with the risk of escalation to war (Brecher and Wilkenfeld 1997, 2000). Coupled with advantage to the offense, crisis conditions create significant opportunity for war to break out.

Final conditions are the purposes that guide change, equivalent to willingness in the language of Most and Starr (2015 [1989]). Relevant in this context are (a) stag hunt preference and (b) deadlock preference. The shift from one preference ordering to the other signals greater willingness to fight.

Efficient causes or movers come last. The conditions are as follows: (i) increasing mobilization, heightened alert, tougher rhetoric, and accident; (ii) overcommitment of reputation; and (iii) high probability of major power war. An interconnected set of confrontational actions, along with determination to head off perceptions of weakness, are sufficient to overwhelm crisis management.

With a graphic portrayal in place and a review of cause and effect, attention turns to the critiques of dynamic differentials theory that appeared earlier in this chapter.

What about the argument that dynamic differentials theory is too parsimonious and incomplete regarding levels of analysis? This point seems off base, at least to some degree; with 13 variables, the theory is within a normal range among realist frameworks about war. In addition, dynamic differentials includes four nodal variables—more than any other realist theory of war included in this volume. At the same time, it should be noted that dynamic differentials theory lacks any purely micro-level connection. The theory also does not include any input from the international system into the region.

Dynamic differentials, according to one critic, should engage further with other theories. Given its more macroscopic orientation, dynamic differentials can benefit from contact with neoclassical realist theories about war. More thereby can be said about the micro level. This elaboration will take place in Chapter 19.

Evidence from across levels of analysis seems to be in short supply. As per above, more emphasis on conditions at the brink of war, notably the roles played by individual leaders, can strengthen dynamic differentials as a theory.

Is dynamic differentials an obsolete theory? To say yes would effectively write off realist theories in general. Instead, a turn toward updating assessment of capabilities would seem worthwhile. This point is explored in Chapter 19.

Reflections on Dynamic Differentials

Dynamic differentials is a theory that recognizes the reality of multiple and complex pathways to war. Destabilizing forces emerge from the process of decline for one or more great powers. Confrontational preferences combine with other variables to produce a crisis. Dangerous policies, such as harsh rhetoric, take hold and increase the probability of major power war. At the same time, the theory points out that great powers can avert war even under crisis conditions. Dynamic differentials is an excellent candidate for elaboration through contact with other realist theories in Chapter 19.

17
Offensive Realism

Overview

Offensive realism is a vision of international relations with an emphasis on great power expansionism as an explanation for war. The theory sees the seeking of power and conquest as immanent realities of world politics. This is an ongoing disposition and constrained only by relative capabilities and geographic realities. Offensive realism focuses on intentions among great powers as a conditioning factor for policy choices and outcomes. Put differently, the international system overwhelmingly reflects the interactions of major powers with each other under conditions that encourage aggression and expansion.

This chapter moves forward in five further sections. The second section presents offensive realism in a gestalt way and identifies its axioms. The third section puts forward offensive realism as a theory about great power war. The fourth section covers critiques. The fifth section offers a graphic representation of offensive realism as a theory about why great power war occurs. This visualization also is used to respond to critics. A sixth and final section reflects upon the accomplishments of offensive realism.

What Is Offensive Realism?

One of the most controversial works of scholarship about international relations over the last few decades is *The Tragedy of Great Power Politics* (Mearsheimer 2014 [2001]), the magnum opus for offensive realism. Among studies of realism, this one definitely is the most reviewed and debated since Waltz (1979).[1]

While not endowed with a graphic presentation, Mearsheimer (2014 [2001])—identified by Elman and Jensen (2014: 8) as the "flagship statement" of offensive realism—nonetheless may be the most praised among realist texts vis-à-vis clear communication of ideas. Gowan (2002: 47; see also Kennedy 2002: 3; Posen 2002: 119) observes that the book "is extraordinarily accessible: forceful, direct and clear, without a trace of the usual academic jargon."

---

[1] Reviews include Baev (2002), Francis (2002), Lord (2002), Rosecrance (2002), Kupchan (2003), Masala (2003), and Schmidt (2004).

Rendall (2006: 523) identifies Mearsheimer as the head of "a school of thought known as offensive realism, which argues that international anarchy drives states to expand whenever opportunity beckons." And Toft (2005: 400) adds that, in comparison to most theories of IR, "offensive realism does pretty well." It probably is fair to say that the offensive variant is the modal topic within realist dialogue in the new millennium.

What is offensive realism? It is a system-oriented theory that focuses on comparative statics. "Offensive realists," according to Leiber (2008: 190–191), assert that "structural factors such as anarchy and the distribution of power among states, as well as inherent uncertainty about state intentions, matter most in explaining the behavior of states." The theory regards power maximization to obtain higher relative standing as the norm among great powers (Snyder 2002: 153; Kupchan 2003: Valeriano 2009: 180). States can be counted upon to seek power in order to "ensure their state's security under conditions of anarchy in the international system" (Valeriano 2009: 180). Survival is pursued through maximization of state power, and "perpetual movement toward hegemonic ambition ultimately leads states to enter into war" (Valeriano 2009: 182, 181).

Table 17.1 offers ideas that establish the identity of offensive realism in a gestalt sense. Anarchy plays a central role in shaping what occurs in the international system. Security is scarce, so competition is intense, and offensive strategies are to be expected among states. Great powers in particular seek enhanced power and vie for regional hegemony. War is to be expected. This process ultimately is contained only by the stopping power of water, which discourages great powers from pursuing world conquest.

How does offensive realism look vis-à-vis the axioms of realism? According to Mearsheimer (2014 [2001]: 29–31), offensive realism entails five assumptions:

1. The international system is anarchic, which does not mean that it is chaotic or riven by disorder.
2. Great powers inherently possess some offensive military capability, which gives them the wherewithal to hurt and possibly destroy.
3. States never can be certain about other states' intentions.
4. Survival is the primary goal of great powers.
5. Great powers are rational actors.

Mearsheimer (2014 [2001]: 31) adds that "states pay attention to the long term as well as the immediate consequences of their actions." This assertion elaborates on the assumption of rationality.

Does the offensive variant fit under the realist umbrella, understood in terms of the four axioms from Chapter 8: anarchy, state-centrism, power seeking, and rationality? The answer is a clear yes. Anarchy and rationality appear explicitly on

Table 17.1 Offensive Realism at a Glance

Frankel (1996b: xv)	Offensive realists posit that security in the international system is scarce, and that the fierce competition to attain security forces states to adopt offensive strategies, which often result in conflict and war. Offensive realists portray the international system as an unregulated free market.
Taliaferro (2000–2001: 128)	Offensive realism holds that anarchy—the absence of a worldwide government or universal sovereign—provides strong incentives for expansion.
Gowan (2002: 67)	If its message is a chilling one—the probability of wars between the major states of the 21st century—it neither conceals nor acclaims it.
Lynn-Jones (2002: 365)	"This quest for survival drives states to seek power aggressively and relentlessly.... The most important component of power is land power, the military capability to conquer territory. As great powers increase their relative power, they become more expansionist."
Rosecrance (2002: 365)	Major powers will seek to expand, and the greatest powers will seek to expand the most, at least on their own continent.
Walt (2002: 207)	"Offensive realists suggest that all major powers are constantly looking for opportunities to improve their relative power position ... and predict that states will normally choose to pass the buck rather than shoulder the burdens of balancing themselves."
Kupchan (2003: 750)	States consistently capitalize on opportunities to increase their power.
Nincic (2003: 239)	"Whether or not states are by nature power hungry, they have no choice but to act as if they were.... Uncertain about the intentions of others, each must assume that their purposes are predatory."
Taliaferro, Lobell, and Ripsman (2009: 18)	Offensive realism departs from Waltz's balance-of-power theory with its contention that states can never be certain how much power is necessary to achieve security for themselves now and in the future.
Valeriano (2009: 181)	The three tenets of offensive realism: (1) the goal is to maximize share of world power, (2) the ultimate aim is to become the hegemon, and (3) since global hegemony is impossible, the world is condemned to perpetual great power competition.
Rosecrance and Steiner (2010: 342)	Offensive realism requires major countries to increase their power and to seek at least regional hegemony.
Fiammenghi (2011: 126)	Offensive realists contend that states have a structural incentive to accumulate power.

Table 17.1 Continued

David (2015: 10–11)	Offensive realism includes anarchy but not chaos; leaders seek survival for their states and are rational.
Person (2017: 48)	Offensive realism: states in the international system aspire to accumulate the maximum amount of power possible.

the list from Mearsheimer (2014 [2001]). State-centrism is implied overwhelmingly by the focus in Mearsheimer (2014 [2001]) on great powers and military capability. In a separate exposition, Mearsheimer (1994–95) refers to the "false promise" of international institutions and emphasizes the persistence of states. What, then, about power seeking? This is the essence of offensive realism. States pursue greater capabilities in order to survive under conditions of uncertainty.

While not mentioned explicitly as an assumption, the stopping power of water plays a key role in offensive realism. "Although global hegemony is the final goal," as Yordán (2006: 129) points out, "Mearsheimer maintains that most great powers can only hope to realize regional hegemony, as global hegemony is difficult to establish because the world's oceans hinder the projecting of power to other parts of the world." Offensive realism emphasizes power on land and occupation of territory in its account of war.

One other axiom is implicit for offensive realism. Like other system-oriented realist theories, this assumption is essential to generate shifts in capability that stimulate aggression among its state inhabitants. The Realist Law of Uneven Growth therefore is added to the list of axioms for offensive realism.

Offensive realism is well connected to the classical tradition. Prominent instances include Morgenthau (1959 [1948]) on balance of power, Wolfers (1962) with respect to aggressive and threat-perceiving states, and Aron (1966) about offensive and defensive considerations. In addition, Toft (2005: 388) points out that offensive realism is sufficiently pessimistic that it resembles what might be labeled the "evil" school of realism. Thus the offensive variant is a throwback in that way, as well, to the classical tradition.

Expositions on the Causes of War

Offensive realism, as Mearsheimer (2014 [2001]: 53) puts it forward, includes an antinomy to set the context: "I do not adopt Morgenthau's claim that states invariably behave aggressively because they have a will to power hardwired into them." The account from offensive realism instead is structural and seeks to explain the causes of great power war, which refers to any conflict that involves at least one such actor (Mearsheimer 2014 [2001]: 334). While anarchy is a deep cause, this alone is not enough to explain why competition over security leads to war in some instances and not others. Anarchy is a constant, while war is not (Mearsheimer 2014 [2001]: 334–335). Mearsheimer (2014 [2001]: 335) therefore acknowledges that "structural theories such as offensive realism are at best crude predictors of when security competition leads to war." Thus it is essential to look at the state level, as well, for a full sense of what causes a specific war. States are not expected, as a matter of course, to fight a war for security-related reasons alone (Mearsheimer 2014 [2001]: 335).

Another structural variable comes into play along the road to war: "the distribution of power among the leading states in the system" (Mearsheimer 2014 [2001]: 335). Principal causes of war are "located in the architecture of the international system," and "the key ratio is that between the two most formidable states in the system" (Mearsheimer 2014 [2001]: 337). A potential hegemon enhances the likelihood of war by "increasing the level of fear among the great powers" (Mearsheimer 2014 [2001]: 345). The presence of an aspiring hegemon, according to Mearsheimer (2014 [2001]: 337), means that the system is unbalanced; absence of such a dominant state indicates the opposite. In addition, a system features either two leading great powers, labeled as bipolarity, or a higher number of greater powers, known as multipolarity. The two dimensions of power, (a) balanced versus unbalanced and (b) bipolarity as opposed to multipolarity, combine to form four profiles: "1) unbalanced bipolarity; 2) balanced bipolarity; 3) unbalanced multipolarity; and 4) balanced multipolarity" (Mearsheimer 2014 [2001]: 337). Unbalanced bipolarity is very unlikely to occur and thus is deemed irrelevant the rest of the way (Mearsheimer 2014 [2001]: 337). The argument producing that conclusion is in line with Waltz (1979) on expectations about bipolar rivalry leading to vigilance and thus a sustained balance of power between the two leading states.

Each type of system is anticipated to have a different propensity toward great power war. "The core of my argument," observes Mearsheimer (2014 [2001]: 335), "is that bipolar systems tend to be the most peaceful, and unbalanced multipolar systems are the most prone to deadly conflict. Balanced multipolar systems fall somewhere in between." War is more likely in multipolarity than bipolarity for three reasons (Mearsheimer 2014 [2001]: 338):

> First there are more opportunities for war, because there are more potential conflict dyads in a multipolar system. Second, imbalances of power are more commonplace in a multipolar world, and thus great powers are more likely to have the capability to win a war, making deterrence more difficult and war more likely. Third, the potential for miscalculation is greater in multipolarity: states

might think they have the capability to coerce or conquer another state when, in fact, they do not.

A bipolar system might contain a large number of states, but prospects for stability remain quite good. This is because the "pulling of minor powers into the orbit of one or the other great power makes it difficult for either great power to pick a fight with minor powers closely allied with its adversary; as a result, the number of potential conflict situations is substantially less" (Mearsheimer 2014 [2001]: 339). In addition, miscalculation is less likely and the relative tightness of a bipolar system obstructs war involving minor powers (Mearsheimer 2014 [2001]: 344, 340).

Multipolar systems, in contrast to bipolar ones, possess a less firm structure (Mearsheimer 2014 [2001]: 340). Thus conflict in multipolarity can "erupt across dyads involving major and minor powers" and more opportunities arise for minor powers to fight each other and ultimately involve great powers (Mearsheimer 2014 [2001]: 339, 340). Under multipolarity, even when threatened states do engage in balancing, diplomacy remains an uncertain process (Mearsheimer 2014 [2001]: 342).

Interesting to consider is the effort by Elman (2004) to extend offensive realism as articulated by Mearsheimer (2014 [2001]). The essential point of elaboration is "that the anarchic international system provides dissimilar cues to different types of states to engage in extraregional balancing" (Elman 2004: 573). The new phase of theorizing focuses on anticipated *extraregional* behavior for types of great powers implicit in Mearsheimer (2014 [2001]): continental great powers and island great powers (unclear, but likely to balance against would-be regional hegemons); and regional hegemons (balance against any would-be regional hegemons) (Elman 2004: 565). Elman (2004: 566) predicts variation in great power behavior under different distributions of power. The possible combinations are as follows: (a) one of multiple great powers in the region, an insular state, the only great power in the region, or a regional hegemon; and acting in another region with (b) more than one continental power, more than one great power (including an insular state), only one great power, or a hegemon. The anticipated outcome varies for each profile when the categories from (a) and (b) are cross-referenced with each other.

Elman (2004: 570) uses the Louisiana Purchase to illustrate the dynamics associated with such extraregional balances. France sold *all* of Louisiana to the United States, a decision that fits the "prediction that extraregional foreign policies are subordinate to local power considerations." French policy changed in March 1803. A deteriorating situation with Britain "forced Napoleon to make a choice between containing American power and pursuing French ambitions in Europe" (Elman 2004: 573). France went with transfer of the entire colony to the

United States "because it provided the largest monetary return and gave France the best chance of befriending the Americans" (Elman 2004: 574). In sum, considerations of power in Europe, not North America, explain French calculations about Louisiana (Elman 2004: 574). Different circumstances in the home region could have produced varying results abroad.

Evidence in favor of offensive realism focuses primarily on major powers, for the most part in Europe, but also including the United States and Japan. Along those lines, the experiences of Italy, which tend to receive less attention in studies that focus on major powers, are covered from 1861 to 1945. Notable also is analysis of Soviet-American nuclear-based rivalry in the Cold War era, which did not culminate in war. Mearsheimer (2014 [2001]) sees the experiences of the great powers over time as quite favorable to offensive realism. Aside from the stopping power of water, major powers seek to make gains at the expense of others and will go to war in order to achieve that goal.[2]

Critiques

Offensive realism is a highly visible and controversial theory. Points of criticism, to be considered in turn, focus on (a) potential falsification, (b) use of logic and gaps in theorizing, (c) how capabilities are assessed, (d) choice of historical evidence, (e) anticipated effects from the stopping power of water, and (f) how great powers act after war concludes.

What evidence, asks Nincic (2003: 239), would refute offensive realism? It would appear that no great power can be content with the status quo. All states are regarded as equally aggressive, leading Rosecrance (2003: 143) to speculate, humorously, on whether Monaco really would like to conquer the world. More explanation is needed for why and when wars occur, along with the cast of state characters involved in a given drama.

Toft (2005: 391–392) claims that multiple problems relate to the role of logic in offensive realism. Do the hypotheses really follow on from the assumptions? "To make its inferences fully consistent with the axioms, Toft (2005: 391) asserts, offensive realism must "identify the conditions that propel states to maximize relative power" or "make unstated assumptions about state motivations of extreme fear or greed." Toft (2005: 392) also sees the role of the rationality assumption as

---

[2] One quantitative analysis of offensive realism, not directly focused on war, also is available. Based on MID data from 1816 to 1992, Valeriano (2009: 192) conducts a statistical test of offensive realism in connection with great power involvement in those events. According to Valeriano (2009: 199), the results say that Mearsheimer is correct to a point: "The rate of conflict for major powers is indeed greater than for minor powers." At the same time, other results are not in line with offensive realism (Valeriano 2009: 200).

problematic: "If the weak are likely to balance against the strong, the resulting cost-benefit analysis of potential hegemons should rarely result in an outcome favouring expansion." In addition, offensive realism does not seem to account in any way for peaceful change (Kupchan 2003: 751).

Some critics identify incomplete specification as a problem for offensive realism. The theory, Walt (2002: 209) observes, "understates the risks of relentless competition and underestimates the possibility that states could increase their security by agreeing (either formally or tacitly) not to compete in certain ways." While offensive realism allows for such arrangements—if the balance of power is not affected—the theory "cannot account for such behavior and suggests it will be quite rare" (Walt 2002: 209). Furthermore, the theory incorporates neither international institutions nor economic interdependence in its network of variables (Nincic 2003: 239). Without such elements, how are war and peace to be explained?

Another line of criticism focuses on how capabilities are assessed in practice (Toft 2005: 384).

> The downside of this extreme focus on military capabilities is, however, that Mearsheimer's analyses are blind to other ways of exercising power—for example, economic warfare. In addition, other realists have shown that states are highly concerned with trends in latent power rather than with actual military capabilities (e.g. Copeland 2000). Thus, the French and British fears of a disarmed Germany in the 1920s are difficult to reconcile with Mearsheimer's argument. Furthermore, the focus on land power leads Mearsheimer to focus narrowly on territorial expansion. This implies a risk that his analyses miss a host of other ways of gaining and exercising influence.

In other words, is it realistic to infer that great powers face an existential threat? One critic sees this as an essential belief of offensive realism—and one for which there is "scant historical evidence" (Gowan 2002: 53). More needs to be said about the unit level.

Some critics of offensive realism question the choice of historical evidence that is claimed to support the theory. Rendall (2006: 524; see also Pashakhanlou 2013: 214) asserts that Mearsheimer has selected biased evidence, with an emphasis on "aggressive states in aggressive periods."[3] A more complete look at the 19th-century Concert of Europe, according to Rendall (2006: 524), is not that friendly to offensive realism. Its members look more like defensive realists

---

[3] In a critique of theorizing from Mearsheimer that culminated in offensive realism, Vasquez (1998: 292–301) points out at length that evidence does not support the presumed greater instability and warlikeness of multipolarity.

and "responded to structural constraints as they did largely because their leaders and domestic regimes were cautious and moderate—in other words, *for unit-level reasons*."[4] Russian restraint in the Near East, 1821–33, is quite noteworthy: "If great powers are as aggressive as Mearsheimer claims, Russia should have taken all it could get away with from its decaying neighbour, the Ottoman empire" (Rendall 2006: 530). Instead, Russia forfeited multiple opportunities to seize Constantinople (Rendall 2006: 530). And how is Russian (in)action to be explained? "Whereas they faced only weak adversaries in the Caucasus, further expansion into Europe would bring them into conflict with other great powers" (Rendall 2006: 534). In addition, the decline of the Ottoman Empire suggests that war can be caused just as easily by weakening rather than strengthening a key actor (Lord 2002: 113).

According to Gowan (2002: 62), the stopping power of water is overstated as an obstacle to expansionism. If the oceans limit hegemony to a regional basis, then why should the United States—secure in its hemisphere—"ever have worried about the prospect of a hegemon in Asia?" Furthermore, Gowan (2002: 62) asks, if the United States has been preeminent in control of the Americas for over a century, can that be explained by the stopping power of water? Pashakhanlou (2013: 213; see also Haslam 2010: 323) adds that offensive realism "cannot account for the actions of the US—*the most* important actor in the international system or the entire region it has operated in since year 1900." Thus, if the critiques about the stopping power of water are on target, the United States stands out as an anomaly for offensive realism.

Consider also the case of Japan, which, according to multiple critics (Posen 2002: 123; Lynn-Jones 2002: 366; Toft 2005: 395), goes against the grain of offensive realism. Recognizing that challenge, Toft (2005: 395) observes, Mearsheimer claims that Japan could have "expand[ed] across the narrow Sea of Japan and acted like a landlocked power because it faced weak opponents." Use of insularity to explain the absence of hegemonic expansion is problematic. Consider, for instance, the aggressiveness of Imperial Japan from 1895 to 1945—a power no less insular than either Britain or the United States (Haslam 2010: 324).

What about great power behavior after conclusion of war? As Posen (2002: 122) observes, following victory in war, the United States and UK have tended to pack up and go home, "or nearly done so." This would seem to go beyond mere geography and looks more like behavior consistent with defensive rather than offensive realism (Posen 2002: 122). With possible continental hegemons eliminated

---

[4] Rendall (2006: 526) focuses specifically on several dangerous crises between the winding down of the Napoleonic era in 1814 and the revolutions of 1848: the Polish-Saxon crisis at the Congress of Vienna, the Greek revolution during the 1820s, the Belgian revolution in 1830, and the Syrian crisis of 1840.

after respective wars, Posen (2002: 122) observes, these insular powers felt secure enough to depart.

Graphic Representation

Figure 17.1 is an effort to convey in graphic form the offensive realist explanation for great power war.[5] A region and the international system as its surrounding environment appear in Figure 17.1a. The story begins at the system level in Figure 17.1b with "ANARCHY" → "SECURITY COMPETITION." As an initial variable, "ANARCHY" appears as an oval. An absence of hierarchy causes states to compete with each other; everyone must take responsibility for their continuing survival under such conditions. The next connection, added in Figure 17.1c, is "SECURITY COMPETITION" → "DISTRIBUTION OF CAPABILITIES." As a divergent variable, the latter appears as a diamond. The Realist Law of Uneven Growth produces a dispersion of power that can vary significantly from one era to the next.

Consider first the simpler pathway out of the diamond, which continues in Figure 17.1d at the macro level with "DISTRIBUTION OF CAPABILITIES" → "BALANCED BIPOLARITY." As a convergent variable, "BALANCED BIPOLARITY" appears as a parallelogram. With time and events, the capability distribution is anticipated to crystallize into a profile that includes a specific and relatively small number of highly identifiable great powers. One such configuration is bipolarity, with two preeminent states. Moreover, rivalry and attendant close attention to each other are expected to produce a sustained balance in such a system.

Depicted in Figure 17.1e, the next step is "BALANCED BIPOLARITY" → "POLARIZATION." States will accumulate under the banner of one preeminent state or the other, which in turn produces a highly polarized system. In the Cold War, for instance, this refers to the Warsaw Pact on the side of the USSR in opposition to NATO and various other alliances involving the United States. This pathway continues in Figure 17.1f with "POLARIZATION → "REDUCED MINOR POWER WARFARE." Once states in the system are identified with one camp or the other, conflicts between them should be more manageable. One further connection is a feedback effect that appears in Figure 17.1g: "REDUCED MINOR POWER WARFARE" → "BALANCED BIPOLARITY." Thus the bipolar world takes the form of a self-reinforcing and stabilizing loop.

---

[5] Figure 17.1 is based on the exposition from Mearsheimer (2014 [2001]: 334–345) and has benefited from a consultation with John J. Mearsheimer.

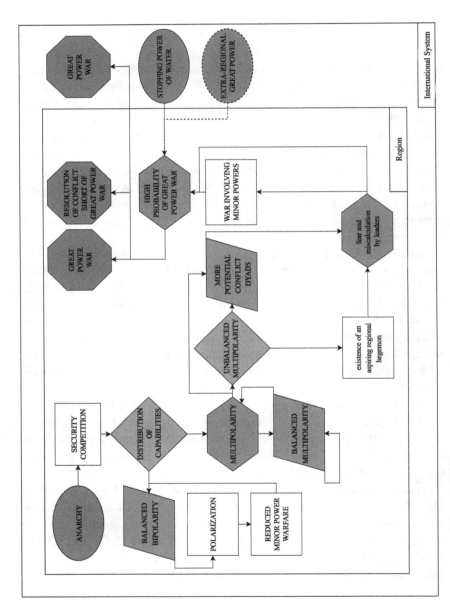

Figure 17.1 Offensive Realism

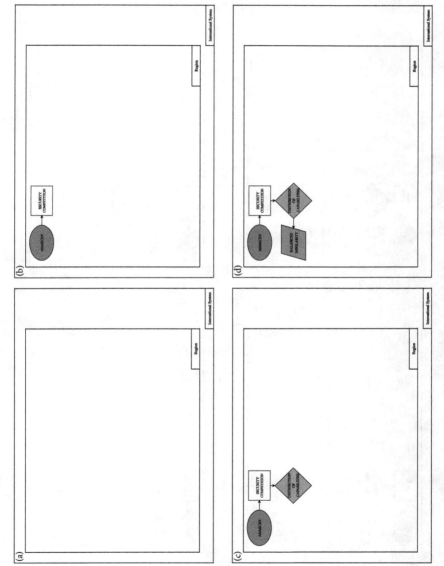

Figure 17.1 Continued

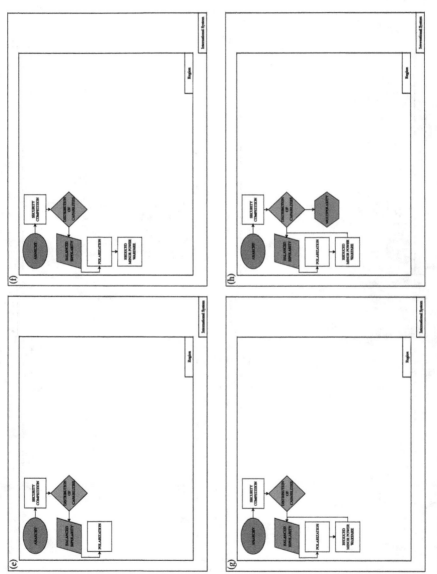

Figure 17.1 Continued

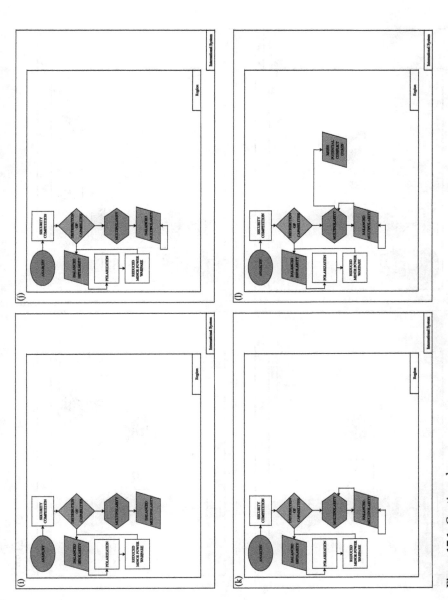

Figure 17.1 Continued

Figure 17.1 Continued

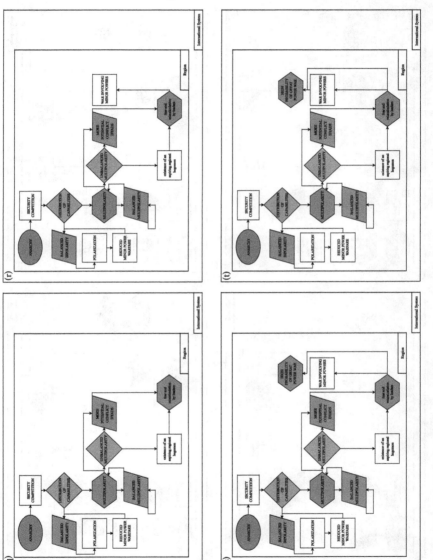

Figure 17.1 Continued

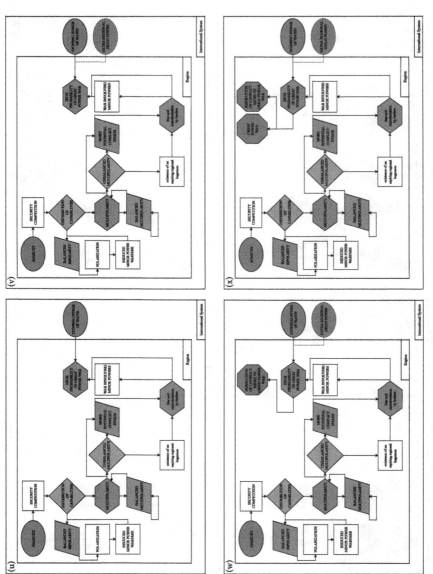

Figure 17.1 Continued

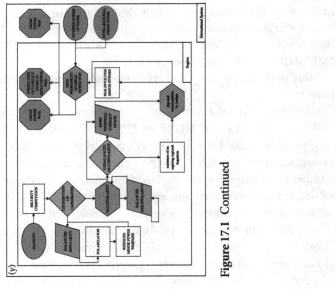

Figure 17.1 Continued

Another pathway emerges from the diamond in Figure 17.1h: "DISTRIBUTION OF CAPABILITIES" → "MULTIPOLARITY." This is the other option with regard to a crystallized profile vis-à-vis the number of great powers. Note that multipolarity, a nodal variable, takes the shape of a hexagon.

One possibility—desirable but unlikely to be achieved—appears in Figure 17.1i as "MULTIPOLARITY" → "BALANCED MULTIPOLARITY." As a convergent variable, the latter appears as a parallelogram. This linkage comes into place only if the great powers, in spite of the challenges faced as a result of coalition politics in particular, are able to maintain a stable system. A feedback loop appears in Figure 17.1k: "BALANCED MULTIPOLARITY" → "BALANCED MULTIPOLARITY." Stability becomes self-reinforcing through skillful management of the complexities inherent in a system with more than two great powers. The archetypal case of this, perhaps, would be the European state system in the era of Bismarck (Bew 2016; Rathbun 2019). At some point, however, the system still is anticipated to return to the overall dynamic leading in the direction of war. Thus the loop is followed by "BALANCED MULTIPOLARITY" → "MULTIPOLARITY" in Figure 17.1k.

More probable are the pathways to the right of multipolarity. Each is traced in turn.

Consider first the pathway that continues in Figure 17.1l with "MULTIPOLARITY" → "MORE POTENTIAL CONFLICT DYADS." As a convergent variable, the latter appears as a parallelogram. This connection also is a byproduct of the system's complexity, but in this context it is about the overall number of pairings that are in place as opposed to the size of the great power subset. The system becomes more conflict prone because of its high number of interaction opportunities in the absence of bipolar-style balancing.

Another pathway ensues in Figure 17.1m with "MULTIPOLARITY → "UNBALANCED MULTIPOLARITY." As a divergent variable, the latter appears as a diamond. This is to be expected, given the potential gyrations associated with affiliations between and among great powers—a problem exacerbated steadily as their number increases.

Figure 17.1n displays a further macro-level connection: "UNBALANCED MULTIPOLARITY" → "MORE POTENTIAL CONFLICT DYADS." As a convergent variable, the latter is depicted as a parallelogram. Complexity of the system, in terms of its range of interaction opportunities, poses a cognitive challenge to leaders among states, who must somehow try to manage potential conflicts in a non-escalatory way. This route continues downward to the micro level in Figure 17.1o with "MORE POTENTIAL CONFLICT DYADS" → "fear and miscalculation by leaders." As a nodal variable, the latter is depicted as a hexagon. This connection reflects the complicated nature of the system itself that induces stress and tension among leaders of its member states. Errors in judgment are an unfortunate byproduct of the high-pressure environment of rivalries and coalitional complications.

Additional movement downward to the state level ensues in Figure 17.1p: "UNBALANCED MULTIPOLARITY" → "existence of an aspiring regional hegemon." Lack of balancing in the complicated multipolar setting gives rise to the dream of hegemony in the region on the part of at least one of its great powers. The next step, depicted in Figure 17.1q, is "existence of an aspiring hegemon" → "fear and miscalculation by leaders." Anxieties and errors associated with them bring the great powers of the region one step closer to open conflict. Rather than a violation of rationality, existence of such errors is in line with its ordinal variant—eventually complications at a sufficient level can overwhelm cognition.

Two pathways lead toward the macro level. The first branch continues upward in Figure 17.1r with "fear and miscalculation by leaders" → "WAR INVOLVING MINOR POWERS." Once again, the sheer number of great powers makes it difficult for them to head off escalation of conflict.

Another pathway upward appears in Figure 17.1s: "fear and miscalculation by leaders" → "HIGH PROBABILITY OF GREAT POWER WAR." As a nodal variable, the latter appears as a hexagon. The routes converge in Figure 17.1t with "WAR INVOLVING MINOR POWERS" → "HIGH PROBABILITY OF GREAT POWER WAR." Reinforcing factors point toward war.

From the international system into the macro level of the region, a connection ensues in Figure 17.1u: "STOPPING POWER OF WATER" → "HIGH PROBABILITY OF GREAT POWER WAR." As an initial variable, the former of these two is depicted as an oval. Put simply, oceans limit the ambitions of hegemonic powers at the brink of war. They pursue great power war within a regional context because world conquest is so difficult for logistical reasons.

Interesting to note is that an effort to extend theorizing from offensive realism produces a further linkage from outside of the system.[6] This connection, depicted as a broken line in Figure 17.1v, is "EXTRA-REGIONAL GREAT POWER" → "HIGH PROBABILITY OF GREAT POWER WAR." As an initial variable, "EXTRA-REGIONAL GREAT POWER" takes the form of an oval.[7] Elman (2004) theorizes that the situation of a great power in its own region will explain what it does elsewhere. Thus one reason why the United States engages in significant interventions in other regions is that it achieved regional hegemony a very long time ago. Unlike other capitals, Washington possesses the opportunity

---

[6] This additional linkage is based on Elman (2004: 565–566).
[7] The border of the variable, introduced by Elman (2004) as an extension of offensive realism, also appears as a broken line.

to engage in balancing behavior outside of North America precisely because nothing it does abroad jeopardizes its predominance in the home region.

Figure 17.1w continues at the macro level with "HIGH PROBABILITY OF WAR" → "RESOLUTION OF CONFLICT SHORT OF GREAT POWER WAR." As a terminal variable, the latter appears as an octagon. Even at the brink of war, some redistribution of resources still can head off that outcome (Coase 1960). Another branch of this pathway also ends, in Figure 17.x, at the macro level: "HIGH PROBABILITY OF GREAT POWER WAR" → "GREAT POWER WAR." As a terminal variable, the latter is depicted as an octagon. A final possibility extends into the international system in Figure 17.1y: "HIGH PROBABILITY OF GREAT POWER WAR" → "GREAT POWER WAR." The latter, a terminal variable, appears as an octagon. While quite rare, general war does occur in spite of obstacles posed by sheer distance across regions.

With 19 variables in its network, offensive realism is the most complex realist theory of war, at least in terms of the sheer number of components. It is the only realist theory with all basic types of connection from systemism in place. The theory features three initial and three terminal variables. In addition, there are two divergent, three convergent, and three nodal variables. Inclusion of two feedback loops reinforces the sense of offensive realism as a comprehensive account of why great power wars occur.

With a graphic presentation in place, consider offensive realism in relation to the framework on cause and effect adopted from Kurki (2002). Formal, material, final, and efficient conditions are explored in turn.

Formal conditions—defining shapes or relations—serve as the background to events. Several items belong in this category: (a) anarchy, (b) security competition, and (c) distribution of capabilities. These are normal conditions within the world according to realism.

What about material conditions—passive potentiality of matter or the opportunity to act (Most and Starr 2015 [1989])? Variables included here are (i) multipolarity, (ii) unbalanced multipolarity, (iii) more potential conflict dyads, (iv) balanced bipolarity, (v) polarization, (vi) reduced minor power warfare, and (vii) stopping power of water. At varying points, each of these factors impacts the opportunity for war. For example, balanced bipolarity and reduced minor power warfare combine to diminish the likelihood of escalation, while multipolarity and unbalanced multipolarity have the opposite effect. The stopping power of water limits the opportunity for extraregional conquest.

Final conditions focus on the purposes that guide change—willingness, as described by Most and Starr (2015 [1989]). Existence of an aspiring regional hegemon—ready to pursue war if feasible—is the variable placed in this category. With intensely revisionist goals, this state will not shy away from war.

Efficient conditions or movers include (i) fear and miscalculation by leaders, (ii) war involving minor powers, (iii) high probability of great power war, and

(iv) extraregional great powers. All of these factors combine in intuitively obvious ways to bring about war and impact its specific characteristics.

With a graphic exposition in place, along with a summary of cause and effect, attention returns to the critiques noted earlier in this chapter.

Lack of potential for falsification emerges as a serious challenge to offensive realism. Threshold effects need to be identified for the efficient conditions in particular. How do these factors combine to bring about war? What are their levels of substitutability for each other in the process of escalation? These and other questions will receive tentative answers in Chapter 19, when offensive realism is engaged with other realist theories.

What about inappropriate use of logic and gaps in theorizing? Scope conditions emerge as a key issue. Most notable is the absence of the offense-defense balance. Beliefs about this balance could help to explain diverse outcomes. This matter also is taken up in Chapter 19.

Saying more about how capabilities are assessed in practice would be a valuable step forward for offensive realism. The theory seems incomplete, especially in the context of the new millennium, and the stopping power of water deserves particular attention. Technologies such as aircraft, rockets, and drones need to be built into this discussion. Interesting to consider, vis-à-vis an overall sense of capabilities, is an ideational turn. What if the stopping power of water, which operates more for land forces than others, possesses a more important psychological than material impact across the board?

What about the choice of historical evidence? Not all cases of war and peace can be explained by offensive realism in its current form. Elaboration to include more of a role for foreign policy emerges as a priority. The theory therefore should engage more with visions cast at the micro level in particular, and that will take place in Chapter 19.

Great power actions after at least some wars seem collectively to pose an anomaly for offensive realism. One way to address this problem is through elaboration at the micro level to permit variation by power endowments. In particular, the marginal utility of further conquest for the leading state in the system is likely to be at a relatively low level. All of that is consistent with rationality and power seeking. The door is open to elaboration of offensive realism to take into account different kinds of states. This will take place through contact with neoclassical realist theories in Chapter 19.

Reflections on Offensive Realism

Offensive realism is an influential theory about the causes of great power war. The theory is cast at the system level and focuses on comparative statics. The great powers, in a word, are players in an ongoing tragedy. Power seeking under anarchy and especially multipolarity, which is likely to be unbalanced, poses danger for any region. Minor power warfare contributes to the likelihood of escalation that involves major powers. The stopping power of water is put forward as an explanation for why efforts toward world domination rarely are witnessed. Offensive realism, in sum, points toward war between and among great powers as an ongoing possibility within the international system. Engagement of the theory with others from realism should prove enlightening in Chapter 19.

18
Predation

Overview

Predation theory focuses on the dynamics of capabilities at the system level in connection to propensity for war. For the first time in nearly two decades, a magnum opus on the causes of international war has appeared within the realist school of thought. The long gap between such book-length expositions—almost two decades going back to Mearsheimer (2014 [2001]) on offensive realism—may be a product of a shift toward the study of civil wars or perhaps any number of other things. Predation theory asks a basic question about world politics: How do great powers treat one of their number when it goes into decline? The answer to this question is contingent upon the strategic value of a state with diminished capabilities to its peers. Important implications exist for international stability and the likelihood of great power war.

Predation theory is well received as a new entrant into realist theorizing about war. Among reviews, a consensus exists on the importance of *Rising Titans, Falling Giants* (Shifrinson 2019a; Lascurettes [Fuji et al.] 2019: 8; Ikenberry 2019; Montgomery [Fuji et al] 2019).[1] For example, Edelstein [Fuji et al.] (2019: 2) describes the book as "a model of how to conduct robust, rigorous empirical tests of arguments using qualitative evidence." MacDonald [Fuji et al.] (2019: 8) assesses the evidence for predation theory quite favorably, noting a combination of archival documents and many interviews with policymakers.

This chapter unfolds in five additional sections. The second section conveys the meaning of predation theory. The third section covers predation as a theory about the causes of war. The fourth section focuses on critiques. In the fifth section, predation theory is presented in visual form. This graphic exposition also will be applied in response to critiques. The sixth and final section reflects upon the accomplishments of predation theory.

---

[1] Items denoted with "[Fuji et al.]" are specific contributions to a roundtable on Shifrinson (2019a).

What Is Predation?

Predation theory is system oriented and focuses on the dynamics of capabilities possessed by the great powers. A great power refers to a "state with the resources to make a good showing in a fight with the strongest state in the international system" (Shifrinson 2019a: 13; see also Shifrinson 2018). Under the challenging conditions of anarchy, these states seek to maximize power, relative to others, and therefore "carefully assess whether the benefits of expansion outweigh the risks involved" (Shifrinson 2019a: 23). Significant shifts in relative capabilities among the great power subset are essential in accounting for (in)stability in the system.

Table 18.1 gives a sense of the main features for predation theory. Great powers are in constant competition with each other. The focal point of the theory is noteworthy change in capabilities. When a great power loses significant ground, how will its peers react? According to predation theory, revisionism is not constant but instead pursued in a strategic way. The approach taken toward a declining

Table 18.1 Predation at a Glance

Shifrinson (2018)	In general, situations favorable to predation appear to be rare.
Shifrinson (2019a: 178)	Predation theory uses assumptions rooted in offensive realism—in particular, that states seek power—to show that even rising states that want to maximize power will sometimes cooperate with declining states—behavior more consistent with defensive realist expectations. It does this by highlighting that power-maximizing states sometimes act as if they were power satisficers out of concern with the distribution of power.
Horowitz (2019: 1171)	"The theory is an important step towards understanding the behaviour of Great Powers in the current era . . . others will have to build on his work to better illuminate the rationales underpinning these states' actions."
Edelstein [Fuji et al.] (2019: 1)	Great powers are always seeking ways to exploit changes in the international system to their advantage.
Montgomery [Fuji et al.] (2019: 11)	"States do not engage in revisionist behavior all of the time. What is needed, therefore, and what this volume begins to provide, is a more complete picture of the conditions under which states will act on this impulse, as well as the considerations that will shape how they do so."
Parent (2020)	Shifrinson's balance-of-power theory depends more on objective environmental shifts than subjective statements of the actors in the system.

state by its peers could include initiation of full-scale war, but also might take more nuanced forms. The strategic value of a declining state, along with its military posture, will impact how its peers will respond.

When a state experiences noteworthy decline, its peers must decide how to respond, and that will be determined by the answers to two questions: (1) What is the military posture of the declining power (robust or weak); and (2) What is its strategic value (high or low)? If that state is weak in military posture and low in strategic value, the harsh strategy of relegation is implemented—assertively treating it as a nonentity and seeking maximum relative gains. If the state is weak in military posture but high in strategic value, a strategy of strengthening is implemented—trying to help the state recover, in a passive way, because of its potential value in league against likely adversaries. If the military posture is robust but strategic value is low, weakening is the preferred approach—assertively seeking to accelerate decline. Finally, a state that is robust in military posture and high in value will stimulate a bolstering policy—an assertive attempt to shore up its position (Shifrinson 2019a: 33). This is because of common interests with one or more peers who see it as being in their interest for the state in question to stay in the great power club.

Predation theory also takes polarity into account in theorizing about great power politics under conditions of significant capability redistribution. With multiple potential threats, rising or stable states are incentivized to work with decliners in some situations. It may be in the overall geostrategic interest of a state to prop up another in decline, notably within the complex world of multipolarity. Bipolarity, by contrast, would seem to build in more direct confrontation between the two leading states (Shifrinson 2019a: 25). One simply would be inclined to take advantage of the other whenever possible.

Does predation qualify as a realist theory? While axioms are not listed explicitly at any single point in Shifrinson (2019a), those associated with realism—anarchy, state-centrism, rationality, and seeking power—clearly are in place. Anarchy and state-centrism are referenced frequently in studies based on predation theory (Shifrinson 2018, 2019a, 2019b, 2020). For example, an assessment of politics in East Asia focuses exclusively on states and the distribution of capabilities among them (Shifrinson 2019a: 182–186). Shifrinson (2019a: 14, 178) asserts that states seek to maximize power and "relative capabilities at a state's disposal constitute the *ultima ratio* of its security." In addition, rational choice is accessed on many occasions in predation theory, for example, during various assessments of nuanced state choices about strategy and tactics (Shifrinson 2019a: 178).

Like other realist theories cast at the system level, predation needs to explain why some states end up in a better position to act than others. Capabilities will shift over time. Thus, once again, the Realist Law of Uneven Growth is incorporated in the list of axioms. This creates the possibility, as per the title of Shifrinson (2019a), of rising titans and falling giants.

Predation focuses on great power decline and how it impacts the stability of the international system. Shifrinson (2019a: 15) puts forward three criteria for decline:

> First, great powers had to lose at least 5 percent of their share of capabilities relative to the other great powers within a ten-year period, compared to the average over the preceding ten years. Second, those losses had to be sustained for at least five consecutive years. Third, the time frame for decline ends when states either began sustained growth or left the ranks of the great powers.

The proportional change, in other words, is deemed sufficient to attract attention from peers and even lesser states. What is anticipated to happen under such conditions? Predation theory resembles other variants of realism in that it anticipates calculated aggression—moving forward but only under specific conditions (Shifrinson 2019a: 6).

Available strategies are distinguished from each other as either (i) more or less intense and (ii) positive or negative toward the declining power. Four possibilities result from combination of the categories from (i) with those of (ii): (a) relegation (negative and more intense), (b) strengthening (positive and more intense), (c) weakening (negative and less intense) and (d) bolstering (positive and less intense). Each of the four strategies is introduced in turn, along with historical and contemporary illustrations.

Relegation refers to when a great power "adopts a predatory goal and challenges a declining state with intense means" (Shifrinson 2019a: 21). One policy encompassed within relegation would be to wage war against a declining state (Shifrinson 2019a: 21). An example is Prussia's decision to go to war against France in 1870. This is because Prussia accelerated its rise, along with the decline of France, by overturning the existing European distribution of power (Shifrinson 2019a: 20).

Less extreme than relegation, but also negative, is the strategy of weakening. A rising state that adopts a weakening strategy seeks to undermine a declining state as a competitor through the use of limited means that gradually shift the distribution of power (Shifrinson 2019a: 21–22). Consider, for example, land reclamation and military deployments from the PRC in the East and South China Seas (Shifrinson 2018). This activity, as Shifrinson (2018) points out, involves primarily territories that the Chinese government had claimed previously—not an expansion of maritime claims. These policies make sense from the standpoint of predation theory. On the one hand, China seeks to gain at the expense of the United States from, most notably, its key client states such as Japan. On the other hand, China exists in a crowded and adversarial neighborhood (Shifrinson 2018). Thus the behavior of a rising China is assertive rather than highly confrontational because escalation of conflict with the United States would not be desirable for the foreseeable future.

Strengthening refers to active support for a declining state "by taking steps to sustain or improve its position" (Shifrinson 2019a: 21). Less extreme than strengthening, but also positive, is bolstering—a judicious move to "maintain the status quo in the declining state's favor while constantly looking over their shoulders to assess others' reactions and to determine whether other interests are being sacrificed" (Shifrinson 2019a: 23). This activity reflects self-interest, in terms of the full set of strategic conditions, and should not be confused with altruism.

Consider, as an example of such positive measures, strategic interaction over the significant relative decline of Great Britain at the end of World War II. War-driven expansion of the United States and USSR and massive debt for Great Britain translated into a highly visible shift in relative power in 1945 (Shifrinson 2019a: 44). Forgotten, many decades later, is the fact that the USSR bolstered Britain from 1945 to 1946 and, early in 1947, implemented a strategy of strengthening (Shifrinson 2019a: 83). The Soviet Union, observes Shifrinson (2019a: 90), "quickly moved to explore a formal military alliance—more than one year before the United States did the same—with the United Kingdom." With the onset of the Marshall Plan, however, it became clear to Moscow that Britain had become unavailable as a partner (Shifrinson 2019a: 93). The case of British decline offers support to predation theory in three important ways: "(1) rising states support declining great powers that offer high strategic value; (2) shifts in the declining state's military posture in these circumstances affect the assertiveness of support, and (3) alterations in a declining state's strategic value affect a rising state's fundamental choice of supporting or preying upon a decliner" (Shifrinson 2019a: 97).

Policies can shift over time in response to changing conditions for one or more great powers, as with the USSR vis-à-vis Great Britain in the aftermath of World War II. Consider, as a more extended illustration, the United States in the final decade of the Cold War. In the early 1980s, the United States faced no great power competitor other than the USSR. When power shifted significantly in favor of the United States, around approximately 1983, it began to prey upon its Soviet rival (Shifrinson 2019a: 119). Tensions reached a high level, as Shifrinson (2019a: 121) points out, with the shooting down of a Korean airliner in September 1983. Consistent with predation theory, this intense crisis caused US leadership to realize that Moscow feared aggression (Shifrinson 2019a: 121). The USSR might even respond favorably to negotiations in key areas, such as arms reductions. By 1983–84, US representatives proposed sequential steps "leading to asymmetric

Soviet reductions over time rather than an all-out dismantlement effort" (Shifrinson 2019a: 123). Predatory logic, but with caution, drove this US policy toward the USSR, which can be summarized as weakening—pursuit of gains in a slow and steady way (Shifrinson 2019a: 131–132).

By 1989–90, the military position of the USSR had collapsed and the unthinkable, German reunification with open US support, suddenly came into being (Shifrinson 2019a: 140). From January 1990 onward, the United States shifted to a relegation strategy, preying upon Soviet vulnerabilities. The most notable actions included "(1) seeking to quickly reunify Germany, (2) disregarding Soviet and other European opposition to this objective, and (3) ensuring that the reunified state remained in NATO so as to guarantee the alliance's survival as a vehicle for U.S. power projection" (Shifrinson 2019a: 142). These decisive actions revealed that Washington saw its long-standing rival in Moscow as too limited in resources to resist effectively and virtually bereft of strategic value.

After achievement of the preceding set of goals, according to Shifrinson (2019a: 153), the United States shifted back to a weakening strategy—challenging the USSR in limited ways and not seeking to accelerate its collapse. This is explained by "the danger of antagonizing a Soviet Union which remained—for now—militarily potent" (Shifrinson 2019a: 155). In a word, the United States had hit its limit in making gains without also taking on a serious risk of escalation to war.

Predation theory shows significant connections to the classical realist tradition. Noteworthy in that context are Wight (1978 [1946]) on seeking gain, Kissinger (1957) concerning alliances, and Wolfers (1962) with respect to aggressive and threat-perceiving states. The theory also resembles classical realist expositions because of its emphasis on in-depth historical research and connection with policy-related concerns.

Expositions on the Causes of War

Pathways to war result from strategies adopted by rising states in response to the decline of one or more great power peers. These strategies vary along two dimensions: (a) *goals* pursued by a rising state towards a peer in decline and (b) *means* selected to achieve those aims (Shifrinson 2020). When considering expansion, a rising state must assess benefits versus cost under conditions of risk. Efforts to maximize power can "elicit retaliation from states with similar concerns about relative power and security" (Shifrinson 2020). War can occur as states react to change in relative capabilities.

Consider, as an illustration, the wars fought by Prussia against Austria in 1866 and France in 1870. Prussia responded to major developing incentives to undermine French and Austrian power (Shifrinson 2019a: 167). Each of these rival states featured robust military postures and low strategic value. Prussia therefore adopted a weakening strategy toward France (Shifrinson 2019a: 167). By contrast, Russia and Britain engaged in bolstering relations with Austria (Shifrinson 2019a: 171). These processes culminated in two limited wars, as opposed to a conflagration that involved all of the European powers. From the late 1890s onward, France's military posture collapsed and German predation intensified (Shifrinson 2019a: 175). These events in the European multipolar system strongly support predation theory: "As predicted, rising states generally supported declining states with high strategic value, preyed upon decliners with low strategic value, and modulated their assertiveness depending on the declining state's military posture" (Shifrinson 2019a: 176). The specificity of these respective results is especially favorable to the theory.

Critiques

Criticism of predation theory focuses on (a) the logic behind respective strategic options and (b) measurement of key components in connection to concerns about potential falsification.

One point of criticism focuses on why strategies such as strengthening or bolstering ever would be implemented. "If a declining power is falling rapidly from the ranks of the great powers so that no amount of assistance could ever make it a valuable ally," MacDonald ([Fuji et al.] 2019: 10) observes, "why would a rising power still offer to help?" From this point of view, a rising great power is expected to "thread the needle"—hoping that declining client states retain enough capabilities to be useful, while not being sufficiently capable to exploit the friendship (MacDonald ([Fuji et al.] 2019: 10). Is this too demanding in terms of expectations for leaders faced with management of what sometimes can be very rapid change?

Consider also the logic behind policies such as weakening and relegation. Is it even worthwhile, Montgomery ([Fuji et al.] 2019: 12) asks, to engage in predation against a state in decline? Assertive efforts to improve relative power will entail risks, so it could seem preferable to wait for the competitor simply to decline on its own (Montgomery ([Fuji et al.] 2019: 12). Would it not be rational simply to wait things out?

What about assessment of key variables, notably with respect to potential falsification of the theory? Consider military posture. Issues arise about operationalization for military posture. Military postures are identified as weak or robust on the basis of "case-specific details" (Lascurettes [Fuji et al.] 2019: 6). In a more general sense, however, what is the demarcation of one bearing from another? Concerns also arise about assessment of high- versus low-intensity actions toward a declining power (Montgomery [Fuji et al.] 2019: 12). What is the specific and a priori threshold for assessing low versus high intensity? Without such specification, the theory can be made consistent with any evidence.

Graphic Representation

Figure 18.1 shows predation theory in graphic form.[2] A region and the international system as its environment appear in Figure 18.1a. Figure 18.1b displays the starting point at the micro level: "great power experiences significant decline in capabilities." As an initial variable, this appears as an oval. Movement from the micro to the macro level occurs in Figure 18.1c: "great power experiences significant decline in capabilities" → "VISIBLE SHIFT IN GREAT POWER CAPABILITIES." As a divergent variable, the latter appears as a diamond.

Two pathways emerge in Figure 18.1d: "VISIBLE SHIFT IN GREAT POWER CAPABILITIES" → "rising state perceives declining state as either high in strategic value or strong in military posture"; "rising state perceives declining state as low in strategic value and weak in military posture." This foundation for positive or negative policies, along with their intensity, follows on from how a declining state fits into the geostrategic situation for each of its great power peers.

Figure 18.1e extends both pathways at the micro level: "rising state perceives declining state as either high in strategic value or strong in military posture" → "rising state adopts strengthening, weakening or bolstering strategy towards declining state," and "rising state perceives declining state as low in strategic value and weak in military posture" → "rising state adopts relegation strategy towards declining state." In a word, is the declining state still deemed worthy of peer status as a great power? The answer to that question will determine policy.

Movement back to the macro level occurs in Figure 18.1f with "rising state adopts relegation strategy towards declining state" → "RISING STATE ADOPTS A PREDATORY GOAL AND CHALLENGES A DECLINING STATE WITH INTENSE MEANS." This pathway continues at the macro level in Figure 18.1g with "RISING STATE ADOPTS A PREDATORY GOAL AND CHALLENGES A DECLINING STATE WITH INTENSE MEANS" → "ASSESSMENT OF BENEFITS OF EXPANSION VERSUS RISKS." As a divergent variable, the latter is depicted with a diamond. The other pathway also moves up from micro to macro with "rising state adopts strengthening, weakening or bolstering strategy towards declining state" → "NON-WAR OUTCOME." As a terminal variable,

---

[2] This diagram is based primarily on Figure 1.3 from Shifrinson (2019a: 37). The figure also has benefited from a consultation with Joshua R. Itzkowitz Shifrinson.

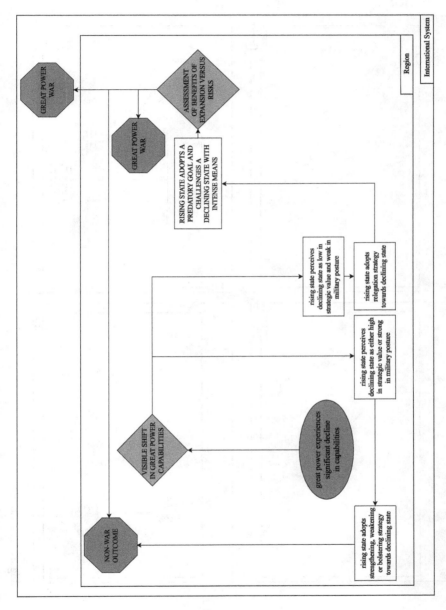

Figure 18.1 Predation

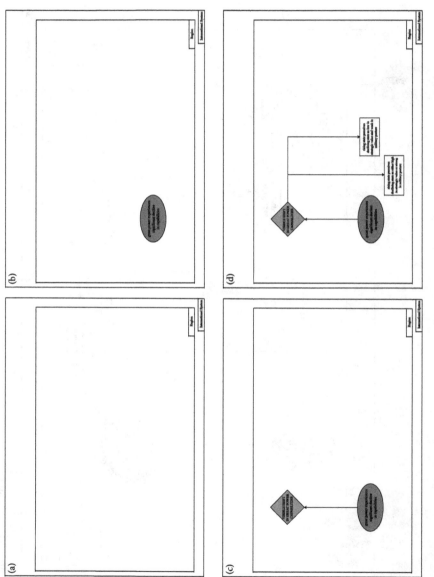

Figure 18.1 Continued

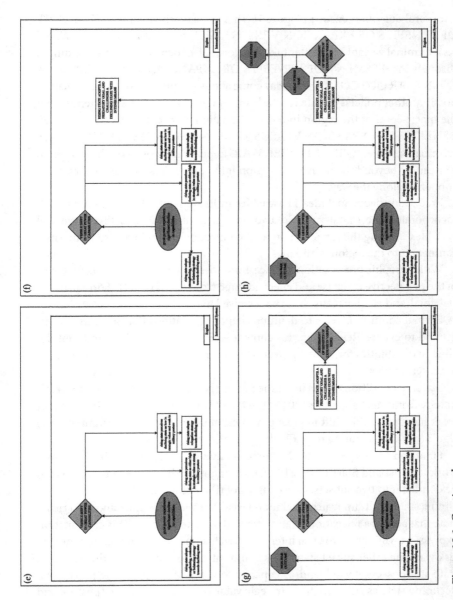

Figure 18.1 Continued

the latter appears as an octagon. The three policies—strengthening, weakening, and bolstering—are alike in that none is directly confrontational toward the state in decline.

Several outcomes ensue in Figure 18.1h. One is reached with "ASSESSMENT OF BENEFITS OF EXPANSION VERSUS RISKS" → "GREAT POWER WAR." As a terminal variable, the latter takes the form of an octagon. Another ending is through "ASSESSMENT OF BENEFITS OF EXPANSION VERSUS RISKS" → "NON-WAR OUTCOME." This may come about as a product of appeasement or possibly other policies pursued at the brink of war. A final outcome extends from the macro level of the region into the international system: "ASSESSMENT OF BENEFITS OF EXPANSION VERSUS RISKS" → "GREAT POWER WAR." As a terminal variable, "GREAT POWER WAR" appears as an octagon. Escalation to war can go beyond the immediate region if the range of issues and actors is not contained along the way.

Predation theory includes 11 variables in its network of cause and effect. It incorporates one initial variable, two divergent variables, and three terminal variables. Among the range of potential connections, only input from the environment into the region is missing.

With a graphic presentation in place, how does predation theory look in terms of the perspective on cause and effect adopted from Kurki (2002)? Formal, material, final, and efficient causes will be reviewed in turn.

Formal conditions refer to defining shapes or relations that serve as a background to events. Relevant in this context is the experience of a significant decline in capabilities for a great power. This is certain to occur under the practice of power politics.

Material conditions focus upon the passive potential of matter—in the terminology from Most and Starr (2015 [1989]), the opportunity to act. The factor at work here is a visible shift in great power capabilities. A power vacuum of some significant size is waiting to be filled.

Final conditions pertain to the purposes that guide change or, in the framework in Most and Starr (2015 [1989]), willingness. The forces that operate can be divided into two subsets. One consists of (i) a rising state that perceives a declining state as low in strategic value and weak in military posture and (ii) a rising state that adopts a relegation strategy toward a declining state. This combination expresses a willingness to push intensively against the declining state and thereby risk war. The other subset shows less commitment to war because the declining state still possesses value and/or capacity to act: (iii) a rising state perceives a declining state as either high in strategic value or strong in military posture and (iv) a rising state adopts a strengthening, weakening or bolstering strategy toward a declining state. While the strategies vary in other ways, none is highly confrontational.

Efficient causes, or movers, complete the process. The mover occurs when a rising state adopts a predatory goal and challenges a declining state with intense means. Either a bargain short of war or escalation will ensue.

With a graphic representation of the theory and an assessment of cause and effective in place, it is time to review the critiques.

One point of criticism focuses on the logic behind the choice of strategic options. Consider this point in the context of ordinal rationality. It is impossible to forecast with high precision the magnitude of change in relative capabilities, so the focus will be on direction of movement. Put differently, short-term trends do not represent long-term laws that encourage forecasting with a focus on anything but the near future. Thus implementation of one of the strategies might seem best in light of existing developments. For example, the idea of waiting things out rather than acting more decisively against a declining rival would make more sense if that trend could be assumed to persist. What, however, if it might stop or even reverse? In sum, observation of decline signals a window of opportunity that, in turn, could close without much notice.

Another critique focuses on measurement of key variables—military posture, strategic value, and intensity of action. In each instance, what is the threshold for classification? This set of concerns must be met in order to meet the requirement of potential falsifiability. A set of answers to this query will be pursued through engagement with other realist theories in Chapter 19.

Reflections on Predation

Among realist theories about war, predation is the most recently articulated. The theory is dynamic and system oriented. Predation focuses on how great powers respond to significant decline in one of their peers. The theory identifies several strategic options—bolstering, strengthening, weakening, and relegation—with the choices among them impacting significantly upon the likelihood of war. The theory is very new, but already features support from some important cases. Thus predation is an excellent candidate for engagement with other realist theories in Chapter 19.

PART V
THE WAY FORWARD

Part V of the book pursues a graphic approach toward a well-integrated version of realism as a contributor to the growth of knowledge and brings together the insights accumulated throughout preceding chapters. This work unfolds in the two chapters that follow.

Chapter 19 engages realist theories about wars with each other. Graphic portrayal of respective theories following on from classical realism, described already in Chapters 11 to 18, facilitates moving forward with this agenda. Realist theories are identified as either complementary or competitive with each other. Opportunities are explored for combination and, when appropriate, more effective competition. Within the context of SIR, this activity is a form of systematic synthesis. Also in line with SIR, the chapter includes bricolagic bridging—engagement of realist theories with ideas from a major work of scholarship beyond this school of thought. This contact takes place in the spirit of analytic eclecticism, but with an eye on logical consistency and coherence as the work is carried out.

Chapter 20 reflects on the project as a whole and gets underway with a review of specific accomplishments from Parts I -IV. This final chapter assesses realism in an overall sense in light of an extensive *graphic* review of its theories in the context of the causes of war. Is realism a scientifically viable research enterprise? This question is answered affirmatively, but tentatively. Potential exists but remains unrealized for realism, which must meet rather than eschew scientific standards in order to move forward. Accomplishment of that goal through adoption of a systemist graphic approach toward communication, in turn, would facilitate comparison to any other research enterprise that subsequently is identified in the same way as realism within this volume. The chapter also offers several ideas about future research, and its final thoughts are on the prospects of realism as a scientific research enterprise.

19
Dialogue for Realist Theories of War

Overview

Realism, so far in this volume, has been assessed either on the basis of individual theories or as a school of thought. Parts I and II of this volume combined to produce a metatheory of progress. Through incorporation of both (a) deductive and rationalist and (b) inductive and sociological criteria, Part III of this volume identified realism as a research enterprise and developed a typology and taxonomy for its theories to facilitate comparative analysis. Part IV then located realist theories about the causes of war and placed each into a graphic format. The present chapter turns to Systemist International Relations (SIR) as articulated in Part II and responds to critiques and opportunities identified through a review of systemist figures. Systematic synthesis and bricolagic bridging from SIR are implemented to promote dialogue for realist theories, with each other and beyond, as a pathway toward scientific progress for the research enterprise as a whole.

Progress, perhaps, could occur in a natural way—so why bother with the preceding set of structured activities for realist theories about war? An answer in favor of implementation for SIR derives from the ambiguous state of realism today. This condition has become clear to see from articulation of the school at a general level in tandem with a review of its respective theories about war in Parts III and IV, respectively, of this volume. At the same time, it has been possible to identify a realist research enterprise that is anticipated to find support from both adherents and those beyond its boundaries. SIR can build on that foundation to move realism forward.

Not surprisingly, in light of current conditions, opinions vary on the viability of realism in the new millennium. These expositions show no signs of converging with each other.

Quite positive in outlook is Wohlforth (2008: 145–146), who sees realism as becoming eclectic, with more productive exchanges, and less competition, with other schools of thought. Wohlforth (2008: 147) summarizes the state of the art as follows:

> Realism's diversity is increasingly transparent, [and] realist scholarship is more problem focused, more empirical, more historically and methodologically sophisticated, and more open to other traditions and disciplines than it ever was

in the heyday of classical or neorealism. As a result, scholars working within the realist tradition are arguably adding more to knowledge about their subject today than ever before.

From that point of view, the volume and range of realist scholarship looks inherently valuable and pointed in the right direction.

Others, however, are less positive about future prospects for realism. For example, Wivel (2005: 356) identifies available options in a quite negative way. Realism seems to offer "two equally unattractive options when attempting to explain foreign policy: either the indeterminate and highly abstract assumptions of structural realism or the context-specific *ad hoc* analyses of neoclassical and postclassical realism." This observation effectively returns to the authoritative expositions from Vasquez (1983, 1998), which identified many logical inconsistencies and contradictions in realism even as it existed over two decades ago. With further expansion in the absence of a graphic means toward communication, issues with the scientific status of the realist research enterprise have not diminished and arguably stand as more challenging than ever. All of that remains true in spite of significant accomplishments from individual realist theories, notably in working on empirical problems related to international conflict.

Qualifications should be offered before moving forward with the tasks at hand. One is that the following exercises in systematic synthesis and bricolagic bridging are intended as a point of departure for continuing work of the same nature. The goal is to set analysis in motion rather than claim in any way to have completed it. A similar qualifying observation concerns pursuit of a series of dialogues as opposed to a grand synthesis for realism. The cautionary tale from Barkin and Sjoberg (2019), recounted in Chapter 4, argues against the quest for a single version of realism. So, too, does the metatheory of scientific progress, within which analytic eclecticism and its search for effective middle-range theory are prominent features. The objective is to improve realist theories through graphic-led exchanges, as opposed to carrying out a process in which one version simply absorbs the others. This conclusion against pursuit of a full synthesis also is in line with Gödel's theorem, referenced earlier in this volume with regard to the likely continuing incompleteness of all explanations in any science.

This chapter unfolds in five further sections. The 14 realist theories of war from Chapters 11–18 are profiled in the second section. This sets the stage for further engagement of these theories with each other and beyond. The third section looks at the realist theories with multiple variants to identify possibilities for combination and begin to address criticism encountered in preceding chapters. After the process of combination, the fourth section engages the eight remaining realist theories with each other through systematic synthesis. The fifth section carries out bricolagic bridging that incorporates a major study of conflict processes from beyond the boundaries of realism. The sixth and final section reflects upon what has been accomplished through this process of contact for realist theories with each other and ideas from outside of the research enterprise.

Profiling Realist Theories of War

Table 19.1 profiles the 14 realist theories about the causes of war. The table shows (i) varieties of realism and associated theories; (ii) assumptions beyond anarchy, state-centrism, rationality, and power seeking; (iii) priorities for improvement; and (iv) the number of variables, contingencies (i.e., inclusion of divergent, convergent, and nodal variables), synergies, and loops. Each of the preceding features is considered in turn.

From a review of additional assumptions in the second column of Table 19.1, several significant properties become visible when viewed in terms of the material versus ideational dichotomy. Multiple system-oriented theories—power cycle, hegemonic stability, offensive realism, and predation—rely on the Realist Law of Uneven Growth to account for emergence of a capability distribution. A few other axioms among those listed in the table are material as well. Structural realism includes a threshold effect for movement from two great powers to three or more. Both variants from balance of threat assume that geographic proximity, distance, and offensive capability and advantages impact policy choices under threat. Dynamic differentials theory asserts that the offense-defense balance and technological costs of war are neutral. Finally, offensive realism entails belief in the stopping power of water.

Additional assumptions of an ideational nature also appear for multiple realist theories. Each version of balance-of-threat theory assumes that perceptions of danger affect policy choice, while the revolution variant asserts that a state going through such an upheaval creates uncertainty in its region. All of the balance-of-interests theories assume that the condition of state and society, in terms of degree of cohesion and motivation, impact foreign policy. Defensive realist theories believe that perceptions of geostrategic setting—in terms of first-mover advantage, impending shifts in relative power, and offensive versus defensive dominance—affect foreign policy. For dynamic differentials, it is assumed that security is a goal for states and uncertainty exists about capabilities and intentions.

Three observations follow on from the preceding summary of additional assumptions. The first point is that the theories do not incorporate a large number of axioms beyond anarchy, state-centrism, rationality, and power seeking. The maximum added for any theory in the table is four assumptions. Second, a few additional axioms are adopted by more than one theory. Each of the preceding observations points toward economy of explanation and thus bodes well from the standpoint of the Performance Ratio. A third point is that a majority among the assumptions added are ideational rather than material in

Table 19.1 Profiling Realist Theories

Varieties of Realism and Associated Theories	Additional Assumptions	Priorities for Improvement	Number of Variables, Contingencies, Synergies and Loops
Power cycle	The Realist Law of Uneven Growth means that states will not remain equal in capabilities.	Elaborate the micro level—foreign policy decision-making; domestic politics; and management of capabilities. Reassess measurement of capabilities.	13, 3, 0
Structural realism	There is a threshold effect from two great powers to three or more because coalitions become possible.	Focus on system-level change. Theorize state level beyond self-help. Address balancing versus other forms of behavior.	13, 3, 1
Structural realism: hegemonic stability	Realist Law of Uneven Growth means that states will not remain equal in capabilities.	Elaborate the micro level to include foreign policy. Identify the threshold for a significant redistribution of capabilities.	9, 2, 0
Balance of threat	Geographic proximity, distance, and offensive capability and advantages impact policy choices under threat. Perceptions of threat affect policy choices.	Explain how the categories of threat—power, proximity, and offensive capabilities—combine to produce escalation versus another outcome. Address lack of variation among states in relation to range of actions observed. Identify the threshold for a weak versus strong state.	13, 9, 2
Balance of threat: revolution	Geographic proximity, distance, and offensive capability and advantages impact policy choices under threat. Perceptions of threat affect policy choices. A state that experiences revolution creates uncertainty in its region.	Explain how the categories of threat—power, proximity, and offensive capabilities—combine to produce escalation versus another outcome. Address lack of variation among states in relation to range of actions observed. Identify the threshold for a weak versus strong state. Explain anomalous nonwar outcomes. Elaborate to include one or more connections from the system to the state level.	13, 6, 0

Balance of interests: additive model	The condition of state and society, in terms of degree of cohesion and motivation, impact foreign policy.	Address the high degree of complexity in enumerating the respective models.	11, 3, 0
Balance of interests: extremely incoherent state model	The condition of state and society, in terms of degree of cohesion and motivation, impact foreign policy.	Address the high degree of complexity in enumerating the respective models.	12, 2, 1
Balance of interests: polarized democratic state model	The condition of state and society, in terms of degree of cohesion and motivation, impact foreign policy.	Address the high degree of complexity in enumerating the respective models.	11, 4, 0
Defensive realism: stability	Perceptions of geostrategic setting, through first-mover advantage, affect foreign policy.	Address the complexity across the three models. Move beyond just one micro variable and no micro-micro connection. Address the fact that one pathway contains more than three variables. Identify threshold for first-mover advantage.	9, 3, 0
Defensive realism: windows	Perceptions of geostrategic setting, through impending shifts in relative power, affect foreign policy.	Address the complexity across the three models. Address the lack of detail about the process of restoring equilibrium. Move beyond a single pathway with no contingencies.	10, 0, 0
Defensive realism: offense-defense	Perceptions of geostrategic setting, through offensive versus defensive dominance, affect foreign policy.	Identify threshold for impending shifts in relative power. Address the complexity across the three models. Move beyond the single pathway with no contingencies. Identify threshold for offense dominance.	12, 0, 0

(*continued*)

Table 19.1 Continued

Dynamic differentials	Security is a goal for states.	There is no micro–micro connection.	13, 5, 1
	Uncertainty exists about capabilities and intentions.	Add analysis of leadership in crisis conditions.	
	The offense-defense balance is neutral.	Reassess the meaning of capabilities.	
	The technological costs of war are neutral.		
Offensive realism	The stopping power of water limits great power conquest to its regional setting.	Develop criteria for potential falsification.	19, 8, 3
		Take into account the offense-defense balance.	
	The Realist Law of Uneven Growth means that states will not remain equal in capabilities.	Reassess the meaning of capabilities.	
		Elaborate on the micro level vis-a-vis the possible role of fear and miscalculation among leaders.	
Predation	The Realist Law of Uneven Growth means that states will not remain equal in capabilities.	Develop a priori measurements for high versus low strategic value, military posture, and intensity of action.	11, 2, 0

nature. From a scientific realist outlook, this is a pattern to be expected. Theories based on power politics are expanding to include unobservables that either will become more credible or be discarded as research accumulates.

What, then, are the priorities for improvement? Several patterns are visible for the entries in the third column of Table 19.1. Analysis will begin with priorities identified for multiple theories and also move consecutively in an approximate way through the contents of the table.

For system-oriented theories—power cycle, structural realism, hegemonic stability, defensive realism, dynamic differentials, and offensive realism—more needs to be said about micro-level connections. For example, in structural realism, what aspects of the state might impact the specifics of self-help? Like other system-level theories, this one so far does not provide an explanation for the fact that a great deal of variety is observed in the conduct of states. From the standpoint of SIR, this type of gap reflects a more general tendency in the field toward use of a ceteris paribus clause rather than more properly completing the story of cause and effect.

Thresholds remain unidentified for multiple key variables from realist theories. These variables are (a) significant redistribution of capabilities for hegemonic stability and the windows variant of defensive realism (b) the offense-defense balance for the offense-defense version of defensive realism, along with offensive realism; (c) strong versus weak states for both versions of balance of threat; (d) first-mover advantage for the stability variation of defensive realism; and (e) high versus low strategic value, military posture, and intensity of action for predation. Without a priori designation, these variables do not provide a basis for effective testing of their respective theories. It becomes possible for an underperforming theory to hide behind an after-the-fact assessment (Vasquez 1983, 1998). For example, if a crisis does not escalate to war, the windows variant of defensive realism could claim that redistribution of capabilities had fallen short of a *significant* level. Other examples would be just as easy to imagine.

Observed versus theorized actions also deserve further attention. Table 19.1 makes that assertion about respective theories—(1) balancing versus other forms of behavior for structural realism and (2) lack of variation among states for both variants of balance of threat.

One issue of measurement comes up for multiple theories, namely, with regard to the meaning of capabilities. Power cycle, dynamic differentials, and offensive realism emerge as priorities in that context. Each offers a different sense of what is meant by capabilities, and an exchange of ideas among these theories and beyond could lead toward a greater consensus on this foundation for key variables throughout realism.

Issues of high complexity, raised in Table 19.1, also should be addressed. Note that three versions exist for both balance of interests and defensive realism. As revealed through the graphics from Chapters 14 and 15, some versions overlap significantly with each other. Various critiques of respective variants in defensive realism help to set an agenda for their combination with each other. Two of three variations for defensive realism—windows and offense-defense—lack any contingent variable. For the stability variant of defensive realism, no pathway contains more than three variables, while the windows version lacks detail about restoring the process of equilibrium.

Several points arise either for a specific theory or within one of the eight types. A greater ability to account for system-level change would be valuable for structural realism. In both variations of balance of threat, it would be helpful to explain how the categories of danger—power, proximity, and offensive capabilities—combine to produce escalation versus other outcomes. For the revolution variant within balance of threat, it would be salutary to account for anomalous nonwar outcomes and elaborate the theory to make one or more connections from the macro level down to the micro level. Offensive realism would be enhanced by identification of criteria that create potential for falsification. Finally, predation, as noted in Table 19.1, faces challenges vis-à-vis potential falsification. Thresholds must be identified for the theory's key components in order to facilitate meaningful testing. For a great power, what is the point of demarcation for low versus high strategic value, weak or strong military posture, and high- versus low-intensity action? Each of the preceding dichotomies is in need of operationalization that permits a priori specification.

Attention turns to the fourth column of Table 19.1, which contains data about variables from respective theories. The range for sheer number of variables is from (i) nine in hegemonic stability and the stability variant of defensive realism to (ii) 19 for offensive realism. The mode is 13 and the mean is just over 11 variables. Recall that defensive realism and balance of interests had been criticized for a high degree of intricacy. None of the theories within either of these types includes more than 12 variables, so concerns about complexity in each instance can and will be addressed through combining versions within each of these theories.

What about contingency within a theory? This trait refers to the total number of divergent, convergent, and nodal variables. The range in Table 19.1 is from zero, in windows and the offense-defense variation of defensive realism, up to nine for balance of threat. The mode is two/three and the mean about midway between three and four. Contingency, perhaps, is the trait for which realist theories exhibit the least uniformity.

Synergies and loops also appear among the theories, although not frequently. Nine theories have neither of these features, so zero is the mode. Five of the theories—structural realism, balance of threat, the extremely incoherent state model for balance of interests, dynamic differentials, and offensive realism—have either a loop or at least one pair of synergistic variables. Only balance of threat and offensive realism include even two such connections.

With SIR in its infancy, a large number of diagrams is not yet available for comparison with those summarized here. Expansion of the VIRP archive to include thousands of figures will take care of that challenge and permit a better sense of context for realist expositions in the near future. It already can be said after the initial effort at profiling, however, that realist theories are neither simplistic nor complicated on an individual basis, at least in terms of additional axioms and number of variables. Most of these theories about war include contingencies. In at least some instances, realist explanations also offer a degree of specificity that includes loops and synergies for respective variables.

Theories in Combination and Competition

Theories from within varieties of realism will be assessed in turn, notably with economy of explanation in mind. This stage of comparison is relevant for structural realism, balance of threat, balance of interests, and defensive realism, each of which features multiple variations. If it becomes possible to combine versions with each other, this streamlining would be desirable from the standpoint of the Performance Ratio. It also is worthwhile to identify zones of competition between and among the respective theories.

With regard to the process that follows, a few words are appropriate about how it looks from the standpoint of principles about method. In line with the deductive and rationalist exposition from Vasquez (1983, 1998), realist theories will be compared to each other to identify possibilities for combination and competition. On the one hand, such an approach might seem to imply that a turn toward formal modeling would be best suited to identifying contradictions and omissions for realist theories about war. On the other hand, an inductive and sociological outlook would point toward a more accessible approach than state-of-the-art formal theory, which relies upon a highly mathematical style of communication. Thus a few simple expressions will appear below—in a technical sense, nothing beyond comparing rates of change and inequalities with each other—to assist in a visual manner with sorting out how and when respective theories apply. Along the way, it will be opportune to respond to some of the priorities identified in Table 19.1.

Consider structural realism and hegemonic stability in juxtaposition with each other. The analysis that follows will identify conditions under which the theories are complementary or competitive.

Refer to the capabilities of the leader and challenger, the two leading states in the system, as L and C. Let the capabilities in the system sum to 1, with $0 < C < L < 1$. The preceding set of inequalities means that no state ever is without at least some capability (i.e., all are greater than zero) or in control of all resources (i.e., all are less than one). For structural realism, the focal point is on stability as a function of bipolarity. The degree of bipolarity in the system is as follows:

$$L+C \quad \text{where } L+C<1 \qquad (19.1)$$

The closer this quantity gets to its theoretical maximum of 1, the more capabilities are concentrated in the two rivals in the stratosphere of the system. If virtually all resources are held by those two states, according to the logic of neorealism, the system should be at its simplest and easiest to manage.

What is expected to happen, however, as changes occur in the capability shares for L and C? Ordinal rationality suggests a focus on the rate of change in two plausible forms. One is velocity and the other is acceleration—familiar terms about motion.[1] Let "Δ" represent change, "t" be time, with "V_{L+C}" and "A_{L+C}" as velocity and acceleration, respectively, for the quantity "L + C":[2]

$$V_{L+C} = \frac{\Delta(L + C)}{\Delta t} \qquad (19.2)$$

$$A_{L+C} = \frac{\Delta V_{L+C}}{\Delta t} \qquad (19.3)$$

When velocity is greater than or equal to zero, this means that the combined capabilities of the two top states are increasing or stable. Thus bipolarity is sustained or even strengthening because $V_{L+C} \geq 0$. The direction of acceleration does not matter under this condition because the overall direction is upward for the share of capabilities possessed by the two leading states.

What if velocity is less than zero? If $V_{L+C} < 0$, then $A_{L+C} < 0$ is essential to prevent a significant shift away from bipolarity. If the share of capabilities for the two rivals at the top is declining, but in a way that is slowing down, this does not threaten the bipolar nature of the system. If, however, $A_{L+C} \geq 0$—meaning that the margin is diminishing at a faster pace—this could produce ambiguity in system structure, potentially even followed by a shift to multipolarity.

Simple metrics can be developed for hegemonic stability as well, using the same notation as above. The key variable, however, now is L − C, which is the margin of superiority for the leading state over the challenger. Expression 19.4 conveys this inequality:

$$L-C \quad \text{where } L-C > 0 \qquad (19.4)$$

---

[1] Higher-order metrics, such as change in the rate of acceleration, could be calculated. These items, however, are deemed irrelevant under the assumption of ordinal rationality.
[2] The expressions that follow could be presented more efficiently through calculus, but this would increase cognitive burdens and make the argument less accessible to a general audience.

Velocity and acceleration are written analogous to as above:

$$V_{L-C} = \frac{\Delta(L-C)}{\Delta t} \tag{19.5}$$

$$A_{L-C} = \frac{\Delta V_{L-C}}{\Delta t} \tag{19.6}$$

For hegemonic stability, it is desirable that $V_{L-C} \geq 0$. This means that the margin in capabilities for the leader over the challenger is increasing or stable. If that condition holds, then the value of A_{L-C} does not matter; it either is speeding up or slowing down the rate at which the leader is gaining ground over the challenger. If, however, $V_{L-C} < 0$, then $A_{L-C} < 0$ is essential. It is not inherently destabilizing for the challenger to gain ground at a rate that is diminishing. However, either a steady or accelerating pace for relative capabilities in favor of the challenger would point toward disequilibrium. Note that $A_{L-C} = 0$ also is problematic because the leader is losing ground to the challenger at a constant rate.

With all scenarios in place, it is possible to identify when structural realism and hegemonic stability are independent, reinforcing, or competing in their expectations. Among the possible combinations for velocity and acceleration in terms of positive, negative, or zero values regarding $L + C$ and $L - C$, the following conditions produce competition versus commonality:

$$V_{L-C} > 0 \text{ and } A_{L-C} \geq 0 \tag{19.7}$$

$$V_{L-C} < 0 \text{ and } A_{L-C} = 0 \tag{19.8}$$

$$V_{L-C} < 0 \text{ and } A_{L-C} > 0 \tag{19.9}$$

$$V_{L-C} < 0 \text{ and } A_{L-C} < 0 \tag{19.10}$$

For expression 19.7, the conditions are favorable for hegemonic stability and dangerous from the standpoint of structural realism. The leader is widening its edge over the challenger, with no sign of slowing down. This bodes well for hegemonic leadership but not persistence of bipolarity if the challenger falls too far behind the leader. The situation reverses in expression 19.8, where the challenger is gaining steadily—a less hegemonic but more bipolar system. Expression 19.9, in which the leader is losing ground to the challenger at an increasing rate, is problematic for both hegemonic stability and structural realism. The leader may not only end up behind the challenger, but could fall out of competition altogether if the trend lasts long enough. Finally, expression 19.10 represents a mildly destabilizing scenario for hegemonic stability; the leader is losing ground to the challenger at a diminishing pace. For structural realism, this points in the direction of greater stability because the challenger and leader are becoming more evenly matched in a gradual way.

Structural realism and hegemonic stability have zones of agreement but also competition, as designated through expressions 19.7 through 19.10. For this reason, each theory will be preserved for development in the ensuing stages of comparison.

One priority for structural realism—an account of system-level change called for in Table 19.1—can begin to be met through a focus on war versus other means of transformation. Consider in this context the dynamics of "L− C" and "L + C" in combination. System-level change can be generated through sufficient movement, upward and downward, respectively, for those expressions. As with other realist theories, the basic question is "How much is enough"? What is meant by a significant decline, in relative terms, for the leading state? At what threshold does the combined power of the two rivals at the top of the international system drop below the level required for bipolarity and shift into either multipolarity or unipolarity? Answers from realism to these questions, at least so far, have taken an inductive and sociological form. For example, Cold War bipolarity shifted into unipolarity, by general agreement, with the decline and fall of the USSR. Scientific advancement, however, requires a turn toward a rationalist and deductive approach in order to meet conditions for potential refutation. Identification of threshold effects is a recurring priority for realist theories in pursuit of testability. This is just one of many instances in which the critique from Vasquez (1983, 1998) about a lack of falsifiability for realism comes into play.

Balance of threat entails two theories. The general balance-of-threat theory is complemented by a version that focuses specifically on revolution as a creator of uncertainty in a regional system. These theories do not compete with each other, but instead can be applied under different scope conditions. The obvious difference is that the revolution variant pertains to situations that include such an event, while the general model does not take into account the intensifying effects from a sudden regime change on perception of threat within a region. These theories therefore are not suitable for a merger with each other.

Balance of threat, whether in its general or specific form, must deal with the problem of testability. Either variant can elude refutation by asserting that one or more of the elements of an external threat—overall power, proximity, or offensive capability—is not at a level essential to produce an anticipated effect. For example, if a war does not occur, the excuse can be made that it is because one or more of the preceding factors had not reached a sufficient degree of intensity.

Two methods, one qualitative and the other quantitative, can be accessed to enhance future testing for balance-of-threat theory. Each is introduced in turn.

With regard to qualitative methods, consider the innovative approach from Harvey (1999), which evaluated deterrence theory using Boolean logic and comparative analysis. This study enumerated conditions that had been put forward for successful deterrence and then implemented a Boolean approach, which focuses on the degree to which members of a set of factors associated with an outcome are present or absent. These steps enabled more effective assessment of a standard model of deterrence based on rational choice. As more conditions are in place, the likelihood of successful deterrence increases, as would be anticipated on the basis of instrumental rationality (Harvey 1999). The same approach could be applied profitably to factors that combine to sum up an external menace in balance-of-threat theory. In other words, war should become more likely when overall power, high proximity, and offensive capability all are present.

This type of model could be elaborated further via quantification. For example, interaction terms could be introduced. What if, to cite one possibility, there is a main effect from high proximity, but also an interaction when that factor is combined with overall capability? In other words, a multiplicative, as well as additive, specification could be put forward for balance-of-threat theory. Results from testing a more extensive set of connections would have the potential to stimulate new ideas about sources and management of threats.

What about balance of interests? This realist theory includes three variants—additive, extremely incoherent states, and polarized democratic. An opportunity for combination exists with regard to the additive and extremely incoherent states models, which thereby produces a more general version. With a focus on one type of regime, the polarized domestic model is specialized and continues on its own. In that sense it resembles the revolution variant from balance-of-threat theory as described earlier. Taken together, the additive and extremely incoherent states models from Schweller (2006) turn out to be consistent with a curvilinear relationship for the likelihood of a defender balancing in connection with its degree of coherence. Combination, in other words, is a viable option.

Once again, some relatively simple notation and expressions will provide a visual aid to analysis of balance-of-interests theories in contact with each other. Let "S" represent internal strife, "E" effective balancing, and "H" a threshold at which a state reaches a condition of incoherence. All of these variables range in value from 0 to 1. Consider the following expressions in the context of balance-of-interests theory:

$$V_E = \frac{\Delta E}{\Delta S} \tag{19.11}$$

$$A_E = \frac{\Delta V_E}{\Delta S} \qquad (19.12)$$

Multiple combinations for velocity and acceleration of balancing as a function of internal strife are possible. The threshold effects are as follows:

$$V_E > 0 \text{ and } A_E < 0 \text{ when } 0 \leq S \leq H \leq 1 \qquad (19.13)$$

$$V_E < 0 \text{ and } A_E > 0 \text{ when } 0 \leq H \leq S \leq 1 \qquad (19.14)$$

In other words, balancing becomes more likely up to the designated threshold of H; beyond that point, its probability declines. This relationship takes an inverted "U" shape. Up to the threshold, the familiar logic of Coser (1956) with regard to conflict and cohesion takes hold. When faced with internal strife, leaders can be anticipated to consider a diversionary approach—rallying the public against an outside enemy up to a point of viability. However, once a certain level of incoherence has been reached, such a response no longer is feasible and becomes less likely as strife ensues.

What, then, to say about "H"? This is where inductive research, following on from examples elsewhere in the social sciences, can play a valuable role for the combined version of balance of interests. Take, for example, ongoing debate over the "Kuznets Curve," which puts forward the idea that an inverted "U" relationship exists for income and environmental damage (Yandle, Vijayaraghavan, and Bhattarai 2002). Up to a certain point, further increases in income are harmful to the environment, with positive effects beyond that threshold. A parallel program of research could be carried out for the threshold of "H" in the context of viability for a policy of diversionary conflict. Moreover, such work is essential in order to move toward a testable version of balance-of-interests theory. Otherwise, the problem identified in an earlier chapter about the unscientific character of phlogiston theory comes back into play. Without an a priori identification of the threshold for incoherence, all results can be accepted as consistent with the theory.

Figure 19.1 displays the combined version for balance of interests. All of its variables are familiar from prior analysis, so sub-figures are not provided. The new variant contains 14 variables—still around the average among realist theories of war. Seven points of contingency exist: two divergent, two convergent, and three nodal variables. The diagram also contains one loop.

Note that the bifurcation with regard to being above or below the threshold of "H" with regard to incoherence appears relatively late in the diagram—toward the end of micro-level processes. An alternative would have been to depict that fork in the road prior to the set of contingent variables that includes "social fragmentation of defender," "government or regime vulnerability of defender," and "elite fragmentation of defender." Then one route, toward incoherence above the identified threshold of H, would depict those three variables as a *sequence*, as in the original model for extremely incoherent states. The alternative pathway would show these three variables as reached separately and then converging with each other, as in the additive model. This is just one example of how, through a diagrammatic exposition, debate could be stimulated that might not occur otherwise and therefore leave ambiguity in place.

Figure 19.1, in sum, offers a more complete version of cause and effect—formal, material, final, and efficient conditions—than either model from balance of interests on its own. Throughout the remainder of the volume, this rendition for balance of interests will be referred to in place of the two versions that have been combined to create it.

Defensive realism exists in three variants—stability, windows, and offense-defense. Given the logical consistency of these versions with each other, along with the fact that all are general in purported application, combination should be pursued. The formal (or background) condition for each variant, respectively, is perceived first-mover advantage, anticipated impending shifts in power, and offense dominance. There is no contradiction posed in bringing these factors together in a single model. Two of the three versions outline a single pathway to interstate war. Only the stability variant possesses multiple routes to that same outcome.

Figure 19.2 displays a defensive realist synthesis. The diagram contains 20 variables. There are four convergent variables and one nodal variable. Several decisions have been made along the way in this initial attempt to combine the three theories with each other. Each is presented in turn.

First, as in the stability rather than windows variant of defensive realism, "concealed grievances, capabilities, plans and misperceptions" appears near the outset. The connection from the offense-defense variant is reflected in "WINDOWS AND FAITS ACCOMPLIS ARE MORE COMMON AND MORE DANGEROUS" → "concealed grievances, capabilities, plans and misperceptions."

Second, because "OFFENSE DOMINANCE" appears at the outset of the offense-defense variant, it is not added later on. This had been the case in the stability version; that is, OFFENSIVE ADVANTAGE appeared further along in the network of variables.

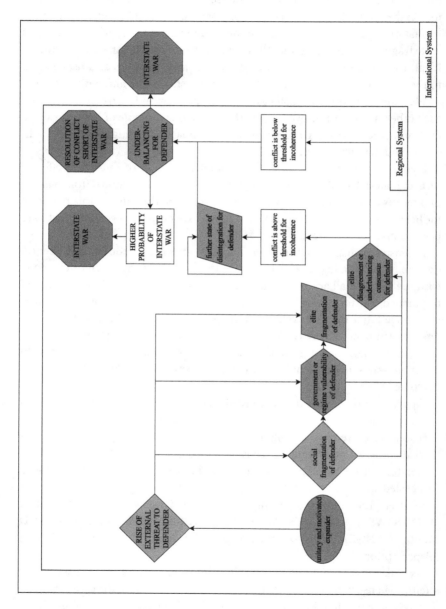

Figure 19.1 Combined Version for Balance of Interests

Third, consider the position of "FIRST MOVER ADVANTAGE"—for the stability variant, a formal (or background) condition. This variable appears in the combined model, of course, but not at the point where it had been in the offense-defense rendition.

Fourth, consider the position of "RECIPROCAL FEAR" in the diagram. In the stability variant, it connects with "PREEMPTIVE STRIKE," while in the combined version it feeds into "WINDOWS AND FAITS ACCOMPLIS ARE MORE COMMON AND MORE DANGEROUS" to achieve simplification.

Fifth, note the placement of "HASTENED OR TRUNCATED DIPLOMACY." This is the same as what the windows version depicts, rather than as a single point between the initial and terminal variables with the stability rendition.

Sixth, and finally, note that "PROCESS OF RESTORING EQUILIBRIUM" leads directly to war in the windows version. It now feeds into a more detailed sequence from "STATES RESPOND TO OTHERS' BLUNDERS FASTER AND MORE BELLIGERENTLY."

Consider Figure 19.2 in the context of priorities for respective versions of defensive realism from Table 19.1. Starting with the stability variant, note that four micro variables now are included, although still no micro-micro connection exists. While stability had no pathway that required three variables to reach the termination point of interstate war, the combined version offers a more complete and intuitively plausible sense of escalation to war. The windows version has been criticized for a lack of detail about the process of restoring equilibrium, but the placement of that variable in the combined version addresses that point to at least some degree. While both windows and offense-defense depicted a single pathway, the new diagram includes five contingent variables.

With its 20 variables, the combined version for defensive realism includes one more than the previous maximum encountered among theories of war in Chapters 11–18. Is this combined theory too complicated for its own good? Given the ability to shift from three versions of defensive realism to just one, intuition says that the answer is likely to be no. A more informed response to the preceding query would have to await accumulation of research findings and hypothesis generation set in motion by the new combined version of defensive realism. This would permit estimation of the Performance Ratio through addition of data for its numerator as well as its denominator.

With the process of combination completed, the list of realist theories is reduced to 10: power cycle; structural realism and hegemonic stability; balance of threat and its revolution variant; balance of interests in a synthesis of the additive and extremely incoherent states models, along with its polarized democratic state model; a defensive realist synthesis; dynamic differentials; and predation. The revolution variant of balance of threat, along with the polarized democratic state model from balance of interests, is deemed as specialized and therefore will

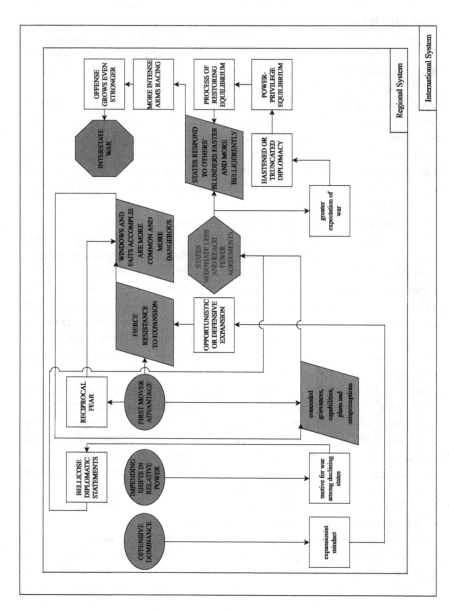

Figure 19.2 A Defensive Realist Synthesis

not be included in the exercises that follow. Each theory, of course, can continue to guide research within those more restricted boundaries. Thus eight realist theories will appear in the analysis from this point onward.

Engaging Realist Theories with Each Other

Before going ahead with systematic synthesis, a few points of qualification are noted. What follows should be regarded as in line with the logic of discovery. Ideas are put forward to improve respective theories, and undoubtedly any number of alternatives could have been pursued instead. No empirical testing will occur; the logic of confirmation therefore is not involved in a direct sense. However, the ensuing exercises are intended to enhance the rigor and testability of respective theories, offering favorable implications in regard to the logic of confirmation. Note also that responses to some points raised in Table 19.1 already have occurred in the preceding section. Others will take place during bricolagic bridging later on in this chapter.

Systematic synthesis can take various forms in engaging studies from a given domain with each other.[3] Consider, for example, combination of cause and effect from 14 statistical studies about crisis escalation to war as carried out in James (2019a). This instance of systematic synthesis combined hypotheses that found support from the above-noted investigations into a single systemist graphic representation. The current application of systematic synthesis, by contrast, focuses on a set of studies that are primarily theoretical and whose testing, when it does occur, tends to be qualitative in nature. The objective of the following exercise is to improve a given theory by inserting ideas from one or more of its peers. Further diagrammatic expositions could ensue as variables from one theory are placed within the account of cause and effect for another. Thus what follows is a prediagrammatic exploration of possibilities to pursue through further research.

Among realist theories about war, it is possible to pursue various types of contact—bilateral and higher order. This activity is essential to any serious response to the compelling critiques from Vasquez (1983, 1998) with regard to contradictions within the corpus of realism. Given the presence of eight theories, at this point it is impossible to do more than begin that process. Thus what

---

[3] Systematic synthesis is intended for application in a localized way, that is, the graphic representation of a sector within a given subject area. This should not be equated with the pursuit of synthesis at the level of the discipline, which is deemed to be a vain pursuit. For a compelling argument along those lines, see Barkin and Sjoberg (2019),

follows will concentrate on direct points of engagement, with a few higher-order contacts in response to priorities identified for three or more theories in Table 19.1.

Even this primarily bilateral approach, allowing for insights operating in both directions for any given pair of theories, produces 112 possibilities (i.e., 8 × 7 × 2). While it also would be valuable to pursue higher-order combinations systematically—three or more at a time—it is beyond the scope of the present investigation to consider anything beyond bilateral engagements for the theories. Thus what follows is an early stage of a process that, if followed consistently, should enhance the rigor of realism as an outlook on the causes of war.

Multiple opportunities can be identified to elaborate power cycle theory in response to priorities from Table 19.1. Each is pursued, in turn, through contact with other realist theories about war.

Interlocking concerns for power cycle theory focus on foreign policy decision-making, domestic politics, and management of capabilities. Attention in this context turns toward existing variables from the micro level of the great power subset as depicted in Figure 11.1 for power cycle theory: (a) explosion of political uncertainty due to nonlinear change and (b) adjustment problems from power-role surplus or deficit. Several ideas from other realist theories can be accessed and combined to expand upon these relatively terse treatments from power cycle theory of coping at the micro level.

Consider the following variables from Figure 19.1, which depicts the synthesis for balance-of-interests theory: (a) social fragmentation of defender, (b) government or regime vulnerability of defender, and (c) elite fragmentation of defender. These variables bring domestic politics into the account of decision-making. Recall the threshold value, H, for internal strife from that model. Below H, balancing is more likely to occur, whereas above that level the state is expected to be impaired in its response to threat. The playing out of suddenly increasing political uncertainty, along with role-related adjustment problems, could be impacted by the level of cohesion in relation to the above-noted threshold. Additional propositions, which add specificity to power cycle theory on the subject of foreign policy choices, can be anticipated as a result of adding variables from balance of interests. For example, a state near a critical point might be more likely to initiate war if it is coherent (i.e., below H) and be the target of an attack if it is incoherent (i.e., above H).

Important also is the tactical situation faced by decision-makers—another opportunity for elaboration of power cycle theory. Of interest here are first-mover advantage and offensive dominance, respectively, from the defensive realist synthesis in Figure 19.2. These variables expand what power cycle theory can say about management of capabilities. Each of these conditions, furthermore, creates more of a "hair trigger" situation for leaders in an international system already challenged by proximity to one or more critical points among them.

Another consideration for the treatment from power cycle theory of decision-making at the brink of war focuses on how one or more peers among the great powers might be viewed in terms of strategic value and military posture, which can be borrowed from predation theory. Along those lines, two combinations of the preceding variables can provide insights for power cycle theory. The following conjunctions appear respectively in Figure 18.1: a rising state perceives a declining state as (i) either high in strategic value or strong in military posture, which produces the choice of a strengthening, weakening, or bolstering strategy; or (ii) low strategic value and weak in military posture, which leads to the choice of a relegation strategy. Scenarios (i) and (ii) introduce policy-related nuances for expected great power reactions to states at either the maximum point and heading downward or the second inflection point on the power cycle, at which the rate of decline begins to slow down. With a focus on strategic value and military posture for a state in proximity to the preceding critical points, it becomes possible to hypothesize about specifics with regard to policy choices. Will peers pursue strengthening, bolstering, weakening, or relegation as described in predation theory? An answer to that multifaceted question must await further research, but even the ability to pose that query is valuable to power cycle theory in going forward with a development of its micro-level account.

Attention turns to priorities identified in Table 19.1 for structural realism. Critiques of structural realism have focused on (a) a lack of theorizing about the state level beyond citing the concept of self-help and (b) the presence of balancing versus other forms of behavior. These points can be addressed together. The ideas that follow also serve as a response to the call for hegemonic stability theory to elaborate its micro level.

Consider ideas available from balance-of-threat theory, notably concerning the characteristics of a menacing state. Figure 13.1 for balance of threat includes (a) aggregate power of external threat, (b) proximity of external threat, and (c) offensive capabilities of external threat. These traits could be used to account for whether balancing, buck-passing, or other forms of behavior occur. Combinations of conditions (a) through (c) would be assessed in terms of variation in the likelihood of balancing in particular. On the basis of simple presence or absence for the preceding traits of the external threat, eight profiles exist, with each frequency noted in parentheses: all (1), two (3), one (3), or none (1) in place. It is not difficult to imagine hypotheses beyond intuitively plausible main effects. Put differently, a state acting in line with ordinal rationality would not have to pursue self-help strictly through balancing. Other options could be preferred on tactical grounds as assessed through combinations of conditions (a) through (c).

Potentially valuable to structural realism and hegemonic stability for identifying specifics about policy are several variables from the combined version of balance-of-interests theory in Figure 19.1: (i) social fragmentation of defender, (ii) government or regime vulnerability of defender, and (iii) elite fragmentation of defender. Balancing should be more likely below the threshold of H, at which incoherence is reached. Above H, a range of other policy options would seem more likely to be selected, with increasing likelihood of incoherence.

Still further engagements with other realist theories can assist with elaboration of structural realism and hegemonic stability. Factors from the defensive realist synthesis and power cycle theory also can play a role in sorting out what specific foreign policy actions should be expected from states that pursue self-help: (1) first-mover advantage, (2) offense dominance, and (3) proximity to critical points. The most dangerous combination is the presence of (1) through (3) together—less so with one or more of the three conditions missing. When these macro-level variables are brought into the story, in tandem with preceding micro-level variables located in balance-of-threat and balance-of-interests theories, pathways can multiply quickly. Process-tracing, guided by systemist figures, would be ideal for pursuing such possibilities with regard to structural realism and hegemonic stability.

What is the threshold for a *significant* redistribution of capabilities? Table 19.1 identifies this as a question to which hegemonic stability and the defensive realist synthesis must reply. Answers are available from two other realist theories about war. For power cycle theory, critical points constitute significant shifts in capabilities among the great powers. When relative capabilities for one or more great powers change in either velocity or acceleration (or both)—the definition of a critical point—this is considered noteworthy in creating the potential for destabilization and war. Consider also the decision rules from predation theory about significant change (Shifrinson 2019a)—a 5% drop in relative capabilities for a great power in one decade serves as the threshold. These and other metrics are worthy of attention for realist theories that refer to change but without inherent falsifiability.

Lack of variation among states is identified in Table 19.1 as an issue for balance-of-threat theory. In particular, how are weak and strong states to be distinguished from each other? It is not acceptable to answer this question after the fact by observing policies selected—say, balancing versus appeasement in some form—and then labeling states at that point. A more appealing option is to access the indicators for the condition of a state from the synthesis for balance-of-interests theory that appear in Figure 19.1: (a) social fragmentation, (b) government or regime vulnerability, and (c) elite fragmentation. While specific metrics are beyond the scope of the present exposition, an index of state strength based on material capabilities could be supplemented with indicators such as (a) through (c). A breakpoint for strong versus weak states, once identified a priori, would facilitate testing.

Defensive realism, as noted in Table 19.1, does not incorporate any purely micro-level connections. One possibility for elaboration focuses on key internal conditions for a state as summarized in balance-of-interests theory: (a) social fragmentation, (b) government or regime vulnerability, and (c) elite fragmentation. The profile of a state, along the preceding lines, could impact variables such as (i) concealed grievances, capabilities, plans, and misperceptions; (ii) the motive for war among declining states; and (iii) an expansionist mindset. Whether a state resides above or below the threshold for coherence, H, will impact its disposition. For example, an incoherent state would seem more likely to suffer from the ill effects of secrecy regarding major issues, while at the same time possessing a greater likelihood of undesired exposure for plans and capabilities. Leaders of an incoherent state, moreover, would be more likely to experience misperception—overwhelmed by the volume of incoming information under already chaotic conditions at home.

Like defensive realism, dynamic differentials theory does not include any micro-micro connection. The preceding ideas would apply equally well here and later on for offensive realism.

For offensive realism, potential for refutation is an essential characteristic to obtain—a basic priority enumerated in Table 19.1. This matter can begin to be addressed through greater specificity about the meaning of balanced versus unbalanced multipolarity in the offensive realist world. To return to the notation applied earlier in this chapter to structural realism, the leading state is "L." The multipolar system of great powers is composed of "L" and $C_1, \ldots, C_N$, a set of challengers, with $N \geq 2$ and the sum of all great power capabilities equal to 1. Let "D" be the threshold for an unbalanced and therefore dangerous international system.

$$L - \sum_{i=1}^{N} C_i > D \rightarrow \text{where } 0 < C_i < L < 1 \qquad (19.15)$$

Offensive realism must identify the threshold in expression 19.15, D, at which the multipolar system is unbalanced due to the presence of a leading state that is just too powerful in relation to its peers combined. The perfectly balanced international system, by contrast, would have all challengers equal to the leader in capability. A widening gap for the leader over a principal challenger, it should be noted, is just the most straightforward way of thinking about danger in the international system. Further queries arise about the profile of capabilities among the set of challengers over and beyond comparison with the leader.

While it is beyond the scope of the present exposition to pursue that preceding point at length, consider triangulation—a pun perhaps intended—with what is identified in some way as a tripolar dispersion of capabilities. Schweller (1998) theorized that tripolarity would be the most dangerous profile of all. This idea could be tested through analysis of the three most powerful states in the system—in the current notation, L, C_1, and C_2—with regard to the degree of stability observed in relation to combined capabilities. It is easy to imagine other possibilities as well, although integration of new ideas must be logically consistent with those in place.

One of the long-standing critiques of offensive realism, noted in Table 19.1, is with respect to scope conditions. Can it really be expected to hold true at all times? This question leads naturally into the connection of defensive and offensive realism with each other. Sustained debate over the merits of these theories in comparison to each other is an exceptional instance within the realist research enterprise. While it is too much to cover in detail, a review of a few highlights from arguments back and forth will assist in moving forward the process of systematic synthesis.

More than two decades ago, Walt (1998: 37) noted an emerging schism between offensive and defensive strands of realist thought. On the one hand, Schweller and Wohlforth (2000: 72) observe that both sides of the debate agree on how "imperatives of anarchy require states to view their gains and losses in relative, not absolute, terms." On the other hand, clear differences can be identified between offensive and defensive realism. The distinction is useful, Freyberg-Inan (2004: 77) asserts, "because it helps explain why realist scholars quite frequently arrive at contradictory judgments with respect to crucial questions" pertaining to the relationship between "structural characteristics of the international system, such as polarity or the distribution of capabilities, and the likelihood of war." For macroscopic realist theories such as defensive and offensive realism, unit-level axioms occupy an essential role in developing explanations and predictions (Freyberg-Inan 2004: 78). At the same time, these micro aspects tend to remain implicit in such system-oriented realist theories.

Differences for offensive and defensive realism with each other are highlighted by Layne (2006). According to Layne (2006: 16), defensive realists assert that states should seek to maximize security, rather than power, in order to avert an inevitable strategic overstretch (Layne 2006: 16). Offensive realists, by contrast, believe that security is scarce (Layne 2006: 17). Thus, to gain security, offensive realists assert that "great powers are impelled to pursue expansionist, offensive strategies that aim at maximizing their power and influence at their rivals' expense" (Layne 2006: 17). Thus defensive and offensive realism remain at an impasse over what states want, when, and why.

Interesting to consider in that context is a multistage parabolic relationship for power with security (Fiammenghi 2011: 128). Cause and effect are impacted through structural incentives that change as a state moves along the continuum of power (Fiammenghi 2011: 131). For a weak state, observes Fiammenghi (2011: 132), an increase in power is "a positive development for both the state and its partners." Past a given point, however, gains from additional power begin to diminish (Fiammenghi (2011: 133). The apex of the Security Curve, which is shaped like a downward-facing parabola, corresponds to the security threshold, a concept implicit in realism. This identifies the maximum for relative power, beyond which additional increments reduce its security (Fiammenghi 2011: 137). A more encompassing argument should be added, with a basis in instrumental reality, about the likelihood of diminishing returns above some threshold value. An analogy might be made with the observed results over a long period for various types of natural resource extraction; difficulty and costs eventually can rise to a prohibitive level.

Security, to continue with this line of reasoning, is a function of relative power. Specific policies are anticipated to vary along the curve (Fiammenghi 2011: 137):

- Up to the security threshold, a state will bandwagon with a rising power and security will increase as a function of relative power.
- After the security threshold, states will balance against a rising power and security will decrease as a function of relative power.
- But after the absolute security threshold is reached, bandwagoning resumes and security once again will increase as a function of relative power.

All of this comes together in a way that is quite informative for long-standing quarrels over offensive and defensive realism. Each should be viewed as a partial hypothesis that can describe behavior given different levels of capabilities or at two distinct times during the political life of an individual state (Fiammenghi 2011: 139).

This mode of reasoning is quite valuable, in and of itself, and also stimulates more specific thinking about thresholds—a key aspect for achievement of testability. According to Fiammenghi (2011: 142–143), balancing should be expected above one-third and below approximately one-half of relative power. Thus a powerful state that does not want to put security at risk can stay near the security threshold and forgo additional capabilities (Fiammenghi 2011: 145). By contrast, some states do aspire to hegemony and might "provide other states with selective benefits or public goods to prevent or, at least, soften their opposition" (Fiammenghi 2011: 146, 149). The specific range of values associated with balancing—one-third up to one-half of relative power—creates obvious potential for testing.

This analysis of functional form for relative power in relation to security ultimately could help to identify scope conditions for offensive realism. So, too, does attention toward the offense-defense balance. Incorporation of this factor into theorizing that also includes the Security Curve can move forward constructively debate over when and why offensive versus defensive realism should be expected to apply. This is a topic beyond the scope of the present exposition, but explicit references to the Security Curve and offense-defense balance point to more specific conditions for relevance of offensive versus defensive realism.

Power cycle theory and predation emerge as competitors with regard to what constitutes *significant* change in relative capabilities in one specific context—decline for a great power. Thus the competition would exist for goodness of fit regarding the two critical points from power cycle theory that focus on decline—the maximum and second inflection (Doran and Parsons 1980). It also becomes interesting to consider further development of predation theory in relation to critical points from power cycle theory. Could predation theory be elaborated to include propositions about how great powers will react to significant increase in capabilities for one among them? Are prospects for adoption of a weakening, predation, bolstering, or strengthening strategy toward one or more peers affected when a state climbs the ladder of power rapidly? Or, instead, is yet some other foreign policy profile more likely? Answers to such questions could expand the engagement of power cycle and predation theory with each other in a potentially very productive way.

After completion of a process of bilateral contact, several combinations of realist theories turn out to compete with each other. First, consider structural realism and hegemonic theory. A review of scenarios based on the sum and difference of capabilities for the two leading states reveals competition under some conditions and not others. Second, offensive and defensive realism clearly apply more or less under different scope conditions. A process of identification is underway but requires much more theoretical work. Third, power cycle and predation compete in putting forward different metrics for what constitutes significant great power decline.

For the most part, however, the eight realist theories are amenable to combination with each other. Insertion of variables from one variant can shore up another, as seen in a number of instances, and this can be accomplished without contradiction. Such a process can and should continue beyond this volume.

Bricolagic Bridging

Bricolagic bridging provides an operational rendering for analytic eclecticism, an element from within the knowledge component of the metatheory for progress developed in Part II. Analytic eclecticism urges thinking beyond the boundaries of any single school of thought (Sil and Katzenstein 2010a). This approach also urges constructive engagement between and among ideas in building middle-range theories with relevance to problems in the real world—in line with what Freyberg-Inan (2016) calls sociable pluralism. What follows is an initial and limited attempt at bricolagic bridging that involves realism—perhaps the first time that anything like this has occurred in a way that includes a graphic approach to communication as well.

What can be said of how realism stands in connection with other ideas that dwell within International Relations? Occasional arguments occur inside and across schools of thought, but this activity is not institutionalized in any way. In some instances, and with hindsight, exchanges deemed to be of overarching importance are designated as great debates (Lapid 1989). These arguments concern more fundamental matters over time and show no sign of resolution (Ruane and James 2012). SIR sees a way forward through engagement, in a graphic format, of theories from realism with others beyond the research enterprise. This activity, labeled as bricolagic bridging, can take various forms. More than two decades ago, Walt (1998: 30) looked favorably on such pursuits for realism, although without calling for a visual emphasis in carrying out the work. However, very little contact for realist theories with others has been seen in practice—a point made quite a while ago by Legro and Moravcsik (1999: 47)—yet still seemingly valid today.

One reason why constructive engagement remains dormant resides in the challenges to communication covered at length in Part II of this volume, which in turn developed a metatheory of progress in IR. In line with analytic eclecticism from that metatheory, a process of bricolagic bridging is instituted for realist theories about war in this section. Emphasis is on the logic of discovery rather than confirmation. Put differently, the goal is to identify new research questions that might not be derived otherwise. In particular, priorities for research identified in Table 19.1 offer guidance for at least some of this process.

For bricolagic bridging that involves realist theories about war, a natural point of contact is with a study of great importance that focuses on the same basic subject matter. From outside of realism, although not produced in opposition to it, *A Study of Crisis* (Brecher and Wilkenfeld 1997, 2000) is an obvious choice to provide a point of departure for bricolagic bridging. *A Study of Crisis* stands as a point of culmination for over two decades of qualitative and quantitative research from the International Crisis Behavior (ICB) Project. The data analysis from that volume may even be the most comprehensive in the field of conflict processes since *A Study of War* (Wright 1942).

A Study of Crisis puts forward models that successfully explain a wide range of characteristics for both international crises and foreign policy crises. An international crisis integrates together the experiences of all participants under a single heading, whereas a foreign policy crisis focuses upon the activities of a single crisis actor in that context (Brecher and Wilkenfeld 1997: 4–5, 3). For example, the Berlin Wall is one of the international crises included in the compendium; it encompasses foreign policy crises for East and West Germany, France, the USSR, the UK, and the United States (Brecher and Wilkenfeld 1997: 350–352). At the time of publication for *A Study of Crisis*, the ICB Project had holdings on 412 international crises and 895 foreign policy crises that spanned the period following the termination of World War I in November 1918 through the end of 1994.[4] It is beyond the scope of this overview even to summarize the models and findings, but origins, crisis management technique, and legacy are just a few important aspects that are explored systematically in *A Study of Crisis*.

Reviews of *A Study of Crisis* see it as a monumental contribution to research on conflict processes (Hegre 1998; Leng 1999). The volume also leans toward a systemist outlook, as witnessed by its comprehensive models for both international crisis and foreign policy crisis (Brecher and Wilkenfeld 1997, 2000). Thus the book makes a great contribution in terms of original theorizing as well. Among many innovations, *A Study of Crisis* should be commended for (a) exploring the interconnectedness of international conflict, protracted conflict, crisis, and war as concepts; (b) linking unit- and system-level components; and (c) offering static and dynamic conceptions of crisis (Brecher and Wilkenfeld 1997: 7–9). These accomplishments, moreover, create excellent resources to access in meeting priorities in place for improvement of representative realist theories.

Figure 19.3 depicts *A Study of Crisis* in graphic form.[5] Figure 19.3a displays a regional system and the international system that serves as the environment for it. Within the regional system, the micro and macro levels, respectively, represent interactions within states and beyond their boundaries.

Initial connections move from the international system into the micro level of the regional system in Figure 19.3b: "SYSTEM STRUCTURE OF POLYCENTRISM" → "high stress"; "trigger violence for first actor." Note that the first variable is exogenous and depicted with an oval, while the latter two variables are convergent and appear as parallelograms. Polycentrism, which consists of two leading powers along with a larger number of centers of independent decision, is the most complex system structure and theorized as therefore the most unstable. Stress and tension and an attendant disposition toward violence are anticipated to be at higher levels for polycentrism than other system structures such as bipolarity or multipolarity.

---

[4] The ICB datasets now include 476 international crises and 1,052 foreign policy crises through to the end of 2015; see Brecher et al. (2017).
[5] This figure is based on material from Brecher and Wilkenfeld (1997: 749, 770, 774, 787, 823) and consultations with the authors. While *A Study of Crisis* contains other models, those that appear on the pages just above are amenable to assembly into the most comprehensive version that can be communicated in a single figure.

Micro-macro and macro-macro connections begin with ovals at lower and center right, respectively, in Figure 19.3c: "ethnic conflict" → "PROTRACTED CONFLICT" and "CRISIS AND ADVERSARIAL LOCATIONS" → "PROTRACTED CONFLICT." As a nodal variable, "PROTRACTED CONFLICT" appears as a hexagon. Ethnic strife, with its emphasis on potentially indivisible issues grounded in identity, creates a significant likelihood of protracted conflict. Crisis and adversarial locations refer, respectively, to degree of proximity for (a) interactions to the home territory of crisis actors, collectively speaking; and (b) states identified by each other as adversaries. In each instance, closeness is deemed more likely to create a lock-in effect from crisis activity to sustained conflict.

Figure 19.3d adds a connection from the international system to the macro level of the region: "SYSTEM STRUCTURE OF POLYCENTRISM" → "PROTRACTED CONFLICT." The logic is the same as in a previous context—polycentrism is expected to be the most conflict-prone structure across the board. One other linkage, macro-micro in nature, appears in the diagram: "CRISIS AND ADVERSARIAL LOCATIONS" → "trigger violence for first actor." This connection is justified in the same manner as the one above regarding location-related effects—proximity to adversaries and the crisis setting both create a greater expectation of violence, which includes the way in which a case begins.

Figure 19.3e shows a macro-macro connection completed at the center of the page: "PROTRACTED CONFLICT" → "VIOLENCE IN CRISIS MANAGEMENT TECHNIQUE." Put differently, protracted conflict aggravates the security dilemma and thus the tendency to employ violence among crisis participants. The other linkage in the diagram goes to the same place: "CRISIS AND ADVERSARIAL LOCATIONS" → "VIOLENCE IN CRISIS MANAGEMENT TECHNIQUE." The latter variable is convergent and appears as a parallelogram. The logic for this connection is the same as above for trigger violence by the first crisis actor. Proximity of actions and adversaries to each other creates a greater likelihood of ensuing violence intended to manage the crisis.

Figure 19.3f adds two macro-micro connections: "PROTRACTED CONFLICT" → "high stress" and "PROTRACTED CONFLICT" → "trigger violence for first actor." Note that the first of these couplings skips over the vertical line that it crosses.

Figure 19.3g includes connections that appear with broken lines (i.e., inferred connections). Each linkage is micro-macro: "high stress"; "trigger violence for first actor" → "VIOLENCE IN CRISIS MANAGEMENT TECHNIQUE." This follows on from intuition; along with violence already in place, high stress puts in place a "hair trigger" situation that is very likely to produce further violence (Wilkenfeld 1973; Boyer and Wilkenfeld 1989).

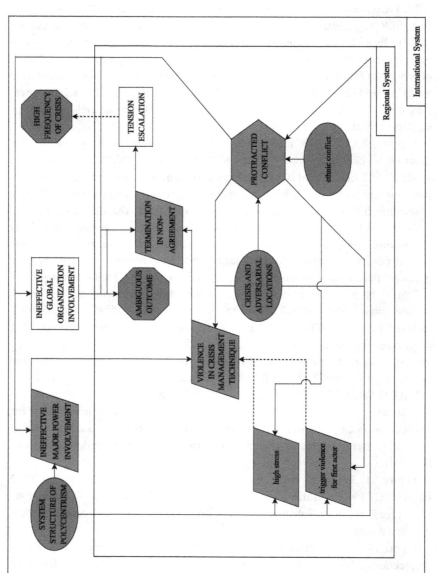

Figure 19.3 A Study of Crisis

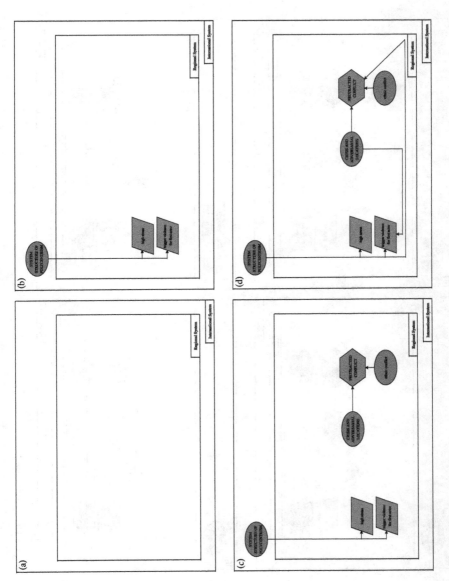

Figure 19.3 Continued

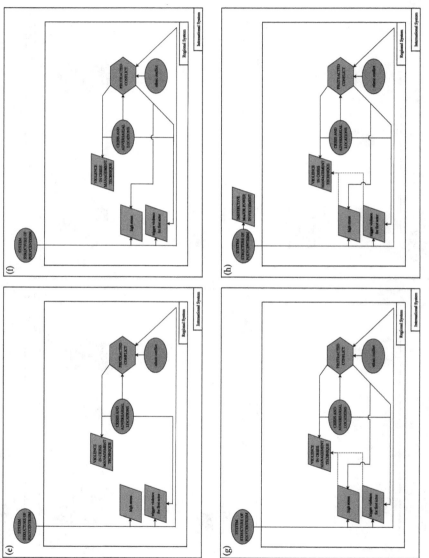

Figure 19.3 Continued

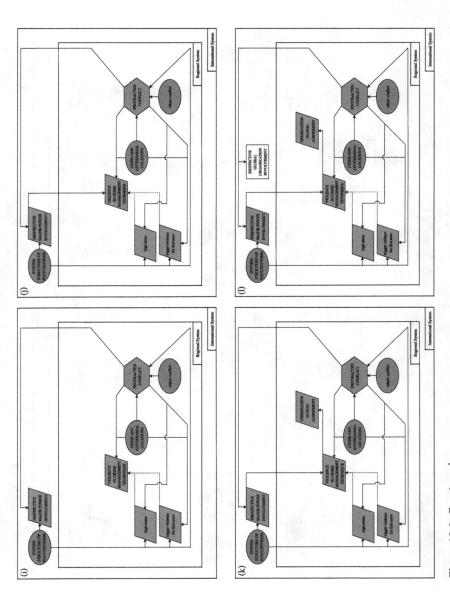

Figure 19.3 Continued

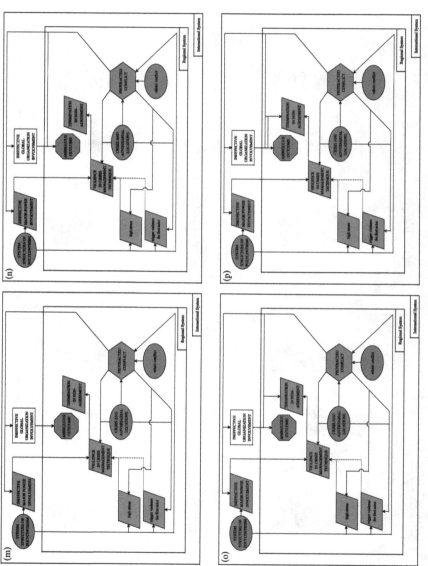

Figure 19.3 Continued

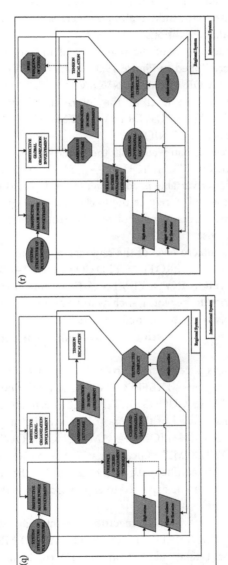

Figure 19.3 Continued

Figure 19.3h starts a pathway in the international system: "SYSTEM STRUCTURE OF POLYCENTRISM" → "INEFFECTIVE MAJOR POWER INVOLVEMENT." The latter, a convergent variable, takes the form of a parallelogram. The decentralized system structure is inherently more complicated than others and thus anticipated to render major power crisis management efforts less effective than under other conditions.

Variables at the macro level of the regional system and the international system, respectively, are linked in Figure 19.3i: "PROTRACTED CONFLICT" → "INEFFECTIVE MAJOR POWER INVOLVEMENT." The pathway continues, back into the macro level of the international system, in Figure 19.3j: "INEFFECTIVE MAJOR POWER INVOLVEMENT" → "VIOLENCE IN CRISIS MANAGEMENT TECHNIQUE."

Figure 19.3k conveys a connection at the macro level: "VIOLENCE IN CRISIS MANAGEMENT TECHNIQUE" → "TERMINATION IN NON-AGREEMENT." The latter variable is convergent and depicted with a parallelogram. Violence is expected to reduce the likelihood of pragmatic bargaining that leads to an agreement because of an obviously greater emotive element than would be present otherwise.

Movement from the macro level of the regional system to the international system occurs in Figure 19.3l: "PROTRACTED CONFLICT" → "INEFFECTIVE GLOBAL ORGANIZATION INVOLVEMENT." This connection brings to mind the most persistent strife in the world, such as India and Pakistan over Kashmir (Brecher 1953). The UN Security Council, with its veto principle and limited resources for peacekeeping, is not well equipped to intervene effectively in such protracted conflicts.

Figure 19.3m conveys a connection from the international system to the macro level of the region: "INEFFECTIVE GLOBAL ORGANIZATION INVOLVEMENT" → "AMBIGUOUS OUTCOME." This tendency is reinforced by a linkage at the macro level of the regional system that appears in Figure 19.3n: "PROTRACTED CONFLICT" → "AMBIGUOUS OUTCOME." Note that "AMBIGUOUS OUTCOME" appears as an octagon—a point of termination. Adversaries locked in conflict with each other, and in the absence of effective outside intervention, can be expected to experience crises that end with no clear substantive outcome.

Figure 19.3o shows a macro-macro connection: "PROTRACTED CONFLICT" → "TERMINATION IN NON-AGREEMENT." Within Figure 19.3p, movement takes place from the international system to the macro level of the regional system and ends up in the same place as just above: "INEFFECTIVE GLOBAL ORGANIZATION INVOLVEMENT" → "TERMINATION IN NON-AGREEMENT." The macro-level pathway continues in Figure 19.3q: "TERMINATION IN NON-AGREEMENT" → "TENSION

ESCALATION." All of these connections follow intuition based on roles played at earlier stages by variables such as global organization ineffectiveness.

Finally, a broken line in Figure 19.3r shows a connection from the macro level of the regional system with the international system: "TENSION ESCALATION" → "HIGH FREQUENCY OF CRISIS." As a point of termination, the latter variable appears as an octagon.

Based on 13 variables, Figure 19.3 provides an account for crisis escalation. The diagram contains three initial variables, five convergent variables, and one nodal variable. In line with the systemist identity of the ICB Project, Figure 19.3 includes five of six basic connections—macro-macro, macro-micro, micro-macro, and back and forth between the region and international system. With an absence of a micro-micro connection—also a feature of some realist theories about war—combination of such variables with each other emerges as a natural priority.

With *A Study of Crisis* fully introduced, bricolagic bridging can get underway. Several points of contact will be introduced for potential development. Each corresponds to a priority for one or more realist theories identified in Table 19.1.

Consider the issues raised with assessment of the offense-defense balance for both defensive and offensive realism, along with defensive realism in connection with first-mover advantage. While obviously many data sets can be used to measure variables and test propositions from realism in a more rigorous way—a point emphasized in the classic exposition by Vasquez (1983, 1998)—ICB is well suited to deal with the role of *perceptions* in particular. Recall that a foreign policy crisis is based on perception of a threat to basic values, finite time for response, and a likelihood of military hostilities. Thus the ICB Project (represented in the direct sense by *A Study of Crisis*) and the above-noted realist theories are well positioned to assist each other in certain ways. Supplemented with other sources, ICB case summaries can be used to code a variable such as the perceived offense-defense balance. Moreover, with its case- and actor-level data, such coding can assess whether the offense-defense balance belongs strictly at the macro level—current practice within the realist school—or also should be measured for individual states as crisis actors. The same can be said for first-mover advantage.

Contact for *A Study of Crisis* with realist theories, in the preceding context, also can create value for the ICB Project. On the one hand, ICB includes hundreds of variables that have appeared in a wide range of research designs about conflict processes (Brecher 1999; James 2019a). On the other hand, consider the absence of a first-mover advantage and the offense-defense balance from those extensive holdings. This gap, along with some others, can be traced to the sociology of knowledge. Within the community of scholars in IR, ICB is based more in the tradition of foreign policy analysis than security studies. Thus variables that focus on decision-making, for example, are more likely to be incorporated than military-oriented metrics that provide detail beyond a basic sense of polarity for the system and type of state in terms of power status. The process of bricolagic bridging therefore can prove beneficial in identifying interesting possibilities for data collection even with regard to a long-standing and comprehensive project. At the same time, a review of realism shows very little activity in accessing the data and insights available either from the ICB Project or research on foreign policy analysis in general. Based on analysis from Kaarbo (2015), this in all likelihood is an example of the more encompassing estrangement of IR from foreign policy.

Defensive realism, as noted in Table 19.1, continues to lack any connection that is purely at the micro level. In Figure 19.2, which depicts the defensive realist synthesis, the micro variables are (a) concealed grievances, capabilities, plans, and misperceptions; (b) motive for war among declining states; (c) expansionist mindset; and (d) greater expectation of war. In Figure 19.3, the micro-level variables from *A Study of War* include (1) high stress, (2) trigger violence for first actor, and (3) ethnic conflict. It is easy to imagine connections back and forth, with an initial concentration on how the preceding variables (1) through (3) might impact (a) to (c). High stress, for example, could explain a turn toward concealed grievances, plans, and misperceptions. Another likely connection is that trigger violence for the first actor in an international crisis could produce greater expectation of war in particular, over and above perception of higher likelihood of military hostilities. Consider, as well, ethnic conflict as either a possible motive for war among declining states or a factor contributing to an expansionist mindset.

Another point raised in Table 19.1 concerns the need for offensive realism to develop more fully the role of fear and miscalculation in its account for war. In Figure 17.1, which depicts offensive realism, just two among 19 variables—existence of an aspiring regional hegemon, along with fear and miscalculation by leaders—appear at the micro level. Consider in that context the potential role of high stress and trigger value for the first actor in an international crisis. As of now, the one micro-level connection in Figure 17.1 is "existence of an aspiring regional hegemon" → "fear and miscalculation by leaders." While plausible, this coupling seems inherently incomplete and leaves obvious space for elaboration to include events in a crisis setting. For instance, how might the above-noted connection be mediated by variables such as perceived level of threat, traits of decision-making units, and so on? Question about both macro- and micro-level patterns also arise. For example, does existence of an aspiring hegemon stimulate more crises in a region than would be expected otherwise? What is the level of threat in such an instance; perhaps most notably, do all crises that involve a would-be hegemon tend toward perceptions among participants of possible grave damage or loss of existence rather than something more contained? ICB holdings are ready to answer these queries once coding is expanded to include the presence or absence of an aspiring regional hegemon and perhaps even a measure for its intensity of commitment to that objective.

Offensive realism also can inform the modeling from *A Study of Crisis* in a way that suggests directions for future research. Consider once again, from Figure 17.1, existence of an aspiring regional hegemon. At least two variables from *A Study of Crisis* in Figure 19.3 could be investigated further in connection with absence or presence of a would-be hegemon in a region. At the micro level, consider trigger violence for the first actor. Is this more likely if an aspiring hegemon exists within a region? If so, does that actor have a greater tendency to use violence when initiating crisis conditions with one or more adversaries? These questions are worth answering because the connection of trigger violence with crisis escalation is well established over decades of ICB research (Brecher and Wilkenfeld 1997, 2000). Another variable from Figure 19.3, VIOLENCE IN CRISIS MANAGEMENT TECHNIQUE, also could be studied in connection with whether or not a would-be regional hegemon exists. Does such an actor, even independent of how a crisis gets underway, have a greater disposition toward violent crisis management? What about the conduct of other states when confronted, under crisis conditions, with an aspiring hegemon in their region? Once again it becomes possible to consult the priorities for realist theories and add interesting research questions to the already expansive agenda of the ICB Project.

For dynamic differentials theory as described in Table 19.1, one priority is to say more about the role of leadership in crisis. Additional ICB holdings—not present in the visualization from Figure 19.3, but easily brought to mind after a review of its contents—become relevant here. Variables of interest would include the size and structure of decision-making units. In addition to the sheer number of participants, ICB identifies whether decision-making took place in an institutional, ad hoc, or combined setting. Other variables could be added, but the basic point is that ICB can handle any number of options identified to expand the micro level of dynamic differentials theory.

Last among the items enumerated in Table 19.1 is the need for predation theory to develop a priori measurements for high versus low strategic value, military posture, and intensity of action. Once again, Figure 19.3 does not contain the specific variables from ICB that become relevant in a context such as this one, but the diagram stimulates thinking about what is relevant from data holdings.

With regard to intensity of action, ICB data include coding for crisis management technique. The measure includes what tentatively could be labeled as low-intensity actions, such as negotiation, adjudication or arbitration, mediation, multiple nonviolent techniques, and nonmilitary pressure. Possible high-intensity categories for crisis management consist of nonviolent military, multiple including violence, and violence. Whether this coding regime ultimately turns out to be appropriate is not the key point for now; instead, what matters is that something can be figured out to assess systematically low- versus high-intensity actions in the context of predation theory.

While geostrategic salience is assessed for the location of a crisis, there is no variable coded in ICB for the strategic value of a particular state. Military posture also does not appear in ICB holdings. The project's detailed case summaries, with some added material, could produce coding for these variables. As with earlier examples, inclusion of such variables would enhance the connection of ICB with security studies in general and some realist theories in particular.

Nearly pervasive among realist theories about war is a lack of precision in specifying regional boundaries, along with an absence of theorizing systematically about cause and effect back and forth with the environment. On the one hand, all of the realist theories mention the behavior of actors beyond a region of immediate concern. On the other hand, these connections tend not to be built into theoretical specifications ahead of time. Even offensive realism, which incorporates the stopping power of water explicitly as an assumption, does not offer specific regional delineations. Coding from ICB exists for regions and subregions around the globe; for example Africa appears along with four subregions within it. Designation of the system and environment before theorizing moves forward is important for purposes of rigor and efficiency.

One additional exercise in bricolagic bridging will be incorporated. This involves realist theories with material other than *A Study of Crisis*. The contact that follows is prediagrammatic and included in order to complete the process of responding to priorities identified in Table 19.1.

One issue from Table 19.1 concerns the need for realist theories—power cycle, dynamic differentials, and offensive realism are noted in particular—to reassess the meaning of capabilities (see also Rosecrance and Steiner 2010). How is power to be measured in the new millennium? This is relevant to both material and ideational aspects of capability and, most notably, in combination with each other over time. The key concern in this sense is the rise of cyber activity on a global basis and its association with any number of ongoing conflicts. Attempts to measure such capability are at an early stage of development. For example, Valeriano, Jensen, and Maness (2018) identify the top 10 most active cyber states, along with latent capacity, and make a comparison with more familiar indicators such as GDP, military spending, and the share of capabilities within the standard index from COW. While the indicators mostly correlate with each other, it is interesting to see South and North Korea in first and 10th place, respectively, for latent cyber capacity (Valeriano, Jensen, and Maness 2018: 59, Table 3.4). The very high standing of these neighboring states, along with their visible difference in rank, undoubtedly reflects the impact of rivalry coupled with vastly different levels of wealth. In sum, the recent work on cyber power possesses important implications for various matters already discussed in the context of realism, notably measurement for the distribution of power and significant changes within it. All of this should be pursued further within realist research on the causes of war.

Summing Up the Realist Dialogue

This chapter placed realist theories about the causes of war in a dialogue with each other and beyond. An effort to profile realist theories about war focused on auxiliary assumptions, priorities for improvement, the number and variety of variables, and specialized connections such as loops and synergies. This exercise created the basis for comparative analysis to follow. Systematic synthesis, implemented through reference to systemist diagrams for respective theories, produced multiple dividends. The original list of 14 theories became consolidated into eight for purposes of further comparison. Realist theories engaged with each other to meet priorities for improvement identified in Chapters 11 through 18. Bricolagic bridging took place through dialogue with a major work of scholarship from outside of the realist research enterprise. Further improvements for respective realist theories about war ensued. All of this in line with the logic of discovery and leads naturally into Chapter 20, which sums up what has been accomplished through a pragmatic approach and identifies new research directions for realism in particular and IR in general.

20
Realism and Progress in International Relations

> If ever there were subjectivist animals, they either died very young from exposure to the world they denied, or they were appointed professors of philosophy.
>
> —Bunge (1993: 233)

Overview

Can there be a science of International Relations? If so, is there a place for realism as a research enterprise within it? The unequivocal answer to both of these questions is yes. This conclusion is in line with the playful yet also insightful epigraph above. Without at least some degree of objective reality to assess arguments back and forth, why talk to each other at all? This is a quick way of summarizing prior arguments in this volume that led to endorsement of scientific realism as the most pragmatic choice among major options available from the philosophy of inquiry. Together with other elements, scientific realism defined a metatheory of progress that found application to research from a major school of thought about international relations. More specifically, assessment has focused on realist theories about the causes of war. After carrying out a great deal of work along those lines, we arrive at the time to look back on what has been done and provide a few ideas for moving forward.

This chapter unfolds in three additional sections. The second section reviews the accomplishments of the volume. Achievements from Parts I–V are enumerated in turn. Given its relatively high level of abstraction, somewhat more detail is provided about the contents of Part II. The third section suggests directions for future research. Ideas range from specific and substantive to general and abstract. The fourth and final section offers a few thoughts about the prospects for realism and scientific progress in IR.

Accomplishments

Several challenging tasks have been completed in this volume. Achievements from Parts I through IV will be summarized in sequence. What follows is a terse retrospective on many preceding pages. Attention then turns to the overarching goals put forward in Chapter 1.

Part I started out in Chapter 1 with the assertion that realism can and must be a scientific venture within the study of international relations. With appropriate reformulation, realism can contribute to both the logic of discovery and that of confirmation. Reassessment of realism has been carried out with five features in place, each being noted near the outset of this volume: (1) the time frame is the post–World War II era; (2) improved explanation, as opposed to direct relevance to policy, is the priority; (3) the causes of war are the substantive matter of interest; (4) suggestions are offered from an internal rather than external point of reference; and (5) concepts are introduced in a gradual way in line with insights from cognitive psychology. Even with these boundaries in place, the investigation of realism as a school of thought and provider of explanations for war has turned out to be vast in scope.

Chapter 2 identified scientific progress for the discipline of IR. This took place through a combination of (a) inductive and sociological and (b) deductive and rationalist criteria. Based on a deductive and rationalist argument, scientific realism is determined to be capable of advancement through the logics of both discovery and confirmation. In comparison, other major outlooks are limited. Among the three alternatives, analyticism and reflexivity would possess value concentrated into discovery, while neopositivism stands as an ideal state rather than a guide to practice. Scientific realism also is in line with desirable characteristics and results for research as identified through a review of prior inquiries that identified aspects of progress in IR—an inductive and sociological exercise. With all considerations in place, scientific realism has emerged as the optimal choice to guide research in a world of finite academic resources.

Part II produced a metatheory of scientific progress as a working system. Introduced in Chapter 3, components based on knowledge, units, and methods appear in this metatheory. Scientific realism (Ö), analytic eclecticism (Æ) and a model of cognition (Χ) are elements within the knowledge component. For the unit component, the elements are rationality (β) and the research enterprise as a system of explanation (Σ). Identification of axioms for a research enterprise (↑) and systemism (∫) are the elements for the methods component. As per insights from cognitive psychology, each element is associated with a visual representation to enhance understanding and retention. Rationality, for example, is associated with the letter beta, for βismarck—a memorable practitioner of foreign policy. Chapters 4–6 then presented each of the preceding sets of elements at greater length.

Chapter 4 introduced scientific realism, analytic eclecticism, and a model of cognition—elements of the knowledge-related component of the metatheory—in detail. Scientific realism combines belief in objective reality and a place for unobservables in theory. From a review based on deductive and rationalist principles, scientific realism emerges as the preferred option among overarching perspectives. Analytic eclecticism goes beyond paradigmatic boundaries. Its focus is on problem-solving rather than an agenda for research associated with a particular school of thought. Analytic eclecticism seeks middle range explanations that possess relevance to policy. The final knowledge-related element, a model of cognition, points toward a graphic turn for IR. The academic study of international relations is vast and, as a result, challenges associated with transforming information into knowledge are not being met sufficiently. The model of cognition also encourages use of relational reasoning—analogy, antinomy, anomaly, and antithesis—to complement and reinforce arguments about cause and effect placed within a visual format. These four techniques have found valuable application throughout analysis in this volume of how realism accounts for war.

Chapter 5 covered units of the metatheory in detail. The two elements are individuals who act on instrumental rationality and systems of explanation for research. In this context, rational choice focuses on decision-making about means rather than ends. Instrumental rationality is ordinal, meaning that people are expected to update their beliefs in a direction compatible with new data. Rationality therefore does not assume that precise calculations take place in the process of decision. The second element, a system of explanation, is a scheme of organization such as a research tradition or paradigm. The research enterprise—the preferred system of explanation—combines the best characteristics of familiar efforts that have been primarily inductive or deductive in nature. The concept of a research enterprise is based upon both (i) deductive and rationalist and (ii) inductive and sociological reasoning about how to identify a school of thought. For a research enterprise, the focus is on developing theories to address and solve empirical problems. Moreover, the properties of a research enterprise facilitate its ability to work in tandem with a graphic approach toward communication.

Chapter 6 identified elements for the methods component of the metatheory of progress. One element is identification of axioms for a research enterprise as a system of explanation. Candidate assumptions are designated on the basis of a process that combines inductive and deductive stages. The goal is to designate axioms underlying a school of thought in a way that is acceptable to both adherents and those outside of its boundaries. Systemism, the other element of methods, translates causal mechanisms conveyed in words into a graphic format. This shift toward visualization is intended to enhance dialogue about empirical problems. Neoclassical realism has been used to highlight the value that can be obtained from applying systemism to theories about international politics. The resulting approach, Systemist International Relations (SIR), is implemented through systematic synthesis and bricolagic bridging between and among works of scholarship. The objective is to identify and solve empirical problems more effectively through such means.

Chapter 7 completed Part II through assembly of the elements from the knowledge, units, and methods components into a working metatheory of progress for IR. This process culminated in presentation of the metatheory in the form of a systemist diagram. The chapter also introduced the Performance Ratio, which compares the track record in solving empirical problems (i.e., numerator) to degree of complexity required to do so (i.e., denominator)—an operational way to assess theories. This metric is put forward as a potential improvement over alternatives from other systems of explanation, such as empirical content within a research program, which have become more normatively oriented with time.

Part III identified realism as a research enterprise. Chapter 8 focused on the meaning of realism in an overall sense and also designated its axioms via the method introduced in Chapter 6. Realism, in a basic sense, corresponds to power politics. Consensus beyond that point is difficult to identify, so attention turns to a process that systematically identifies its assumptions. Criteria implemented in four stages are required to designate axioms for the realist research enterprise. Stages I and IV are inductive and sociological, and Stages II and III are deductive and rationalist. Anarchy and state-centrism at the system level, along with power seeking and rationality at the state level, are the assumptions that emerge from the four-stage process.

Chapter 9 also adopted a hybrid approach—inductive and sociological, along with deductive and rationalist—to classify realist theories about war. To facilitate comparative analysis in this study and beyond, both a typology and a taxonomy have been developed in that chapter. The typology is based on two dimensions: (1) system versus state and (2) dynamic or static specification for variables. Characteristics of capability-based variables form the basis of the taxonomy. The preceding dimensions and characteristics are plausible starting points for classification of realist theories in light of underlying assumptions for the research enterprise.

Chapter 10 found classical realism, a prescientific foundation for work continuing to this day, to be in compliance with the preceding set of axioms for the research enterprise. A sample of prominent works from the classical realist era, once converted to systemist graphics, have revealed a more complex and interesting set of studies than might have been remembered on the basis of words alone. In terms of the logic of discovery, classical realism can be deemed successful and a worthwhile point of departure for future research.

Part IV applied systemism to create graphic portrayals for realist theories of war. Power cycle, structural, balance of threat, balance of interests, defensive, dynamic differentials, offensive, and predation have been introduced as varieties of realism in Chapters 11 to 18. In each instance, a magnum opus is identified as a point of origin for a full-fledged theory. Some of these theories contain more than one variant, so Chapters 11–18 created a total of 14 systemist visualizations. Each graphic facilitated analysis of a theory in terms of cause-and-effect relations, with formal, material, final, and efficient conditions combined into an overall account for war. This visual approach also helped when responding, in an initial way, to critiques of the respective theories. Priorities for elaboration have been identified for each theory when placed in communication with its peers and ideas from beyond realism about why wars occur.

Part V engaged the preceding set of realist theories about war with each other and ideas from beyond the research enterprise. Chapter 19 profiled the realist theories and thereby identified general versus specialized versions, along with opportunities for combination. From the original 14 theories, the process of review derived a set of eight for further analysis. Systematic synthesis and bricolagic bridging have been carried out for those theories in response to priorities for elaboration that had been identified in preceding chapters.

Put forward at the outset of this volume, three basic goals have been achieved through carrying out the tasks just summarized:

- Implementing a scientific realist foundation to promote progress.
- Taking a graphic turn, via systemism, to facilitate communication within the vastness of the discipline.
- Focusing on political realism as the most long-standing school of thought in order to demonstrate the value of scientific realism in combination with a graphic approach toward subject matter.

Scientific realism has been adopted as an element of the knowledge component within a metatheory of progress. Consistent with a scientific realist standpoint, a visual approach toward communication, systemism, has been implemented to meet challenges produced by the vastness of power politics as a research enterprise. Thus realist theories about war now are available in a graphic format that enhances prospects for dialogue within and beyond the research enterprise. Taken together, scientific realism, the graphic turn, and other developments in this volume should increase the likelihood that realism can address and solve empirical problems, notably the causes of war, effectively. In that sense, the volume is intended as a work on scholarship on realism but also as a "user manual" for further application of SIR regardless of subject matter.

Priorities for Future Research

While additional lines of inquiry could be suggested, the ideas that follow should be sufficient to establish that the work carried out in this volume can stimulate significant new lines of inquiry. Potential directions for research are presented in approximately descending order of abstraction and generality. Along the way, one prominent exposition from within realism, Walt (2002), is referenced at times with regard to various ideas that previously have been identified as priorities yet still seem in need of greater attention.

What is excluded from the agenda of realism as a research enterprise? In other words, what is the *antithesis* of realism? The axioms of realism—anarchy and state-centrism at the system level, along with rationality and power seeking at the state level—establish boundaries for theory construction. Some violations will be easier to detect than others. For example, realism is concerned with the logic of consequences rather than appropriateness with regard to actions taken in line with ordinal rationality. Moral arguments should not intrude because the agenda of realism consists of developing explanations based on its axioms and auxiliary assumptions adopted in respective theories. Another obvious departure from realism would arise from insertion of transnational actors into any purported solution to an empirical problem. International institutions, along with nonstate actors, are not permitted in realist theory except as entities to be manipulated and controlled by states. Thus international law, identified by Walt (2002: 222–228) as a priority for future realist research, should be designated as entirely outside of the research enterprise. Any research enterprise that incorporates international law would stand as a competitor for realism.

One point of confusion concerns whether both ideational and material variables are welcome in future realist research. All the way back to classical realism, each of these types has played a role in explanations based on power politics. The key point is that actions are assessed on the basis of instrumental rather than normative rationality. Thus perceptions, along with concepts such as risk propensity and uncertainty, can continue to be included in realist accounts. Norms, moral arguments, and the like exist outside of realism—not because of their ideational nature but instead as a result of referencing the logic of appropriateness.

How is the metatheory expected to guide future research about international relations? Even two decades ago, Walt (2002: 222–228) had identified testing of causal mechanisms as a priority for realism. Consider potential interactions involving qualitative and quantitative research about cause and effect. SIR tilts toward neither quantitative nor qualitative methods. Therefore, SIR can guide movement back and forth between iterations of qualitative and quantitative analysis through an ability to portray theories in graphic form, revised on the basis of case studies, statistical analysis, or other methods.

Systemism, as applied in this volume, has yielded value in relation to realism but also awaits further development. Two aspects of systemism readily come to mind. First, the diagrams so far used to represent theories do not include any time scale. In other words, the length of a given arrow connecting variables to each other in a systemist visualization provides no information about the time lag for ostensible cause and effect. Exploring the temporal aspects for a network of variables would be valuable in enhancing falsifiability over and beyond what can be obtained from graphic portrayal. Second, consider the issue of functional form. With significant work required to transform realist theories about war into systemist graphics, the default position is to assume incremental connections between and among variables. Only a few instances of nonlinearity, such as the threshold effect for connection of domestic incoherence with the likelihood of balancing against a foreign menace, have been considered in the preceding review of realism. Thus further theorizing about realism should explore the possibility that variables, such as those just mentioned for balance of interests, are connected to each other in nonlinear ways. And identification of such specifics once again would enhance falsifiability.

This volume has developed a metatheory for scientific progress in the context of IR and identified realism as a research enterprise. What about application of the metatheory beyond the boundaries of realism? Such a process could begin through engagement, based on the metatheory from this volume, between the realist research enterprise and what is known as *critical* realism.[1] Adherents of critical realism accept some aspects of power politics as identified in this volume, but would reject certain restrictions, such as the assumptions of anarchy and state-centrism. Critical realists allow roles for both hierarchy and anarchy in developing theories. In addition, this way of thinking replaces state-centrism with a sovereign-centric frame of reference. Since these scholars identify as critical more than problem-solving—their focus is more on understanding than explanation within the well-known dichotomy from Hollis and Smith (1992)—moral commitments such as emancipation would have to be added to the list of axioms. A natural point of departure for identifying critical realism as a research enterprise would be the exposition from Bell (2008) on international relations and political thought. With completion of such a process, critical realism could be compared more effectively to realism. Through

---

[1] The possibilities noted in this paragraph have been identified in Buxton (2018).

systemist graphics, points in common and differences in outlook could be identified to facilitate collaboration or competition, where appropriate, for realism and critical realism.

Advocates of realism might argue that the approach to designation and comparative analysis of theories adopted in this volume leaves something to be desired. Is it appropriate to focus exclusively on how well realist theories, which may have other priorities, perform in accounting for the causes of war? What about achievements in other areas? Structural realism, for instance, contributes significantly to understanding the degree of competition observed in world politics. In the case of balance of threat, a major priority is to explain the origins of alliances. Many more examples of the preceding type could be offered. While acknowledging that the assessment of realism conducted in this volume may seem unfair to some, it responds to the generally unheeded call for rigorous reflection made famous by Vasquez (1983, 1998). Future systemist evaluation of realist theories can and should be extended to subjects other than the causes of war, which has received pride of place because of its position at the origin of the discipline over a century ago.

Another potential point of controversy is the presence of domestic politics within respective realist theories—identified by Walt (2002: 222–228) as a topic in need of more attention. Factors related to domestic politics do not contradict realism; rather, accessing such variables assists in figuring out capabilities for a *state*. Thus neoclassical theories, such as balance of threat and balance of interests, can play a role in the realist research enterprise going forward.

Consider again the typology and taxonomy developed for realist theories about war. The initial versions, respectively, feature two dimensions and one characteristic. This relatively simple approach toward classification awaits refinement and possibly expansion as more realist theories about war are identified. Put differently, the typology and taxonomy offered in this volume serve a purpose analogous to the one associated with classical realism earlier in another context, namely, a foundation for further work that is put forward more in line with the logic of discovery than confirmation.

Realist theories have been engaged with each other and ideas beyond the research enterprise to provide a more effective foundation for further research. Thus achievements so far with regard to war as an empirical problem are more in the logic of discovery than confirmation. In terms of the two dimensions for any empirical problem identified in Chapter 5—diachronic versus synchronic, along with system versus state focus—what has been covered so far remains quite limited. All of the realist theories focus on escalation to war in synchronic terms—more like a picture than a video. Some theories pertain to states in general, while others zero in on the great power subset. Thus a priority for future research, to cite perhaps the most neglected aspect within realism so far, would be on research designs that are diachronic and focused on either the warlikeness of states or the system as a whole.

Assessment of capabilities emerges as a major priority for realism—identified as a point of emphasis even two decades ago within this school of thought (Walt 2002: 222–228). Respective theories about war, as this volume makes clear, have not been relying upon any uniform metric. Thus further bricolagic bridging should be pursued to identify measurements that are most valid for use in the new millennium.

Consider also any number of critiques posed to realism that have focused on how it seems to struggle with explaining some of the major and even transforming events in world politics. The end of the Cold War, perhaps, is the most-recognized instance (Vasquez 1998). Thus a reinvigorated realism should set an agenda for dealing with events that are of great importance for either continuity or change at the level of the system. An initial list would include the end of the Cold War, 9/11, events pulled together under the label of the Arab Spring, and the pandemic still underway at this time of writing. Over and beyond accounting for interstate war, realism must take on such challenges and compete, as a research enterprise, against whatever alternatives are put forward to explain momentous events.

Final Thoughts

This volume started out with conflicting epigraphs from Mearsheimer and Vasquez. After an extensive review of realism, each observer somehow manages to end up being right. Mearsheimer emphasizes the logic of discovery, while Vasquez focuses on the logic of confirmation. Mearsheimer accurately described realism as interesting and based on long-standing intuition about how the world works, while Vasquez is right to say that power politics has yet to live up to the standards of modern science. This volume has relied upon both (i) deductive and rationalist and (ii) inductive and sociological reasoning to learn as much as possible about realist theories of war and find a way toward progress. The conclusion is that implementation of SIR can improve realism, scientifically speaking, across the board—meeting the demands of both the logic of discovery and that of confirmation more effectively than before.

Consider one last time the pod of hippopotamuses in front of Chapter 1. Their size and lack of overall direction in movement offers a sense, figuratively speaking, of how IR looks at present. This study has put forward a metatheory that is intended to facilitate progress, with scientific realism and an approach toward communication based on systemist graphics, among other aspects, deemed essential. A review of realism, the most long-standing school of thought in the discipline, has served as the natural starting point for application of such a metatheory. Given the vastness of realism, a focus on the empirical problem of most long-standing interest, interstate war, provided a point of departure for graphic communication based on systemism. The visual turn pursued in this study has produced a range of benefits, perhaps most importantly an improved foundation for realist research on conflict processes. In this way, it is hoped that the work carried out in the present volume will enhance prospects for more coordinated and productive movement for the IR "pod" as it explores the world.

References

Acharya, Amitav. 2014. "Global International Relations and Regional Worlds: A New Agenda for International Studies." *International Studies Quarterly* 58: 647–659.
Albertini, Luigi. 1953. *Origins of the War of 1914*. 3 vols. Isabella Massey, trans. London: Oxford University Press.
ALIAS. 2019. www.isanet.org/ISA/Sections/ALIAS.
Allison, Graham T. 1971. *Essence of Decision: Explaining the Cuban Missile Crisis*. Boston: Little, Brown.
Allison, Graham T., and Philip Zelikow. 1999. *Essence of Decision: Explaining the Cuban Missile Crisis*. 2nd ed. New York, NY: Pearson.
Almond, Gabriel A., and Stephen J. Genco. 1977. "Clouds, Clocks, and the Study of Politics." *World Politics* 29: 489–522.
Ambrose, Susan A., Michael W. Bridges, Michele DiPietro, Marsha C. Lovett, and Marie K. Norman. 2010. *How Learning Works: Seven Research-Based Principles for Smart Learning*. San Francisco, CA: Jossey-Bass.
Anderson, Lorin W., David R. Krathwohl, Peter W. Airasian, Kathleen A. Cruikshank, Richard E. Mayer, Paul R. Pintrich, James Raths, and Merlin C. Wittrock. 2001. *A Taxonomy for Learning, Teaching, and Assessing: A Revision of Bloom's Taxonomy of Educational Objectives*. New York, NY: Longman.
Angell, Norman. 1911. *The Great Illusion: A Study of the Relation of Military Power in Nations to Their Economic and Social Advantage*. New York, NY: G. P. Putnam's & Sons.
Aradau, Claudia, and Jef Huysmans. 2014. "Critical Methods in International Relations: The Politics of Techniques, Devices and Acts." *European Journal of International Relations* 20: 596–619.
Archer, Margaret A. 1996. *Culture and Agency: The Place of Culture in Social Theory*. Rev. ed. Cambridge: Cambridge University Press.
Aron, Raymond. 1966. *Peace and War: A Theory of International Relations*. Richard Howard and Annette Baker Fox, trans. London: Weidenfeld and Nicolson.
Aronow, Peter M., and Cyrus Samii. 2015. "Does Regression Produce Representative Estimates of Causal Effects?" *American Political Science Review* 60: 250–267.
Arrow, Kenneth J. 1951a. *Social Choice and Individual Values*. New York, NY: Wiley.
Arrow, Kenneth J. 1951b. "Mathematical Models in the Social Sciences." In Daniel Lerner and Harold Lasswell, eds. *The Policy Sciences*. Stanford, CA: Stanford University Press, 129–154.
Ashley, Richard K. 1984. "The Poverty of Neorealism." *International Organization* 38: 225–286.
Axelrod, Robert. 1973. "Schema Theory: An Information Processing Model of Perception and Cognition." *American Political Science Review* 67: 1248–1266.
Ayres, William R. 2016. "Naïve Scientists and Conflict Analysis: Learning through Case Studies." *Learning and Teaching* 9: 29–49.
Ba, Alice D. 2010. "Symposium: Beyond Paradigms and Research Programs—Reflections on Analytic Eclecticism and the Field." *Qualitative and Multi-method Research* 8: 14–17.

Babbie, Earl. 2001. *The Practice of Social Research*. 9th ed. Belmont, CA: Wadsworth.
Babst, Dean. 1972. "Elective Governments—a Force for Peace." *Industrial Research*, April, 55–58.
Baev, Pavel. 2002. "Review of *The Tragedy of Great Power Politics*." *Journal of Peace Research* 39: 641.
Baker, Linda. 2016. "Metacognition." www.education.com.
Baldwin, David, ed. 1993. *Neorealism and Neoliberalism: The Contemporary Debate*. New York, NY: Columbia University Press.
Ball, Terence. 1976. "From Paradigms to Research Programs: Toward a Post-Kuhnian Political Science." *American Journal of Political Science* 20: 151–177.
Banchoff, Thomas. 1999. "Review of *Deadly Imbalances*." *German Politics & Society* 17: 134–137.
Barkin, J. Samuel. 2003. "Realist Constructivism." *International Studies Review* 5: 325–342.
Barkin, J. Samuel. 2010. *Realist Constructivism*. Cambridge: Cambridge University Press.
Barkin, J. Samuel, and Laura Sjoberg. 2019. *International Relations Last Synthesis? Decoupling Constructivist and Critical Approaches*. Oxford: Oxford University Press.
Barnett, Michael. 2003. "Alliances, Balances of Threats, and Neorealism: The Accidental Coup." In John A. Vasquez and Colin Elman, eds. *Realism and the Balance of Power: A New Debate*. Upper Saddle River, NJ: Prentice Hall, 222–249.
Barnett, Michael, and Raymond Duvall. 2008. "Power in International Politics." *International Organization* 59: 39–75.
Barnoschi, Miruna. 2017. "Perspectives on the Problem of Community and the Problem of Dirty Hands: Anglo-American Realists and Continental Humanists in the Context of the Syrian Crisis." Evanston, IL: Northwestern University. Unpublished manuscript.
Basu, Soumita. 2013. "Emancipatory Potential in Feminist Security Studies." *International Studies Perspectives* 14: 455–458.
Basu, Soumita, and Maya Eichler. 2017. "Gender in International Relations: Interdisciplinarity and the Study of Conflict." In Steve A. Yetiv and Patrick James, eds. *Advancing Interdisciplinary Approaches to International Relations*. New York, NY: Palgrave Macmillan, 189–228.
Bauer, Harry, and Elisabetta Brighi. 2009. "Conclusions: On the Obstacle and Promises of Pragmatism in International Relations." In Harry Bauer and Elisabetta Brighi, eds. *Pragmatism in International Relations*. New York, NY: Routledge, 159–166.
Beach, Derek. 2016. "Symposium: Causal Mechanisms and Process Tracing—What Are We Actually Tracing? Process Tracing and the Benefits of Conceptualizing Causal Mechanisms as Systems." *Qualitative and Multi-method Research Section Newsletter* 14: 15–22.
Bell, Duncan, ed. 2008. *Political Thought and International Relations: Variations on a Realist Theme*. Oxford: Oxford University Press.
Bennett, Andrew. 2010. "Symposium: Beyond Paradigms and Research Programs—from Analytic Eclecticism to Structured Pluralism." *Qualitative and Multi-method Research* 8: 6–9.
Bennett, Andrew. 2013. "The Mother of All Isms: Causal Mechanisms and Structured Pluralism in International Relations Theory." *European Journal of International Relations* 19: 459–481.
Bennett, Andrew, Aharon Barth, and Kenneth Rutherford. 2003. "Do We Preach What We Practice? A Survey of Methods in Journals and Graduate Curricula." *PS: Political Science and Politics* 36: 387–389.

Benson, Oliver. 1988. "Review of *The Origins of Alliances*." *Annals of the American Academy of Political and Social Science* 500: 132–133.

Berenskoetter, Felix, and Michael J. Williams, eds. 2007. *Power in World Politics*. New York, NY: Routledge.

Bertucci, Mariano E., Jarrod Hayes, and Patrick James. 2018a. "A New Look at Constructivism." In Mariano E. Bertucci, Jarrod Hayes, and Patrick James, eds. *Constructivism Reconsidered*. Ann Arbor, MI: University of Michigan Press, 1–14.

Bertucci, Mariano E., Jarrod Hayes, and Patrick James. 2018b. "Moving Forward." In Mariano E. Bertucci, Ewan Jarrod Hayes, and Patrick James, eds. *Constructivism Reconsidered*. Ann Arbor, MI: University of Michigan Press, 243–261.

Best, Jacqueline, and William Walters. 2013. "'Actor-Network Theory' and International Relationality: Lost (and Found) in Translation." *International Political Sociology* 7: 332–334.

Bew, John. 2016. *Realpolitik: A History*. Oxford: Oxford University Press.

Black, Duncan. 1958. *The Theory of Committees and Elections*. Cambridge: Cambridge University Press.

Blagden, David. 2016. "Induction and Deduction in International Relations: Squaring the Circle between Theory and Evidence." *International Studies Review* 18: 195–213.

Blagden, David. 2018. "Realism, Uncertainty, and the Security Dilemma: Identity and the Tantalizing Promise of Transformed International Relations." In Mariano E. Bertucci, Jarrod Hayes, and Patrick James, eds. *Constructivism Reconsidered*. Ann Arbor MI: University of Michigan Press, 197–226.

Blaug, Mark. 1980. *The Methodology of Economics*. Cambridge: Cambridge University Press.

Bleiker, Roland. 2018a. "The Aesthetic Turn in International Relations." Oxford Bibliographies in International Relations. http://www.oxfordbibliographies.com/page/international-relations.

Bleiker, Roland, ed. 2018b. "Mapping Visual Global Politics." *Visual Global Politics (Interventions)*. New York, NY: Routledge, 1–29.

Bobrow, Davis B. 1996. "Complex Insecurity: Implications of a Sobering Metaphor." *International Studies Quarterly* 40: 435–450.

Bock, Andreas M., Ingo Henneberg, and Friedrich Plank. 2015. "'If You Compress the Spring, It Will Snap Back Hard': The Ukrainian Crisis and the Balance of Threat Theory." *International Journal* 7: 101–109.

Boehmer, Charles. 2010. "Economic Growth and Violent International Conflict: 1875–1999." *Defense and Peace Economics* 21: 249–268.

Boehmer, Charles, and David Sobek. 2005. "Violent Adolescence: State Development and the Propensity for Militarized Interstate Conflict." *Journal of Peace Research* 42: 5–26.

Booth, Ken. 1982. "Review of *War and Change in World Politics*." *International Affairs* 58: 507.

Booth, William James, Patrick James, and Hudson Meadwell, eds. 1993. *Politics and Rationality*. Cambridge: Cambridge University Press.

Boudon, Raymond. 1991. "What Middle-Range Theories Are." *Contemporary Sociology* 20: 519–522.

Boyer, Mark A., and Jonathan Wilkenfeld. 1989. "The Superpowers as Crisis Managers." In Michael Brecher and Jonathan Wilkenfeld, eds. *Crisis, Conflict and Instability*. Oxford: Pergamon, 75–90.

Brady, Henry E., and David Collier, eds. 2004. *Rethinking Social Inquiry: Diverse Tools, Shared Standards*. Lanham, MD: Rowman and Littlefield.

Brams, Steven J. 1993. *Theory of Moves*. Cambridge: Cambridge University Press.

Branch, Jordan. 2014. *The Cartographic State: Maps, Territory and the Origins of Sovereignty*. Cambridge: Cambridge University Press.

Branch, Jordan. 2018. "Technology and Constructivism: Interrogating the Material-Ideational Divide." In Mariano E. Bertucci, Jarrod Hayes, and Patrick James, eds. *Constructivism Reconsidered*. Ann Arbor, MI: University of Michigan Press, 103-115.

Braumoller, Bear F., and Benjamin Campbell. 2018. "The Logics of Systemic Theory." In William R. Thompson, ed. *Empirical International Relations Theory*. Vol. 2. Oxford: Oxford University Press, 445-467.

Brawley, Mark. 2009. *Political Economy and Grand Strategy: A Neoclassical Realist View*. New York, NY: Routledge.

Brecher, Michael. 1953. *The Struggle for Kashmir*. New York, NY: Oxford University Press.

Brecher, Michael. 1972. *The Foreign Policy System of Israel: Setting, Images, Process*. London: Oxford University Press, 1972.

Brecher, Michael. 1999. "International Studies in the Twentieth Century and Beyond: Flawed Dichotomies, Synthesis, Cumulation." *International Studies Quarterly* 43: 231-264.

Brecher, Michael. 2016. *The World of Protracted Conflicts*. Lanham, MD: Lexington.

Brecher, Michael. 2018. *A Century of Crisis and Conflict in the International System: Theory and Evidence*. New York, NY: Palgrave-Macmillan.

Brecher, Michael, Patrick James, and Jonathan Wilkenfeld. 1990. "Polarity and Stability: New Concepts, Indicators and Evidence." *International Interactions* 16: 49-80.

Brecher, Michael, and Jonathan Wilkenfeld. 1997. *A Study of Crisis*. Ann Arbor, MI: University of Michigan Press.

Brecher, Michael, and Jonathan Wilkenfeld. 2000. *A Study of Crisis*. 2nd ed. Ann Arbor, MI: University of Michigan Press.

Brecher, Michael, Jonathan Wilkenfeld, Kyle Beardsley, Patrick James, and David Quinn. 2017. *International Crisis Behavior Codebook, Version 12*. Durham, North Carolina. http://sites.duke.edu/icbdata/data-collections/.

Bremer, Stuart A. 1992. "Dangerous Dyads: Conditions Affecting the Likelihood of Interstate War, 1816-1965." *Journal of Conflict Resolution* 36: 309-341.

Bremer, Stuart A., and Thomas R. Cusack. 1980. "The Urns of War: An Application of Probability Theory to the Genesis of War." Discussion Paper IIVG/dp 80-128. West Berlin: Wissenschaftszentrum Berlin.

Bremer, Stuart A., J. David Singer, and Urs Luterbacher. 1973. "The Population Density and War Proneness of European Nations, 1816-1965." *Comparative Political Studies* 6: 329-348.

Brooks, Stephen G. 1997. "Dueling Realisms." *International Organization* 51: 445-477.

Brown, Chris. 2012. "Review Article—Realism: Rational or Reasonable?" *International Affairs* 88: 857-866.

Brzoska, Michael. 1993. "Review of Charles F. Doran, *Systems in Crisis*." *Politische Vierteljahresschrift* 34: 381-382.

Buchanan, James M., and Gordon Tullock. 1962. *The Calculus of Consent: Logical Foundations of Constitutional Democracy*. Indianapolis, IN: Liberty Fund.

Bueno de Mesquita, Bruce. 1980. "Theories of International Conflict: An Analysis and an Appraisal." In Ted Robert Gurr, ed. *Handbook of Political Conflict: Theory and Research*. New York: Free Press, 361-398.

Bueno de Mesquita, Bruce. 1981. *The War Trap*. New Haven, CT: Yale University Press.
Bueno de Mesquita, Bruce. 2003. "Neorealism's Logic and Evidence: When Is a Theory Falsified?" In John A. Vasquez and Colin Elman, eds. *Realism and the Balance of Power: A New Debate*. Upper Saddle River, NJ: Prentice Hall, 166–199.
Bueno de Mesquita, Bruce, and David Lalman. 1992. *War and Reason: Domestic and International Imperatives*. New Haven, CT: Yale University Press.
Bueno de Mesquita, Bruce, Alistair Smith, Randolph M. Siverson, and James D. Morrow. 2003. *The Logic of Political Survival*. Cambridge, MA: MIT Press.
Buhaug, Halvard. 2005. "Dangerous Dyads Revisited: Democracies May Not Be That Peaceful After All." *Conflict Management and Peace Science* 22: 95–111.
Bull, Hedley. 1966. "International Theory: The Case for a Classical Approach." *World Politics* 18: 361–377.
Bull, Hedley. 1977. *The Anarchical Society: A Study of Order in World Politics*. London: Macmillan.
Bunge, Mario. 1993. "Realism and Antirealism in Social Science." *Theory and Decision* 35: 207–235.
Bunge, Mario. 1996. *Finding Philosophy in Social Science*. New Haven, CT: Yale University Press.
Bunge, Mario. 1997. "Mechanism and Explanation." *Philosophy of the Social Sciences* 27: 410–465.
Bunge, Mario. 1998. *Social Science under Debate: A Philosophical Perspective*. Toronto: University of Toronto Press.
Bunge, Mario. 2003. *Philosophical Dictionary*. Enlarged ed. Amherst, NY: Prometheus Books.
Bunge, Mario. 2004. "How Does It Work? The Search for Explanatory Mechanisms." *Philosophy of the Social Sciences* 34: 182–210.
Burch, Robert. 2014. "Charles Sanders Peirce." *Stanford Encyclopedia of Philosophy*. https://plato.stanford.edu/entries/peirce.
Buxton, Angharad. 2018. Personal communication.
Buzan, Barry, and Richard Little. 2003. "Reconceptualizing Anarchy: Structural Realism Meets World History." *European Journal of International Relations* 2: 403–438.
Buzan, Barry, Ole Wæver, and Jaap de Wilde. 1998. *Security: A New Framework for Analysis*. Boulder, CO: Lynne Rienner.
Carr, E. H. 1964 [1939]. *The Twenty Years' Crisis, 1919–1939: An Introduction to the Study of International Relations*. London: Macmillan.
Cashman, Greg. 2013. *What Causes War? An Introduction to Theories of International Conflict*. New York, NY: Rowman & Littlefield.
Cha, Victor D. 2000. "Abandonment, Entrapment, and Neoclassical Realism in Asia: The United States, Japan, and Korea." *International Studies Quarterly* 44: 261–291.
Chakravartty, Anjan. 2007. *A Metaphysics for Scientific Realism: Knowing the Unobservable*. Cambridge: Cambridge University Press.
Chakravartty, Anjan. 2011. "Scientific Realism." In Edward N. Zalta, ed. *Stanford Encyclopedia of Philosophy*. Summer 2017 ed. http://plato.stanford.edu/entries/scientific-realism/.
Celucci, Carlo. 2019. "Diagrams in Mathematics." *Foundations of Science* 24: 583–604.
Checkel, Jeffrey T. 2010. "Theoretical Synthesis in IR: Possibilities and Limits." Simons Papers in Security and Development, No. 6. September. Vancouver: School for International Studies, Simon Fraser University.

Checkel, Jeffrey T. 2016. "Mechanisms, Method and the Near-Death of IR Theory in the Post-paradigm Era." IR 2030 Workshop. Laramie, WY: University of Wyoming.
Chernoff, Fred. 2007. "Critical Realism, Scientific Realism, and International Relations Theory." *Millennium* 35: 399–407.
Chernoff, Fred. 2009. "Defending Foundations for International Relations Theory." *International Theory* 1: 466–477.
Chernoff, Fred. 2013. "Science, Progress and Pluralism in the Study of International Relations." *Millennium* 41: 346–366.
Chernoff, Fred. 2014. *Explanation and Progress in Security Studies: Bridging Theoretical Divides in International Relations*. Stanford, CA: Stanford University Press.
Chernoff, Fred. 2017. "Bounded Pluralism and Explanatory Progress in International Relations: What We Can Learn from the Democratic Peace Debate." In Annette Freyberg-Inan, Ewan Harrison, and Patrick James, eds. *Evaluating Progress in International Relations: How Do You Know?* New York, NY: Routledge, 89–108.
Chiu, Daniel Y. 2003. "International Alliances in the Power Cycle Theory of State Behavior." *International Political Science Review* 24: 123–136.
Choi, Hyunsun. 2011. "Systemism." In John T. Ishiyama and Marijke Breuning, eds. *21st Century Political Science: A Reference Handbook*. Vol. 1. Los Angeles, CA: Sage, 29–33.
Choi, Seung-Whan, and Patrick James. 2005. *A New Quest for International Peace: Civil-Military Dynamics, Political Communications and Democracy*. New York, NY: Palgrave.
Choucri, Nazli. 2012. *Cyberpolitics in International Relations*. Cambridge, MA: MIT Press.
Christensen, Thomas, and Jack Snyder. 2003. "Progressive Research on Degenerate Alliances." In John A. Vasquez and Colin Elman, eds. *Realism and the Balance of Power: A New Debate*. Upper Saddle River, NJ: Prentice Hall, 66–73.
Claude, Jr., Inis L. 1962. *Power and International Relations*. New York, NY: Random House.
Cleveland, William S. 1985. *The Elements of Graphing Data*. Monterey, CA: Wadsworth Advanced Books and Software.
Coase, R. H. 1960. "The Problem of Social Cost." *Journal of Law and Economics* 3: 1–44.
Cohen, Raymond, and Raymond Westbrook, eds. 2002. *Amarna Diplomacy: The Beginnings of International Relations*. Baltimore, MD: Johns Hopkins University Press.
Coleman, James S. 1990. *Foundations of Social Theory*. Cambridge, MA: Belknap Press of Harvard University Press.
Collingwood, R. G. 1946. *The Idea of History*. Oxford: Oxford University Press.
Cooper, Scott. 2003. "State-Centric Balance-of-Threat Theory." *Security Studies* 13: 306–349.
Copeland, Dale C. 1996. "Neorealism and the Myth of Bipolar Stability: Toward a New Dynamic Realist Theory of Major War." In Benjamin Frankel, ed. *Realism: Restatements and Renewal*. London: Frank Cass, 29–89.
Copeland, Dale C. 2000. *The Origins of Major War*. Ithaca, NY: Cornell University Press.
Cornut, Jérémie. 2015. "Analytic Eclecticism in Practice: A Method for Combining International Relations Theories." *International Studies Perspectives* 16: 50–66.
Correlates of War Project. 2017. http://www.correlatesofwar.org/data-sets.
Coser, Lewis F. 1956. *The Functions of Social Conflict*. New York, NY: Free Press.
Cozette, Murielle. 2008. "What Lies Ahead: Classical Realism on the Future of International Relations." *International Studies Review* 10: 667–679.
Cristol, Jonathan. 2017. "Realism." Oxford Bibliographies on International Relations. http://www.oxfordbibliographies.com/obo/page/international-relations.

Dahl, Robert A. 1957. "The Concept of Power." *Systems Research and Behavioral Science* 2: 201–215.

Danielson, Robert W., and Gale M. Sinatra. 2017. "A Relational Reasoning Approach to Text-Graphic Processing." *Educational Psychology Review* 29: 55–72.

David, Steven R. 2015. *Obama: The Reluctant Realist*. Ramat Gan, Israel: Begin-Sadat Center for Strategic Studies, Mideast Security and Policy Studies No. 113.

Deutsch, Karl, and J. David Singer. 1964. "Multipolar Power Systems and International Stability." *World Politics* 16: 390–406.

Diehl, Paul F., and Frank W. Wayman. 1994. "Realpolitik: Dead End, Detour, or Road Map?" In Frank W. Wayman and Paul F. Diehl, eds. *Reconstructing Realpolitik*. Ann Arbor, MI: University of Michigan Press, 247–265.

Donnelly, Jack. 2000. *Realism and International Relations*. New York, NY: Cambridge University Press.

Donnelly, Jack. 2008. "The Ethics of Realism." In Christian Reus-Smit and Duncan Snidal, eds. *The Oxford Handbook of International Relations*. Oxford: Oxford University Press, 150–162.

Doran, Charles F. 1971. *The Politics of Assimilation: Hegemony and Its Aftermath*. Baltimore, MD: Johns Hopkins University Press.

Doran, Charles F. 1980. "Modes, Mechanisms, and Turning Points: Perspectives on the Transformation of the International System." *International Political Science Review* 1: 35–61.

Doran, Charles F. 1983. "War and Power Dynamics: Economic Underpinnings." *International Studies Quarterly* 27: 419–441.

Doran, Charles F. 1989a. "Systemic Disequilibrium, Foreign Policy Role, and the Power Cycle: Challenges for Research Design." *Journal of Conflict Resolution* 33: 371–401.

Doran, Charles F. 1989b. "Power Cycle Theory of Systems Structure and Stability: Commonalities and Complementarities." In Manus I. Midlarsky, ed. *Handbook of War Studies*. Ann Arbor, MI: University of Michigan Press, 83–110.

Doran, Charles F. 1991. *Systems in Crisis: New Imperatives of High Politics at Century's End*. Cambridge: Cambridge University Press.

Doran, Charles F. 2003. "Economics, Philosophy of History, and the Single Dynamic of Power Cycle Theory: Expectations, Competition, and Statecraft." *International Political Science Review* 24: 13–49.

Doran, Charles F. 2007. "Review of *Unanswered Threats*." *International History Review* 29: 465–467.

Doran, Charles F. 2012. "Power Cycle Theory and the Ascendance of China: Peaceful or Stormy?" *SAIS Review* 32: 73–87.

Doran, Charles F., and Wes Parsons. 1980. "War and the Cycle of Relative Power." *American Political Science Review* 74: 947–965.

Doty, D. Harold, and William H. Glick. 1994. "Typologies as a Unique Form of Theory Building: Toward Improved Understanding and Modeling." *Academy of Management Review* 19: 230–251.

Downs, Anthony. 1957. *An Economic Theory of Democracy*. New York, NY: Harper.

Doyle, Michael. 1986. "Liberalism and World Politics." *American Political Science Review* 80: 1151–1169.

Easton, David. 1953. *The Political System: An Inquiry into the State of Political Science*. New York, NY: Alfred A. Knopf.

Easton, David. 1965a. *A Framework for Political Analysis.* Englewood Cliffs, NJ: Prentice Hall, Inc.

Easton, David. 1965b. *A Systems Analysis of Political Life.* New York, NY: Wiley.

Easton, David. 1990. *The Analysis of Political Structure.* New York, NY: Routledge.

Eckstein, Harry. 1975. "Case Study and Theory in Political Science." In Fred I. Greenstein and Nelson W. Polsby, eds. *Handbook of Political Science.* Vol. 7. Reading, MA: Addison-Wesley, 79–137.

Eichler, Maya. 2012. *Militarizing Men: Gender, Conscription, and War in Post-Soviet Russia.* Stanford, CA: Stanford University Press.

Elman, Colin. 2003. "Introduction: Appraising Balance of Power Theory." In John A. Vasquez and Colin Elman, eds. *Realism and the Balance of Power: A New Debate.* Upper Saddle River, NJ: Prentice Hall, 1–22.

Elman, Colin. 2004. "Extending Offensive Realism: The Louisiana Purchase and America's Rise to Regional Hegemony." *American Political Science Review* 98: 563–576.

Elman, Colin, and Miriam Fendius Elman. 2003a. "Lakatos and Neorealism: A Reply to Vasquez." In John A. Vasquez and Colin Elman, eds. *Realism and the Balance of Power: A New Debate.* Upper Saddle River, NJ: Prentice Hall, 81–86.

Elman, Colin, and Miriam Fendius Elman, eds. 2003b. *Progress in International Relations Theory: Appraising the Field.* Cambridge, MA: MIT Press.

Elman, Colin, and Michael A. Jensen. 2014. "Introduction." In Colin Elman and Michael A. Jensen, eds. *Realism Reader.* New York, NY: Routledge, 1–30.

Elman, Colin, and John A. Vasquez. 2003. "Closing Dialogue." In John A. Vasquez and Colin Elman, eds. *Realism and the Balance of Power: A New Debate.* Upper Saddle River, NJ: Prentice Hall, 280–303.

Elman, Miriam, ed. 1997. *Paths to Peace: Is Democracy the Answer?* Cambridge, MA: MIT Press.

Evans, Peter B., Dietrich Rueschmeyer, and Theda Skocpol, eds. 1985. *Bringing the State Back In.* Cambridge: Cambridge University Press.

Fearon, James D. 2011. "Two States, Two Types, Two Actions." *Security Studies* 20: 431–440.

Feaver, Peter, Gunther Hellman, Randall L. Schweller, Jeffrey W. Taliaferro, William C. Wohlforth, Jeffrey W. Legro, and Andrew Moravcsik. 2000. "Correspondence: Brother, Can You Spare a Paradigm? (or Was Anybody Ever a Realist)?" *International Security* 25: 165–193.

Ferguson, Yale H. 2015. "Diversity in IR Theory: Pluralism as an Opportunity for Understanding Global Politics." *International Studies Perspectives* 16: 3–12.

Ferrarotti, Franco. 1999. "The Social Character of Science: The Lessons of Positivism." *International Journal of Politics, Culture, and Society* 12: 535–553.

Feyerabend, Paul. 1975. *Against Method.* London: Verso.

Fiammenghi, Davide. 2011. "The Security Curve and the Structure of International Politics: A Neorealist Synthesis." *International Security* 35: 126–154.

Finnemore, Martha. 2003. *The Purpose of Intervention: Changing Beliefs about the Use of Force.* Ithaca, NY: Cornell University Press.

Fisher, John R. 2011. "Systems Theory and Structural Functionalism." In John T. Ishiyama and Marijke Breuning, eds. *21st Century Political Science: A Reference Handbook.* Vol. 1. Los Angeles, CA: Sage, 71–80.

Fisunoğlu, Ali. 2019. "System Dynamics Modeling in International Relations." *All Azimuth* 8: 231–253.

Fordham, Benjamin O. 1998. *Building the Cold War Consensus: The Political Economy of U.S. National Security Policy, 1949–51*. Ann Arbor, MI: University of Michigan Press.
Fordham, Benjamin O. 2005. "Strategic Conflict Avoidance and the Diversionary Use of Force." *Journal of Politics* 67: 132–153.
Fox, William T. R. 1982–83. "Review of *War and Change in World Politics*." *Political Science Quarterly* 97: 684–685.
Fozouni, Bahman. 1995. "Confutation of Political Realism." *International Studies Quarterly* 39: 479–510.
Francis, Michael J. 2002. "Review of *The Tragedy of Great Power Politics*." *Review of Politics* 64: 560–563.
Frankel, Benjamin, ed. 1996a. *Realism: Restatements and Renewal*. London: Frank Cass.
Frankel, Benjamin. 1996b. "Restating the Realist Case: An Introduction." In Benjamin Frankel, ed. *Realism: Restatements and Renewal*. London: Frank Cass, ix–xx.
Frankel, Benjamin. 1996c. "Introduction." In Benjamin Frankel, ed. *Roots of Realism*. Portland, OR: Frank Cass, ix–xxiii.
Frankel, Benjamin, ed. 1996d. *Roots of Realism*. Portland, OR: Frank Cass.
Freeden, Michael. 2013. "The Morphological Analysis of Ideology." In Michael Freeden and Mar Stears, eds. *The Oxford Handbook of Political Ideologies*. Oxford: Oxford University Press, 115–137.
Freyberg-Inan, Annette. 2004. *What Moves Man: The Realist Theory of International Relations and Its Judgment of Human Nature*. Albany, NY: State University of New York Press.
Freyberg-Inan, Annette. 2006. "Rational Paranoia and Enlightened Machismo: The Strange Psychological Foundations of Realism." *Journal of International Relations and Development* 9: 247–268.
Freyberg-Inan, Annette. 2016. "Rationality." In Felix Berenskötter, ed. *Concepts in World Politics*. London: Sage, 57–72.
Freyberg-Inan, Annette. 2017. "The Role of Knowledge Creation for Theory in IR: A Sociable Pluralist Discussion." In Annette Freyberg-Inan, Ewan Harrison, and Patrick James, eds. *Evaluating Progress in International Relations: How Do You Know?* New York, NY: Routledge, 74–85.
Freyberg-Inan, Annette. 2020. Personal communication.
Freyberg-Inan, Annette, Ewan Harrison, and Patrick James, eds. 2017. *Evaluating Progress in International Relations: How Do You Know?* New York, NY: Routledge.
Freyberg-Inan, Annette, Ewan Harrison, and Patrick James. 2017b. "Conclusion: Different Standards for Discovery and Confirmation." In Annette Freyberg-Inan, Ewan Harrison, and Patrick James, eds. *Evaluating Progress in International Relations: How Do You Know?* New York, NY: Routledge, 173–184.
Friedberg, Aaron L. 1988. *The Weary Titan: Britain and the Experience of Relative Decline, 1895–1905*. Princeton, NJ: Princeton University Press.
Friedberg, Aaron L. 1992. "Why Didn't the United States Become a Garrison State?" *International Security* 16: 109–142.
Friedman, Gil, and Harvey Starr. 1997. *Agency, Structure, and International Politics: From Ontology to Empirical Inquiry*. New York, NY: Routledge.
Fritsch, Stefan. 2017. "Technology, Conflict and International Relations." In Steve A. Yetiv and Patrick James, eds. *Advancing Interdisciplinary Approaches to International Relations*. New York, NY: Palgrave Macmillan, 115–152.
Galtung, Johan. 1971. "A Structural Theory of Imperialism." *Journal of Peace Research* 8: 81–117.

Gansen, Sarah, and Patrick James. 2021. "A Graphic Turn for Canadian Foreign Policy: Insights from Systemism." *Canadian Foreign Policy Journal* 27: 271–291.

Gartzke, Erik. 1998. "Kant We All Just Get Along? Opportunity, Willingness, and the Origins of the Democratic Peace." *American Journal of Political Science* 42: 1–27.

Gartzke, Erik. 2002. "Review of *Causes of War*." *Journal of Policy Analysis and Management* 21: 723–725.

Gartzke, Erik. 2005. The Affinity of Nations. http://www.columbia.edu/ eg589/datasets.htm.

Gartzke, Erik. 2007. "The Capitalist Peace." *American Journal of Political Science* 51: 166–191.

Gastfriend, Eric. 2015. "90% of All of the Scientists That Ever Lived Are Alive Today." http://futureoflife.org/2015/11/05/90-of-all-the-scientists-that-ever-lived-are-alive-today/.

Gat, Azar. 2009. "So Why Do People Fight? Evolutionary Theory and the Causes of War." *European Journal of International Relations* 15: 571–599.

Geller, Daniel S., and J. David Singer. 1998. *Nations at War: A Scientific Study of International Conflict*. Cambridge: Cambridge University Press.

George, Alexander L., and Andrew Bennett. 2005. *Case Studies and Theory Development in the Social Sciences*. Cambridge, MA: MIT Press.

Gerring, John. 2007. *Case Study Research: Principles and Practices*. Cambridge: Cambridge University Press.

Gerth, H. H., and C. Wright Mills, trans. and eds. 1946. *From Max Weber: Essays in Sociology*. New York, NY: Oxford University Press, 77–128.

Gibler, Douglas M. 2009. *International Military Alliances, 1648-2008*. Washington, DC: CQ Press.

Gibler, Douglas M. 2012. *The Territorial Peace: Borders, State Development, and International Conflict*. Cambridge: Cambridge University Press.

Gilpin, Robert G. 1981. *War and Change in World Politics*. Cambridge: Cambridge University Press.

Gilpin, Robert G. 1984. "The Richness of the Tradition of Political Realism." *International Organization* 38: 287–304.

Gilpin, Robert. 1996. "No One Loves a Political Realist." In Benjamin Frankel, ed. *Realism: Restatements and Renewal*. London: Frank Cass, 3–26.

Glaser, Charles L. 1996. "Realists as Optimists: Cooperation as Self-Help." In Benjamin Frankel, ed. *Realism: Restatements and Renewal*. London: Frank Cass, 122–163.

Glaser, Charles L. 2003. "The Necessary and Natural Evolution of Structural Realism." In John A. Vasquez and Colin Elman, eds. *Realism and the Balance of Power: A New Debate*. Upper Saddle River, NJ: Prentice Hall, 266–279.

Glaser, Charles L. 2010. *Rational Theory of International Politics: The Logic of Competition and Cooperation*. Princeton, NJ: Princeton University Press.

Glenn, John. 2009. "Realism versus Strategic Culture: Competition and Collaboration?" *International Studies Review* 11: 523–551.

Golding, William. 1954. *The Lord of the Flies*. London: Faber and Faber.

Goldman, Emily O. 2011. *Power in Uncertain Times: Strategy in the Fog of Peace*. Stanford, CA: Stanford University Press.

Gourevitch, Peter. 1978. "The Second Image Reversed: The International Sources of Domestic Politics." *International Organization* 32: 881–912.

Gowan, Peter. 2002. "A Calculus of Power." *New Left Review* 16: 47–67.

Graham, Benjamin A. T. 2017. Personal communication.
Graham, Benjamin A. T. 2018. *Investing in the Homeland: The Political Economy of Diaspora Direct Investment*. Ann Arbor, MI: University of Michigan Press.
Green, Leslie. 1985. "Support for the System." *British Journal of Political Science* 15: 127–142.
Grieco, Joseph M. 1988. "Anarchy and the Limits of Cooperation: A Realist Critique of the Newest Liberal Institutionalism." *International Organization* 42: 485–507.
Grieco, Joseph M. 2019. "The Schools of Thought Problem in International Relations." *International Studies Review* 21: 424–446.
Griffiths, Martin. 1992. *Realism, Idealism and International Politics: A Reinterpretation*. New York, NY: Routledge.
Grzymala-Busse, Anna. 2011. "Time Will Tell? Temporality and the Analysis of Causal Mechanisms and Processes." *Comparative Political Studies* 44: 1267–1297.
Guilhot, Nicolas. 2016. "The Kuhning of Reason: Realism, Rationalism, and Political Decision in IR Theory after Thomas Kuhn." *Review of International Studies* 42: 3–24.
Gunnell, John G. 2011. "Social Scientific Inquiry and Meta-theoretical Fantasy: The Case of International Relations." *Review of International Studies* 47: 1447–1469.
Guzzini, Stefano. 1998. *Realism in International Relations and International Political Economy: The Continuing Story of a Death Foretold*. New York, NY: Routledge.
Guzzini, Stefano. 2000. "A Reconstruction of Constructivism in International Relations." *European Journal of International Relations* 6: 147–182.
Guzzini, Stefano. 2004. "The Enduring Dilemmas of Realism in International Relations." *European Journal of International Relations* 10: 533–568.
Haas, Michael. 2017. *Political Science Revitalized: Filling the Jigsaw Puzzle with Metatheory*. Lanham, MD: Lexington Books.
Haas, Peter M. 2010a. "Symposium: Beyond Paradigms and Research Programs—Introduction." *Qualitative and Multi-method Research* 8: 5.
Haas, Peter M. 2010b. "Symposium: Beyond Paradigms and Research Programs—Practicing Analytic Eclecticism." *Qualitative and Multi-method Research* 8: 9–14.
Hafner-Burton, Emilie M., and Stephan Haggard. 2017. "The Behavioral Revolution and International Relations." *International Organization* 71: S1–S31.
Hafner-Burton, Emilie, Stephan Haggard, David A. Lake, and David G. Victor. 2017. "The Behavioral Revolution and International Relations." *International Organization* 71: S1–S31.
Haglund, David G. 2015. *Ethnic Diasporas and the Canada-United States Security Community: From the Civil War to Today*. New York, NY: Rowman & Littlefield.
Hall, Todd H., and Andrew A. G. Ross. 2015. "Affective Politics After 9/11." *International Organization* 69: 847–879.
Halliday, Fred. 1997. "Review of Stephen M. Walt, *Revolution and War* (Ithaca, NY: Cornell University Press, 1996)." *Millennium* 26: 230–232.
Hamilton, Eric J., and Brian C. Rathbun. 2013. "Scarce Differences: Toward a Material and Systemic Foundation for Offensive and Defensive Realism." *Security Studies* 22: 436–465.
Hardin, Garrett. 1968. "The Tragedy of the Commons." *Science* 162, 3859: 1243–1248.
Harrison, Ewan, Annette Freyberg-Inan, and Patrick James. 2017. "Introduction: Progress, Consensus, and Cumulation in IR Scholarship?" In Annette Freyberg-Inan, Ewan Harrison, and Patrick James, eds. *Evaluating Progress in International Relations: How Do You Know?* New York, NY: Routledge, 1–14.

Harrison, Ewan, and Sara Mitchell. 2014. *The Triumph of Democracy and the Eclipse of the West*. New York, NY: Palgrave Macmillan.

Harvey, Frank. 1999. "Practicing Coercion: Revisiting Successes and Failures Using Boolean Logic and Comparative Methods." *Journal of Conflict Resolution* 43: 840–871.

Haslam, Jonathan. 2010. "John Mearsheimer's 'Elementary Geometry of Power': Euclidean Moment or an Intellectual Blind Alley?" In Ernest R. May, Richard Rosecrance, and Zara Steiner, eds. *History and Neorealism*. Cambridge: Cambridge University Press, 322–340.

Hayes, Jarrod. 2009. "Identity and Securitization in the Democratic Peace: The United States and the Divergence of Response to India and Iran's Nuclear Programs." *International Studies Quarterly* 53: 977–999.

Hayes, Jarrod. 2015. *Constructing National Security: U.S. Relations with India and China*. Cambridge: Cambridge University Press.

Hayes, Jarrod, and Patrick James. 2017. "Systemism, Analytic Eclecticism, and the Democratic Peace." In Annette Freyberg-Inan, Ewan Harrison, and Patrick James, eds. *Progress in International Relations: How Do You Know?* New York, NY: Routledge, 109–124.

He, Kai, and Huiyun Feng. 2010. "'Why Is There No NATO in Asia?' Revisited: Prospect Theory, Balance of Threat, and US Alliance Strategies." *European Journal of International Relations* 18: 227–250.

Hebron, Lui, Patrick James, and Michael Rudy. 2007. "Testing Dynamic Theories of Conflict: Power Cycles, Power Transitions, Foreign Policy Crises and Militarized Interstate Disputes." *International Interactions* 33: 1–29.

Hegre, Håvard. 1998. "Review of *A Study of Crisis*." *Journal of Peace Research* 35: 647.

Hempel, Carl G. 1965. *Aspects of Scientific Explanation: And Other Essays in the Philosophy of Science*. New York, NY: Free Press.

Herz, John H. 1951. *Political Realism and Political Idealism*. Chicago, IL: University of Chicago Press.

Hirschman, Albert O. 1970. *Exit, Voice, and Loyalty: Responses to Decline in Firms, Organizations, and States*. Cambridge, MA: Harvard University Press.

Hobbs, Heidi. 2016. "The Research Poster as a Pedagogical Tool in International Relations." Paper presented at the International Studies Association (West), Pasadena, CA, September 23–24.

Hobbes, Thomas. 1982 [1651]. *Leviathan*. London: Penguin.

Hoffmann, Stanley. 1977. "An American Social Science: International Relations." *Daedalus* 106: 41–60.

Hollis, Martin, and Steve Smith. 1992. *Explaining and Understanding International Relations*. Oxford: Oxford University Press.

Holsti, Ole R. 1972. *Crisis, Escalation, War*. Montreal: McGill-Queen's University Press.

Holsti, Ole R. 1995. "Theories of International Relations and Foreign Policy: Realism and Its Challengers." In Charles W. Kegley Jr., ed. *Controversies in International Relations Theory: Realism and the Neoliberal Challenge*. New York, NY: St. Martin's Press, 35–66.

Homer-Dixon, Thomas, Jonathan Leader Maynard, Matto Mildenberger, Manjana Milkoreit, Steven J. Mock, Stephen Quilley, Tobias Schröder, and Paul Thagard. 2013. "A Complex Systems Approach to the Study of Ideology: Cognitive-Affective Structures and the Dynamics of Belief Systems." *Journal of Social and Political Psychology* 1: 337–363.

Hughes, Barry B., and Evan E. Hillebrand. 2006. *Exploring and Shaping International Futures.* New York, NY: Routledge.

Huth, Paul K. 1998. *Standing Your Ground: Territorial Disputes and International Conflict.* Ann Arbor, MI: University of Michigan Press.

Ikenberry, G. John. 2001. "Review of Dale C. Copeland, *The Origins of Major Wars*." Ithaca, NY: Cornell University Press, 2000." 80: 167.

Ikenberry, G. John. 2019. "Review of Joshua Shifrinson, *Rising Titans, Falling Giants: How Great Powers Exploit Power Shifts.* Ithaca, NY: Cornell University Press, 2018." *Foreign Affairs Capsule Review,* May–June.

Ikenberry, G. John, and William C. Wohlforth, eds. 2002. *America Unrivaled: The Future of the Balance of Power.* Ithaca, NY: Cornell University Press.

Imai, Kosuke. 2017. *Quantitative Social Science: An Introduction.* Princeton, NJ: Princeton University Press.

Inoguchi, Takashi. 2003. "Conclusion: Generating Equilibrium, Generating Power Cycles." *International Political Science Review* 24: 167–172.

Jackson, Patrick Thaddeus. 2011. *The Conduct of Inquiry in International Relations: Philosophy of Science and Its Implications for the Study of World Politics.* New York, NY: Routledge.

Jackson, Patrick Thaddeus. 2016. *The Conduct of Inquiry in International Relations: Philosophy of Science and Its Implications for the Study of World Politics.* 2nd ed. New York, NY: Routledge.

Jackson, Patrick Thaddeus. 2017. "The Bias of 'Science': On the Intellectual Appeal of Neopositivism." In Annette Freyberg-Inan, Ewan Harrison, and Patrick James, eds. *Evaluating Progress in International Relations: How Do You Know?* New York, NY: Routledge, 17–30.

Jackson, Patrick Thaddeus, and Daniel H. Nexon. 2009. "Paradigmatic Faults in International-Relations Theory." *International Studies Quarterly* 53: 907–930.

James, Carolyn C. 2016. "Canada, Sovereignty and the Alaska Boundary Dispute." Paper presented at the Annual Meeting of the International Studies Association (West), September 23–24.

James, Carolyn C. 2021. "Canada's Arctic Boundaries and the United States: Binational vs. Bilateral Policy Making in North America." In Geoffrey Hale and Greg Anderson, eds. *Navigating a Changing World: Canada's International Policies in an Age of Uncertainties.* Toronto: University of Toronto Press, 355–377.

James, Carolyn C., and Patrick James. 2017. "Systemism and Foreign Policy Analysis." In Steve A. Yetiv and Patrick James, eds. *Advancing Interdisciplinary Approaches to International Relations.* New York, NY: Palgrave Macmillan, 289–321.

James, Patrick. 1987. "Conflict and Cohesion: A Review of the Literature and Recommendations for Future Research." *Cooperation and Conflict* 22: 21–33.

James, Patrick. 1988. *Crisis and War.* Montreal: McGill-Queen's University Press.

James, Patrick. 2002a. "Systemism and International Relations: Toward a Reassessment of Realism." In Michael Brecher and Frank P. Harvey, *Millennial Reflections on International Studies.* Ann Arbor, MI: University of Michigan Press, 131–142.

James, Patrick. 2002b. *International Relations and Scientific Progress: Structural Realism Reconsidered.* Columbus, OH: Ohio State University Press.

James, Patrick. 2012a. "Deterrence and Systemism: A Diagrammatic Exposition of Deterrence-Related Processes Leading to the War in Iraq." *St. Antony's International Review* 7: 139–163.

James, Patrick. 2012b. *Canada and Conflict.* Don Mills: Oxford University Press.

James, Patrick. 2019a. "What Do We Know about Crisis, Escalation and War? A Visual Assessment of the International Crisis Behavior Project." *Conflict Management and Peace Science* 36: 3–19.

James, Patrick. 2019b. "Systemist International Relations." *International Studies Quarterly* 63: 781–804.

James, Patrick, and Randall J. Jones. 2018. "IR's Crystal Ball: Prediction and Forecasting." In Andreas Gofas, Innana Hamati-Ataya, and Nicholas Onuf, eds. *The Sage Handbook of the History, Philosophy and Society of International Relations.* Thousand Oaks, CA: Sage, 252–265.

James, Patrick, and Michael Lusztig. 2003. "The US Power Cycle, Expected Utility, and the Probable Future of the FTAA." *International Political Science Review* 24: 83–96.

James, Patirck, Eric Solberg, and Murray Wolfson. 1999. "An identified Systemic Model of the Democracy-Peace Nexus." *Defence and Peace Economics* 10: 1–37.

James, William. 1907. *Pragmatism: A New Name for Some Old Ways of Thinking.* New York, NY: Longman Green.

Jeffreys, Diarmuid. 2005. *Aspirin: The Remarkable Story of a Wonder Drug.* New York, NY: Bloomsbury.

Jervis, Robert. 1976. *Perception and Misperception in International Politics.* Princeton, NJ: Princeton University Press.

Jervis, Robert. 1992. "Review of *Systems in Crisis.*" *International History Review* 14: 861–863.

Jervis, Robert. 1998. *System Effects: Complexity in Political and Social Life.* Princeton, NJ: Princeton University Press.

Joseph, Jonathan. 2007. "Philosophy in International Relations: A Scientific Realist Approach." *Millennium* 35: 345–359.

Kaarbo, Juliet. 2015. "A Foreign Policy Analysis Perspective on the Domestic Politics Turn in IR Theory." *International Studies Review* 17: 189–216.

Kahler, Miles. 1998. "Rationality in International Relations." *International Organization* 52: 919–941.

Kang, David C. 2012. *East Asia before the West: Five Centuries of Trade and Tribute.* New York, NY: Columbia University Press.

Kaplan, Morton A. 1957. *System and Process in International Politics.* New York, NY: John Wiley & Sons.

Kaplan, Morton A. 1966. "The New Great Debate: Traditionalism vs. Science in International Relations." *World Politics* 19: 1–20.

Katzenstein, Peter, and Rudra Sil. 2008. "Eclectic Theorizing in the Study and Practice of International Relations." In Christian Reus-Smit and Duncan Snidal, eds. *The Oxford Handbook of International Relations.* Oxford: Oxford University Press, 109–130.

Kaufman, Robert G. 2001. "On the Uses and Abuses of History in International Relations Theory: Dale Copeland's *The Origins of Major War.*" *Security Studies* 10: 179–211.

Kaufman, Stuart J. 2017. Personal communication.

Kautilya. 1992 [n.d.] *The Arthashastra.* London: Penguin.

Keck, Margaret E., and Kathryn Sikkink. 1998. *Activists beyond Borders: Advocacy Networks in International Politics.* Ithaca, NY: Cornell University Press.

Kecskemeti, Paul. 1960. "Review of Lewis Fry Richardson, *Arms and Insecurity* and *Statistics of Deadly Quarrels.* Pittsburgh, PA: Boxwood Press." *Science* 30: 1931–1932.

Kennedy, Paul. 2002. "The Modern Machiavelli." *New York Review of Books*, November 7.

Keohane, Robert. O. 1984. *After Hegemony: Cooperation and Discord in the World Political Economy*. Princeton, NJ: Princeton University Press.

Keohane, Robert O. 1989. *International Institutions and State Power: Essays in International Relations Theory*. Boulder, CO: Westview Press.

Keohane, Robert O., and Joseph S. Nye. 1977. *Power and Interdependence: World Politics in Transition*. Boston, MA: Little Brown.

Kertzer, Joshua D. 2017. "Microfoundations in International Relations." *Conflict Management and Peace Science* 34: 81–97.

Kesgin, Baris. 2011. "Foreign Policy Analysis." In John T. Ishiyama and Marijke Breuning, eds. *21st Century Political Science: A Reference Handbook*. Vol. 1. Thousand Oaks, CA: Sage, 336–343.

Kessler, Oliver. 2016. "The Failure of Failure: On Constructivism, the Limits of Critique, and the Socio-Political Economy of Economics." *Millennium* 44: 348–369.

Kessler, Oliver, and Brent Steele. 2018. "On Constructivism, Realism and Contingency." In Mariano E. Bertucci, Jarrod Hayes, and Patrick James, eds. *Constructivism Reconsidered*. Ann Arbor, MI: University of Michigan Press, 47–66.

Khong, Yuen Foong. 1992. *Analogies at War: Korea, Munich, Dien Bien Phu, and the Vietnam Decisions of 1965*. Princeton, NJ: Princeton University Press.

King, Gary. 1989. *Unifying Political Methodology: The Likelihood Theory of Statistical Inference*. New York, NY: Cambridge University Press.

King, Gary, Robert O. Keohane, and Sidney Verba. 1994. *Designing Social Inquiry: Scientific Inference in Qualitative Research*. Princeton, NJ: Princeton University Press.

Kirschner, Paul, Femke Kirschner, and Fred Paas. 2016. "Cognitive Load Theory." www.education.com.

Kirshner, Jonathan. 2010. "The Tragedy of Offensive Realism: Classical Realism and the Rise of China." *European Journal of International Relations* 18: 53–75.

Kissinger, Henry. 1957. *A World Restored: Metternich, Castlereagh and the Problems of Peace, 1812–22*. Boston, MA: Houghton-Mifflin.

Knutsen, Torbjørn. 2016. *A History of International Relations Theory*. Manchester: Manchester University Press.

Knutsen, Torbjørn. 2017. "Substance, Form, and Context: Scholarly Communities, Institutions, and the Nature of IR." In Annette Freyberg-Inan, Ewan Harrison, and Patrick James, eds. *Evaluating Progress in International Relations: How Do You Know?* New York: Routledge, 51–73.

Krasner, Stephen D. 1999. *Sovereignty: Organized Hypocrisy*. Princeton, NJ: Princeton University Press.

Krebs, Ronald R., and Patrick Thaddeus Jackson. 2007. "Twisting Tongues and Twisting Arms: The Power of Political Rhetoric." *European Journal of International Relations* 13: 35–66.

Kugler, Jacek, and Douglas Lemke. 1996. *Parity and War: Evaluations and Extensions of "The War Ledger."* Ann Arbor, MI: University of Michigan Press.

Kugler, Jacek, and Ronald L. Tammen, eds. 2012. *The Performance of Nations*. New York, NY: Rowman & Littlefield.

Kugler, Jacek, and Paul J. Zak. 2017. "Trust, Cooperation and Conflict: Neuropolitics and International Relations." In Steve A. Yetiv and Patrick James, eds. *Advancing Interdisciplinary Approaches to International Relations*. New York, NY: Palgrave Macmillan, 83–114.

Kuhn, Thomas S. 1970 [1962]. *The Structure of Scientific Revolutions*. 2nd ed. Chicago, IL: University of Chicago Press.

Kupchan, Charles A. 2003. "Review of *The Tragedy of Great Power Politics*." *International History Review* 25: 750–751.
Kurki, Milja. 2002. "Causes of a Divided Discipline: A Critical Examination of the Concept of Cause in International Relations Theory." *Global Politics Network*. www.globalpolitics.net. Accessed on 15 April 2022.
Kurki, Milja. 2007. "Critical Realism and Causal Analysis in International Relations." *Millennium* 35: 361–378.
Kurki, Milja, and Hidemi Suganami. 2012. "Towards the Politics of Causal Explanation: A Reply to the Critics of Causal Inquiries." *International Theory* 4: 400–429.
Kydd, Andrew H. 2008. "Methodological Individualism and Rational Choice." In Christian Reus-Smit and Duncan Snidal, eds. *The Oxford Handbook of International Relations*. Oxford: Oxford University Press, 425–443.
Labs, Eric J. 1997. "Beyond Victory: Offensive Realism and the Expansion of War Aims." *Security Studies* 6: 1–49.
Lakatos, Imre. 1970. "Falsification and the Methodology of Scientific Research Programmes." In Imre Lakatos and Alan Musgrave, eds. *Criticism and the Growth of Knowledge*. Cambridge: Cambridge University Press, 91–196.
Lake, David A. 1982. "Review of *War and Change in World Politics*." *American Political Science Review* 76: 950–951.
Lake, David A. 1992. "Powerful Pacifists: Democratic States and War." *American Political Science Review* 86: 24–37.
Lake, David A. 2002. "Beyond Paradigms in the Study of Institutions." In Michael Brecher and Frank Harvey, eds. *Millennial Reflections on International Studies: Realism and Institutionalism in International Studies*. Ann Arbor, MI: University of Michigan Press, 135–152.
Lake, David A. 2008. "The State and International Relations." In Christian Reus-Smit and Duncan Snidal, eds. *The Oxford Handbook of International Relations*. Oxford: Oxford University Press, 41–61.
Lake, David A. 2009. *Hierarchy in International Relations*. Ithaca, NY: Cornell University Press.
Lake, David A. 2011. "Why 'Isms' Are Evil: Theory, Epistemology, and Academic Sects as Impediments to Understanding and Progress." *International Studies Quarterly* 55: 465–480.
Lake, David A. 2013. "Theory Is Dead, Long Live Theory: The End of the Great Debates and the Rise of Eclecticism in International Relations." *European Journal of International Relations* 19: 567–587.
Lapid, Yosef. 1989. "The Third Debate: On the Prospects of International Theory in a Post-positivist Era." *International Studies Quarterly* 33: 235–254.
Larson, Deborah Welch. 1997. "Review of *Revolution and War*." *International History Review* 19: 491–492.
Lasswell, Harold D. 1941. "The Garrison State." *American Journal of Sociology* 46: 455–468.
Laudan, Larry. 1977. *Progress and Its Problems*. Berkeley, CA: University of California Press.
Law, Kenneth, Chi-Sum Wong, and William H. Mobley. 1998. "Toward a Taxonomy of Multidimensional Constructs." *Academy of Management Review* 23: 741–755.
Layne, Christopher. 2006. *The Peace of Illusions: American Grand Strategy from 1940 to the Present*. Ithaca, NY: Cornell University Press.
Lebovic, James H. 2010. *The Limits of U.S. Military Capability: Lessons from Vietnam and Iraq*. Baltimore, MD: Johns Hopkins University Press.

Leeds, Brett Ashley. 2017. The Alliance Treaty Obligations and Provisions Project (ATOP). http://atop.rice.edu/.
Legro, Jeffrey W., and Andrew Moravcsik. 1999. "Is Anybody Still a Realist?" *International Organization* 24: 5–55.
Leiber, Keir. 2008. "Correspondence: Defensive Realism and the 'New' History of World War I." *International Security* 33: 185–194.
Lemke, Douglas. 2002. *Regions of War and Peace*. Cambridge: Cambridge University Press.
Lemke, Douglas. 2003. "African Lessons for International Relations Research." *World Politics* 56: 114–138.
Leng, Russell J. 1999. "Review of Michael Brecher and Jonathan Wilkenfeld, *A Study of Crisis*. Ann Arbor, MI: University of Michigan Press, 1997." *American Political Science Review* 93: 746–747.
Leroi-Gourhan, Arlette. 1982. "The Archaeology of Lascaux Cave." *Scientific American* 246 (6): 104–113.
Leslie, Peter. 1972. "General Theory in Political Science: A Critique of Easton's Systems Analysis." *British Journal of Political Science* 2: 155–172.
Levine, Daniel J., and Alexander D. Barder. 2014. "The Closing of the American Mind: 'American School' International Relations and the State of Grand Theory." *European Journal of International Relations* 20: 863–888.
Levy, Jack S. 1983. "Review of *The War Trap*." *Social Science Quarterly* 64: 215–216.
Levy, Jack S. 1985. "Theories of General War." *World Politics* 37: 344–374.
Levy, Jack S. 1989. "The Diversionary Theory of War: A Critique." In Manus I. Midlarsky, ed. *Handbook of War Studies*. Boston, MA: Unwin Hyman, 259–288.
Levy, Jack S. 2003. "Balances and Balancing: Concepts, Propositions, and Research Designs." In John A. Vasquez and Colin Elman, eds. *Realism and the Balance of Power: A New Debate*. Upper Saddle River, NJ: Prentice Hall, 128–153.
Levy, Jack S. 2004. "What Do Great Powers Balance Against and When?" In T. V. Paul, James J. Wirtz and Michel Fortmann, eds. *Balance of Power: Theory and Practice in the 21st Century*. Stanford, CA: Stanford University Press, 29–51.
Levy, Jack S. 2008. "Preventive War and Democratic Politics." *International Studies Quarterly* 52: 1–24.
List, Christian, and Kai Spiekermann. 2013. "Methodological Individualism and Holism in Political Science: A Reconciliation." *American Political Science Review* 107: 629–643.
Little, Richard. 2007. "The Balance of Power in *Politics among Nations*." In Michael C. Williams, ed. *Realism Reconsidered: The Legacy of Hans Morgenthau in International Relations*. Oxford: Oxford University Press, 137–165.
Lizée, Pierre P. 2011. *A Whole New World: Reinventing International Studies for the Post-Western World*. New York, NY: Palgrave Macmillan.
Lobell, Steven E., Norrin M. Ripsman, and Jeffrey W. Taliaferro, eds. 2009. *Neoclassical Realism, the State, and Foreign Policy*. Cambridge: Cambridge University Press.
Lopes, Dominic. 1995. "Pictorial Realism." *Journal of Aesthetics and Art Criticism* 53: 277–285.
Lord, Carnes. 2002. "Review of *The Tragedy of Great Power Politics*." *Naval War College Review* 55: 112–113.
Lowenthal, Mark M. 2017. *Intelligence from Secrets to Policy*. 7th ed. Thousand Oaks, CA: Sage.
Lowi, Theodore J. 1969. *The End of Liberalism*. New York, NY: Norton.

Luard, Evan. 1992. "The International System." In Evan Luard, ed. *Basic Texts in International Relations: The Evolution of Ideas about International Society*. London: Macmillan, 516–519.
Lucidchart. 2022. www.lucidchart.com. Accessed 15 April 2022.
Lusztig, Michael. 2004. *The Limits of Protection: Building Coalitions for Free Trade*. Pittsburgh, PA: University of Pittsburgh Press.
Lynn-Jones, Sean M. 2002. "Review of *The Tragedy of Great Power Politics*." *International Affairs* 78: 365–366.
Machiavelli, Niccolò. 2003 [1532]. *The Prince*. George Bull, trans. London: Penguin.
Macdonald, Douglas J. 1989. "Book Review: *The Origins of Alliances*." *Journal of Politics* 51: 795–798.
MacDonald, Paul K. 2003. "Useful Fiction or Miracle Makers: The Competing Epistemological Foundations of Rational Choice Theory." *American Political Science Review* 97: 551–565.
Mahnken, Thomas G. 2000. "Review of *Causes of War*." *Naval War College Review* 53: 207–208.
Mahoney, James, and Rodrigo Barrenchea. 2016. "The Logic of Counterfactual Analysis in Historical Explanation." Ann Arbor, MI: Paper presented to the Department of Political Science, University of Michigan, April 15.
Mansbach, Richard. W. 1992. "Review of *Systems in Crisis: New Imperatives of High Politics at Century's End*. Cambridge: Cambridge University Press, 1991." *American Political Science Review* 86: 839–840.
Maoz, Zeev. 2003. "Paradoxical Functions of International Alliances: Security and Other Dilemmas." In John A. Vasquez and Colin Elman, eds. *Realism and the Balance of Power: A New Debate*. Upper Saddle River, NJ: Prentice Hall, 200–221.
Maoz, Zeev, ed. 2012. "Network Analysis in International Relations." Special issue of *Conflict Management and Peace Science* 29, 3.
Maoz, Zeev, and Nasrin Abdolali. 1989. "Regime Types and International Conflict, 1816–1976." *Journal of Conflict Resolution* 33: 3–35.
Maoz, Zeev, and Bruce M. Russett. 1993. "Normative and Structural Causes of Democratic Peace, 1946–1986." *American Political Science Review* 87: 624–638.
Maradi, Alberto. 1990. "Classification, Typology, Taxonomy." *Quality & Quantity* 24: 129–157.
March, James G., and Johan P. Olsen. 2011. "The Logic of Appropriateness." In Robert E. Goodin, ed. *The Oxford Handbook of Political Science*. Oxford: Oxford University Press. https://www.oxfordhandbooks.com/view/10.1093/oxfordhb/9780199604456.001.0001/oxfordhb-9780199604456-e-024.
Masala, Carlo. 2003. "Review of John J. Mearsheimer, *The Tragedy of Great Power Politics*. New York: W. W. Norton, 2001." *Vierteljahresschrift* 44: 442–444.
Mastanduno, Michael. 1997. "Preserving the Unipolar Moment: Realist Theories and U.S. Grand Strategy After the Cold War." *International Security* 21: 49–88.
Mastanduno, Michael, David A. Lake, and G. John Ikenberry. 1988. "Toward a Realist Theory of State Action." *International Studies Quarterly* 33: 457–474.
Matheson, Carl, and Justin Dallmann. 2014. "Historicist Theories of Scientific Rationality." In Edward N. Zalta, ed. *Stanford Encyclopedia of Philosophy*. Spring 2021 ed. http://plato.stanford.edu/entries/rationality-historicist/.
Mayer, Richard E. 2010. *Applying the Science of Learning*. Boston, MA: Pearson.

McCourt, David M. 2018. "The Future of Constructivism." In Mariano E. Bertucci, Jarrod Hayes, and Patrick James, eds. *Constructivism Reconsidered*. Ann Arbor, MI: University of Michigan Press, 33–46.

McNeill, William H. 1982. *The Pursuit of Power: Technology, Armed Force, and Society since A. D. 1000*. Chicago, IL: University of Chicago Press.

Mearsheimer, John J. 1994–95. "The False Promise of International Institutions." *International Security* 19: 5–49.

Mearsheimer, John J. 2009. "Reckless States and Realism." *International Relations* 23: 241–256.

Mearsheimer, John J. 2014 [2001]. *The Tragedy of Great Power Politics*. Updated ed. New York, NY: Norton.

Mearsheimer, John J. 2018. *The Great Delusion: Liberal Dreams and International Realities*. New Haven, CT: Yale University Press.

Mearsheimer, John J., and Stephen M. Walt. 2013. "Leaving Theory Behind: Why Simplistic Hypothesis Testing Is Bad for International Relations." *European Journal of International Relations* 19: 427–457.

Melbauer, Gustav. 2019. "Interests, Ideas, and the Study of State Behaviour in Neoclassical Realism." *Review of International Studies* 46: 20–36.

Menon, Rajan, and Hendrik Spruyt. 1999. "The Limits of Neorealism: Understanding Security in Central Asia." *Review of International Studies* 25: 87–105.

Mercer, Jonathan. 2005. "Rationality and Psychology in International Politics." *International Organization* 59: 77–106.

Merton, Robert K. 1957. *Social Theory and Social Structure*. Glencoe, IL: Free Press.

Mickolus, Edward F. 2006. *International Terrorism: Attributes of Terrorist Events*. Dunn Loring, VA: Vinyard Software.

Migdal, Joel. S. 2001. *State in Society: Studying How States and Societies Transform and Constitute One Another*. Cambridge: Cambridge University Press.

Miller, Lee Ryan. 2004. *Confessions of a Recovering Realist: Toward a Neo-liberal Theory of International Relations*. Bloomington, IN: AuthorHouse.

Milner, Helen. 1991. "The Assumption of Anarchy in International Relations Theory: A Critique." *Review of International Studies* 17: 67–85.

Mintz, Alex, and Karl DeRouen Jr. 2010. *Understanding Foreign Policy Decision Making*. Cambridge: Cambridge University Press.

Mitchell, Sara McLaughlin. 2012. "Norms and the Democratic Peace." In John A. Vasquez, ed. *What Do We Know About War?* 2nd ed. New York, NY: Rowman and Littlefield, 167–188.

Mitchell, Sara McLaughlin, and Brandon C. Prins. 2004. "Rivalry and Diversionary Uses of Force." *Journal of Conflict Resolution* 48: 937–961.

Molloy, Seán. 2003. "Realism: A Problematic Paradigm." *Security Dialogue* 34: 71–85.

Monroe, Kristen Renwick. 2001. "Paradigm Shift: From Rational Choice to Perspective." *International Political Science Review* 22: 151–172.

Monteiro, Nuno P. 2011–12. "Unrest Assured: Why Unipolarity Is Not Peaceful." *International Security* 36: 9–40.

Monteiro, Nuno P. 2012. "We Can Never Study Merely One Thing: Reflections on Systems Thinking and IR." *Critical Review* 24: 343–366.

Montgomery, Evan Braden. 2014. "Breaking Out of the Security Dilemma: Realism, Reassurance, and the Problem of Uncertainty." *International Security* 31: 151–185.

Moravcsik, Andrew. 1997. "Taking Preferences Seriously: A Liberal Theory of International Politics." *International Organization* 51: 513–553.
Morgan, Stephen L., and Christopher Winship. 2015. *Counterfactuals and Causal Inference: Methods and Principles for Social Research*. 2nd ed. Cambridge: Cambridge University Press.
Morgenthau, Hans J. 1946. *Scientific Man versus Power Politics*. Chicago, IL: University of Chicago Press.
Morgenthau, Hans J. 1959 [1948]. *Politics among Nations: The Struggle for Power and Peace*. 2nd ed. New York, NY: Alfred A. Knopf.
Morgenthau, Hans J. 1964. "The Intellectual and Political Functions of a Theory of International Relations." In Horace V. Harrison, ed. 1964. *The Role of Theory in International Relations*. Princeton, NJ: D. Van Nostrand, 101–118.
Morrow, James D. 1994. *Game Theory for Political Scientists*. Princeton, NJ: Princeton University Press.
Morrow, James D. 2007. "When Do States Follow the Laws of War?" *American Political Science Review* 101: 559–572.
Mosca, Matthew W. 2013. *From Frontier Policy to Foreign Policy: The Question of India and the Transformation of Geopolitics in Qing China*. Stanford, CA: Stanford University Press.
Most, Benjamin A., and Harvey Starr. 2015 [1989]. *Inquiry, Logic, and International Politics*. Columbia, SC: University of South Carolina Press.
Mousseau, Michael. 2005. "Comparing New Theory with Prior Beliefs: Market Civilization and the Democratic Peace." *Conflict Management and Peace Science* 22: 63–77.
Mousseau, Michael. 2013. "The Democratic Peace Unraveled: It's the Economy." *International Studies Quarterly* 57: 186–197.
Mueller, Dennis C. 1979, 1989, 2003. *Public Choice I, II, III*. Cambridge: Cambridge University Press.
National Eye Institute. 2019. https://www.nih.gov/about-nih/what-we-do/nih-almanac/national-eye-institute-nei.
Niebuhr, Reinhold. 2010 [1952]. *The Irony of American History*. Chicago, IL: University of Chicago Press.
Nincic, Miroslav. 2003. "Review of *The Tragedy of Great Power Politics*." *Perspectives on Politics* 1: 239–240.
Niou, Emerson M. S., Peter C. Ordeshook, and Gregory F. Rose. 1989. *The Balance of Power: Stability in International Systems*. Cambridge: Cambridge University Press.
Nurmi, Hannu. 1974. *Causality and Complexity: Some Problems of Causal Analysis in the Social Sciences*. Turku, Finland: Turun Yliopisto.
O'Loughlin, Conor. 2008. "Irish Foreign Policy during World War II: A Test for Realist Theories of Foreign Policy." *Irish Studies in International Affairs* 19: 99–117.
Olson, Mancur. 1965. *The Logic of Collective Action*. Cambridge, MA: Harvard University Press.
Olson, Mancur, and Richard Zeckhauser. 1966. "An Economic Theory of Alliances." *Review of Economics and Statistics* 48: 266–279.
Oneal, John R., and James Lee Ray. 1997. "New Tests of the Democratic Peace: Controlling for Economic Interdependence, 1950–85." *Political Research Quarterly* 50: 751–775.
Oneal, John R., and Bruce M. Russett. 1997. "The Classical Liberals Were Right: Democracy, Interdependence, and Conflict, 1950–1985." *International Studies Quarterly* 41: 267–293.

Onuf, Nicholas Greenwood. 1989. *World of Our Making: Rules and Rule in Social Theory and International Relations.* New York, NY: Routledge.
Organski, A. F. K. 1958. *World Politics.* New York, NY: Alfred A. Knopf.
Organski, A. F. K., and Jacek Kugler. 1980. *The War Ledger.* Chicago, IL: University of Chicago Press.
Ostrom, Elinor. 1990. *Governing the Commons: The Evolution of Institutions for Collective Action.* Cambridge: Cambridge University Press.
Overy, Richard. 2000. "Review of *Deadly Imbalances*." *English Historical Review* 115: 507–508.
Oxford Bibliographies in International Relations. 2019. https://www.oxfordbibliographies.com/page/international-relations.
Özdemir, Haluk. 2015. "An Inter-subsystemic Approach in International Relations." *All Azimuth* 4: 5–26.
Parasiliti, Andrew T. 2003. "The Causes and Timing of Iraq's Wars: A Power Cycle Assessment." *International Political Science Review* 24: 151–165.
Parent, Joseph M. 2020. "Review of Joshua Shifrinson, *Rising Titans, Falling Giants: How Great Powers Exploit Power Shifts.* Ithaca, NY: Cornell University Press, 2018." *Air University Press.* August 26.
Parent, Joseph M., and Joshua M. Baron. 2011. "Elder Abuse: How the Moderns Mistreat Classical Realism." *International Studies Quarterly* 13: 193–213.
Park, Hun Joo. 1998. "The Problem of Scientific Progress and Major Schools of Thought in Contemporary International Politics Theory." *Journal of International and Area Studies* 5: 1–20.
Parsons, Craig. 2015. "Before Eclecticism: Competing Alternatives in Constructivist Research." *International Theory* 7: 1–38.
Pashakhanlou, Arash Heydarian. 2013. "Back to the Drawing Board: A Critique of Offensive Realism." *International Relations* 27: 202–225.
Pashler, Harold, Mark McDaniel, Doug Rohrer, and Robert Bjork. 2009. "Learning Styles: Concepts and Evidence." *Psychological Science in the Public Interest* 9: 105–119.
Paul, T. V. 2010. "Symposium: Beyond Paradigms and Research Programs—a Plea for Puzzle-Driven International Relations Research." *Qualitative and Multi-method Research* 8: 17–19.
Paul, T. V. 2018. *Restraining Great Powers: Soft Balancing from Empires to the Global Era.* New Haven, CT: Yale University Press.
Pearl, Judea. 2009. *Causality.* Cambridge: Cambridge University Press.
Person, Robert. 2017. "Balance of Threat: The Domestic Insecurity of Vladimir Putin." *Journal of Eurasian Studies* 8: 44–59.
Pfonner, Michael, and Patrick James. 2020. "The Visual International Relations Project." *International Studies Review* 22: 192–213.
Pickel, Andreas. 2007. "Rethinking Systems Theory: A Programmatic Introduction." *Philosophy of the Social Sciences* 37: 391–407.
Pickering, Jeffrey, and Emizet F. Kisangani. 2010. "Diversionary Despots? Comparing Autocracies' Propensities to Use and to Benefit from Military Force." *American Journal of Political Science* 54: 477–493.
Popper, Karl R. 2002 [1959]. *The Logic of Scientific Discovery.* New York, NY: Routledge.
Popper, Karl R. 2002 [1963]. *Conjectures and Refutations: The Growth of Scientific Knowledge.* New York, NY: Routledge.

Porter, Brian. 1972. *The Aberystwyth Papers: International Politics, 1919–1969*. London: Oxford University Press for the University College of Wales.
Posen, Barry R. 1984. *The Sources of Military Doctrine*. Ithaca, NY: Cornell University Press.
Posen, Barry R. 2002. "Review of John J. Mearsheimer, *The Tragedy of Great Power Politics*. New York, NY: W. W. Norton, 2001." *National Interest* 67: 119–126.
Powell, Robert. 1991. "Absolute and Relative Gains in International Relations Theory." *American Political Science Review* 85: 1303–1320.
Powell, Robert. 1999. *In the Shadow of Power*. Princeton, NJ: Princeton University Press.
Prange, Gordon W. 1982. *At Dawn We Slept: The Untold Story of Pearl Harbor*. London: Penguin Books.
Priest, Graham. 2017. *Logic: A Very Short Introduction*. 2nd ed. Oxford: Oxford University Press.
Putnam, Robert D. 1988. "Diplomacy and Domestic Politics: The Logic of Two-Level Games." *International Organization* 42: 427–460.
Putnam, Robert. D. 1993. *Making Democracy Work: Civic Traditions in Modern Italy*. Princeton, NJ: Princeton University Press.
Quackenbush, Stephen L. 2015. *International Conflict: Logic and Evidence*. Los Angeles, CA: Sage.
Quinn, Adam. 2013. "Kenneth Waltz, Adam Smith and the Limits of Science: Hard Choices for Neoclassical Realism." *International Politics* 50: 159–182.
Rathbun, Brian. 2008. "A Rose by Any Other Name: Neoclassical Realism as the Logical and Necessary Extension of Structural Realism." *Security Studies* 17: 294–321.
Rathbun, Brian C. 2019. *Reasoning of State: Realists, Romantics and Rationality in International Relations*. Cambridge: Cambridge University Press.
Rathbun, Brian C., and Rachel Stein. 2020. "Greater Goods: Morality and Attitudes toward the Use of Nuclear Weapons." *Journal of Conflict Resolution* 64: 787–816.
Ray, James Lee. 1995. *Democracy and International Conflict: An Evaluation of the Democratic Peace Proposition*. Columbia: University of South Carolina Press.
Ray, James Lee. 2002. "Does Interstate War Have a Future?" *Conflict Management and Peace Science* 19: 53–80.
Raymond, Mark. 2019. *Social Practices of Rule-Making in World Politics*. Oxford: Oxford University Press.
Raymond, Mark, and Laura DeNardis. 2015. "Multistakeholderism: Anatomy of an Inchoate Global Institution." *International Theory* 7: 572–616.
Reed, William. 2001. "Review of Dale C. Copeland, *The Origins of Major War*. Ithaca, NY: Cornell University Press, 2000." *American Political Science Review* 95: 513–514.
Reiter, Dan. 2000. "Review of *Causes of War*." *Journal of Politics* 62: 1259–1261.
Rendall, Matthew. 2006. "Defensive Realism and the Concert of Europe." *Review of International Studies* 32: 523–540.
Rengger, Nicholas. 1998. "Review of *Revolution and War*." *International Affairs* 74: 203–204.
Rengger, Nicholas. 2015. "Pluralism in International Relations Theory: Three Questions." *International Studies Perspectives* 16: 32–39.
Resende-Santos, Joao. 2007. *Neorealism, States, and the Modern Mass Army*. New York, NY: Cambridge University Press.
Resnick, Evan. 2007. "Review of *Unanswered Threats*." *Perspectives on Politics* 5: 417–418.
Rhamey, J. Patrick, Jr., and Bryan R. Early. 2013. "Going for the Gold: Status-Seeking Behavior and Olympic Performance." *International Area Studies Review* 16: 244–261.

Richards, Michael. 1997. "Review of Stephen M. Walt, *Revolution and War* (Ithaca, NY: Cornell University Press, 1996)." *American Historical Review* 102: 1447–1448.

Richardson, Lewis Fry. 1960. *Arms and Insecurity*. Pittsburgh, PA: Boxwood Press.

Riker, William H. 1962. *The Theory of Political Coalitions*. New Haven, CT: Yale University Press.

Riker, William H., and Peter C. Ordeshook. 1973. *An Introduction to Positive Political Theory*. Englewood Cliffs, NJ: Prentice Hall.

Ripsman, Norrin M. 2005. "Two Stages of Transition from a Region of War to a Region of Peace: Realist Transition and Liberal Endurance." *International Studies Quarterly* 49: 669–693.

Ripsman, Norrin M. 2010. "Domestic Practices and Balancing: Integrating Practice into Neoclassical Realism." In Vincent Pouliot and Emanuel Adler, eds. *International Practices*. Cambridge: Cambridge University Press, 200–228.

Ripsman, Norrin M., and Jack S. Levy. 2008. "Wishful Thinking or Buying Time? The Logic of British Appeasement in the 1930s." *International Security* 33: 148–181.

Ripsman, Norrin M., Jeffrey W. Taliaferro, and Steven E. Lobell. 2009. "Conclusion: The State of Neoclassical Realism." In Steven E. Lobell, Norrin M. Ripsman, and Jeffrey W. Taliaferro, eds. *Neoclassical Realism, the State, and Foreign Policy*. Cambridge: Cambridge University Press, 280–299.

Ripsman, Norrin M., Jeffrey W. Taliaferro, and Steven E. Lobell. 2016. *Neoclassical Realist Theory of International Politics*. Oxford: Oxford University Press.

Rogers, Matt. 2012. "Contextualizing Theories and Practices of Bricolage Research." *Qualitative Report* 17: 1–17.

Rohrer, Doug, and Harold Pashler. 2012. "Learning Styles: Where's the Evidence?" *Medical Education* 46: 634–635.

Rosato, Sebastien. 2011. "Europe's Troubles: Power Politics and the State of the European Project." *International Security* 35: 45–86.

Rose, Gideon. 1998. "Neoclassical Realism and Theories of Foreign Policy." *World Politics* 51: 144–172.

Rose, William, and Eliza van Dusen. 2002. "Sudan's Islamic Revolutions as a Cause of Foreign Intervention in Its Wars: Insights from Balance of Threat Theory." *Civil Wars* 5: 1–64.

Rosecrance, Richard N. 1974. "Review of Charles F. Doran, *The Politics of Assimilation: Hegemony and Its Aftermath*. Baltimore, MD: Johns Hopkins University Press." *American Political Science Review* 68: 860–861.

Rosecrance, Richard N. 2002. "War and Peace." *World Politics* 55: 137–166.

Rosecrance, Richard N. 2003. "Is There a Balance of Power?" In John A. Vasquez and Colin Elman, eds. *Realism and the Balance of Power: A New Debate*. Upper Saddle River, NJ: Prentice Hall, 154–165.

Rosecrance, Richard N. 2007. "Review of *Unanswered Threats*." *Political Science Quarterly* 122: 512–514.

Rosecrance, Richard N., and Zara Steiner. 2010. "History and Neorealism Reconsidered." In Ernest R. May, Richard Rosecrance, and Zara Steiner, eds. *History and Neorealism*. Cambridge: Cambridge University Press, 341–365.

Rosenau, James N. 1966. "Pre-theories and Theories of Foreign Policy." In R. Barry Farrell, ed. *Approaches to Comparative and International Politics*. Evanston, IL: Northwestern University Press, 27–92.

Rosenau, James N. 1990. *Turbulence in World Politics: A Theory of Change and Continuity*. Princeton, NJ: Princeton University Press.

Roth, Ariel Ilan. 2006. "Review of *Unanswered Threats*." *International Studies Review* 8: 486–488.

Rothstein, Robert L. 2005. "On the Costs of Realism." In Richard Little and Michael Smith, eds. *Perspectives on World Politics*. 3rd ed. New York, NY: Routledge, 368–374.

Ruane, Abigail, and Patrick James. 2008. "The International Relations of Middle-Earth: Learning from the *Lord of the Rings*." *International Studies Perspectives* 9: 377–394.

Ruane, Abigail, and Patrick James. 2012. *The International Relations of Middle-Earth: Learning from the Lord of the Rings*. Ann Arbor, MI: University of Michigan Press.

Rubin, Lawrence. 2014. *Islam in the Balance: Ideational Threats in Arab Politics*. Stanford, CA: Stanford University Press.

Russett, Bruce M. 1963. "The Calculus of Deterrence." *Journal of Conflict Resolution* 7: 97–109.

Russett, Bruce M. 1969. "The Young Science of International Politics." *World Politics* 22: 87–94.

Russett, Bruce M., and John R. Oneal. 2001. *Triangulating Peace: Democracy, Interdependence, and International Organizations*. New York, NY: Norton.

Saideman, Stephen M. 2018. "The Apparent Decline of the IR Paradigms: Examining Patterns of Publications, Perceptions, and Citations." *International Studies Review* 20: 685–703.

Samuelson, William, and Richard Zeckhauser. 1988. "Status Quo Bias in Decision Making." *Journal of Risk and Uncertainty* 1: 7–59.

Sandal, Nukhet. 2017. *Religious Leaders and Conflict Transformation*. Cambridge: Cambridge University Press.

Sandler, Todd, and Walter Enders. 2004. "An Economic Perspective on Transnational Terrorism." *European Journal of Political Economy* 20: 301–316.

Sarotte, Mary Elise. 2011. *1989: The Struggle to Create Post–Cold War Europe*. Princeton, NJ: Princeton University Press.

Sarotte, Mary Elise. 2014. *The Collapse: The Accidental Opening of the Berlin Wall*. New York, NY: Basic Books.

Schelling, Thomas C. 1960. *The Strategy of Conflict*. Cambridge, MA: Harvard University Press.

Schelling, Thomas C. 2006. *Micromotives and Macrobehavior (with a New Preface and the Nobel Lecture)*. New York, NY: Norton.

Scheuerman, William E. 2007. "Was Morgenthau a Realist? Revisiting *Scientific Man vs. Power Politics*." *Constellations* 14: 506–530.

Schmidt, Brian C. 2001. "Review of Dale C. Copeland, *The Origins of Major War*. Ithaca, NY: Cornell University Press, 2000." *International Affairs* 77: 409.

Schmidt, Brian C. 2004. "Realism as Tragedy." *Review of International Studies* 30: 427–441.

Schmidt, Brian C. 2007. "Realism and Facets of Power in International Relations." In Felix Berenskoetter and M. J. Williams, eds. *Power in World Politics*. New York, NY: Routledge, 43–63.

Schmidt, Brian C., and Thomas Juneau. 2012. "Neoclassical Realism and Power." In Alse Toje and Barbara Kunz, eds. *Neoclassical Realism in European Politics: Bringing Power Back In*. Manchester: University of Manchester Press, 61–78.

Schroeder, Paul W. 1994. "Historical Reality vs. Neo-realist Theory." *International Security* 19: 108–148.

Schroeder, Paul W. 2003. "Why Realism Does Not Work Well for International History (Whether or Not It Represents a Degenerate IR Research Strategy)." In John A. Vasquez and Colin Elman, eds. *Realism and the Balance of Power: A New Debate*. Upper Saddle River, NJ: Prentice Hall, 114–127.

Schuker, Stephen A. 1999. "Review of *Deadly Imbalances*." *International History Review* 21: 1080–1082.

Schumacker, Randall E., and Richard G. Lomax. 2010. *A Beginner's Guide to Structural Equation Modeling*. 3rd ed. New York, NY: Routledge.

Schutz, Alfred. 1967. *The Phenomenology of the Social World*. Evanston, IL: Northwestern University Press.

Schweller, Randall L. 1994. "Bandwagoning for Profit: Bringing the Revisionist State Back In." *International Security* 19: 72–107.

Schweller, Randall L. 1996. "Neorealism's Status-Quo Bias: What Security Dilemma?" In Benjamin Frankel, ed. *Realism: Restatements and Renewal*. London: Frank Cass, 90–121.

Schweller, Randall L. 1997. "New Realist Research on Alliances: Refining, Not Refuting, Waltz's Balancing Proposition." *American Political Science Review* 91: 927–930.

Schweller, Randall L. 1998. *Deadly Imbalances: Tripolarity and Hitler's Strategy of World Conquest*. New York, NY: Columbia University Press.

Schweller, Randall L. 2003a. "The Progressiveness of Neoclassical Realism." In Colin Elman and Miriam Fendius Elman, eds. *Progress in International Relations Theory: Appraising the Field*. Cambridge, MA: MIT Press, 311–347.

Schweller, Randall L. 2003b. "New Realist Research on Alliances: Refining, Not Refuting, Waltz's Balancing Proposition." In John A. Vasquez and Colin Elman, eds. *Realism and the Balance of Power: A New Debate*. Upper Saddle River, NJ: Prentice Hall, 74–79.

Schweller, Randall L. 2004. "Unanswered Threats: A Neoclassical Realist Theory of Underbalancing." *International Security* 29: 159–201.

Schweller, Randall L. 2006. *Unanswered Threats: Political Constraints on the Balance of Power*. Princeton, NJ: Princeton University Press.

Schweller, Randall L. 2018. "The Balance of Power in World Politics." In William R. Thompson, ed. *Empirical International Relations Theory*. Vol. 1. Oxford: Oxford University Press, 143–157.

Schweller, Randall L., and David Priess. 1997. "A Tale of Two Realisms: Expanding the Institutions Debate." *Mershon International Studies Review* 41: 1–32.

Schweller, Randall L., and William C. Wohlforth. 2000. "Power Test: Evaluating Realism in Response to the End of the Cold War." *Security Studies* 9: 60–107.

Scott, Joan Wallach. 2005. "Against Eclecticism." *Differences* 16: 114–137.

Selten, Reinhard. 1974. "The Chain Store Paradox." Institute of Mathematical Economics Working Papers no. 18. Bielefeld: Center for Mathematical Economics.

Sending, Ole Jacob. 2002. "Constitution, Choice and Change: Problems with the 'Logic of Appropriateness' and Its Use in Constructivist Theory." *European Journal of International Relations* 8: 443–470.

Senese, Paul D., and John A. Vasquez. 2008. *The Steps to War: An Empirical Study*. Princeton, NJ: Princeton University Press.

Sheetz, Mark S., and Michael Mastanduno. 1997–1998. "Debating the Unipolar Moment." *International Security* 22: 168–174.

Shifrinson, Joshua R. Itzkowitz. 2018. "The Rise of China, Balance of Power Theory and US National Security: Reasons for Optimism." *Journal of Strategic Studies* 43: 175–216.

Shifrinson, Joshua R. Itzkowitz. 2019a. *Rising Titans, Falling Giants: How Great Powers Exploit Power Shifts*. Ithaca, NY: Cornell University Press.

Shifrinson, Joshua R. Itzkowitz. 2019b. "Should the United States Fear China's Rise." *The Washington Quarterly* 41: 65–83.

Shifrinson, Joshua R. Itzkowitz. 2020. "Partnership or Predation? How Rising States Contend with Declining Great Powers." *International Security* 45: 90–126.

Shuell, Thomas. 2016. "Theories of Learning." www.education.com.

Sil, Rudra. 2000a. "The Foundations of Eclecticism: The Epistemological Status of Agency, Culture, and Structure in Social Theory." *Journal of Theoretical Politics* 12: 353–387.

Sil, Rudra. 2000b. "Against Epistemological Absolutism: Toward a 'Pragmatic' Center?" In Rudra Sil and Eileen M. Doherty, eds. *Beyond Boundaries? Disciplines, Paradigms and Theoretical Integration in International Studies.* Albany, NY: State University of New York Press, 145–176.

Sil, Rudra. 2002. *Managing Modernity: Work, Community and Authority in Late-Industrializing Japan and Russia.* Ann Arbor, MI: University of Michigan Press.

Sil, Rudra. 2009. "Simplifying Pragmatism: From Social Theory to Problem-Driven Eclecticism." *International Studies Review* 11: 648–652.

Sil, Rudra, and Peter J. Katzenstein. 2010a. *Beyond Paradigms: Analytic Eclecticism in the Study of World Politics.* New York, NY: Palgrave Macmillan.

Sil, Rudra, and Peter J. Katzenstein. 2010b. "Analytic Eclecticism in the Study of World Politics: Reconfiguring Problems and Mechanisms across Research Traditions." *Perspectives on Politics* 8: 411–431.

Sil, Rudra, and Peter Katzenstein. 2010c. "Eclectic Theorizing in the Study and Practice of International Relations." In Christian Reus-Smit and Duncan Snidal, eds. *The Oxford Handbook of International Relations.* Oxford: Oxford University Press, 109–130.

Sil, Rudra, and Peter J. Katzenstein. 2010d. "Symposium: Beyond Paradigms and Research Programs—Analytic Eclecticism: Not Perfect, but Indispensable." *Qualitative and Multi-method Research* 8: 19–24.

Sil, Rudra, and Peter J. Katzenstein. 2011. "De-centering, Not Discarding, the 'Isms': Some Friendly Amendments." *International Studies Quarterly* 55: 481–485.

Simon, Herbert A. 1969. *The Sciences of the Artificial.* Cambridge, MA: MIT Press.

Singer, J. David. 1961. "The Level-of-Analysis Problem in International Relations." *World Politics* 14: 77–92.

Sjoberg, Laura, and J. Samuel Barkin. 2018. "If It Is Everything, It Is Nothing: An Argument for Specificity in Constructivisms." In Mariano E. Bertucci, Jarrod Hayes, and Patrick James, eds. *Constructivism Reconsidered.* Ann Arbor, MI: University of Michigan Press, 227–242.

Small, Melvin, and J. David Singer. 1982. *Resort to Arms: International and Civil Wars, 1816–1980.* Beverly Hills, CA: Sage.

Smith, Kevin B. 2002. "Typologies, Taxonomies, and the Benefits of Policy Classification." *Policy Studies Journal* 30: 379–395.

Smith, Michael Joseph. 1986. *Realist Thought from Weber to Kissinger.* Baton Rouge, LA: Louisiana State University Press.

Snidal, Duncan. 1985. "The Limits of Hegemonic Stability Theory." *International Organization* 39: 579–614.

Snidal, Duncan. 1991. "Relative Gains and the Pattern of International Cooperation." *American Political Science Review* 85: 701–726.

Snidal, Duncan. 2018. Personal communication.

Snidal, Duncan, and Alexander Wendt. 2009. "Why There Is *International Theory* Now." *International Theory* 1: 1–14.

Snyder, Glenn H. 1991. "Alliances, Balance, and Stability." *International Organization* 45: 121–142.

Snyder, Glenn H. 2002. "Mearsheimer's World—Offensive Realism and the Struggle for Security." *International Security* 27: 149–173.

Snyder, Jack. 1991. *Myths of Empire*. Ithaca, NY: Cornell University Press.

Snyder, Jack., and Keir A. Lieber. 2008. "Correspondence: Defensive Realism and the 'New' History of World War I." *International Security* 33: 174–185.

Souva, Mark. 2018. "Power Shifts and War." In William R. Thompson, ed. *Empirical International Relations Theory*. Vol. 3. Oxford: Oxford University Press, 138–153.

Spruyt, Hendrik. 1996. *The Sovereign State and Its Competitors: An Analysis of Systems Change*. Princeton, NJ: Princeton University Press.

Stam, Allan C. 2001. "Review of *Causes of War*." *American Political Science Review* 95: 265–266.

Starr, Harvey. 1984. *Henry Kissinger: Perceptions of International Politics*. Lexington, KY: University Press of Kentucky.

Starr, Harvey. 2002a. "Visions of Global Politics as an Intellectual Enterprise: Three Questions without Answers." In Donald Puchala, ed. *Visions of International Relations: Assessing an Academic Field*. Columbia, SC: University of South Carolina Press, 42–61.

Starr, Harvey. 2002b. "Cumulation from Proper Specification: Theory, Logic, Research Design and 'Nice' Laws." *Conflict Management and Peace Science* 22: 353–363.

Steele, Brent J. 2013. *Alternative Accountabilities in Global Politics: The Scars of Violence*. New York, NY: Routledge.

Sterling-Folker, Jennifer. 1997. "Realist Environment, Liberal Process, and Domestic-Level Variables." *International Studies Quarterly* 41: 1–25.

Sun Tzu. 1963 [500–450 BCE]. *The Art of War*. Samuel B. Griffith, trans. Oxford: Oxford University Press.

Taliaferro, Jeffrey W. 2000–2001. "Security Seeking under Anarchy: Defensive Realism Revisited." *International Security* 25: 128–161.

Taliaferro, Jeffrey W. 2004. *Balancing Risks: Great Power Intervention in the Periphery*. Ithaca, NY: Cornell University Press.

Taliaferro, Jeffrey W. 2006. "State Building for Future Wars: Neoclassical Realism and the Resource-Extractive State." *Security Studies* 15: 464–495.

Taliaferro, Jeffrey W. 2009a. "Neoclassical Realism: The Psychology of Great Power Intervention." In Jennifer Sterling-Folker, ed. *Making Sense of International Relations Theory*. Boulder, CO: Lynne Rienner, 38–54.

Taliaferro, Jeffrey W. 2009b. "Neoclassical Realism and Resource Extraction: State Building for Future War." In Steven E. Lobell, Norrin M. Ripsman, and Jeffrey W. Taliaferro, eds. *Neoclassical Realism, the State, and Foreign Policy*. Cambridge: Cambridge University Press, 194–226.

Taliaferro, Jeffrey W. 2019. *Defending Frenemies: Alliance Politics and Nuclear Nonproliferation in US Foreign Policy*. New York, NY: Oxford University Press.

Taliaferro, Jeffrey W., Steven E. Lobell, and Norrin M. Ripsman. 2009. "Introduction: Neoclassical Realism, the State, and Foreign Policy." In Steven E. Lobell, Norrin M. Ripsman, and Jeffrey W. Taliaferro, eds. *Neoclassical Realism, the State, and Foreign Policy*. Cambridge: Cambridge University Press, 1–41.

Tammen, Ronald L., et al. 2000. *Power Transitions: Strategies for the 21st Century*. New York, NY: Chatham House Publishers.

Tammen, Ronald L., and Jacek Kugler, eds. 2020a. *The Rise of Regions: Conflict and Cooperation*. New York, NY: Rowman & Littlefield.

Tammen, Ronald L., and Jacek Kugler. 2020b. "The Rise of Regions." In Ronald L. Tammen and Jacek Kugler, eds. *The Rise of Regions: Conflict and Cooperation*. New York, NY: Rowman & Littlefield, 1–18.

Tammen, Ronald L., Jacek Kugler, and Douglas Lemke. 2017. "Foundations of Power Transition Theory." In *Oxford Research Encyclopedia of Politics*. Oxford: Oxford University Press, 1–59.

Tang, Shiping. 2008. "Fear in International Politics: Two Positions." *International Studies Review* 10: 451–471.

Tang, Shiping. 2009. "Taking Stock of Neoclassical Realism." *International Studies Review* 11: 799–803.

Taylor, Michael. 1976. *Anarchy and Cooperation*. New York, NY: John Wiley & Sons.

Tellis, Ashley J. 1996. "Reconstructing Political Realism: The Long March to Scientific Theory." In Benjamin Frankel, ed. *Roots of Realism*. Portland, OR: Frank Cass, 3–100.

Thompson, William R. 1996. "Democracy and Peace: Putting the Cart Before the Horse?" *International Organization* 50: 141–174.

Thompson, William R. 2002. "Review of Dale C. Copeland, *The Origins of Major War*. Ithaca, NY: Cornell University Press, 2000." *Journal of Politics* 64: 333–335.

Thucydides. 1972 [431 BCE]. *History of the Peloponnesian War*. Rex Warner, ed. London: Penguin.

Tickner, Arlene B. 2013. "Core, Periphery and (Neo)Imperialist International Relations." *European Journal of International Relations* 19: 627–646.

Toft, Peter. 2005. "John J. Mearsheimer: An Offensive Realist between Geopolitics and Power." *Journal of International Relations and Development* 8: 381–408.

Toulmin, Stephen E. 1953. *The Philosophy of Science: An Introduction*. London: Mayflower Press.

Toulmin, Stephen E. 1970. "Does the Distinction Between Normal and Revolutionary Science Hold Water?" In Imre Lakatos and Alan Musgrave, eds. *Criticism and the Growth of Knowledge*. Cambridge: Cambridge University of Press, 39–50.

Tufte, Edward R. 2006. *Beautiful Evidence*. Cheshire, CT: Graphics Press.

Uslaner, Eric M. 2002. *The Moral Foundations of Trust*. Cambridge: Cambridge University Press.

Valeriano, Brandon. 2009. "The Tragedy of Offensive Realism: Testing Aggressive Power Politics Models." *International Interactions* 35: 179–206.

Valeriano, Brandon, Benjamin Jensen, and Ryan C. Maness. 2018. *Cyber Strategy: The Evolving Character of Power and Coercion*. Oxford: Oxford University Press.

Valeriano, Brandon, and Ryan C. Maness. 2015. *Cyber War versus Cyber Realities: Cyber Conflict in the International System*. Oxford: Oxford University Press.

Vancouver, Jeffrey B. 1996. "Living Systems Theory as a Paradigm for Organizational Behavior: Understanding Humans, Organizations, and Social Processes." *Behavioral Science* 41: 165–204.

Van Evera, Stephen. 1999. *Causes of War: Power and the Roots of Conflict*. Ithaca, NY: Cornell University Press.

van Gelder, Tim. 2015. "Using Argument Mapping to Improve Critical Thinking Skills." In Martin Davies and Ronald Barnett, eds. *The Palgrave Handbook of Critical Thinking in Higher Education*. New York, NY: Palgrave Macmillan, 183–192.

Vasquez, John A. 1979. "Colouring It Morgenthau: New Evidence for an Old Thesis on Quantitative International Politics." *British Journal of International Studies* 5: 210–228.
Vasquez, John A. 1983. *The Power of Power Politics: A Critique.* New Brunswick, NJ: Rutgers University Press.
Vasquez, John A. 1998. *The Power of Power Politics: From Classical Realism to Neotraditionalism.* New York, NY: Cambridge University Press.
Vasquez, John A. 2003a. "The Realist Paradigm and Degenerative versus Progressive Research Programs: An Appraisal of Neotraditional Research on Waltz's Balancing Proposition." In John A. Vasquez and Colin Elman, eds. *Realism and the Balance of Power: A New Debate.* Upper Saddle River, NJ: Prentice Hall, 23–48.
Vasquez, John A. 2003b. "The New Debate on Balancing Power: A Reply to My Critics." In John A. Vasquez and Colin Elman, eds. *Realism and the Balance of Power: A New Debate.* Upper Saddle River, NJ: Prentice Hall, 87–113.
Vasquez, John A. 2003c. "Kuhn versus Lakatos: The Case for Multiple Frames in Appraising International Relations Theory." In Colin Elman and Miriam Fendius Elman, eds. *Progress in International Relations Theory: Appraising the Field.* Cambridge, MA: MIT Press, 419–454.
Thorstein. 1899. *The Theory of the Leisure Class.* New York, NY: B. W. Huebsch.
Vernon, Raymond. 1971. *Sovereignty at Bay: The Multinational Spread of U.S. Enterprises.* New York, NY: Wiley.
Viterale, Francisco Del Canto. 2019. "Developing a Systems Architecture Model to Study the Science, Technology and Innovation in International Studies." *Systems* 7: 46.
von Hlatky, Stéfanie. 2013. *American Allies in Times of War.* Oxford: Oxford University Press.
von Hlatky, Stéfanie. 2015. "Cash or Combat? America's Asian Alliances during the War in Afghanistan." *Asian Security* 10: 31–51.
Wæver, Ole. 2009. "Waltz's Theory of Theory." *International Relations* 23: 201–222.
Wagner, R. Harrison. 2007. *War and the State: The Theory of International Politics.* Ann Arbor, MI: University of Michigan Press.
Walker, Thomas C. 2018. "Theoretical Diversity in International Relations: Dominance, Pluralism, and Division." In William R. Thompson, ed. *Empirical International Relations Theory.* Vol. 4. Oxford: Oxford University Press, 179–209.
Walker, Thomas C., and Jeffrey S. Morton. 2005. "Re-assessing the 'Power of Power Politics' Thesis: Is Realism Still Dominant?" *International Studies Review* 7: 341–356.
Walt, Stephen M. 1990 [1987]. *The Origins of Alliances.* 2nd ed. Ithaca, NY: Cornell University Press.
Walt, Stephen M. 1996. *Revolution and War.* 1996. Ithaca, NY: Cornell University Press.
Walt, Stephen M. 1998. "International Relations: One World, Many Theories." *Foreign Policy* 10: 29–46.
Walt, Stephen M. 2002. "The Enduring Relevance of the Realist Tradition." In Ira Katznelson and Helen V. Milner, eds. *Political Science: The State of the Discipline.* New York, NY: Norton, 197–230.
Walt, Stephen M. 2003. "The Progressive Power of Realism." In John A. Vasquez and Colin Elman, eds. *Realism and the Balance of Power: A New Debate.* Upper Saddle River, NJ: Prentice Hall, 58–65.
Waltz, Kenneth N. 1959. *Man, the State, and War: A Theoretical Analysis.* New York, NY: Columbia University Press.

Waltz, Kenneth N. 1964. "The Stability of a Bipolar World." *Daedalus* 93: 881–909.
Waltz, Kenneth N. 1979. *Theory of International Politics*. Reading, MA: Addison Wesley.
Waltz, Kenneth N. 1988. "The Origins of War in Neorealist Theory." In Robert I. Rotberg and Theodore K. Rabb, eds. *The Origin and Prevention of Major Wars*. Cambridge: Cambridge University Press, 39–52.
Waltz, Kenneth N. 1995. "Realist Thought and Neorealist Theory." In Charles W. Kegley Jr., ed. *Controversies in International Relations Theory: Realism and the Neoliberal Challenge*. New York, NY: St. Martin's Press, 67–82.
Waltz, Kenneth N. 2002. "Structural Realism After the Cold War." In John G. Ikenberry, ed. *America Unrivaled: The Future of the Balance of Power*. Ithaca, NY: Cornell University Press, 29–67.
Waltz, Kenneth N. 2003a. "Thoughts about Assaying Theories." In Colin Elman and Miriam Fendius Elman, eds. *Progress in International Relations Theory: Appraising the Field*. Cambridge, MA: MIT Press, vii–xiv.
Waltz, Kenneth N. 2003b. "Evaluating Theories." In John A. Vasquez and Colin Elman, eds. *Realism and the Balance of Power: A New Debate*. Upper Saddle River, NJ: Prentice Hall, 49–57.
Ward, Michael D. 2018. "Do We Have Too Much Theory in International Relations or Do We Need Less? Waltz Was Wrong, Tetlock Was Right?" In William R. Thompson, ed. *The Oxford Encyclopedia of Empirical International Relations Theory*. Vol. 1. Oxford: Oxford University Press, 554–570.
Wayman, Frank W., and Paul F. Diehl. 1994a. "Realism Reconsidered: The Realpolitik Framework and Its Basic Propositions." In Frank W. Wayman and Paul F. Diehl, eds. *Reconstructing Realpolitik*. Ann Arbor, MI: University of Michigan Press, 3–26.
Wayman, Frank W., and Paul F. Diehl, eds. 1994b. *Reconstructing Realpolitik*. Ann Arbor, MI: University of Michigan Press.
Weeks, Jessica L. P. 2014. *Dictators at War and Peace*. Ithaca, NY: Cornell University Press.
Welch, David A. 2003. "Why International Relations Theorists Should Stop Reading Thucydides." *Review of International Studies* 29: 301–319.
Wendt, Alexander. 1999. *Social Theory of International Politics*. Cambridge: Cambridge University Press.
Whewell, William. 1840. *The Philosophy of the Inductive Sciences, Founded upon Their History*. 2 vols. London: John W. Parker.
Wight, Colin. 1996. "Incommensurability and Cross-Paradigm Communication in International Relations Theory: 'What's the Frequency Kenneth?'" *Millennium* 25: 291–319.
Wight, Colin. 2007. "A Manifesto for Scientific Realism in IR: Assuming the Can-Opener Won't Work!" *Millennium* 35: 379–398.
Wight, Colin. 2017. "Maps, Models, and Theories: A Scientific Realist Approach toward Validity." In Annette Freyberg-Inan, Ewan Harrison, and Patrick James, eds. *Evaluating Progress in International Relations: How Do You Know?* New York, NY: Routledge, 31–50.
Wight, Colin. 2019. "Bringing the Outside In: The Limits of Theoretical Fragmentation and Pluralism in IR Theory." *Politics* 39: 64–81.
Wight, Martin. 1978 [1946]. *Power Politics*. Hedley Bull and Carsten Holbraad, eds. New York, NY: Holmes & Meier.
Wilkenfeld, Jonathan, ed. 1973. *Conflict Behavior and Linkage Politics*. New York, NY: David McKay.

Williams, Michael C. 2004. "Why Ideas Matter in International Relations: Hans Morgenthau, Classical Realism, and the Moral Construction of Power Politics." *International Organization* 58: 633–665.

Williams, Michael C. 2005. *The Realist Tradition and the Limits of International Relations.* Cambridge: Cambridge University Press.

Williams, Michael C. 2007. *Realism Reconsidered: The Legacy of Hans Morgenthau in International Relations.* New York, NY: Oxford University Press.

Wivel, Andreas. 2005. "Explaining Why State X Made a Certain Move Last Tuesday: The Promise and Limitations of Realist Foreign Policy Analysis." *Journal of International Relations and Development* 8: 355–380.

Wohlforth, William C. 1993. *The Elusive Balance: Power and Perceptions during the Cold War.* Ithaca, NY: Cornell University Press.

Wohlforth, William C. 2003. "Measuring Power—and the Power of Theories." In John A. Vasquez and Colin Elman, eds. *Realism and the Balance of Power: A New Debate.* Upper Saddle River, NJ: Prentice Hall, 250–265.

Wohlforth, William C. 2008. "Realism." In Christian Reus-Smit and Duncan Snidal, eds. *The Oxford Handbook of International Relations.* Oxford: Oxford University Press, 131–149.

Wohlstetter, Albert. 1968. "Theory and Opposed Systems Design." *Journal of Conflict Resolution* 12: 302–331.

Wolfers, Arnold. 1962. *Discord and Collaboration: Essays on International Politics.* Baltimore, MD: Johns Hopkins University Press.

Yandle, Bruce, Maya Vijayaraghavan and Madhusudan Bhattari. 2002. "The Environmental Kuznets Curve." PERC Research Study 02-1. May.

Yarhi-Milo, Keren. 2013. "In the Eye of the Beholder: How Leaders and Intelligence Communities Assess the Intentions of Adversaries." *International Security* 38: 7–51.

Yetiv, Steve, and Patrick James, eds. 2016. *Advancing Interdisciplinary Approaches to International Relations.* New York, NY: Palgrave Macmillan.

Yoo, Hyon Joo. 2012. "Domestic Hurdles for System-Driven Behavior: Neoclassical Realism and Missile Defense Policies in Japan and South Korea." *International Relations of the Asia-Pacific* 12: 317–348.

Yoon, Young-Kwan. 2003. "Introduction: Power Cycle Theory and the Practice of International Relations." *International Political Science Review* 24: 5–12.

Yordán, Carlos L. 2006. "America's Quest for Global Hegemony: Offensive Realism, the Bush Doctrine, and the 2003 Iraq War." *Theoria* 110: 125–157.

Young, Oran R. 1968. *Systems of Political Science.* Englewood Cliffs, NJ: Prentice Hall.

Young, Oran R. 1969. "Professor Russett: Industrious Tailor to a Naked Emperor." *World Politics* 21: 486–511.

Zagare, Frank C. 2019. *Game Theory, Diplomatic History and Security Studies.* Oxford: Oxford University Press.

Zakaria, Fareed. 1992. "Realism and Domestic Politics: A Review Essay." *International Security* 17: 177–198.

Zakaria, Fareed. 1998. *From Wealth to Power: The Unusual Origins of America's World Role.* Princeton, NJ: Princeton University Press.

Zinnes, Dina A. 1967. "An Analytical Study of the Balance of Power Theories." *Journal of Peace Research* 4: 270–288.

Zinnes, Dina A. 1976. *Contemporary Research in International Relations, A Perspective and a Critical Appraisal.* New York, NY: Free Press.

Zinnes, Dina A. 1980. "Three Puzzles in Search of a Researcher." *International Studies Quarterly* 24: 315–342.

Index

For the benefit of digital users, indexed terms that span two pages (e.g., 52–53) may, on occasion, appear on only one of those pages.

Tables and figures are indicated by *t* and *f* following the page number

9/11 attacks (2001), 82, 94, 582

Aberystwyth University, 109
Active Learning in International Affairs Section (ALIAS), 120
Alaska border disputes, 88–89
Alexander I (tsar of Russia), 102
Allison, Graham, 82–83, 203
Almond, Gabriel, 7
American Political Science Association, 120
analytic eclecticism
   axiom identification and, 258–59
   bridge building and, 63, 65, 558–59
   causes of war and, 104–5
   critiques of, 106–7
   interdisciplinary borrowing from, 109–10
   middle-range causal arguments and, 98–101, 122, 220–21, 226, 534, 558–59, 576
   model of cognition and, 221
   open-ended approach of, 98–100
   policy relevance and, 32, 64–65, 98–99, 122, 576
   Systemist International Relations and, 207
   value added from, 103–8, 122
analyticism, 34, 36–39, 42, 45–46, 74, 219, 575
anarchy
   balance of threat theory and, 388–89
   classical realism and, 261–62, 288, 293–94, 298, 313–18
   defensive realism and, 268, 449
   definition of, 257
   neoclassical realism and, 195, 268
   offensive realism and, 495
   power cycle theory and, 333, 343
   structural realism and, 270
antirealism, 83–84
Arab Spring, 82, 582
Argentina, 422
Aron, Raymond, 41, 238, 294, 318–22, 319*f*, 323*t*

Arrow Impossibility Theorem, 69, 163–64
Austria, 102, 310–13, 393–94
axiom identification
   abstract statement condition and, 164
   Anti-Brutus Criterion and, 164–65
   distinctiveness criterion and, 166, 177–78
   economy of expression condition and, 163–64, 165, 252–53
   external validation and, 162–63
   internal validation and, 161–63
   logical consistency condition and, 163–64, 165, 251–52
   model of cognition and, 225
   primitive statement condition and, 164, 250
   rationalist and deductive approach to, 163–66
   research enterprise and, 147–49, 155, 158–68, 160*t*, 223, 576–77
   scientific realism and, 222–23
   sociological and inductive approach to, 159–63, 166–67, 168
   universal assumption condition and, 164, 250–51
   visual representation and, 162

Baghdad Pact, 393
balance of interests theory
   additional noncore assumptions in, 536*t*
   causes of war and, 421–22
   combination between subvariants of, 545–47, 548*f*
   critiques of, 423
   defining qualities of, 279, 282*t*, 417–21, 420*t*
   domestic politics and, 420–21
   efficient conditions and, 430, 438, 445–46
   final conditions and, 430, 438, 445
   formal conditions and, 430, 438, 445
   instrumental rationality and, 258
   material conditions and, 430, 445
   Munich Conference (1938) and, 419
   priorities for improvement in, 536*t*, 539–40

balance of interests theory (cont.)
   range of variable types and, 431t, 536t, 540
   visual representations of, 423–46, 424f, 433f, 439f
   World War II and, 422
balance of power theory
   as analogy, 117
   falsification and, 395
   inconsistent uses of the term, 44
   international law and, 301–6
   state centrism and, 395
   structural realism and, 366–67
   visual representation of, 187–88
   world public opinion and, 301, 306
balance of threat theory. *See also* revolution-based balance of threat theory
   additional noncore assumptions in, 536t
   anarchy and, 388–89
   balancing and, 328, 387
   bandwagoning and, 328, 387–88
   causes of war, 393
   critiques of, 394–95
   defining qualities of, 279, 328, 386–93
   geographical proximity and, 389–90
   instrumental rationality and, 258
   perceptions of danger and, 535
   priorities for improvement in, 536t, 539
   range of variable types and, 536t
   testability of, 544–45
   variable types in, 405t
   visual representations of, 396–415, 397f
Balkan Wars, 131–32, 350–51
Barkin, J. Samuel, 64, 90, 92–93, 102, 191, 235t, 245t
Bauer, Harry, 7
Bayes, Thomas, 80, 111, 127–28, 130–31, 132–33, 257
Ben-Gurion, David, 219–20
Bennett, Andrew, 26–27, 78, 176t
Berlin Wall, 132, 559–60
biological realism, 270
Bismarck, Otto von, 67, 491–92
Brazil, 422
Brexit vote (2016), 117
Brighi, Elisabetta, 7
Bull, Hedley, 114–15
Bunge, Mario, 77, 173–74, 574
Bush, George W., 129–30

Canada, 88–89, 118
Carr, E.H., 278, 290
Castlereagh, Lord (Robert Stewart), 101, 293
Castro, Fidel, 22–23

Central America, 23
Chamberlain, Neville, 422, 484
Chernoff, Fred, 54, 135–37, 389t, 420t
China, 3, 260, 377, 384, 392, 520–21
classical realism
   anarchy and, 261–62, 288, 293–94, 298, 313–18
   causes of war and, 289–95
   Cold War and, 284
   critiques of, 295–97
   general systems theory and, 311–12
   logic of discovery and, 278, 324–25
   political equilibrium and, 306–11, 312–13
   range of variables included in, 323t, 324, 536t
   rationality and, 288–89
   state centrality and, 288
   state focus on power and, 288
   systemism and, 324
   view of human nature in, 231, 284, 288–89
   visual representations of theories of war in, 297–322, 299f, 302f, 307f, 577–78
Coase Theorem, 429–30
cognitive load theory, 75, 108, 113, 116–20, 195–202
Cold War
   Berlin Wall and, 132, 559–60
   end of, 81–82, 541, 544, 582
   Latin America and, 22–23
   mutually assured destruction (MAD) and, 203
   polarity and, 544
   realist typologies of war and, 263–64
Congress of Vienna, 99–100
constructivism
   analyticism and, 36–37
   causes of war and, 86
   ideational analysis and, 27–28
   norms of, 57
   proliferation of theoretical mechanisms in, 6
   social constructivists and, 86
Copeland, Dale C., 266t, 269–70, 294, 480t, 482
Correlates of War (COW) data set, 14, 81, 154–55
Covid-19 pandemic, 117
Crimean War (1853–56), 232–33, 366
Crimean War (2014), 464
critical realism, 580–81
Cuba, 22–23, 395–96
Cuban Missile Crisis (1962), 78–79, 82–83, 182, 202–3, 390

Dahl, Robert, 41
Danielson, Robert W., 112

David, Stephen R., 235t, 240, 287t, 496t
defensive realism
    additional noncore assumptions in, 536t
    anarchy and, 268, 449
    bellicose diplomatic tactics and, 464–69, 470
    causes of war and, 451–53
    combination between subvariants of, 547–49, 550f
    critiques of, 423
    defining qualities of, 268, 279, 282t, 328–29, 448–51, 450t
    degrees of complexity for, 477
    efficient conditions and, 464
    false perceptions and, 452
    final conditions and, 464
    first-mover advantage and, 328–29, 461–62, 549
    formal causes and, 462
    material conditions and, 464
    offense-defense and, 470–77, 471f
    power-privilege disequilibrium and, 469–70
    priorities for improvement in, 536t, 539–40, 555, 570
    range of variable types in, 463t, 536t, 540
    rationality and, 449–50
    reciprocal fear and, 452, 461–62, 464, 549
    relative power and, 275
    secrecy and, 452
    stability and, 454–64
    state centrism and, 449
    visual representations of, 454–64, 455f, 465f, 471f
    windows of opportunity and, 452, 464–70, 465f
democratic peace theory, 138–39, 232–33
Diehl, Paul F., 16–17
Dominican Republic, 22–23
Donnelly, Jack, 266t, 270
Doran, Charles F., 89–90, 331–32, 335t, 336–37, 338
dynamic differentials theory
    additional noncore assumptions in, 536t
    bipolarity and, 483
    causes of war and, 482–83
    critiques of, 483–85
    defining qualities of, 279–80, 282t, 329, 479–81, 480t
    efficient causes and, 492
    final conditions and, 492
    great power decline and, 329, 480
    material conditions and, 492
    parsimony of, 493
    priorities for improvement in, 536t, 539, 555, 571, 572–73

range of variable types and, 536t, 540
state security goals and, 535
visual representation of, 485–93, 486f

Easton, David, 169–71, 173, 312–13
Edward VIII (king of England), 78–79
Egypt, 82, 240, 393
Elman, Colin
    on balance of power, 44
    on classical realism, 287t
    on explanatory power of realism, 5
    on international relations' lack of metatheory, 54–55
    realism summarized by, 235t
    on research programs, 58, 144–45
Elman, Miriam, 58, 144–45
English school, 111, 142, 233, 272
European Union (EU), 117, 186–87

falsification
    commensurability and, 87
    deductive reasoning and, 136t
    power cycle theory and, 342
    realism and, 32
    research enterprise and, 124
    scientific progress and, 29t, 32
    systems of explanation and, 135–37
Feng, Huiyun, 391
First Punic War, 483
France
    French Revolution and, 312–13, 393–94
    interwar years and, 422
    Napoleonic Wars and, 100, 310
    Suez War and, 393
    World War I and, 131–32, 178, 223–24
Freyberg-Inan, Annette, 26, 28, 235t

Genco, Stephen, 7
general systems theory, 169–70, 311–12
Germany
    Berlin Wall and, 132, 559–60
    US-Germany wiretapping scandal (2013) and, 186
    Versailles Treaty and, 332
    World War I and, 131–32, 178
    World War II and, 422
Gilpin, Robert
    hegemonic stability theory and, 269–70, 357t, 360–63, 368
    power cycle theory summarized by, 335t
    realism summarized by, 235t, 245t
Glaser, Charles L., 94–95
Gödel's theorem, 89–90, 220, 224, 534

Gorbachev, Mikhail, 446
grand strategy, 154, 186, 231, 444–46
graphic turn. *See* visual representation
Great Britain. *See* United Kingdom
Great War. *See* World War I
Greece, 3, 186–87
Gulf Cooperation Council, 391
Guzzini, Stefano, 8, 166, 235*t*, 287*t*, 292–93, 295

Harrison, Ewan, 28
He, Kai, 391
hedged realism, 270
hegemonic stability theory
  additional noncore assumptions in, 536*t*
  causes of war and, 363
  critiques of, 368
  defining qualities of, 282*t*, 360–62
  efficient causes and, 384
  formal conditions and, 384
  material conditions and, 384
  priorities for improvement in, 536*t*, 539, 553–54
  range of variable types and, 536*t*, 540
  Realist Law of Uneven Growth and, 535
  structural realism and, 541–44, 553–54
  visual representation and, 379–85, 380*f*
Hitler, Adolf, 204, 298–301, 484
Hobbes, Thomas, 3–4, 250–52, 286, 298
Hoffman, Stanley, 11–12, 295

India, 57, 475, 568
Inoguchi, Takashi, 335*t*, 341–42
instrumental rationality
  balance of threat and, 258
  as baseline position on behavior, 125–28
  definition of, 67
  incorrect information and, 132
  self-interest and, 68, 126, 132
International Crisis Behavior (ICB) Project, 181, 559–60, 569–72
International Security, 16, 120, 192
International Studies Association, 109, 120
Iran, 240, 341, 390–92, 406–13
Iraq, 41, 129–30, 258, 341, 393, 406–13
Ireland, 186–87, 388
ISIS (Islamic State), 258
Israel, 62–63, 219–20, 240, 393
Italy, 186–87

Jackson, Patrick Thaddeus
  neopositivism critiqued by, 13
  on progress in international relations, 33–34
  on science and international relations, 12–13
  on scientific status of knowledge claims in international relations, 54
James, William, 6–7
Japan
  classical realism and, 324
  interwar period and, 340
  offensive realism and, 502
  Pearl Harbor attack and, 133, 379–84
  predation theory and, 520–21
  Russo-Japanese War (1905) and, 338
Jensen, Michael A., 235*t*, 266*t*, 271, 287*t*, 357*t*, 449
Jervis, Robert, 335*t*
Johnson, Lyndon, 204
Journal of Conflict Resolution, 192
Journal of Political Science Education, 120

Kaplan, Morton A., 114–15
Katzenstein, Peter
  on analytic eclecticism, 63–64, 103, 105*t*
  on multimethod approaches, 38
  on social science and research traditions, 159–61
Kautilya, 3–4
Kennedy, John F., 182, 202–3
Keohane, Robert, 69–70, 158, 232
Kessler, Oliver, 37
Khrushchev, Nikita, 202–3
Kissinger, Henry
  analytic eclecticism and, 99–103
  on causes of war, 293–94
  on Metternich, 100, 311–13
  Nixon Administration and, 99
  on political equilibrium, 310
  systemism and, 179
  visual representations of classical realism's theory of war by, 306–13, 307*f*
Knutsen, Torbjørn, 14–15, 119
Korean War, 392, 395–96
Kuhn, Thomas
  falsification and, 137–38
  international relations theory and, 140
  paradigm shifts and, 81–82, 138–39
  paradigms in scientific research and, 57–58
Kurki, Milja, 176*t*
Kuwait, 341
Kuznets Curve, 546

Lakatos, Imre
  on empirical content of theories, 242
  metatheory and, 54
  paradigm concept critiqued by, 141–42
  research program concept and, 57–58, 69, 141–42

INDEX 621

Lake, David, 27–28, 82
Latin America, 21f, 22–23, 174
Laudan, Larry, 135, 136t, 145–49
Legro, Jeffrey W.
   on axiom identification, 161–62
   balance of interest theory critiqued by, 421
   on failings of realism, 5, 161–62, 239, 256
   on neoclassical realism, 196t
Levy, Jack S., 335t, 357t
liberalism
   bottom-up view of politics and, 111
   democratic peace theory and, 213
   interdependence and, 232, 286
   rationality and, 255–56
   realism and, 232–33, 254
Little, Richard, 296
Lobell, Steven E., 195, 196t, 235t, 496t
London cholera outbreak (1854), 117
Louisiana Purchase, 499–500
Louis XIV (king of France), 340, 366

Machiavelli, Niccolò, 3–4, 128–29, 234, 286, 293
Malthus, Thomas, 137
Marshall Plan, 186, 521
Marxism, 145, 166, 235t
Mearsheimer, John
   on appeal of realism, 3, 4–5, 582
   offensive realism and, 268, 329, 494
   on polarity, 498–99
   realism summarized by, 235t
   research program concept critiqued by, 143
   on Waltz and rational choice, 134
Merkel, Angela, 186
metacognition, 110–15
metatheory
   analytic eclecticism and, 76–77
   comprehensiveness and, 74
   definition of, 17
   epistemology and, 76
   international relations and, 53–54, 577
   knowledge and, 56
   as means to move beyond fads, 55
   methods and, 55, 58
   performance ratio regarding theory performance and, 225–27, 577
   rationality and, 67, 126–27
   research enterprise and, 69, 155
   scientific realism and, 43, 74, 574, 578–79
   skepticism regarding, 224–25
   systems of explanation and, 68
   visual representation and, 225
   as working system, 213–24, 214f

Metternich, Klemens Wenzel von, 100–2, 293, 311–13
Middle East, 82, 174, 240–41, 390, 393
Miller, Lee Ryan., 10
model of cognition
   analytic eclecticism and, 221
   axiom identification and, 225
   ordinal rationality and, 133–34
   relational reasoning and, 65, 576
   systemism and, 222
   visual representation and, 65–66, 76–77, 576
Moravcsik, Andrew
   on axiom identification, 161–62
   balance of interest theory critiqued by, 421
   on failings of realism, 5, 161–62, 239, 256
   on neoclassical realism, 196t
Morgenthau, Hans
   analytic eclecticism and, 99
   on balance of power, 291
   on causes of war, 291–93
   on challenges of writing international relations theory, 289
   critiques of the work of, 295–96
   on democratic control and foreign policy, 125–26
   on domestic politics and international relations, 101–2
   flexibility of power and interest concepts in work of, 95, 187–88
   history as a series of conflicts for, 15
   on indices of national power, 41
   on liberalism and rationality, 255–56
   rationalism and, 128
   realism summarized by, 235t
   visual representations of classical realism's theory of war by, 301–6, 302f
Morsi, Mohamed, 240
Most, Benjamin, 326, 377, 384
Multimedia Principle, 112
Munich Conference (1938), 419
Muslim Brotherhood, 240
mutually assured destruction (MAD), 203

Napoleon Bonaparte, 310–13, 499–500
Napoleonic Wars, 100–2, 179, 310
Nasser, Gamal, 393
neoclassical realism
   anarchy and, 195, 268
   causation and, 205
   contingency and, 205
   definition of, 194
   domestic politics and, 194–95, 240–41
   mathematical models and, 206

neoclassical realism (*cont.*)
  policy relevance and, 205
  the state and, 194–95
  systemism and, 157, 194–206
  visual representation of, 197*f*, 202–6
neopositivism
  consensus and, 28
  dualist view of world in, 34
  "end of history" and, 89
  highly confirmed empirical referents and, 12–13, 40, 88, 575
  hypothesis testing and, 42
  international relations and, 12, 45–46
  metatheory and, 74
  reflexivity and, 37*f*, 37–38
  rhetoric and, 13
  world as empirically comprehensible in, 34, 44, 62
neorealism. *See* structural realism
The Netherlands, 340
Newton, Isaac, 62, 89n.14, 141
nonaligned-states movement, 57
normative rationality, 125–26
North Atlantic Treaty Organization (NATO), 186, 390, 503, 522
North Korea, 377, 572–73
Nye, Joseph, 232

Obama, Barack, 129–30, 186, 240–41
offensive realism
  additional noncore assumptions in, 536*t*
  anarchy and, 495
  balanced bipolarity and, 498, 503, 514
  causes of war and, 497–500
  critiques of, 500–3
  defensive realism and, 556–57
  defining qualities of, 268, 280, 329, 494–97, 504*f*
  efficient conditions and, 514–15
  falsification and, 515
  final conditions and, 514
  formal conditions and, 514
  incomplete information and, 495
  material conditions and, 514
  maximization of relative power and, 275
  polarity and, 498–99, 512–13
  priorities for improvement in, 536*t*, 539–40, 555–56, 557–58, 570–71, 572–73
  range of variable types and, 536*t*, 540
  rationality and, 495
  Realist Law of Uneven Growth and, 535
  state survival and, 495
  visual representation and, 503–15, 504*f*
Ottoman Empire, 388, 501–2

Papal State, 367
paradigms
  commensurability and, 139–41
  constructive engagement across, 97–99
  converge and, 138
  critiques of concept of, 140–42
  defining qualities of, 68
  democratic peace theory, 138–39
  Gödel's theorem and, 90
  inductive reasoning and, 136*t*
  international relations theory and, 57–58, 90, 145
  paradigmatic pragmatism and, 93
  problems with, 91–97
  scientific research and, 57–58, 137–38
  shifts in, 81–82, 138–39
  as a system of explanation, 134–35
  World War I and, 139–40
Paraguay, 422
Pashler, Harold, 111
Peace Science Society, 120
Pearl Harbor, Battle of (1941), 133, 379–84
Peirce, Charles Sanders, 6
Peloponnesian War, 3–4, 202, 285–86
polycentrism, 57, 560–61
Popper, Karl von, 135–37, 136*t*, 140–42, 143, 147, 149–50
Portugal, 186–87
positivism, 34–35. *See also* neopositivism
postmodernism, 42, 83–86
power competition, 290, 294, 313–18
power cycle theory
  additional noncore assumptions in, 536*t*
  anarchy and, 333, 343
  causes of war and, 336–42
  critiques of, 342–43, 352–53
  defining qualities of, 278, 282*t*, 327, 331–34
  domestic politics and, 343
  efficient causes and, 352
  falsification and, 342
  final causes and, 352
  formal causes and, 352
  material causes and, 352
  mathematical models and, 334
  priorities for improvement in, 536*t*, 539, 552–53, 572–73
  range of variable types and, 536*t*
  rationality and, 333–34
  Realist Law of Uneven Growth and, 535
  relative capability of great powers and, 332, 337–38, 350
  Russo-Japanese War (1905) and, 338
  state centrism and, 333

state focus on power in, 333
visual representation of, 339f, 343–53, 344f
pragmatism, 6–7, 28, 64, 93, 98
predation theory
additional noncore assumptions in, 536t
causes of war and, 522–23
critiques of, 523–24
defining qualities of, 280, 282t, 329–30, 518–22, 518t
great power decline and, 522–24
incomplete information and, 329–30
priorities for improvement in, 536t, 539–40, 558, 571
range of variable types and, 536t
Realist Law of Uneven Growth and, 535
visual representation of, 524–29, 525f
Priess, David, 273t, 274
Prussia, 67, 311, 393–94, 520, 522–23
Putin, Vladimir, 390
Putnam, Robert, 83, 96

Quinn, Adam, 273t, 275

radical realism, 270
rationality
classical realism and, 288–89
cultural context and, 129–30
liberalism and, 255–56
metatheory and, 67, 126–27
power cycle theory and, 333–34
rational choice theory and, 67
realism and, 128–30, 256, 577, 579
research enterprise and, 68, 124
scientific realism and, 129, 219
self-interest and, 67–68
Raymond, Mark, 6
realism. *See also specific realisms*
anarchy and, 234–37, 252–53, 281, 577, 579
axiom identification and, 242–59, 245t, 577
bricolagic bridging and, 533, 534, 558–73
combination of and competition between variations of, 541–51
comprehensiveness and, 32
critiques of, 238–42
falsifiability and, 32
genealogy of theories for, 276–82, 277f
identifying causal mechanisms and, 32
instrumental rationality and, 258
liberalism and, 232–33, 254
neo-Kantianism and, 253–54
pessimistic view of human life in, 234–37
political psychology and, 254
power transition theory and, 253–54

predictive value and, 32–33
priorities for future research in, 579–82
public exchange of views and, 32–33
rationality and, 128–30, 256, 577, 579
Realist Law of Uneven Growth and, 333, 361–62, 379, 384, 497, 503, 519–20, 535, 536t
as research enterprise, 231, 533, 574, 579, 580–81
salience in international relations theory of, 231–32
state centrism and, 258, 281, 577, 579
state focus on power in, 252–53, 258, 577, 579
states as principal actors in, 252–53
states' predisposition to conflict and, 252
systematic synthesis and, 533, 534, 551–58
taxonomies of, 272–75, 577, 581
typologies of, 265–72, 577, 581
realpolitik, 4n.5, 99, 293
reflexivity, 34, 37–39, 42, 45–46, 74, 213, 219, 575
relational reasoning, 65, 108, 116, 119, 121–22, 212, 576
research enterprise
analytic eclecticism and, 69
axiom identification and, 147–49, 155, 158–68, 160t, 223, 576–77
falsification and, 124
inductive and deductive reasoning in, 124–25, 136t, 147, 155, 212, 231, 576
metatheory and, 69, 155
paradigm compared to, 69
rationality and, 68, 124
systemism and, 223
as a system of explanation, 135
value of theory in, 150–51
research program
critiques of, 143–45
deductive reasoning and, 136t
defining qualities of, 57–58, 68
"hard core" and, 142–43
heuristics and, 142
novel fact concept and, 144
"protective belt" and, 142
serial approach to assessing performance in, 143
research tradition concept, 145–47
revolution-based balance of threat theory
additional noncore assumptions in, 536t
causes of war and, 393–94
critiques of, 395–96
defining qualities of, 391–93
efficient causes and, 415

revolution-based balance of threat theory (*cont.*)
  final conditions and, 415
  formal causes and, 414
  material conditions and, 414–15
  priorities for improvement in, 536*t*, 540
  range of variable types and, 536*t*
  regional uncertainty and, 535
  testability of, 544–45
  visual representation of, 406–15, 407*f*
  windows of opportunity and, 413
Ripsman, Norrin M., 195, 196*t*, 235*t*, 496*t*
Roman Empire, 3, 260, 483
Rose, Gideon, 194
Rose, William, 266*t*, 389*t*, 392
Rosecrance, Richard N., 10, 99, 343, 420*t*, 496*t*, 500
Rousseau, Jean-Jacques, 485–91
Russell, Bertrand, 182
Russia
  Napoleonic Wars and, 310–12
  Ottoman Empire and, 501–2
  revolution (1917) in, 13, 392
  Russo-Japanese War (1905) and, 338
  Triple Entente and, 178
  Ukraine and, 240, 390, 464
  World War I and, 178, 484

Saudi Arabia, 341, 393
Scheuerman, William E, 291–92
Schroeder, Paul W., 366–67
Schweller, Randall
  balance of interests theory summarized by, 418–19, 420*t*
  on bandwagoning, 115
  on causes of war, 421
  on differences between traditional realism and neorealism, 274
  on realism and rationality, 256
  realism summarized by, 235*t*
  tripolarity and, 151–53, 555–56
scientific progress
  comprehensiveness and, 28, 29*t*, 31
  concept formation and, 26
  convergence in thinking and, 26–27
  epistemology and, 26–27
  falsifiability and, 29*t*, 32
  identifying causal mechanisms and, 29*t*, 31, 32
  international relations and, 26, 574–75
  ontology and, 26–27
  pragmatism and, 7, 28
  predictive value and, 29*t*, 31–32
  public exchange and, 28, 29*t*, 31–32
  range of explanation and, 29*t*

  realism and, 10, 15–19, 53
  scientific realism and, 224, 578
  systemism and, 223
  transfactualism and, 33–34
scientific realism
  analyticism and, 37*f*, 37–38
  antirealism and, 83–84
  axiom identification and, 222–23
  comprehensiveness and, 43
  dualist view of world in, 34, 42–43, 62
  falsifiability and, 43
  identification of causal mechanisms and, 43, 45
  logical consistency and, 53
  logic of confirmation and, 39
  metatheory and, 43, 74, 574, 578–79
  objective reality and, 19–20, 53, 76–77, 122, 576
  predictive value and, 43, 87–88
  public exchange of views and, 43
  range of explanation and, 43
  rationality and, 129, 219
  scientific progress and, 224, 578
  scientism and, 78
  transfactualism and, 40, 42–43
  unobservables and, 19–20, 24, 35–36, 44, 45–46, 53, 62, 76, 78–79, 87, 122, 134–35, 219, 221, 576
Second Punic War, 483
Shifrinson, Joshua, 329–30, 363, 518*t*, 519–23
Sil, Rudra
  on analytic eclecticism, 63–64, 97–98, 103, 105*t*
  on multimethod approaches, 37
  on rational choice, 129
  on scientific realism and unobservables, 87
  on social science and research tradition, 159–61
Sinai War (1956), 393
Sinatra, Gale M., 112
el-Sisi, Abdel-Fattah, 240
Six Day War (1967), 178, 393
Smith, Adam, 67
Smith, Michael Joseph, 9–10, 235*t*
Snow, John, 117
sociable pluralism, 96, 146–47, 558–59
social capital, 96
Social Darwinism, 223–24
South China Sea, 384
South Korea, 572–73
Soviet Union
  Cold War and, 523–24
  collapse of, 332, 388, 524, 544
  Suez War and, 342–43, 393

Spain, 186–87
Spanish-American War, 232–33
Stalin, Josef, 48
Starr, Harvey, 38–39
structural realism
   additional noncore assumptions in, 536*t*, 539
   alliance entrapment and, 375, 377–78
   anarchy and, 270
   balance of power and, 366–67
   causes of war and, 362–63
   completeness and, 365
   critiques of, 364–68
   deductive theory and, 356–58
   defining qualities of, 278–79, 282*t*, 327–28, 356–60
   efficient causes and, 352
   formal causes and, 377
   hegemonic stability theory and, 541–44, 553–54
   material conditions and, 377
   parsimonious nature of, 364, 377
   polarity and, 362–63
   priorities for improvement in, 536*t*, 540, 544, 553–54
   range of variable types and, 536*t*, 540
   rationality and, 359–60, 365, 377
   states efforts to ensure survival in, 359
   system-level change and, 378
   variable range and, 376*t*
   visual representation and, 368–78, 370*f*
A Study of Crisis (Brecher and Wilkenfeld), 559–72, 562*f*
Sudan, 379–84, 392
Suez Canal, 393
Sun Tsu, 3–4
Switzerland, 118
Syria, 258, 393
systemism
   bricolagic bridging and, 207–8
   causation and, 71, 173, 175–77, 176*t*, 187, 576–77
   ceteris paribus clause and, 71
   classical realism and, 324
   complexity and, 177–79
   composition and, 174
   concept mapping and, 71–72
   critiques of, 193
   denials of, 179–80
   environment and, 174
   model of cognition and, 222
   neoclassical realism and, 157, 194–206
   regression models and, 188–89
   research enterprise and, 223

   scientific progress and, 223
   Systemist International Relations (SIR) and, 206–8, 531, 533, 539, 540–41, 559, 576–77, 578–80, 582
   systems analysis and, 169–71
   visual representation and, 20–22, 21*f*, 108, 121, 169, 182–93, 185*f*, 190*t*, 576–77, 578–79, 580

Taliaferro, Jeffrey, 195, 196*t*, 235*t*, 287*t*, 496*t*
Tang, Shiping, 266*t*, 271
Tellis, Ashley, 266*t*
Thucydides, 3–4, 128–29, 202, 285–86
Toft, Peter, 500–2
traditional realism, 273*t*, 274, 356
transfactualism, 33–34, 40, 42–43, 76–77, 122
Trieste, 396–403
Trujillo, Rafael, 22–23
Truman, Harry S., 484
Turkey, 174, 388, 392

Ukraine, 240, 390
United Arab Emirates (UAE), 341
United Kingdom
   Alaska border disputes of nineteenth century and, 88–89
   Brexit vote (2016) in, 117
   interwar period and, 422
   Napoleonic Wars and, 310–11
   power cycle theory and, 349
   Suez War and, 393
   World War I and, 131–32, 178
United Nations, 388
United States
   Civil War in, 177
   Latin America and, 22–23
   US-Germany wiretapping scandal (2013) and, 186
   World War II and, 133

Van Evera, Steven
   on causes of war, 451–52
   on classical realism, 287*t*
   defensive realism and, 448
   typologies of realism and, 266*t*, 268–69
Vasquez, John A.
   on balance of power, 44
   balance-of-threat theory and, 115
   comprehensive critique of realism by, 238–39, 581
   on falsifiability and realism, 3, 5, 582
   on international relations' lack of metatheory, 54–55

Vasquez, John A. (*cont.*)
  on realism and conventional standards for scientific inquiry, 11
  on realism's lack of internal consistency, 16, 534
  research program concept critiqued by, 143
  Walt and, 241–42
Versailles Treaty, 332
Vietnam War, 41, 204, 232
Visual International Relations Project (VIRP), 207–8, 210
visual representation
  axiom identification and, 162
  balance of interests theory and, 423–46, 424*f*, 433*f*, 439*f*
  balance of power theory and, 187–88
  balance of threat theory and, 396–415, 397*f*
  causal mechanisms and, 121–22
  classical realism and, 297–322, 299*f*, 302*f*, 307*f*, 577–78
  cognitive load theory and, 116
  game theory and, 120
  metatheory and, 225
  model of cognition and, 65–66, 76–77, 576
  natural sciences and, 66
  neoclassical realism and, 197*f*, 202–6
  poster sessions and, 120
  structural realism and, 368–78, 370*f*
  systemism and, 20–22, 21*f*, 108, 121, 169, 182–93, 185*f*, 190*t*, 578–79, 580

Walt, Steven
  balance-of-threat theory and, 115, 387, 389*t*
  on classical realism, 287*t*
  on disagreements within realism, 241
  on explanatory power of realism, 4–5
  on neoclassical realism, 196*t*
  offensive realism summarized by, 496*t*
  on priorities for future research in realism, 579–82
  realism summarized by, 235*t*
  research program concept critiqued by, 143
  structural realism and, 357*t*
  on theory and fast-paced information, 112
  Vasquez and, 241–42
Waltz, Kenneth
  on bipolarity *versus* multipolarity, 180
  rational choice theory and, 130–31, 134
  research program concept critiqued by, 144
  structural realism and, 165–66, 327–28, 355
Wayman, Frank W., 16–17
Weber, Max, 80, 83, 171
Wight, Martin, 290–91, 298–301, 299*f*
Williams, Michael, 231–32
Wilson, Woodrow, 18
Wivel, Andreas, 534
Wohlforth, William C., 235*t*, 272–75, 273*t*, 533–34
Wolfers, Arnold, 293–94, 313–18, 314*f*
World War I
  aerial battles in, 131–32
  causes of, 130–31
  France and, 131–32, 178, 223–24
  Germany and, 131–32, 178
  multipolarity and, 174–75, 178
  paradigm shifts regarding, 139–40
  Social Darwinism and, 223–24
  United Kingdom and, 131–32, 178
World War II, 133, 379–84, 422

Yoon, Young-Kwan, 335*t*, 357*t*

Zakaria, Fareed, 296